CHARLES ROYSTER

THE DESTRUCTIVE WAR

Charles Royster was born in Nashville, Tennessee, in 1944.
He was educated at the University of California, Berkeley.
From 1977 until 1979 he was a Fellow of the Institute of
Early American History and Culture. Since 1981 he has
taught history at Louisiana State University, where he is
T. Harry Williams Professor of American History. He has
previously published *Light-Horse Harry Lee and the Legacy
of the American Revolution* (1981) and *A Revolutionary People at War: The Continental Army and American Character,
1775–1783* (1979), which received the Francis Parkman Prize
and several other awards.

Also by Charles Royster

A Revolutionary People at War:
The Continental Army and American Character, 1775–1783
(1979)

*Light-Horse Harry Lee and the Legacy of
the American Revolution*
(1981)

EDITOR
Memoirs of General W. T. Sherman
(1990)

THE DESTRUCTIVE WAR

WILLIAM TECUMSEH SHERMAN,
STONEWALL JACKSON,
AND THE AMERICANS

CHARLES ROYSTER

VINTAGE CIVIL WAR LIBRARY

Vintage Books
A Division of Random House, Inc.
New York

FIRST VINTAGE CIVIL WAR LIBRARY EDITION, JANUARY 1993

Copyright © 1991 by Charles Royster

All rights reserved under International and Pan-American Copyright Conventions.
Published in the United States by Vintage Books, a division of Random House, Inc.,
New York, and simultaneously in Canada by Random House of Canada Limited,
Toronto. Originally published in hardcover by Alfred A. Knopf, Inc.,
New York, in 1991.

Owing to limitations of space, all acknowledgments of permission to use material
will be found following the index.

Library of Congress Cataloging-in-Publication Data
Royster, Charles.
The destructive war: William Tecumseh Sherman, Stonewall Jackson, and the
Americans / Charles Royster. — 1st Vintage Civil War library ed.
p. cm.
Originally published: New York: Knopf, 1991.
Includes bibliographical references and index.
ISBN 0-679-73878-9
1. United States—History—Civil War, 1861–1865. 2. Sherman, William T.
(William Tecumseh), 1820–1891—Military leadership. 3. Jackson, Stonewall,
1824–1863—Military leadership. I. Title.
[E468.9.R69 1993]
973.7—dc20 92-56370
CIP

Manufactured in the United States of America
10 9 8 7 6 5 4 3

To

THAD TATE
FRANK SMITH
GALE PAGE

CONTENTS

LIST OF ILLUSTRATIONS

Following page 210

LIST OF MAPS

(Courtesy of the Department of Geography and Anthropology, Louisiana State University)

PREFACE

THIS book deals primarily with one aspect of the Civil War: the scale of destruction to which the participants committed themselves. The lives and property swept away, as well as other forms of harm, far exceeded most early predictions. Americans surprised themselves with the extent of violence they could attain. I have explored some of the ways they reached this condition and the ways they accounted for it. I have given particular attention to the careers and reputations of two officers: William Tecumseh Sherman and Thomas Jonathan Jackson. For large numbers of their contemporaries these men epitomized the waging of successful war by drastic measures justified with claims to righteousness. Many people trying to explain the war did so in part by telling stories of and giving opinions about Jackson and Sherman.

A study of growing destructiveness in the Civil War properly touches on two of the questions most widely discussed by participants and historians: Why was the war fought? Why did the North win? Neither of these questions, however, is the main concern of this book. Nor have I undertaken to write a full survey of the military engagements in which Sherman and Jackson took part. My book is a long essay, touching on many aspects of war experiences and on postwar memories of them, in an effort to understand Americans' ways of making their war destructive.

No one needs to be reminded—and in the course of my research I have not been allowed to forget—that the Civil War generation contained a complex multiplicity of opinions and aspirations. In using the customary imprecise words "Northern" and "Southern" as they apply to people waging war, I have of course meant to refer to the proponents of war that would preserve the union and the proponents of war that would sustain secession. People in both camps often said that they thought of themselves as Americans. Perhaps no public question impressed them more deeply than the efforts to define a nation, to make explicit in public life the bases for banding together as Americans. Obviously, some of the definitions were incompatible, not to mention internally inconsistent. To call oneself an American was to raise more questions than the word answered. The word is not less useful or important on this account, but more so. Millions of self-styled Americans set out to win assent to one or another definition by hurting or killing those who disagreed.

I have arranged the subjects discussed in this book with an intent to look as carefully as I could at the paths by which Americans came to seek more destructive war, the diverse results they anticipated from it, and the ways they understood what they had done. I have examined these topics with more than one approach to representing the versions of experience I found in the Civil War generation's writings. The destructive war grew from small beginnings; yet it was also present or incipient at the start of the fighting. The people who made it surprised themselves, but the surprise consisted, in part, of getting what they had asked for.

THE DESTRUCTIVE WAR

CHAPTER 1

THE DESTRUCTION OF COLUMBIA

BRIGADIER GENERAL BENJAMIN H. GRIERSON, commander of the famous cavalry raid through Mississippi to Baton Rouge, accompanied Ulysses S. Grant to the White House on February 11, 1865. They were calling on the president, whom Grierson had known during the Illinois senatorial campaign of 1858. President Lincoln looked in excellent spirits as he sat with Grierson and talked, while General Grant studied a military map spread on a nearby table. The president said that the Confederacy was nearing its death struggle, and he seemed to be thinking mostly about the process of reconstruction that would follow the war. But he considerately complimented Grierson on several cavalry operations and approved Grierson's promotion to brevet major general. As usual, the president told a funny story, which amused even the silent General Grant.

Then Grant walked to where Lincoln sat and suggested that they review the military situation. The three men gathered around the map. Grant pointed out the positions of the armies over which he, as lieutenant general, had supreme command. Meade's army, which Grant accompanied and commanded in person, faced the Confederate forces under Lee along a thirty-five-mile entrenched front from Richmond to Petersburg, Virginia. Thomas's army in Tennessee had defeated and scattered the Confederates last December. Canby would soon move against Mobile, Alabama. Terry's capture of Fort Fisher in North Carolina during January had closed the Confederacy's last port. And Sherman's army, having marched easily from Atlanta to Savannah, was moving northward through South Carolina. By breaking rail lines it would reduce Charleston, isolate the munitions works at Augusta, Georgia, and cut Lee's connection with the lower South.

Grierson noticed the ease with which Grant spoke and the confidence with which he planned the simultaneous correlated movements of large, dispersed armies. Grant expressed only one fear—that Lee would abandon the Virginia trenches to march against Sherman more rapidly than Grant could follow. Grant had promised his friend Sherman that he would try to prevent such a movement. It alone might disrupt the concerted operations for defeating the Confederacy in the coming spring. This was "the only apprehension in the General's mind," Grierson observed, as Grant "pointed to Columbia, S.C. on the map and stated that Gen. Sherman would be there with his army between the 15th and 20th of February."

EVEN AS Grant was speaking, part of Sherman's army was approaching Orangeburg, South Carolina. Once the men had waded through the icy cypress swamps enclosing the channels of the north fork of the Edisto River, they could march on firm ground. The roads rolled over the low hills east of the piedmont, past acres of prairie grass, among pine, fir, and magnolia trees. From a rise men could see large fields for cotton and corn with plantation houses scattered among them. Four long columns of soldiers—60,000 men—followed the weaving roads. The easternmost column, the 17th Army Corps, was usually about thirty miles from the westernmost, the 14th Army Corps. Still farther west the cavalry held to a parallel route northward. The track of the columns was clear at a glance. Fat pillars of dense black smoke rose from many fires that soldiers constantly were starting. Burning cotton bales, corn cribs, gins, barns, houses, fences, crops, and pine woods sent up dark clouds that the upper air currents spread over the countryside. They turned the sun red.

During the second week of February the soldiers, some sooner than others, figured out the army's destination. Of course, they had all known for a month that they would eventually wind up in Virginia and show Grant how to beat Lee. But, for obvious reasons, Sherman did not say what route he would take. At first, the two corps of the right wing seemed to be heading northeast toward Charleston, while the two corps of the left wing seemed to be marching up the Savannah River toward Augusta, to the northwest. Then the right wing turned northwestward, too. After both wings crossed the Edisto and headed north, anyone could see that General Sherman was taking them all to Columbia.

Most of the men were enjoying their march into South Carolina. To go to Columbia would make it even better. After three years of combat, leaving dead men on the ground from Shiloh and Vicksburg to Atlanta, these soldiers had reached two conclusions about the Confederacy: Southerners hated the United States of America, and South Carolinians hated it most—so much that they had started the war. While still in Georgia, the men had talked about South Carolina. They would have been disappointed if their commander had not taken them into the state; the trip would reward their achievements. Men in the left wing threatened: "Carolina may dread us, she brought the war on and shall pay the penalty"; "I hope we may be able to exterminate the whole breed of Carolina, she is too overbearing and should be wiped out from the Earth." A soldier in the right wing said: "I am certain that South Carolina will smoke . . . if we march through it for the soldiers have a big gruge against the hot Bed of treason." General Sherman knew their minds. "The truth is," he wrote in Georgia, "the whole army is burning with an insatiable desire to wreak vengeance upon South Carolina. I almost tremble at her fate, but feel that she deserves all that seems in store for her."

To march into South Carolina was one thing; to know where to go was another. Cold rains, swollen rivers, broad swamps, and narrow, muddy roads might have given pause to an invading army. But Sherman, who had roamed these regions before many of his soldiers had been born, always seemed to know what lay ahead. He had proven this gift during the fighting in northwest Georgia, and his men trusted him. Most were in their early twenties and thought of Sherman, who had just turned forty-five, as an old man. They made allowances for his favoritisms. Clearly, he liked the right wing—the 15th and 17th Corps—better than the left, and he favored the 15th Corps, the one he had commanded at Vicksburg, above all. In Tennessee, Mississippi, and Georgia the men of the 15th Corps had shown, as Sherman said, "that they generally do their work up pretty well." They knew that secession had begun in Columbia, and as they marched toward the city many of them sang new words to one of America's unofficial national anthems:

Hail Columbia, happy land;
If we don't burn you, I'll be damned.

The capital of South Carolina lay at the confluence of the Broad River and the Saluda River, where they met to form the Congaree River. Travelers praised the city's beauty. True, there were brothels near the river, ramshackle houses and slums, and the dirty quarters of the female operatives who worked at the Saluda Factory, making cloth. But the center of the city, laid out on gentle hills above the Congaree, pleased the eye. Streets 100 feet wide, lined with trees, intersected to form residential blocks, each of which covered four acres. Many homes were surrounded by magnolia and orange trees, as well as flower gardens full of jasmine, oleander, and solfaterre roses. Sidney Park attracted evening promenaders across its sixteen acres; the city itself seemed parklike. Business was largely confined to Main Street, which led from the northwestern precincts, known as Cottontown, to the state capitol and continued to the south. Hotels and the post office were on the parallel street to the west, Assembly Street, in which stood the Market building. The parallel streets to the east of Main, Sumter and Marion, led to most of the churches and, below the capitol, to the grounds of South Carolina College. Columbians took pride in their substantial brick houses, stores, manufacturing establishments, and churches. They had academies for the young, an Ursuline convent school, the state Lunatic Asylum, and the depots of two main railroad lines. Dominating all, in the center of the city, stood the unfinished new state house, which was being built of granite and marble. The old wooden capitol was still in use nearby, but, despite the many memories it evoked of eminent South Carolinians who had spoken in its chambers, it was getting dingy.

War had changed Columbia. The city had never been large, numbering about 8,000 people in peacetime; but the war had more than tripled its population. Many Southerners, including the Confederate authorities in Richmond, had concluded that it was one of the safest places in the South. Columbia became the site of the Confederacy's currency printing, an operation employing many young women to sign bills. The government used the city as a depot for military supplies. Professor Joseph LeConte of South Carolina College operated a chemical laboratory for the Niter and Mining Bureau, testing nitrous earth to aid in the production of gunpowder. Manufacture of munitions was one of Columbia's largest industries. Bankers in Charleston and elsewhere had moved their most valuable holdings to Columbia. The city had at least seventeen banks, instead of the three of prewar days. Their vaults contained the silver services, jewels, title deeds, bonds, and other valuables of prosperous South Carolinians. Families near the coast had sent their most prized objects to friends and relatives for safekeeping. Paintings, furniture, other heirlooms, and the best vintages from wine cellars lay stored in Columbia. With all of these came thousands of new residents—refugees, especially women, seeking a safe place. During Sunday, February 12, a new set of fugitives began to enter the city. They were families, bringing livestock and wagons loaded with furniture, running northward away from Sherman's army.

Some people were forced into Columbia: slaveowners moved their human property. The number of black people in Columbia, usually about one-third of the population, swelled with the influx of slaves. Some blacks had escaped during the relocation, had hidden in swamps, and were greeting the approaching Federal soldiers with descriptions of the roads ahead. Blacks in the city felt sure of Sherman's destination sooner than his own men did. On January 29, a white man who heard them noted: "The niggers sing hallelujahs for him every day." Some of the slaves concentrated in Columbia grew restive, and white people reacted harshly. They set up a whipping post near the Market in Assembly Street, where floggings took place daily. A black man caught smuggling news to Federal prisoners in the city received 100 lashes and a promise that, if he repeated the offense, he would be killed. Afterward, he told the prisoners: "Dey may kill dis nigger, but dey cain't make him hate de Yankees." The daily whippings aroused bitter resentment among young black men. Some of them called the Market post "Hell" and agreed among themselves to make a hell of the city once the Yankees came.

By Monday, February 13, the Yankees' approach was becoming clear. Federal prisoners of war, confined on the grounds of the Lunatic Asylum, had more practiced ears and detected the distant rumble and thud of Sherman's artillery fire a day earlier than did Columbia's citizens. The Federals also had other reports. On Monday an old black man, who delivered the camp's firewood but was not allowed to speak to the prisoners, developed sudden trouble with the rear gate of his wagon as he turned it around in the middle of the camp. He jumped down from the driver's seat to fix the tailgate. Without raising his head as he worked among the white men, he muttered over and over: "Sherman is within thirty miles. He'll be here in a few days."

All 1,200 prisoners of war were officers. Though the Confederacy had much worse prison camps, the men in the Asylum Camp found it bad enough. On two acres they lived in shacks, in the open, and in holes in the ground. They ate, irregularly, only cornmeal and sorghum molasses. At a previous camp outside the city they had seen men shot without provocation. On the way to Columbia from Charleston they had watched a lieutenant die after bloodhounds stopped his escape by catching him and tearing him apart. Marching through the city to the Asylum Camp, they had heard hoots and hisses from men, women, and children. One Columbian asked them whether they were "Sherman's wagon-train." Some people called for the guards to let citizens hang the Yankees. The officers knew that the sound of Sherman's guns meant that the Confederates would soon move the prisoners again. Some decided to escape. When guards came to take the men to the railroad depot, fifty or more were missing, hidden in holes and rafters and in the asylum hospital. As soon as these men could safely move, they found friends in Columbia. Ira B. Sampson, William Baird, S. H. M. Byers, and other officers entrusted themselves to blacks' households and waited in the families' attics, hoping that Sherman would not decide to go around Columbia.

Columbians had among them more military experts than usual. Major General Matthew Calbraith Butler had brought his cavalry to help defend his native state; the senior cavalry officer, Major General Wade Hampton, a leading citizen of Columbia, had come from Lee's army with Butler. General P. G. T. Beauregard commanded all Confederate forces in the region. General Joseph E. Johnston, former commander of the Army of Tennessee, had held no command since the previous July but was living in Columbia, meditating on the mistakes that Jefferson Davis and Robert E. Lee were making. Johnston was accompanied by Major General Mansfield Lovell, who was still in official disgrace for having lost New Orleans in 1862. Lieutenant General Joseph Wheeler was nearby, commanding the Confederate cavalry that skirmished with the fringes of Sherman's army. Before February 12, Beauregard and Hampton said they could keep Sherman from crossing the Congaree. Even so, Beauregard ordered that the many bales of cotton stored in Columbia be stacked in the center of the wide streets, ready to be burned if they seemed likely to fall into Federal hands. Each day, some of the well-mounted generals gathered, rode out to study the perimeter, then adjourned to the home of James and Mary Chesnut, where they looked at military maps and expertly identified the points of Sherman's vulnerability. However, Beauregard had only lately detected Sherman's intentions and, before returning to Columbia, could not tell whether Sherman was heading for Charleston or Augusta or some intermediate point; so Confederate forces in those cities remained stationary and useless against Sherman's advance.

Beauregard had at most 800 men in Columbia and 1,500 under Butler, retreating before Sherman. People in Columbia might hope for General Hardee to march from the coast or for General D. H. Hill to come from Augusta. They might admire Beauregard's and Hampton's confidence. Still, they faced the question of what to do. The Columbia newspapers published inspirational editorials. On the 11th, the Columbia *Tri-Weekly South Carolinian* promised a concentration of Confederate strength that would make Sherman tremble. "If he comes forward, a reception awaits him unlike that which he encountered in his career through Georgia." South Carolinians were the boldest Confederates, as an editorial the following day implied: "Long before Columbia falls we look for a battle and a victory" which would prove that God "has vouchsafed to South Carolina the proud privilege of closing as she began this war—in triumph." The streets where these papers were distributed grew busier each day with the traffic of people leaving the city. Wagons, buggies, and other vehicles headed for Laurens Street in the northeastern corner of town, site of the Charlotte & South Carolina Railroad depot. William Johnson, president of the company, took rolling stock from other lines—the South Carolina Railroad and the Greenville & Columbia Railroad—onto the Charlotte track. Thereafter, at all hours, shrill steam whistles told Columbians of departures of loaded trains.

Officials of the Treasury Department with their engraving plates; officers of the Commercial Bank, the Bank of South Carolina, and the Planters and Mechanics Bank with their banks' books and some valuables; wealthy citizens with wagonloads of furniture, huge crates, and household slaves; ladies wearing several layers of dresses, stockings, and undergarments, among which were concealed gold watches, pins, rings, and bracelets; Professor LeConte with his boxes of chemicals—the urgent refugees packed the depot. The press of people near the tracks grew thicker on Monday and Tuesday, still greater on Wednesday. Trains arrived already loaded with families fleeing Charleston. Departing trains were surrounded by screaming, cursing, fighting crowds. Abandoned and broken furniture lay on muddy ground under trees sheathed in sleet. Women and children begged to be taken aboard the cars, which slowly rumbled away from the station on sagging rails, unable to go faster than ten miles per hour. In the afternoon of the 14th and on Wednesday, the 15th, the sound of Sherman's cannons grew louder and nearer. More citizens abandoned their earlier intention to stay in the city. For a while it had seemed plausible to some that Confederate troops would finally come from Charleston or that Sherman would go around Columbia or that the fall of Columbia might be like the occupation of Savannah, controlled and orderly. But the rush to the Charlotte depot, the locomotives' incessant whistles, and the approach of Yankee guns changed people's minds. More Columbians, in a "contagious panic," decided to join the escape. The Confederate government showed what it thought: special cars carried away the young women who worked for the Treasury, and a special train removed the Federal prisoners of war toward North Carolina.

Other departing refugees did not try the railroad. The roads toward Winnsboro and Alston filled with people on foot and in a mixed collection of vehicles. Lacking the money and influence needed to board the trains, they still had ways to escape. In their midst, prominent people also took to the highway. Campbell Bryce, who had joined and helped to finance the Congaree Troop of South Carolina Cavalry earlier in the war, and the Reverend Benjamin M. Palmer, a leader of the movement for secession in Louisiana, were induced by their wives, who remained in Columbia, to flee from the Yankees' vengeance in a broken-down vehicle. A woman helped them on the road and recalled later: "They were two miserable, unhappy men, accusing themselves of cowardice in leaving their families to the mercy of the vandals."

Artillery fire from the direction of Sherman's army disclosed that the small Confederate force of infantry, with Butler's cavalry, was trying a delaying action against the closest Federal troops, General Charles R. Woods's First Division of the 15th Corps. Woods called the fighting "stubborn." Wounded Confederates were sent back to Columbia. Still, the Southerners could not stop even two of Woods's brigades, much less the whole division or a corps. To the east, General Frank Blair's 17th Corps had destroyed the railroad to Charleston, burning ties and twisting rails. To the west, the two corps of the left wing had done the same to the railroad to Augusta. By Tuesday, February 14, all four columns were ready to converge on Columbia.

The 15th Corps approached the city from the southwest. All day on Wednesday, under a cold rain, Woods's skirmishers exchanged fire with Butler's slowly retreating cavalry. After cautiously advancing in this manner for five miles, Woods saw what the Confederates had waiting for him. At the crossing of Congaree Creek, a tributary of the Congaree River, stood an entrenched bridgehead on the south bank and a well-designed fort on the north bank, manned by artillery and infantry. A body of water on the Confederates' left, a cypress swamp on their right, and level open fields in front, covered with two to four feet of water, presented to Federal soldiers a sight "to appal the stoutest heart." The long causeway bridge crossing the flooded fields lay in the Confederate artillery's field of fire. General Woods, imitating General Sherman on a small scale, turned to flanking. He sent his Third Brigade left through the cypress swamp and his Second Brigade right, downstream, to look for a crossing of the creek. To hold the Confederates' attention in front, he also ordered his skirmishers directly forward. They coolly advanced under fire, waist deep in mud and water. The Third Brigade's crossing of the swamp upstream made the Confederates' bridgehead on the south bank unsafe; they withdrew back across the creek to their fort. Then both flanking brigades reached the north bank of the creek and converged on the fort. During the fighting, General Butler, in the fort, told his aide that he probably would retreat into Columbia and burn the bridge across the Congaree River. In the afternoon he abandoned the position and moved back toward the city. When Woods's division made camp that night, it was three miles from Columbia. The men could hear locomotive whistles from the Charlotte depot.

In the evening the sky cleared and the air became pleasant, but the men of the First Division, and many in the Second, did not sleep well. While a long Confederate army wagon train headed north out of Columbia and

Butler's men withdrew into the city, a Confederate battery on the edge of the Congaree River began to throw artillery shells among the soldiers of the 15th Corps. Their campfires made them easy night targets. From midnight until nearly dawn the shells kept coming, killing several men and wounding many more. The veterans knew what to do: they quickly threw up earthen traverses for shelter; but the shrieking of shot in the darkness had its effect. A soldier in the 53d Ohio Regiment said: "There was more profanity at the shelling that night than on any previous night of our army history."

Morning on Thursday brought a temperate, springlike day. Word came that the 20th Corps and the 14th Corps had arrived upriver, just as General Sherman had planned. Advancing from the northwest, the west, and the southwest, the whole army came to Columbia, though the left wing remained several miles out of town. The best view of the city belonged to the 15th Corps. The Confederates had abandoned the previous day's entrenchments. A short march took the Federals to an open plain on an elevation above the right bank of the Congaree. The swollen, rapid river separated them from the city. For the first time the men saw Columbia's church steeples, capitol buildings, white houses, railroad stations, and tree-lined streets. The sight reminded an Illinois soldier of Peoria. The remains of the bridge across the Congaree smoldered; only its supports still stood. On the heights, the 15th Corps announced its arrival to the South Carolinians. It marched onto the open ground in review formation: shredded regimental battle flags waving, shiny fixed bayonets swaying in cadence, brass bands playing—especially "Yankee Doodle." The First, Second, Fourth, and Third divisions, in that order, with their artillery, ambulances, and supply wagons—a complete Army Corps, 15,000 men, all within sight at one time: even veterans were impressed with themselves. As they looked across the river, along Gervais Street, at the conspicuous South Carolina state house, "the soldiers," according to an army surgeon, "all were cursing that spot as the cause of our being here."

No one in Columbia could still hope or fear that Sherman would pass by the city. More people decided to go. Colonel Ellis paid $600 for a pair of wheels so that he could take his family and slaves by wagon toward Camden. The trains leaving the Charlotte depot could not keep up with the confused crush of desperate passengers and delayed government goods. General Joseph E. Johnston, who in 1864 had faced the same Federal soldiers and heard the same brass bands from Dalton, Georgia, to Atlanta, put his wife and her sister aboard a train containing 300 women. Johnston, a short, trim man, took pride in his military bearing and self-control. This day, however, his face was pale and his eyes were moist.

The train rolled away; he remained behind with the soldiers. Wade Hampton had just learned of his promotion to lieutenant general and of his assignment to command the cavalry in South Carolina. He also knew that the Federals had cut the rail line to Charleston. Since they would not be able to ship cotton out, there would be no need to burn it in the streets. He ordered some of the bales removed. General Hampton remained calm; he showed his impressive physique and easy horsemanship while riding about the city, promising citizens that there would be no fighting in the streets. He could not, however, prevent all disorder. Before dawn and during the day, Wheeler's cavalrymen broke into stores along Main Street to plunder Columbia's merchants. White people and black people joined the troopers in stealing. Then the Confederate government warehouses near the river were thrown open, and a crowd soon gathered, grasping and struggling with each other, mainly for food. Nearby, on the riverbank, boys of the Arsenal Academy were digging hard to throw up earthworks for firing positions to prevent the re-laying of the bridge. They were within easy rifle range of the opposite bank, but the Federals let them dig. Obviously, Confederate soldiers would not be in Columbia long. A black man, after walking downtown and back home, described Hampton's men to the escaped Federal prisoners concealed in his garret: "They stands round on the sidewalks, and they looks mighty sullen. I's bound to b'lieve they's gwine to run away."

The 15th Corps waited on the heights. Captain Francis DeGress, well known throughout the army as commander of a battery of four accurate Parrott artillery pieces, could not resist the target that the city offered to a marksman. He unlimbered a section of his guns and began to drop shells expertly along Main Street, among the cavalrymen and others loaded with loot. The street quickly emptied. While DeGress was firing, General Sherman came up to him. The soldiers knew the general by sight; his idiosyncrasies were famous. He was tall, thin, and small-chested. He moved constantly—walking, shifting, jerking, pointing, glancing, smoking cigars, rubbing his uncombed red hair or his short, wiry red beard. The intricate lines and wrinkles of his face were always moving and changing, partly because he seldom stopped talking for long and partly because his fleeting expressions registered the rapid jumps of his mood and attention. His dark eyes looked sharply at everything, missing little and never resting. He wore a regulation blue uniform that was dirty and rumpled, and a wide-brimmed, round-topped hat which made him look like a sunburnt farmer or a cattle dealer. Sherman ordered DeGress to cease fire.

The captain had just started to enjoy himself. He showed Sherman where looters were carrying bags of cornmeal from the Confederate supplies at the South Carolina Railroad depot—food that the army could use. The general looked through his field glasses, then told DeGress to burst a few shells above the depot. The guns fired; white puffs of smoke suddenly appeared in the air across the river; and the people under them scattered. The sight of the great granite capitol building caused Sherman to relent a little further. Before the war, on a day more than four years past, he had been in his office in Louisiana, where he had received his mail with the newspapers that announced the secession of South Carolina. A forty-year-old man, he had cried like a child and talked on and on about a long, bloody war. Sherman ordered DeGress to put a few twenty-pound solid shot into the capitol. Five hit it. DeGress also fired explosive shells, some of which struck nearby houses. Mayor Thomas Jefferson Goodwyn and his family lived across Gervais Street from the capitol grounds; they heard the front steps of their house blow up. Another shell took a corner off the house in which lived the family of John Niernsee, the state architect. There and in other nearby homes women, children, and household slaves ran fearfully to basements. Niernsee's daughter watched her mother, her governess, and the black maids fall to their knees and pray. General Sherman soon left DeGress, and his firing stopped. Later in the day, other batteries of the 15th Corps and the 17th Corps, irritated by the sniping of Confederate sharpshooters, sent more shells into the city. The artillery also fired at the railroad yards, where Confederate officials were trying to remove the armory's most essential machinery. Some Columbians, having stored cotton in their basements as a form of savings or investment, feared that the explosions would start a fire; they moved more cotton out into Main Street with the other bales.

The Federal engineers decided that the Congaree was too wide and swift for their pontoon bridge. Sherman ordered the 15th Corps to move three miles up the Saluda. The engineers could lay their bridge across the Saluda near the Factory; and, if General William B. Hazen and some of his Second Division pushed fast enough, they might get across the neck of land east of the Saluda in time to capture intact the covered bridge across the Broad River. For these men, crossing rivers had become a well-drilled routine. During the afternoon, boatloads of skirmishers and sharpshooters reached the left bank of the Saluda and drove back the Confederate rear guard. As firing continued around the stone factory building, the women workers rushed among the looms, grabbing as much cloth and yarn as they could carry away. They knew that their employment had ended. General Hazen quickly led a mounted infantry regiment to the Broad, but the Confederates had made the bridge highly flammable with resin and light wood. They set it on fire so hastily that some of their retreating men were burned. From a distance Sherman knew what the fire meant and ordered that extra pontoons be borrowed from the engineers of the left wing and that both rivers be bridged. General Charles Woods set up a ferry to get the Third Brigade of his division across the Broad during the night so that he could move against the city in the morning, while the engineers were still working on the pontoons. During the day, Sherman had issued special orders for the march beyond Columbia toward Fayetteville, North Carolina. Troops of the right wing, Sherman wrote, were to "occupy Columbia, destroy the public buildings, railroad property, manufacturing and machine shops, but will spare libraries and asylums and private dwellings."

In Columbia, people who could not get out of the city and those who wanted to stay worked hard to conceal food and valuables. Some slave-owners entrusted silver to house servants, in the hope that Yankees would not plunder the blacks whom they were liberating and that the blacks would keep the silver safe. Hams, bacon, cornmeal, clothes, jewels, silver flatware, gold and silver coin went into attics, mattresses, false-bottomed chairs, baby cribs, or homemade money belts. The depot and the northbound roads continued to attract refugees. Departures continued after sunset of Thursday the 16th. In the evening General Hampton conferred with General Beauregard at Hunt's Hotel near the capitol; they made plans for the departure of their forces from the city. Hampton would command the rear guard. Beauregard told him not to burn the cotton in the streets. Then Beauregard met with Mayor Goodwyn to tell him that the army was leaving and that he would have to surrender the city in the morning. Most of the Confederate troops marched out during the night; Beauregard accompanied the bulk of his small force. The last boxcars leaving the Charlotte depot contained women refugees and gunpowder. Governor Andrew G. Magrath, three weeks before, had begged in vain for Jefferson Davis to send more reinforcements from Virginia; he rode out of the city at 2:00 A.M. with a military escort. At the same hour Sallie Coles Heyward and her family drove away in carriages containing changes of clothing and a trunk of silver. The streets were not quiet. Mayor Goodwyn ordered the Market opened so that people could take the food stored there. A crowd quickly cleared it out. Blacks and whites returned to the government supplies at the South Carolina Railroad depot, where by torchlight they hurried to get as much as they could. The depot also contained a stockpile of gunpowder and ammunition—during the rush the building exploded with a force that shook the ground throughout the city. Twenty or thirty looters died in the blast; others were severely hurt. At dawn the long brick building was a shell, still burning.

Friday morning's sky was clear; a hard, steady wind blew from the northwest. Near the Congaree, the ruins of the depot warehouse and station sent up smoke. On the right bank of the river men of the 17th Corps watched eagerly for signs that the city had been taken; upriver, the Saluda had been bridged with pontoons, and engineers were working hard to complete the bridging of the Broad. From a bluff above the river many soldiers watched. One group consisted of the commanding generals. Sherman walked around biting an unlit cigar. He stopped to talk; he sat down to whittle on a stick; he stood up to walk again. General Oliver Otis Howard, commander of the right wing, read a newspaper, making remarks as he read and answering Sherman's questions. Despite having lost his right arm in 1862, Howard was always ready for action yet remained soft-spoken and even-tempered. General Frank P. Blair and General John A. Logan, commander of the 15th Corps, were nearby; they bore little resemblance to Howard. Logan stood out with his dark complexion and his black hair and large mustache; his intensity in combat or in speech-making showed that he was a good hater. Blair, a member of a political family, divided the world into loyal friends and bitter enemies. General Hazen, the first to have reached the spot, and the other officers and soldiers saw the canvas-and-plank bridge being slowly extended across the noisy overflowing river. From four o'clock until eight o'clock in the morning, Colonel George A. Stone ferried his brigade, the Third of Woods's division, across the Broad. After capturing some Confederate skirmishers and chasing others, the men entrenched to wait for the next brigade to start to cross.

The streets of Columbia showed the effects of the night's unrest. Confederate soldiers, slaves, and citizens had continued to grab goods and food. Some stores on Main Street stood broken open, their windows smashed and their merchandise scattered. Many of the cotton bales, piled three high in an intermittent row down the street, had been split open. Their bagging had broken, and cotton was blowing from them into tree branches and onto buildings. Fewer white people than usual but a much larger proportion of black people gathered outdoors in the business section of the city. Among the private hoards that the night's activities had brought out were large quantities of whiskey and brandy—barrels of liquor that had run the naval blockade but, like cotton, had suddenly begun to look like a bad investment.

Mayor Goodwyn called some of the aldermen to City Hall on Main Street, two blocks from the capitol, where they discussed the situation soon after dawn. They wanted to run up a white flag on the tower, cross the Congaree by boat, and find Sherman in order to surrender. General Hampton sent an officer to stop the raising of the white flag. Soon, however, he learned that a Federal brigade had reached the left bank of the Broad River north of town. At 8:30, in front of City Hall, the general told the mayor that the Confederate troops were leaving and that the civilians could go surrender the city. Hampton shook hands with Good-wyn and said: "Good-bye and God bless you."

As Hampton and his staff rode out of Columbia to the northeast, the mayor and the aldermen, riding in a carriage and carrying a white sheet, headed up Main Street toward the Yankees. A half mile out of town they met General Joseph Wheeler. His cavalrymen were trying to harass the Yankees while running. Colonel Stone's brigade was moving forward from its temporary entrenchments, and Wheeler assured the city officials that, despite the intermittent gunfire they heard, the Confederate cavalry would soon be gone.

While waiting for the surrender of Columbia, a few of the 17th Corps soldiers across the Congaree grew impatient. They decided to jump ahead of the 15th Corps. Not enough men could get over the river to occupy the city, but a few could cross in boats and try to be the first to raise the Stars and Stripes above the citadel of treason, South Carolina's old state house. Twenty-one men of the 13th Iowa Regiment, with their young commander, Lieutenant Colonel J. C. Kennedy, crossed the river and entered the city at the same time that Wheeler's cavalrymen were retreating through the streets. They saw blacks and whites drinking and Confederate soldiers pouring turpentine on cotton bales and setting them afire. The men headed for the old state house. Once inside, they got up through the musty cupola onto the roof, pulled down the Palmetto Flag, and hung out the United States flag. From this height they could see, beyond the northern edge of town, the advancing skirmish line of Stone's brigade.

Having held the mayor's carriage until after ten o'clock, Wheeler allowed it to go on. A patrol of Wheeler's men rode down Main Street telling their fellow troopers in the city to get out. Goodwyn and the aldermen continued along the road toward the Broad River until they met a captain commanding the Federal skirmishers. He sent them with another captain to meet Colonel Stone, who insisted on the unconditional surrender of the city. Stone sent back to Sherman the mayor's request for guards to keep private property secure, and he promised that the Third Brigade would protect the city. After a brief alarm over some unexpected gunfire, the colonel rode into Columbia with the mayor and the aldermen in their carriage, soon followed by his brigade of Iowans.

With a hard wind at their backs blowing up clouds of dirt and debris, the men marched down Main Street. They saw many black people of all ages, as well as white men in butternut jeans, taking goods from the stores. As the soldiers had often experienced before, many slaves greeted them as bringers of freedom and instruments of God's will. Blacks and whites, many already drunk, urged the men to drink. Colonel Stone hurried on to the state house to raise the flag, unaware that other Iowans were already there. During the hour around noon while he was at the capitol, his brigade broke up. The soldiers had gone without much sleep or any food for more than twenty-four hours; liquor gave them a quick jolt. One officer later said: "I saw men who never drank before in their lives, drunk that day." Some broke into stores to show the Columbia novices how experienced men tore a place apart. Others ripped open cotton bales and watched the tufts blow away, covering more of the city with the appearance of a snowfall. Several soldiers headed for homes to begin what they called "foraging," which meant taking not only food, clothing, and guns, but also watches, silver, and jewelry—sometimes at gunpoint. Part of the cotton on Main Street burst into dangerous flame, and fire-alarm bells were rung. Volunteers of the Independent Fire Company wheeled out their engines and, with the help of some soldiers, pumped water onto the bales, reducing the blaze to a less alarming level. A fire in the jail, two blocks west of the Market, was also suppressed, but soldiers stuck bayonets into the fire hoses and quickly made one engine useless. Stone still had some disciplined soldiers. At City Hall he assured the aldermen that private property would be safe. He sent guards to homes in response to requests; he posted sentries at intersections and ordered all liquor destroyed. His orders were partially carried out; yet he could not present a peaceful city to his superiors—Woods, Logan, Howard, and Sherman—who were coming.

Soon after a detail of Stone's men cleared some of the debris from Main Street at two o'clock, the sound of military bands came from the direction of Broad River. While the left wing of the army stayed well outside the city and the 17th Corps went around it, the 15th Corps marched through Columbia. General Logan, mounted, led his men; Sherman and Howard rode together behind him. The even ranks looked full; few soldiers wanted to miss the occasion. Battle flags stood out in the whipping wind. One after another, the brigade bands played "Hail Columbia," then varied their tunes with "The Star-Spangled Banner," "The Red, White, and Blue," "Yankee Doodle," and other marches before playing "Hail Columbia" again. Along the sidewalks and intersections a dense crowd made noise to rival the bands and the wind. In front of the stores, soldiers of Stone's brigade cheered Sherman more loudly than usual, but less coherently. Black people let out their glee in many ways: shaking each other's hands, laughing, dancing to the music, marching alongside in step; some old men took off their hats and bowed. Many people shouted to the soldiers: "God bless you; I'se free now!" "T'ank de Almighty God, Mister Sherman has come at last. We knew it; we prayed for de day, and de Lord Jesus heard our prayers." A few of Columbia's white people hung out the Stars and Stripes. In the middle of the street General Sherman was suddenly stopped by a soldier who stepped out from the sidewalk and moved unsteadily in front of Sherman's horse. The man wore a long, figured silk dressing gown with his army gear buckled around it, a shiny plug hat, and a string of epaulets as a necklace. Carrying his musket at shoulder shift, he stepped up to Sherman, lifted his hat, and said: "I have the honor (hic), General, to present (hic) you with (hic) the freedom of the (hic) City." Sherman turned his head away to hide a grin. The man was quickly taken under guard, and the head of the column moved on to City Hall. Sherman and Howard stayed there while the corps marched through the city to its new camps a mile outside. In camp an Illinois soldier of the First Division deplored the stealing and drunkenness he had seen among Stone's brigade. He wrote in his diary: "I think the city should be burned, but would like to see it done decently."

At City Hall, Sherman met Mayor Goodwyn, asked him for a house to serve as headquarters, and promised him that the city would be safe. Many of the officers who had escaped from the prison camp had gathered there. Sherman greeted them, heard accounts of their treatment, and invited them to visit him at his headquarters. While the rest of the 15th Corps marched along Main Street, Sherman and Howard rode to the smoldering South Carolina Railroad depot, where they saw soldiers salvaging unburnt grain, then continued uptown to look at the arsenal and returned to the Market. Sherman believed that the city was under control, but Colonel Stone soon asked General Woods for reinforcements to patrol the streets. None came.

During the afternoon the wind gusted still harder, steadily making "a weird and gloomy sound." Outside the city, a division of the 17th Corps had to move its camp away from the woods into an open field when a fire in the underbrush quickly grew too big to fight. Even in the field, the air was full of smoke, blowing sand, and flying leaves. In the afternoon and the evening, many soldiers left their camps to go into Columbia. The 15th and 17th corps were near, but men also came from the 14th and 20th corps northwest of town and even from Kilpatrick's cavalry, which was twenty miles away. Private Michael Griffin of the 15th Corps said: "You better believe there was a rush to see the City and get Trophies." Soldiers and blacks moved through the streets in pursuit of private purposes or to no purpose. Some soldiers dispersed among the prosperous-looking houses and gardens, growing whiter from flying bits of cotton, and began to search for food and valuables. About fifty men broke into the Bank of Charleston and the Commercial Bank of Columbia and began to fill bags with silver. Many houses had guards who kept other soldiers out, and officers walked around, ready to interfere with a private's fun. Even so, other Columbia homes received a visit, sometimes several, from wandering groups of soldiers. The men said they were looking for food and firearms but snatched whatever caught their fancy. Soldiers did not assault civilians during their afternoon wanderings, yet some did enjoy scaring those whom they blamed for the war— waving weapons, damning South Carolina, and warning that Columbia was going to suffer after dark. Most, a Columbian noticed, were "civil and pleasant spoken, but there was a marked air of absence from all restraint and control, and the soldiers evidently knew that it was general holiday." Not long after soldiers found the half block of brothels on Gervais Street, fire broke out in those frame buildings, which burned quickly in the wind. Cotton bales near the center of the city continued to burn inside, throwing out flaming fragments. In the suburbs, the mansions of Wade Hampton and George Trenholm, Confederate secretary of the treasury, went up in smoke that citizens in town could see.

Other stragglers went to the arsenal to look at British cannon captured at Yorktown in 1781 and to bend musket barrels over the old prizes of war. The unfinished new capitol building offered many targets to anyone who hated South Carolina. Hard work went into breaking off the beaks of stone eagles and smashing marble fasces, as well as other decorative devices. A bronze statue of George Washington served as a target for bricks and rocks. As usual, soldiers left graffiti everywhere: their names, numbers and names of their companies and regiments, and some "foul comments." Close by, in the old state house, men found documents from South Carolina's attempt to nullify federal law in 1832. Thirty or forty soldiers gathered in the senate chamber and organized themselves as the South Carolina senate. They voted repeal of the ordinance of secession and passed a resolution of censure against John C. Calhoun. Then they bombarded Hiram Powers's marble bust of Calhoun with inkstands and spittoons. Finally, they sang with great enthusiasm:

> John Brown's body lies a-mouldering in the grave
> But his soul goes marching on.

The "senate" adjourned to reconvene at Raleigh, North Carolina. Captain John J. Safely walked out of the chamber with the clock, the thermometer, the state surveying instruments, and, he said, "several other trophies too numerous to mention."

At dusk, soldiers were wandering throughout the city, under no control. Several buildings in the center of the business district caught fire. The volunteer firemen brought out their remaining engines and tried to bring the hoses to bear on the flames, but soldiers quickly smashed the machinery with axes. The constant straining wind caused the stores to burn fast. With shouts and cheers men moved through the broken and discarded merchandise in the street, the sober as excited as the drunk. Lieutenant Colonel Jeremiah W. Jenkins, the provost marshal who was supposed to police the city, found the task too great. His "youthful, tall lithe and elegant form, in his officers suit and high topped boots" caught the eye of a Columbia woman who sought from him a guard for her house. He walked along the street with her restlessly, rushing into buildings to stamp out small fires. He tried to apologize to her for the disorder, but she denounced the North for making war on women and children after having failed in fair combat. At last Jenkins told her: "The women of the South kept the war alive—and it is only by making them suffer that we can subdue the men."

Not long after sunset, several rockets shot up above the city, leaving bright trails of color. To the soldiers this was a common sight, since rockets were the usual nighttime signals among the separated columns of Sherman's army. But citizens of Columbia read a more frightening meaning into the signal. Some of them had heard warnings about a plan among the soldiers to burn the city. Harriott Horry Ravenel suspected that her slave Martha knew more than she had revealed, because Martha reacted to the rockets by saying: "That's it Miss. Lord hab mussy on us—it's beginning!"

On Main Street a large fire was burning near City Hall. A block north and on the other side of the street, the office of the Southern Express Company was burning. Around the corner, on Taylor Street, A. R. Phillips's store was on fire. In the other direction from City Hall, the buildings on the west side of Main Street in the next block, where the cotton was still burning, also caught fire. Soon fires appeared in many places in the city, especially the upper, northern section, the quarter from which the wind blew. On the east side of town, the Charlotte railroad depot seemed to burst into flame all at once, fire shooting out its doors and windows, quickly spreading to the abandoned furniture and household possessions near the tracks.

New fires were started by some of the soldiers going from house to house, carrying pots of turpentine, balls of cotton, pine sticks aflame, bundles of straw, and lightwood torches. They tossed burning cotton balls in windows and doors, doused furniture with turpentine and lit it. Their shouts and laughter and jokes showed they were having a good time, but the keenest enjoyment belonged to the officers who had escaped from the Confederate prison camp. One of them later bragged that he had fired seventeen houses. Black men led groups of soldiers through the streets to show them hidden valuables, wine cellars, and the homes of certain Columbians. The league of young black men carried out their plan to start fires. The day before Sherman's army arrived, twenty slaves had been flogged at the Market whipping post. This night brought revenge. The father of two of the young men tried to persuade his sons not to take part, but he failed; so he followed them and put out two of the fires they had set. Soldiers knew of specific citizens who deserved punishment and went in search of their homes, asking: "Is this the home of Mr. Rhett?" "Is that the dwelling of Mr. Middleton?" Two aged Charlestonians, Arthur P. Hayne and Alfred Huger, were pulled about and struck. Officers tried to learn from Louisa Cheves McCord the whereabouts of Dr. John Cheves; they blamed him for the land mines that had wounded Federal soldiers outside Savannah and said they would hang him. The devoted secessionist Maxcy Gregg had been killed at the battle of Fredericksburg, but his house was accessible. Soldiers took his gold-headed cane, his gold epaulets and crimson sash, and the trousers he had worn in his last battle. Some former prisoners of war knew which houses they wanted to burn—those of Columbians who had spat on the captured Yankees. A group of soldiers, led by black men and freed prisoners, went to the home of a man who ran a pack of bloodhounds for the capture of escaping slaves and Federal soldiers. They killed the hounds, burned the house, tied the man to a tree, and let the biggest black men flog him.

Men threw burning cotton into the McCord home even after General Howard had made it his headquarters. Howard put out small fires and drily commented that it was remarkable how the cotton was blowing about. Mayor Goodwyn returned home after the fire engines were broken near City Hall and found his house burning. He tried to save some possessions by taking them into the street; but soldiers made fun of him, put pistols to his head and knives to his throat, tore things from his hands and smashed them. People in their homes heard soldiers in the street shout, "Your house is on fire." As the residents rushed out, the soldiers went in to loot. Drunken men ranged through Harriott Ravenel's house on Henderson Street, trying to beat one another to the trunks and closets. They took trinkets, pictures, china, clothing, blankets, and food, then started fires before leaving. The house servants helped put out the fires after the men had gone. Some soldiers seemed to admire the composure of the women in the Ravenel home and stopped long enough to say that they "were sorry for the women and children, but South Carolina must be destroyed." Others were just having a good time: one man left the house wearing a blue silk dress and carrying a lace parasol.

The streets grew more crowded as people fled from burning houses and as more soldiers came in from the surrounding camps. In an arc north and west of the city, thousands of campfires lit the darkened countryside. Sections of the pine woods were burning. The wind pushed those fires: flames jumped among the trees, which threw up streams of sparks within columns of thick smoke. Inside the city, at ten o'clock, all the buildings along Main Street, from the north edge of town to the capitol, were burning. The flames leaned eastward under the steady blast of wind, creeping along Washington Street and other parallel cross streets, toward the churches and the academies. Pulsing globes of fire rose from burning buildings, rushed through the air, and seized more structures. Frantic chickens and pigs, caught by the flames, burned alive. Bursting bales of cotton threw masses of crackling fibers into the air. Burning shingles and fiery debris followed the upward draft of black smoke and hot air hundreds of feet above the city, then fell on roofs, in gardens, and among people in the streets. The branches of shade trees, now bare and black, writhed and snaked under the intense pressure of the heat and the wind.

No one knew which way was safe. The crowds in the streets—white women and children, a few older white men, and black people of all ages—milled in different directions, at cross purposes, trying to safeguard possessions. Hundreds of yelling, smoky-faced young soldiers were enjoying themselves. They snatched bundles and blankets, stole or broke valuables, made jokes, and celebrated their revenge on South Carolinians, a vengeance so long delayed and so costly. The Reverend Peter J. Shand lost the sacred vessels of Trinity Church to five men who took them from him at gunpoint in the street. Another man cursed Shand and expressed a wish to lay the entire city in ashes and sow the ground with salt. Soldiers shouted derisively at passing women: "The aristocrats! The chivalry!" Stamping their feet, clapping their hands, and gritting their teeth to look menacing, the agitated soldiers shouted jokes, obscenities, and political remarks interchangeably; "the damned den of rebels in South Carolina had been plotting this thing for years," they said, "and now they had determined to exterminate it, root and branch, even if . . . every man, woman and child had to be burned with the town." One young soldier, "in a hilarious mood," asked a merchant whose store was burning: "Say, did you and your folks think of this when you hurrahed for secession before the war? How do you like it, hey?" Eliza Goodwyn, the mayor's wife, told a soldier who approached her as she watched her house burn, that she had sent six sons into the Confederate army—two had been killed—and she wished she could send six more. "Yes," he answered, "damn you women, you are the ones keeping up the war." The Niernsee family encountered drunken men of the 15th Corps in a vacant lot. The soldiers fired pistols, chased girls while carrying knives, and grabbed blankets from children, saying: "Let the d——d little rebels suffer as we have had to do for the past four years."

Some men grew more and more frenzied with the destruction; it became their sole purpose. They seized possessions only to throw them into the flames. While one group gave finery and valuables to passing black people, another pillaged slave quarters and destroyed blacks' belongings. While one set of men looted banks systematically and extracted buried silver with an experienced touch, others smashed mirrors, slashed paintings, and broke furniture that women had hauled into the streets. A soldier played a piano in the street as another soldier chopped the instrument with an axe. A group of soldiers set fire to a piano, then one played it while the others danced around it until the flames forced the pianist to step back. Men who were too drunk and too intent on spreading the fire passed out in burning buildings, and the flames closed over them. A few men murdered. They caught black women, whom they stripped, raped, and killed.

Columbians still in their homes could not be sure when or whether they would have to take to the streets. To stay might save the house; to go might be the only way to save the lives of the family. In the Bachman household a woman went into labor and gave birth while the building shook from nearby explosions of stored artillery shells the fire had reached. In the Henry home three daughters sat in a room with the body of their mother, who had died on Thursday. They watched the corpse, expecting soon to have to run out of a burning house. In Moses C. Mordecai's ample brick house, people waited for the fire to reach them. Mordecai served sherry in delicate glasses to a group of Federal officers, while his daughter played the piano. They calmly entertained their guests until the shutters started to burn. Then Mordecai said: "My daughter, it is time to go," and they all walked out into Sumter Street, chatting pleasantly. In the streets, women watched the destruction of their homes silently, with pale, expressionless faces. Others moved among the crowd, frantically weeping and begging soldiers to save their property. Defiant women laughed bitterly and threatened their enemies with the vengeance that the Confederate army would take. Some people refused to go into the streets without a guard, explaining to Captain Jacob Ritner: "Why, niggers will kill us." Scared, reluctant people were carried out of their endangered houses.

Despite its reputation for ferocity, the 15th Corps included many men who denounced the burning and looting. These soldiers guarded houses from plunderers, helped to put out fires, and protected families from being robbed in the streets. But they were outnumbered. Men who did not want to steal and destroy stayed in their camps; the men who went into Columbia were not the disciplined ones. After dark General Charles R. Woods ordered his First Brigade, commanded by his brother, William B. Woods, to come into the city as a replacement for Stone's brigade. The First Brigade was supposed to fight the fire and restore order, but many of its men soon found liquor and joined the looting and burning. Some men, with their officers, worked hard to save homes from the fire, but the powerful wind overcame their efforts.

In small groups soldiers from all four corps went back and forth between their camps and the city by the light of the mounting fire. In the camps excited, drunken men compared their plunder and went back for more. Private Willie Baugh got a silver napkin ring, three silver nut-pickers, and pearl opera glasses. His friends in the 76th Ohio, Briggs and Nettleton, got jewelry from the Commercial Bank, including a lady's gold watch, gold rings, sets of silver tea spoons, earrings, and many other things. Not long after ten o'clock the camp of the 1st Minnesota Light Battery in the 17th Corps was almost empty. One of its artillerymen said: "All hands are in for a good time and they are having it." The Second Brigade of the First Division in the 20th Corps did not get across the Saluda until midnight; the brightly lit sky showed the men that Columbia was burning. On the riverbank the First Brigade band played "Hail Columbia," "The Star-Spangled Banner," and "Yankee Doodle" while the soldiers shouted and sang.

At midnight the largest fire covered an area nine blocks long and almost four blocks wide. The wind veered between the northwest and the southwest but did not slacken its blasting force. The noise of the wind and the fire rose to a loud droning monotone—an unceasing roar like that of the greatest waterfalls. Musket ammunition and artillery shells detonated irregularly when the flames ignited them, giving off the sounds of battle within the burning buildings. Muffled explosions sent up columns of fire and sprayed hot metal in all directions. Beneath black clouds of smoke the blaze roiled and heaved in turbulent waves. Wreaths of flame shot up with flying burning objects and showers of bright sparks. Brick walls collapsed and brought down burning rafters amid the rubble. As buildings along both sides of the streets were consumed together, the flames joined from 100 feet apart in an arch of fire. The heat made the air like the blast of a furnace, and the fire cast an intense, vivid light, brighter than day. Minute objects could be seen distinctly from unusual distances, and the fire itself could be followed as it moved eastward: first sending out projectiles—burning cotton balls, shingles, and litter—then enveloping more houses. General Charles Woods's men tried to contain the fire by tearing down buildings in its path, but the wind carried the flames across the streets, and the fire leaped easily over gaps. At two o'clock in the morning houses were burning on Bull Street, five blocks east of Assembly Street. Just short of Bull Street, on the north side of Laurel Street, stood the impressive home of T. B. Clarkson. The large house, set back from the sidewalk, was surrounded by thirty-nine tall columns joined in an arched colonnade. These remained standing as the house burned, framing the destruction within until nothing remained but the columns, their blackened brickwork exposed. The churches along Marion Street produced towers of flame rising above the fires in the houses near them. Between Marion and Sumter, on Plain Street, lived Dr. Robert W. Gibbes. He had an income of $20,000 a year from the rent of his properties and from hiring out black mechanics whom he owned. He devoted much of his time to scientific, artistic, and historical pursuits. His large brick house, with high arched windows and tall chimneys, was a museum, a library, and an archive. It contained thousands of fossils and other specimens, paintings by Allston, Sully, Inman, and others, a collection of ancient coins, and many eighteenth-century manuscripts concerning the Revolutionary War in South Carolina. Everything was destroyed in a fire started in Gibbes's presence by soldiers who broke into his basement and answered his protests by saying: "That is the way the boys do, old man." Professor Joseph LeConte and his brother John had sent their lecture notes and scientific papers to a home on Main Street. All, including Joseph's thesis at Harvard, "The Homologues of the Radiata," burned. Pages of poetry in the handwriting of its author, Edgar Allan Poe, once submitted to the *Southern Literary Messenger* and belonging to the Confederacy's leading poet, Paul Hamilton Hayne, disappeared as Hayne's bank crumbled. Another block to the west, in the middle of Assembly Street, the Market building, which had open sides, burned quickly, only its archways still standing. After its steeple caught fire, the Market bell went down, ringing as it fell among the embers—a familiar bell, called "Secessia," it had rung to celebrate each Southern state's secession from the union. Three blocks away, the old state house burned as fast and hot as tinder. Next to it, the granite of the new capitol's walls blistered under the heat. The architect's library and drawings went into the flames. Marble sculptures—forty Corinthian capitals, unfinished statues, bas-reliefs of Robert Y. Hayne and George McDuffie, Powers's bust of Calhoun, a statue of Calhoun in the toga of a Roman senator, a statue personifying the Genius of Liberty—all dissolved into a quicklime puddle.

Lieutenant Matthew H. Jamison walked through the streets as the fire spread. He saw people, black and white, carrying children and possessions. He met an old man and three daughters arguing about whether to leave their house and what to take with them. As he moved on, a woman with eight children asked him what she should do. He saw General Giles A. Smith, commander of the Fourth Division of the 17th Corps, sitting on horseback and lifting a flask to drink damnation to the Confederacy. Irish soldiers were helping Irish civilians save their property. Black people came up to Jamison to beg. Soldiers walked by with a sack full of cigars. Another soldier carried an immense silver platter. A family passed, carrying a poodle and leading a hound. In Main Street, crowded with hurrying people and lit by burning stores, the lieutenant asked an old black man: "What do you think of the night, sir?" The man replied: "Wall, I tell you what I dinks, I dinks de Day of Jubilee for me hab come." Walking east from Main Street, Jamison looked into a house and saw a woman sitting on a staircase surrounded by her trunks, while her soldier guard lay stretched on the floor asleep. He found more people in the streets with their household effects, and he put out one small fire. Meeting a heavily burdened fat man walking with a family, he heard the man say: "Alas, that we should suffer so on account of our rulers!" The lieutenant walked on, talking to a couple whose house had burned, watching a soldier lead away a small white pony and another soldier parade with a window curtain as a banner. He met an Irish woman who was carrying a baby and blessing General Sherman.

Sherman had spent the afternoon walking through the city and visiting families he had known as a young lieutenant stationed at Charleston. While walking with Mayor Goodwyn, he had seen the body of a black man, shot by soldiers who took offense at the man's impudence; but Sherman had not arrested the soldiers. In the evening he had remained at the house that served as his headquarters, near the east end of Gervais Street, until eleven o'clock. After supper, he and General Hazen went into the yard and saw the light from the fire. Sherman said: "They have brought it on themselves."

As the light grew brighter, Sherman decided to go into the center of the city. Dressed in the civilian suit and dirty dickey that he often wore in the evenings, he walked around the eastern edge of the blaze. He saw burning balls of cotton blown across two blocks and burning shingles carried 100 yards by the wind. He found that Generals Howard, Logan, and Woods were all giving orders for fighting the fire. In the McCord house, Howard's headquarters, the girls of the family looked out the window and saw what one of them called "a dreadful looking creature . . . red headed, stubby bearded and fierce eyed." Sherman left his subordinates and walked along the north side of Blanding Street a few blocks west of the Charlotte railroad. A guard called him to the home of Harris Simons, whose wife was the niece of an old army friend of

Sherman's. She persuaded him to write orders of protection for the house; he wrote similar orders for her neighbors, told the guard to be vigilant, and left. He saved one house by ordering nearby soldiers to put out burning shingles. About three o'clock in the morning, at an intersection, Sherman met the Reverend A. Toomer Porter, whom he recognized in the brilliant light from the burning buildings. Sherman said: "This is a horrible sight." "Yes," Porter replied, "when you reflect that women and children are the victims." "Your Governor is responsible for this," Sherman said. When Porter asked how, Sherman continued: "Who ever heard of an evacuated city to be left a depot of liquor for an army to occupy? I found one hundred and twenty casks of whiskey in one cellar. Your Governor being a lawyer or Judge, refused to have it destroyed as it was private property, and now my men have got drunk and have got beyond my control, and this is the result." Sherman sent an officer with an order to bring one brigade from Hazen's division into the city to help Woods restore order. Then he left Porter and continued his pacing through the streets.

As the movement of the fire became apparent to all, people headed for open areas where the fire might not reach. Sidney Park, west of Assembly Street, and the grounds of the Methodist Female Seminary and the Charlotte railroad right-of-way on the east end of the city filled with blacks and whites. Sitting or lying among bundles and trunks, they felt the cold winter night as they watched the city burn. Friends compared possessions they had saved. Families were escorted to safety by soldiers who protected their belongings. Other wandering soldiers mocked the people who had fled the fire. "Ladies, it is a cold night," a mounted officer said. "Why don't you go into your burning town and warm yourselves?" Near the Female Seminary, Edwin Scott met a soldier who asked: "Well, old man, what do you think of the Yankees now?" Scott said: "I think they have done their work pretty thoroughly this time." The soldier replied: "Yes, if you want a job well done put a Yankee at it!" In the places of refuge, as on the streets, excited men snatched things and jeered at the "first families" and the "aristocrats": "Where now is all your pride—see what we have brought you to," they said. "This is what you get for setting yourselves up as better than other folks." The army educated South Carolinians, a 20th Corps man said; it "left them houseles to test a Soldier life."

Across Taylor Street from Sidney Park, among the gravestones in the cemetery behind the Catholic church, the nuns of the Ursuline convent watched over their sixty schoolgirls, as soldiers going by in the street shouted: "We are just as holy as you are!" The convent, an imposing three-story brick building at the intersection of Main and Blanding streets, had quickly attracted looters; it had no hope of surviving the fire. Yet the nuns had stayed as long as they dared. By ten o'clock, when they were forced to leave, the surrounding fire was intense. Between burning warehouses on both sides of Blanding Street, the Mother Superior, the black-robed nuns, and the girls, in a column of twos, had followed Father J. J. O'Connell, who led the way holding up a crucifix. After their left turn into Assembly Street, mounted officers had escorted them the rest of the way to the churchyard. From the cemetery, at about three o'clock, the nuns and the girls could see the cross above the convent topple.

At the same time, other Columbians, including Mayor Goodwyn, watched the fire from the South Carolina College grounds, a block south and east of the capitol. The Common was crowded with women and children, some wrapped in blankets. The adjacent college buildings served as a temporary hospital for Federal soldiers and Confederates who had been left behind because of their severe wounds. To the people who watched the fire move toward the college walls, everything northward seemed to be burning; the sky looked the color of copper, and across it black smoke filled with sparks flowed rapidly; standing apart, closest among the undulating waves of flame, the old state house was burning on all sides at once. Doctors, nurses, and a few of the soldiers sent to guard the college stood on the hospital roofs and struggled to knock off or put out the sparks, coals, and burning debris the wind threw down on them. In the wards, the wounded men expected the hospital to burn. Some crawled out into the Common; those unable to move lay waiting.

In the northeastern corner of the city, about 500 people had reached the enclosed grounds of the Lunatic Asylum, which the superintendent, Dr. J. W. Parker, opened to them. Pallets for the sick were laid in the halls. One room was filled with babies; they had cried so much that they sounded hoarse. In the outer yard, covered with families and their bundles, everyone could see houses burning within two blocks of them, both to the west and to the south. Passing soldiers shouted that the asylum would soon be burned or blown up. From within the asylum building rose the constant shrill screams of the inmates.

After three o'clock, obeying Sherman's order, General John M. Oliver's brigade marched from its camp to the northern edge of Columbia. All three brigades of Woods's division were already in the city. His Second Brigade had stayed in better order than the Third and the First, fighting fires but not controlling the streets. Oliver's brigade had orders to restore discipline. He reported afterward: "Did so." The regiments deployed across the streets and in unison moved southward amid the fire and rubble. In a wide dragnet the soldiers marched steadily, stopping only to arrest men in their path. Those who resisted were shot. By the time the brigade reached the southern end of the city, it had shot 32 men, two of whom died, and had arrested 370. Patrols eventually rounded up 2,500 soldiers and civilians.

During Oliver's sweep through the city, the wind changed direction and began to come from the northeast. Citizens on the streets near the asylum watched the fire being blown back toward blocks it had already burned. By six o'clock the wind had died; efforts to control the fire succeeded.

Dawn brought a mild, sunny day. In parts of the city smoke still rose from low fires in the rubble. Occasionally a wall or a free-standing chimney crashed. A long section of Columbia consisted only of brick shells, blackened columns, and smoldering mounds, facing streets lined with bare, blistered trees. The streak across the city covered thirty-six blocks, from the grounds of the hollow stone capitol to Cottontown at the north end of Main Street. Though dotted with other scattered ruins, most of the city remained standing. But the business district, most churches, and the richest residential streets had been destroyed. The refugees on the college grounds, in Sidney Park, at the asylum, and along the railroad tracks dispersed in search of shelter. Several surprised people learned that their houses still stood, while families without homes began to leave the city. Despite the tightened discipline, soldiers still got into town to prowl for treasure and to start more small fires. Columbians were treated to samples of army humor: "Why do you build your chimneys before you build your houses?" "I suppose you call your town Chimneyville." Soldiers threatened to burn the asylum and other surviving structures.

General Sherman spent Saturday, the 18th, at his headquarters, receiving a series of petitioners with their complaints. In his journal for the day he wrote: "Columbia burned fire high wind. Cotton in the streets fired by the enemy, and the general animosity of our own men—great distress of people." However, this was not the version of events that he wanted to impress upon South Carolinians. They needed to learn the folly of making war against the government. When women came to request guards for their homes, he reminded them of the Confederate promises to fight and die in the last ditch. To Mrs. Campbell Bryce, who had pushed her husband out of Columbia, he said: "Where are your fathers and husbands and sons? Why are they not here to protect you?" To Mayor Goodwyn he expressed regret that the fire had occurred, but concluded: "It was your fault Mr. Mayor," and reminded Goodwyn of the liquor. Sherman sent an ambulance to bring the Simons family from the asylum grounds. In his headquarters he gave them breakfast, cutting up the food on the children's plates, and told them that they "must not give way, it was not half as bad as it seemed." Yet to all who complained he spoke of the responsibility that Columbia and South Carolina bore for the war. He told one woman: "You have suffered much already, but if I have to come back again!" Citizens told him of their hardships, and he replied: "Such is the fortune of war." They would remember this day if they ever again thought of rebelling against the authority of the United States. John Caldwell welcomed the general, assuring him: "I have always been a Union man, have always done what I could against the war." Sherman asked: "Well, how could you have remained here in your own country and been a good Union man? Were you not in that acting the traitor?" Southerners needed to understand that allegiance imposed obligations. The Reverend Porter asked that the college library not be burned. Sherman replied: "Far from destroying books, I will send them here. If there had been a few more books in this part of the world there would not have been all this difficulty."

All day and night on Saturday and again on Sunday intermittent explosions boomed across the city. Men of the 15th Corps were destroying the stockpiles of Confederate arms and ammunition, as well as munitions works, factories and their smokestacks, locomotives and boxcars, a rolling mill, and the city gas works. Battering rams leveled the arsenal. The 1st Michigan Engineers gutted the remaining railroad buildings. Tons of machinery in the rail yards and the powder mills were smashed or disabled. Controlled fires consumed more than 1,000 bales of cotton and two warehouses full of official stationery. Reams of currency in the printers' warehouses turned Yankee soldiers into Confederate millionaires; they gambled away fortunes after demolishing the presses. Other regiments resumed the familiar labor of lifting railroad tracks in segments hundreds of yards long, then turning the rails into large corkscrews. At the end of their work, the lines from Wilmington, Charlotte, Greenville, Augusta, and Charleston all ended abruptly twenty-nine miles or more from Columbia. Large quantities of Confederate army supplies were destroyed, but some of the most useful items became United States government property, including a battery of four sophisticated Blakely artillery pieces from England, each bearing a plate that read: PRESENTED BY THE MANUFACTURERS TO THE SOVEREIGN STATE OF SOUTH CAROLINA.

Burial details pulled charred corpses from piles of bricks and coals. Some severely burned soldiers who were still alive were taken to the hospital at the college. The bodies and body fragments of people killed in the explosion of the South Carolina depot warehouse were extracted and buried. Three more men died and twenty were wounded when carelessly handled artillery shells blew up near the river.

Mayor Goodwyn, Edwin Scott, and several ministers and businessmen visited Sherman on Sunday. They were anxious about the condition of the city's residents once the army had gone. They would need food, and they would have no way to protect whites from any blacks who might be, Scott said, "disorderly." Sherman courteously welcomed the men into his headquarters house. In his quick movements and glances, as he pulled his vest down and looked at himself, he seemed very pleased. He was inclined to joke and told them that they ought to be in church on a Sunday. After they all sat down, Goodwyn explained their concerns. He asked the general to leave a supply of food, arms, and ammunition. Sherman replied excitedly. Southerners had only themselves to blame for their present condition; it had been folly for them to start this war. Of course, the issue was slavery. Slaveholders had once had warm friends in the North. He himself, he said, favored domestic servitude and objected only to "plantation slavery." He launched into a history of past political conflict, declaring that the most important event had been Southerners' attempt to force slavery on Kansas, which had alienated Northern friends of the South and done more than anything else to strengthen abolitionism. He also explained how Beauregard had mismanaged the defense of South Carolina, and he described conditions in Georgia.

Goodwyn and the others listened silently until Sherman spoke of the fire. He neither excused it nor apologized for it. He said: "It is true our men have burnt Columbia, but it was your fault." Goodwyn had gone through this exchange before; he again asked: "How so, General?" He again heard Sherman say: "Doctor you brought all this on yourselves. There was too much liquor in your town and your people distributed too much of it to my soldiers it is all your own fault." James J. McCarter told the general that a soldier had demanded his watch at gunpoint. Sherman laughed and replied that McCarter ought to have resisted. He promised that no more houses would be damaged and that a rear guard would make sure that no stragglers remained behind when the army left the next day. He concluded by agreeing to leave 500 head of cattle, tierces of salt for curing the meat, wire for a ferry across the Congaree, medicine, and 100 muskets with ammunition. Sherman sent Goodwyn to General Howard for these, remarking: "He will treat you better than one of your own generals."

While the army stayed in Columbia, hundreds of black people came to the city from the surrounding countryside. Families, complete with infants and the very old, planned to leave South Carolina by following the soldiers. Many black Columbians and at least 800 whites prepared to go, as well. Northern-born people, unionists, citizens who had helped Federal prisoners or fraternized with the army, poor people fearing starvation, men escaping the Confederacy's widening conscription, women with no homes or livelihoods, others who feared disorder: a mixed crowd gathered with wagons, buggies, horses, and mules. Their baggage ranged from small bundles to heavy trunks. Howard's officers spent Sunday apportioning the refugees among the divisions of the 15th Corps and organizing wagon trains so that the columns could move in good order.

At seven o'clock on Monday morning, February 20, another mild day of beautiful weather, Sherman, Howard, the soldiers of the 15th Corps, and the refugees began their departure from Columbia. They moved in three columns: one going north on Main Street to the Winnsboro Road, one following the twisted rails and burnt ties of the Charlotte railroad, one going out Taylor Street to the Camden Road. Small groups of Columbians gathered along the wrecked streets to watch. For the last time they saw the nervous, talkative, red-haired general and the mild-mannered one-armed general riding sleek, muscular horses. Again they heard lively march tunes from military bands; they saw the stained, ripped battle flags and the Stars and Stripes—which a Columbia girl called "their horrid old gridiron of a flag"—waving above even ranks of soldiers marching with a rhythmic tramp. Limbered artillery pieces and caissons went by, behind teams of horses. Long trains of canvas-topped supply wagons driven by black teamsters followed the soldiers. Then came the mixed array of wagons, buggies, and open carriages containing the refugees. Families of black people wearing their Sunday clothes; Yankee mechanics who had worked in the factories; the artist Halpin with his wife and daughter; the slave Hannibal, who once had accompanied the Niernsee boys with the Confederate army as a faithful body servant but now was driving away the Niernsees' traveling carriage; a pregnant woman, three days short of delivering a baby she would name Liberty Sherman; a friend of the Cheveses' and the Middletons'—Mrs. Crafts—whose departure on her own in an open wagon shocked everyone, especially her husband; riding in a carriage, a stately old black woman, wearing a large once-fashionable hat and waving a palmetto fan, who said—when a white woman asked where she was going—"La, honey! I'se gwine back inter de Union"; elegantly displaying herself in a huge landau, the most beautiful white woman in Columbia, Marie Boozer— one of those a black man described as "not real ladies, but second-hand ladies"—who had found for herself among Sherman's young officers a husband who would do until she met a wealthy New York businessman; and the "gloriously handsome" Italian opera star Eugenio Torriani— stranded in Columbia since 1860—who had been reduced to giving voice lessons to rich girls and holding evening musicales until he had become "a soul-starved man": all these and hundreds of others rolled out of town to the jaunty tune of "Hail Columbia, Happy Land," going with Sherman and his army northward, toward freedom and civilization.

At two o'clock a mounted patrol completed their ride through the city to roust out the last stragglers. The remaining residents commented on the sudden strange silence all around them. Smoke still rose from some of the ruins. People walking by the skeletons of buildings stayed in the middle of the streets in fear of the sudden crumbling of brick walls. Their first concern was food. Until supplies could come from beyond the Federal army's path, Columbians would depend on the decrepit cattle General Howard had left, many of which died before they could be butchered. Only a few of the army muskets worked; but, James G. Gibbes later said, they "did faithful service in guarding our city." Gibbes replaced Goodwyn as mayor. He sent committees of men to the homes of blacks to seize food, weapons, and personal effects claimed by whites. Many blacks were "severely punished"; some were shot. More white men came back from their hiding places in the country, and a few Confederate cavalrymen showed up. People raked through the ashes of their houses to find a few things: melted silver and other valuables that the Yankees had missed. They also found more burnt and blackened corpses of soldiers. Emma LeConte wrote in her diary: "How I rejoice to think of any of them being killed. . . . if only the whole army could have been roasted alive." Soon the last of the bodies, those missed by the burial details and the citizens, were found by buzzards.

Dr. William Reynolds had managed to save his house intact amid the surrounding ruins. His daughter Lottie was standing in front of it when she saw a man driving ahead of him a Federal soldier—a captured straggler. As the two passed by, the guard asked her: "What shall I do with this man?" A wave of hatred hit her. She answered, deliberately: "Kill him." The silent look that the prisoner gave her stayed in her mind's eye from then on. The man was not killed, and afterward, she said, she felt glad of it; but "in that moment all she had to suffer seemed to burn out every feeling of pity and she knew what war was."

CHAPTER 2

THE AGGRESSIVE WAR: JACKSON

DURING SEPTEMBER 1862, Harriott Horry Ravenel heard in Columbia that Lee's army had entered Maryland. Expressing her hopes for Confederate independence though using the wrong words, she commented to her mother: "I believe that Washington in ruins would give peace to both sections of the country." She was not alone in her choice of methods. From the beginnings of secession until the last surrender, and in wishful thinking thereafter, many Southerners called for devastation of the North. The shock of ruin would show misguided Yankees that they must accept Confederate independence or risk still greater destruction. Faced with such a drastic threat, Northerners would learn, sooner than many distant battles could teach them, that war cost more than they were willing to pay. Before leaving the United States Senate, both Jefferson Davis and Louis T. Wigfall warned that Northern wealth might be destroyed by the burning of Northern cities, while Southern prosperity lay safe in crops produced by incombustible land. Davis said on January 10, 1861: "The torch and sword can do their work with dreadful havoc, and starving millions would weep at the stupidity of those who had precipitated them into so sad a policy."

Throughout its brief history the Confederate States of America depended on its ability to wage war. Without proof of that ability, everyone knew, the Confederate nation would vanish. Though convincing European governments was important, independence could be secure only when Yankees conceded the superior power of Southern warmaking; the sooner they felt its strength the sooner they would acknowledge the Confederacy. Advocates of hurting the Yankees in their homes began to make their case before the Federal army had moved into the South. A month after the firing on Fort Sumter, Annie R. Maney wrote: "I only pray God may be with us to give us strength to conquer them, to exterminate *them*, to lay waste every Northern city, town and village, to destroy them utterly." The Memphis *Avalanche* suggested in August 1861: "The bombardment of a few Northern cities would bring our enemies to their senses." As Northern soldiers started to damage the South, Confederates called for retaliation by their own army. Advocating "desolations of the firesides," the Norfolk *Day Book* said in February 1862: "Such a war would thrill the South from the Potomac to the Rio Grande." During the spring Governor John Letcher of Virginia and the editor J. D. B. DeBow pressed the same case. Attacks on civilians would be designed not simply to restrain the enemy's army but to punish the populace for its audacity in supporting an assault on the Confederacy. Long before Federal soldiers had grown purposeful and efficient in de- structive work, Southerners urged the Confederate government to strike decisively at Northerners, who had set a precedent for a war of invasion against civilians. For many Southerners aggressive war offered the best means of establishing their new nation swiftly and conclusively. After decades of sectional crises, years of threats to secede, and months of debate between eager and reluctant secessionists, an assault on the North would demonstrate at once the reality of the Confederacy and the power of its new citizenry.

The Confederate army's main movements into the North came later in the war and failed. Nevertheless, they rested on the original argument that Southerners' best hope for independence lay in taking the war to Yankees. Lee's invasions of Maryland and Pennsylvania in 1862 and 1863 did not go far or last long, but he undertook them in hope of great results. In both instances he expected to keep his army in Pennsylvania for months, preferably until late in the fall, when bad weather ended the season for active campaigning. In addition to relieving Virginia of the armies' presence and finding rich supplies, the Confederates, Lee believed, could influence Northern politics. A prolonged invasion would show how far from success the Lincoln administration's effort to defeat seces- sion had fallen. Democrats opposing war against the South and against slavery would gain support from other Northerners who suddenly would realize how strong the Confederates remained. If enough people gave up on coercion, they might force an armistice on the government. A cease- fire would lead to Confederate independence despite Northern peace men's professed hope for ultimate reunion. Lee's calculations for a success- ful campaign depended on his army's influence on the minds of civilians.

Most Southerners welcomed this policy in 1862. In the Confederate

THE EASTERN THEATER OF THE WAR

House of Representatives, William Porcher Miles, eager to "make the enemy feel the horrors of war," won passage of a resolution applauding Lee's invasion by a vote of 63–15. Five days later the *Richmond Dispatch* said: "We hope the troops will turn the whole country into a desert, as the Yankees did the Piedmont country of Virginia." Edward A. Pollard, an editorial writer for the *Richmond Examiner,* recalled after the war that Lee's designs for his advance into the North "were much more moderate than those commonly entertained by the Confederate public." In the west Elise Bragg, with many others, urged her husband, Braxton, to take his army to Cincinnati and "make our enemies feel . . . what it is to have our homes invaded, property destroyed." Though he did not get beyond Kentucky, he boasted afterward that he had subsisted his army on the enemy's countryside for two months.

When Lee reached Pennsylvania in 1863, he issued an order forbidding plunder. After the war, former Confederates never tired of quoting the order to contrast the South's civility with the ruthlessness of Yankees. Yet, while he was in Carlisle, Alexander Pendleton, former aide to Stonewall Jackson, said of the Pennsylvanians: "The only way to touch them is to burn their property, and much as I deplore the horrors of war, I am ready to begin it." Lee did not want this kind of devastation. He thought that looting would undermine his army's cohesion. But anyone who had observed the marches of 60,000-man armies could have predicted the effect of a summer's sojourn by such a force among the prosperous farms of Pennsylvania. The ruin wrought by both armies in Virginia had given Lee one of his motives for taking the war out of that state. He issued his order forbidding plundering only after looting had begun; house-breakings, thefts, destruction of property, and the private seizure of food continued despite the order. No matter what superior level of discipline or decency the Army of Northern Virginia might aspire to maintain, invasion brought depredation. Many soldiers were not sorry to see Yankees suffer. The army's damage seemed almost to happen of its own accord. Louis T. Wigfall's son commented: "One feels much more like a spectator and doesn't have any sense of regret at the unavoidable destruction in the line of march of an army." Without a supply line from the South, Lee's army could not stay long in one place, because the nearby food would soon be consumed. The army would have to move to fresh fields or widen the range of its confiscations. Lee's original plan, cut short by the unexpected battle of Gettysburg, entailed the stripping of swaths through eastern Pennsylvania.

In 1863 and 1864, as Northern armies combined greater success with greater destruction, Southerners demanded reprisal. The *Savannah Republican*—having said on June 23, 1863, "Let Yankee cities burn and their fields be laid waste"—noted with satisfaction three days later that a large majority of Southern newspapers shared the *Republican*'s eagerness for retaliation. Like many others, John S. Foster concluded in May that, to achieve peace, Confederates must invade the North "and let the negro worshipers have a taste of what we have experienced for two years." Desire for revenge pushed some Southerners toward fantasy. Captain Elijah Petty wanted to form one grand army which would "cut & thrash and lay wast as we go" until it reached Boston and eradicated every seed of abolitionism. Newspaper editors' fertile imaginations thrust 40,000 men into Pennsylvania, columns of 50,000 into various sectors, and an army of 200,000 into the North, desolating as it advanced. All of these strategists could agree in 1864 that the Confederates, during their brief opportunity in Pennsylvania, had shown what the *Mobile Tribune* called "mistaken philanthropy." As Sherman marched through Georgia, Howell Cobb, Jr., consoled himself with the hope of returning the devastation tenfold: "It would be a joyous sight to see the homes of the Villains . . . crumbling beneath devouring flames."

Davis's government tried to bring fire to Northern cities. Confederate agents entered New York City in November 1864 and started simultaneous fires in ten hotels in different parts of Manhattan on November 25. The original plan, authorized by Jacob Thompson, intended these as a diversion while antiwar Democrats seized control of the city. Though the New Yorkers withdrew from this scheme after Lincoln's re-election, the Southerners went ahead with arson. Captain Robert C. Kennedy, a Confederate officer who set four fires, afterward explained: "In retaliation for Sheridan's atrocities in the Shenandoah Valley we desired to destroy property, not the lives of women and children, although that would of course have followed in its train." Reporting the incendiaries' failure to Secretary of State Judah P. Benjamin, Thompson blamed it on the use of phosphorus: "Reliance on the Greek fire has proven a misfortune. It cannot be depended on as an agent in such work." Other plans for sabotage also had little plausible claim to be steps toward stopping the Northern war effort. Aggressive war, first conceived as a means to expedite Confederate independence, lost its aura of political promise as Southern prospects faded. Yet doing damage in the North retained its appeal even when it no longer offered security to the Southerners' nation. Visions of attack became primarily sour thoughts of wreaking revenge on the Yankees.

On July 30, 1864, after Jubal Early's diversionary raid north of Washington, his subordinate, General John McCausland, burned Chambersburg, Pennsylvania, obeying Early's orders which named several Virginians whose homes Yankees had destroyed. Early offered to spare the city in return for a payment of $100,000 in gold or $500,000 in greenbacks. The citizens had no such sum and refused to pay anything. The fire destroyed more than 300 buildings, while Confederate soldiers rifled houses and robbed people. A cavalryman wrote in his diary that night: "There were some who having become drunk seemed to glory in spreading destruction." Lieutenant Fielder C. Slingluff later recalled that soldiers welcomed the order: "We had long come to the conclusion that it was time for us to burn something in the enemy's country." On the way out of town they set fire to the home of the county superintendent of public schools, telling his family that they did so because "he had taught negroes." Unlike Atlanta and Columbia, Chambersburg was neither a fortified, defended city nor the site of munitions plants and other military manufacturing. It was just a city the Confederates could reach. Its destruction, for which Early continued to claim credit long after the war, was an act of revenge preceded by an attempt at terror. In Richmond, General Josiah Gorgas noted: "The burning of Chambersburgh by Early gives intense satisfaction."

The justness of revenge, the principal Confederate argument for hurting Northern civilians after the first year of war, was the same proposition Northerners invoked in support of punishing rebels for starting the war and sabotaging the union. From the first, the prevalent public voices calling for victory defined no clear break in the continuum of revenge, no categorical distinction between firing on Fort Sumter and burning Chambersburg or Columbia. The South did not have a distinctive approach to war. Though many Southerners thought invasion of the North morally or militarily unsound, the most popular images of Confederate independence were compatible with images of attacks on the civilian population of the North. Southerners often contrasted the humane Lee with various vicious Federal generals. But to want to harm more Yankees than Lee had hurt did not make one less of a Confederate. Historians often have traced the changing character of the Civil War, starting as a conflict restricted to armies and increasingly becoming a war against Southern civilians as well. Extensive and successful use of invasion, devastation, and terror belonged to the Federal army. The conception belonged to civilians and soldiers of both the North and the South. Americans did not invent new methods of drastic war during the Civil War so much as they made real a version of conflict many of them had talked about from the start. Despite their differing fates in this kind of war, people in both sections understood it to be their means to vindicate a nation. Northerners and Southerners, especially Southerners, found that destructive war embraced not only the enemy but also its advocates.

A CONFEDERATE GENERAL, Thomas Jonathan Jackson, epitomized for many of his contemporaries the pursuit of Confederate independence through aggressive warfare. The sobriquet "Stonewall," which he and the First Virginia Brigade acquired by virtue of their stand during the first battle of Bull Run, did not fit with Jackson's approach to fighting in later campaigns. Movement and risk pervaded his operations. To stop the Federal war effort, Jackson believed, Southerners should quickly make its cost as high as possible. He would have preferred that Confederates take no prisoners but kill every Yankee soldier they could reach. In January 1861 he wrote that, if Virginia were invaded, its people should "defend it with a terrific resistance—even to taking no prisoners." Governor Letcher recalled later in the war that a week after the state seceded, Jackson had urged on him the policy of flying the black flag, "proposing to set the example himself." This policy would also make Southerners fight desperately because they would know that capture meant death.

From 1861 until his death in May 1863, Jackson sought a war of invasion. He and his closest political ally, Congressman A. R. Boteler, repeatedly recommended taking the Confederate army into the North. During February 1862 Jackson wrote to Boteler: "In one of your letters you spoke of our moving on Philadelphia to do this would require well disciplined troops. If the move could be successfully executed it would be of vast service to us." In March he was eager to advance: "Let us make thorough work of it. . . . Now we may look for war in earnest." The Reverend James R. Graham, Jackson's host in Winchester during the winter, afterward quoted the general as saying that, to fight the enemy, armies should "invade his country and do him all possible damage in the shortest possible time." Boteler pressed the idea of invasion on Jefferson Davis in May, and it appealed, in principle, to General Lee, who wrote: "It would change the character of the war. . . . Jackson could in that event cross into Maryland and Penn." Lee still liked the plan a year later. On February 23, 1863, Jackson ordered his cartographer, Jedediah Hotchkiss, to draft a map extending to Harrisburg and Philadelphia. A week later he wrote to Boteler: "I am cordially with you in favor of carrying the war North of the Potomac." He envisioned a campaign different from that which Lee undertook in June. Lee acknowledged that he could not hope for a lasting military occupation of Pennsylvania. Jackson agreed; instead of speaking, as Lee did, of living off the land and relieving Virginia for several months, Jackson talked about cities and about making the North feel the war.

The evidence for describing Jackson's conception of war in Pennsylvania comes from postwar recollections of those who heard him. Their accounts agreed that he wanted the army not just to subsist itself but to wreak destruction. He said in September 1862 that "he desired to get in Pennsylvania & give them a taste of war . . . they were so near and yet so bitter." To the objection that the enemy army could then get in the Confederates' rear, Jackson "replied there was t[w]o rears." Early in the war he told General Gustavus W. Smith that Confederates should "destroy industrial establishments wherever we found them, break up the lines of interior commercial intercourse, close the coal mines, seize and, if necessary, destroy the manufactories and commerce of Philadelphia, and of other large cities within our reach; take and hold the narrow neck of country between Pittsburg and Lake Erie, subsist mainly on the country we traverse, and making unrelenting war amidst their homes, force the people of the North to understand what it will cost them to hold the South in the Union at bayonet's point."

Almost every assessment of Stonewall Jackson by those who knew him during the war, both admirers and detractors, stressed one quality: relentlessness. He ordered hard marches; he denied applications for furloughs; he severely punished infractions of discipline; he arrested officers who departed from his instructions; he ordered soldiers absent without leave to be brought back to the army in irons; he had deserters shot—during three days in August 1862, thirteen of his men were executed; he tried to kill as many of the enemy as possible, and he did not shrink from getting his own men killed doing it. Jackson did not go through the Civil War's often-described transition from notions of chivalric gallantry to brutal attrition. For him the war was always earnest, massed, and lethal. His preference for invasion across the Mason-Dixon line complemented, in strategy, his preference for the tactical offensive in battle. He favorably endorsed John D. Imboden's proposal to form a regiment of rangers to fight a guerrilla war in western Virginia, where, Imboden said, "I shall expect to hunt Yankees as I would wild beasts." Jackson cautioned Robert L. Dabney about this partisan warfare: "The difficulty consists in finding sufficient patriotic nerve in men to join in such service."

Before Virginia seceded, Jackson assumed that coercion by the North would include turning the slaves against Southern whites. Congressman Boteler predicted "black revolution" in the South if Lincoln ruled uncontested. While Lincoln was still denying that the North was fighting to abolish slavery, Jackson said the war would become one for abolition whether Lincoln knew it or not. The war was, "for our people, *a struggle for life and death,* and it would have been best for the people to have its true character unmasked to them from the first." If his recommendation had been followed, soldiers would have known "that when they went into action it must be victory or death literally for them, as it is going to be for their country." Jackson's analogy suggested that the citizen's life

belonged to the nation, deriving its significance from the nation's continued existence. The Confederacy would prevail because its fighting men
showed that their devotion and aggressiveness knew no limit. The enemy,
less fully identified with his country, would concede the Confederates'
superiority and national independence. This emphasis on the primacy of
public duty, which could make a soldier execute disarmed prisoners and
risk the same fate if he did not die in combat, found some support from
William Tecumseh Sherman. In March 1865 a staff officer told Sherman
"what Stonewall Jackson said as to not taking prisoners. 'Perhaps he was
right,' said the General. 'It seems cruel; but if there were no quarter given,
most men would keep out of war. Rebellions would be few and short.' "
Many Northerners besides Sherman saw in Jackson's version of patriotic
war a model for defeating Jackson's cause. In the contest between Northerners' and Southerners' devotion to their respective nations, Yankees
turned out not to be so inferior as Jackson had hoped. Northerners
respected Jackson's severity so much that they first exaggerated it, then
emulated it, finding in him a kindred spirit.

As an evocative figure, Jackson attained a unique stature in the North
by his success in the Shenandoah Valley Campaign in May and June 1862.
With 17,000 men, he chased 8,000 Federals down the valley to the
Potomac, then used the forks of the Shenandoah and the terrain of the
valley to keep separated the superior forces converging to pursue him.
Fighting three small armies sequentially, he inflicted twice as many
casualties as he sustained, and he helped induce Lincoln to withhold
45,000 men from the Federal forces approaching Richmond. Southerners
liked to believe that Jackson's advance to the Potomac had caused panic
in the North and thrown fear into Lincoln and Secretary of War Stanton.
This greatly overstated the case. Nevertheless, the name of Stonewall
Jackson thereafter carried vivid associations. Confederate sympathizers in
Baltimore celebrated his approach. On the afternoon of May 25, in the
street outside the War Department's offices, Senators William Pitt Fessenden and James W. Grimes kidded their antislavery colleague, Senator
Charles Sumner, by telling him that Federal troops were fleeing in the
valley and he would be among the first to be executed when Jackson
reached the capital. Baltimore and Washington were in no danger, but
Jackson, by his audacity, had established himself in Northerners' eyes as
"a genuine general." Newspapers promised that he would have to retreat
or get caught. Still, a Federal soldier wrote home a week after the Valley
Campaign: "Jackson . . . is a second Napoleon and . . . to be feared."

In the last week of June, Lee's repulse of George B. McClellan's army
in the Seven Days battles east of Richmond confirmed this view of
Jackson. Though Jackson wanted to go into Pennsylvania, Lee called him

from the valley to join the Army of Northern Virginia and help bring superior numbers to bear against the right wing of the Army of the Potomac. Lee's poorly coordinated attacks met strong resistance. For reasons that have been much debated, Jackson and his men were slow to take aggressive action—too slow, Lee complained in a postwar conversation. Northern supporters of the war, however, had expected McClellan to take Richmond. When, instead, the Army of the Potomac fell back to the bank of the James River and gave up the offensive, a popular explanation in the North spoke of the sudden flanking onslaught of Stonewall Jackson, who had swooped down from the Blue Ridge, sowing terror in his track. A woman working in the Army of the Potomac's field hospitals described her situation on June 26: "Running away down the Pamunkey again as fast as we can go, escaping from Stonewall Jackson!" The *New York Times* explained that "Stonewall Jackson rushed from the Valley of the Shenandoah . . . and got in the rear of our whole army" by a *"coup de guerre." Harper's Weekly* described his "sudden appearance" and "the furious attacks of enormous rebel armies." Confederate strength seemed to come from audacity; an editorial in the *Times* urged the Federals to follow Jackson's example. Henry W. Bellows, head of the United States Sanitary Commission, hoped that a rumor of Jackson's death was true: "He has evinced more genius & more real adequacy to military success than any body on either side."

The second battle of Bull Run at the end of August and the Confederate invasion of Maryland in September enhanced Jackson's reputation as a threat to the safety of Washington and the North. Writing about "the ubiquitous Jackson," one Northern soldier said that he "turned both flanks" of the Federal army at Bull Run. Though all of Lee's army participated in these operations, Jackson was the general who outmaneuvered John Pope's army, who took Harpers Ferry and its garrison, who attracted the most sensational notice as an invader. The day before Confederates started to cross the Potomac, the Associated Press reported that Jackson was headed for Baltimore, while Federal soldiers near Washington heard that 200,000 rebels were coming and were "swearing they would enter Washington or pile the ground with their men." Private Samuel E. Radcliffe warned his father: "Look out or Jackson will soon take Harrisburg and then Philadelphia." Jackson had become the Confederate perhaps most widely known in the North, certainly the most vividly described.

Northerners were learning from the battles of 1862 that Southerners would fight more bitterly and successfully than most people in the North had imagined. Confederate weaknesses apparent by 1862 attracted less comment than the unexpected instances of Confederate audacity and dedication. Jackson embodied this newly discovered Southern wrath. Jackson, Northerners said, was sincere. He hit the Federals as hard as he could, again and again, because he wanted to win the war and break up the union. The specter of him as an invader took on a sinister cast because he might do anything to accomplish his purposes. Talking to people in Maryland, a Federal soldier found that "the greatest horror is entertained of Jackson whom they seem to regard as a species of demon." Some residents of Harrisburg spoke to a *New York Herald* correspondent as if Jackson would "drop into their midst like a fallen angel, and devour them." Later in the autumn, in response to another alarm about Jackson marching northward, General John W. Geary warned his wife, who lived in Harrisburg: "Escape if you can, for he is a cold blooded rascal." Black people in the Shenandoah Valley fled before his army during the May campaign because they expected him to massacre them.

Wendell Phillips exploited Jackson's reputation for his own purposes. He preached vigorous Northern prosecution of the war as the quickest way to destroy the slave system. With his customary knack for the most provocative way to publicize his arguments, he called for a Northern general and a Northern war effort as single-minded as the Southerners'. Speaking at the Cooper Institute on January 21, 1863, he said: "No man can fight Stonewall Jackson, an honest fanatic on the side of slavery, but John Brown, an equally honest fanatic on the side of freedom." Even people lacking Phillips's enthusiasm for emancipation saw in Jackson the illustration of a connection between radical ruthlessness and victory. On the evening of January 24, Jedediah Hotchkiss took a copy of the *New York Herald* to Jackson's headquarters and read Phillips's speech to the general, who in 1859 had witnessed John Brown's execution. The abolitionist and the slaveholding secessionist had found common ground in methods of waging war: no quarter.

At the same time that Jackson showed he could roam, like Satan, to and fro, he reminded Northerners of Oliver Cromwell. Thomas Carlyle had helped make Cromwell an emblem of power achieved through certitude and fighting. Descriptions of Jackson fit him to the type Carlyle had defined. Writers repeatedly used the word "fanatic" in suggesting that Jackson's belief in a "God of vengeance" gave him extraordinary influence over his soldiers, making their attacks, according to a *New York Times* correspondent, "unique and irresistible." His piety—"the bluest kind of Presbyterian"—complemented his secessionist dedication and his aggressive combat: they were interlocking attributes of a consistent personality.

Confederates, too, likened Jackson to Cromwell, meaning to praise him; and even the Northern portrait of a malevolent zealot contained, as in Phillips's speech, backhanded praise. Jackson epitomized qualities Yankees admired. He was direct, competent, courageous, devout, and patriotic; it was just that, unfortunately, like his fellow rebel Americans, he perverted the national virtues that he simultaneously exemplified. Catherine Cooper Hopley told her British readers in 1863 that most people in the North "pride themselves that he was a fellow-citizen of the republic, an AMERICAN, independent of Northern or Southern birth." *Harper's Weekly* described him as "an honorable and conscientious man" who had long hesitated when secession forced him to choose sides. Federal prisoners taken by his troops sometimes cheered Jackson; army diaries and letters praised his dedication and looked for comparable qualities among Federal commanders. After the fighting at South Mountain in September 1862 and after the battle of Fredericksburg in December, units of the Army of the Potomac prided themselves on being called "Stonewall." Yankees might fear Jackson, but it was hard to hate him; he was like them. Jackson showed how a democratic society ought to fight a war for the nation.

In later years General Thomas Church Haskell Smith of Massachusetts argued that Jackson ought to have been a Federal general because he had the makings of a popular leader in a republic. Alone among Confederates he was suited to be the founder of a nationality. But he and the South were prisoners of the antirepublican institution of slavery and of the "caste" or "faction" of slaveholders. If Jackson's mind could have escaped this thralldom, he would have fought on the side more compatible with his egalitarian nature. To Smith, Jackson represented the antebellum South's temporarily thwarted potential for fully embracing American progress. He was "a man of the future of the South—not of its maddened self destroying present . . . American not sectional in his character." He and his fellow Confederates had died in defense of a doomed aristocracy which dared not entrust supreme power to a man of the people. If he had sided with the union, the North would have won the war quickly. Jackson's popular appeal, derived in large part from his military aggressiveness, made him best suited for uniting war and modern democracy, as the North succeeded in doing.

John Greenleaf Whittier's wartime poem "Barbara Frietchie" drew for its appeal on this confidence that Jackson was an American. If Jackson had not seemed a ruthless invader—ordering his men, Whittier wrote, to fire into the only house in Frederick, Maryland, showing the Stars and Stripes—his confrontation with the gray-haired Barbara Frietchie would have had little significance, since the patriotic woman would not have been risking her life. Had Jackson not also been fundamentally an American, Barbara Frietchie's call to him to spare "your" country's flag would not have evoked in him, as it did, a "shade of sadness, a blush of shame," thereby stirring his "nobler nature." Then he turned his ferocity on his own men and said that anyone who hurt the old woman would die like a dog. Confederates discredited the poem's story, adding that no Southerner, least of all Jackson, would have offered violence to a woman. Whittier's Jackson, though, was not deferring to a lady when he changed his order; he was responding to "that woman's deed and word," recalling him to his former respect for the American flag. The episode was fiction. Yet Whittier insistently defended the truth of the poem's dramatic situation, even after its narrative had been discredited. He wanted to memorialize the woman, "a hater of the Slavery Rebellion," who had aroused the irrepressible Americanism of the rebellion's fiercest champion. In the years since the Civil War, the proposition that Stonewall Jackson embodied distinctively American qualities has appealed to people with an array of diverse motives. But it first found currency among Northerners devoted to the defeat of the Confederacy and to the abolition of slavery. They detected in Jackson's fervent, efficient war-making a gift native to the United States which could be employed for the country's preservation.

After Virginia seceded, Jackson never lamented the lost union. Sometimes he spoke about the future of the new Confederate republic; occasionally he suggested that he might not survive its war for independence. The notion of his posthumously becoming a hero of the reunited union would have surprised him. He had given himself wholly to the Confederacy. In this new allegiance Jackson broke with an important part of his past. Some of his relatives sided with the unionists in western Virginia, and his sister Laura Jackson Arnold became an outspoken supporter of the Northern cause, greeting and nursing Federal soldiers. From the war years through the first decade of the twentieth century she denounced the Confederacy. First the soldiers visiting her home in Beverly, then the veterans meeting her at reunions in Ohio, found in Stonewall Jackson's sister the same courageous resolve as the Confederate general's—in her case, devoted to the United States. Brother and sister, orphaned at an early age, had grown up separately in the homes of relatives but had remained closely tied to each other. Thomas's frequent letters to Laura were rivaled in expressions of love and solicitude only by his wartime letters to his wife. For ten years he worked to convert Laura from unbelief to Christianity, which she accepted in 1858. He took a strong interest in the upbringing of her children, and she visited the Jacksons in Lexington in 1859. Thomas assumed in 1855 that, "in the event of trouble between N. & S.," he and Laura would side with the South and that, if their half-brother Wirt Woodson moved to a free state, "he would stand on one side and we on the opposite." However, in 1861 Thomas's correspondence with Laura stopped. During the war, Jackson asked travelers who had recently come from western Virginia for news about her. One of them recalled in 1863: "He regretted that his sister Mrs. Arnold entertained union sentiments, but his expressions about her were kind but brief." He named his second daughter, born in 1862, Julia Laura, after his mother and his sister.

By September 1861, Laura Arnold was being praised in the *Cincinnati Commercial* for her "unremitting attention" to sick Federal soldiers. A Federal surgeon described her: "Almost alone, amidst a disloyal community, she unflinchingly declared her devotion to the flag, not only by word but act." Soldiers calling on her in the summer of 1862 found that "she was staunch for the Union and gave us her blessing as we left." She seldom spoke of her brother as he grew in fame, "except to regret that he had taken up arms against his country." In later years she remained a fervent "union patriot." She did not want to hear the sobriquet "Stonewall"; she told a reporter that her brother had gained admission to the United States Military Academy by cheating on the entrance examination. When General Jackson rejected applications for furloughs, telling his men that they must put their country before their family, he did not surpass the implacable patriotism of his sister.

FAR MORE than most of his admirers realized, T. J. Jackson had constructed by his own design the public character that brought him fame. His friend and brother-in-law D. H. Hill later said: "The biographer of Stonewall Jackson is a poor philosopher who does not point out the connection between the severe struggles of the *man* with himself & the giant wrestling of the *General* with his enemies." Before Jackson became "Stonewall" he had found an identity through filling the public roles of patriot and evangelical Christian. By making his behavior consistent enough to carry conviction to others, he strove to persuade himself that the consistency arose from an inner harmony of his thoughts and desires. His effort had to be constant; no degree of success could quiet it. Finally it sought to create a nation. Not only would God validate the Confederacy through war, but the Confederacy would also, in the process, validate the man Jackson had made. Both in his own mind and in the minds of many Southerners his character, his beliefs, and his methods seemed inseparable from the new nation's success. This striving on a continental scale brought to a climax the two concerns that long had pervaded his life: his Christian faith and his worldly ambition.

Jackson was born in Clarksburg, Virginia, about January 21, 1824, though he never knew the exact date. His father died in 1826, and his mother in 1831. He was reared in the home of an uncle, Cummins Jackson. Thomas felt grateful to his uncle, but seems always to have expected to make his own way in the world. For this purpose his appointment to the United States Military Academy in 1842 was crucial. There he had to work harder than other cadets to repair the deficiencies of his early education. As a young artillery officer in the war with Mexico, Jackson rose from brevet second lieutenant to brevet major, advancement won in combat and unsurpassed by any other junior officer. After the war he did garrison duty in New York and Florida until 1851, when he left the army to accept a professorship at the Virginia Military Institute. He taught natural philosophy, optics, and artillery tactics until the start of the Civil War. While living in Lexington, Virginia, he married Elinor Junkin, a daughter of the president of Washington College, in August 1853. Her death in October 1854 caused in Jackson a deep depression from which he did not emerge until he toured Europe in the summer of 1856. Not long after his return he married Mary Anna Morrison, daughter of the president of Davidson College in North Carolina. By 1860 their life together had become a comfortable routine, divided between the academic year in Lexington and summer travel.

None of these developments came easily for Jackson. The outwardly stable existence he left for war in 1861 had been achieved at the cost of great anxiety and strivings. His father, Jonathan Jackson, a kind, amiable man, was a lawyer but not a successful one. He lost property and left his wife and three surviving children poor when he died of typhoid fever on March 26, 1826. After supporting herself for a while with the help of her husband's Masonic lodge brothers, Julia Neale Jackson remarried in November 1830. Thirteen months later, afflicted with a fever and severe dysentery, she too died. Her first husband's relatives had opposed her marriage to Blake B. Woodson, an older widower. They evidently pressed her to give up custody of her children; for a while during her pregnancy in 1831 the children stayed with Jonathan Jackson's half-sister but returned to their mother before her death. Afterward, Woodson kept them with him; however, he soon died, and his son W. C. Woodson wrote to Thomas Neale, Julia's father, "to Come after the Children or they would be Bound out." Much to Neale's disgust, Cummins E. Jackson arrived first and took his nephew and niece, Thomas and Laura, to live with their father's relatives. In 1835 the Jacksons gave Laura to the custody of the Neales.

By the age of eleven, Thomas had seen the deaths of an infant sister, his father, his mother, and his stepfather and had been separated from his brother and surviving sister. While a young man, he imagined heaven as "a land where care and sorrow are unknown there with a mother a brother a sister . . . and I hope a father to live in a state of felicity uncontaminated by *mortality.*" Out of the flux of his earliest years, he most vividly recalled his mother, especially the pain of his first parting from her and her death. He thought of her as "the impersonation of sweetness, grace, and beauty." He believed that his and his sister's coming to Christ was the answer to their mother's prayers. When naming his daughter for her, he wrote: "My mother was mindful of me when I was a helpless, fatherless child, and I wish to commemorate her now."

Thomas Neale wanted in 1833 to compel Cummins Jackson to give up Thomas and Laura, suspecting that Jackson wanted "to make drudges of them." Nevertheless, Thomas stayed with his uncle until he left for West Point in 1842. Though he worked for his uncle—driving oxen, hauling logs to the Jackson sawmill, plowing, and tending the mill—he afterward had happy memories of the time. To competitors, creditors, and enemies, Cummins Jackson seemed unscrupulous and vindictive, a shrewd, grasping businessman prone to litigation. At his death he left an estate worth more than $25,000. To those he befriended, he was generous. Three years after Thomas left what he called "my adopted home" he recalled his days there as a life of freedom. His uncle took him bear hunting and made him a jockey in scrub races that Thomas usually won on his uncle's horses. Cummins Jackson joined the gold rush to California, where he died of typhoid fever on December 4, 1849. "This is news which goes to my heart," Thomas wrote. "Uncle was a father to me."

At the age of fifteen or sixteen, Jackson began to experience intense gastrointestinal pains which recurred for almost twenty years. They then bore the general name of "dyspepsia" and may have been caused by ulcers. According to some who knew him, he had a parasitic worm, of which he was eventually cured; but he did not mention this in his frequent lists of his disorders. Hearing about a man driven to suicide by the pain of dyspepsia, Jackson said "he could understand that and thought if a man could be driven to suicide by any cause, it might be from dyspepsia." From the age of eighteen and probably earlier he spent a great deal of time thinking about his health and experimenting with ways to improve it. His familial isolation was mirrored by a physical isolation expressed in the conviction that his body was extraordinarily susceptible to disease.

As an army officer and as a faculty member at the Virginia Military Institute, Jackson worried about his vision, his hearing, his throat, his digestion, his liver, his kidneys, his nervous system, his musculature, and the circulation of his blood. He undertook varying regimens in pursuit of health. On the advice of Dr. Lowrey Barney, a water-cure specialist in New York, he made brown bread a staple of his diet. For a while he gave up butter, which he formerly had relished; then he switched to using butter freely; finally he quit eating brown bread. When his eyes hurt he treated them by putting his face in a basin of cold water six times a day while holding his eyes open. He dosed himself externally with eye medicine, wet cloths, and chloroform liniment; he tried glycerine and nitrate of silver, taken through the nostrils, and inhaled the smoke of burning mullein. He took an ammonia preparation internally. He studied such works as the phrenologist Orson Squire Fowler's *Physiology, Animal and Mental: Applied to the Preservation and Restoration of Health of Body and Power of Mind* and Andrew Combe's *The Principles of Physiology Applied to the Preservation of Health and to the Improvement of Physical and Mental Education.* An avid gardener, Jackson copiously marked his copy of Robert Buist's *The Family Kitchen Gardener* in places where the book described healthful properties of vegetables. When one of his wartime aides remarked that beans were the most nutritious food, Jackson corrected him, saying: "No, rice was 95 per ct & beans only 92." Jackson took notes at temperance lectures; because he enjoyed the taste and the effect of whiskey he hardly ever drank alcohol. He told his sister-in-law that he had absolute control over his appetite. He walked at least five miles a day and did exercises "of a violent character"—so much so that in 1860 he increased the pain he was trying to cure. He became a connoisseur of mineral waters, patronizing resorts and hydropathic establishments from Virginia to Brattleboro, Vermont, and Northampton, Massachusetts. From the Rockbridge Alum Springs he wrote: "This water I consider the water of waters." Sometimes he thought one of his arms was bigger than the other. He raised the heavy arm so that the blood would flow back into his body. Jackson's preoccupation with his body, leading to strenuous efforts to control it and improve its condition, arose in part from his keen empathetic imagination. His sister-in-law later recalled: "He had an incredible natural impatience of, and shrinking from pain." In both the Mexican War and the Civil War he could not stand to visit hospitals. While suffering from an illness he would say that he wished God might let him die. Yet, in praising the teachings of the sixteenth-century Italian writer Luigi Cornaro, Jackson said that "he would not be surprised if, like Cornaro, he lived to be very old."

Jackson never fully outgrew his adolescent awkwardness. As a West Point cadet he found the simplest movements of artillery drill hard to perform. His instructor described him as "raw boned, stiff jointed, and totally devoid of all grace of motion." On the command "Load," Jackson "would go all to pieces" again and again, then return to the position of attention, his sweaty face bearing an expression of "sorrow & suffering." Later he commanded a battery under heavy fire in Mexico and became an artillery instructor. Yet people still said he looked awkward. As a rider, he was secure in the saddle, but other horsemen could never quite see how. In ordinary social intercourse he channeled his inelegant self-consciousness into a set of routinized postures and gestures, never crossing his legs, never letting his back touch the chair in which he sat, holding his spine rigid in order to keep his alimentary canal straight, striving for a precise and polite correctness which made his uneasiness all the more conspicuous. Parts of Jackson's anatomy grew out of proportion: he had big feet, long legs, and long arms. His constrained demeanor, though apparent to most who described him, came not so much from the construction of his body as from his making every movement by deliberate calculation. He seemed always to be thinking about himself.

From the time of his mother's death through his arrival in Lexington, Jackson found himself friendless in a series of new scenes. Uncle Cummins would provide for him; the army would teach him its rules; the Virginia Military Institute would employ him. Jackson found new connections in all these settings, but in all of them he began alone. To loneliness, awkwardness, physical pain, and obsessive uncertainty about his health, Jackson responded with a thoroughgoing effort to make his life orderly. He wrote to his sister in 1850: "It is probable that I am more particular in my rules, than any person of your acquaintance." In addition to his stringent, though changing, dietary restrictions and his exercise regimen, he adhered to strict punctuality, moving through the day with a resolve to be neither late nor early to any appointment. He strove for exact truth and precise meaning in all words written or spoken and worked diligently to avoid errors in grammar or spelling. Despite extreme nervousness and repeated failures, he forced himself to overcome his fear of speaking in public and of offering extemporaneous public prayer. Etiquette was for him as rigorous as military regulations; he determined not to break its rules. In all aspects of his life Jackson wanted never to make a mistake.

Matching the outward coherence of his conduct with his spiritual state, Jackson asserted that God had saved his soul, that God disposed everything that happened to him for the ultimate purpose of his eternal happiness. The beginnings of Jackson's religious faith remain hard to specify. In adulthood he "traced his first sacred impression" back to his mother's lessons. While living with Uncle Cummins, he went to some church services, though his relatives did not. He later recalled that "before the age of maturity, I too endeavored to lead a Godly life, but obstacles so great presented themselves as to cause me to return to the world, and its own." Rumors recorded after his death said he had fathered an illegitimate child while home on furlough from West Point. Before he left the academy he knew he was a Christian, though he waited until 1851 to join the Presbyterian Church. In Mexico he studied Roman Catholicism; during his stay at Fort Hamilton, New York, he was baptized by an Episcopal priest. He admonished his sister for her lack of religious faith. Looking into the infinite future, he warned, "Whilst I am 'to shine like a star in the firmament for ever and ever,' you are to be assigned to *unending misery.*" At the age of twenty-six, Jackson interpreted his earlier afflictions as God's "punishment for my offences against his *Holy* Laws." Thus his pain had turned him "from the path of eternal death to that of everlasting life."

Although Jackson found Presbyterianism to be the denomination most congenial to him, he resisted the doctrine of predestination in the Presbyterian Confession of Faith. He did not want to believe that God, before time began, had chosen the souls to be saved and those to be damned. "His views," the Reverend William S. White said, "were strongly tinctured with Arminianism." Even after joining the church, Jackson felt an aversion to the notion that man could neither choose nor earn salvation: "His repugnance to predestination was long and determined." He eventually brought himself to accept the doctrine; yet the wording of his efforts to bring people to Christ continued to suggest that one could attain grace by an act of will. The sinner who, after being exposed to the gospel, does not "turn to God," he wrote, "deserves the *agonies* of perdition." Contrary to subsequent descriptions of Jackson the Puritan fanatic and narrow-minded dogmatist, he encouraged all forms of Christian faith. He also expressed interest in other religions, even attending a performance by a touring troupe which purported to re-create the rites of the Druids.

Once Jackson had concluded that God loved him and had promised him eternal salvation, this certitude became central to every part of his life—in fact, to his every waking hour. Beyond church services, prayer meetings, and family worship, he surrounded all his routine actions with prayer. As he sealed letters, drank water, took walks, taught classes, or greeted acquaintances, he commended his actions to God in brief prayers. So pervasive did these rituals become that he hardly had to remind himself to perform them. His minister in Lexington later wrote: "Jackson's faith not only made him brave, but gave form, order, direction and power to his whole life." In the army and in Lexington he found other Christians with whom he enjoyed long talks about points of doctrine, worship practices, and evangelizing. He especially enjoyed conversations with ministers, whose calling he deemed the highest to which a man could aspire. He said that, "had his education fitted him for it, and had he more of the gift of speaking, he would have entered the pulpit." In these talks with fellow believers and in communal prayer, much of Jackson's awkwardness fell away. He surprised people with the articulateness of his views on matters of faith, and he moved others with the earnestness and eloquence of his spontaneous prayers. His manner of speaking in prayer, one minister noticed, was *"wholly* unlike his common quick & stern emphasis: on the contrary, tender, soft, pleading, almost plaintive." The intensity of religious feelings shared with others gave some intimation of the coming millennium and the end of the troubles Jackson knew well. He put a special marking by the fourth verse of the twenty-first chapter of the Book of Revelation and underlined the crucial words: "And God shall wipe away all tears from their eyes; and there shall be no more *death,* neither *sorrow,* nor *crying,* neither shall there be any more *pain:* for the former things are passed away."

Jackson strictly observed the Sabbath as a day of rest devoted to God. He abstained from secular activities. The government's practice of transporting and delivering mail on Sunday offended him; he never opened letters on Sunday and always sent mail early enough that it would not travel on the Sabbath. Jackson's lyrical descriptions of Sundays revealed how much he enjoyed departing from the rigorous routine of the other six days, devoting his time instead to worship, to thinking and reading and talking about religion, and to enjoying the natural beauties with which God had surrounded him. He felt ashamed that in one respect he took the day of rest too far: he often slept through the sermon.

Unlike those many anxious Christians who constantly examined the state of their souls and expressed fears that they were damned, Jackson categorically asserted that he had no doubts, that he lived in serene confidence of God's favor. During the war he told Dr. Hunter McGuire: "I have no fears whatever that I shall ever fall under the wrath of God. I am as certain of my acceptance & heavenly reward, as that I am sitting here." He asserted this confidence so strenuously that one wonders why serenity needed such iteration. In any case, it had not always been thus. Upon first coming to Lexington, Jackson found a friend in John Lyle, a bookdealer and an earnest Christian. He confided to Lyle that, although he had felt much concern about salvation for some time, he "had almost despaired of mercy." He said he was willing to "follow the Saviour," but when Lyle advised him to begin family prayer, he replied: "I am not fit to pray in my family. I am not religious yet." Lyle persuaded him, and Jackson reported within days that "peace had followed." Even so, Jackson's spiritual certainty had to be continually won through constant effort. In his Bible he marked the colloquy between Jesus and the father of the boy who was possessed: "Jesus said unto him, If thou canst believe, all things are possible to him that believeth. And straightway the father of the child cried out, and said with tears, Lord, I believe; help thou mine unbelief." Jackson underlined the last four words. His markings in religious books suggested a special interest in the pains suffered by those who did not believe. After his sister became a Christian, Jackson told her not to tolerate for a moment the thought that temptations might yet cause her to be cast away; "God withdraws his sensible presence from us to try our faith." Jackson's evangelical intensity in bringing others to conversion, his frequent declarations of happiness, and his exulting in spiritual superiority over the unregenerate revealed his awareness of the strength of the enemy, despair. He wrote in 1859: "I have been taught never to despair, but to wait, expecting the blessing at the last moment."

Jackson came nearest to despair in life, if not in the soul, after his first wife died. Elinor Junkin Jackson left much less of a record than her sister, Margaret Junkin Preston, a prolific poet and memoirist. Elinor and Margaret had an intense attachment to each other. They shared the same room, dressed alike, and spent much of their time together doing the same things. Jackson described Elinor as "an intellectual, pure, and lovely lady." A woman who knew her said that her "vivacity and beauty" had brought her other suitors, but Jackson was the first to win her love. D. H. Hill thought that his wife had played matchmaker; she mediated between Thomas and Elinor to renew the engagement after Elinor had ended it, leaving Thomas distraught. As the wedding day approached, Margaret Junkin reacted unhappily to the prospect of losing part of her sister's attention. Thomas evidently accused her of trying, at least unconsciously, to prevent the marriage. She acknowledged to Elinor, "I deserved the reproof," and concluded: "Instead then of letting *you* go, I will try & add *him.*" In fact, she accompanied Elinor and Thomas on their honeymoon trip to Niagara Falls. Elinor did not move out of her parents' house; instead, Thomas lived in the Junkin home. The Junkins had been surprised at first that Elinor felt attracted to "such a grave and ungraceful person" but soon approved her judgment. She found a conscientious, appealing man behind his awkwardness and idiosyncrasies. They shared their Christian faith, and she recognized, as she playfully told him, "that Duty was the goddess of his worship." Within fifteen months of their wedding she died in childbirth and was buried with her dead baby.

In marriage Jackson escaped much of his isolation. Ten weeks after the wedding he wrote to his sister: "The weather here is beautiful and I am enjoying life. To me my wife is a great source of happiness." He enjoyed her telling him her thoughts, "joyous as well as afflictive." He looked forward to her welcome at the end of his working day, when she soothed his "troubled spirit by her ever kind, sympathizing heart, words, and love." Then, unexpectedly, he again found himself alone. On the cold day of her burial, after a cadet honor guard and the mourners had left the gravesite, Jackson remained by the open grave, holding his uniform cap in his hand and looking extremely pale. The Reverend White slowly walked back from the gate of the cemetery and led him away. He continued to live in the Junkin home after his wife's death and persevered in his duties at the Institute and his activities in Lexington. But he repeatedly thought of death, Elinor's and his own. He visited her grave daily, experiencing almost irresistible impulses to dig up her coffin and open it. More than a year after the funeral he wrote: "I look forward with delight to the day when I shall join *her.*" He scrupulously avoided defying God's will by wishing she had not died. He repeatedly insisted that God intended this affliction, too, for his good. But he grieved for almost two years, and people in Lexington thought he might lose his reason. Jackson afterward said that, by taking a trip to Europe, he had torn himself away "from that state of mind which I feared." More than any other experience, his wife's death strained his assurance that God's will was beneficent. He often told his second wife, "with the greatest fervor and tenderness," that he did not want to outlive her; he hoped, "whatever trial his Heavenly Father sent upon him, *this* might be spared."

Jackson met Mary Anna Morrison when she and her sister visited Lexington during his engagement to Elinor Junkin. He considered Anna the "more beautiful" and "more fascinating" of the two sisters and called on them, at least briefly, almost every day of their six-week stay. He renewed the acquaintance in 1857, and they were married on July 16. Within two weeks of the wedding she became pregnant. For the first time, Jackson acquired his own home in Lexington, where he and his wife enjoyed their life together. He showed his love by speaking endearments in Spanish, which he thought a more romantic language, by encouraging her good spirits and affectionate disposition, by constantly restating his love, and by demonstrating it physically—including his often hiding behind a door in order to surprise her with what she called "a startling caress." She later wrote: "He luxuriated in the freedom and liberty of his home, and his buoyancy and joyousness of nature often ran into a playfulness and *abandon* that would have been incredible to those who saw him only when he put on his official dignity." She conformed her daily life to his undeviating routine, and her only surviving expression of distress in marriage arose from their being apart. In January 1863 she told a friend: "I can never cease missing my precious Husband, & his wealth of love & tenderness." Like Elinor Junkin, Anna Morrison was the daughter of a minister who was also a college president. She admired her husband's "deep *fervent piety*"; she called him "my spiritual guide, my *comforter* in all trials. I went to him with every thought almost of my heart." In turn, she found him "as confiding as possible." During the war he wrote to her frequently. Alone in his quarters, he talked aloud to her as if she were present. One of his letters from camp said: "I am in a Sibley tent, which is of a beautiful conical shape, and I am sure you would enjoy being in it for a while."

The first child of Anna and Thomas, a girl named Mary Graham Jackson, died of jaundice less than a month after her birth. Their second daughter, born on November 23, 1862, first saw her father during Anna's visit to the army in April 1863. If possible, he was even more demonstrative as a father than as a husband. While with the child "he rarely had her out of his arms, walking her, and amusing her in every way that he could think of." Most of all he feared that he and his wife would love their daughter so much that God would let the child die in order to show them the error of seeking happiness in earthly love.

By the end of the 1850s T. J. Jackson was a lucky—or, as he would have said, a blessed—man. Whether or not his life proved, as he believed, that God destined his happiness, Jackson based his trustworthiness, around which he ordered his personality, on his assurance of God's love. His recurring preoccupations did not differ greatly from those of many other evangelical Christians, determined self-improvers, and troubled seekers of healthful elixirs. Jackson's distinctiveness lay not so much in the substance of his concerns as in the degree to which he depended in every aspect of his life on the certainty of his sanctity. This determination never to give God cause to abandon him defined Jackson as a man who would perform what he promised, or threatened, to do.

EVIDENTLY writing after his first wife's death, Jackson added to the entries in his notebook:

> Objects to be effected by Ellie's D
> To eradicate ambition
>   "   "   resentment
>   " produce humility.

Neither then nor later did Jackson eradicate his ambition; despite his continual striving for humility, a hunger for advancement pervaded his conduct. Robert L. Dabney, Jubal Early, Hunter McGuire, James Power Smith, John Warwick Daniel, and Thomas J. Arnold—Jackson's nephew—all testified to what McGuire called "his natural appetite for glory, until corrected by grace." Americans of Jackson's time often boasted that their country of freedom and equality opened wider than did any other nation the avenues for advancement. Jackson, however, did not treat his ambition as a virtue. To devote himself to it unreservedly would place earthly concerns in competition with God, thereby provoking divine punishment. In his last conversation with D. H. Hill, Jackson said: "The manner in which the press, the army and the people seem to lean upon certain individuals is positively frightful. They are forgetting God in the instruments He has chosen. It fills me with alarm." By cultivating humility even while winning fame he would evade God's wrath because all his advancement would be God's glory and not man's. Richard Taylor, in his clever memoirs, sketched a vivid but caricatured portrait of Jackson during the Civil War. Yet for Jackson's ambition Taylor found an apt figure, perhaps suggested by Nathaniel Hawthorne's story "Egotism; or, the Bosom Serpent." Jackson, with his ambition, was like a man with a "foul serpent" growing out of his body: "He loathed it, perhaps feared it; but he could not escape it—it was himself—nor rend it—it was his own flesh."

The large Jackson family in western Virginia held a leading place in the politics and society of the region. Most were Whigs. One modern historian of West Virginia has described Thomas Jackson as the "scion of the antebellum elite." The business failure of his father left the orphaned boy dependent on relatives, but they were "very numerous and influential." Thomas often said that he hoped to restore the prominence of the Jackson name. When he applied for a professorship at the Virginia Military Institute, he told his sister: "I consider the position both conspicuous and desirable." In the same letter he expressed his pleasure in the news that cousin William L. Jackson would be in the Virginia Constitutional Convention and concluded: "Indeed I have some hopes that our ancient reputation may be revived."

From Lexington he followed his relatives' political efforts. The Jacksons were allied with the Bennetts and the Arnolds; in 1860 the family secured the election of William L. Jackson to the supreme court of appeals. For Thomas this was only a beginning, as he wrote Jonathan M. Bennett: "I am anxious to see us possess that influence in our section of the State that will enable us to secure any office there, by merely nominating a suitable person and concentrating our strength upon him." In fact, the Jacksons, though they might not wield the same power as in the early days of settlement, had not decayed. Thomas was raising himself, not his well-known kin, from obscurity and was joining them as another successful Jackson. Members of his family and their allies helped push him forward from his youth, securing him an appointment as a constable and recommending him for appointment to the United States Military Academy. Their letter to the secretary of war said that Jackson came "from a family which has deserved much of the country," though he had "nothing but his individual exertions to advance him in life." According to one report—which Jackson's friend and biographer R. L. Dabney marked "true" but did not publish—Congressman Samuel Hays, who appointed Jackson to West Point, was an illegitimate son of John G. Jackson. John G. Jackson had served six terms in Congress and had been appointed the first judge of the United States Court for the District of Western Virginia. He was a cousin of Thomas's father. Politically, Hays was allied to the Jacksons and may therefore have seen Thomas's merits more readily. When a boy whom Hays had first appointed left the academy soon after arriving, Jackson became his replacement. Afterward Jackson called Hays "my *best friend*" and told Hays's son: "I am indebted to your father more than to any other man for the deep interest he has taken in my success."

While at West Point, Jackson several times told his sister that he did not intend to make the army a career but wanted to return to western Virginia and enter business. Yet in his copy of one textbook he wrote imaginary orders, addressed to "Brig. General T. J. Jackson, U. S. Army," by which headquarters gave him command of "the Southwestern division of the Army" on December 17, 1884. Either way, the academy would take him from the sawmill to a profession. He later said he had passed the entrance examination "by the skin of his teeth," and he narrowly escaped elimination at his first January examinations. He mastered lessons with great difficulty, sweating profusely while standing at the blackboard, studying after hours by the light of a coal fire. His laborious perseverance became well known among the cadets. The system of memorization, computation, and recitation, though tedious, yielded to diligence. He rose steadily in academic ranking and graduated seventeenth in the Class of 1846. Eight years later, his teacher Dennis Hart Mahan said that Jackson would advance himself in any profession he entered.

Jackson's reputation, based on his courageous conduct and rapid promotion during the war with Mexico, spread in western Virginia and in Lexington after he moved there. He was among the regulars assigned to General Winfield Scott's army, which took Mexico City. At first, assigned to garrison duty, he fretted at not being in action. He speculated that God might be chastising him as a "means of diminishing my excessive ambition," but he still wanted God to "gratify my desire." When he was later asked how he had felt during his first experience of combat, he replied: "Afraid the fire would not be hot enough for me to distinguish myself." By getting a transfer from heavy artillery to Captain John B. Magruder's light artillery battery, Jackson saw action in the Mexico City campaign, especially in the assault on Chapultepec on September 14, 1847. He wrote to his sister in October that he had been "within full ran[ge] and in a road which was swept by grape and canestor and at the same time thousands of muskets from the Castle itself above pouring down like hail upon you." While most of his artillerymen took cover, Jackson kept one piece in action. In response to General William J. Worth's order to fall back, "I sent him back word that with one company of regulars as a support I could carry the work on which he moved forward a whole brigade." Jackson won commendation in his superiors' reports—he made copies of the relevant passages—and promotion to brevet major. Years later, applying for a Confederate commission, he informed Judah P. Benjamin: "At the time of forwarding the resignation of my commission in the U. S. Army my Brevet rank was superior to that of any other West Point graduate who did not enter the Academy previous to myself." Jackson had warned his sister in March 1847 that junior officers did not get their names published in the newspapers. By December the *Harrison Republican* of Clarksburg, Virginia, announced that the conduct of Thomas Jackson in the fighting near Mexico City had been favorably mentioned in official reports.

The peacetime army was a small establishment in which officers' promotions by seniority came slowly; most assignments were to small, remote posts. Many young officers resigned their commissions to pursue position and money in civilian life. Jackson got an unpleasant sample of tedious garrison duty at Fort Meade in Florida. His stay there was embittered by a prolonged quarrel with his superior officer, William H. French, against whom he preferred charges. Jackson had hoped to be sent to Florida "should there be a war of any importance. . . . There is not much glory . . . in fighting Indians: but there is still less in remaining out of the theatre of war." But Fort Meade had little even of that kind of fighting in 1850. Nor did the United States invade Cuba in 1849, though Jackson had anticipated such an expedition in the event that friction with Spain led to war. At Havana, he imagined, "glory could be acquired in facing the veteran troops of Castile."

Still, in 1851, he did not want to leave the military profession. His sister told him that, if he stayed in the army, he would have to live on fame for the present. He replied: "I say not only for the present but during life." Applying for a professorship at the Virginia Military Institute, Jackson called on all of his connections to help him get the appointment. In deciding to leave the army, he reasoned that his professorship would in effect continue a military career, making him at least as likely as regular army officers to receive a high-ranking commission in the next war. Meanwhile, in a country whose people often scorned career soldiers as parasites, he had a conspicuous professorship, for which other West Point graduates had applied and in which he could, he said, "cultivate his mind." Nor was the Institute the limit of his academic ambition. In 1854 he unsuccessfully sought the chair of mathematics at the University of Virginia. His letters of recommendation by Robert E. Lee, Dennis Hart Mahan, and others dwelt on Jackson's strength of character and determination to advance himself. When asked whether such an appointment would take him away from a military career, he said: "It will only prepare me better for it." Jackson intended to distinguish himself in Virginia in peacetime, but he had not abandoned the hope of being a great leader in war.

During his ten years in Lexington, Jackson transformed himself from a peculiar young stranger wearing large, old artillery boots and living upstairs in the Lexington Hotel to a homeowner, a slaveholder, a church deacon, and an investor. Many people, especially Institute cadets, still thought him peculiar, but he had become an established, respected citizen. He accomplished this by persistence. An entry in his notebook read:

will
"You may be what ever you resolve to be.

This maxim, preceded but not followed by quotation marks in the manuscript, often has been attributed to Jackson. But in fact it came from a small book entitled *Lectures to Young Men, on the Formation of Character &c,* published in 1851 by Joel Hawes, a minister in New Haven, Connecticut. Hawes wrote: "My friends, *you may be whatever you resolve to be. Resolution is omnipotent.* Determine that you will be something in the world, and you shall be something. Aim at excellence, and excellence will be attained. This is the great secret of effort and eminence." Jackson remained loyal to Hawes's injunctions to strict observance of the Sabbath, to his argument for Christianity, and to his confidence in the earthly benefits of self-improvement. Jackson often said he could do anything to which he set his mind. In the 1850s he resolved to establish himself and to educate himself. His public life revolved around the Virginia Military Institute and the Reverend William S. White's Presbyterian congregation.

During the Civil War, Jackson said that he was fond of teaching. Unless he was lying, as he almost never did, this remark testifies to his ability to draw enjoyment from mortification. Even the most admiring witnesses agreed that Jackson was a poor teacher. He taught in the way he learned: by rote. He memorized lessons, rehearsing them the night before in the dark or with his eyes closed and his face to the wall, then presented them to the cadets verbatim and seriatim. His notes for one lecture may give some hint of his classroom manner: "In order to explain the physical constitution of bodies we shall adopt the views of Boscovich so far as may be necessary for understanding the subjects which may come under our consideration. According to his theory an atom is an indivisible and inextended element of matter. When two atoms are in sensible contact the forces they exert on each other are called atomic or molecular forces." From the cadets he wanted the same literalness in recitation. Alumni of the Institute remembered his classes in natural philosophy vividly, but not for the reasons teachers usually wish to be remembered. "Discussions in the class-room were unknown, and even explanations were infrequent, and when they did occur they usually left the matter where they found it." Jackson called his first examination period at the Institute a "trying ordeal."

The cadets probably caused Jackson more discomfort than he did them. The principal reason for establishing such military schools was not to provide military training but to impose discipline while trying to educate. Aside from the inevitable unruliness of teen-aged boys in general, many sons of well-to-do Southern families had known little restraint at home. They had learned to regard any curtailment of their freedom of action as an offense to their honor and an insult to their budding freeborn American manhood. According to the Institute's adjutant, a large number of the boys had been sent to the school to be disciplined. The only form of external control to which a gentleman could honorably submit was military authority. Even so, the Institute succeeded only partially in controlling the cadets. Jackson, whom they saw both in class and in artillery exercises, became the butt of practical jokes. Though his Mexican War record won him respect among the boys, his idiosyncrasies—stiff bearing, painfully studied demeanor, strict adherence to regulations, tediousness of instruction, big feet—provoked ridicule and mischief. One person recalled that "he was looked on as being slightly 'cracked.' "

Cadets drew a caricature of Jackson or the picture of a big foot on the blackboard before he entered the section room; they mimicked him when they thought he was not looking; they threw paper pellets at each other behind his back; from hiding they threw or dropped bricks and other projectiles as he walked by. With a serious face, Cadet Davidson Penn asked: "Major, can a cannon be so bent as to make it shoot around a corner?" Adjutant Thomas T. Munford later said: "Major Jackson's *time,* was fully *occupied to maintain himself,* from the *word go.* . . . Jackson was *sick* and *tired & slow* of motion, with great *big* eyes. He would stare at them, I could never tell *whether* in *sympathy* or was disgusted." In artillery drill, they mocked the drawn-out drawl of his regular army method of giving commands. Some cadets went through the motions carelessly, tacitly defying him. Others tried to whirl the artillery pieces in such a way as to make him jump or to trip him with the drag ropes. They loosened the linchpin in the axle of a piece so that a wheel would fall off during maneuvers. Through all of this Jackson persevered, pretending not to notice unless a cadet committed an offense before his eyes. He answered frivolous questions with a straight face. He did not flinch or swerve from the falling objects, though some would have hurt him severely if they had hit him. He gravely suggested that there must be a defect in the manufacture of the linchpins, while the boys marveled at his dull wits. He patiently made careless cadets repeat an exercise until they did it right. As D. H. Hill remembered, "They played tricks upon him, they made sport of him, they teased him, they persecuted him. All in vain."

After five years of experience, Jackson's teaching still left him subject to criticism. In 1856 "no small number" of the Institute's supporters, mainly alumni, told the Board of Visitors "that Professor Jackson wanted capacity adequate to the duties of his chair." The Board of Visitors did not act on the complaint or on Jackson's request for an investigation. Though attempts to have him dismissed failed, he felt slighted by the superintendent, Francis H. Smith, who doubted his qualifications. Smith was a skillful politician, good at getting money for his school from the Virginia legislature. Anna Jackson, however, subsequently recalled him as one who had "never appreciated" her husband. Jackson's position as a professor, like his other achievements, came at the cost of sustained self-control. If he did not eradicate resentment, as he admonished himself to do, he had to swallow a great deal of it.

The church Jackson joined in 1851, after his decision in favor of Presbyterianism, had the largest and most socially prominent congregation among Lexington's churches. As John S. Wise recalled many years later, Lexington was dominated culturally by Scots-Irish Presbyterians of a dour cast. They found Jackson to be a serious, responsible, godly man—an exemplary Christian except for his unfortunate habit of sleeping in church. He reported to the Reverend White as to his spiritual commanding officer and made himself well known by his diligence in church affairs: raising money, tithing from his own income, serving as a deacon. Greatly impressed by one of White's remarks—"in our country the man who could speak multiplied himself by five"—Jackson resolved to make himself a speaker. During a visit to his sister he delivered public lectures on the evidences of Christianity. In Lexington he led a Sunday school class for young men on this subject. His most conspicuously praiseworthy act was his founding of a Sunday school for black children. In 1858 the school had ninety-one children in it. Supervising several teachers, including his wife, he ran it along his usual pedagogical lines: he insisted on punctuality, kept careful attendance records, expounded biblical passages, administered examinations on the children's catechism, reported misconduct to the children's owners, and rewarded good performances with the gift of a New Testament or a Bible. Despite his having no ear or voice for singing, Sunday after Sunday he led the children in the same hymn:

> Amazing grace, how sweet the sound
> That saved a wretch like me.

Some black people later recalled gratefully his sincere concern for their spiritual welfare; others may have responded less enthusiastically. A young black named John, whom Jackson greeted in camp during the war, commented cryptically to one of the general's aides, somewhat in the manner of former Institute cadets: "Oh, I know the major; the major made me get the catechism." The Sunday school, like Jackson's other church activities, manifested piety and selflessness, thereby giving him increased stature in his community. The day after the first battle of Bull Run, Jackson mailed a contribution to the Reverend White. But the accompanying letter from Lexingtonians' newly famous fellow townsman, arriving so soon after the Confederacy's first victory, only said: "In my tent last night, after a fatiguing day's service, I remembered that I had failed to send you my contribution for our colored Sunday-school. Enclosed you will find my check for that object, which please acknowledge at your earliest convenience, and oblige yours faithfully." What a magnificent display of modesty, people commented afterward: no mention of his wounded hand, no account of the heroic stand of the Stonewall Brigade, no more than a hint of his fatigue—only a humble solicitude for God's work. To his wife Jackson wrote on the same day: "Whilst great credit is due to other parts of our gallant army, God made my brigade more instrumental than any other, in repulsing the main attack. This is for your information only—say nothing about it. Let others speak praise—not myself."

Throughout his adult life, Jackson worked to educate himself. Encouraging his niece to strive for perfect grammar and spelling, he recalled the embarrassment he had experienced as a result of his own youthful ignorance. He urged Laura Arnold to let her children live in Lexington to go to school. "Without a good education they must ever fall short of that position in life which they ought to occupy." Jackson read eclectically. He had studied French at West Point; he afterward taught himself Spanish and began to study Latin. Many of his books are preserved in the library of the Virginia Historical Society. Although they do not contain many written marginalia, they are full of markings; some multiple strokes apparently emphasize important passages, while other underlinings seem to show Jackson at work increasing his vocabulary. Religious volumes are conspicuous, including sermons, biblical exegeses, explications of church doctrine, and, of course, Bunyan's *Pilgrim's Progress.* Short, popularized histories and biographies appealed to him, especially those describing the triumphs of leaders. His markings suggest that he took special notice of the rise to power of men and women who made themselves great. He was equally intrigued by those who ruled virtuously and by those who ruined themselves through excess. The careers of Mohammed, Cleopatra, Julius Caesar, Mark Antony, Xerxes, and Cyrus had clear moral lessons, especially in the simplified works of Jacob Abbott. Jackson also read Plutarch, Bancroft, Hallam, von Humboldt, Rollin, Macaulay, Allan Cunningham's *Lives of the Most Eminent British Painters and Sculptors,* H. H. Milman's *History of the Jews,* John Cormack's translation of Fénelon's *Lives of the Ancient Philosophers,* books on Andrew Jackson and Henry Clay, and John Marshall's *Life of George Washington.* He appears not to have read fiction, except Cervantes, but enjoyed the plays of Shakespeare, which he and his wife read together. His library included books that he used in his teaching, as well as books on gardening, diet, and health.

Jackson used books to help make himself a gentleman. He not only tried to expand his learning, he also studied advice on correct demeanor. George Winfred Hervey's *The Principles of Courtesy: with Hints and Observations on Manners and Habits* taught him, as Jackson noted with a marginal marking, that charity "endeavors to sink beneath the notice of the world, and yet its very self-abasement excites the wonder and wins the praise of all." He was ready to profit socially from Lord Chesterfield's cynical letters to his son, as well as from studiously Christian works like Hervey's. Jackson's disparate reading—from military field manuals to biblical commentaries, from *The Principles of English Grammar* to *The New Hydropathic Cook-Book*—all centered on his determination to improve himself.

Jackson's tour of Europe in the summer of 1856 resembled his reading program in its energetic inclusiveness. He had first wanted to go to Europe in 1851 but had deferred the trip to move to Lexington. Five years later, travel had become a way to take his mind off the loss of his wife. He tried to absorb the maximum amount of cultural stimuli. He set himself a fast pace and an exacting schedule in order to see as many cathedrals, museums, castles, statues, and natural wonders as possible. In London and probably in the other cities as well—including Brussels, Cologne, Bonn, Strasbourg, Basel, Geneva, Milan, Verona, Venice, Florence, Naples, Rome, Genoa, and Paris—he devoted sixteen hours a day, from five in the morning until nine at night, to sightseeing. He prepared himself with guidebooks and at each stop took copious notes, filling notebooks with detailed, hastily written memoranda about paintings, sculpture, churches, and other wonders. Descriptions and statistics mingled promiscuously with summary aesthetic judgments. From every gallery, edifice, or vista Jackson wanted to retain as much as possible, to add it all to the store of erudition and sophistication he had been painstakingly building since his departure from Jackson's Mill for West Point. While stationed at Fort Hamilton, New York, after the Mexican War, he had visited an art gallery each time he went into New York City. During the Civil War he reminisced about the National Gallery in London and the Louvre. He enjoyed and fondly remembered many of the creations he had so quickly and diligently studied. Some wartime English visitors to Jackson's camp near Fredericksburg, expecting to meet an aged backcountry rustic named Old Stonewall, were surprised to find a well-mannered, articulate thirty-nine-year-old man, who conversed with them about the architecture of English cathedrals.

When they set up housekeeping by themselves, Thomas and Anna Jackson filled their two-story home with the solid furniture, the piano, and the decorative luxuries appropriate to well-established citizens. They owned six slaves: two women, Amy and Hetty, Hetty's sons Cyrus and George, an orphan girl named Emma, and a man named Albert, who was repaying his purchase price to Jackson by working as a hotel waiter to earn his freedom. Hetty, Cyrus, and George had come with Anna from North Carolina. Jackson required the household slaves to attend family prayers and to conform to his inflexible routine. His corrections of what he considered negligence apparently were strict, but surviving accounts do not say what he did. Jackson respected Amy as a Christian woman; hearing of her death in 1861, he believed that she had gone to heaven, "where I hope that we among the ransomed of the Lord may be privileged to join her." He seldom spoke of the institution of slavery. He neither apologized for it nor proclaimed its virtues. Many years later Anna Jackson recalled hearing her husband say "that he would prefer to see the negroes free, but he believed that the Bible taught that slavery was sanctioned by the Creator." He took slavery for granted as a fixture of the social and economic order in which he was rising. In 1860 and 1861 he defined the Republican threat to the South as an attack on the rights of slaveholders.

Jackson placed some of his investments in the North. In 1854 he inquired about bank stock in Ohio yielding 10 percent interest. In 1855 and 1856 he made plans to buy land in Illinois and Kansas, then decided against doing so: "I have rather concluded to keep my money invested in stocks of different kinds and thus get my dividends regularly and trust to the blessing of Providence for gradually increasing my worldly goods." For a while he owned stock in a Northern railroad company. He also profited from the growth of industry in Virginia by buying shares in the Lexington Tannery. At his death he owned, in addition to the tannery stock and government bonds, $600 worth of shares in the Bank of the Commonwealth of Virginia and $2,000 worth of shares in the Bank of Rockbridge. Before the Civil War opened to Jackson a new, continent-wide theater in which to test the reach of his ambition, he was successfully turning to account the opportunities offered by an expanding American economy.

Ever since the Civil War, admirers of Jackson—like those of Lee, Davis, and other Confederates—have stressed the reluctance with which their hero joined the South's secession. Though thrust into high station and immortal fame by the war, the Southern leader must not be suspected to have sought such glory by eagerly embracing a cause which, his later admirers know, was a bloody failure. Nor must the man honored by patriotic citizens of the postwar United States have shown an unseemly haste to help lead in the destruction of the union. The best Confederate patriot did not rush after new rank in a new country but went slowly along the painful, inescapable path of duty and conscience. Yet Jackson's reaction to the sectional crisis showed little if any anguish over the disruption of the union. Once war began, he prayed for peace only in the form of disunion. And he found in the defense of the Confederacy an outlet and a reward for his most strenuous exertions.

In 1856 Jackson hesitated to invest in Northern land because he feared that "a dissolution of the union" would lead to confiscation of Southerners' property in the North. In the 1860 presidential election he joined a small group in Rockbridge County supporting the Southern Democratic candidate, John C. Breckinridge. Most of his neighbors supported either John Bell or Stephen A. Douglas. At a Breckinridge meeting in the county courthouse Jackson spoke for fifteen minutes about "the dangers threatening the South, the duty of taking a firm stand." He interpreted Northerners' election of Lincoln as an attack on slaveholders' rights, and he endorsed Breckinridge Democrats' assertion of Southerners' right to take their slaves into all western territories. In the early months of 1861 he neither wanted nor expected Virginia to secede, because he thought the North would yield to the Southern position. "I feel pretty well satisfied," he wrote on January 26, "that the Northern people love the Union more than they do their peculiar notions of slavery." But he told his sister on February 2 that, if the free states were determined to deprive the South of rights confirmed by the Supreme Court—alluding to the

Dred Scott decision opening the territories to slaveholders—"I am in favor of secession." Unlike Robert E. Lee, he expressed no qualms, either constitutional or emotional, about secession. Unlike Jubal Early, he did not deny the right of secession or oppose the movement until its support- ers prevailed. Just after the presidential election, Jackson dismissed a Lynchburg minister's lament over the country's ominous prospects: " 'Why,' said he, 'should Christians be at all disturbed about the dissolu- tion of the Union? It can only come by God's permission, and will only be permitted, if for his people's good.' " He endorsed a concert of prayer for peace in January, but he had already written to a friend in Washing- ton, requesting a copy of a work on heavy artillery—saying, as his friend wrote him a year later, "that if Virginia should become involved in a war, you wished to be ready for the issue and to fly to her rescue." After Jackson marched the Institute cadets off to war on April 21, 1861, he spoke only of the new revolution and the new nation.

Jackson's choice was costly but not hesitant. It alienated him from his sister and other relatives, as well as from the family of his first wife. The Reverend George Junkin's relations with Jackson, Junkin's brother re- called, "were those of a fond father and an affectionate son." Junkin, a Pennsylvanian, had long opposed abolitionism and in 1846 had received a letter of praise from John C. Calhoun for his biblical defense of slavery. Yet he vehemently denounced disunion. At a public meeting after South Carolina's secession he said: "The traitor deserves hemp, and South Caro- lina is a traitor." In February he told restive seniors at Washington College: "The pseudo right of secession is a national wrong." He resigned the presidency of the college on April 18, 1861, after the faculty unani- mously refused to support him in his demand that the students remove a secessionist flag. Leaving behind three of his children who sided with the Confederacy, he headed down the valley toward Pennsylvania. In Winchester he told the Reverend James Graham: "I am escaping from a set of lunatics. Lexington is one vast mad-house." His son-in-law Major Jackson, he said, "is the best and bravest man I ever knew, but he is as crazy as the rest."

During the war, Junkin preached and published denunciations of what he called "the false political maxims of Calhounism, which break down all the barriers of moral truth." The *New York Herald* contrasted his loyal sermons with Jackson's rebellion. In Junkin's book *Political Fallacies,* a copy of which he sent to Jackson in 1863, he wrote of the death of Elinor Junkin Jackson: "The Lord took her away from the evil to come." Jackson had been deeply affected by Ellie's death, her father well knew. Now her father was telling him that Ellie's death had been a blessing because she did not have to see Jackson become a traitor. Not even this reproof—no alienation, however painful—evoked from Jackson any sign of doubt as he identified himself with the Confederacy. His faith and his ambition pointed the same way. God clearly meant the Confederacy to flourish in service to His purposes, and Jackson knew that God ordered events to benefit His dutiful servant. The South as an independent nation was the next step in Christian history, and Jackson would glorify God by doing His work as strenuously and as conspicuously as he could. Neither Laura Arnold nor George Junkin nor anyone else who loved him but stayed with the union could understand that Jackson now needed the Confederacy as much as it needed him.

AS A Confederate officer Jackson won rapid promotion from colonel to lieutenant general; the victories justifying this advancement made him extraordinarily widely known among Southerners. For almost two years, beginning with an account of the battle of Bull Run in the *Richmond Dispatch* of July 29, 1861, newspapers helped make Jackson famous throughout the Confederacy. In January and February 1862, before his spectacular operations began, the *Richmond Examiner* and the *New Orleans Daily Crescent* were praising "this intrepid general." The *Richmond Whig* explained the battle of Kernstown in March: "His object was to give the enemy a foretaste of what they had to expect in the valley, and if they were satisfied with the result, I am sure 'Old Stonewall' is." After the Shenandoah Valley campaign in May and June, Jackson stories became a staple of the press. In January 1863, P. W. Alexander wrote in the *Southern Literary Messenger:* "He is the idol of the people, and is the object of greater enthusiasm than any other military chieftain of our day."

The influence of this publicity appeared in wartime letters and diaries. Catherine Edmonston commented after the Valley Campaign: "He is the only one of our generals who gives the enemy no rest." Two weeks later, W. Henry Sullivan, upon learning that Jackson was attacking the Federals near Richmond, wrote to a friend: "Hurrah for old Stonewall!!!! . . . What can save their army from annihilation. Isn't it delightful to think about?" In Cheneyville, Louisiana, Mary Cornelia Wright recorded her delight at receiving a picture of Jackson: "Bless his dear old war-worn face—he has led our brave troops through many a stormy field! He is better looking than I expected." People who had never seen Jackson and had only vague ideas of his operations spoke of him as a familiar character for whom they felt affection and solicitude. His fame, they said, rivaled that of his namesake Andrew Jackson; he was the George Washington of the Confederate revolution: "Their souls, their deeds, their cause the same!" No two figures in the history of the American republic represented more fully than George Washington and Andrew Jackson the union of the strong-willed man, the triumphant general, and the country's divinely decreed destiny. They had led in the direction history moved. Stonewall Jackson could be such a man for the Confederate nation, its publicists said. His aggressiveness embodied his confidence that, when the destruction to which he committed himself stopped at last, his cause would prove to have been God's.

General Lafayette McLaws believed that Richmond newspapers, with the widest distribution in the South, only grudgingly praised generals from other states, while inflating the deeds of Virginians. He privately complained that Virginia generals engaged in shameless self-promotion. Without naming him, McLaws said that Jackson "panders to the religious zeal of a puritanical Church, and has numerous scribes writing fancy anecdotes of his peculiarities, which never existed." Anna Jackson, concerned about inaccurate descriptions of her husband, apparently suggested to him that she arrange for publication of a correct account. He replied in October 1862 that she should not do so. "These things are earthly and transitory. . . . It is best for us to keep our eyes fixed upon the throne of God and the realities of a more glorious existence beyond the verge of time. It is gratifying to be beloved and to have our conduct approved by our fellow-men, but this is not worthy to be compared with the glory that is in reservation for us in the presence of our glorified Redeemer." Yet, as McLaws cynically suggested, Jackson's constant public restatements of his humility and of his complete dependence on God for success enhanced his worldly fame. Southern Christians noted with approval that Jackson's dispatches after victories gave all the glory to God. The *Knoxville Register* reported that he administered the sacrament of communion to church members in the army, commenting editorially that such an incident gave "an explanation of General Jackson's invincibility." Citizens privately echoed public praise of his humility: "Gen. Jackson is one of the purest men I ever knew. He is far above all political or personal considerations. He is a Christian patriot." Fabricated stories and corrections of fabrications built his reputation for piety. The correspondent of the *Charleston Courier* said that Jackson prayed in front of his army after battle, showing by his faith how "he can lead his army to certain victory." The *Southern Literary Messenger* contradicted this report: "He is too sincere a Christian to indulge in such ostentatious display of his piety."

Jackson's aide Henry Kyd Douglas said after the war that the general eventually had stopped reading newspapers: "He was so modest that their broad compliments embarrassed and annoyed him." As public praise for his success in the valley swelled, Jackson wrote to the Reverend White, telling him to warn people that ascribing victories to anyone but God would ruin the cause. Yet Jackson disseminated evidence of the triumphs God gave him and of the humility for which he strove. Although he was too busy to write full reports of his battles, he regularly took time to write letters of thanks to Southerners, especially women and ministers, who had sent him gifts or had offered to help the soldiers. He thanked his correspondents for their prayers, told them God would bless them for their efforts, and redirected the compliments they paid him: "You must not over-estimate me in the work. I have been but the unworthy instrument whom it pleased God to use in accomplishing His purpose." At the same time, he hinted at more victories to come. Shortly before he took the offensive in the valley, he wrote to Anna Castleman in Winchester that he hoped God would soon enable him to return to her town. While he was planning an invasion of the North, he wrote to Mary Matilda Hademan that he looked forward to seeing Maryland join the Confederacy. Even his simple hope that God would "soon bless us with an honorable and lasting peace" implied imminent defeat of the Federals. In turn, he praised his correspondents, assuring Mary Tucker Magill: "I feel a deep & abiding interest in our female soldiers. They are *patriots in the truest sense of the word,* and I more than admire them." If Jackson had never read a newspaper he still would have known from his mail, which he faithfully answered, that he was the hero of the war.

The famous Stonewall politely received newspaper correspondents—including one from the *New York Herald* whom he briefly held as a prisoner—and patiently submitted to the attentions of citizens eager to meet him. In the lower Shenandoah Valley, after the battle of Antietam and before his move to Fredericksburg, he attracted much notice, especially from women, and he gave autographs. As usual, he impressed people with his humility. Cornelia McDonald saw him at Sunday service in the Kent Street Presbyterian Church in Winchester. To her he looked "so quiet and modest, and so concerned that every eye was fixed on him. His manner was very devout, and he attended closely to every word said." Though wearing "a splendid new uniform," he seemed to wish to be inconspicuous.

Jackson helped make himself a distinctive, beloved public figure. He did so in much the same way he had become a respected citizen of Lexington: by assiduous attention to duties likely to win him public respect. D. H. Hill predicted early in 1862 that, if the war lasted six years and if Jackson survived, he would attain supreme command. Congressman A. R. Boteler told Jackson that people were speaking of him as a future president of the Confederate States of America. Jackson said he would never accept the office. Despite his rapid rise to prominence his admirers believed him to be oblivious to his own greatness. According to Edmund Ruffin, Jackson "never did or said anything to direct attention to any act or opinion of his own"; he thought of himself only as a subordinate doing his duty. After the war, "if his countrymen did not prevent," Jackson would contentedly have become "an unobtrusive & obscure citizen." Thus Jackson's demeanor promoted his fame by a paradox aptly summarized in the *Savannah News* as "the magnificent plainness of 'Stonewall.'"

Writing one of the *Richmond Examiner*'s many tributes to Stonewall, Edward A. Pollard remarked in passing to the editor, John M. Daniel, that Jackson ignored public opinion and probably would never read what Pollard was writing. Daniel, one of Jackson's most enthusiastic admirers, replied: "You are utterly mistaken; he is to-day the most ambitious man within the limits of the Southern Confederacy." Jackson's ostentatious self-abasement neither disproved Daniel's assertion nor contradicted Jackson's own professions. Winning glory and apparently enjoying it aroused anxiety in him. He acknowledged divine direction of Confederate victories no less sincerely than he warned Anna against focusing too much love on their daughter—as he had on his first wife, Ellie. Selfish fulfillment of earthly ambition might provoke the wrath of a jealous God. He kept reminding himself that he would not give up the slightest part of his future glory in heaven for all that this world could give him. "My prayer," he wrote to his wife, "is that such may ever be the feeling of my heart." In this prayer he implied that love of fame was the one temptation to which he felt in danger of succumbing. This struggle between his desires created tension. He channeled it into aggressive pursuit of duty.

The fight to triumph with the Confederacy was only the last and largest of Jackson's efforts to avoid becoming lost in preoccupation with himself and his afflictions. Such isolation would be morbid and dangerous, he had seen after Ellie's death. As a public figure he could prove that God blessed him through God's blessings on the Confederate cause. People whom he awed saw the great exemplar—the patriot and the Christian—but did not see and did not want to know the sad man with whom Stonewall was struggling. A Confederate officer wrote in August 1862: "All admire his genius and great deeds; no one could love the man for himself. He seems to be cut off from his fellow-man and to commune with his own spirit only, or with spirits of which we wot not." To function and prosper in the antebellum army and in Lexington, Jackson had constructed a public figure. His ability to impose that public figure on the minds of others was the main source of confidence and continuity in his life. As his fame grew in wartime, so did Southerners' expectations. If he deserved his reputation, he must ever more fully demonstrate the power of will to dominate men and events. Popular enthusiasm for Stonewall, heralding the success of Jackson's ambition, placed an ever greater burden on the man who had created Stonewall.

The admiration Jackson sought and won among Southerners linked his public character, his success, and Confederate victory. Confederates often exaggerated his personality and overstated his achievements. Doing so, they conveyed their support for the kind of war Jackson wanted to wage. The Valley Campaign evoked an unusually intense reaction by proving Confederate strength amid reverses elsewhere. Federals had occupied Tennessee and northern Mississippi, in addition to taking New Orleans, Baton Rouge, and Natchez. McClellan's huge army lay within sight of Richmond. General Joseph E. Johnston and his successor after the battle of Seven Pines, General R. E. Lee, seemed preoccupied with defense as McClellan tried to strangle the city. Into this transcontinental scene of Confederate withdrawal and irresoluteness, Jackson suddenly introduced pleasing images of Yankees fleeing across the Potomac and Lincoln's secretary of war calling for troops to protect Washington. Though Jackson's strategy was directed by Johnston and Lee, he usually received the greatest public credit for his accomplishments. For the next eleven months Southerners heard of Jackson suddenly hitting and crushing the enemy. Even when he was not so sudden—as at the start of the Seven Days—or not so crushing—as at Cedar Mountain—or stood on the defensive—as at Antietam—his reputation for relentless audacity remained intact. Jackson chases the Federals out of the valley; Jackson hits McClellan's right near the Chickahominy; Jackson surprises Pope and threatens Washington; Jackson takes Harpers Ferry and 11,000 prisoners; Jackson breaks Federal assaults at Antietam and Fredericksburg; Jackson routs Hooker's right at Chancellorsville—the cumulative message was clear: Stonewall Jackson's aggressiveness brought Confederate success.

Praising the attributes that enabled their hero to win, Southerners, if anything, exaggerated his self-disciplined perseverance. The demeanor which cost him much labor often looked innate and monolithic to his admirers. Some of those closest to Jackson fostered this view of him. Robert L. Dabney, who soon afterward, as a biographer, revealed an understanding of Jackson's struggle with ambition, presented in his memorial sermon a portrait of uncomplicated patriotism: "No thought of personal advancement, of ambition or applause, ever for one instant divided the homage of his heart with his great cause." Jackson had become, in the words of Secretary of War James A. Seddon, "the very type and model of the Christian and hero." Confederates made the way to triumph, led by Jackson, look easier than it was. Jackson's long marches and lethal battles came at the cost of great pain to his men. He had felt pain since adolescence, had withstood and overcome it. Jackson was ready to die; his soldiers must live or die on the same principle. He never forgave General Richard Garnett for withdrawing the Stonewall Brigade during the battle of Kernstown on March 23, 1862, when the Confederates were fighting twice their number. Jackson had known times when he had wanted to die. On December 2, 1859, commanding the artillery detachment of Virginia Military Institute cadets, he had carefully scrutinized the bearing of John Brown as the violent abolitionist, going through the ritual of being hanged, showed that a revolutionary could die well. Jackson felt little tolerance for supporters of the Confederate revolution who were not willing to die equally well. Patriots should set no limits on their fighting for the cause. A troubled man, in conflict with himself, and a troubled people, striving for unity in self-defense, sought purpose and cohesion through attacking the Yankees.

Southerners who praised Jackson gave many signs of wanting him to carry out the offensive war he had come to represent. To follow his exploits, celebrate his victories, and cheer him as he passed often meant more than wishing for Confederate independence. In Ouachita County, Arkansas, Mary E. Boddie, after learning of the Valley Campaign, wrote: "I hope our army there may follow them even to New York, & make them realize the misery of houses laid waste & people hunted up like beasts. . . . We hear now that . . . Stonewall Jackson is encamped on the ashes of Washington City." She was one of many Confederates for whom Jackson epitomized victory through invasion and devastation. Southerners believed overblown accounts of the terror evoked in the North by the movements and the reputation of Stonewall. If Jackson were about to do to Yankees what his admirers wanted him to do, such reports of panic would seem plausible enough. Though Jackson did not take his army across the Potomac in the spring of 1862, the *Richmond Dispatch* jumped to conclusions: "The fact that Jackson is the first man to lead an army into Maryland will stamp him as the hero of the war." Men in the army and women at home knew that Jackson had recommended taking no prisoners. To J. B. Jones in Richmond, news that Jackson's corps was being reorganized to march on Washington in July 1862 had a clear meaning: "By their emancipation and confiscation measures, the Yankees have made this a war of extermination." The Confederacy should accept the challenge. Again and again in Southerners' fantasies, Stonewall—more than Lee or Longstreet or Bragg or Johnston—was the general hoisting the black flag, blowing up the United States Capitol, seizing Northern cities, and ending the war by the massive use of force. "Let Stonewall have one lick" at Washington, "give Jackson half our present army," and the enemy would soon be destroyed. In the *Richmond Whig*'s version of the battle of Cedar Mountain, Jackson made his men impetuous and irresistible: "The ground over which they passed was almost literally covered with slaughtered Yankees." The Army of Northern Virginia began to enter Maryland on September 4, 1862, and a Virginian commented two days later: "The people are in high spirits now as Jackson has crossed the river." Imagining a triumphant Confederacy included imagining a victorious Stonewall. He did not have occasions to do all the things Southerners pictured him doing. If he had not been denied those opportunities, many people said, his cause would not have failed.

After 1865, a recurrent refrain in Southern war writing contended that, if Jackson had lived, the Confederacy would have won its independence. General Lee said in private conversation that the presence of Jackson would have brought him victory at Gettysburg in 1863 and in the Wilderness in 1864. After Jackson's death and the Confederate defeat at Gettysburg seven weeks later, Southern strategy was largely confined to the defensive; Confederate prospects appeared to have shifted suddenly from inflicting bold strokes to suffering slow attrition. Retrospective fantasies about a surviving Jackson and a triumphant Confederacy were hazy. They did not define an alternative Southern strategy so much as they suggested simply that Jackson was an abler commander than most of those who outlived him. The versions of what Jackson would have done did not seek internal consistency. They thrust Jackson into battles that took place after his death, then thrust him again into later ones that would not have occurred, given the hypothetical victories he would have won earlier. Fitzhugh Lee imagined Jackson in command of the Confederate left, taking Cemetery Hill at Gettysburg on July 1—and in command of the Confederate right, taking the Round Tops on July 2. The Reverend J. William Jones imagined Jackson's presence assuring a complete success at Gettysburg, followed by Confederate independence. Yet Jones also knew that, if Jackson had lived, he would have taken command of the Army of Tennessee and would have fought much better in the west than Bragg or Johnston did later in 1863 and 1864. P. G. T. Beauregard confidently asserted that Jackson in command of the Army of Tennessee late in 1864 and early in 1865 would have swept into Ohio and Pennsylvania or would have joined Lee to defeat Grant at Petersburg. At the same time, as commander of the Trans-Mississippi Department, he would have done more than Kirby Smith. Others put him in Stuart's place on the second day at Chancellorsville, in A. P. Hill's place in the operations against Meade on the Rapidan, in Bragg's place at Chattanooga, in Early's place in the Shenandoah Valley, in Hood's place at Spring Hill, Tennessee. Many former Confederates evidently agreed with Jedediah Hotchkiss's statement to Jackson's British biographer G. F. R. Henderson: "I never saw a great battle subsequent to Jackson's death in which I did not see the opportunity which, in my opinion, he would have seized and routed his opponents."

The postmortem victories that Southerners attributed to Jackson came from his aggressiveness more than from any other quality. When the *Chattanooga Rebel,* published in Atlanta in October 1863, said that "one signal Stonewall Jackson campaign" would drive the Federal army to the Ohio River, the editor implied that the offensive, properly executed, could still save the South. After the Confederacy's defeat, Jackson remained the one commander "in whose lexicon 'there was no such word as fail,' for whom the impossible did not exist." Jackson's death, Southern generals' abandonment of or failure in the offensive, and Confederate defeat came together in people's reflections on the war. To break retrospectively through the war's tightening ring of circumstance closing in Federal victory, Southerners argued that one man could have reversed the outcome. In this vaguely formulated suggestion, they tried to deal with the way the war had changed by denying the necessity of the changes. The fighting need not have become a story of defense, entrenchment, and attrition. The popularly acclaimed methods of bold attack and invasion only required the proper leader to break the Federal lines and give the Confederacy victory. These Southerners used their faith in Confederate war-making to refute the course of events. They wrote the history of what had not occurred in order to show that they had not judged wrong in resorting to war.

Contemptuous of such a form of argument, John S. Mosby, writing about the battle of Gettysburg in 1877, sarcastically suggested the uselessness of imagining men who did not exist: "Probably if Stonewall Jackson had been there the issue would have been different. . . . Very probably if Stuart could have been in front and rear of Hooker at the same time or if we had had two Stuarts the battle would have gone differently." W. T. Sherman found this Southern penchant for revising reality the greatest weakness in Jefferson Davis's *The Rise and Fall of the Confederate Government*— "his taking refuge in possibilities . . . if Stonewall Jackson had been in Hood's place, there would not have been a March to Sea &c. History deals with what was and is, and tis folly to discuss what might have been." The course of the war disclosed the insufficiency of the public figure Stonewall Jackson, implacable destroyer and ubiquitous mastermind, as a representative and an agent of Confederate independence. Neither by making himself God's instrument nor by making God the guarantor of his earthly and spiritual triumph could Jackson attain the power over war which Stonewall was supposed to possess. Virtuosity led to disaster. Wielding power ended in being destroyed. The history of the

Confederacy, promising as it first unfolded to narrate Jackson's conspicuous deeds in making a nation, could later sustain belief in Stonewall's destiny only by resorting to the imaginary and the hypothetical. Confederate narrative of a larger-than-life figure dominating actual events became narrative of a mythical figure—Stonewall Jackson fighting on after May 10, 1863—shaping fictional events.

Emulation of Jackson's methods after his death hurt the Confederates more than it helped. Lee's greatest problem at Gettysburg was not that he lacked a Jackson who would have pressed forward and seized the high ground on July 1, whereas Ewell did not, or a Jackson who would have promptly and energetically hit the Federal left on July 2, whereas Longstreet did not. Rather, the Army of Northern Virginia again confronted a fact Lee could not overcome: breaking up a corps of the Army of the Potomac did not destroy the Federal army, though it did get many Confederates killed. Lee and Jackson had agreed upon daring tactical offensives. These had not won and gave no promise of winning the war with the conclusive stroke many Confederates envisioned.

General John Bell Hood tried to be a Stonewall Jackson at Atlanta on July 20 and 22, 1864. Having succeeded Johnston in command with the understanding that the Confederates would take the offensive, Hood drew on plans made by Johnston and modeled his assaults, especially William J. Hardee's flanking attack, on the examples set by Jackson. Sherman was surprised by Hardee on July 22 but, in the ensuing combat, did not use reinforcements from the rest of his army. He let the Army of the Tennessee recover the ground it had lost. In his memoirs, Hood argued that his orders had been right because they were like Jackson's. Long marches, followed by assaults, "improved the *morale* of the army" even when they failed. Blame for failure lay with Johnston and with the soldiers because the army had not "been previously handled according to the Lee and Jackson school." Subsequently explaining his failure to stop Schofield's march to join Thomas at Nashville, Hood suggested that he could have been another Jackson at Gettysburg, at Atlanta, and at Spring Hill with assaults on the Federal armies' flanks. "I had beheld with admiration the noble deeds and grand results achieved by the immortal Jackson in similar manoeuvres; I had seen his Corps made equal to ten times its number by a sudden attack on the enemy's rear, and I hoped in this instance to be able to profit by the teaching of my illustrious countryman." Hood knew the mystique of the relentless, irresistible Jackson better than he understood the situation of the Army of Tennessee. While Hood was delayed in Alabama preparing to head north, General Nathan Bedford Forrest, a commander as aggressive as any, correctly predicted that "Hood would come out of Tennessee faster than he entered."

Stonewall Jackson was not at Gettysburg or Chattanooga or Atlanta because he had died after being severely wounded by gunfire from his own men on the night of May 2, 1863, in the act of reconnoitering to achieve a more conclusive stroke against the Federals. He was the victim not only of his men's mistake but also of his own commitment to the offensive. Five months earlier, on the evening of December 13, 1862, Jackson's troops, after driving back the Federal left at Fredericksburg, "had gotten into such confusion in the plain as to fire into each other," Lee said after the war. Though Jackson had recommended against a further attack then, he had not abandoned the effort to resolve confusion by aggressive action, as he showed on his last night in command.

In fact, Jackson's movements and attacks, linked in public praise with his monolithically consistent character as Christian, patriot, and commander, had false starts and shortcomings—just as his character, far from being monolithic, strove to supplant frailties with perfection. John Cheves Haskell later commented: "He certainly never doubted he was right and the man who differed was wrong. . . . I can never be a blind admirer of Jackson. No man as positive as he was could ever hope to escape grievous errors." Jackson had a reputation for obsessive secrecy; yet he lost important papers, including a letter from Joseph E. Johnston which made clear the purpose of the Valley Campaign and was published in the *New York Herald*. With little tact or trust and much censoriousness, Jackson tried to mold his subordinate officers to his will by peremptory orders and court-martial charges. He wanted to make his men an extension of his certitude. Yet, in ordering assaults, he overreached at Port Republic and at Cedar Mountain; he overestimated the pace at which he could come to Lee's aid at Richmond; he privately complained about Lee's favoritism toward Longstreet and spoke of resigning.

Like all generals, Jackson made mistakes. His errors often flowed from his ambition to overcome all impediments, to miss no opportunity to take the war to the enemy. H. E. Gourdin, who served under Longstreet, wrote just before the battle of Antietam that "one very well able to judge" had said of Jackson: "A month uncontrolled and he would destroy himself and all under him." The Confederate fantasy of Jackson the war-winner, like Jackson's ambition, put faith in an ever more violent effort at self-creation. Jackson convinced many people, including soldiers whose lives he risked and lost, that God favored his every move. He succeeded so well that his accomplishments seemed more thorough than they were, just as the celebrations of his methods obscured the vulnerabilities his determination had tried to override. With Jackson, Confederates embraced a false premise for their war of independence. It was not true that they could be whatever they resolved to be.

CHAPTER 3

THE AGGRESSIVE WAR: SHERMAN

SECESSION and Confederates' persistence in fighting made many Northerners so angry that they demanded the thorough and final obliteration of sectional defiance of the nation. An aggressive attack on rebellion seemed inevitable and beneficial. To many of its strongest supporters war for the union looked progressive. It would free the country from the backwardness and obstructionism they saw in long-standing Southern resistance, which they attributed to aristocracy and slavery. Free society and a republican nation would attain security through the prostration of their domestic enemies. Indeed, the war's capacity for effecting progress through violence struck civilians and private soldiers more forcibly than it did many generals of the regular army. The fate that came upon the Confederacy in the last two years of the war had been sketched out, prayed for, and urged onward by Northerners during the first two years.

As in the South, a popular call for destructive measures arose at once in the North. In December 1860, while the southernmost states moved toward secession, Senator Benjamin F. Wade of Ohio was already talking about *"making the south a desert."* As soon as the Confederates fired on Fort Sumter, a member of the Ohio legislature wrote to John Sherman: "We propose an appropriation of *one million dollars* to pay for the *scalps of rebels."* Vehement public reactions to the fall of Fort Sumter and to the Federal defeat at Bull Run included visions of mayhem equal to anything the Federal army later enacted. Speaking in Philadelphia, Judge Levi Hubbell, a Democrat from Milwaukee, said in April 1861 that, if the war continued, the North must "restore New Orleans to its native marshes, then march across the country, burn Montgomery to ashes, and serve Charleston in the same way.... We must starve, drown, burn, shoot the traitors." After the battle of Bull Run it was easy to see, Wendell Phillips said, that "General Scott might have burned over Virginia months ago, and left no woods to conceal the masked batteries of Manassas." Like Phillips's call for defoliation or the first demands for a quick march on Richmond, the early proposals had an air of unreality, assuming that some spectacularly aggressive stroke would soon subdue the rebels. Invasion and devastation would not be so easy as Northerners supposed; but when the army found adequate methods, the people were ready.

One of the most striking, widespread expressions of public support for more drastic war-making arose in the North after the Shenandoah Valley campaign and the battles of the Seven Days. Federal defeats in the valley and the repulse of McClellan from Richmond disappointed people who had confidently expected the fall of the Confederate capital to match Federal victories in the west and end the war. *Harper's Weekly* had said in April: "The keys of the so-called Confederate states are Richmond and New Orleans. When we have taken these our task will be done." But Richmond did not fall, and the Confederate war effort did not collapse under the reverses early in 1862. Reacting to this disappointment, many Northerners resolved to mount a more ruthless attack on the rebels. Two British writers, Edward Dicey and Catherine Hopley, one sympathetic with the North, the other with the South, noticed the growing bitterness in their travels through the North. Hopley said that she often heard men and women "firmly and resolutely say of the Southerners, 'We must annihilate them,' with as little remorse as they have before displayed in destroying the Indians." This hostility loomed large in patriotic rallies devoted to recruiting volunteers for the army. In New York, Washington, Pittsburgh, Cincinnati, and other places, speakers equated raising an army with sending destruction into the South. Governor Andrew Curtin anticipated the later aphorisms of General Sherman when he told a crowd in Pittsburgh: "War means violence, and in time of war man relapses into barbarism. The property, nay, even the life of the enemy, everything he has, we must take and use against him." Northerners' visions of unlimited war owed much to hostility or rage provoked by the rebels' daring to resist and refusing to succumb to Northern superiority at once. Such a challenge, seeming to vindicate Southern bravado, was intolerable.

Stonewall Jackson's successes, as well as the invasion of the free states he urged but did not live to see, had unforeseen effects on Yankees. Northerners decided that they should not confine their armies' activities to countering Stonewall's flanking games but should change the rules. In Northern summaries of the 1862 Virginia campaigns, Federal soldiers had preserved rebels' houses in Winchester; then Jackson had driven them out of the town, and citizens had fired on the retreating men from those same houses. During McClellan's Peninsular Campaign, the Federal army had hesitated to destroy what was supposed to be its own country, but such leniency invited defeat, again at the hands of Jackson, and obviously had been a mistake. In the first week of September, Confederates conclusively proved the error of Northern restraint by crossing the Potomac into Maryland. For a cheering crowd in Union Square in Manhattan, L. E. Chittenden drew the clear moral: "I say it is time to proclaim to every Winchester in the so-called Southern confederacy that there shall not be left one article above ground in such a town that fire can consume." After the war, looking back on Confederate defeat, Jackson's first biographer, John Esten Cooke, discerned a pattern: "From the summer of 1862, the war became a war of wholesale devastation. From the spring of 1864, it seemed to have become nearly a war of extermination."

Northern expressions of support for intensified war-making assumed that the Confederate army was an instrument of the Southern populace and that the populace was a legitimate object of attack. Reacting to news of Lee's entry into Maryland, John W. Davenport made the connection explicit: "Oh for a lawles and relentless Dictator for a seazon to scourge with fire and sword the southern soil, and render it unfit to support the Armies of the *rebels*. That is the only way." The proposed measures varied widely: legislation authorizing confiscation of rebels' property, demands for destruction of crops and cities, threats of extermination and of deportation. As usual, Thaddeus Stevens went farther than most. Drafting a speech, he wrote: "The necessities of state require that all the inhabitants of a hostile country should be treated as enemies whether in arms or not. Even women and children are enemies. . . . The humanity of modern civilization does not justify putting them to death unless absolutely necessary." Pronouncements in this spirit, if not this sweeping, became commonplace. They accustomed Northerners to think of quelling the rebel armies by hurting civilians. Senator John Sherman, a careful, temporizing politician, said on July 9, 1862: "You cannot conduct warfare against savages unless you become half savage yourself. . . . I would practice every mode of warfare that is prescribed in either ancient or modern history."

Alongside their readiness to wage drastic war, many Northerners, primarily Republicans, welcomed proposals for remaking the South's society and economy. The ideas differed in scope, ranging from plans for redistributing property to vague notions about the regenerative effect of Northern settlers in the South. Some envisioned small farms for ex-slaves, poor whites, and Federal veterans. Others spoke of repeopling the South. The wife of an Ohio soldier wrote to Secretary Stanton that soldiers' wives and sisters, if they controlled the rebels' fate, "would banish them forever . . . and confiscate their property to the use of the government or to the use of poor loyal citizens." The planners and dreamers, in their several ways, imagined that war could make the South more like the North. Carl Schurz predicted a dismantling of great estates. Instead of mansions, slave cabins, and poor whites' hovels, the landscape would reveal "the neat white cottage in the midst of small but flourishing fields." An influx of Northerners with tools, machinery, capital, knowledge, and "a spirit of progressive improvement" would give the South a "progressive civilization." In 1865, during a visit to Columbia, Schurz told a South Carolinian "that a new people (Yankees) will make the south 'the Eden' of the known world." These visions of a transformed society often set no limits on the destruction that might have to precede it. Since secessionists and their world were obsolete, the Federal army would render a service by sweeping away whatever obstructed the victory of progress. Talk of regeneration included talk of extermination and depopulation. Colonel Horace Binney Sargent of the 1st Massachusetts Cavalry wrote to Charles Sumner: "What matters it, even if the lands were left uninhabited & a desert? . . . the country would be the more ready to receive the new civilization, that the North, sooner or later, must precipitate upon it." Successful war-making demonstrated the superiority of Northern society, and this demonstration must be conclusive, preparing Southerners' minds for the new order. The Reverend Thomas Starr King had only one doubt: "Does the South *deserve* to be regenerated & lifted up into noble prosperity by the triumph of the North & the Nation?"

Such plans and expectations were far from universal among Northerners. Many people, especially Democrats, objected to reformers' plans almost as bitterly as Southerners did. However, the dissenters did not have an influence on Federal war-making proportionate to their numbers. Furthermore, Democrats often wound up helping to suppress the rebellion with measures they deplored. They were among the first to undergo an experience that became nearly universal: talking about purposes and stating principles to which they could not make the war conform. Democrats who opposed the Lincoln administration's war effort used the growing bloodshed and the prospect of unrestrained war against all Southern whites as their main evidence of the war's evil. They also saw connections between bitter war and Republican policies they opposed. Implicit in the call to defeat treason by all available means was the prospect of an American government, economy, and social order remade on the Republican model. During the 1864 presidential campaign a Democrat in St. Louis simplified the issue for a European traveler, saying: "This war is the conquest of America by Massachusetts." Democrats' criticism of harsher war denounced departures from Christian, civilized principles. And they warned that, if Lincoln were allowed to persevere in it, the republic would be ruined. Only a Democratic president could restore the "good old Jeffersonian days of domestic concord and tranquility." "Jeffersonian," in this setting, meant restricting the power the federal government could wield. That goal, directed toward the North's means of waging war, dominated Democrats' opposition to Lincoln. General George B. McClellan in effect announced his candidacy for the presidency in an open letter to Lincoln on July 7, 1862. According to Francis P. Blair, Sr., McClellan first had prepared a "military proclamation" intended to guide the army's treatment of civilians. He substituted for it a "political letter . . . proposing *delicate treatment* of the rebels," written "as a programme for his canvass as a Presidential candidate." The government, McClellan said, should not subjugate, expropriate, destroy, proscribe, or execute. It should not forcibly end slavery. Only the Confederate army should be attacked. To act differently would lead to disintegration of the Federal army. McClellan's Democratic supporters and those Democrats who thought him too warlike agreed in portraying the Federal army's invasion as the epitome of Lincoln's evil policies for the nation's future. In the House of Representatives, Samuel S. Cox equated the removal of McClellan from command with the administration's refusal to seek reunion through compromise. "Will you compromise with desolation and call it peace? Will you glory in the unity and indivisibility of a territory denuded by the besom of war?"

Denouncing the Republicans' war, Democrats portrayed its effects the same way the war's supporters did on at least one score: the war, they said, served purposes beyond preservation of the union. Intensifying conflict would change society, but for Democratic critics this dynamic was progress toward a sinister end. The war's effects were all the more alarming because, though many people denounced it, they seemed powerless to turn aside the movement toward a Republican war. Democrats opposing the administration most often used one or more of three appeals: the Republican war sacrificed Northern and Southern whites in order to exalt blacks, who would move north in great numbers; Lincoln's expansion of governmental power threatened to destroy liberty and self-government; and the Republican war was enriching industrialists, speculators, and Eastern plutocrats at the expense of producers, who were whip-sawed by the protective tariff, inflation, and extortionate railroad and shipping rates. For the most strident critics, these designs complemented one another in a conspiracy: the competition of former slaves would degrade all laboring men; subjugation of the South would put the producers of both sections in the power of the manufacturing, transportation, and financial interests; the capitalists would maintain their control with a conscripted army, an arbitrary centralized government, and taxation to pay interest on a bloated national debt largely owed to them and to foreigners—all of which had been excused by the goal of freeing the slaves and subduing the South.

A war for union that was also an attack on Southern society and a solidification of Republican power presented Democrats with a dilemma that handicapped their opposition to Lincoln's administration. Most Democrats supported a war for the union, if not the kind of war Lincoln was conducting. Few were prepared to accept disunion, and those who seemed willing to do so knew that their view did not have much support. Democrats could denounce Republican war aims, war methods, and economic and racial policies but could not effectively obstruct them as long as Republicans won voters' support for the war. Democrats spent much of their energy fighting one another, especially over the question of whether they should promise to continue the war or cling to the hypothetical assurance that an armistice would lead to reunion, not to permanent disunion. Their strong opposition to Republican policies could not hope to become effective politically unless they could plausibly argue that Democrats would restore the union. Since even most Democrats believed that this could be done only by war, those who did not call for an armistice and who did not support the Lincoln administration were reduced to claiming that Democrats could defeat the rebellion by not augmenting federal power, not attacking Southern society, and not undermining slavery. Events of the war, especially the intensity of Confederates' fighting, made this proposition less and less credible. Indeed, the main threat to Republicans' electoral success lay in the prospect that they might fail to win the war even with their more severe measures. Democrats opposed to Lincoln's methods for maintaining union were caught in a dilemma by the connection between union and harsher war, a link they often tried to break but failed to dispel from most voters' minds.

Still, Democrats' attack on a Republican war and on a Republican conspiracy to transform America did manage to win the support of a large minority of the Northern electorate. But what proved to be the crucial difficulty they could not overcome was identified by Francis P. Blair, Sr., Seward, and the pro-war Democratic governor of Ohio, John Brough. In 1863 Brough reminded young Democrats what had happened to loyalists who opposed the Revolution, Federalists who opposed the War of 1812, Whigs who opposed the Mexican War: "Beware how you tread on that platform. It is unsound, and the reproach will follow you in all your future years." The phenomenon that antiadministration Democrats made their central symbol of Republican radical design—the terrible momentum of the war—was their undoing. Most Americans in the North were more attached to the union than alarmed by the war's evils. The election of McClellan would mean the triumph of the rebellion, Blair wrote: "The nation's instinct sees this & the army sees it—& little Mac is a doomed man." Soldiers of the United States Army voted overwhelmingly Republican. The imbalance was so great not because soldiers supported all Republican policies but because the Lincoln administration's measures were more likely to smash the rebellion. A Democratic soldier from Wisconsin wrote to his father in the summer of 1863: "I feel as *conservative,* Pa, as ever I did, but you know there is a difference between *army* conservatism and Northern. We are here and can see where the excuse is for many things that you call abuses. . . . I cannot but believe that you and a large portion of the Democratic party are mistaken in your views, and are retarding instead of hastening the end of this horrible war."

In the latter half of 1862 more than 500,000 new recruits joined the Federal army. From the start of their service, many of these soldiers acted as if terrorizing Southern civilians were well-established policy. A staff officer said of Sherman's new troops in Mississippi: "They have come down here with the intention of burning and destroying, and well are they carrying out their intentions." During 1862 most commanders worked to restrain their troops from plunder, relying on supply lines from the North rather than on Southern civilians' produce. At the start of his brief tenure as commander of the Federal Army of Virginia in the summer of 1862, General John Pope, in accordance with new attitudes in Washington, announced a more stringent policy toward Southern civilians, including seizure of supplies without payment and expulsion from Federal lines of people who refused to swear allegiance to the United States. Though Pope's order was not systematically implemented, soldiers approved of it. Ulysses S. Grant later wrote that renewal of the Confederate war effort in the spring and summer of 1862 had convinced him that the only way to save the union was by "complete conquest." To that end, he recalled, he had changed from protecting civilians' property to ordering that his army "consume everything that could be used to support or supply armies." However, Grant was slower to turn his army against Southern resources and morale than he afterward remembered. An officer wrote from Mississippi on December 1, 1862, saying that most regiments enforced a very strict order against burning and plundering, though soldiers did burn fences and outhouses. Soldiers' letters in 1862 called for devastation and extermination, deploring their commanders' practice of guarding Southerners' property. By November, men in

both western and eastern armies defied restraint with increasing frequency. As one veteran later explained, "the ideas of the soldiers upon
the subject of 'confiscation' were, during the first months of the war, a
long way in advance of those held by the double-starred generals, and
the statesmen at Washington who were steering the ship. It was about
two years before the latter caught up with the procession."

Experienced soldiers believed that ruining rebels would more quickly
end the war. New soldiers brought from home the assumption that
ruining rebels was the purpose of the war. In the Army of the Potomac,
William Thompson Lusk complained that officers' efforts to check destruction, insult, and injury were "completely neutralized by the accursed
conduct of the Press with its clamor for a vigorous prosecution of the
war." Soldiers' eagerness to make the populace suffer, often expressed in
the spring and summer of 1862, did not just indulge a love of violence
but explicitly conveyed a political design. "We have treated them as
misled long enough," Rufus Mead, Jr., wrote to his family in May. "Now
then let us treat them as the Rebels they are." Cyrus Clay Carpenter,
writing from Iuka, Mississippi, in August, wanted the army to go through
Alabama leaving "a desert waste" behind: "I believe that this war before
it ends will become a 'violent and remorseless revolutionary struggle' try
to avoid as Presidents and cabinets may." When their generals, especially
Sherman, caught up with their attitudes, the soldiers were ready to do
the work thoroughly.

One of Sherman's soldiers who usually sympathized with suffering
women said of the wife of the railroad agent at Madison, Georgia: "I did
not much pity her. She was a regular secesh and spit out her spite and
venom against the dirty Yanks and mudsills of the north." Women, who
were supposed to embody the noncombatant's exemption from war,
instead became the objects of special hostility from Northern citizens and
soldiers. Among Northerners, Southern women gained a reputation for
being the most devoted supporters of the Confederacy. By 1862 the
venomous Southern virago was a commonplace in Northern discussion
of the war. S. M. Stevens, wife of a Federal soldier, asked Edwin M.
Stanton whether such "female hyenas" were worthy to live in America,
then answered her own question: "I say no." In *Harper's Weekly,* Thomas
Nast included among his war drawings a picture of "Southern Women
Gloating Over Dead Union Soldiers." Hardly anyone questioned the
power of women's influence over men; but, in the conventions of the
time, women were supposed to use their power to ennoble and civilize—
whereas, Southern women, it seemed, were serving what Elizabeth Cady
Stanton called "mere pride of race and class." By promoting war against

the union and by showing their hatred of Federal soldiers, they imitated Lady Macbeth and "unsexed themselves to prove their scorn of 'the Yankees.' " Thus they forfeited their exemption as ladies and noncombatants. Working partly in public—through rallies, handsewn flags, cheers, and organized efforts on behalf of the Confederate army—but even more insidiously in private society, seducing or shaming or driving men to go to war, Confederate women showed themselves to be the most fanatical and powerful rebels. Federal soldiers in the South repeatedly said that women showed more bitter secessionist spirit than men. Their demeanor represented resistance that must be crushed. In July 1862, S. J. F. Miller wrote to his parents about Huntsville, Alabama: "The *ladies* of the place allow no opportunity to pass, to insult our soldiers & our flag. If I had the managing of the place I would *burn* the town."

Despite women's defiance, Federal armies, especially Sherman's, saw many women reduced to crying and begging. George H. Cadman wrote to his wife that in Mississippi, Alabama, and Tennessee he had seen hundreds of women come to camp to beg for food, "their poor, pale, emaciated faces too plainly speaking what they have suffered." Women exchanged sexual intercourse for food. Though soldiers often commented, in other connections, on the disparity between rich Southerners and poor ones, their gratification at the subduing of Southern women cut across lines of class. In most soldiers' eyes, the female sex among Southern whites had committed itself to rebellion and would learn that women's influence was not omnipotent when turned to treason. In Lancaster, South Carolina, General Smith D. Atkins gave the home of Virginia Wade a guard; but, before doing so, he lectured her: "We shall soon see the women of Carolina as those of Geo. with tears begging crusts from our men for their famishing children. O it was glorious to see such a sight. . . . you women keep up this war. we are fighting *you.*"

Federal soldiers' hostility toward Southerners dwelt with special bitterness on Southern criticism of the North's free-labor society. In 1858 a famous speech by Senator James H. Hammond of South Carolina put a word into Northerners' political vocabulary—"mud-sill"—that came back to the Confederates in mockery as their nation collapsed. Hammond asserted that every social system needed an underclass to do menial work: the "mud-sill of society and of political government." By consigning blacks to this role, the Southern system, according to its admirers, avoided the conflicts among whites incipient in a society where some whites were laborers while others were capitalists. Hammond said to Northerners: "Your whole hireling class of manual laborers and 'operatives,' as you call them, are essentially slaves." This argument, part of a larger celebration of a privileged white people's civilization made possible by enslaving blacks, convinced many Northerners that secessionists held themselves to be superior to any man who worked with his hands.

Editorials and speeches in the Confederacy scorned Federal soldiers, whose fighting ability and courage surely had been vitiated by their subservience in a mechanically minded, commercially minded, materialistic society. These strictures impressed Northern soldiers as the outgrowth of decades of Southern arrogance and hostility. Returning to Detroit in August 1862 after some time as a prisoner of war, General Orlando B. Willcox, a Democrat, told a public gathering: "The ignorant and prejudiced and interested classes of the South hate the North, hate all her institutions, hate her enterprising spirit, hate her free schools, hate her colleges, hate her manufactures, hate her machinery and hate that enterprise of her[s] which has given to the South as well as the North that grand character of American nationality which they enjoyed." And Southerners, in their wartime efforts to justify and define their new nation, continued to give offense by predicting the disintegration of the North in what the *Richmond Enquirer* called "the inevitable revolution which is to tear to pieces that most rotten society." All the while, their contemptuousness won them more enmity. For the most part, people who worked with their hands turned violently against the rebels, not against the capitalists. They detected in Southerners' insults the outlook expressed privately by C. L. Burn of South Carolina while he was eagerly awaiting secession: "The Southern States ought to split this glorious Union and leave Old Lincoln to preside over the white niggers at the North."

This proposition—that Southerners were better than Northerners—crudely, vaguely, but forcefully defined secession for Federal soldiers and for citizens cheering them on. In February 1865, the *Daily Missouri Democrat* enjoyed the humiliation of the Charlestonians: "In their arrogance they branded their oppressors as 'mudsills' and 'greasy mechanics,' and a class universally their inferiors." Suppression of the rebellion seemed a way to vindicate the North's egalitarian society, not so much by proving that it was egalitarian as by assuming that it was, then proving that it was stronger. Emancipation of the slaves—"It just brings these proud southerners down to a level with other people"—combat on the battlefield—"The chivalry of the South met the mudsills of Michigan and learned to respect them"—and punishment of civilians all refuted the intolerable idea that free labor could be subordinated to an elite. "The people feel now the effects of war," a Federal soldier wrote from Tennessee in January 1863. "So shall the whole rebellious race of Aristocrats bite the dust and bow before the victorious march of Northern freemen."

The Northern defense of free labor through war interpreted secession as a conspiracy by a small group of rich men. They "count laborers as their capital," George Bancroft warned. They wanted to engross the western territories for the benefit of the "capitalist slaveholder"; they tried to dominate the nation or, failing that, to ruin it. Recognizing that political power in the hands of "the laboring class" would obstruct their plan, they set out to destroy popular institutions. Soldiers repeated these arguments. But the Southern army's strong resistance, compounded by Southern civilians' hostility, persuaded Federal soldiers that the rich were not their only enemies. Humbling the proud always gratified Northern men; their conception of the arrogant Southerner widened beyond conspirators and slaveholders to include all rebels: the populace. In order to overthrow the principle "that capital ought to own labor" and to show the hollowness of "rebel cavaliers who claim to be better stuff than Puritan mud-sills," it finally seemed necessary to ruin the Confederacy, not just defeat its armies and government. Southerners could hardly have found a more irksome taunt, goading Northerners to disprove it, than the charge that Yankees were hirelings and Southerners were not. Southerners' rhetoric assumed that they had a superior society; Northerners were prepared to destroy that society in order to refute the rhetoric. Making their vision of the country an extension of their pride in their own success, unionists vindicated free labor through combat and devastation.

THE NORTHERNER best known by the end of the war for his success at drastic war-making was General William Tecumseh Sherman. His victories and his methods won widespread acclaim in the North. To large numbers of people his public character embodied the severity needed for crushing the rebellion; his name became synonymous with war that punished all rebels. He owed his notoriety not only to his destructive marches through the South but also to his pungent letters and reports. Widely reprinted and often praised, these documents made him the clearest exponent of winning by a willingness to use any means. However, Sherman did not advocate this policy early in the war. He came to it through experience, after civilians long had urged it on the government. During the first two years of the war Sherman, who revered national unity and federal authority, learned new means for quelling resistance to these uncompromisable principles. For him, instability in the body politic was a personal as well as a public threat. The equanimity of his mind was upset by disorder in society, portending anarchy. When the traditional manner of war he had originally learned and at first tried to practice proved inadequate, he grew steadily more willing to gratify Northern civilians and soldiers who demanded more aggressive war. As he learned how to wage it, his confidence in the nation's future waxed stronger.

When the states of the lower South passed ordinances of secession, Sherman was professor of engineering and superintendent of the Louisiana Seminary of Learning and Military Academy. He had a wide acquaintance among Red River planters and Louisiana politicians, who praised his accomplishments during the new seminary's first year of operation. He shared their distaste for abolitionists and for Northern politicians who made hostility to slaveholders a political platform. Still, he told Louisianians that secession was treason and that he would not collaborate with it by remaining in the state.

Secession surprised Sherman. He assumed that it would lead to "civil war of the most horrible kind" and would thereby imperil the institution of slavery more quickly than anything Northern Republicans could do in peacetime. He could not believe, he said in June 1860, that "any one even Yancey or Davis would be rash enough to take the first step." In the days following the election of Lincoln, he hoped that agitation might die down, as it had done in previous crises. By the third week of November he could not miss seeing Louisiana's movement toward secession: "Many gentlemen who were heretofore moderate in their opinions now begin to fall into the popular current and go with the mad foolish crowd. . . . I had no idea that this would actually begin so soon." Sherman found their constitutional argument empty, but he scorned even more their blithe assurance that the South could establish its independence without war. When newspapers reporting South Carolina's secession on December 20 arrived at the seminary, Professor David F. Boyd was with Sherman. Boyd afterward recalled that Sherman *"burst out crying like a child,* and pacing his room in that *nervous way* of *his,* he turned to me & exclaimed: 'Boyd, you people of the *South* don't know *what you* are *doing!* You think you can tear to pieces this great Union without war! But I tell you there will be *blood-shed*—and plenty of it! and *God only knows how it will end!'* " He talked for more than an hour in the same vein.

Secessionists, Sherman thought, suffered from two mutually enhancing delusions: believing that the Northern public wanted to end slavery and believing that Northerners would not fight to preserve the union. He often said that secession was accomplished by a conspiracy among a comparatively small group of politicians. Yet he also understood that, for the most part, opinion in Louisiana was divided only between those favoring immediate secession and those favoring cooperation among Southern states in making demands on the North for the security of slavery in the states and the territories—demands he knew to be futile.

He saw that the spreading delusion could not be checked. It extended even to two Northern women who recently had moved to Alexandria: "The cruel fanatic north came from their lips as easily as though they had not just come from Ohio." Politicians were "hearing the prejudices and moving with the current." Governor Moore seized the federal arsenal at Baton Rouge, and Sherman submitted his resignation on January 18, 1861, to take effect when the state convention voted to secede, as it did on January 26. Several of Sherman's Louisiana friends later remembered his comments during his last days in Alexandria and New Orleans. He foresaw "a terrible internecine war" and predicted that the South "would be subjugated by the north, *in time.*" One of them wrote to him in the summer of 1865: "The wounds of the vanquished South, bleeding at every pore, give fatal proof of your prescience." He was among the few Americans in 1860 and 1861 whose imagination portrayed a civil war worse than the one that followed.

In the secession winter a series of shocks made the future look even worse than he had predicted in Louisiana. President Buchanan failed to support Major Robert Anderson in Fort Sumter with more troops and a strong naval force; Buchanan's State of the Union message disavowed coercion; and Sherman's travels to Ohio and Washington in February and March showed him a heedless, apathetic Northern populace whose indignation seemed to have subsided since the first outburst in response to secession. "I was amazed," he later wrote. "Everybody was attending to his business as in time of profound peace." He met Lincoln; the president seemed to underestimate the crisis and did not request Sherman's military services. Sherman told his brother "that the country was sleeping on a volcano that might burst forth at any minute." Unless Northerners let the union disintegrate, as he briefly feared they might do, this popular torpor would only worsen the ensuing war by giving the seceding states greater initial advantage from their preparation and determination.

Far from being eager to lead in subjugation of the South, which looked ever more distant, Sherman vacillated. He told his Louisiana friends that he hoped to stay out of the war; he wrote to his wife in January: "I see every chance of a long, confused and disorganizing civil war, and I feel no desire to take a hand therein." He blamed politicians both for the coming of the crisis and for the weak Northern response to secession. He doubted the usefulness of serving in an army controlled by such men. After unsuccessfully seeking a federal patronage appointment as subtreasurer in St. Louis, he took charge of a small streetcar company there. Still considering government service, he thought himself best suited to an administrative position, such as quartermaster general. He was not willing to become only the chief clerk in the War Department, even as a step to greater responsibilities. Through these fleeting, conflicting thoughts about possible courses of action ran his anxiety to find a place to ride out the coming upheavals. Sherman recalled sitting in the Senate gallery on August 1, 1850, hearing Henry Clay declare that if Kentucky took up arms against the union he, in his old age, would volunteer to help put down the rebellion. Ten years later, Clay's hyperbole was Sherman's evidence that peaceable secession was "an absurd impossibility."

In returning to the army after the firing on Fort Sumter, Sherman still took the long view. He declined an invitation to become a major general of volunteers, preferring a regular army commission as colonel of the 13th United States Infantry Regiment. The Federal victory would not come quickly from the rush of civilian volunteers to the colors. It demanded a sustained effort. Lincoln's call for men serving three years showed some understanding of the war's dimensions. Sherman wrote to Secretary of War Simon Cameron that such an army "would enable an officer to prepare his command, and do good service." Entering the war from which he had flinched, Sherman expected it to be bigger and longer than most people realized. He planned to focus, at first, on the discipline of his troops.

Sherman commanded the Third Brigade of General Daniel Tyler's Division in the first battle of Bull Run, his first experience of combat. Most of his men were recent recruits with no experience and little training, like the Confederates whom they fought. In the week before the march to Manassas, Sherman had drilled his men in brigade movements three times. His regiments carried out several charges during the disorganized fighting along the Warrenton Pike. As the Federal soldiers in mounting numbers left the battle in the afternoon, Sherman and other officers tried to get his brigade to re-form but failed: "The men kept edging off in masses toward the rear." One of Sherman's men afterward wrote to his father: "They cleaned us out and we were obliged to leave in hot haste." Although Sherman rallied his brigade at Centreville, he called them and the rest of the Federals "an armed mob" and thereafter blamed the defeat on the inexperience and panic of the privates.

The lesson of Bull Run was clear to Sherman: the army must train and discipline. Only military expertise and pride could sustain it in the years of combat that lay ahead. He was appalled by his inability to keep volunteer soldiers from stealing civilians' property and burning houses. These actions made the populace hostile. "No goths or vandals ever had less respect for the lives & property of friends and foes, and henceforth we ought never to hope for any friends in Virginia." In Fort Corcoran, part of Washington's defenses, Sherman drilled his men and imposed stricter discipline, quelling unrest among members of the 69th New York Regiment who claimed that their enlistments had expired. "I was severe," he wrote two months later, "but endeavoured to be just, for I knew if we could not command our men, we had no business to attempt invasion." President Lincoln and Secretary of State Seward, in their tour of the camps, noticed that Sherman had taken more pains than other commanders. Lincoln nominated him for promotion to brigadier general of volunteers before the Ohio congressional delegation recommended him.

Later in the war Sherman said that the defeat at Bull Run was "the best lesson a vain & conceited crowd ever got. Up to that time no one seemed to measure the danger, the necessity of prolonged preparation and infinite outlay of money." In the summer of 1861 he could not imagine how the United States would prevail in the war. He was willing to lead a brigade, but he did not want the responsibility of an independent command. With such an unreliable army and unperceptive populace, the North had not demonstrated the strength on which one could calculate in devising means for victory. A commander might make sound plans and give wise orders yet be ruined by the unreliability of Northerners' war effort. For that reason, Sherman doubted his ability to guide strategy. He preferred to lead only as many men as he could watch all at one time.

Those wishes were overruled when Lincoln assigned General Robert Anderson, hero of Fort Sumter, to command the Federal forces in Kentucky. In mid-August, Anderson asked that two of his subordinates be W. T. Sherman and George H. Thomas, brigadier generals who had served as lieutenants under Anderson in the 1840s. Stipulating that he should remain a subordinate, Sherman went west as Anderson's second-in-command, moving in the western part of central Kentucky, while Thomas operated in the eastern part. On the way to Louisville in September, Sherman stopped in Indianapolis and Springfield to talk to Governors Oliver P. Morton and Richard Yates. Both told him that they did not know how they would arm the recruits who were enlisting. Morton feared that Louisville would fall to the enemy and Indiana would be defenseless. Yet Lincoln wanted part of the Federal force to march into eastern Tennessee and help unionists there free the region from Confederate control.

In the fall of 1861 the military situation in Kentucky was confused and fluctuating. Governor Beriah Magoffin sympathized with the secessionists. The legislature in effect committed the state to the union. Confederate forces commanded by General Albert Sidney Johnston occupied Bowling Green; yet Johnston thought himself to be on the defensive, buying time until he could obtain more recruits. He had no more than

13,000 men before the end of November. The force at Bowling Green was a small brigade under General Simon Bolivar Buckner. Farther east General Felix Zollicoffer had only about 3,500 men and an equal number of reserves. Johnston later wrote of the populace: "No enthusiasm as we imagined & hoped but hostility was manifested in Kentucky." He reported his weakness to the Confederate War Department and the state governors, but the "aid given was small." The Federal forces in Kentucky were in similar disarray. Untrained and unarmed regiments arrived from Northern states. Sherman took 5,000 men to Muldraugh's Hill on the Louisville & Nashville Railroad line more than forty miles south of Louisville toward Bowling Green. He considered his position indefensible by a force of this size, and he expected an attack by Buckner, whose strength he estimated at between 8,000 and 15,000 men, "all actuated by a common purpose to destroy us." Yet he also assumed that, if Federals did not make a show of strength, they would have no hope of enlistments or support by Kentuckians and would lose the state.

The last week of September passed. No reinforcements came from the eastern army, and few recruits gathered from the countryside. Meanwhile, Sherman imagined, "All the secessionists are armed and flocking to Buckner's command." The citizens seemed to be growing more hostile because, despite Sherman's orders and entreaties, Federal troops were stealing livestock and "committing depredations that will ruin our cause." Retreat under fire would be impossible; "the whole country would rise round about us, leaving us with an ambush all the way." Expecting Buckner to attack, he told his regimental commanders: "Make up your minds to die right here, and we will fight them down to the stubs." No

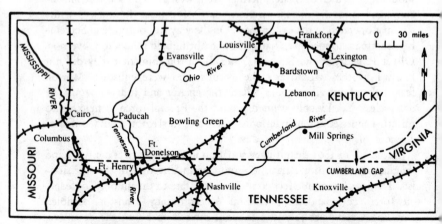

CENTRAL AND WESTERN KENTUCKY

attack came, but Sherman's anxieties soon increased. General Anderson decided that his own nerves and health could no longer bear the strain of such responsibility. He resigned his command, leaving Sherman in charge, on October 8, 1861.

Though Sherman lacked confidence in his soldiers, who had left home only a few days or weeks earlier, he persevered in trying to discipline them. He received from citizens many complaints about damaged property. He punished soldiers for their offenses and paid for what the army took, despite his belief that the people were hostile. His standard of conduct was the West Point ideal of a regular army, keeping warfare away from noncombatants for the sake of both humanity and strict discipline. He did not want to drive Kentuckians further toward supporting the Confederates by letting the state's defenders become pillagers. Sherman ordered the forcible return of escaped slaves to their masters, respecting the peacetime order of civilian society. Meanwhile, the *New York Times,* the *Cincinnati Commercial,* and the *Louisville Journal* praised Sherman. "His mind is calm, quiet, vigorous, comprehensive, and resolute"; he was "the superior of any military man in the West—clear headed and strong headed." "He performs his business with a Napoleonic dispatch." These newspapers expected him to take the offensive. The *Times* wanted "a brilliant dash on Bowling Green" and punishment of Kentucky for her citizens' equivocal behavior. "The least penalty she can expect to suffer is to see her beautiful territory devastated by fire and sword, before the invaders can be driven from her soil." Senator Garrett Davis wrote to Sherman, congratulating Kentucky for having such a commander and expressing confidence that Sherman, once furnished with men and arms, "will not only drive back Buckner & all his confederates, but reduce Middle & Eastern Tennessee." While Sherman worried about the survival and discipline of his forces, public expressions of trust in him anticipated his army's penetration and chastisement of the South under his aggressive, clear-minded leadership.

Sherman found himself in the very position he had most wanted to avoid: the senior officer for the longest and most vulnerable line between North and South. By his calculations, Johnston could easily unite with Zollicoffer, defeat Thomas, then march into Louisville. The fall of Kentucky would imperil St. Louis and Cincinnati. Sherman doubted the federal government's ability to defeat the rebellion unless Northern forces controlled Kentucky and Tennessee. Thus, failure in Kentucky meant the end of the union. Two days after taking command Sherman telegraphed to Lincoln: "The force now here or expected is entirely inadequate." He wrote to the adjutant general on October 8 that he would need 60,000 men. Yet he had fewer than one-third that number and no arms for recruits. Kentuckians, instead of enlisting, demanded that Federal troops protect them.

During his first week as commander Sherman decided that an expedition to help unionists in East Tennessee would be unwise, for lack of men, supplies, and transportation. He assumed that the army would have to carry its own rations, not take food from citizens. He worried about Thomas's ability to avoid being destroyed in Kentucky, even without going farther south. Sherman pictured destruction of the Kentucky River bridge or part of the Kentucky Central Railroad in Thomas's rear, leaving the Federal force isolated and vulnerable. Convinced that the president, the secretary of war, and General McClellan failed to realize the danger and neglected his warnings and requests for reinforcements, Sherman grew more harried. He went without food for much of the day, eating only an evening meal. He spent most of the night at the Associated Press office in Louisville because the government used the AP cypher for telegraph messages. He paced constantly, chain-smoking cigars and appearing to be deep in thought. When the office closed at three o'clock in the morning, he returned to his rooms on the ground floor of the Galt House hotel, where he continued to walk and smoke and think. As he later told his wife and his brother, he began to drink too much.

Secretary of War Cameron visited Missouri in October, intending to relieve General John C. Frémont of command of the Western Department. During Cameron's trip back to Washington, Sherman met him and Adjutant General Lorenzo Thomas in Louisville on October 16, eager to make them understand the extreme peril in which Kentucky lay. Cameron told Sherman to speak freely in the presence of the secretary's entourage, and Sherman surprised Cameron with a gloomy view of the military situation. "I then said," Sherman later recalled, "that Sidney Johnston was a fool if he did not move from Bowling Green and take Louisville; that our troops could not prevent it; that we were too weak for that space." He told Cameron he had no plans because he did not have enough men to execute a campaign. He estimated Confederate forces in Kentucky at 35,000 men. Expecting their advance toward the Ohio River, he anticipated that 20,000 Kentuckians would join them, while the effective Federal forces numbered no more than 14,000 out of a total of about 20,000. He repeated the estimate he had written for Adjutant General Thomas the previous week: expelling the rebels from Kentucky would require 60,000 men. Sherman added that the theater would eventually need 200,000 men. Cameron was shocked. Like many others, he had expected Federal troops to be attacking the rebels. He believed that Sherman was overestimating the enemy's numbers, and he criticized Sherman's lack of plans for aggressive action. Cameron said that he "was tired of this defensive war, and that the troops must assume the offensive and carry the war to the firesides of the enemy."

Stopping in Cincinnati as he continued eastward, Cameron met General Ormsby M. Mitchel, who had expected to lead the Federal advance into East Tennessee. Mitchel complained about Sherman's cancellation of it. Cameron promised that, when he got back to Washington, he would "bring order out of confusion." He and Adjutant General Thomas reported to Lincoln that Sherman was overstating the enemy's strength and mistrusting everyone. Postmaster General Montgomery Blair wrote on October 22: "Sherman is playing the fool in Ky. He is believing the most exaggerated stories & not doing any thing till he can get reinforcements to the most extraordinary amts." On the same day, Sherman was telegraphing to the adjutant general: "I again repeat that our force here is out of all proportion to the importance of the position. Our defeat would be disastrous to the nation." Cameron and Thomas apparently decided to discredit Sherman by making his alarmist views public. The secretary's entourage in Louisville had included Samuel Wilkeson, the Washington correspondent of the *New York Tribune*. After the conference Wilkeson told another reporter, Henry Villard, that Cameron believed Sherman's mind had become unbalanced by his fears and he must not be left in command. On October 30, the *Tribune* published the adjutant general's official report of the discussion between the general and the secretary. Its wording contrasted Cameron's desire for offensive war with Sherman's demand for 200,000 men, clearly implying that Sherman was unreasonable and defeatist.

Publication of Thomas's report heightened Sherman's anxiety. He had already shown his hostility toward newspaper correspondents, whom he considered parasites and sensation-mongers. Most important, he feared that their reports would reveal to the enemy the Federals' vulnerability. The *Tribune* did so and seemed to Sherman a proof that neither the public nor officials in Washington realized the danger. On November 4 he telegraphed to the adjutant general a reiteration of his warning about the enemy, "whose force and numbers the country never has and probably never will comprehend. I am told that my estimate of troops needed for this line, viz. 200,000, has been construed to my prejudice and therefore leave it to the future." This was one of the dispatches Lincoln called "desponding, complaining, and almost insubordinate." It may have been the one Thomas read to a member of Congress "with some ridicule," calling the troop request "unnecessary" and Sherman "crazy."

Feeling isolated and misunderstood, Sherman grew still more alarmed during the early days of November. On October 20 he had said the enemy's forces outnumbered the Federals three to one. Six days later he had concluded that the ratio was five to one. By November 1 reports coming to him fluctuated in their estimates of enemy strength from 25,000 to 60,000. The coming disaster loomed ever more vividly: Confederates, "at the signal," would attack; the Federal force south of Louisville would be wiped out; the Confederates would drive on to the Ohio, joined by the Kentucky populace, who could "shoot us all down like dogs"; the river cities would fall, and the Northern states would lie open to invasion. Sherman wrote to his wife: "The idea of going down to history with a fame such as threatens me nearly makes me crazy, indeed I may be so now."

On November 3, Sherman heard that Confederates at Bowling Green were gathering a large number of wagons from the countryside. Day after day his mind returned to the report on the wagons, certain that they presaged the imminent assault. In fact, Albert Sidney Johnston had no intention of advancing. He told one of his engineers that he was "determined to move cautiously—risking no disaster." The Federal forces were "too strong to make an advance prudent." Johnston afterward reported that, to conceal the Confederates' weakness, "I magnified my forces to the enemy." In Louisville, Sherman, unable to sleep, paced and smoked and imagined the capture of the volunteer railroad guards, the breaking of the rail lines, and the isolation and destruction of his dispersed camps. He telegraphed to General McClellan: "Our forces too small to do good, and too large to sacrifice." On November 6, he wrote to the governor of Ohio to warn him that the enemy, if in the strength reported, could not be stopped. "You should have some good men ready for any emergency."

Two days later he could stand the strain no longer and asked McClellan to appoint a new commander for the department. A week passed before General Don Carlos Buell arrived to replace him. During those days, Sherman received still more distressing news. While watching for the irresistible Confederate onslaught, he learned that the unionists in East Tennessee, unwilling to continue waiting for the Federal invasion Sherman had withheld, had started their uprising on November 8. They burned five bridges on the rail lines east and west of Knoxville and fired on Confederate troops. The futile effort was quickly crushed by the Confederates, who arrested many unionists and summarily hanged five men near the burned bridges. For months afterward Sherman repeatedly explained how he had been unable to send troops into Tennessee, despite the urgings of Lincoln, Secretary Chase, Senator Andrew Johnson, and Representative Horace Maynard. Even so, he kept thinking about the execution of the unionists, telling his brother that it "has been the chief source of my despondency as I may be mainly responsible for it."

In response to a telegram from one of Sherman's officers, Ellen Sherman arrived in Louisville on November 10 with her brother and the Shermans' two sons. Before seeing her husband, she had feared that he might have succumbed to the melancholic depression that had afflicted some members of Sherman's mother's family. Though she called this disorder "insanity," its symptoms in Sherman's uncle and grandmother had been "extreme depression of spirits" or "morbid melancholy which never deranges the intellect or incapacitates for business." She found her husband to be in "a morbid state of anxiety," troubled by "melancholy forebodings," but she soon concluded that he did not suffer from the familial disorder. His problem was that he "gives himself too much concern & takes the dangers too much to heart." Ellen said that his spirits were improving and that he would be as well as ever when Buell arrived, yet Sherman kept writing warnings about the "vast force" of Confederates preparing for a "concentric and simultaneous" advance "along the whole line." In the week before Buell reached Louisville, the *Cincinnati Commercial* began to compare Sherman unfavorably with his successor. Buell "has the *go* in him, and does not want two hundred thousand men," while Sherman "seems to lack . . . the boldness of conception and dash of execution, that always distinguishes great commanders." On Buell's first full day in command, the *Commercial* headed one of its editorials: "Forward to East Tennessee!" In Washington, Alexander McClure asked Assistant Secretary of War Thomas A. Scott what the appointment of Buell meant. Scott answered: "Sherman's gone in the head."

Sherman went to Missouri to serve without a command under General Henry W. Halleck, who replaced Frémont in command of the department. Though Sherman had been freed from responsibility, he could not escape the depressing conviction that the North had lost its chance to defeat the rebellion. In St. Louis, where most of his old friends were Confederate sympathizers, he saw more evidence of Missourians' hostility to the Federals. Thinking Southerners to be united, bitter, and capable of any atrocity, he continued to anticipate disaster and feared that conquest of the South was impossible. He expressed these opinions in conversation, predicting that the Confederates would take St. Louis. Halleck sent him on an inspection trip to Sedalia, authorizing him to take command of the troops there if John Pope were absent and if the enemy threatened. Lieutenant Colonel Alfred West Gilbert noted in his diary that Sherman "took command" on November 26: "From the manner in which the Commanding general acts many think he is out of his head." Officers at Sedalia sent warnings to Halleck that Sherman was "stampeded" and was "stampeding" the army. Halleck countermanded some troop movements Sherman had ordered—movements that later proved to have been correct but premature—recalled him from the field, and sent him home to Ohio for a twenty-day rest. Halleck wrote to McClellan: "General S[herman's] physical and mental system is so completely broken by labor and care as to render him for the present entirely unfit for duty."

In Lancaster with his family, Sherman improved in health and spirits until he read the *Cincinnati Commercial* on December 11. One item began: "The painful intelligence reaches us in such form that we are not at liberty to discredit it that Gen. W. T. Sherman, late commander of the Department of the Cumberland, is *insane*. It appears that he was at times when commanding in Kentucky, stark mad." Murat Halstead wrote the article, relying on what he had been told by Henry Villard. Villard repeated Samuel Wilkeson's description of the meeting between Cameron and Sherman in Louisville and evidently also obtained a copy of Halleck's report to McClellan about Sherman's condition. Villard urged Halstead to publish the story in order to prevent a catastrophe, which might result from Sherman's retaining a command. Halstead recalled meeting Sherman in Washington before the battle of Bull Run and hearing him say that, if the army were defeated, the people of Washington would show their Southern sympathies "by cutting the throats of our wounded with case knives." The paragraph in the *Commercial,* though ostensibly written in sympathy, studiously repeated such phrases as "out of their wits," "his mad freaks," "a madman," "his strange conduct," and "loss of the mind." The story was quickly reprinted from New York to St. Louis.

Members of Sherman's family went to work to refute the story and to reassure Lincoln. Soon satisfied that Sherman was not insane, Halstead expressed his regrets; for the rest of the war the *Commercial* often praised Sherman. Lincoln had not abandoned the favorable opinion of Sherman he had formed during the summer. But Sherman, back in St. Louis after his furlough, was dejected. Halleck put him in charge of a training installation at Benton Barracks, a bleak set of buildings that one visitor called "foul hovels" in "a sea of mud." Trying to impose strict discipline, he provoked the hostility of the soldiers, who thought him "a very morose and gloomy sort of a man." He concluded that in Kentucky he had been "sadly mistaken in the power and plans of the enemy" and that he ought not to have given up his command. He brooded about the shame his disgrace would bring on his brother, his father-in-law, his wife, and their children. He wrote to his wife: "I feel as though I should cast myself into the Mississippi."

Twice within six weeks Sherman had seen himself ridiculed throughout the North: once for the military estimate he had given to Cameron and once for his conduct in Kentucky and Missouri. The public comments assumed that Sherman had been too timid and cautious. The rebels could be defeated by an aggressive general who did not make them more formidable in fantasy than they really were. Five days before reporting that Sherman was insane, the *New York Times* was looking forward to the invasion of Mississippi: "It will not be many months before one hundred thousand Federal troops will be upon the soil of the State, to carry with them all the horrors and devastations of war." John Sherman argued to his brother that Sherman's prewar acquaintance with secessionists had warped his judgment, causing him to "overlook the enormity of their crime" and thereby depriving him of the necessary relentlessness. "They will only be beaten by men who regard them as Rebels—Traitors . . . who as such deserve the punishment of Death." Senator Sherman received letters from constituents supporting this view: "What has kept our armies back in Kentucky? Slavery! . . . The rebels will *never* submit till *forced* to do by military subjugation"; "go ahead and *conquer* the Rebellion in the *shortest* and most effectual way possible—regardless of *means* and of *consequences!*" Edwin M. Stanton replaced Cameron as secretary of war and surpassed his predecessor in his eagerness to take the offensive: "We should have . . . one hundred thousand men thrusting upon Nashville and sweeping rebellion & treason out of Kentucky with fire & sword."

Sherman had thought that the only way to save the union was to hold the upper South and eventually regain control of the Mississippi. This would require, he believed, a large, well-disciplined, well-supplied army. Only a large force could confront the united, bitter secessionists; only a disciplined army could win the support of Southern unionists by refraining from disorder and plunder. He found himself in Kentucky with a small, undisciplined force unfit to fight but given to depredations that alienated the populace. This gave him the feeling of "riding a whirlwind unable to guide the storm." He gave up his command, he explained in December, because "I was convinced in Kentucky that I could not guide events. . . . To guide I had not the faith which would inspire success." Yet all around him politicians, soldiers, and organs of public opinion expressed a different kind of faith: a trust in the inherent efficacy of war-making, a belief that fighting and punishing rebels wherever possible was the best and quickest way to save the union.

During his weeks at Benton Barracks he continued to write pessimistically, seeing no hope in the war and wondering whether he were crazy. Sherman had mistaken Kentuckians' state of mind, as well as the strength and intentions of the Confederate army in Kentucky. His miscalculation of the military situation in the Department of the Cumberland was humiliating. But, unlike people urging him to the offensive, he had foreseen the difficulty of overcoming the rebellion by force of arms. His

intimations of the fierceness of Southern resistance and of the scale of
Northern effort needed to defeat it had been valid, but he had projected
these amorphous intuitions about the future on the initial movements in
Kentucky, expecting of the small armies there a violent climax that
instead eventually spread over dozens of months and more than a thousand miles. In 1861 some people thought Sherman insane or unbalanced
because of his excessive alarm about an exaggerated enemy threat. He
doubted his own sanity when the prevailing heedless overconfidence left
him no grounds for faith that the North could quell the rebels. From both
points of view—Sherman's alarmist one and his critics' eager one—sanity
was equated with waging massive war against the South. For war's
purposes, the question "What is real?" became, in effect, "What is the
strength of the Confederacy?" and "What effort is needed to destroy it?"
As Sherman's answers and the public's answers grew more congruent, the
former problems in Kentucky seemed petty. The way to victory was
increasingly clear to all. A new theme began to appear in his comments.
The great problem was still the readiness of the Southern populace to "rise
up and commit havoc. The restoration of the Union can only occur after
this feeling on the part of the people subsides, and that it will never do
unless great success attend our armies." Instead of achieving such success,
undisciplined soldiers' "acts of trespass & violence" were converting
unionists into enemies. Under these circumstances, how could the South
be subjugated? He could think of only one way: that "the people of the
north actually obliterate all in their progress south and fill up by settlement." If one were going to trust to the momentum of war, it would
have to be almost unimaginably terrible. As Sherman had said when the
Commercial's article appeared, "In these times tis hard to say who are sane
and who insane."

A few months later, Sherman established in his own eyes his courage
and his competence to lead men. He did so in the battle of Shiloh. While
Grant opened the Tennessee and Cumberland rivers by taking Fort Henry
and Fort Donelson in February 1862, Sherman worked at Paducah, Kentucky, forwarding men and supplies. When Grant's army headed toward
Corinth, Mississippi, Sherman commanded a division in it. The battle of
Shiloh took place on April 6 and 7, just north of the Mississippi state line,
along the west bank of the Tennessee River. It became the subject of
intense, prolonged dispute. Northerners and Southerners argued among
themselves and with their opponents about what had happened and who
was responsible. The size of the paper controversy rivaled that connected
with the battle of Gettysburg. Sherman always insisted that the Confederates' morning attack on the unentrenched Federal camp was not a surprise.
He admitted that he, Grant, and other generals had not expected an attack.

Sherman had assumed that the Confederates would not leave their base on the railroad to hit the Federals in their base on the river. His pickets' encounters with Confederate cavalrymen in the days before the battle he had dismissed as minor skirmishing. Not until he saw massed Confederate infantry on the morning of April 6 did he realize that an assault was imminent. Still, the Federal divisions had enough time to form their lines. Sherman also denied that Grant's army owed its survival on the 6th to the long-awaited arrival of Buell's Army of the Ohio in the afternoon.

These controverted questions provoked especially passionate debate because the battle was bitter, lethal, and confused. Most men on both sides came new to combat, yet fought all day on the 6th, Confederates repeatedly assaulting, Federals repulsing them while moving back toward the river. At the same time, large numbers of green soldiers headed for the rear in panic. This happened in both armies but was more prevalent and memorable on the Federal side. Thousands of men huddled along the river under the protection of the low bluff on the left bank, while nearby their fellow soldiers continued to fight. Sherman estimated that half of his 8,000 men "disappeared to the rear." Some Federal units remaining on the field lost their cohesion; soldiers fired in line with strangers from other regiments. Under these volatile conditions, successful defense depended partly on the generals' ability to hold their mixed forces together and direct their fire despite the disarray of the structure of organization and command. Grant did not reach the battlefield until two hours after fighting had started, and he afterward gave Sherman the principal credit for maintaining the line. While General Benjamin M. Prentiss's division withstood Confederate assaults on the center until it was flanked and surrounded, Sherman's men held the right. He moved his line back three times and took a final position more than a mile from the river at four o'clock. He directed both his own division and that of General John A. McClernand, who hung around Sherman, allowing him to give the orders though McClernand was the senior brigadier general. In the sustained fire, Sherman had three horses shot under him, saw many men near him fall, received a slight wound in his hand and a bruise where a spent ball hit him. Several other shots that could have killed him narrowly missed. He gave no sign of panic, did not succumb to awful imaginings of disaster, and in fact looked calmer than usual. He persuaded regiments out of ammunition to remain on the firing line in order not to alarm other troops by falling back separately. Grant visited his line but gave him no orders until late in the afternoon. One officer wrote to John Sherman later in the month: "I was not out of sight of your brother on the 6 or 7th and never saw a braver man."

General P. G. T. Beauregard had taken command of the Confederates after Albert Sidney Johnston's death on the battlefield; he decided not to assault the Federals' line during the last hour of daylight. By then the Confederates, according to Braxton Bragg, were "disorganized, demoralized, and exhausted." Another Confederate commander, Leonidas Polk, later reported that Sherman's and McClernand's men had "fought with determined courage and contested every inch of ground." Grant ordered preparations for a counterattack the next day. Although Buell's army had begun to arrive on the east bank of the river and a few regiments crossed on the 6th, Grant and Sherman insisted for the rest of their lives that the Army of the Ohio had not "saved" them and that the fighting on the 6th was their army's victory. With the help of Buell's men and General Lew Wallace's belatedly arrived division, driving back the Confederates on the 7th seemed easier than the work of the previous day.

Both Grant and Halleck, who afterward came from St. Louis to assume command, publicly praised Sherman. Halleck reported to Secretary Stanton: "It is the unanimous opinion here that Brig. Gen. W. T. Sherman saved the fortune of the day on the 6th instant, and contributed largely to the glorious victory on the 7th." He was promoted to major general of volunteers. His conduct during the battle had made his name. Halleck's report meant, Sherman said, that "at last I stand redeemed from the vile slanders of that Cincinnati paper." Sherman used the battle to justify his earlier alarm. By concentrating their forces to attack the most advanced Federal outpost, the Confederates "performed the very thing which Johnson should have done in Kentucky last October." If the Federal army had been defeated at Shiloh or were yet defeated in Mississippi, the border states of Kentucky, Tennessee, and Missouri still lay open to Confederate invasion. The dangers of which he had warned in the fall of 1861 loomed in the spring of 1862. He wrote to his brother: "I suppose you and all are now convinced that I never over estimated the strength resources and dreadful determination of our enemy." By its very ferocity the battle of Shiloh struck Sherman as an acting out of his ominous predictions and as a demonstration that he could remain steady in the face of their fulfillment. The grounds for his growing confidence could only be the North's increasing resolve to destroy the enemy's resources and determination.

Despite this evidence of his foresight and stability, Sherman again found himself under public attack. Shiloh was the first great battle of the war—20,000 men killed or wounded in thirty-six hours. Long casualty lists had not yet grown familiar. Northerners had not adequately envisioned the cost of subduing the rebellion. They had not expected such a show of Confederate strength; nor had they accepted Sherman's belief that war's end would not come "for a long long time." Such surprising and inconclusive violence demanded explanation. Newspaper reporters blamed the generals, especially Grant but also Sherman and others. The best-known dispatch came on April 9 from Whitelaw Reid, correspondent of the *Cincinnati Gazette*. With retrospective comprehensiveness of vision and with a profusion of circumstantial detail, Reid exploited the disorder of the battle to magnify the triumph of the narrator's art. He contrasted Grant's grounds for anticipating an attack with Grant's failure to fortify his camps or otherwise prepare. Reid described his own arrival on the battlefield after the fighting had begun, when he saw the frightened men under the river bluff and found Sherman's, McClernand's, and Prentiss's divisions "falling back in disorder." Though he had not seen the start of the battle, he described the first contact as a complete rout, Confederates suddenly appearing in the Federal camps, shooting and bayoneting unsuspecting soldiers caught dressing, washing, cooking, and eating. In contrast with this "wild disorder" among the Federals, he depicted "the serried columns of the magnificent rebel advance." Commending Sherman's personal courage, Reid nevertheless made the story of Sunday, April 6, one of almost complete ruin, thereby heightening the drama—accentuated with his exclamation points—when he narrated the arrival of Buell's army. Praising soldiers who had stayed to fight, Reid kept reminding his readers that the generals had disposed the troops haphazardly, had failed to entrench, and had shown no plans, no "generalship." Correspondents reaching the army after the battle and some who never came near it reported on Shiloh in a tone similar to Reid's. Some reporters faked eyewitness narratives. The *Cincinnati Commercial*'s correspondent recalled the following year that he had arrived in camp on April 13 and had heard soldiers complaining about Grant. "Of course I could but echo the popular sentiment." The *New York Tribune* blamed Sherman for the Confederates' capture of Prentiss. The *Cincinnati Gazette* denounced the promotion of Sherman after the battle and set out to expose his "spurious reputation." Although the heaviest censure fell on Grant, Sherman took it all personally: once more his critics were pointing to his weakness—not lack of courage but lack of ability to handle an invading army so as to hurt the enemy without losing many men.

Grant's principal supporter, Representative Elihu B. Washburne, received reports of public opinion warning him that the Shiloh stories would stick: "Who ever is to blame for the surprise of Sunday & the great loss of life &c at that battle . . . will have to go under." Senator James Harlan of Iowa said that those who allowed Grant to retain a command "carry on their skirts the blood of thousands of their slaughtered countrymen." In this censure, Sherman saw a pattern, as he suggested in his letter to the Forest City Union Association of Cleveland: "Our people are at fault." There was, Sherman knew, "constant pressure on the army to attempt something bold & rash." Yet the casualties sustained by untrained, unreliable troops brought condemnation from the very politicians and reporters who had urged the army forward to the combat for which it was ill prepared. "The political leaders dare not lay the blame where it belongs," and the reporters "like vultures hang around after the carnage is done, when they are safe to gloat over the death & ruin of their own creation." However, the sacrifice of scapegoats, in lieu of facing the difficulty and the magnitude of the war, originated not with correspondents but with their readers. "So greedy after victims are our people that newspapers must provide victims to suit the market.—The people are the ultimate cause. When public opinion changes a better condition of things will result & not before." Sherman relied on the war to effect that change, to teach citizens the need for a regular army. Reacting to the outcry after Shiloh, he put his trust not in sudden bold strokes or in a collapse of secessionist spirit among the Southern populace but in preparation for a long, severe conflict between the armies. Sherman said of the newly combined force of Grant and Buell: "Figures begin to approximate my standard." Two weeks later he wrote: "We must sally forth and have a more bloody battle than that of April 6 & 7. . . . According to my notion the war will soon begin."

Sherman denounced the follies of his critics, but his approach to the war changed in response to some of their concerns. After taking Corinth, Mississippi, Halleck dispersed his large army, leaving Sherman in command at Memphis, Tennessee, beginning in July. Federal occupation of west Tennessee brought out some unionists, true or feigned, but encountered mostly resentment, concern for property, bushwhacking of isolated soldiers, and potshots at boats on the Mississippi River. Civilians with cotton to sell were in many cases helping the Confederate war effort by procuring blankets, shoes, food, medicine, salt, and munitions from the North. The coin, currency, and treasury notes Southerners received for cotton enabled the Confederacy to buy military supplies. Sherman ordered that the purchase of cotton stop, but the authorities in Washington, responsive to heavy demand and high prices, overruled him. The busy commercial activity of Memphis, ostensibly civilian, supported the Confederate armies.

During his five months in the city, Sherman's thinking about the war moved more rapidly toward military action against the Southern populace. At the beginning he seemed reluctant. As his division marched through Mississippi and Tennessee in June and July, he paid for supplies and refused to help slaves leave their masters. He repeatedly ordered that pillaging be prevented, warning that, if it did not stop, "the country will rise on us and justly shoot us down like dogs and wild beasts." Upon arriving in Memphis, he talked tough. To suggestions that he encourage unionist sentiment he replied that the army "didn't come here to visit their friends. The people of the city were prisoners of war." But he restored the mayor and council to office under his supervision and wrote to his daughter that, even though Southerners wanted to kill him, "I cannot but look on these people as my old friends." The *New York Herald* at first reported that Sherman would govern "with an iron hand." Soon, however, Northern newspapers started to censure him for showing too much kindness. In August, John Sherman sent him examples and warned him: "The only criticism I notice of your management in Memphis is your leniency to the rebels." According to the senator, "the popular idea" was that the rebels must be "conquered, by confiscation, by the employment of their slaves by terror, energy audacity rather than by conciliation."

Guerrillas' activities gave the immediate provocation for General Sherman's increased severity. On the way to Memphis in July he had arrested twenty-five prominent men near Moscow, Tennessee, after a Federal forage train had been shot at. He intended "to hold the neighborhood fully responsible, though the punishment may fall on the wrong parties." When riverboats carrying civilian passengers and food for Tennesseeans came under fire from the banks of the Mississippi, Sherman extended this policy. On September 24 he sent the 46th Ohio Regiment to level the town of Randolph, Tennessee. Three days later he announced that, for each boat fired on in the future, the families of ten Confederate soldiers would be evicted from the city and sent beyond Federal lines. Sherman knew that Memphis had sent sixty-two companies of men into the Confederate army; he had a roster of their kin. For more than two weeks after the burning of Randolph and the publication of the expulsion order, the sniping stopped. When it resumed in mid-October, Sherman carried out his threat, ordering forty families to move twenty-five miles out of Memphis and sending the 46th Ohio to destroy all houses, farms, and corn crops on the west bank of the Mississippi for a distance of fifteen miles downriver from Memphis. These punishments were not simple cases of reprisal for unprovoked attacks. Before they occurred Sherman had sent out many patrols. Soldiers committed what he called "great atrocities"; citizens killed soldiers; soldiers "burned many homes and killed citizens." Early in September he had worried that the commander of the 52d Indiana was so "energetic and full of zeal" that the regiment might provoke firing on boats. A woman in the area wrote about Sherman: "He is the wiriest rat of them all he keeps the Yankees raiding around in every direction so that the people in the surrounding country can't have a minutes peace or rest."

Sherman's patrols and the river traffic evoked from Southerners violent reactions, confirming the opinion he had held before coming to Memphis: "We cannot change the inveterate hatred of these people." While Sherman's officers were congratulating themselves on a change from protecting property to the practice of "burn, sink, and destroy," Sherman could imagine the war's worsening until "no life or property would be safe in the regions where we do hold possession and power." He clung to notions of restraint because he saw no necessary limits. As his confidence in Federal power increased, his warnings to rebels grew more peremptory. He replied to complaints about pillage by saying that he would punish individually identified soldiers who had not acted under orders. Nevertheless, the Southern people, "who made the war," must expect waste and damage: "generally war is destruction and nothing else." The only question was: at what point on the scale of increasing violence would Southerners give up their resistance? Expelling families from Memphis gave the rebels only a hint of his far more drastic vision of repeopling the South. And he found that it worked. Two months after acting on his order he reported to Secretary Stanton that firing on boats had not resumed.

So far, Sherman would only risk raids launched from a secure base on the river. He threatened to "land troops on unexpected points and devastate the country into the interior." Such comparatively small-scale ideas arose from the same assumptions underlying his later, much larger operations. He learned from his Memphis experience that the rebellion could not be quelled with garrisons of occupying forces and that the citizenry would side with the Confederacy until the United States hurt them enough to make them quit doing so. Before his stay in Memphis the limits on Sherman's army included rules sharply differentiating civilians from combatants; thereafter he was limited only by his troops' power, his own imagination, and the scruples he and his men chose to observe. To reassure his daughter and, by extension, himself that he was not a "brutal wretch," he repeated: "I feel that we are fighting our own people." At the same time, his images of Southerners' hostility toward him drew no distinctions of age or sex. He told his daughter: "Hundreds of children like yourself are daily taught to curse my name, and each night thousands kneel in prayer & beseech the almighty to consign me to perdition." As if to confirm this view, the *Chattanooga Rebel* predicted that expulsion of families from Memphis would "make him personally an object of particular revenge."

Against his own predisposition, Sherman had grown ready to make war on Southern society. He had no deep-seated objections to the social order, no desire to transform it forcibly in pursuit of greater morality, democracy, or enterprise. In this respect he agreed with McClellan and Buell, both of whom Lincoln relieved from command while Sherman was in Memphis. Like them, he would have preferred to leave the South unchanged if its people would forgo secession. But, unlike them, he had abandoned hope for preserving the union by conciliating Southerners and confining the war to soldiers' combat. To win, the North would have to attack the society Sherman once had found congenial. After coming to this conclusion, he still moved slowly. He talked of "extermination," "universal confiscation and colonization": "Enemies must be killed or transported to some other country." Still, he came nowhere near such measures. His hyperbole expressed his conviction that the main obstacle to Federal success was Southern unity. He set out to sap that unity by raising the cost of rebellion until Southerners turned from the Confederate cause to protect what was left of their private interests. He explained in January 1864: "Three years ago by a little reflection and patience they could have had a hundred years of peace and prosperity. . . . Last year they could have saved their slaves, but now it is too late. . . . Next year their lands will be taken . . . and in another year they may beg in vain for their lives."

In Sherman's rudimentary analysis of the Southern social order, the "laborers & mechanics," with whom he also grouped "smaller farmers" and "merchants," had acted with the wealthy planter class in the erroneous belief that both groups shared the same interests. These "poorer & industrious classes" could be made neutral, tired of war, and ultimately obedient to the federal government by showing them that the planters had led them to ruin. The "rich and slave-holding" were not united in their secessionist purpose, either. Some remained so stubborn that they would have to be killed. Others could learn in much the same way that the poorer people did. "I know we can manage this class," Sherman wrote in September 1863, "but only by action; argument is exhausted, and words have not their usual meaning. Nothing but the logic of events touches their understanding." When the landowners of Warren County, Mississippi, complained about depredations, he explained the meaning of the army's action: a commander "may take your house, your fields, your everything, and turn you all out, helpless, to starve. It may be wrong, but that don't alter the case. In war you can't help yourselves, and the only possible remedy is to stop war. . . . Our duty is not to build up; it is rather to destroy both the rebel army and whatever of wealth or property it has founded its boasted strength upon." The poorer people, to end their suffering, and the richer people, to preserve some of their property, would give up war rather than allow destruction to run its full course.

As with his movement toward harsher treatment of civilians, Sherman developed this threat of societal disintegration during his stay in Memphis. He acknowledged that "as Belligerents we ought to seek the hostile Army and fight it and not the people." Somewhat disingenuously, he argued that the Confederate army had excused the Federals from this limitation by declining battle at Corinth. Then he came to his main conclusion, on which he acted for the rest of the war: "We are not bound to follow them, but rightfully make war by any means that will tend to bring about an end and restore Peace. . . . one of the modes of bringing People to reason is to touch their Interests pecuniary or property." In his mind's eye Sherman still saw the united, warlike South that had spooked him in Kentucky. He wrote to his brother in August: "Don't expect to overcome such a country or subdue such a people in one two or five years, it is the task of half a century." In Memphis he found the way to break the enemy eventually: by striking at society's cohesion, which he had long said was strong but was based on the delusion of serving the interests of all through secession.

The Federal campaign to take Vicksburg, Mississippi, lasting from December 1862 until July 4, 1863, concluded Sherman's turn to a new conception of the war. This campaign made him confident of ultimate victory, and it showed him the means whereby victory could be won. But it began with failure and another round of newspaper censure of Sherman. He and Grant hoped to take Vicksburg by a quick strike while it was lightly defended. The Federal army had reached Oxford, Mississippi. Grant decided to move overland along the Mississippi Central Railroad; he sent Sherman back to Memphis to bring another force downriver on transports, thus converging on Vicksburg from two directions. By the time Sherman reached the Yazoo River north of the city on December 26, Grant had decided not to continue his advance. The Confederates had destroyed his supply depot at Holly Springs, Mississippi, and he did not think he could rely on the countryside for supplies. Knowing that Grant had turned back, the Confederates reinforced Vicksburg, while Sherman still expected to break through the defenses and be met by Grant. He wrote to Admiral David Dixon Porter on December 20: "I want to get ashore in Yazoo before they can concentrate." On December 28 he told Porter he would go "into Vicksburg if it be in human possibility."

The next day Sherman ordered an assault on part of the Confederate works along bluffs overlooking Chickasaw Bayou. It failed. The bodies of water and the terrain confined the Federals' movements so that, as the

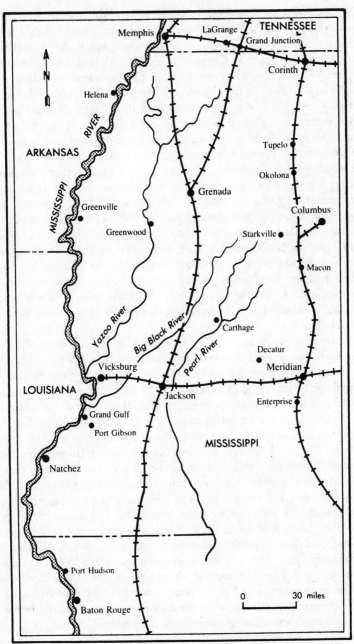

THE MISSISSIPPI THEATER

Confederate General Stephen D. Lee reported before the battle, "There is scarcely a place around the lines where they could advance with company front 75 yards." Sherman afterward argued that the assault could have succeeded if General George W. Morgan had been more aggressive. But Grant, having looked over the Confederate positions after the Federals took them from the rear in May, said that a successful frontal attack would have been impossible. More than 500 of Sherman's men were captured or missing. More than 1,200 were hit during the short battle. Many of these lay exposed for fifty hours in a cold rain, moaning, calling out, and dying. Admiral Porter later recalled Sherman's visit to his flagship on the night of December 29: "This was the only occasion during the war that I saw Genl. Sherman despond." Sherman was uncharacteristically silent and seemed "all unhinged." Soon, however, the two men began to plan another attack. The weather forestalled the attempt, and Sherman received word that Grant had withdrawn, which meant that the Confederates could concentrate many more troops against him than he had expected. Taking Vicksburg would have put him in a worse position than he was already in. Instead of renewing the assault, he re-embarked his force on the transports. Three months later he contended: "The only mistake I made was in not waiting to see the signs of Grants approach."

Again newspapers in St. Louis, Chicago, Cincinnati, New York, and other cities denounced Sherman. They said that, in ordering an assault, he threw away his men's lives in a vain attempt to win glory by taking Vicksburg before Grant or McClernand could arrive; they said that his orders and troop dispositions were confused; they accused him of panic in withdrawing after the battle; and they revived the suggestion, directly or by innuendo, that he was insane. The *Daily Missouri Democrat* commented: "A stupid blunder, and an ignoble attempt to forestall another general's laurels, have brought shame and calamity to our country, desolation and woe to more than two thousand households, and peril to the cause of liberty and free government." All the correspondents' mentioning insanity did not occur by coincidence. They had agreed to use the charge to discredit Sherman. His hostility to reporters was well known. He had tried to exclude them from the Vicksburg expedition, though five accompanied it. Then one of his officers had removed reporters' dispatches from the mail. Sherman arrested Thomas W. Knox of the *New York Herald,* court-martialing him on charges of publishing false accusations and disobeying orders. The reporters took their revenge. Knox admitted as much to Sherman and explained that if a reporter "cannot get at the truth, he must publish falsehood."

In subsequent weeks, Knox acknowledged the errors in his report. The

Missouri Republican, which had published one of the most scathing accounts, made a "full and apologetic retraction." Lincoln, Stanton, and Grant retained their confidence in Sherman, and his public standing was not appreciably hurt. His brother and several friends tried to persuade him that his preoccupation with reporters and with censure in the press was futile and self-defeating. By kindness he could win their support. By ignoring criticisms he could spare himself unnecessary anxiety. Sherman still brooded. He insisted on expelling Knox from the Mississippi theater. He talked about suing the *Missouri Republican* for libel, and he alarmed John Sherman by saying he would resign. He was especially irritated by being subordinate to McClernand. In the second week of January, Sherman, co-operating with Porter, directed Federal forces that captured Fort Hindman fifty miles up the Arkansas River. McClernand held command, but the plan came from Sherman. Porter provided naval support on the condition that Sherman, not McClernand, lead the troops. The fort fell to a combined naval artillery barrage and infantry assault. Confederates could no longer use it as a base for vessels raiding river traffic on the Mississippi. With reporters' co-operation McClernand took all the credit for the victory. The *New York Herald*'s correspondent contrasted Sherman with McClernand: "The one leader brought us defeat and disgrace, the other has brought us honor and success."

The battle at Chickasaw Bluffs was Sherman's first large independent operation and his first clear defeat; it could not be blamed on the soldiers, as at Bull Run. Though the casualties troubled him and he privately admitted his error in attacking too soon, he interpreted the outcome as a vindication of his earlier comments on the war. The rebels again had proven that they were as strong and dedicated as Sherman had often said. The casualties were only beginning—"Say Vicksburg will cost us 10000, Port Hudson 5000, Jackson 30000 & so on." The public and the press clamored for a sweep down the Mississippi, but citizens failed to mount an adequate, united effort. Instead, they recruited too few men, allowed reporters to publish information for the enemy, and destroyed generals by newspaper attacks. Though his complaints sounded like the ones he had made in Kentucky, this time Sherman did not resign his command. By early 1863 he had concluded that Northern victory was possible and that he could help achieve it. He wanted the federal government to unite the North forcibly in order to defeat the South. He recommended large-scale conscription, suppression of newspaper criticism, a turn from the pen to the sword. He told Murat Halstead: "Discussion must cease and action begin." The federal government would have to become much more coercive because the rebels had shown "their ability to prolong this war indefinitely." Consequently, "to subdue the rebellion you must obliterate a whole race, our equals in courage, resources, and determination."

As usual, Sherman's conduct was less drastic than his words. He did not again try to exclude reporters from his operations. In the war's last two years he received increasingly favorable attention in major Northern newspapers. With growing success he did what the press had long been urging. He swept across broad sections of the South in a manner he originally had deemed both unjustifiable and unfeasible. In turn, reporters, editors, and their readers more fully accepted the truth of some of Sherman's admonitions: that the success they wanted would require far more resources, men, and casualties—including those from generals' mistakes—than most people had admitted during the first two years of war. Instead of ending his career, Sherman's failure at Chickasaw Bluffs made him more eager for an overpowering Northern war effort that would spare him another such mortification.

To take Vicksburg, Grant needed to get his army east of the city, where he could prevent the Confederates from reinforcing the garrison or uniting their divided forces against him. He also needed a supply line from the North, preferably the secure one provided by the Mississippi and Yazoo rivers. During the first three months of 1863, Grant's men worked on a variety of engineering projects designed to open a water route to the south or east of Vicksburg without exposing vessels to Confederate artillery in the city's fortifications. All of these were frustrated either by the water or by the Confederates. With Admiral Porter's co-operation, Grant decided to march down the west bank of the Mississippi and cross the river below Vicksburg. This required that naval vessels run past the guns of Vicksburg and Grand Gulf.

Sherman advised Grant against this movement, which violated sound military principles by abandoning the supply line. Sherman said that the obligation to maintain a base of supplies was "an axiom in war." He "quoted Jomini in favor of the policy of concentration," recommending that Grant's army return to Memphis and advance overland to Vicksburg along the rail line by way of Grenada. Grant believed that such a retrograde movement, appearing to Northern civilians to be a defeat, would impair public support for the Lincoln administration and for conscription. Conforming to one of his long-standing superstitions, he refused to retrace his steps. To divert Confederates' attention from his real purpose, he ordered Sherman to feint an attack near Vicksburg while the rest of the army crossed to the east bank downriver from Grand Gulf. Four days before this movement Sherman wrote: "I feel in its success less confidence than any similar undertaking of the war." But he carried out his part and rejoined Grant near Grand Gulf.

Grant learned that Nathaniel P. Banks would not be immediately available for a joint offensive against Port Hudson, Louisiana, the other Confederate fortification commanding the river. Grant decided to operate independently against Vicksburg, first marching to Jackson, Mississippi, to disrupt Confederate forces and rail lines that would be in his rear when he turned west toward Vicksburg. Sherman urged him to wait until he had gathered wagons for carrying supplies from the river, but Grant ordered the march toward Jackson. The army not only seized food and livestock along the route but also engaged in what Sherman called "universal burning and wanton destruction," which he deemed "not justifiable in war." Knowing that Halleck in Washington would disapprove of the plan on the same strategic principles invoked by Sherman, Grant sent word of his intended movements, then hurried to accomplish them before he could be overruled. He did not receive countermanding orders until after he had taken Jackson and defeated the Confederate force which had come out of Vicksburg. He ignored the orders directing him to take Port Hudson first. He instead continued to advance on Vicksburg.

On May 18, when Grant and Sherman rode to the crest of the hills above the Yazoo, from which the Confederates had repulsed Sherman's attack in December, the two generals knew the army could re-establish its supply line. Grant's unconventional strategy had worked. Sherman made "exclamations of joy," saying that this "was the end of one of the greatest campaigns in history." On May 19 and 22, Grant ordered general assaults on the city's steep, powerful defensive works. These failed at heavy cost, but he could assure Halleck on May 24: "The fall of Vicksburg and the capture of most of the garrison can only be a question of time." General Joseph E. Johnston, still gathering men and wagons with some thought of moving against the Federal rear, did not expect to be able to relieve the garrison. He wrote on June 7: "The only imaginable hope is in the perpetration by Grant of some extravagant blunder, & there is no ground for such a hope." The city held out until July 4, when General John C. Pemberton surrendered it and 31,600 men. Five days later the Confederates at Port Hudson also surrendered, and the United States government controlled all of the Mississippi River. Grant afterward regretted having ordered the assault on May 22. Even so, he said: "I see fewer mistakes in the Vicksburg campaign than in any other."

The Federal success, achieved in defiance of Sherman's cautionary recommendations about supplies and his scruples about devastation, converted Sherman to the method of war he had been approaching. On the day after Pemberton's surrender, Sherman wrote to his wife: "The capture of Vicksburg is to me the first glance of daylight in this war." He would not have taken the risks Grant took. Having seen their efficacy, he at once imagined far larger incursions into the Confederacy. The Army of the

Tennessee and the Army of the Cumberland "could also, acting in concert drive all opposing masses into the recesses of Georgia & Alabama, leaving the Atlantic slopes the great theatre of war." The Federal army could repeat and redouble marches like Grant's until Southerners admitted the futility of further resistance. Late in July, Sherman wrote of Vicksburg's fall: "It settles the whole question. The people of the South cant deceive themselves any longer. They see & feel if we make up our mind and set ourselves to work, we will in the end make it." Not long before, Sherman had tried to alert people in the North to the rebels' desperate resolve. The quick turnaround had occurred more in his mind than in the Confederacy. He saw why Southerners ought to give up, and he spoke as if all of them saw it, too. In later years, looking back on continued resistance, he said that their defeats at Vicksburg and Gettysburg "should have ended the war; but the rebel leaders were mad, and seemed determined that their people should drink of the very lowest dregs of the cup of war."

Grant was promoted to major general in the regular army, and, on his recommendation, Sherman and James Birdseye McPherson were promoted to brigadier general in the regular army. The tie of mutual trust among these men, especially that between Grant and Sherman, was thus publicly embodied in their military success and in recognition of them by the president and the Senate. Sherman learned from Grant a greater confidence in ultimate victory, received rewards—in contrast with former censure—for using new methods, and introduced into his own view of the war a new tone of assurance, even arrogance. For the subsequent conduct of the war Sherman deprecated all suggestions for conciliating Southerners or restoring the union through "civil compromises" rather than through conclusive military victory. Three months after the fall of Vicksburg he wrote to Grant: "I would make this war as severe as possible, and show no symptoms of tiring till the South begs for mercy. . . . The South has done her worst, and now is the time for us to pile on our blows thick and fast."

Sherman still fretted about his soldiers' undisciplined destructiveness. In August he showed his disgust when a court-martial acquitted a soldier of the 35th Iowa whom Sherman had caught in the act of burning a cotton gin. The soldier said that an officer had ordered him to do it; the officer, too, was acquitted, but Sherman urged Grant to have him dismissed. Otherwise, "you and I and every commander must go through the war justly chargeable with crimes at which we blush." Yet Sherman blushed less and less. A year later he looked back wryly at his behavior in Kentucky in 1861, when secessionists burned the homes of unionists and "I, poor innocent, would not let a soldier take a green apple or a fence rail." The experiences eroding his innocence by the end of 1863 encouraged the methods of war he subsequently used.

The most vocal Northern supporters of the war demanded aggressive punishment of rebels but protested heavy Federal casualties. The most dedicated Confederates demonstrated that major strategic setbacks and heavy losses in battle would not persuade them to give up in order to minimize the cost of foreseeable defeat. The Vicksburg campaign, like Bragg's earlier march through Kentucky and Lee's invasion of Pennsylvania, demonstrated that a large army could move easily through a hostile countryside by living off the resources of the enemy populace. After the war Grant said: "If the Vicksburg campaign meant anything, in a military point of view, it was that there are no fixed laws of war which are not subject to the conditions of the country, the climate, and the habits of the people." In defying the strategic "law" that armies should always maintain a supply line, Grant speeded the already rapid erosion of the moral "law" confining an army's attacks to the soldiers and the public property of the enemy. Sherman had experienced a series of singularly intense frustrations, failures, and hostile criticisms in his efforts to make the war a conventional conflict between disciplined combatants. These experiences in the first two years, working on his original expectation of a vast war over fundamental issues, prepared him to become, for the last two years, the main exponent of war without indefeasible laws. Frightened by the scale of rebellion, he conceived a thoroughgoing method to suppress it. Subjected to civilians' impatience with military professionalism and their censoriousness toward generals, he eventually departed spectacularly from old West Point ways.

In purposely bringing hardship to civilians and threatening far worse, such as deportation or extermination, Sherman gave a military application to his understanding of the political and societal bases of secessionism. He contended that the rebellion could not persevere without public support, secured through demagogic political manipulation and slaveholders' dominance of Southern society. From this premise he argued that Southerners bore a collective responsibility for the war. There was no enemy nation divided between peaceable, innocent civilians and military combatants employed by a hostile government; there were only rebels whose diverse means of resistance to the United States government formed a continuum of treason. To strike it at any point or at all points was equally legitimate. Though Southerners might have been gulled into supporting a cause which did not serve their interests, their delusion did not diminish their complicity. He wrote to Salmon P. Chase in August 1862: "The government of the United States may now safely proceed on the proper rule that all in the South are enemies of all in the North."

The moral argument that appealed to many Northerners—that ante-bellum Southern society was shot through with evil and deserved to be razed—had little appeal for Sherman. Nor did he see the army's increasing severity as solely a quantitative calculation in pursuit of tangible results: steadily adding increments of pain to induce alterations in behavior. Rather, the army would inflict on the rebels some of the just effects of a moral choice they had made. Sherman instructed one of his subordinates in November 1863: "It is none of our business to protect a people that has sent all its youth, and arms and horses, and all that is of any account to war against us. . . . The people have done all the harm they can, so let them reap the consequences."

After his early disappointments, Sherman set little store by the residual Southern unionism in which Lincoln and other Northerners had faith. Most so-called unionism amounted in his eyes only to expedient, deceitful efforts to save property after the Federal army had arrived in overwhelming force. Loyalty oaths were worthless. Southerners had to be defeated, not liberated. To those who had lived under Confederate rule but called themselves unionists when it was safe to do so, Sherman reacted more scathingly than to rebels. During the march to Savannah he often said to such people: "If it is true that you are Unionists, you should not have permitted Jeff. Davis to dragoon you, until you are as much his slaves as once the niggers were yours." The secessionist conspiracy had prevailed partly because those Southerners who knew it was wrong knuckled under to it. A unionist ought to avow his loyalty to the government and fight for it. By quiescently acceding to the rule of Jefferson Davis, a unionist did the work of a traitor, betraying both his country and his conscience. At the end of the war, looking back at the scenes of destruction through which he had passed, Sherman said: "I attribute these to a failure on the part of the Union men of the South to stand by their country in that dread day of danger when the South arose to enforce a disunion."

To dramatize his conclusion, Sherman cited his own case. When Louisiana seceded, he had been far from friends and family, alone among secessionists who wanted him to stay at the seminary and collaborate with the new order. After a series of business failures, he had no other prospects of employment. Yet he resigned and thereafter regarded his letter of resignation as the most important document in his life. Faced with a costly choice, he had remained loyal to the United States. The rebellion, he believed, confronted every Southerner—indeed, every American—with a comparable choice. Sherman's resignation, judged by outward circumstances, was less risky than he later liked to make it appear. It is hard to imagine him leaving his wife, children, and relatives, none of whom

sympathized with secession, in order to stay in the Confederacy. He had
never shared disunionist sentiment. Despite his public opposition to secession, he stood in little danger of the violence and intimidation many
Northerners and unionists suffered in the South. He stayed in Louisiana,
unmolested, during most of February 1861. Although his decision to
resign may look to others less suspenseful and less perilous than it did to
Sherman in retrospect, it remained a crucial moment for his subsequent
definition of collective responsibility in war. Every Southerner he and
his soldiers met on their marches had once had the same chance that
Sherman had when surrounded by secessionists in 1860 and 1861. Unlike
Sherman or George H. Thomas of Virginia or the commander of Sherman's cavalry escort, Lieutenant George Snelling of Georgia, they were
not fighting for the union. They were, therefore, parties to the attempt
to destroy it. Sherman's emphasis on the power of manipulative Southern
leaders to precipitate secession and to arouse support for war did not
exculpate people who followed or only watched. Even when he acknowledged, as he did in 1864, that "a few individuals cannot resist a
torrent of error and passion such as swept the South into rebellion," he
insisted that Southerners who "desire a government" could separate themselves from "those who insist on war and its desolation." He praised the
South Carolina unionist James L. Petigru for standing "almost alone a
rock against which the wave of treason beat in vain." For Sherman
loyalty to the United States was both a sign and a source of consistent,
stable character. He found his coherence and identity in the security of
the nation. The alternative was madness. The people who abandoned the
nation were not creating a different form of order but were abandoning
reason. Not to resist them betrayed weakness. Fifty men, he claimed,
could have prevented the secession of North Carolina. By this formulation he deepened the guilt of the vast majority: they drifted passively or
they unthinkingly joined "the senseless howl of the crowd." The more
one believed they could have effectively acted otherwise, the more rigor-
ously one could hold them to account.

SHERMAN'S distress over the coming of civil war, followed by his
finding in greater violence a basis for confidence, were not the only
origins of his vehement attachment to the United States government's
authority. Though he said in 1861 that he wanted to stay out of the war,
he hardly considered doing so. Many aspects of his life before 1861
pointed toward his accepting an opportunity to make himself a defender
of the nation. From his earliest political observations until his death,
Sherman dwelt on the threats to order in American life. Secession was

only the greatest of many tendencies toward anarchy in a society constantly subject to the pull of centrifugal forces. Insofar as the Civil War pointed toward increased centralization of political and economic power in the United States, especially through the agency of a stronger federal government, it accomplished purposes Sherman was eager to promote. His varied life before the war had exposed him to many proofs that America was never far from dissolution. He traced his failures and disappointments in those years not only to his own mistakes but also to the disordered condition of his country. America's finding a basis for cohesion through civil war coincided with Sherman's finding a career and an optimism based on securing America's future.

Sherman's father and mother, Charles R. Sherman and Mary Hoyt Sherman, moved from Norwalk, Connecticut, to Lancaster, Ohio, in 1811. Charles Sherman was a popular circuit-riding attorney, well known throughout Ohio. In 1823 the legislature elected him a judge of the Ohio Supreme Court, on which he served until his death at the age of forty-one in 1829. He won the affection and respect of many of his fellow attorneys. An obituary said: "Firmness, without the least appearance of dogmatism, was his peculiar trait. . . . he never lost his temper." After his death some who had known him held him up to his sons as a leading figure in the golden age of the Ohio bench and bar. John Sherman wrote many years later: "I gladly acknowledge that I have received many a kindness, and much aid in business as well as political and social life, from the kindly memory of my father." The elder Sherman was learned, eloquent, and conscientious. His friend Thomas Ewing always said in later years that none of Judge Sherman's sons "approached him in capacity or ability."

Charles Sherman named his third son Tecumseh—the "William" came years later—because he admired the Shawnee statesman who had tried to build a federation of tribes from the Great Lakes to Florida. The political and legal acumen of Tecumseh—properly, Tecumtha or Tekamthe—in defense of Indian lands, as well as his eloquence, his courage, and his abstention from ruthless cruelty in war, won him respect from at least some whites, even though they opposed his plan for a separate Indian nation. The historian Alvin M. Josephy, Jr., has called Tecumseh "the greatest of all the American Indian leaders." During and after the Civil War, comments on Sherman's given name associated the famous chief, killed in battle in 1813, with ferocity. Charles Sherman, in reply to remonstrances about giving his son a "savage Indian name," said only: "Tecumseh was a great warrior." Tecumseh Sherman, known in the family as "Cump," was nine years old when his father died.

The stories Sherman later told about his childhood portrayed a family with no serious discontent, though he was unruly as a boy, a trait which continued through his years at West Point, where he amassed many demerits. Charles Sherman evidently did not use physical punishment with his children, just as W. T. Sherman, when a father, used none with his. Young Cump once took offense at his father's orders and decided to run away from home. He went to live with the family of a friend, the Kings. His father responded by greeting him on the street as "Cumpy King." Sherman's family persisted in using the new name for some time after Cump came home of his own accord. Mary Hoyt Sherman was a gentle, amiable woman, to whom Cump remained emotionally close. The strictest disciplinarian in the family was Charles Sherman's mother, Elizabeth Stoddard Sherman. She moved from Connecticut to Ohio in 1816 and lived until 1848. Though she intimidated her daughter-in-law and "never spared the rod or broom" among her grandchildren, they remembered her for her "square solid sense." She told them stories of the Revolutionary War, of the rivalry between Federalists and Republicans, and of the War of 1812. John Sherman recalled her as a "strong-willed, religious Puritan of the Connecticut school," and W. T. Sherman said that he and his brothers inherited from her "what little sense we possess."

When Charles Sherman died, he left his widow and eleven children a house in Lancaster and bank stock yielding an income of $200 or $300 per year. Although he had high standing in public life, Sherman had suffered financial stringency since 1817. While serving as a federal collector of internal revenue, he had taken responsibility for his deputies' defaults when the government suddenly stopped accepting Ohio state bank notes. This obligation took the proceeds of his property and a large part of his salary. Without her late husband's income, Mary Sherman could not support all her children in her own home. To relieve her, several of her husband's friends and relatives offered to raise her children, one in each of their homes. Thus Cump, at the age of nine, joined the household of Thomas Ewing on the same block of Main Street as his mother's residence in Lancaster.

Now largely forgotten, except by political historians, Ewing was a national figure in politics and law during the decades before the Civil War. A pioneer settler of Ohio, a self-made man who rose from salt-boiling to extensive real estate investments, he started his legal career riding circuit with the adventurous, cheerful young men of the Ohio bar and ended it as the grand old man of the United States Supreme Court bar. Ewing was a leader of the Whig party and served as senator from Ohio in the years 1831–1836 and 1850–1851. He became William Henry Harrison's secretary of the treasury, but his tenure was cut short by Harrison's death and the subsequent break between the new President, John Tyler, and the Whigs. In Zachary Taylor's administration he was secretary of the interior. A friend of Daniel Webster's, Ewing held a wide range of information and reading in an orderly mind. He was a large man with a gift for stately oratory. Murat Halstead said of him: "I have never met a man who would better bear the application of the word grandeur than Mr. Ewing."

John Sherman, who went to Mansfield, Ohio, after his father's death, believed in later years that his brother's political outlook had been shaped by the dominant influence of Thomas Ewing. Certainly, W. T. Sherman had long exposure to such influence. He acquired the name William when he received a Catholic baptism in the Ewing home in 1830. Ewing chose a West Point education and a military career for Sherman, saying that Charles Sherman had often expressed a wish that Cump enter the army or the navy. Sherman was commissioned in 1840; four years later Sherman and Ewing's daughter Ellen agreed to marry. The long-delayed wedding took place on May 1, 1850, in Ewing's Washington home—the Blair house—on Pennsylvania Avenue near the White House. The ceremony was attended by President Taylor, members of the cabinet, Senators Webster, Clay, Benton, and Douglas, and other important men paying their respects on the occasion of the marriage of Secretary Ewing's daughter to Secretary Ewing's foster son. The festivities lasted until three o'clock in the morning. Cump and Ellen headed for Niagara Falls three hours later. As a dependent and as a son-in-law, Sherman remained close to Ewing for forty years.

Always loyal to Ewing and eager for his good opinion, Sherman nevertheless bridled at his magisterial, somewhat condescending solicitude. As soon as he had a cadet's pay, Sherman stayed with his mother, not with the Ewings, when home on furlough. A year after leaving West Point, Sherman said that army life was better than "falling back into a state of dependency." Ewing pressed him with loving advice and, during his eight years out of the army, continually held out to Sherman the prospect he most dreaded: living in the Hocking Valley of Ohio and working as Ewing's employee. After marrying, Ellen Sherman spent long periods away from her husband, living with her parents. She even seemed to regard her honeymoon trip to Niagara Falls as a circuitous route from Washington to Lancaster. Living with Cump in St. Louis, New Orleans, or San Francisco, she looked forward to her visits home. In 1852 Sherman wrote: "I think she has been at Lancaster too much since her marriage, and it is full time for her to be weaned." But fourteen years later he acknowledged to Ewing: "Of course her chief desire is to be near you." One of the Shermans' granddaughters recalled the general's saying that if he were to blindfold Ellen, spin her around, and set her down, "she would make a direct line for Lancaster." During the war Sherman still depended on Ewing to help refute critics in the newspapers and protect him from political enemies. No matter what remote and adventurous exploits Sherman undertook—moving to California twice, moving to Louisiana twice, commanding large bodies of men in combat—he saw Thomas Ewing waiting in Lancaster, taking care of Ellen, and hurrying to assist as soon as Sherman faltered. Sherman had two fathers: a great man whom he could not know and a great man whom he could not escape.

When John Sherman entered politics, campaigning for the Whigs in 1844, Cump was appalled to find his brother among the "travelling demagogues," though he, too, wanted Henry Clay to win the presidency. He did not give up trying to persuade John to abandon a political career until ten years later, after John joined what Cump called "the new black republican party." Still Cump was advising him "to follow the example of Clay, Jefferson, Ewing and others whom he must respect" by refraining from provocative challenges to Southerners' anxiety about the security of slavery. It is hardly surprising that John Sherman believed that his brother had fallen under Ewing's influence. Ewing left the Senate in 1851, and retired from politics after the election of 1852. With Ohio sending antislavery men like Salmon P. Chase and Benjamin F. Wade to the Senate, Ewing's day was over. In many respects he and his foster son, not in political office, remained Whigs long after the party's collapse. Though the Civil War brought many new men, including John Sherman, to prominence, W. T. Sherman's list of eminent patriots remained for years afterward men like Clay, Ewing, Robert C. Winthrop, Reverdy Johnson, and Henry Stanbery. Supporting the union without seeking to transform Southern society, they defended order against both rebellion and radicalism. In 1864 John wrote in a testy mood: "Mr Ewings opinions grew out of old political contests & nothing can change it."

Cump's heroes were men of the past. But, after the rebels triumphed for a while and after the radicals triumphed for a while, Sherman was still, in the last third of the nineteenth century, promoting a vision of America that had much in common with the views of Whigs he had long admired. He often said that the normal condition of national life was harmony sustained by complementary economic ties among the sections and by a corresponding emotion of national sentiment, a reverence for unity. He expected not forcible consolidation but equilibrium, not drastic conversions of society and economy but increasing congruence of interest accompanied by firmer attachment to the union. Notwithstanding his complaints about the volatility of democratic politics, agitated by demagogues, Sherman spoke as if disharmony were deviant and temporary, disrupting a customary stability. At the same time that he imagined sectional and societal equilibrium, however, he anticipated not stasis but the nation's rapid progress: expansion of settlement, growth of market agriculture, acceleration of manufacturing, extension of transportation systems. For fifty years he encouraged these radical changes, always seeing them as bringers of unity, prosperity, and order.

Sherman preferred the Whigs, but did not become an active partisan. He shared with many of his fellow army officers and with many other elitist-minded Americans a contempt for the disorderliness of American politics. While he was still at West Point the "humbuggery" of Harrison's presidential campaign in 1840 disgusted him. Instruction at the military academy, devoted to conventional subjects and to training in engineering, did not overtly inculcate a militarist or antidemocratic ethos, and the curriculum included little study of war as a political or strategic phenomenon. Yet four years as a cadet isolated the young men from civilian society and encouraged them to form their closest attachments to one another. As Sherman explained to Ewing in 1844, the cadets "are easily convinced of the vast superiority of themselves over everybody else, acquire a sort of contempt for civil pursuits and live in the hope of one day acquiring the glorious fame of a Military Hero." When Sherman was a lieutenant, 554 of the army's 733 officers were graduates of the academy. Those who set themselves apart from other Americans had incentives besides their experience as cadets. For one thing, West Point and the officer corps had many critics. Two years after Sherman graduated, the legislature of Connecticut resolved that the academy ought to be abolished: it was "aristocratic and anti-republican." Members of Congress and state legislatures, including that of Ohio, had made similar charges in the 1830s, and criticism continued throughout the nineteenth century. The attacks called the academy expensive, authoritarian, and an engine of political patronage for the rich and the powerful. Censure also fell on the officer corps; they wondered every year whether Congress would further cut their perquisites or the size of their units. Hostility to professional military men had a long history among Americans. Since before the Revolution, suspicious citizens had seen in a standing army the makings of a parasitic elite exalting rank, discipline, and executive power at the expense of civic virtue and equality. Recalling his youth, Sherman wrote in 1866: "An officer of the army could not wear the U.S. uniform in Columbus Ohio without being sneered at as an incubus on the industrious."

The exclusivity instilled at West Point, combined with opprobrium from many civilians, encouraged among officers what Sherman called "that intense mistrust of politicians, to which the Old Army was bred." In him this outlook became an aversion to the messy mixture of greed, ambition, expediency, and claptrap that he saw in American politics. He wanted a government that was "firm & independent" and a citizenry that obeyed all laws implicitly. Instead, he witnessed bombast, corruption, and fickle popular clamor manipulated in pursuit of political patronage. He thought it a disgrace to serve in the House of Representatives. Early in the war he reminded his wife that no one knew better than Thomas Ewing "that our government has gradually been tending to anarchy." For Sherman, intensifying sectional controversies were less a transformation of political issues than a worsening of the longtime evil: political agitation "calculated to break down all governments." The "real trouble," he said just before the war, "is not slavery, it is the democratic spirit which substitutes mere popular opinion for law." Similarly, another West Point graduate, the Federal general Gouverneur Kemble Warren, reminisced in 1863 about his prewar conversations with fellow officers from the South: "Together we deplored the political debasement and malignity that was bringing on this war."

To show the fate of a republic that failed at self-government, many Americans cited the history of Mexico. During the war with Mexico, soldiers and citizens of the United States often said that the defeated nation might be politically regenerated under the control of the conquerors. Assuming that the United States was essentially Anglo-Saxon and that the Indian, Hispanic, and *mestizo* peoples of Mexico were inferior, these Americans explained Mexico's political decline by saying that the populace was unfit for self-government or could be made fit only by emulating Americans, who had a special cultural genius for republican liberty. The Civil War, however, suggested to Northerners a more ominous meaning in the Mexican experience: the United States might soon become as pitiable a failure as Americans held Mexico to be. Losing an election or disliking the government in office, partisans in Mexico resorted to armed resistance and grasped for power in violation of constitutional forms. Governments compromised with revolutionaries; presidents were deposed; and, in the words of one American congressman, "Civil war became the normal condition of the people." Americans who did not share Sherman's pessimistic view of democratic politics nevertheless gave signs, in their mentions of Mexico, that they thought their own republic in danger of lapsing into a mockery of their pretensions to have solved the problem of liberty and government.

The underlying failure of Mexican politics, according to these warnings, lay in the disparity between grand rhetoric about saving the republic and inability to make self-government work. Talking about the success of revolution and independence might be only a mask for their collapse. The grandiloquence Americans loved could not entirely overcome their suspicion that it was illusory, that manifestos and *pronunciamientos* tended toward hyperbole which became self-parody, vainly trying to conceal anarchy or dictatorship with republican forms and words. For Northerners the Southern states' secession made this threat more acute. Unless quelled, Confederates would make republicanism look ridiculous. Denouncing secession, Daniel S. Dickinson said that Mexico "has been seceding, and dividing, and pronouncing, and fighting for her rights, and in the self-defence of aggressive leaders, from the day of her nominal independence, and she has reaped an abundant harvest of degradation and shame." The Confederates' instant republic—based, as far as Northerners could see, on prolix speeches, high-sounding public documents, newly created titles and ranks, newly designed uniforms and flags, and colorful worthless paper money—would turn North America into another Central America. Such diverse public figures as Joseph Holt, Stephen A. Douglas, Charles Sumner, and Wendell Phillips, with many others, gave similar warnings. The Confederate States and the United States would be in perpetual war. Further political division would follow, burdening the continent with "jarring, warring, fragmentary States," armies, and "a race of chieftains, who will rival the political bandits of South America and Mexico." Believing that American politics already had grown ridiculous, Sherman still wanted the United States to avoid "the fate of Mexico, which is eternal war." The failure of Mexico was for Sherman not simply an edifying contrast with the success of the United States. It was the fate which the United States could never be sure of escaping.

After he had moved out of the South for the last time Sherman often reminisced about his years there and professed his attachment to the antebellum South. He did not take planters and politicians at their own valuation, but he thought that he had found in the South an enviable social stability—until, amazingly, almost inexplicably, the society's principal beneficiaries threw it all away. Army assignments to Florida, South Carolina, and Louisiana kept him in the section for seven years between 1840 and 1853, and he returned in 1859. As an army officer and as a seminary superintendent, he was welcome in the circles of the wealthiest planters. He made many friends and found their life congenial. In 1860 he was prepared to spend the rest of his life in Louisiana if sectional peace lasted. Sherman formed social ties mainly with slaveholders and accepted slavery as a fixture. "I would not if I could abolish or modify slavery," he wrote in 1859. "I dont know that I would materially change the actual or political relation of master & slave." According to the South Carolina historian Yates Snowden, whose mother knew Sherman in the 1840s, the young lieutenant once brought balls and chains to the Poyas plantation on the Cooper River, recommending that they be put on two "refractory runaway negroes." In 1860 he assumed that after Ellen joined him in Louisiana they would have to buy slaves as household servants. He accepted some of the geographical and economic arguments of slavery's defenders: only blacks could do the labor that produced the South's staple crops; blacks would do so only under compulsion; the products of their labor were "necessary to the civilized world"; hence Northerners should refrain from provocative censure of the institution.

Sherman enjoyed the company of men and women of the planter class, but he was not so impressed by the South's grandeur and power as they were. He always regarded them as a people on the defensive, indulging inflated notions of their society's importance. In 1843 he told his brother that South Carolinians boasted of "this state, the aristocracy their age, the patriotism chivalry & glory—all trash. No people in America are so poor in reality." More enterprising Southern entrepreneurs might turn the plantation system to more profitable account. Nevertheless, throughout Sherman's antebellum exposure to the South, he regarded slavery as a backward labor system, doomed to minority status within a union politically dominated by free states. So obvious did this destiny seem, and so subsidiary the moral concerns, that he wanted John Sherman and the Republicans who opposed territorial expansion of slavery to let Southerners down easily, defeating their expansionist schemes without belaboring the opprobrium. Slave states prospered more slowly than free states, and the disparity would become ever clearer, he thought. Still, slaveholders could not brook any threat to their security. Perversely, like the fox in Aesop's fable who lost his tail in a trap and tried to get the other foxes to cut off theirs, Southerners felt compelled to insist that their deformity was a virtue. "I would indulge them in their delusion," Sherman said in 1859.

More keenly than most slaveholders he knew, Sherman, like the abolitionists, saw slavery's dependence on Northern assent. Its security lay in union, the Constitution, federal law, and the collaboration of Northerners in its continuance. If Southerners rejected these, he said after the 1860 election, "it will be of course only the beginning of the end." This was the offense for which he could not forgive his former friends. He liked to recall "the sweet jessamin of Mount Pleasant" in South Carolina, where he could "gather the Magnolia blossom for some fair girl, or drape the linen to make a picnic." But his wartime protestations of affection for Southerners heaped coals on those who had forsaken him while he was laboring to defend their interests. He said that he "would have resisted, even with arms, any attack upon their rights—even their slave rights" if they had stayed in the union. He knew that Southern politicians regarded relegation of their section to that of a minority subsisting on sufferance as a "crisis so long approaching and so certain to come." And he knew that the "mere dread of sedition, revolt, or external interference makes men ordinarily calm, almost mad." He could "indulge" their conceit of a superior slave society, but he could not abide disruption of the union, a futile attempt to repudiate the clear truth that the North must be predominant. Sherman thought they could see as well as he that the "South had no cause, not even a pretext" to rebel. He had befriended Southerners, had cast his lot among them, had defended their society even against his brother's strictures. By abandoning him and by remaining stubborn in their error, they freed him to do his worst. Whatever the defects of antebellum Southern society, it had attained what Sherman valued most: order. The bitterest irony he saw in secession was Southerners' betrayal of their greatest accomplishment.

Among the examples of disorder showing Sherman that American society might at any time dissolve, nothing before secession matched the California gold rush. Sherman saw its first phase while he was a lieutenant stationed in California from 1847 until the end of 1849. In 1853 he resigned his commission and returned to manage a bank in San Francisco, where he lived until 1857. He went back to the state for a brief visit in 1858. In his later years Sherman decided that California finally had attained the prosperity combined with extraordinary progress that discovery of gold had seemed to promise at once. At the end of the 1850s, however, he was reproaching himself for having believed in that promise enough to stake almost everything on it. He concluded then that California's progress, its economic activity, the structure of its society—the relation of citizen to citizen—all were an illusion. He had treated them as a reality and had come to grief. During the Civil War and afterward Sherman meant to establish that America, unlike California, was real.

As an officer on the staff of Colonel Richard B. Mason, military governor of California, Sherman helped establish the authority of the new government, suppressing resistance from Mexican inhabitants and from American immigrants who wanted to elect their own officials at once. He wrote on April 18, 1848: "A more quiet community could not exist." Years later, far from California, he fondly recalled hunting, exploring the coast range, and seeing the broad valley vistas of the sparsely populated "pastoral land." In 1847, on his first visit to the village of Yerba Buena, which became the city of San Francisco, he could not get a room, a meal, or food for his horse, so small was the outpost.

During the spring and summer of 1848, everything changed rapidly. Gold had been discovered in the riverbeds of the Sacramento Valley in January. Lieutenant Sherman wrote the draft of Colonel Mason's report of the find, dated August 17. Before the new riches had become generally known, some men, with the usual American schemes for newly acquired lands, already had envisioned for California "palaces and spires rising up in a very few years." The effects of the gold, for once, rivaled the fantasies of dreamers. For eighteen months Sherman watched what he later called "the chaos of 1849–50." By this he did not mean violence—in 1852 he enjoyed his memories of "the wild scenes of the gold mountains"—so much as the instant sundering of all formal bonds between men in the race for selfish advantage. Soldiers deserted; sailors jumped ship; workers left their jobs; farmers abandoned their fields: all headed for the diggings. "The aged have called for their crutches, and children have caught the common infection," Sherman wrote. "Even the ragged indians are on their knees worshipping the common idol." He made two trips to the diggings, where he saw people arrive, "look about, swear at the high prices and disappear in the grand vortex."

Those who did not take up placer mining nevertheless turned to money-making. Prices rose 300 percent in less than four months. Laborers could get wages of one dollar an hour; tradesmen took in $15–$20 a day. Sherman later recalled: "The fabulous reports of the mines unsettled everybody. No one kept his contract." Thousands of anxious men fanned out over land held by uncertain title or no title. At first, the army was the only legally constituted authority, but soldiers' desertions left it with little coercive power. Seeing that "there is no law or compulsory process here," Sherman pictured the ease with which new resistance to the federal government's rule could arise. Only obsession with getting gold distracted people from political mischief. He anticipated that, eventually, "the Democracy" would turn on Colonel Mason and denounce him as a military despot. Sherman thought it possible that, without military government, "every body in California would turn to rob steal and murder each other." But the gold rush scared him not so much with the prospect of killing, excess, and summary miners' law as with the spectacle of a society in which no man's word was good and no one served any cause or revered any authority other than himself.

Sherman, too, felt the attraction of the bonanza. Rapid inflation made a first lieutenant's pay inadequate. He took two months' leave to work as a surveyor, helping to lay out the lines of visionaries' future cities and ranchers' land claims. He was paid in land, which he sold for several thousand dollars. While deploring the chaotic rush, he spoke with awe of its magnitude. Miners continued to pour out gold. More thousands of men joined them, and trade multiplied behind them. John Sutter, holder of a large Mexican grant in the Sacramento Valley, including the site where gold had first been found, asked Sherman to become his agent for selling city lots in Sacramento. Sherman had other "splendid offers of employment and of partnership." Attracted by these and unhappy at having missed combat and promotion in the war with Mexico, he tried to resign his commission in the spring of 1849. General Persifor Smith, commander of the Division of the Pacific, dissuaded him. Meanwhile, he wrote in April, "I believe the gold mines are as yet barely touched, and that many will realize fortunes."

Smith agreed to send Sherman back east. On January 2, 1850, he sailed out through the Golden Gate, leaving behind a harbor crowded with derelict vessels, abandoned by those who had come to get rich. Lieutenant Sherman believed that his assignment outside the combat zone in wartime had blighted his military career. He thought that, apart from its gold, California was an unpromising waste. He denounced the promiscuous chase after gold and feared its social consequences. Still, he missed California. For the first time he had been an important person in great affairs. Like his father and Thomas Ewing, he had pioneered in expanding American settlement and introducing government to the frontier. He had witnessed in 1849 the formation of a state constitution. California was as attractive as it was alarming. In 1853 he came back through the Golden Gate to become a San Francisco banker.

In antebellum America, banking was a controversial activity; debating its merits and practices, Americans expressed their differing views of enterprise and virtue, of commerce and the country's future. Upon coming to power in 1841, the Whigs in Congress, collaborating with Secretary of the Treasury Thomas Ewing, set out to revive a modified form of the national bank Democrats had dismantled. Lieutenant Sherman, less than a year out of West Point, understood that one of the purposes of the new institution, if it had been established, would have been to exert a regulatory influence on the state-chartered banks, on the supply of currency and credit, and hence on the economy's development. But he took a jaundiced view of all banks: "There is no set of men in the world who deserve the halter more than the brokers bankers & hangers on of our citi[es]." He abandoned these simplistic views to become a banker, then returned to them, in part, after he failed. The strong emotions aroused by banks partly found expression in politics. State-chartered banks, by their high-risk loans and speculative issuing of notes, expanded the credit available for growth of commerce and industry. Many people denounced all banks for profiting from manipulation of the proceeds of productive labor and for facilitating concentration of wealth in fewer hands. No matter whose part they took, Americans saw banks as agents of a promising or an ominous future they wished to promote or to forestall. Sherman launched himself into the cutthroat world of high-risk banking because the gold rush seemed to promise sure success. Having missed glory in war, he wanted to triumph as a capitalist.

Sherman expected to make himself famous and independently wealthy through California's sudden growth. As soon as he and Ellen set their wedding date in 1850, she wrote to her brother: "He will of course leave the army and establish himself in business." Though she accompanied him to army posts in St. Louis and New Orleans during the next two years, she knew that, if he remained in the army, he would have to spend much of his time at remote western forts where she would not wish to go. Cump found that his salary of $136 per month in New Orleans could not support Ellen with comforts like those in Lancaster. In December 1852 the St. Louis banker James H. Lucas and Sherman's friend Henry S. Turner invited Sherman to become the manager of a bank they were opening in San Francisco, where Lucas's banking rivals in St. Louis— Page, Bacon & Company—reported large profits. Cump left the decision to Ellen. She chose the bank over the army, agreeing to live in San Francisco until 1860, she told her mother, "with the prospect of getting home for *good* in six years." Home, of course, was Lancaster.

Though Sherman took a six-month leave of absence from the army rather than resign his commission at once, he undertook the banking venture with confidence. When he returned to San Francisco in April 1853 the city had topped the crest of its sudden prosperity as an entrepôt for the gold rush. "This is the most extraordinary place on earth," Sherman wrote; "large brick & granite houses fill the site where stood the poor contemptible village." He worried mainly that Lucas and Turner would be "too cautious & timid for California" and would "leave me no room to *experience* absolute success." If Lucas would agree to start the branch with a capital of $300,000, "we stand a chance of making money fast." Lucas settled on $200,000. Sherman told Thomas Ewing that he expected to clear $50,000 in six years from his salary and commission. After a year in the city he wrote to Turner: "Neither Mr. Lucas, yourself desire to be small bankers, and I assure you that I am ambitious of making our name famous among the 'Nations of the Earth.'"

The San Francisco branch of Lucas & Simonds—Lucas, Turner & Company—lasted four years. Late in 1856 the owners decided to close it in the spring of 1857, and Sherman, at first surprised, agreed that the decision was wise. Unlike a number of others, including Page, Bacon & Company and the banking operations of the express firm Adams & Company, Sherman's bank did not fail. It met all its obligations, even during a run on deposits in 1855 which he called "the Battle of 23 Feby." But it did not realize the anticipated profits for the owners or for

Sherman. Banking proved more complex and less safe than Sherman foresaw. An older, more experienced banker warned him: "Look out, you go to sleep thinking just nothing whilst a thousand men are dreaming how they can cheat you." Louis McLane, Jr., who also went to California in 1853 to make profitable investments, described San Francisco as a city "where men sleep with their eyes open." Banks in San Francisco charged a commission for shipping gold to the east; Sherman found that the system enriched the insurance companies, the steamship companies, and the New York banks, but not his. The bank made a better profit from commissions on bills of exchange. Though the prevailing interest rate was 3 percent per month, Sherman ultimately found that the risk of bad loans, even with his conservative lending policy, was commensurate with this seemingly high return. The most blatant proof appeared when San Francisco's biggest speculator, Henry ("Honest Harry") Meiggs, suddenly sailed for South America, leaving behind unpaid debts totaling at least $800,000. Sherman lost $18,000 of his own money because he sold land in St. Louis and Illinois in order to reimburse his bank after Meiggs's collateral for a loan fell short.

For a while, business was good. Real estate rose in value; construction continued; rents were high. In January 1854 Sherman estimated the bank's profits at $10,000 a month. He persuaded Lucas and Turner to authorize a new building for the bank, which would cost more than $90,000, and he spent $10,000 of his own money on a house for his family. He wrote afterward: "Without a knowledge of business or an appreciation of the dangers incident thereto, I . . . made extraordinary efforts in San Francisco to build myself & business on a *big scale.*" He also agreed to invest the money of friends living in other parts of the country who wanted to profit from California's boom. He took responsibility for a total of about $130,000 in addition to the bank's outstanding loans of about $450,000. He told his brother in June 1854: "All parties seem to have confidence in me." Behind the devious intricacy of San Francisco's many enterprises to exploit high prices, quick profits, and the flow of people, goods, and gold, the city was exceeding the limits of expansion its commerce could sustain. The number of miners, hence of consumers, leveled off and began to drop, as did the yield of gold. Increased production of food in California reduced demand for imports. Competition among merchants created an oversupply, and diminished returns could not support exorbitant rents and an interest rate of 36 percent per year. Contraction became unmistakable early in 1854 and continued for the rest of Sherman's stay in California. Investors withdrew capital from San Francisco. Prudent merchants stopped borrowing, and imprudent ones who borrowed were likely to default. While taxes remained high, property values and rents fell steeply. Warehouses and stores stood empty. City, county, state, and corporate bonds were repudiated. Banks failed. Sherman recalled three years later: "At that instant of time 1855 San Francisco exploded— property, bonds stock and all sorts of securities vanished from sight like the baseless fabric of a dream."

Though Sherman kept his bank solvent, hoping to outlast the depression, he began to see mistakes in his loans and investments. Men and institutions apparently substantial turned out to be unreliable. "In a strict sense there is no banking here," he wrote in 1857. "All is speculation. . . . Nobody feels a fixed interest here, and all are ready to bolt as soon as a good chance offers." He worried that his naïveté was hurting Lucas and Turner. The "magnificent" bank building, still at the northeast corner of the intersection of Montgomery and Jackson streets after 135 years of earthquakes, was the only stable feature of the enterprise, and its expensiveness mockingly reminded Sherman of his early extravagance. He had even guessed wrong about the development of the financial district and in 1856 had to move his banking operations to a rented office at Battery and Washington streets. Far from amassing capital of his own, he spent more than he made, maintaining a household with three servants and a carriage. The family's expenses in 1854 were one-third more than double his salary, or about $13,000. In October his personal account in the bank was overdrawn by $8,000.

Preferring outdoor activity and exercise, Sherman found that office work and anxiety, as well as San Francisco's fogs, aggravated his asthma. Always a light sleeper, he spent many night hours awake, coughing and struggling to breathe. Sometimes he got no sleep before returning to the bank in the morning. He took what he called "debilitating medicines" constantly. His sickness left him "quite depressed at times"; with each new asthma attack he wondered whether it was the one that would kill him. Ellen Sherman may have been thinking of this combination of depression and anxiety when she later said that she had seen Cump in the siege of insanity in California. After he left the state she wrote to him: "I trust you may not be soon again troubled with the terrible night mare that oppressed you during your entire stay in San Francisco." Years later, perhaps alluding to his recurrent nightmares, Sherman wrote to a California friend: "I . . . have with my eyes closed, seen things that human eyes and ears could not reach."

Belatedly, Sherman recalled his earlier aversion to the anarchical greed and pervasive bad faith he had seen at the start of the gold rush. After closing his bank he denounced the "cursed land" of gamblers and bankrupts: "There seems to be no reliance on any body or thing here." He reflected bitterly on the ruin of his ambitious optimism: "I shall never recover my self respect, after having allowed myself to be taken in by California, of which I ought to have known better." After the fall of Atlanta in September 1864, he asked a friend in California to sell a city lot which had been given to his daughter Lizzie and had continued to run up a tax bill. Sherman said: "I can handle an hundred thousand men in battle, and take the 'City of the Sun,' but am afraid to manage a lot in the swamp of San Francisco."

Further humiliation awaited Sherman. As if to extend the lesson of California to the rest of the country, the Panic of 1857 began in New York not long after Sherman went there to open a branch bank for Lucas and Turner. He watched a run on every bank in the city and expected all to fail. Lucas's bank in St. Louis suspended payments, and Lucas met its obligations out of his personal fortune. In the process he closed Sherman's New York office, which had lasted less than three months. Two years later, after receiving yet another offer of banking work, this time in London, Sherman said: "I suppose I was the Jonah that blew up San Francisco, and it only took two months residence in Wall Street to bust up New York, and I think my arrival in London will be the signal of the downfall of that mighty empire." He returned to California in 1858, attempting to recover debts owed to Lucas, Turner & Company and salvage investments he had made for friends. Unable to recoup all of these, he reimbursed his friends from his own dwindling funds, leaving him with less than $1,000 in assets. People in San Francisco urged him to reopen Lucas, Turner & Company to take advantage of the failure of other banks, forgetting that he, too, represented a broken bank. Though he applied to regain a commission in the army, he expected to have to work for his father-in-law in the Hocking Valley at the salt-wells and the coal mines. In California he acted despondent, looked unwell, wore seedy clothes, and told people that he would be "compelled to go into a log cabin."

With a jaded eye Sherman observed two more gold rushes in 1858. Many miners who had passed through San Francisco on their way to the interior of California passed through again, going the other way, when they heard that gold had been discovered in British Columbia. Their "mad rush" made Sherman think of "a flock of sheep." After returning to Ohio he decided to join Hugh Ewing and Thomas Ewing, Jr., in their law firm in Leavenworth, Kansas. The new town struck him as "a shabby place," but it became a way station for the Pike's Peak gold rush to Colorado. "I have seen so many gold stampedes," Sherman said, "that I am incredulous always." He spent less than a year in Kansas, working mainly on land transactions and the management of property. Again he was surrounded by a carnival of speculation and self-promotion, amid which he made little money. "It is California all over." In 1859, on the recommendation of Sherman's army friends, the governor of Louisiana offered him the superintendency of the state's new military academy, and he accepted. He was at last reduced to teaching planters' unruly sons. From Rapides Parish he wrote to a friend: "Financial crisis of 1857 threw me flat on my back without a profession, and I am now down here."

Had he set out to do so, Sherman could hardly have contrived a range of experiences better calculated to intensify his preoccupation with social stability, governmental power, and the rule of law. Southerners' secession and Northerners' unreliable response to it showed him that he still had underestimated Americans' capacity for folly. But he saw in the turn to mass violence in 1861 a climax to the dissolution of societal cohesion in the 1850s. Though Americans had to have a war to teach them their lesson, they could have seen it all in California: the collapse of civic virtue into self-interest, mob action, and defiance of government would eventually destroy a society.

Of all his California adventures—of all his experiences before the Civil War—Sherman attributed the greatest importance to his stand against the San Francisco Committee of Vigilance in 1856. From May until October the Committee made itself an extra-legal government of the city. It defied the governor, punished its political enemies, and entrenched its leaders in power lasting long after its disbandment. It included many businessmen and won the support of newspapers and, apparently, of most citizens. The vigilantes had won, Sherman often acknowledged afterward; but their success was dangerous. If the institutions and forms of law could be repudiated by those claiming to represent popular opinion or public welfare, no government could forestall anarchy.

During the Vigilance Committee's rule, San Franciscans knew that Sherman opposed it. After it dissolved and after Sherman left San Francisco, he often emphasized his stand against it. Yet he became involved in the confrontation inadvertently and withdrew from it quickly. As with his refusal to join Louisiana's secession in 1861, he later exaggerated his lonely stand for law against the crowd. Although the vigilantes represented themselves as an organization of decent citizens determined to establish order in a violent city misgoverned by corrupt politicians, their membership and their conduct revealed them to be a political organization—Whigs, nativist Know-Nothings, and Republicans—seeking to wrest political power from Democrats, especially Irish Catholic Democrats of the Tammany faction in the California party.

The immediate provocation or excuse for the Committee to mobilize was the shooting of the virulent anti-Democratic newspaper editor James

King of William by the equally virulent editor James Patrick Casey. Sherman despised both men for their sensationalism and for their editorial posturing as defenders of depositors against the machinations of sinister bankers. If Casey had been suddenly killed after shooting King, Sherman would have welcomed the outcome. Instead, Casey surrendered to the sheriff, and King lay mortally wounded but alive for several days. The Democrats' opponents took this opportunity to be shocked and to say that murder would go unpunished if Casey were entrusted to the ordinary course of the law in the hands of his cronies. With an efficient haste that suggested prior concert, the vigilantes mobilized to supersede the city and county government. Before these events Sherman, who was friendly with William Gwin and the Chivalry, or pro-Southern, wing of the Democratic party, had accepted the seemingly nominal position of major general of militia from the newly elected Know-Nothing governor of California, J. Neely Johnson. Though Johnson's political allies were, in many cases, among the vigilantes and though Sherman had no troops and no arms, the two men tried to dissuade the Vigilance Committee from taking extra-legal action. They failed.

As soon as King died, the vigilantes hanged Casey and Charles Cora, who was awaiting retrial for killing a United States marshal. In the following weeks the Vigilance Committee forcibly shipped out of San Francisco people it deemed criminals, a proceeding which bore a strong resemblance to sabotaging the Democratic organization in the city. Two more men were hanged. During most of these activities, Sherman, who was not sorry to see the banished people go, remained only an observer. Casey and Cora were hanged on May 22. Sherman resigned his militia command on June 6. Publicly, he did so because the local United States Army commander, General John Wool, reneged on an oral promise to supply arms with which the militia might have overawed the vigilantes. But Sherman's ability to raise an adequate force was uncertain. Unlike Judge David S. Terry of the state supreme court and some of Governor Johnson's other advisers, Sherman wanted to prevent combat. He held what he called "moderate ideas," in contrast with Terry's and Edward Baker's desire to call miners from the mountains and "sweep the damned pork sellers into the bay." On June 21 Terry became a prisoner of the Vigilance Committee after he stabbed a vigilante who was trying to arrest him.

Sherman also had private reasons for resigning. He anticipated that, by seeking conflict with the Committee, he would bring the business leaders' revenge down on Lucas and Turner's bank. He saw that the businessmen—"the mob in broadcloth," a Californian called them later—"have regarded those who favored the cause of Law and Order as enemies of the people, and withdrawn their patronage from newspapers and all other interests controlled by Law and Order men." On the day of King's funeral Sherman had crepe hung on his bank because he did not want it to be conspicuous as the only building not draped in mourning. Convinced that General Wool's refusal of arms made further resistance futile and concerned about the harm he already had done to Lucas and Turner by his banking mistakes, Sherman chose discretion. He explained to his brother: "Being in a business where large interests are at stake I cannot act with that decision otherwise that would suit me."

Six months after the Vigilance Committee had disbanded, its leaders having won control of the city's regular government in the fall election, Sherman admitted that Governor Johnson "had a right to have some little feeling against me for deserting him at a critical moment." Yet when Sherman mentioned "the Vigilance War" in later years, as he often did, he reiterated that he had then first clearly seen and staunchly opposed the forces of disorder that crested in the Civil War and persisted thereafter. He wrote in 1861: "I am and always have been an active defender of law & the constitution. Twice have I sacrificed myself thereto. In San Francisco to a Northern mob, and in Louisiana to a Southern rebellion." If Sherman could stand firm against popular madness, so should the nation. The San Francisco of the 1850s remained his most expressive example of the turbulent tendencies in democratic society. Economic depression amid mountains of gold, greed and fraud checked only by stupidity, a governor without power, an army general without honor, militiamen without guns, men of property sabotaging the rule of law which alone made property secure, former convicts in public office and a violent judge in illegal detention, libel and slander and murder and lynching all done in the name of the people—the days of the Vigilance Committee reappeared in Sherman's mind whenever he encountered opposition to government.

Thomas G. Cary attacked Sherman in a defense of the Committee written thirty years afterward, arguing that its extra-legal actions carried out "the republican theory" instead of statute law, or the "despotic theory": "The republican theory is that the citizens of San Francisco erected a Government in that State, for their own security, profit, and advantage; and that as they originally erected it to fulfill these purposes, so they have the full right to pull it down again when it ceases, in their opinion, to fulfill them." William T. Coleman, leader of the Committee, later claimed that its conduct, "while technically outside the law," embodied the principle that every citizen was part of the workings of government, a proposition which was "one of the great strongholds of self-government." Hence the Vigilance Committee had put into practice Americans' fundamental political beliefs. To Sherman these arguments, like the Committee's actions, showed how easily the shibboleths of democracy and equality could sabotage the rule of law. Such opportunistic doctrines eroded all fixed standards and invited anarchy.

The prevailing historical interpretation of the Committee during Sherman's lifetime, embodied especially in Josiah Royce's study of California and in the work of Hubert Howe Bancroft, portrayed the vigilantes as "cautious and conscientious men" who had redeemed the city from pervasive political corruption and violent crime. Like Sherman, Royce deplored an atomized society of greed, in which people failed to serve an ideal of community. Unlike Sherman, he believed that an extra-legal movement, though an evil, could "regenerate the social order" if its leaders restrained the "natural tendencies" of vigilantism. Bancroft wrote an even more laudatory account. Sherman argued that the Vigilance Committee had been essentially political, that government and crime in San Francisco had not been significantly worse than in other American cities, and that the Committee's political victory had brought no transcendent moral reformation. Instead, the vigilantes had established a precedent of usurpation to which any Americans, not just businessmen, could appeal. The interests of his bank had somewhat compromised Sherman's stand against lawlessness in 1856. For more than thirty years after leaving California he made up for that defeat, fighting the vigilantes as they reappeared in new guises.

President Buchanan's failure to reinforce the garrison at Charleston in 1861 reminded Sherman of "Johnsons abandoning the jail in San Francisco"; guarding the jail in Washington holding the assassin who had shot President Garfield reminded Sherman of "California at the time of the King-Casey affair"; he likened both the Ku Klux Klan and the Knights of Labor to vigilance committees. In 1884 he wrote from St. Louis to an old friend in California: "The influence of that committee is more wide spread than even you can comprehend. It is quoted here and every where as an example to justify mob violence. . . . the claim of the Vigilance Committee was *all sham.*" One could not understand the Civil War or postwar America without acknowledging that the "Law and Order" partisans in San Francisco had been right. Throughout the war Sherman complained that participants failed to understand the central question underlying the war, which only the war could resolve. This question, he insisted, was not slavery, despite sectional differences over its future. Nor was the issue one of race relations, in which he could imagine no great change. In the economic order he saw no provocation to war but rather a complementary prosperity, each section benefiting the other. The political cultures of the two sections might invite internecine violence, but only because they were so similar, beset by preachers, editors, demagogues, and the propensity of all Americans to exalt their own will above the law. The central question was whether or not citizens would place loyalty to the nation and obedience to its government ahead of all other loyalties.

Sherman made law as absolute an ideal as Josiah Royce made the communal ethos. Both men sought order. Sherman put his trust not in the community's capacity to regenerate itself but in the government's power to regulate citizens' behavior. Sherman summarized American society's many assaults on his conception of law: "This universal system of credit & worthless bank paper. This reckless taxation of real property by non property owners—this right of mob law, for any state, county, town, or village to do as they d—n please, hang, steal & rob, and call it the Peoples Law—Sewards Higher Law—southern mob law, and California Vigilance Committees are all now the common law of the United States taking precedence of the enactments of legislatures or judgment of courts." Secession had to be defeated not only to subordinate the South to the nation but also to deter, by proof of the government's power, the rebelliousness lurking in all Americans. The alternative he imagined was the apotheosis of anarchy, in which the only power honored by all was violence. The more drastic war measures he began to use in 1862 and 1863 seemed to him a way to prevent this outcome. To have defeated the threat was for him the main justification of the Northern war effort and the central legacy of the war.

LIVING in New Orleans in 1852, Sherman admitted that his imagination wandered back to the wildness of nature in the west and the excitement of adventure as the gold rush started in California. But his reason told him "that it is a barren region as compared with the great valley of the Mississippi." The river and its vast network of tributaries always represented for him the unity and complementary harmony toward which America must aspire. On his first boat trip from St. Louis to New Orleans in December 1843, he had watched with fascination as he moved in six days from snow and barrenness to blooming roses and waving fields of sugar cane. In August 1860 he traveled in the opposite direction, going from drought in upstate Louisiana to bumper crops in Ohio. The experience evoked an allusion to God, whose providence thereby demonstrated "the mutual dependence of one part of our magnificent country on the other" and who "has made a natural avenue between. This is a glorious fact." The Mississippi Valley promised fertility, perpetuity, and growing prosperity. Its promise became for Sherman all that California was not, all that he wanted America to be.

With the coming of the Civil War, Sherman, like many others in the west, argued that control of the Mississippi ought to be the North's preeminent strategic goal. Western politicians who supported the war promised their constituents that the North would reconquer the river; they warned Lincoln that failure to do so would strengthen disaffected Democrats. In October 1862 Frank Blair, Jr., told his brother, the postmaster general, that the people were impatient for a military movement down the Mississippi: "Unless it's done speedily you will hear murmurs from the north west which will be more fearful than the thunders of Stonewall Jackson's cannon." The river's commercial importance for shipment of western produce to the east had declined rapidly in the 1850s, largely supplanted by a growing rail network. However, trade up and down the river between North and South was thriving before the war. Westerners believed that a foreign power in control of the lower Mississippi could choke off their livelihood, notwithstanding the Confederate promise of free trade. They had evidence of their vulnerability in a sudden wartime rise of freight rates charged by railroad companies and Great Lakes shippers, whose customers had no alternate outlet. Farm prices fell; banks failed; workers found their paper wages worthless. Governor Oliver P. Morton of Indiana, fearing that Democrats' denunciation of eastern capitalists in the election campaign of 1862 portended a western separatist movement, told Lincoln: "Even the most ignorant are impressed by the importance of the Mississippi River." Editorials, campaign speeches, and recruiting rallies demanded that the North regain and hold the valley at all costs. Governor Richard Yates of Illinois promised in October 1863: "We stand prepared to swear that the foaming tide of the Mississippi shall run blood from its source to its mouth before we give up that river to traitors."

This scene of disruption and discord violated Sherman's cherished vision of harmony. For him the river was "the grand artery of America." The confluent waters, like the human circulatory system, made an organic whole which to sunder was to destroy. He also called the valley "the spinal column of America." More simply, he wrote to Halleck in 1863: "The valley of the Mississippi is America." When the war ended he was glad to make his headquarters in St. Louis, saying in 1866: "It is a beautiful dream to think of this valley, cultivated by an educated & refined people, from its spring lakes of Minnesota to the Nile like alluvium of Louisiana." During the war Sherman's fears dwelt on the threat to his dream. If the Confederacy could keep the valley divided, perpetual war would ensue. His obsession with its importance exposed him to ridicule late in 1861 and early in 1862. His imagination of the difficulty and the risk caused him to shrink from responsibility, and the shame of his perplexity led him to think of casting himself into the river whose waters he could not see how to reunite. Two days before the battle of Shiloh he again said that the valley must be under one government, "but the task is so gigantic that I am staggered at its cost."

To find faith that the river could be rewon, Sherman relied on the confidence shown by others, especially Halleck and Grant. He was sorry to see Halleck transferred to Washington in July 1862, fearing the consequences for the western campaign. "You took command in the Valley of the Mississippi at a period of deep gloom," Sherman wrote, "when I felt that our poor country was doomed to a Mexican anarchy, but at once arose order, system, firmness, and success in which there has not been a pause." Sherman detested John A. McClernand partly because McClernand spoke loosely of "cutting his way to the sea" but was incompetent to do so. He trivialized the campaign for the river by making it an instrument of his political ambition. When Grant became lieutenant general in March 1864, Sherman urged him to keep his headquarters in the west and make the Mississippi Valley "dead sure." He told Grant that, until the victory at Fort Donelson had opened the Tennessee and Cumberland rivers, "I was almost cowed by the terrible array of anarchical elements that presented themselves at every point; but that admitted the ray of light which I have followed since." Sherman derived confidence from Grant's "simple faith in success . . . which I can liken to nothing else than the faith a Christian has in a Savior." This had given Grant victory at Shiloh and at Vicksburg, restoring the river to the union. Sherman was not a Christian and did not have a simple faith in the nation's success. He built his expectations on the growing, irresistible power of the federal government. To Halleck he had said: "The man who at the end of the war holds the military control of the Valley of the Mississippi will be the man." He reminded Grant: "Here lies the seat of the coming empire." Finally, with Grant's departure for the east, Sherman took command of the Military Division of the Mississippi. Though he was campaigning in Georgia in July 1864, he could say: "I represent the Great Valley."

The military conquest of the lower Mississippi completed only one phase in Sherman's long effort to convince himself and others that the nation had an auspicious future, centered in the valley and guided by natural laws of progress, moving like the flow of the river itself. He argued that "the nature of our people" had made American settlement and possession of the valley inevitable. If Jefferson had not purchased the Louisiana Territory, the people would have seized it. The Mississippi served Sherman as a trope conveying the interconnected design of America. The unity of the valley bespoke an ineluctable purpose in history. John W. Draper, studying the war with Sherman's aid, wrote to him:

"On two great points I perceive we agree—that the course of this nation and indeed of all nations, is under the dominion of irreversible law—and that in a political sense the Valley of the Mississippi is America." For Sherman the bane of the United States was Americans' making a virtue of being isolated and autonomous—as individuals, groups, states, or sections. That propensity could yield only an aberrant momentum to a meaningless end. Then the waters would be terrible. Reproving an old friend who had sided with the South, Sherman wrote in 1862: "You like others have been blown up, and cast into the Mississippi of Secession doubtful if by hard fighting you can reach the shore in safety, or drift out to the Ocean of Death."

Sherman's turn to increasingly harsh war against Southerners during the Mississippi Valley campaign drew on his eagerness to prove the existence of a beneficent national destiny. Late in 1863 he said: "To secure the safety of the navigation of the Mississippi I would slay millions. On that point I am not only insane but mad." His willingness to destroy towns on the riverbank had the same origins as his postwar appeal to "the new men of the South," who he hoped would "cultivate a pride in the whole United States of America." No violence could be so bad as the chaos that would follow a loss of belief in unity. "The great sin of the South, the great cause of all her woes, has been the localism of her brilliant minds." To this isolation Sherman offered an alternative vision. "How much more sublime the thought," he wrote to George H. Braughn of New Orleans, "that you live at the root of a tree whose branches reach the beautiful fields of Western New York, and the majestic cañons of the Yellowstone, and that with every draught of water you take the outflow of the pure lakes of Minnesota and the dripping of the dews of the Alleghany and Rocky Mountains."

Sherman called St. Louis his home; he moved to the city six times but never stayed longer than four years, usually less. His remains are buried there but had to be shipped from New York, where he spent his last five years. After leaving Lancaster, where he never wanted to live again, he had no lasting home. He intensely disliked the political world of Washington, D.C., and while commanding general frequently escaped for long trips. No matter which city he resided in, he left it several times a year on travels taking him all over the United States again and again. He seemed to be trying to incorporate America into himself, or to reassure himself that it was still one, as if he were holding it together by the promise that he would return to every part of it. He sought confirmation of his faith that maintaining the union kept the country in the main channel of history's movement. In this concern he shared the outlook of the Reverend Truman M. Post, speaking on "National Regeneration" in

St. Louis in 1864: "History is no eddy, though embracing many such. It is a Mississippi, bearing all eddies with refluent or affluent whirl, ever to the great ocean. . . . The forces of social progress are immortal; and by properly applying them, society may itself become immortal." Fixed homes were ephemeral, compared to the growing nation defined by the flowing river. With this, rather than with any one place, Sherman most fully identified himself. On the same day that he praised Grant's faith in success he wrote to Ellen Sherman from the vicinity of Memphis: "As soon as the spring campaign is over I want to come here and look after the Mississippi. Like the story in Gil Blas—'Here lies my soul.' . . . I want to live out here & die here also, and dont care if my grave be like DeSotos in its muddy waters."

CHAPTER 4

THE ANOMALOUS WAR

LOOKING BACK on the Civil War, John Esten Cooke recalled with ironical bitterness how confidently Americans in both sections had predicted, right through 1860, that there would be no war. "The world was too 'civilized and enlightened,'" they had said, "too commercial and religious; too intelligent and averse to that folly of follies, war, to permit for a single day, such incredible nonsense." They had been wrong. Cooke could not improve on the plain statement in the second inaugural address of Abraham Lincoln, whose government he had fought. He repeated Lincoln's words: "And the war came." Seemingly a straightforward piece of narrative, those four words gave the war an existence distinct from the people who enacted it. They did not create it. How could they have done so? They did not expect it. It came. War did not mean that the republic had failed; citizens had not proven incapable of self-government in turning to violence; they were not responsible for what they had been forced to do. Americans' killing one another after having deemed such a thing unthinkable led Cooke to conclude: "It was in every point of view the most tragic, unprecedented and anomalous of contests."

How could Americans accept the war's results as the fruition of history's plan for the nation while representing its events, its violence, as an anomaly, a kind of behavior Americans did not choose, from which they were supposed to be exempt? They all had claimed to be guarding the legacy of the American Revolution. They all had professed to be acting under compulsion, defending their nation and its principles. And they had killed one another. For a time, they had experienced disjunctions in their understanding of the nation or nations involved in the war. Had there been only one nation, the United States, which established its existence conclusively by suppressing rebels? Or had there been two, a United States and a Confederate States of America, the former having conquered and obliterated the latter? Or had three nations existed sequentially: the old republic, the Southern Confederacy, and a new consolidated nation, destroyer and supplanter of its predecessors? Perhaps one could even find four by detecting a postwar version of the Confederate nation, still surviving within the United States despite the death of both the antebellum republic and the short-lived Southern republic. Defense of a nation was the ultimate justification for war, but this unquestionable principle somehow had led to unaccountable confusion. In the supposedly anomalous war, Northern nationalists fought for a union whose perpetuity and supremacy they were newly discovering in the middle of the nineteenth century, yet were tracing back to political principles of the eighteenth century. Southern secessionists fought for a state sovereignty whose continuous existence they traced back to the American Revolution; it had not been compromised, they said, by the states' membership in a contingent, expedient union; but, they found, it could be maintained only by creating a new supreme, perpetual nation. Two internally contradictory stories of nation-making thus became justifications for a bitter war to establish which myth was true.

The anomalous war, then, was not just combat between belligerents who denied they were bloodthirsty. Nor was it simply a contest of rival definitions of nationhood with a common origin. It included an interior struggle on each side, an effort to make the newly forming conceptions of nationality inclusive and lasting while they were still controversial and nebulous. In this undertaking Northern unionists fared better than Southern secessionists with durable myth-making, as well as with war-making. For decades unionists had been developing a version of American history which demonstrated to their satisfaction how republican self-government found its fullest development and its sole security in the union. Northerners took inspiration from the American Revolution. In the nineteenth-century history of the early republic, Revolutionary founders lost much of the distinctiveness of their time and their views. The later generation infused the Revolution with modern concerns. Pro-war Irish Democrats hostile to abolitionists believed themselves to be fighting Confederates in order to defend "the most precious fruits of the Revolution," while self-styled antislavery radicals announced that Washington, Jefferson, Adams, Hancock, and Paine all were radicals, too. The Revolutionary generation, which had reinterpreted its seventeenth-century forebears to make them proponents of liberty and republican self-government, was itself reinterpreted to serve purposes of the nineteenth century. Lincoln in his first inaugural address and Federal soldiers recalling their school lessons about Valley Forge equated the War for Independence with the subsequent inseparable unity of the American nation. Private Terah W. Sampson of the 6th Kentucky Regiment, U.S.A., said that he had no mercy for rebels: "The ider of a nation fighting against one another is what tryes me. . . . I want to live under the flag of Gorge Washington the flag of our four fathers or not at all." Northerners imagined that heroes of the Revolution, if they could return to life, would be appalled by secessionists' attack on the union because the Revolutionaries had meant to create a permanent republic.

Eighteenth-century Americans who won independence and supported the Constitution saw republics as vulnerable and short-lived. Everywhere tyrants worked to increase their power. Citizens' capacity to put public good above private interests faced many threats, including economic dependence of the poor on the rich and the prevalence of selfishness and faction. The United States had no promise of perpetuity as an independent nation or as a republic able to preserve its people's liberty. Any generation might, by its divisions or by its corruption, lose what the Revolution had won. Late in the eighteenth century and early in the nineteenth, some surviving leaders of the Revolution who had identified themselves most fully with its enduring success grew pessimistic about the nation's future. Partisan agitation, sectional friction—Americans' susceptibility to passions more powerful than their attachment to unity—foreshadowed failure to maintain the United States through its institutions of self-government, which the Revolution had established only tenuously. George Washington, at the end of his career, thought failure inevitable. His farewell address advised Americans how to preserve the republic but said of his own parting words: "I dare not hope they will make the strong and lasting impression I could wish—that they will control the usual current of the passions or prevent our nation from running the course which has hitherto marked the destiny of nations." For him and his contemporaries, history showed that the destiny of nations, especially republics, was to disappear through fragmentation, conquest, and despotism. Washington was telling Americans, unobtrusively but explicitly, that the United States enjoyed no exemption from the pattern of history. This cyclical view of history was ultimately fatalistic. Members of the founding generation had felt the competing attraction of believing instead that human power could be expanded sufficiently to ensure the republic's perpetual progress or that American history could lead directly to the Christian millennium. By the time of the Civil War, defenders of the union insisted that the Revolutionaries had created a republic that could be made immortal. George Bancroft, the foremost historian of the

United States, assured an audience on Washington's birthday in 1862 that Washington had understood the union's perpetuity better than Chief Justice Roger B. Taney did eighty years later. Other public speakers associated the Revolution with "the progress of democracy, its consolidation and ascendancy, the glory of the New World," "the unity, growth, and destiny of the nation." As Americans had done for decades, Northerners gave the Revolution their own imperatives, replacing the Revolutionaries' cyclical view of history with a progressive one which many people in the previous century would have deemed naive.

Eighteenth-century heroes reappeared in discussion of the Civil War less often as political thinkers and students of ancient history than as bleeding patriots. Their example of courage and sacrifice in combat seemed larger than life. As *Harper's New Monthly Magazine* suggested in 1867, the Northern public had formed its idea of the soldier under the influence of "its schoolboy impressions of our Revolutionary demigods." The battles fought against the British were the republic's foundation. Henry Ward Beecher called them "our constitutions and source of moral power." When secession threatened the nation, true Americans had to vindicate the Revolution by emulating their predecessors in combat. Sometimes they drew a direct familial connection. The father of a soldier killed in the summer of 1862 justified having allowed his son to enlist at the age of sixteen on the grounds that the boy's great-grandfather had enlisted in the Continental Army at the same age. Clara Barton explained her dedication to battlefield nursing by writing to Secretary Stanton: "My father was a soldier following Mad Anthony Wayne . . . he charged me with a dying patriots love to serve and sacrifice for my country." For rhetorical purposes, the whole populace figuratively became descendants of the heroes of the Revolution, of those whom the *Detroit Free Press* called "our Revolutionary sires." The fathers' example taught the virtue of service to the nation through bloodshed.

Though commemorating Americans who had overthrown British rule, Northerners did not make a virtue of revolution. The people's right of revolution as an ultimate recourse was a staple of antebellum political rhetoric, but the Civil War brought out among Northerners a patriotic theme that had entered popular speech since the American Revolution—a reverence for government, country, and flag as ends in themselves. Mention of these carried a heavy freight of emotion. Government, which the founders had regarded as an instrument, became an ideal. The outburst of belligerent patriotism following the attack on Fort Sumter showed how far Northerners already had gone in making loyalty a passion. The war for the union was afterward labeled the great divide between the era of the contingent republic and the era of the permanent nation. However, the death of the old republic had not been so abrupt as this distinction implied. Unionists' war against secession drew on a national sentiment already in existence. That sentiment did not allow loyalty to depend simply on citizens' political opinion or choice. Unionists' version of American history and the American nation presupposed readiness, even eagerness, for bloodshed and coercion to stamp out deviance.

In the spring of 1861, Southerners and their remaining Northern friends bitterly noted the quick collapse of once insuperable objections to maintaining the union by force. Strict constructionist constitutional views, threats in the North to resist federal coercion of the South, abolitionists' professed willingness to let the South go, doubts about the feasibility of conquering a vast territory—principled, rationally chosen positions apparently promising a consistent line of conduct—proved weaker than popular resentment of an attack on the United States. Many politicians and editors who had deprecated war turned around quickly. Both great rivals in New York, Horace Greeley of the *Tribune* and James Gordon Bennett of the *Herald,* with different objectives, changed their editorial course to support coercion enthusiastically. Parts of their editorials became almost indistinguishable: "The chief business of the American people must be proving that they have a Government," said one; "one question—'Shall there be a government and a Union?' absorbed all minor considerations and differences," said the other. Three weeks after the firing on Fort Sumter a resident of New York who sympathized with secession wrote to a friend in Virginia: "You ask where are the conservative hosts who voted against Lincoln last fall. Ah where, dissolved into thin air, gone, gone and now all men vie with each other in preaching up a crusade of fire & sword against the heathen. . . . And all this is done under the boast of Law & order, upholding the Union and Constitution—the Stars & Stripes. The question 'Have we a government,' is to be answered by inaugurating a civil war and subjugating and murdering the citizens of a large section of the Country." This letter overstated the new Northern unity, and the initial enthusiasm did not last in full force. Still, the New Yorker's complaint identified an essential element of the Northern cause throughout the war: an emotional attachment to vague but numinous symbols of national solidarity. More and more Northerners were ready to surrender to the union at the moment that Southerners chose to deny its hold on them.

One of the most popular evocations of this sentiment in the North was Edward Everett Hale's short story, "The Man Without a Country." Hale wrote it for publication in the autumn of 1863 to encourage Northerners' support of the war and especially to persuade Ohioans to vote against the antiwar Democrat Clement L. Vallandigham in their gubernatorial election. Vallandigham had been arrested for disloyal speeches in May 1863 and later forcibly ejected into Confederate lines; he went to Canada and campaigned for governor while in exile. *The Atlantic* belatedly published Hale's story in December, after John Brough had been elected by a large majority. In subsequent months the story fulfilled its larger patriotic purpose. More than 500,000 copies were printed within a year; Federal soldiers and sailors wrote to Hale after reading it. It remained a fixture of classroom readings and popular anthologies in the twentieth century.

The story described the fate of a fictional United States Army officer, Lieutenant Philip Nolan, convicted during Jefferson's administration of participating in Aaron Burr's scheme to establish a new empire in the west. Before being sentenced, Nolan said to the court: "Damn the United States! I wish I may never hear of the United States again!" The fulfillment of his wish became his punishment. He was sentenced to spend the rest of his life at sea aboard American vessels, never allowed to read about or hear any mention of the United States. In a series of scenes portraying Nolan's plight through decades, Hale exploited the reader's empathy with the terror of isolation in order to dramatize an inborn need to belong to a country. Despite comfortable subsistence and the friendly companionship of naval officers, Nolan suffered the painful spiritual consequences of his treason. He had no home. No countrymen acknowledged him. He was alone. Unable to bear this state of mind, he secretly turned to passionate patriotism. Eking out his memory with conjecture, he drew a map of the United States, which he revered in the privacy of his cabin, alongside a portrait of George Washington, a painting of an eagle overshadowing the globe, and an American flag whose stars revealed to him the nation's growth. He survived spiritually during his long exile and became a noble figure in death by rejoining the country he had damned, overcoming the most nearly complete separation imaginable. Hale equated Nolan's rash curse in court with Vallandigham's readiness "to throw away a country" and with Confederates' eagerness to do "all that in them lay that they might have no country" by breaking up the United States. A nation, he implied, held its people with a force greater than material interest or rational choice. It gave them an identity they could not repudiate without destroying themselves. A traitor, by sabotaging the United States, undercut every loyal citizen. Treason had to be suppressed, or all Americans would be men and women without a country.

Hale's sentimental story touched a theme which pervaded the writings of Northern unionists. Even the least literate could say, as did the father of a soldier from DeWitt County, Illinois: "I am in for my Country evry time Right or rong." Hale reached so large and receptive an audience probably because he was confirming what many people already felt.

Urging a New York audience to support the war in 1861, Joseph Holt asked: "Is it nothing to live without a country and without a flag ... and to stand forth the degenerate and abased descendants of a great ancestry?" Government and country transcended the politicians in power and took on a separate existence in the imagination, associated with benign parental guarantees of security. Northerners called the Confederate attack parricide. An Indiana couple rebuked their nephew, who had joined the Confederate army: "I want you to tell me why you are in a Rebellion against our Government? When you was little the Government protected you, and now I want to know what the matter is with you, that you turned against it. The Government has raised you." Appeals to government, country, and flag in political campaigns relied on the aura of beneficence emanating from these indistinct ideas.

Advising Salmon P. Chase on ways to defeat Vallandigham in the Ohio election, Murat Halstead wrote: "The essential thing is to keep the administration out of sight as much as possible, and talk of the cause of nationality and nothing else." Such an approach could bring together large numbers of people who held divergent views not so much by fooling them as by tapping the sentiment that moved them more strongly than did their opinions on matters of policy. Private Henry Spaulding, a New Jersey Democrat, put rhetorical questions to his wife: "What though the party in power differ widely from my views, & commit acts I think unconstitutional, & are actuated by unpatriotic & selfish & sectional & fanatical views & motives, can I love my *country* less? . . . Can I consent to let that 'political heresy,' that country destroying principle, *Secession* prevail?" Confederates and Democrats, deploring the federal government's tyranny, usually talked past such beliefs rather than to them. Studied constitutional arguments and appeals to material, sectional, and racial interests could not disprove the validity of an emotion. Directed toward emblems of patriotism, as in its other forms, love did not depend on reasons, and it flourished on notions of sacrifice. Finding their own worth in the vision of one America, unionists could muster many arguments for it but could not be reasoned out of it.

Supporters of war for the union assumed that the republic was or could be made immortal. As Southern states began to secede, Nathaniel P. Banks, leaving office as governor of Massachusetts, told the legislature that the government could not be broken: "It has been sanctified by the sacrifice of the best blood of the people and that sacrifice has made it a nation, indissoluble and eternal." Although a few Americans in the early years of the republic had asserted its perpetuity, the main expression of this ideal arose later in response to nineteenth-century constitutional and historical analyses proclaiming the sovereignty of the states and the right of secession. The doctrine that the union could not be lawfully dissolved became a promise that the United States must exist eternally. The Reverend Alexander H. Vinton formulated perhaps the best characterization of this conceit. Instead of basing it on reason or precedent, he called it "both a prayer and a prophecy: 'My country, be thou perpetual as the ages.' " Neither history nor law could make such a promise. Its plausibility lay in repetition and in successful use of force. America had the best government in the world, William Henry Seward said in Gettysburg before Lincoln's address; it "must be, and, so far as we are concerned, practically will be, immortal." No one surpassed Lincoln's gift for rhetorically transmuting soldiers' mortality into the nation's immortality. To an interpretation of its past, unionists added a prophecy of America's future, defining the nation by apostrophizing it. They attributed to the union the same permanence, supremacy, and presumptive right to prevail that they ascribed to all unquestionable moral and political truths.

In his dedicatory address at the Gettysburg cemetery, Lincoln spoke from a premise congenial to Northerners of a metaphysical turn of mind: he assumed that nationality inhered in an idea. People were one because their minds were occupied by a common image or definition. James McKaye took it for granted that a nation "must, from the very nature of things, incorporate its own distinctive organic force or Idea. Indeed, it is only in virtue of this distinctive organic idea, that it becomes a nation at all." Lincoln confined himself to stating the idea as "the proposition that all men are created equal." A month earlier, campaigning for Republican candidates in Indiana, Secretary Chase had used a more specific formulation derived from natural rights doctrine, saying that the war was giving birth to "a great nation . . . that shall respect the rights of every human being." The Unitarian minister James Freeman Clarke of Boston sought a less controversial idea, one with a "commanding presence," which "all people" could share. He settled for "the idea of 'Our Country.' " Whatever proposition such nationalists chose for summarizing the nation's essence, they in effect said that the nation existed by virtue of its pervading idea. This definition implicitly or explicitly detached the nation's identity from a dependence on anything temporary or adventitious, such as political arrangements, revocable compacts, or states' proximity or similarity to one another. The nation's life, "filled with an idea," was "self-directed." Citizens gave themselves up to it. To try to do otherwise, as the Confederates did in denying a transcendent America and in supposing themselves able to manage a new political arrangement for their own interests, was not to divide one nation into two nations; it was to repudiate the basis on which the United States existed.

Northerners who studied the growing power of nationality and the state in Europe often said that the United States must follow history's movement toward consolidation of political entities and centralization of power. They recognized that idealization of the nation was neither unique to America nor altogether of native origin. Two immigrant scholars, Francis Lieber and John W. Draper, both of whom began their American academic careers in the South, argued that the idea of the nation as the supreme political good had come to the United States from Europe. In his lectures on the Constitution at Columbia University's school of law, Lieber especially enjoyed teaching about what he called "the period of *nationalisation* . . . when the national government became the normal type (and God's great blessing) of modern civilisation—the period when that great process of Europeanizing America began." As a central part of this process, both men relegated states to the category of "convenient political fictions," in Draper's words. Yet the United States thereby became more than an aggregation of such fictions. By suffusing Northerners with "the Idea of Nationality," the new way of thinking gave the United States its first intellectually legitimate claim to reality as a nation-state. George Bancroft presented the prospect in simple language to a Massachusetts regiment in 1861: "We have heard much talk about the power of the people; it is left to you to demonstrate that there is in existence a people of the United States." Using oratorical syllepsis he shifted the meaning of the word "people" from one which implicitly counterpoised "the" people against a government or an elite to one which incorporated all Americans into "a" people, defined by their nationality in contrast with that of other peoples. The entity whose existence the soldiers demonstrated with their coercive power was the oneness of the inhabitants of the United States.

Unionists believed, as did Confederates, that the spirit of the age militated in favor of creating nations. For unionists such creation required defeat of centrifugal politics. This proposition seemed obvious to Louis Moreau Gottschalk, a native of New Orleans who had freed his slaves in the 1850s. After studying in Paris and attaining international celebrity as a pianist, he toured the North during the war, giving nearly 1,000 concerts that always included his patriotic composition "The Union." He explained his allegiance by his rejection of slavery and by his understanding of political progress: "In the nineteenth century nationalities are no longer broken—the general movement tends to unification." Americans had boasted since the Revolution that they were the vanguard of history. They could not lead by falling into disorder. Fragmentation would be fatal to their ambition to show that a republic could endure. In his Gettysburg address, Lincoln, like Bancroft in his speech to the soldiers, could play on the word "people" to conflate the citizenry, the federal government, and the nation. The life which, in perishing, would lose all else was the life of the nation. The more fully it became the source of identity, the more nearly it became an absolute, in America as elsewhere. Speaking in the Seventh Street Synagogue in Philadelphia, Rabbi Sabato Morais said in the spring of 1863: "An Israelite by faith, and an Italian by birth, I would blush to utter in your presence the word 'dissolution.' With the lessons of history stamped on my mind, can I advocate the death of a nation?"

When Lincoln dated the fathers' bringing forth of the nation at a point eighty-seven years before 1863, he took as a premise for his address the familiar unionist contention that the Declaration of Independence and the Revolutionary War had created an indissoluble United States. Secessionists, in explaining the Constitution's text, describing its ratification, and assessing interpretations of it, used false history, unionists said. The union was not a revocable compact among sovereign states. The United States, in the words of Secretary Seward, "would be a nation, if we had no Constitution." The nation not only antedated the charter of government and existed independently of governmental forms, but also, by its self-evident need to exist, empowered its defenders to defeat its enemies without necessarily confining their actions by constitutional restraints. The war accustomed Northerners to hearing that an ideal could override ambiguous or obsolete provisions of fundamental law. Representative John William Noell, a Democrat, echoed in Congress what other politicians, such as Seward, Oliver P. Morton, and Henry Winter Davis said in speeches or in private: "The Constitution of the United States was not framed in full contemplation of the present condition of things. . . . the people of the United States have a right to live as a nation, and they have a right to use the means necessary to save this nation's life." The war, as many people have argued since, enabled Lincoln and his supporters to make the United States the nation unionists said the American Revolution already had made it. The soldiers could help George Bancroft demonstrate that his historical evidence and argument were sound.

Of course, politicians of the Revolution had thought about assertions of state sovereignty, divisions among the states, and the bearing of the central government's powers on the republic's unity. In their debates over the ratification of the Constitution they had revealed a vivid imagination of the prospects for civil war, despotism, anarchy, and fragmentation of the United States. So intensely did these concerns register on their minds that they refrained from making the claim that mattered most to their nineteenth-century unionist successors: the claim that the United States was a permanent, indivisible nation. Secessionists and antiwar Democrats charged, and a variety of unionists conceded, that the preeminence of nationality, sustained by force, did not appear in the teachings of the Revolution. At a Federal veterans' reunion in 1868, General Durbin Ward told his fellow soldiers that only by war could they have settled the doubts formerly raised by political theorists who denied that the founders had created a supreme, perpetual government. The Revolutionary generation, with its political machinery designed to offset citizens' vices, had failed to give conclusive answers. In fact, those answers could not come from theorists or constitutional conventions. "It is a severe but just commentary on the dominion of passion and prejudice over reason, that great and revolutionary changes in political organization are rarely made except through bloodshed." For Ward the new nation was obviously better, purged of secession and slavery, despite the violence of its birth. In 1887 E. L. Godkin, departing from the contention that war for the union merely enforced the founding fathers' design, argued, as many historians have done since, that the North's military victory transformed the Constitution from the founders' provisional, experimental, ambiguous document to the basis for a nation whose government was for the first time the ultimate authority.

Unionists appealed not only to their history of the Revolution but also to their history of their own times as a refutation of Southerners' case for a dissoluble union. Shortly after the firing on Fort Sumter, *Harper's Weekly* offered a tautological argument against the right of secession. Instead of saying that an indissoluble nation began with the Revolution, *Harper's* conceded that the nation had been an experiment at first and that states had reserved the right to withdraw. However, that right, the argument ran, had ended by 1861; eighty years of success had rendered the union no longer an experiment. It had undergone "consolidation . . . into a great and wealthy nation." Hence, no state could leave the union in 1861 because no states had left the union before. *Harper's* begged the question but did so not much more blatantly than did those who said that a perpetual nation had been founded in 1776. The burden of *Harper's* argument lay in its emphasis on experience and on a necessary surrender to the momentum of success.

In this appeal—or, rather, in acting on this assumption—the unionists used war as a sort of *a priori* argument, the nation's successful existence being the premise and its successful use of force being the proof of the proposition to be demonstrated: that the nation had a right to exist. Between the Revolution and the Civil War, the United States had changed, they said, under the influence of forces consolidating the nation. A former Federal officer, Charles Francis Adams, Jr., and a former Confederate officer, E. Porter Alexander, could agree in later years that by 1860 America had become a nation, no matter what the Constitution said.

Antebellum political evolution had perforce accompanied material evolution: the extension of transportation, communication, and industry. What Alexander called "forces as irresistible as those of a volcano" had made eighteenth-century political ideas irrelevant. The resort to war thus came not as a single cataclysmic crisis but as the continuation of a historical process wherein events made nationality seem ineluctable. "From the moment the people of the United States constituted a great nation," *Harper's* said, without specifying the moment, "a political and military necessity for union came into existence." Basing this assurance solely on the union's victory in civil war might suggest that the nation was debatable, tenuous, or arbitrary; basing it on evolution placed it beyond challenge.

Many Northerners, magnifying sentiments expressed after the Revolutionary War, the War of 1812, and the war with Mexico, rejoiced that the United States could prove its power in war. War showed that the American nation had strength equal or superior to all others. Americans must maintain their standing among nations, not throw it away by fragmenting. From standpoints as diverse as those of W. T. Sherman, Thaddeus Stevens, and the workers whom the British writer James Dawson Burn met, people united their own self-respect with the country's newly demonstrated military strength. Early in 1864 Private Jacob Behm told his friends that the war "has proved that the United States have more military resources, and can put into the field greater armies than any nation on earth." Such an esteem for power made union all the more imperative. Only by keeping its resources under one government could the United States surpass the enemies of republican institutions. At the same time that the republic preserved liberty it must also refute the condescending opinions of those who said that a republic could not last long or consolidate its force. By defeating secession, the North would continue what the Baltimore *American* called "our rapid advance to power as a people," which European monarchies wanted to arrest. Burn regretted that so many workingmen supported aggrandizement of the United States through territorial expansion; they failed to see that the consolidated government required for such a purpose would destroy the republic. They were seduced, he believed, by imagining themselves to be the beneficiaries: "They are vain enough to pique themselves upon being citizens of the greatest nation of modern times." It was a vanity common among Americans.

John W. Draper closed his history of the Civil War with a vision of America's "imperial future," when the United States would serve as the new Rome, the disseminator of civilization, but with an advantage Romans had lacked: an understanding of "the progressive improvement of mankind." The war had assured political unity and established "a centre of power," thereby making the United States "the Republic of the future." Nationalists' retrospective definitions made them the masters of war, the outcome of which made the nation great. If Draper rightly predicted that Americans would "desire to put aside the remembrance of this war," they would do so, treating it as an anomaly, because it would later be hard to realize that mastery and progress had ever been imperiled. Europeans must learn that, in the words of the *Daily Missouri Democrat,* "war has been Americanized by Americans." In nothing did nationalists count themselves more progressive.

SOUTHERNERS' JUSTIFICATIONS of the Confederate nation came in several phases. The antebellum secessionist version was predictive, anticipating benefits from nationhood. The wartime version was prescriptive, telling Southerners what they ought to be doing to make the Confederacy whole. The postwar version was defensive, explaining the Confederacy's right to exist, notwithstanding its collapse. These arguments labored under a common difficulty: at the time they were put forward, events had not conformed to them. Measured against the aspirations of its apologists, the Southern nation had no history; it had, instead, a theory or a fantasy of what it should have been. These conceits not only came to grief in the face of Federal armies but also failed to compel Southerners, even in the realm of memory. After the war many Southerners treated the Confederacy's four-year claim to independence as an anomaly in America's history and in Southern life. While they commemorated wartime courage and praised secessionists' integrity of conscience, they did not perpetuate the ideal of Confederate independence. They separated the memory of the fighting from the purpose of the war and often neglected both.

A Louisianian born in 1872, the son of a Confederate veteran, later recalled that, though his father told war stories, "the meaning of the war itself was never discussed enough for the children to realize it or understand it. . . . we never heard much talk about Stuart, Johnston, Jackson or Lee. The war was over—and the new born generation was making a start at forgetting it." Southern schools in the postwar decades used history books written by Northerners, with the result that the "Southern schoolboy is more familiar with the history of the Massachusetts Bay Colony and its petty Indian quarrels, than he is with the great dramas of the national life that have been enacted on Southern fields." Magazines commemorating the Confederacy survived precariously; memoirs and biographies did not have large sales. Anna Jackson's book about her husband, which she published twice, made little money. Margaret Junkin Preston was cynical even about *Century Magazine*'s successful series of articles on the war. She told the editors in 1886 that she wanted her reminiscences of Jackson to be published "before the revived interest in War matters subsides." The longstanding antebellum belief that abolition of slavery would destroy Southern civilization, a threat which had helped sustain the Confederate war effort, quickly faded in most quarters. Southerners could publicly say that they would fare better without slavery and that slavery had formed no necessary part of their society's struggle against the federal government. Beliefs which once had seemed unquestionable already seemed irrelevant. A year after Lee's surrender E. Porter Alexander, planning to write a history of Longstreet's corps, said that the South had won "on the *great* question," which was: "Who is the best man?"—though "we lost the minor point of separate govt." In one sense, the war itself was irrelevant to the future. The clearest lesson to be learned from four years of fighting and the deaths of a quarter million Southerners was how not to promote the interests of a sectionalist South. No matter what their definitions of those interests, Southerners turned to other tactics. Stories of heroism, divorced from the lost ends it had served, grew indistinct—grand memories of a mistake not to be repeated.

The combination of respect and neglect in Southerners' treatment of the Confederate past made the memory of the war extraordinarily malleable. It could be invoked in support of disparate, competing concerns originating not in fidelity to the motives for secession but in divergent plans for the South in the late nineteenth century and the twentieth century. Postwar discussion of Stonewall Jackson in the South showed how plastic the remembered Confederate experience could become. In 1939 the sponsors of an equestrian statue of Jackson to be erected on the Manassas battlefield held a design competition for which sculptors submitted small-scale studies. An exhibition of the models at the Virginia Museum of Fine Arts in Richmond disclosed a remarkably varied array of conceptions of Jackson. Depending on the artist, he looked like Ivanhoe, Wotan, Daniel Boone, Prince Murat, a stylized Soviet or fascist State Hero, or one of the Four Horsemen of the Apocalypse. Interpretations of Jackson's character and significance published after his death did not cover so wide a range, but they did similarly use him as a protean figure, taking new shapes according to the writers' differing outlooks.

Though Robert E. Lee stood as the preeminent Confederate soldier, Jackson had the posthumous advantage of having been Lee's most celebrated lieutenant and of not having been linked with Confederate defeats after May 1863. The figure of Jackson vindicated Confederates' character and taught moral lessons applicable to the new society which emerged after his death. With few exceptions, the differing portraits of Stonewall implicitly accepted a proposition Jackson himself hardly would have shared: that he could honorably have survived the Confederacy's defeat. A few weeks before Jackson died, a friend raised in conversation the possibility that the South might lose the war and fall again under the authority of the United States government. Jackson, like many other Southerners, said "that if he could have his choice in view of such a contingency, he would prefer the grave as his refuge." After the armies' surrender, few of Jackson's fellow Southerners or their descendants sought the grave rather than live without independence, but they insisted that they were acting in the spirit of his heroic example, when they thought about the war at all. Postwar efforts to compile a record of consistent Southern conduct embraced many divergent forms of behavior and belief without reconciling them. The contradictory renderings of the Confederacy's life and legacy in the postwar years did not arise solely from flawed or flexible memory. The wartime struggle to attach Southerners to the Confederacy had never formulated a clear, compelling definition of the nation. Southerners thus were freer to remember what they chose to remember.

No concern connected with recalling the war had more weight than Southerners' eagerness to differentiate secession from treason. Having turned against the federal government and then having left the Confederate government behind them, they remained extremely testy about being called traitors. It was one of the bitterest epithets in the language. Yankees' use of it—even the suspicion, decades after the war, that Yankees might still be thinking it—provoked a heated response. A traitor had no honor; a traitor conspired secretly, professing loyalty but intending betrayal; a traitor acted not from principle but for private advantage; a traitor resembled Benedict Arnold. Such a characterization, the opposite of Southerners' view of themselves, they insisted could not apply to them. They pointed to their great men, especially those who had died for the cause, and said that such men self-evidently could not have been traitors. Nor were the people who revered them. Former Confederate privates, as well as generals and politicians, included in their memoirs and speeches a digest of the secessionist interpretation of the United States Constitution. If, in forming the union, sovereign states had remained sovereign, retaining their right to withdraw, their subsequent exercise of that right involved no betrayal, since their attachment to the union had always been voluntary and contingent. The union had no historical necessity to exist; Southerners had an obligation to defend themselves; free citizens need never submit to coercion.

Though Southerners liked to rewin the constitutional debate long after the question was dead, they placed their greatest emphasis on the integrity of Confederates' character. Proving sincerity discredited the charge of treason. Stonewall Jackson, whose honesty even Northerners praised, embodied with others the South's claim to have a clear conscience. He had believed in the right of secession, and he had faithfully served his state. Henry A. Wise, in a testimonial for John Esten Cooke's *Wearing of the Gray,* said that the great Confederates in the book had been "pure patriots, loyal citizens . . . who proved their faith in their principles by their deaths." After the war these reminders of wartime Confederates' sincerity helped Southerners reassert their equal standing as citizens of the United States. Not having been rebels, they were not paroled felons but loyal Americans. In the 1890 edition of her *History of Virginia for the Use of Schools,* Mary Tucker Magill, who had known Jackson, portrayed him as an exemplary Confederate and Christian. She urged on the young generation the "sacred trust" of saving the Confederate cause from dishonor—such as the idea that Confederates had been " 'Rebels' against the government to which they had sworn allegiance"—and she assured her young readers that they could do so "in perfect consistency with the truest patriotism to the government to which we all belong." Thus Jackson posthumously reassured Southerners that they were as principled as he had been. Like him, they could not have base motives no matter which nation they swore loyalty to.

Jackson's character could also help refute two other insults Southerners heard from the North: that they had rushed into secession, eager to gratify their ambition on the ruins of the union, and that they had seceded and fought mainly to promote slavery. His admirers did not apologize for having defended the right to hold slaves and to secede; Jackson had shared their beliefs. But he had gone to war reluctantly, only because the federal government had turned to "injury and oppression," in the words of Fitzhugh Lee. As a slaveholder, Jackson was kind, Southerners said. Like them, he thought that the two races could survive together only if slavery were preserved. Yet anyone who thought that defending slavery motivated Jackson's fight for the Confederacy must be, William C. Chase wrote, "blind with prejudice." Jackson and other secessionists had been "innocent in conscience." If Northerners' sordid explanation of Southern resistance were wrong about the quintessential Confederates, it could not stand. Speaking to veterans about Lee and Jackson, Bishop George William Peterkin gave his listeners their vindication against the Yankees: "When they tell us, as they do, those wiser, better brethren of ours, and tell the world to make it history, that this our Southern civilization was half barbarism, we may be pardoned if we answer, Behold its product and its representatives!"

Southerners who talked and wrote about the war returned, probably more often than to any other theme, to the courage and skill of the Confederate soldier, epitomized by Jackson. They said that the South's defeat did not demonstrate Northern soldiers' superiority or discredit Southerners as fighters. Only the Federal army's overwhelming numbers could have beaten down the valiant Confederates. This contention, often accompanied by intricate calculations designed to heighten the numerical disparity, reassured Southerners that the enemy's material force, not their own spiritual weakness, had defeated them. When postwar reconciliation grew more important in Southerners' accounts, they tempered invidious sectional distinctions, acknowledging Federals' courage but still dwelling on Confederate prowess, which failure did not dim. Stonewall Jackson showed this strength best; he had succeeded partly because he "knew the value of the Southern volunteer better and sooner . . . than any other of our great leaders." Hence, his victories were the Southern people's victories.

Speaking in 1868 about Jackson's audacity in battle, John Warwick Daniel said: "A country in praising its hero, praises itself." The memory of Jackson gave any former Confederates who needed it an assurance of latent strength belied by the South's postwar subordination to and collaboration with the North. The more that reminiscences dwelt on combat the more easily one could accommodate them to the South's postwar departures from its antebellum order and its wartime purpose. Combat was glorious, though life after the war had no place for the goal that fighting had served: independence. General James A. Walker, former commander of the Stonewall Brigade, told a gathering of Confederate veterans in 1892 that future historians would dwell on achievements of the Southern armies, hardly noticing the civil record of the Confederate government. "In fact if you take out of the Confederate history the deeds of her armies and the devotion and sacrifices of the Southern women there is nothing left." Southerners could achieve greatness through combat without achieving autonomy. They were as selfless as their hero. Though they survived and adapted, they could, in honoring him, see themselves as a faithful, united Stonewall Brigade. The dead Jackson was the perfect Confederate.

While Stonewall Jackson stood, uncompromising, in a heroic past, his example spoke to Southerners about the late nineteenth century and the twentieth. One persistent description of Jackson portrayed him as a man of the people, an ordinary man who happened to be an extraordinary general. His Scots-Irish ancestry, his obscure birth in Virginia's western mountains, his ungainliness and lack of poise, his taciturnity, his worn and faded clothing, his simple evangelical fervor, his popularity among the

soldiers all became parts of a legendary Stonewall Jackson. This legend
dramatized devotion to the Confederacy on the part of Southerners who
owned no slaves and little property. For some writers Lee and Jackson
symbolized the South's unity in its struggle: Marse Robert and Old Jack,
the tidewater aristocrat and the humble mountaineer, the Episcopalian
whose family came from England in the seventeenth century and the
Presbyterian whose family came from Ireland in the eighteenth century.
They had worked together harmoniously and thereby had given the
Confederacy its greatest victories. Quaint anecdotes about Jackson's being
mistaken for a private and Jackson's doing the duty of a private and
Jackson's solicitude for privates first appeared during the war and lasted
long afterward. The *Confederate Monitor and Patriot's Friend* said in 1863:
"Jackson . . . having sprung from the same class of society with the soldiers
who compose his army, appreciates them as equals, loves them, and
associates with them." Though the famous story of Jackson's standing
guard as a lone sentinel while all his soldiers slept was an absurd fiction,
D. H. Hill complained after the war, it continued to be "constantly
repeated by press and pulpit."

The image of Old Stonewall the plain man often supplanted the record
of the ambitious General T. J. Jackson, who had no disposition to tolerate
the failings of his subordinates, much less to be their peer. The labor of
his life was to make himself more than a plain boy from the hill country.
He would not have felt flattered to hear that he represented a different
segment of Confederate society from that which Robert E. Lee exemplified. To speak anachronistically, Jackson was a West Virginian trying to
become a Virginian second to none. To this end he directed rigorous
self-discipline and the determination to withstand any hardship that did
not kill him. He expected others to do likewise in the war, since they
had, in the defense of Confederate independence, a cause worthy of
intense devotion like that which Jackson long had demonstrated in better-
ing himself. An undercurrent of grim satisfaction ran through Jackson's
arrests, executions, hard marches, desperate combat, and orders to sweep
the field with the bayonet. Careless, cocky, worldly men full of vain
self-regard, the likes of whom had condescended to or ridiculed Jackson
all his life, must show whether they had his strengths and his willingness
to die rather than fail. He found many who did, but he was unforgiving
toward those who fell short. His popularity in the army did not come
from his being the privates' friend or from his resemblance to the privates
or from his solicitude for their comfort or their lives. It came from his
leading them to victories. But for him to be the representative Southerner
in postwar efforts to unite the South politically and to win concessions
from the North, he looked better as a democrat. A Jackson of humble

origins and modest demeanor represented a Confederacy that no one could call arrogant toward others or unjust toward its own, that no one could rightly deny an honorable place in the reunited nation.

Some former Confederates found Stonewall Jackson speaking to practical needs of the twentieth century. According to Colonel R. P. Chew in 1912, Jackson offered a model to "all the men of our country," especially "ambitious and aspiring youths." Through self-control and assiduous application he had become a self-made man. His virtues should serve well in modern business. Randolph Barton, a veteran of the Stonewall Brigade who became president of the Maryland Bar Association, said in 1915 that Jackson's career showed "what earnestness, resolution and energy will accomplish. What a splendid rail-road manager he would have made." Such appeals separated Jackson's virtues from the cause to which he had turned them and assimilated him into doctrines dominating the later society. The result looked all the more plausible because in the single-mindedness of his development of himself, reaching a climax in his creation of the character Stonewall, Jackson had been a self-made man. He had turned to the literature of self-cultivation to help him become a disciplined, correct, efficient, distinguished person. Later preachers of success through strength of character and effort found in him a man who fit their prescriptions because he had used similar, earlier prescriptions to shape his own personality. He was a product of the school of thought that claimed him. James Power Smith told Virginia Military Institute cadets in 1906 that young men looking to the future in twentieth-century America should find "a strong bidding and appeal" in Jackson's motto: "You may be whatever you resolve to be."

Long after the disappearance of the Confederacy, Jackson's life served as an argument for believers trying to bring people to Christ. His godliness lived on as an inspiration, separated from the political cause God had blessed so briefly. His humility and his faith, not the outcome of his political beliefs, held the crucial message. At the dedication of a statue of Jackson in 1891, the Reverend A. C. Hopkins prayed: "Thy hand has written his name imperishably among the world's great captains and thrown over it the halo of sanctity, that men may learn the beauty and power of Christian faith." Though accounts differed in fixing the time when he had turned to religion, his life held a full complement of edifying episodes: his orphaned youth, his godless upbringing, his discovery of Jesus, his circumspect conduct, his diligence in the church, his Sunday school class for slaves, his trust in the Lord after his first wife's death, his respect for ministers, his strict observance of the Sabbath, his complete submission to God's will, his deference to God in battle, his evangelizing in the army, and his serenity on his deathbed.

J. J. Clopton, echoing earlier testimonials to Jackson's faith, said in 1913: "To the South today no ideal should stand higher than this life. Great in his bravery, great in his inspiring leadership, but in nothing so great as his religion." Such a litany, celebrating politically vague merits like "bravery" and "leadership," while calling Southerners to share Jackson's religious faith, abstracted him from the concerns of his lifetime. God's plan for Confederate defeat had been unknown to him. He refused to imagine God's disfavor. Everything that happened to him, he thought, formed part of a beneficent divine scheme. He pressed on with political and military assurance that he was serving predestined purposes. To have told him that his labors were doomed but his sincerity was admirable would have confronted him with the paradox he most wanted to avoid. It would have suggested a disjunction between devoted, humble effort and a glorious reward in this world, as well as in the life to come. For later propagandists, his unswerving belief outlived his work that failed. Jackson's death spared him that questionable consolation. While he lived, he insisted that he had no doubt of his eternal salvation and that his life corroborated this promise by overt signs of divine favor for his earthly undertakings, including God's promise of Confederate independence. Jackson often said that his afflictions were part of God's plan to increase his blessings. But he had joined himself to the Confederacy too closely for him to imagine its failure as a means of his improvement. He thought he would die before the new nation did, and he preferred it so. The Christian Stonewall who was not a Confederate did not exist.

Despite Stonewall Jackson's attachment to the Confederacy, he appeared often in the rhetoric of reunification, especially during the last quarter of the nineteenth century, as an exemplary American. In this guise he could help Southerners speed the end of reconstruction by assuring Northerners that the Redeemers were trustworthy. For Governor James L. Kemper and Virginians organizing the dedication of a statue of Jackson in 1875, this concern predominated. The Reverend Moses Drury Hoge's oration dwelt on Jackson's admirable character, promised that the South was loyal, and called for an end to the section's "subjugation." Governor Kemper said that the monument, as a tribute to Jackson's "virtue and genius," would be cherished by every American "with national pride as one of the noblest memorials of a common heritage of glory." If Northerners could honor the perfect Confederate, they could not justly persist in mistrusting their fellow Americans who had fought alongside him. In other words, Northerners should vote Democratic in 1876 or at least take steps to have the remaining army garrisons withdrawn from a political role in the South. By the turn of the century, Southerners claiming a part in America's rising power in the world agreed with Northerners who said that the war had taught Americans their national strengths. In his *Story of Stonewall Jackson* published in 1901, William C. Chase contended that, if Jackson had survived, the Confederacy would have won its independence, and Jackson would have become "the first President of the re-united States." Chase merged Confederate patriotism with twentieth-century American patriotism. "The conditions to-day that enable the people of the re-united country to meet and join in the common cause of making a greater Union were made possible by the life of Jackson and his example." Southerners, accommodating themselves to American national-ism, took Jackson with them back into the union and made him and them-selves the best Americans.

For some Southerners, however, Stonewall Jackson and the Confeder-acy lived on in spirit, with a message of resistance to the accelerating changes in late nineteenth-century America. Most conspicuous among these changes was the consolidation of economic power in the hands of "capitalists" or "monopolists." Aggrandizement of industrial and finan-cial power carried with it, in the minds of these Southern critics, the very dangers secession had tried to avert: "alien and demoralizing speculation," antagonism between capital and labor, subjugation of the South to North-ern plutocrats, erosion of belief in fixed moral laws, and the spread of atheism. According to their warnings, one should honor Jackson for having fought what his onetime subordinate Bradley T. Johnson called in 1891 the "civilization of industrialism." Southerners ought not to be doing what many of them were doing: ingratiating themselves with Yankees, calling both sides noble in the war, saying that they would not change the war's outcome if they had the power to do so.

Berkeley Minor, another veteran who had marched with Stonewall, deplored the illogical position of those Southerners who said they ad-mired Confederate soldiers but also welcomed the survival of the union. For him, erecting monuments to Jackson and other great Confederates should remind people that those heroes had served constitutional liberty, while Northerners, knowingly or not, had fought for tyranny—as, by 1903, the trusts, the protective tariff, and the standing army made clear. Only by rejecting the prevailing materialist argument from success, the false doctrine that power justifies itself, could Southerners resist moral degradation. In this cause, a former chaplain imagined, Jackson's posthu-mous influence might make Confederate veterans and their descendants "a 'stone wall' against all tides of social or political corruption, of moral decay and religious apostasy, unbelief or irreverence." Jackson's character and achievements served this purpose especially because they showed that a great man was not a bubble on the tides of history but a God-made creator of history. "Herbert Spencer applies his theories of evolution and

makes the great man no more than a product of converging influences";
but, the Reverend H. Melville Jackson concluded in 1883, the workings
of Spencer's impersonal forces could not account for Stonewall Jackson.
His greatness was God's handiwork. Some intransigents who wanted
the South to persevere in opposing Yankees' false gods tried to rally
Southerners behind an uncompromised Confederacy and the immov-
able Stonewall.

Many Southerners—many Americans in all sections—looked with
growing alarm on concentrations of economic power or threats to social
order and to fixed moral codes. But they did not usually address these
concerns by reverting to the Civil War and finding an ideal society
in the Confederacy. Southerners, especially young ones, paid too little
attention to the war during the decades that followed it, the purists
complained. Three of the most voluble and intransigent former
Confederates—D. H. Hill, Robert L. Dabney, and Jubal Early—com-
miserated with one another on Southerners' heedlessness. Dabney agreed
with Early that Mrs. Jackson would not make money from a book about
Stonewall: "I don't think that the Southern people care for Jackson or
for any thing much except an opportunity to finger Yankee money." Hill
was disgusted by New South rhetoric and by sentimental effusions about
reunion following the death of Grant. "Why has the South become so
toadyish & sycophantic?" he asked Early, then answered his own question: "I think it is because the best and noblest were killed off during the
war and that the scum element is now in the ascendancy." All three men
had ties to Stonewall Jackson. Hill had been his brother-in-law and
longtime friend; Dabney had been his chief of staff and biographer; Early
had been a brigade and division commander under him. After the war
Early practiced law, while Hill and Dabney held academic appointments.
Still, they devoted much time to memories of the Civil War. Thirty years
after publishing a biography of Jackson, Dabney helped G. F. R. Henderson with his. For a few years, Hill edited *The Land We Love,* a magazine
designed, he said, "to preserve a record of the grand heroism of our
soldiers." As memoirist, controversialist, and president of the Southern
Historical Society, Early started writing about the war in 1865 and did
not stop until he died in 1894.

For these men no detail was too minute to dwell on; no debate ever
died. In their speeches and writings they called wayward Southerners to
return to the lessons of the war experience. Hated modern changes they
made Northern. The war had shown with what skill and devotion
Confederates resisted Northern aggressors; later collaborations with
modernity betrayed the South and repudiated its heroes' example. The
appeals of the three men to the past dwelt less on preserving a unique

society, which they saw Southerners failing to do, than on the climactic struggle for independence. The moral force inherent in memories of killing Yankees ought still to unite Southerners against the Northern future. The fervor of the three veterans' recollections of the bygone Confederate years, by its uncommon passion, made their war look anomalous to Southerners whom they reproved. Not surprisingly, most people found it more congenial to hear that their postwar lives were consistent with those of war heroes than to be accused of decadence. The figure of Stonewall Jackson as an example for the times had wider appeal than that of Jackson as a judgment against the times. Honoring great Confederates made sense; continually refighting the war did not. The intransigents, especially Early and Dabney, addressed their fellow Southerners knowing that, to their audience, especially to younger people, they sounded like old fogies. They eventually thought of themselves, in Dabney's words, as "we old Confederates," who had lived through the heroic days and survived to warn a thoughtless generation of its decline.

Calling Southerners to emulate Jackson, Jubal Early had a unique handicap. As commander in the Shenandoah Valley in 1864 he had been overwhelmed by the Federals under Philip Henry Sheridan not only because of the enemy's greatly superior numbers but also because of his own inferior generalship. Widespread complaints led Lee to remove him from command, and he had to endure invidious comparisons between Jackson's brilliant success against superior numbers in the valley and his own failure. He protested in 1871: "It is not fair to compare me with General Lee and General Jackson. The world has produced few such men as they were and I am certainly not one of them." Instead of rivaling them, Early made himself a spokesman for the dead heroes, a living voice warning against degeneracy. In 1866 Lee read Early's account of the 1864 Valley Campaign and advised him to "omit all epithets or remarks calculated to excite bitterness or animosity between different sections of the country." But Early nurtured bitterness and animosity, wishing that he could excite more of those feelings in the South.

As a young man, Jubal Early had been a Henry Clay Whig. He represented Franklin County in Virginia's secession convention, where he denied the right of secession and wept after the ordinance was passed. He decided to stay with Virginia, justifying his choice by the people's right of revolution, and threw himself into the war. Early, a sardonic unbeliever, and Dabney, a sardonic Presbyterian theologian, both waxed caustic at the expense of eager secessionists who later evaded sacrifice after having rushed the South into war. Learning of proposals in February 1862 to elect only original secessionists to public office, Early wrote: "I a 'submissionist' pray that God may grant that those who, safely ensconced at home in comfort & ease, pride themselves upon their early advocacy of secession as a remedy for all political evils, may not live to rue the day they ever dreamed of it." He spent the rest of his life trying to convince himself and others that he did not rue joining the secessionists.

When the Confederacy collapsed, Early fled to Mexico, hoping to fight the United States in the service of Napoleon III and Maximilian. When that war failed to develop, he moved to Canada, anticipating that Fenian raids across the border might lead to war between Britain and the United States. He wrote to his friends: "I shall never return to the states unless I come back under the Confederate flag of which I do not yet despair." He was ready to fight on the side of any nation that would make war on the United States. He even pictured himself in command of western Indians, devastating the land of the oppressor. "It would afford me the highest gratification to lead a band of 20,000 or 30,000 Comanches and appaches through Kansas, Nebraska Iowa & across the Mississippi—I would leave a trail behind me that would not be erased in this century." Meanwhile, he was writing a rebuttal to accusations that he had been incompetent in his fighting for the Confederacy. His bravado did not altogether conceal his depression. His brother supported him financially in his "unprofitable life" in exile; Early said that only the expectation of America's breaking up made him "care to live," and he toyed with thoughts of settling in Brazil, Venezuela, or New Zealand. News of Republican reconstruction distressed him. He wished Southerners could "take up arms and fight until they were exterminated." Yet he returned to Virginia, testy about the charge that he "did desert the Confederacy in its death agonies." He proclaimed: "I have not deserted the *cause* of the Confederacy." Having painfully abandoned his loyalty to the United States, Early found his repatriation through defeat doubly galling. By making himself the defender of Lee, Jackson, and the Confederacy, smiting with verbal blows Yankees and Southern backsliders, he avoided the shock of a second reversal and remained the Confederate he had not wished to become.

In 1872, speaking on behalf of those called "fossils, fogies and Bourbons," Early set "the utilitarian spirit of the age" against the graves of Confederate war heroes, the most famous of which were in Lexington, Virginia, where he spoke. To "adopt the spirit of progress from our enemies" was to deprive the war of meaning. In 1875 and 1876 Governor Kemper, Fitzhugh Lee, Senator R. E. Withers, and Representative J. R. Tucker tried to get Early to shut up. They patiently explained to him that a Democratic victory in the presidential election was the essential goal, that Northern Democrats wanted to suppress the subject of the war, while Republicans could win votes by pointing to continued Southern belligerence. To "rid this country of the horrors of Radical misrule" Southerners should give no occasion for "recrimination & warlike experiences & reminiscences." But Early, incorrigible and idiosyncratic, made himself what John S. Wise later called "a social and political Ishmaelite." To any hint of the New South heresy, to anyone in danger of joining the "renegades" who betrayed the Confederate cause, Early was quick to say: "Let the memory of Jackson save you!"

Instances of Southerners' willingness to entertain the civilization of industrialism were all too common. Robert M. T. Hunter argued to the recalcitrant Robert L. Dabney in 1866 that Virginia could lead in the defense of what remained of states' rights only by "the development of her physical resources." Hunter agreed that moral character was more important than railroad mileage, but he tried to persuade Dabney that both were necessary. The case for Southern strength through industry had been made by some secessionists before and during the war, and the Confederacy had shown a remarkable capacity for manufacturing under adverse conditions. Postwar growth would entail closer ties with Northern capitalists. A month after fighting ended, the editor of the *Atlanta Intelligencer* told a Northern reporter that he hoped Northern investors would help rebuild Atlanta. He was starting almost at once the city leaders' long drive for development. In 1871 the Board of Trade of Columbia, South Carolina, emulating other cities, published a sixty-five-page booklet proclaiming the city to be "The Future Manufacturing and Commercial Centre of the South." The text complemented the many advertisements for the city's businesses; a brief account of the city's history emphasized its growth, its energetic resurgence from the fire of February 17–18, 1865, and its advantages for future development. The booklet promised: "When the water power of the city has been made ready for utilization, the manufactories of all descriptions will doubtless be multiplied to an almost unlimited extent." It assured potential investors and emigrants: "The nationality or nativity of no man is questioned." Though Northern capital and industry did not flow into the South, Southerners joined the national rush to extract and process nature's riches, concerns which superseded the defunct Confederacy. A description of Charleston, West Virginia, in the summer of 1865 captured a spirit that grew widespread, even in regions where it did not lead to success: "To be sure this community is made up of returned Confederates, Yankees, Federal soldiers, Negroes, rebel sympathizers and intensely union men. But the war being over, the energies of all are being turned to making money, in search of oil, coal land, etc." By the 1890s Southerners were accustomed to speakers and writers who honored wartime sacrifices for the lost cause while celebrating the South's Americanism. Former Confederates proudly recalled that the South had demonstrated its aptitude for industry and enterprise before and during the war, not just in imitation of Northerners, and that it continued to do so in what Clement A. Evans called not the New South but "the Greater South."

Like Early, Dabney deplored these signs of backsliding. During the war he had written a defense of slavery, intended for a European audience. Dedicating the work to General T. J. Jackson, he explained: "I have endeavoured to assail the insolent errors of our detractors with the weapons of truth, as you taught us to attack their forces in the field, with all our strength, and in the name of God and the Right." His biography of Jackson held the general up as proof of the rightness of slaveholding and the righteousness of war for Confederate independence. Dabney's vision of the ideal Southern society, doomed by the war's outcome, shaped his memories of the Confederacy's brief life, especially its fleeting apogee in Jackson's last year. His preoccupation with the war long after its end derived a tone of strong emotion from his reckoning of what the South had lost. A hierarchical, patriarchal, agricultural republic of freeholders governing the propertyless and the enslaved could have withstood the Yankee world of materialism. In Dabney's vocabulary the word "develop" was ugly. By 1882 he was ready to acknowledge reluctantly that the younger generation had to accept a New South. To protect itself in the modern world the South must develop industries, while avoiding the Northern error of idolizing wealth. This regrettable necessity was only part of America's general decline, accelerated by Northern predominance.

Dabney's speeches and writings on the war recalled Confederate failure starkly. The South had lost constitutional liberty forever. His was the last generation to have known true freedom. In its place he saw efforts to lift black people from their proper status as uneducated laborers, efforts on behalf of women's rights which flowed from the same egalitarianism of false natural-rights doctrine, the nation ruled from Wall Street by a capitalist oligarchy, the prospect of revolution by a "hireling proletariat" that ought not even to have votes. Defeat of the Confederacy had removed the last obstruction to "the radicalism of the age," and Dabney kept returning to that defeat partly because he blamed it on Southerners. If they had been a nation of men like Jackson, they would have remained "unconquerable and free." Instead, as Dabney recalled telling Jackson early in the war, too many people shrank from the necessary sacrifices, while the Confederate government unimaginatively settled into a conventional war, which played to the enemy's strengths, rather than undertaking the revolutionary war that Jackson wanted and the Confederacy's circumstances demanded. God justly had humbled a people not fit to be free.

Dabney seemed surprised, almost disgusted, that Southerners consented to stay alive under Yankee rule. People asked "what Jackson would have done at our final surrender." Dabney replied: "In no event could Jackson have survived to see the cause lost. . . . I believe that as his clear eye saw the approaching catastrophe, his faithful zeal would have spurred him to strive so devotedly to avert it that he would either have overwrought his powers or met his death in generous forgetfulness (not in intentional desperation) on the foremost edge of the battle. For him there was destined to be no subjugation!" Though Dabney was harshest on Confederate veterans who cooperated with Republicans, he saw all the postwar expedients of Southerners as merely degrees of decline from the South's moral peak: combat for independence. Ostensibly trying to inspire his listeners to defend what remained, he sounded elegiac. Lecturing on "Stonewall Jackson" in 1872, he began: "The subject sounds remote, antiquated in these last days. How seldom does that name, once on every tongue, mix itself now-a-days, with the current speech of men? Is it not already a fossil name, almost?" He could explain such neglect only in one of three ways. Jackson's fame had been "an empty *simulacrum,*" or Jackson's devotion had been a blunder, or Southerners had changed "so as to be no longer able to appreciate that devotion." Dabney obviously did not accept the first two possibilities. Of the third he said: "We hope not"; but his lecture, as well as his other writings, clearly pointed to that answer. With everything at stake, including, Dabney thought, orthodox religion, the war had given Southerners an opportunity to create a sanctuary for themselves. Having flagged while greater effort could have succeeded, they conveniently forgot the war or made it the instrument of their modern devices.

Jackson's posthumous career as a fighter against the future did not end with the deaths of those who had known him. At the same time that some Southerners found in him a model for success in the twentieth century, he could also appear to others as its implacable enemy. In 1928 Allen Tate made Stonewall a representative of a lost society—the antebellum South—and a scourge for the new world of industrialized production and capitalist finance. Tate's book, *Stonewall Jackson, The Good Soldier: A Narrative,* contained careless errors in its treatment of Jackson's life and the Civil War. He often resorted to his imagination or to tenuous inference for his descriptions of motives and thoughts. While ridiculing psychoanalytical reductionism for not taking a historical figure such as Jackson at his word, Tate imposed his own sociocultural concerns on his subject. He was trying to find in Jackson an antimodernist outlook, a state of mind with origins in a twentieth-century modernity unknown to Jackson but crucial to Tate and his contemporaries. He created a stark conflict. The Old South dealt in tangibles: property was real, could be seen and touched; people were joined by the mutual obligations of fixed classes; religion and morality were public, social; political thought rested on the text of the Constitution. The North and, by extension, the twentieth century dealt in abstractions: property consisted of numbers measuring invisible, "metaphysical" wealth; people dealt with one another by exploitation and by assertions of abstract rights in a selfish struggle; religion was mystical and private, or nonexistent, while morality consisted in individual, arbitrary judgment; political thought put faith in numbers and machinery. These contrasting systems had fought the Civil War. Given the opportunity, Stonewall Jackson could have changed the outcome.

Tate made Stonewall the preeminent aggressive fighter for the Southern way. Jackson would have taken Washington and ended "the so-called Civil War" immediately after First Manassas. Davis should not have overruled Jackson's plans for invasion of the North. Lee fell short of Jackson as a soldier because Lee's greatness as a man—his humility, self-restraint, and political sensitivity—kept him from seizing every means to win the war, as Jackson would have done. Tate's eagerness to see Jackson unleashed for an invasion of the North that would have brought woe to the agents of commerce, industry, abolitionism, and tyranny enlivened his pages again and again. But it was a fantasy of power, created to beguile the powerless. A dream of Jackson's winning the war, thereby making the South self-sufficient in social organization and in cultural folkways—just as Tate imagined plantations to be self-supporting economic units—was the ultimate criticism of the modern world of abstraction, oppression, revolution, and chaotic self-interest. Of course, to revise the past was even more obviously impossible than to arrest the trends of the present. *Stonewall Jackson, The Good Soldier* came near to being a piece of whimsy. The threats Stonewall boldly attacked in the book were the more ominous for having grown so much more dominant in the twentieth century—indeed, for having threatened Tate's mind, too. Still, it was not always possible to take T. J. Jackson seriously for his own sake.

Tate's resort to counterfactual speculations tacitly conceded, almost in spite of his intentions, what Dabney and Early had tried to refute: revivals of the Civil War did not make effective weapons against the modern world. The Old South—still looming in the intransigent veterans' memories as resilient, antithetical to the new Yankee ways, and, in 1863, close to attaining perpetuity—had vanished with a strange rapidity after Jackson died. Those loyal to a belief in its necessary separateness waved Stonewall's banner but saw their fellow Southerners rushing in different directions. The intransigents explained this not by questioning their belief in the Old South's unity, its stability, or its rejection of change, but by concluding that something went wrong during or after the war. Tate ended his hypothetical argument on behalf of Jackson's commanding the Army of Northern Virginia or the western armies: "Beyond this, speculation, however indirect, must end, though regret, which lies in the province of poetry and has no place here, may proceed without limit." Southerners who regarded the Civil War as the beginning of the cultural and economic convergence of North and South and who deplored the nation's rapid changing found that the memory of the Civil War lent itself to regret better than to any other use. It was a story about bygone days, a narrative whose truth, like its fantasy, was poetic. It was a lament, invoking an era of heroes who must have been giants because they had fought forces their descendants took for granted. Writing her reminiscences, a North Carolina woman affectionately recalled her Cousin Ann, who had lived through the war, then had become in her latter years a garrulous terror to the unwary. Having once survived a visit by Yankee bummers, the old woman thereafter, to her dying day, was "never better entertained than when set to Shermanize a stranger." Those had been noble and terrible times, still living only in the memory of a few.

IN THE last third of the nineteenth century Southerners found it easy, or at least expedient, to forget a great deal of what they had known about the Confederacy, to reshape its history, and to remember things that had not occurred. They had no monopoly on retrospective vision that was partial or blurred. Unlike unionists, however, they had no enduring nation around which they could build a cumulative record of triumph, compiled from stories always recounting progress. Had the Confederacy been overwhelmed? Such a fate once had seemed unthinkable. Had the Confederacy collapsed from within? Had it been betrayed? The answers were contradictory, like the postwar legacy. What had happened during the war to the ideal of a unique, perpetual nation? Southerners' reactions to the war's mounting hardships and defeats called into question many of the premises underlying secession—for example, the tractability of slaves, the solidarity of slaveholders with nonslaveholders, the enthusiasm of all Confederate women for war. And the South had more impediments to establishing a well-defined nationality than invasion from the North and delinquencies in the behavior of Southerners. Explanations of Confederate nationality and rhetorical appeals on its behalf were themselves flawed by hyperbole, by a strain of defeatism, and by a formulaic rigidity detached from events. Advocates of the Confederacy had one main response to every challenge: they said that what they wanted to be true must be true and that Southerners must act as if it were true. The plasticity of Confederate days in Southerners' memory had ample precedent in Confederates' wartime efforts to imagine a nation of their own. Their creation was divided against itself.

In seceding, Southerners often proclaimed their inviolability as a people. They put the question in stark alternatives. Either the South had equal standing with the North or the South was degraded by remaining in the union. Either Southerners defended their honor or they were contemptible. Either the South kept intact the principles of the American Revolutionaries or it succumbed to alien despotism. Such definitions of the Confederacy tried to make it sacrosanct. The respect Southerners demanded did not consist simply of the states' sovereignty or of the equal rights of Northern and Southern citizens, including slaveholders' right to take their chattels into western territories. It entailed, too, respect for their assertion of the moral superiority of slaveholding society over free society. In the words of Senator Robert M. T. Hunter, "The social system of a people is its moral being." For Southerners to claim equal standing did not suffice; Northerners must also acknowledge it. This the North had grown less and less willing to do, finally electing Abraham Lincoln, who, with his party, called the slaveholding system wrong, obsolete, permanently confined, and ultimately doomed. Southerners found this intolerable, as Anthony Trollope explained to British readers: "It is no light thing to be told daily by your fellow-citizens, by your fellow-representatives, by your fellow-senators, that you are guilty of the one damning sin that cannot be forgiven. All this they could partly moderate, partly rebuke, and partly bear as long as political power remained in their hands; but they have gradually felt that that was going, and were prepared to cut the rope and run as soon as it was gone." Political power in the hands of Southerners and their allies among Northern Democrats could be construed as a tacit Northern acknowledgment of the South's righteousness. Once predominance passed to critics of Southern society, slavery and all who approved of it would stand condemned by the nation, existing only on sufferance. In 1861 the Reverend James H. Thornwell summarized for the South the result of continued union on that new basis: "The North becomes the United States, and the South a subject province."

Americans in the South, as in the North, wanted to belong to a nation that embodied their claims to greatness as a unique and powerful people. Without Northern deference to Southerners' pretensions to have attained a successful, permanent social system, Southerners would not be able to see themselves in their nation unless they created one of their own. Schemes for political means to protect a slaveholding society's interests during a Republican administration did not adequately address this concern. In the eyes of secessionists the South could command respect for the equal stature of its society only by forcing the North to recognize Southern states as an independent nation. The question turned from one of majorities and minorities within the union to one of Southerners' escape from a country in which their countrymen condemned them. To free themselves from subordination they must make Yankees foreigners. Four weeks after the presidential election of 1860, Senator Thomas L. Clingman of North Carolina said: "The people of the United States would not submit for one moment to the treatment from a foreign nation that the southern States have suffered at the hands of the North." If Southerners could persuade themselves that Clingman's analogy was valid—that they were being attacked by aliens—they could find unity in repudiating censure that came from those who had no right to utter it. The first premise of Confederate nationhood was Yankees' hostility.

As soon as Lincoln won the election, Senator Joseph Lane, the Southern Democrats' vice-presidential candidate, said in private conversation that, if the South failed to resist, "she would have to make up her mind to give up first her honor & then her slaves." For the North to deny the South's equality and to use force against states exercising their right to secede struck Southerners as an affront they could not endure peaceably and still maintain self-respect. The *Jackson Mississippian* argued during the war that Southern states "were literally compelled to secede" by the prospect of dishonorable subordination. If Southerners submitted, they would be "the hissing and by-word of the earth," confirming the Republican taunt that they were braggarts in show and cowards in reality. A proper sense of honor knew no degrees of temporizing, no calculations of expediency. It had an absolute claim: one must lose one's life rather than let its sanctity be infringed. Yankees' attack on the South revealed how oblivious they were to the sentiment they offended. Louis T. Wigfall of Texas, likening Southerners to the defenders of the Alamo, said in December 1860: "Those who regard a sense of honor as one of the relics of barbarism and the incident of the institution of slavery, I know do not understand, or comprehend, or appreciate the feelings which influence the people of the slaveholding States." The demands of honor were not venal; they dictated defensive action regardless of results.

Contrary to prevalent secessionist assumptions, however, obedience to a sense of honor as an inducement to fight the North did not necessarily connote belief in a new national identity or expectation of Confederate success. Among Southerners who, unlike Wigfall, came to secession reluctantly, sometimes foreseeing defeat, their sense of honor told them that they could not abandon their kin or their fellows under attack. These people believed that they must stand with men whose wisdom they doubted. At the end of the war a Confederate staff officer, Benjamin S. Ewell, former president of the College of William and Mary, said of the Confederacy's try for independence: "What a humbug except the brave armies, & the earnest women has this whole affair been. I opposed it ab initio but, even with a halter in the distant prospect for I have never thought myself anything but a rebel, I did not think it honorable to leave my own state in such a time." Honor, a standard defying constraint or reproof, simplified Southerners' complex, costly choice, seeming to banish both ambivalence and remorse. It was an ethos well suited to pride in defeat. No matter what the scale or outcome of the war, no matter whether it made the South weaker than peace in the union would have done, survivors could say that the times had given them no choice, that retaining honor outweighed all the ill consequences. Not long after Robert E. Lee died, Wade Hampton told a biographer that Lee had said after the war: "I could have taken no other course without dishonor & if all was to be done over again I should act precisely in the same manner." This sentiment, later a staple of veterans' rhetoric, showed that personal honor could survive the South's ruin, could join in it fatalistically rather than break familial and local bonds. No one can know whether Lee foresaw the defeat his conception of honor led him to embrace. But some who did anticipate it agreed with him that they acted under the compulsion of their ideal. Jonathan Worth, who opposed secession in the North Carolina legislature, wrote in May 1861: "I think the South is committing suicide, but my lot is cast with the South and being unable to manage the ship, I intend to face the breakers manfully, and go down with my companions."

Claiming inalienable independence, Confederates linked their cause with the American Revolution. They reminded one another that Southerners and slaveholders had taken the most conspicuous places in the movement for American independence and in the early republic. Obscuring the slaveholding founders' reservations about slavery, they argued from the founders' example that the American Revolution's guarantee of liberty did not conflict with chattel slavery. The greater promise of the Revolution for Confederates lay in their confidence that they, like their predecessors, were fighting for the right of self-government. Surely a people inspired by such a cause could withstand the power of an enemy's superior numbers and greater wealth. To Jefferson Davis, as to most Southerners, it seemed irrefutable that the Declaration of Independence meant that "every community may dissolve its connection with any other community previously made." The American Revolution inhered not in events of the Revolutionary War—that is, in a contest of strength between Britons and Americans—but in the assertion of this inalienable right. Natural rights could not be abrogated by force. How could anyone believe in American independence without accepting this self-evident truth? Use of military power in the Revolutionary War had been necessary, to overcome Britain's refusal to recognize the political principle Americans proclaimed. But combat had conformed to truth. The political abstraction was the reality on which the nation rested.

Davis could not see how "any man reasoning *a priori*" could deny that the American Revolution demonstrated the right of peaceable secession and the folly of making war to contradict the law of the universe. It was difficult, if not impossible, to put oneself in the state of mind of anyone who professed to be rational yet denied that secession was constitutional. After the war George Cary Eggleston, a Confederate veteran, wrote of Southerners' demand for nationhood: "They had never been able to understand how any reasonable mind could doubt the right of secession, or fail to see the unlawfulness and iniquity of coercion, and they were in a chronic state of surprised incredulity, as the war began, that the North could indeed be about to wage a war that was manifestly forbidden by unimpeachable logic." Yankees might ruin the federal government; they could not deprive Southerners of what God and the Revolutionary founders had bestowed. Davis anticipated war, but he wanted Northerners to know that Southern independence existed as soon as Southerners proclaimed it, just as all Americans dated the creation of the United States from the Declaration of Independence, not from the treaty ending war in 1783. The Confederacy would rest on right, which Northerners, had they been logical, would have recognized.

While Northerners continued to reinterpret the American Revolution, making it an emblem of national sentiment, of obedience to government, and of perpetual mystical union, Davis kept asserting to Southerners that they had the right of self-determination, "the freedom, equality, and State sovereignty which were the heritage purchased by the blood of your revolutionary sires." As he left the United States Senate, he denied that disruption of the union doomed self-government for all peoples. Institutions protecting liberty operated mainly in the states. He made for the Confederacy the same plea Lincoln made for the union. On the Confederacy's success, Davis said in October 1864, "Now alone depends the existence of constitutional liberty in the world.—We are fighting for that principle—upon us depends the last hope." But the Confederacy's effort to make a nation secure behind the Revolution's precedents did not work.

Davis's confidence, like his presumption that a Confederate nation had been established at once by fiat, betokened not resilience so much as desperation. If Southerners had God-given rights no government could take away, and if the United States were about to try to do what no human power could do, then Southerners could derive from this faith an assurance not readily verifiable in other ways, such as weighing the facts of sectional power or the course of events.

Events ultimately showed their confidence to be groundless. If Southerners expected to retain their rights, they would have to find some other defense. As assurance of the Confederacy's national future flagged, Southerners ceased to make it the repository of their liberty. Resuming their identity as Americans in the United States, they did not go down with the sinking ship of their lost cause. Most Southerners were convinced at the end of the war that, back in the union, they still possessed rights secured to them by American independence. Their conception of the American Revolution inhabited the Confederate revolution only temporarily, then reappeared as Southerners' contribution to the United States in postwar political contests. William C. Oates, Confederate veteran and Alabama politician, said of the 1868 Democratic campaign: "It is but a continuation of the great conflict—with this difference: the other was for constitutional liberty as bequeathed to the American people by Washington & his compeers, outside of the union—the present issue is for the same principle within it." Claiming to be the true legatee of the American Revolution did not make the Confederacy sacrosanct, as Davis had proclaimed—not even in the minds of its own citizens. They did not entrust all their hopes for self-government to the survival of the Confederacy. So certain were they of their American liberty, they believed that they still possessed it after the Confederacy fell.

Secessionists often declared that no power could conquer the Confederacy. The South's vast extent and the united resolve of its seven million white people made the new nation impregnable. Politicians said that history had no record of the overthrow of so powerful a society. Before states had begun to secede, Alfred Iverson, an eager secessionist from Georgia, boasted that five gulf states could defy the world in arms, let alone the North. Southerners did not analyze their politico-military strength so much as they assumed it to be obvious. Writing from New Orleans in August 1861, I. V. Duzanse told his Northern correspondent that "the conquest of the South by any Army from whatever part of the world they may come is the most preposterous idea that can possibly be brought forward." What they could not conceive they need not fear. The Confederate nation used a special vocabulary, as Jefferson Davis suggested to the Confederate Congress: "To speak of subjugating such a people, so united and determined, is to speak a language incomprehensible to them."

Secessionists' defiant new language included many superlatives to depict the South's unique greatness but no antonyms for those words, no way to conceive of a reality other than triumph. The South already was or soon would be greater than all other peoples in all things: its citizens more privileged and harmonious, its Protestant Christianity purer, its men of letters the beneficiaries of a social order conducive to the highest attainments of civilization, its prosperity secure and capable of untold growth. The Confederacy showed, in the words of the *Augusta Constitutionalist*, that "where freemen and slaves live in the same community there the freeman attains his very highest and noblest development." The Confederacy had economic power comparable to its cultural superiority. Slavery, the social system underlying its culture, was also the economic system producing cotton, which the world could not do without. Most Confederates assumed that "the South is essential to the civilized world." Since it was essential, it could command recognition. The British demurred, and Jefferson Davis never forgave them for failing to see their own interests as clearly as he did. Contrary to Southern pretensions, the Confederacy needed help more than any nation needed its existence. In the mind's eye, secessionists redressed the vulnerability of their enterprise by imagining themselves to be the center of the world. Southerners' ability to visualize their new nation consisted, in substantial part, of this conceit.

Believers in a unique, superior Southern civilization that could forestall the corruptions of secularism, materialism, and economic subjugation to distant, alien capitalists tried to fulfill their expectations by creating a new nation-state. It could protect the culture whose origins they traced to the earliest English colonists. The history of the South, if not progressive in the Yankee manner, was still to be purposeful, enacting a distinctive society's destiny in a separate republic. The old South, tolerated by the North or exploited by the North or simply overshadowed by the North, died in secession, no matter what followed. Southern nationalists meant to do something new, realizing a people's thwarted promise. At the same time that secessionists were portraying the United States as a contingent entity of convenience, they were counting on Southerners' supposed lasting cohesiveness. The basic societal premise of independence lay in possession of a unity that the North—polyglot, atomized, moving toward class warfare—could not rival. Embodying their claim to greatness in nationhood, they also entrusted it to war, asserting that the same design in history making them unique also made them powerful. Secessionist rhetoric about Southern grandeur promised success for the Confederacy, based on two unquestioned features of Southerners' behavior:

joint action arising from shared interests and physical might surpassing numerical strength. These propositions pervaded the special Confederate vocabulary, though wartime Confederate behavior more and more often failed to conform to the superlatives.

The Confederate language turned out to be unintelligible to those who did not accept its words' meanings. When a secessionist congressman said that his constituents "know they are clothed in the armor of Virginia's sovereignty, which cannot be penetrated," he alluded to a form of knowledge that depended upon his listeners' sharing his notions of sovereignty and impenetrability. After the Confederacy was invaded, as Northerners kept repudiating Southern assumptions, a closed secessionist vocabulary grew less useful in defining the nation, even for its supporters. The impregnable South had existed only in the mind. In 1866 Braxton Bragg recalled that he had begun to despair of Southern independence as soon as he saw the new Confederate government seized by familiar politicians—"Men who seemed to have but *one idea*—viz—'That eight millions of people resolved to be free could never be conquered,' and accordingly went to glorifying over the result, not yet accomplished, and to dividing the spoils not yet secured." Bragg thought they had doomed their cause by believing their own rhetoric. In denying that Confederates accomplished the creation of a nation by proclaiming it, Bragg rejected the politicians' definitions. Not surprisingly, his outlook disposed him to expect defeat. By January 1864 the *Memphis Appeal,* long in flight from its home town, had begun to perceive that declarations, even widely accepted ones, could not necessarily make reality. The Confederacy's misfortune, the editor wrote, "has been, that we have been enjoying independence before we had achieved it, and enjoying history before we had made it."

While proclaiming an impregnable South, Confederates also promised that they would die in the last ditch rather than surrender. The two truths were fundamental to the Confederacy's existence, though they were incompatible with each other. Yankees were not supposed to get near any last ditch—by definition, there was not supposed to be a "last" ditch—yet Confederates frequently said they would never surrender, regardless of how far the Yankees came. Men would fight on in the mountains, living on acorns; women would torch their own homes to deny them to the enemy. In January 1862 the *Richmond Dispatch* declared that "the South will battle till there is no longer a man within her borders capable of defending his country and his liberty." Incursions by the Federal army and desertions from the Confederate army soon showed that large numbers of Southerners would not conform to this austere standard of conduct. When heard with skepticism, the words lost their meaning. In

Richmond, less than two weeks after the *Dispatch*'s editorial appeared, Sally Grattan said she wished that she could avoid hearing news of the war. People censured her for saying so; "they tell me that is very *unpatriotic* & that I should be willing to see the whole country devastated, all the men, women & children killed &c rather than *submit*. I hold that such a result would be worse than submission. . . . Patriotism is a curious thing, & is beyond my comprehension."

As the Confederates fell back under the pressure of greater defeats in the summer of 1863, the contrast between initial promises and subsequent behavior grew starker. The original definitions of the Confederacy began to lose their hold on Southerners' minds. The *Richmond Enquirer* complained in August: "It has become common to talk sarcastically of the 'last ditch' men, and the 'last-drop-of-blood' men. . . . Has this become a ridiculous sentiment, then?" Admitting that not all Southerners who used the words to describe their intentions would act accordingly, the *Enquirer* warned that, if the Confederacy did not have several hundred thousand "last-drop" men and "last-ditch" men, "it is ill with us this day—with us and our heirs forever." Belief in such men's existence was essential for belief in the Confederacy. The editor tried to rehabilitate the promise to accept death before surrender by separating that resolve from the words used to describe it. "The phrases may have become cant, and may mean nothing in the mouths of those who use them; but the thing itself—the firm resolution to perish rather than submit upon any terms whatever, is precisely what is wanted." Yet the Confederate vocabulary had no way of asserting the nation's existence without using those discredited phrases or their synonyms. There were no Confederate words for a general failure to stand in the last ditch. And there was no Confederacy when its special words became meaningless. Decay of the phrases was decay of "the thing itself," because the thing existed for most Southerners only in the words.

The vehement expressions of Confederate resolve included a frightening vision of Federal victory. Though conquest of the South was officially inconceivable, Southerners imagined it vividly. They made defeat look far more catastrophic in prospect than the North finally made it in practice. Men would be banished or executed; women would be raped and reduced to servitude; all property would be confiscated; with Yankees' encouragement slaves would murder whites; cities and plantations would be leveled; the populace would be exterminated or enslaved. Unless the Confederacy established itself as the newest and proudest country, the *Enquirer* warned, "our name and nation will be extinguished in a night of blood and horror." The intensity and specificity of this catalogue of atrocities could not have been heightened had Southerners been expecting such a result rather than defying the supposed threat of it. Confederates were fascinated by phrases evoking their degradation. In the mind's eye an "appalling desolation" spread over the South like the "ravages of Louis XIV in the valleys of the Rhine"; slaves indulged their "vilest passions"; there were "southern white men working the cotton fields under Yankee overseers"—or, worse, "subordinate to their own negroes"—while the people's hardships far exceeded "the sufferings and miseries of the Poles & Hungarians." Without success in their revolution, Confederate heroes would be "the criminals of a defeated rebellion."

When war or reconstruction gave any sign of acting out Southerners' dread thoughts, however, they said they felt amazed and appalled. Yankees were not supposed to take Southerners at their word and act as cruelly as the menacing fantasies had foretold. Their specter of defeat was an inverted, mutilated image of honor and power—a dream to alarm themselves with, not a scene to be lived. It had the perverse effect of making Northern armies' destructive marches look almost familiar as soon as they began. Confederates comprehended their ruin before they admitted that it could happen. A few had from the start dismissed the rhetoric of impregnability. Years before Sherman's army did its damage, John Copeland had predicted that 50,000 Yankees would go where they pleased through the South. Most scenarios of catastrophe were designed to disprove such prophecies by stimulating Southerners' urge to fight. Yet, while relying on the effectiveness of this appeal, bold Southerners imagined the same terrors that gloomy ones expected. Whether or not Federals' marches had been inevitable, they took on the appearance of inevitability in many Southerners' minds, partly because Confederates had amplified such a lurid schema for a people who failed. As Sherman's army left Atlanta, heading across Georgia, the *Atlanta Intelligencer,* published in Macon, said: "What we have long looked for has come at last."

Southerners were often preoccupied with Yankees' view of the South. Confederates dwelt on the need to make Yankees admit the justness of Southern aspirations to nationhood. This concern resembled the long-standing American impulse to defy Great Britain and to wrest from foreigners, especially Britons, their envious assent that all things American were superior. Just as Americans often saw the United States soon supplanting in the world's respect the obsolete British empire, Southerners tried to find part of their nationality by drawing invidious distinctions between South and North. According to the Austin *State Gazette,* Northern capitalists wanted exclusive control of the western territories in order to expand their empire of "white slaves" because they feared that Southern agrarians' predominance in the west and, by extension, in the nation would ruin their fortunes. An independent South would stand as a perpetual defiance of the capitalists. With an inversion of unionist appeals, James H. Thornwell said that the Confederates were fighting not just for their own interests but "for the salvation of this whole continent." Their defeat of the federal government would arrest the movement toward "a supreme irresponsible democracy" in the North, which if continued would lead to anarchy followed by despotism. Though the Confederacy's triumph might thus benefit Northerners, who otherwise were about to lose their liberty, the Confederacy's destined national greatness must come at the North's expense.

Southerners said they had made the North rich by providing from their fields most of America's exports and by purchasing at inflated prices manufactured goods made or imported by Northerners. Writing from North Carolina in the fall of 1861, James D. Greenlee said of Southerners' economic relations with the Yankees: "We are not dependent as they supposed merely granted them the privilege of working for us & paid them a good price for their Labor." In the absence of these concessions, the North, according to James H. Hammond, would be "the poorest portion of the civilized world." By establishing its independence the Confederacy would explode the hollow pretensions of Yankees who dared to assign to the South a subordinate role in American prosperity and power. After the firing on Fort Sumter, the Georgia *Christian Index* predicted a prompt uniting of the South in secession, followed by Confederates' capture of Washington, D.C. As soon as victorious Southerners dictated the terms of their independence, "the North will sink at once to the position of a third-rate power." The Confederacy, with its capital in Washington, would take the place of the United States as "the valiant American Government," standing "among the first nations of the earth." In the words of the *Richmond Whig,* "We must rule this continent, or be the most degraded people on the earth." Having lost their controlling hold on the American government, Southerners decided to leave the union, but they never fully freed their idea of their new nation from a compulsion to prove that the South had been the best part of the American nation. They still needed the North in order to see who they were.

Another guarantee of Confederate nationality embodied in language comprehensible only to secessionists said that the people of the South differed as much from those of the North as did the people of one European nation from another that was distant and dissimilar. "The lines of demarcation arise from the character of the people." Southerners' lists of their cultural qualities that made Yankees alien could be lengthened almost indefinitely—from the old division between seventeenth-century Puritans of New England and cavaliers of Virginia, through the stark contrast between the South's Anglo-Saxon homogeneity and the North's multicultural Babel, on to an array of admirable personal traits supposedly possessed by Southerners and lacked by Northerners. John Izard Middleton wrote in 1861: "No two peoples are more foreign to each other than are we and the Lincolnites." The notion that two such peoples could lastingly form one nation was ridiculous, a mark of Yankee delusion.

Confederates' dubious historical and sociological arguments, questionable in the categorical extremes to which they were taken, if in nothing else, were ancillary to the main ever-present message: the North was evil. Confederates tried to superinduce a nationality through denunciation of a foreign enemy. Promoting Southern nationalism, secessionists had warned that the South, if it stayed in the union, stood in danger of succumbing to the modes of thought and character that had ruined the North. The attainment of the ideal Confederacy required not only separation from the North but also suppression of Southerners' supposedly Northern proclivities—materialism, pursuit of wealth, selfishness portending chaos. Yet those dangerous tendencies never had been absent from the South and in the 1850s had reached new extremes of indulgence amid unprecedented prosperity for part of the populace and newfound ambition by more people to share more wealth in a more powerful and larger South. Whatever the prospects for Confederate political independence, Southerners could not secede from themselves. Under the pressures of war, they kept slipping out of character, failing to behave like the people they imagined themselves to be. Confederates' writings contained frequent general denunciations of subversives: speculators and extortioners, rich planters, expatriate Yankees, and greedy Jews. But by 1863 the disparity between citizens' selfishness and patriots' calls for service to the cause of independence was too glaring to look like an effect only of foreigners' and elites' machinations. In December, Louis T. Wigfall said on the floor of the Senate: "Talk of speculators, extortioners and Dutch Jews! The farmers have been the worst speculators, extortioners and Dutch Jews of this war. . . . of late a wild spirit of speculation ha[s] seized upon the people which bid[s] fair to work our ruin." Depending on whom one believed, Richmond or Wilmington or Charleston or Atlanta or Mobile or Vicksburg was the most corrupt city in the Confederacy, its inhabitants given over to profiteering. Looking back on Southerners' extortion of high prices in order to come out ahead of their currency's rapid depreciation, William W. Bennett wrote after the war: "All classes, all trades, all professions, and both sexes alas! seemed infected by the foul contagion."

As more Southerners shrank from bearing war's costs, they took on an ever closer resemblance to their stereotype of the alien. If they did not behave like Confederate patriots, who were they? Speaking in Atlanta in

January 1864, Howell Cobb called on Georgians to supply the army and to stop hoarding like speculators and extortioners: "I tell you and the history of this war will bear me out in the assertion, that many true hearted Southern men were born at the North, and some of the vilest Yankees that ever disgraced this earth have been born at the South." Cobb was referring not to individuals who had moved from one section to the other but to people whose behavior conformed to the supposed national character of their nation's foreign enemy. Southerners could turn themselves into Yankees by their delinquencies. Cobb thus had two meanings for "North" and two meanings for "South," one meaning for each word consisting of persons, the other consisting of attributes. He was trying in his speech to fix a true definition of what was Southern by inverting a double set of discrete meanings—definitions which he, in the process, tacitly acknowledged to be unfixed or arbitrary. His appeal dissolved the categorical standard of character it meant to invoke. Perhaps suspecting that his attempted paradox might lead his audience to wonder whether he were a true Southerner, Cobb prefaced his admonition by stating his credentials: "If there is any one in this wide world who hates the Yankee race worse than I do, I am sorry for him, because he must have devoted his whole heart to the work." That was what was supposed to make a Southerner a Confederate: hating Yankees. For its popular appeal, the ideal of a Confederate nation returned consistently to this energizing emotion. Hatred, however, preceded and outlasted Southerners' war and their separate nation. Such intense emotion did not necessarily attach Southerners lastingly to Confederate independence; nor did it assure that they would follow any consistent line of conduct. They could not find an enduring identity in hatred. Events confirmed what George Washington had told Americans in his farewell address: passionate aversion, like passionate attachment, deprived a people of their independence of thought and action, making them poor judges of their own interests because they were in thrall to their emotions. Passion could make a war but not a nation.

Notwithstanding their confidence in the divergence of antebellum Southern society from the Yankee pattern, Confederates meant to clinch their case by saying that the mounting intensity of combat, as well as Yankees' atrocities, enhanced Southerners' attachment to nationhood day by day during the war. Deprecating any hint of reunion, the *Richmond Enquirer* said early in 1863: "Two years, and an abyss of horror and hatred, and the blood of our slaughtered brothers crying aloud from the ground, all prohibit that impious union." Eight months earlier, praising Stonewall Jackson at the end of the Valley Campaign, a Confederate soldier reassured his wife: "The breach is widening every day that divides us from the North we are a distinct people." Supporting secession at the start, the *Mississippi Baptist* promised its readers that "revolutions never move backwards." Just release Southerners' passion of resentment, excited by "a long series of oppression," and their behavior would know no restraint. The further appalling Yankee cruelties of the war years only made Southerners more unlike the people who were hurting them.

This unarguable appeal, taking for granted that violence intensified hatred and that hatred fostered national identity, failed the Confederates. By the summer of 1863 Southern testimony, especially from the president's home state of Mississippi, often said that Confederate casualties and Federal cruelties produced the opposite of their promised patriotic effect. Davis received a variety of reports, all saying that Federal soldiers' abuses made people quiescent, inducing many property owners to show "a readiness to return to the Union" in order to save what they still had. One of Davis's most loyal supporters in the Confederate Congress, Senator James Phelan of Mississippi, warned him after traveling through the South in July: "The day I ever dreaded, *has come*. The *enthusiasm* of the masses of the people is *dead!* . . . Base neither hope nor action upon its supposed existence." Davis continued to do so—other than giving up, he had little choice—but he followed Phelan's advice and also relied on "the *strong, bare arm of military power*." Many historians have examined the ways in which war fractured rather than cemented Southerners' political and societal cohesion. Confederates' original picture of the South as a powerful section or a powerful nation had been predicated on its rich resources and its people's ability to secure and extend antebellum prosperity through national independence. Instead of increased wealth, war brought mounting adversity. Hating the Yankees for causing hardship did not effectively unite Southerners in a nationhood whose main promise was being systematically destroyed. The lengthening lists of battles and casualties foretold not a more defiant, distinctive South but a decimated one. While Confederates, on the crest of their military fortunes, patriotically celebrated the victory at Chancellorsville, they saw, George A. Mercer noted, "that we are merely submitting to a process of extermination, and everyone asks how long will our army and Govnt last under this system." The bloodshed and destruction that, in Confederate rhetoric, were supposed to alienate the two peoples made this question inescapable.

In the spring and summer of 1865 a number of former Confederates attributed the failure of their attempt at nationhood to the lack of intelligence, dedication, and "serious endurance" in the Southern populace. J. W. Yale wrote in May: "And now we are a subjugated People. . . . How did it befall us, that is [the] worst part. We conquered ourselves, committed Suicide—Such a people does not deserve independanc." Reflecting on defeat, General Lee blamed the war and the fate of America on what he called "the absence of virtue in the people." In Richmond, soon after the surrender, a *New York Herald* reporter interviewed Lee and quoted him saying: "The South was never more than half in earnest in this war"—a judgment Lee's official letters often had hinted at. Such defects meant to some Southern leaders that, even if the Confederacy could have won its independence, the basis for an enduring nationality had collapsed during the war. Critics of Jefferson Davis were so disgusted with his creation of a strong central government that, according to the treasurer of North Carolina, Jonathan Worth, "many men having large influence over public opinion, do not take pains to conceal their conviction that the establishment of our Independence would be no permanent blessing to us." The government of the Confederate States of America had become or would have become as oppressive as that of the United States of America, with the extra disadvantage that things did not work so well in the South. The authorities grew increasingly dictatorial, yet the populace more frequently defied them with impunity. Edward A. Pollard wrote of the Confederate government: "Richmond was a Chinese copy of Washington." With broad coercive powers, with unprecedented success in military mobilization, with war-making industrial resourcefulness hardly conceivable a few years earlier, with the loyalty of most officials at all levels, the Confederate government spun its gears and pulleys vigorously as it slowed down and fell apart. It suffered a government's most ignominious fate: issuing demands and orders to citizens who no longer believed in its power to protect, reward, or punish them. A nation relying on appeals was doomed when it could no longer convince. A nation relying on coercion was doomed when it could no longer coerce.

At the same time, some of Davis's friends concluded from the war experience that an independent Confederacy would have failed in its aspiration to be a great republic. Unlike his critics, who contended that successful centralization was self-defeating, his admirers said that Davis and his government had been denied a full trial of the South's ability to maintain a separate nation, falling victim to the obstructionism of petty, local-minded politicians. William Preston Johnston, who had been close to Davis during the war, wrote in July 1865: "We were not fit for Independence or we would have had it. Many of our wisest & truest men, thought, after seeing the results in the war, that we would with our doctrine of Secession & State Rights, be at the mercy of such pestiferous demagogues as Joe Brown & such agitators & destructives as Toombs and Wigfall." Those who used the Confederacy's own doctrines as grounds for refusing to sustain a selfless statesman like Davis could not create a country worth having. They would have ruined it if the Yankees had not. In later years, replicating the wartime mutual lack of faith between Davis's friends and enemies, former Confederates writing about the war spent much of their energy criticizing one another. Their recriminations portrayed a divided wartime leadership, consisting of men who doubted colleagues' competence and distrusted their motives. Such views tended to confirm retrospectively the gloomy conclusion drawn by one of Alexander H. Stephens's correspondents after the fall of Atlanta: "I am not one of those who desire to see the last dollar spent, and the last man killed in setting up the Independence of the Southern states, that I have no assurance will last as many years as we will spend in obtaining it." Differing fundamentally about the flaws revealed by war, these antagonistic pessimists agreed that Confederates had ruined the nation in trying to create it.

As the Confederacy suffered invasion and demoralization in the last two years of the war, losing more of its plausibility as a nation, Southern patriots put greater trust in their army. Soldiers still had the capacity both to repel the enemy and to embody the South's aspirations to cultural and political independence. Men's willingness to fight on under ever greater adversity must come from a belief in the nationality for which they fought and must go far to demonstrate that it existed. In September 1864 the *Richmond Enquirer* said that the dead heroes of the army, such as Stonewall Jackson and Robert Rodes, had shown their love of country by their deeds in battle. They "are our guarantee of success. . . . The nation that gave birth to such hearts, that can boast such devotion, such heroism as our noble troops have displayed in every campaign, on every battlefield, has already proved that she has men worthy of liberty and men capable of directing her destinies." Four months later, William C. P. Breckinridge, a Confederate officer, clung to that assurance. "The people in parts of Georgia, Alabama & the Carolinas are ready to submit; but the real country is the army—it & the vast majority of the women are unconquered & unconquerable."

Amid these reverses, however, most soldiers needed a source of resolve beyond an assurance that they represented the nation. A Federal soldier reported in July 1863: "Many of the Rebel Prisoners that we have taken admit that they now have no hopes of accomplishing their object, but intend to fight us as long as they have a man left able to carry a gun." Holding or failing to hold this intention to fight may have been the main distinction between Confederate soldiers who stayed in the war and men who deserted in growing numbers. Both groups could see Confederate defeat coming. One resolved to fight it out, while the other went home or to the enemy. If the nation inhered in the army, it did so primarily as a desperate hope. George Cary Eggleston recalled after the war: "Our hearts went on hoping for success after our heads had learned to expect failure." Once Grant's bloody offensive began in 1864, "we had to shut our eyes to facts very resolutely, that we might not see how certainly we were to be crushed. And we did shut our eyes so successfully as to hope in a vague, irrational way, for the impossible, to the very end." Soldiers detached their combat from political purposes as the prospects for independence grew faint. When Sherman simultaneously started his offensive in Georgia, one of the Confederate soldiers facing him wrote home: "My motto is to fight them as long as we can and then sell out to France and still fight them." Confined to a dwindling group of Southerners, fighting Yankees, though it was a prerequisite for Confederate nationhood, could not alone define or create nationality. The South could not vindicate with its armies' combat a belief in the nation's future it could not sustain among civilians or soldiers. Before the final defeat they had foreseen that hope would not suffice. The Confederate army outlived the purpose for which it had been created. After the disastrous battle of Sayler's Creek on April 6, 1865, General Henry A. Wise, former governor of Virginia and a leader of the state's secession, urged Robert E. Lee to disband his army and send the soldiers home. Lee asked: "What would the country say of that?" Wise replied: "There is no country. There has been none for many a day. You are all the country there is."

Efforts to give the Confederacy enduring existence by talking about it approached the hallucinatory during Sherman's marches through Georgia and South Carolina. Editors and politicians tried to persuade people in Sherman's path to defy his army and tried to convince people elsewhere that the invaders were doomed. Soon after the fall of Atlanta, Judge Andrew G. Magrath, who was elected governor of South Carolina in December, advised President Davis how to rally forces for the defeat of Sherman and how to revive the populace from its state of "moral atrophy." Like the editors calling for a revival of the spirit of 1861 he said: "We can preach the expulsion of the foe as we preached the disruption of the Union." He and Davis and the editors did so, resorting as usual to perception through exhortation, a way of thinking that had been essential to creating the Confederate nation and that, in these last months, moved farther and farther from what most Southerners in Sherman's path, or perhaps anywhere, regarded as reality.

During the first phase of the Federals' march, as the army went from Atlanta to Savannah in November and December 1864, editors predicted Sherman's ruin, saying that he would suffer the fate of Napoleon in Russia. They called on Georgians and South Carolinians to rise en masse, to harass Federals on all sides, and to leave a stripped, scorched earth in the oncoming army's path. The *Richmond Sentinel* said: "Break in upon his array, and there will soon be a grand hunt, free for everybody, in which we hope everybody will join." The *Augusta Constitutionalist* promised that "our own citizens, without guns, can conquer the enemy," and the *Savannah News* pointed the way to his "utter annihilation." The editors explained that Sherman was retreating in desperation. This call for Southerners to burn their own cities, crops, and homes while civilians fought to the last man was as old as the Confederacy; Georgians had heard it from Howell Cobb and Robert Toombs in February 1862. Southerners never had acted that way in any great numbers when the Federals advanced, and they did not do so in the face of Sherman. Editors gave some signs of knowing how far-fetched their predictions were by adding a warning that, if the Federal army survived, the fault would lie with the people. The *Richmond Examiner* tacitly acknowledged the prevalence of defeatism when it wishfully suggested that Sherman was not conquering Georgia but instead converting wayward Georgians to the true Confederate faith.

Despite the Federals' successful completion of their march to the sea, Sherman's movement through South Carolina in February 1865 evoked from Confederate officials and editors even bolder assertions of confidence. Governor Zebulon Vance, in a speech at Goldsboro, North Carolina, promised that Sherman would be stopped and that the Confederacy would win its independence within a year. The *Richmond Whig* said that on the march Federal forces would dwindle while the Confederate forces grew stronger; the Yankees eventually would be surrounded and captured. "Sherman's doom may be looked upon as sealed." Those Southerners who could not persuade themselves that Sherman would be defeated but who still insisted that the South would win simply defined away the marches' significance. "His expeditions are destructive but not subjugating," the *Richmond Examiner* declared. According to the *Richmond Sentinel,* it did not matter for the security of the Confederacy what Sherman did or where he went: "His track will be that of a bird through the air or a ship over the waters. Our people will rise up behind him everywhere more defiant and unsubdued than ever." Whether the people were surrounding him, in one version, or evading him, in the other, he had no effect on them or on the nation's military fortunes. As late as April 12, 1865, the *Daily South Carolinian,* published in Chester after having been burned out of Columbia, said: "Notwithstanding all our losses, the advantages of position and ability are still with us. . . . if the South will be as much a unit now in her determination and spirit, as she was in the beginning of the struggle, we shall achieve our independence."

The only way to sustain faith in the Confederacy was to move one's

mind ever more fully out of the world of military events and of Southerners' defeatist behavior, into the world of rhetorical events where
declamation prevailed over any contradiction. This was the ultimate state
toward which Davis and others were tending when they argued that no
military reverse could defeat the Confederacy because nationality lay in
the spirit of the people, not in such material manifestations of power as
cities, fortifications, or military positions. From Danville, Virginia, Davis
issued a proclamation on April 4, 1865, describing the fall of Richmond
and Lee's retreat before Grant as "a new phase" of the war. The armies'
movements across the South without bases of supplies would destroy the
enemy; "nothing is now needed to render our triumph certain, but the
exhibition of our own unquenchable resolve. Let us but will it, and we
are free." Davis was making substantially the same case that secessionists
had made in 1861. Aptly, editors and politicians, as they retreated farther
into the world of rhetorical events, invoked the memory of the public's
state of mind in 1861. The arguments making Sherman's movements
meaningless recapitulated the arguments by which Southerners created the
Confederacy, a nationality brought into existence and made indestructible
through *a priori* reasoning. Even in resorting to force, the arbiter beyond
reason, Confederates relied on their powers of persuasion to prove that
they were unconquerable. Like their other weapons, it failed them. But
it was the last one they surrendered.

On May 4, 1865, General Josiah Gorgas, until recently the Confederate
chief of ordnance, wrote in his journal: "It is marvelous that a people that
a month ago had money, armies, and the attributes of a nation should
today be no more, and that we live, breathe, move, talk as before—will
it be so when the soul leaves the body behind it?" With this question
Gorgas suggested, as had Edward Everett Hale in "The Man Without a
Country," that partaking of nationality gave citizens their "soul." The
fictional Philip Nolan had been banished from his country, but the
Confederates' nation disappeared while they stayed at home. As "a people" they no longer existed, Gorgas said; yet, as individuals, their bodies
continued to move in a living political death. Having said many times
that the new nation was eternal, that revolutions never go backward,
Southerners found themselves without a country, obliged to seek another
one by going into exile or by reaccepting the United States.

The Civil War was fought by people who needed a nation. Emotional
exaltation of nationhood had grown in the first half of the nineteenth
century within an American political structure first designed by men who
did not conceive of republics as permanent entities. A new conception
of national independence had replaced the founders' emphasis on reasoned
choice among imperfect institutions and on the mortality of all govern-

ments. Yet this new transcendent nationality was supposed to inhabit institutions that had been created with an expectation that they would be finite in their authority and their duration. Northerners, especially Republicans, made nationality an ultimate value and made governmental powers absolute in cases of violent resistance. The North's myth of the permanent nation subordinated claims to autonomy made by citizen, state, or region and gave that subordination the sanctions of history and of force. Southerners took with them into their Confederacy the contradiction between the eighteenth-century republic and the nineteenth-century United States, which the North was resolving. Southerners exacerbated that contradiction both by re-emphasizing the citizen's liberty and autonomy and by combining with this re-emphasis a newly fabricated supreme, transcendent, perpetual nation. They were forcibly trying to make a modern state, resting its claim to allegiance on citizens' right to resist the forcible creation of a modern state.

Some historians have argued that the Civil War came as a plausible climax to and fulfillment of American political life since the Revolution, especially of the three decades before the war. Antebellum America was pervaded by an uncompromising insistence on personal autonomy, an expectation that opportunity and wealth must steadily expand, a demand that government directly serve citizens' wishes, a growing impatience with restraints on the ambitions of individuals or of groups. These tendencies to reject limitations and to defy unwelcome authority knew no certain means to resolve competing demands other than violence. Parties and the mechanics of government thrived on confrontation and on winner-take-all outcomes, but were far less suited to restrain than to agitate. People so determined to have their own way and so certain of possessing right and power could not readily stop short of war or stop war, once convinced that they were threatened on matters they deemed crucial. All professing to be Americans, they found that America did not keep them together but told them to kill Americans who sought to control them. By doing so they could make history accede to their ethos. If the Revolutionary founders had not promised a perpetual union or indefeasible self-government, if Southern unionists were not so numerous or dedicated as many Northerners supposed (portent of a difficult, bloody war), if the preponderance of numbers and resources weighed heavily against the South (portent of the South's defeat), if the armies' campaigns were not following predictions and intentions—if history or facts or events conflicted with the desire for a lasting country of one's own, citizens could ignore them and fight to prove that their version of America was true. Both Northerners and Southerners were trying to overcome the finiteness of their legacy from the founders without admitting that it had been finite, that they and not the Revolution created their nation, and that they were doing in blood a nation-making that also could be undone by bloodshed. This reliance on force implied the polity's mortality, a truism in the eighteenth century which the Revolution's nineteenth-century descendants were trying to escape. Often, as with John Esten Cooke, when Americans called the war a tragedy they used the word loosely, meaning instead that they thought the war an anomaly—one unique outburst, perhaps "tragic" because avoidable or perhaps "tragic" because necessary in order to resolve a single fundamental difference, such as the fate of slavery. Though they spoke of tragedy, they could not accept the war as intrinsic to Americans' nation.

CHAPTER 5

THE DEATH OF STONEWALL

LYING in bed in a small building near the tracks of the Richmond, Fredericksburg & Potomac Railroad, T. J. Jackson spoke his last audible words. Afterward, his wife told Robert L. Dabney that he had said: "Let us pass over the river, & rest under the shade of the trees." Dabney quoted her account in his biography of Jackson begun during the war. Dr. Hunter McGuire remembered instead the words: "Let us cross over the river, and rest under the shade of the trees." Mary Anna Jackson, writing a book about her husband years after "the beautiful sentence" had become "immortal," adopted the doctor's version. In both forms, or with other variations, the words moved many people to quote them in speeches, poems, and reminiscences. The actions urged by the dying general seemed full of moral meaning. Did Jackson see a specific river in his mind's eye? If so, which one? Or, if he spoke in metaphor or symbol, how should he be interpreted?

Perhaps during his final moments he thought of the Shenandoah, in whose harmonious valley, between the Blue Ridge and the Allegheny Mountains, he had settled until war had called him away. Margaret Junkin Preston asked in her commemorative verse whether her brother-in-law the general had been thinking of the Shenandoah; and Dabney speculated in his biography: "Was his soul wandering back in dreams to the river of his beloved valley?" It seemed fitting to link Jackson with the land, to imagine him in sympathy with its beauty and simplicity, a thought with which a Confederate veteran, before quoting the last words, capped his Memorial Day speech: "His face to heaven, he talks of elemental nature."

For others no natural body of water could convey Jackson's message. Even Preston and Dabney mentioned the Shenandoah only to contrast it with the river parting earthly life from the afterlife. His last vision must have been supernatural. He saw paradise, suggesting to Bible readers images of Eden, of the river that watered the garden, and of the tree of life. The Northern clergyman Henry M. Field, who revised Anna Jackson's draft of her book, suggested in a magazine article that "a gleam from the river of life caught his dying eye." On the other hand, it was the river of death for those who did not want to paraphrase the Book of Genesis or the Revelation of Saint John. From its waters Stonewall emerged on the other side, the farther shore. Aging veterans quoted Jackson to express the tie between their dead comrades and the living who soon would follow. Their general had attained immortality. William A. Swank brought his memorial verse to its climax by saying of Jackson: "Victory over the grave is the last of thy triumphs!"

What lay on the other side of the river? The mention of rest led men to imagine the dead Stonewall in a place of peace. In his final days of sickness he spoke as if he were still on the battlefield, sending orders to his commissary officer and to General A. P. Hill. Yet one could hope that, at the last, he had what Field called "a vision of the unseen" and passed "from a world of conflict to that in which war comes no more." The river separated those two worlds, and Jackson happily crossed it. Dr. McGuire recalled the general's disciplined face taking on an expression "as if of relief." Jackson's aide James Power Smith knew twenty years afterward that his general had gone to "a land where warfare is not known or feared." It was an appealing notion. The Confederate editor Edward A. Pollard, writing in 1868; Bishop George William Peterkin, speaking at a Lee-Jackson birthday observance in 1905; Stephen Vincent Benét, rendering the war in poetry in 1928: each understood Jackson's words to mean a welcome escape from combat. Long after the war Jefferson Davis felt so moved by the image of the once terrible general become "peaceful as a lamb" that he forgot that Dr. McGuire had cut off Jackson's left arm. Davis described to proud former Confederates the inspiring moment of the deathbed scene when the hero "calmly folded his arms, resigning his soul to God and saying: 'Let us cross over the river and rest under the shade of the trees.' " How could Northerners fail to respect or Southerners to revere a man who, in his last moments, had been so free from malignity? His last vision proved his benevolence; for he passed from conquest to serenity. A Northern writer in a Democratic newspaper, the *Detroit Free Press,* censured partisans who still remained bitter toward the South fifteen years after the war: "The man whom they hate died forgiving all. . . . With malice toward none—with forgiveness for all, his life went out as his pale lips whispered: 'Let us cross over the river and rest under the shade of the trees!'"

Yet Jackson had other admirers who pictured him crossing rivers as a victorious general. Dabney's images of the Shenandoah River, as he saw them reappearing in the mind of the dying man, were pastoral only insofar as love for the valley stimulated violent resistance to the invader. For Jackson the river was a body of water "across whose floods he had so often won his passage through the toils of battle." Perhaps his last words were a continuation of the military orders he had imagined himself to be giving; or, as one postwar poet suggested, perhaps Jackson at the moment of death was exulting in a new, imagined success, crowning his memory of earlier ones:

> Those conflicts are over, triumphant at last,
> The warrior may dream of the battle-fields past,
> And cry now in vict'ry, as bright visions please,
> 'We'll cross over the river and rest under the trees.'

Was Jackson thinking of the Potomac River? Word of Lee's entering Maryland in September 1862 excited Paul Hamilton Hayne to write "Beyond the Potomac." The army's northward march to the river formed the urgent refrain of each stanza until at the end the Confederates safely reached the northern bank, where they could attack the oppressor.

> 'Neath a blow swift and mighty the tyrant may fall;
> Vain, vain! to his gods swells a desolate call;
> Hath his grave not been hollowed, and woven his pall,
>   Since they passed o'er the river?

The invasion and the Confederacy failed. Hayne, in an ode written after the war, dated the disappointment of his earlier dream from the day of Jackson's death:

> Our staff, our bulwark broken, the fine clew
> To freedom snapped, his hands had held alone,
> Through all the storms of battle overblown.

Only Jackson's aggressive fighting could have saved the Southern cause. For some who read what he had said, his last words showed that he knew this truth.

Toward whatever shore—pastoral, spiritual, or strategic—Jackson's words may have been yearning, they were a summons, not a narrative.

No one could know whether he had made or could have made the passage he was proposing. General John B. Hood described after the war a conversation with Jackson during December 1862: Jackson "without hesitation" had told Hood "that he did not expect to live through to the close of the contest. Moreover, that he could not say that he desired to do so." Although he did not know it when death came, Jackson had erred in supposing that God had foreordained Confederate independence; he might also have erred in his vision of crossing the river. He seemed to be remembering, yet inverting, a vision of the prophet Ezekiel: "And it was a river that I could not pass over: for the waters were risen, waters to swim in, a river that could not be passed over. And he said unto me, Son of man, hast thou seen this? Then he brought me, and caused me to return to the brink of the river. Now when I had returned, behold, at the bank of the river were very many trees on the one side and on the other."

From first hearing of the wounds Jackson had received on the night of May 2, 1863, until learning that he had died on May 10, many Southerners felt deep anxiety about his condition. Confederate soldiers showed their worry on their saddened faces. Men of the Stonewall Brigade asked about Jackson's health each day. Captain R. E. Wilbourn told General Lee about Jackson's injuries as Lee lay in bed, propped up on one elbow. "Ah! Capt.," Lee said, "any victory is dearly bought that deprives us of the services of Jackson even for a short time." Wilbourn described the wounds and said they had been inflicted by fire from Confederate troops. Lee "seemed ready to burst into tears, gave a moan & after a short silence said, 'Ah Captain don't let us say any thing more about it; it is too painful to talk about' & seemed to give way to grief." Citizens showed almost as much solicitude as soldiers did. As Jackson was moved from a field hospital to Guiney's Station, men and women living along the road came to the ambulance to give him food and to pray for his recovery. In Winchester, still occupied by Federal troops, friends of the Confederacy feared that they would lose the man who once had chased the Yankees away and would, they hoped, return to do so again. Cornelia McDonald wrote in her diary on May 8: "No man was ever better loved by a people than Jackson." So intense was the concern in Lexington that the arrival of the Sunday mail on May 10 broke up the Presbyterian worship service, which had just begun, and the congregation left the church. Southern newspaper editorials described a united public emotion; the *Savannah Republican* said on May 5: "Every heart is ago-nized lest his injuries may prove fatal, and one universal prayer will ascend that his precious life may be spared to the country." The wounds alone made the whole Confederacy mourn, according to the *Charleston*

Courier. In the west, the captain of a company of sharpshooters in the Army of Tennessee wrote on May 6: "My prayers go up to Heaven for our cause and our great and good Chieftain Genl Jackson." God had prospered Jackson so many times, showing His favor to the Confederacy—would He not do so again?

There was hope. Word spread that Jackson was doing well; he could expect to recover. People clung to this wish, knowing what his return to command meant. He would demolish more Yankees. The *Savannah Republican* wanted his stern eye to have another chance to "lighten with a warrior's joy" while his brigades broke the columns of the enemy, who would once again run "with the vengeful Confederate cheer ringing in their ears." William Cabell Rives wrote to assure Jackson that every Confederate felt gratitude for the general's "noble & unremitting services" in a "struggle involving everything dear to humanity." Rives prayed that Jackson would long live to enjoy the appreciation of a grateful people. An officer later said of the men in Jackson's corps: "We all looked forward to a time not far distant when he would again lead us to other victories." Some people, refusing to imagine the alternative, decided that he must survive. Colonel Stapleton Crutchfield told anxious people that "he could not & would not believe that Jackson was going to die." General Lee said: "God will not take him from us, now that we need him so much." On May 5 the *Richmond Examiner* concluded: "We cannot afford to lose this man. He has been the good genius of the war. His extraordinary ability, and the astonishing prestige which attends him everywhere, is a power of the republic." Stonewall Jackson's successes proved that the Confederacy could maintain its independence. Southerners wanted their hero to live; he was uniquely useful. Dr. McGuire knew how much the life of his patient meant to so many people and "seemed weighed down by the care & responsibility."

To the fearful, the hopeful, and the confident, news of Jackson's death came as a blow. Jefferson Davis seemed to think he had been misled during the early days of May; he wrote to Lee: "The announcement of the death of General Jackson followed frequent assurances that he was doing very well, and . . . the shock was increased by its suddenness." At a distance from Guiney's Station and Richmond, Southerners tried to convince themselves that the first report of his death was one of the false war rumors to which they had grown accustomed. But confirmation followed, suspense ended, and disbelief reluctantly gave way.

On May 10 and the following days, especially among Lee's soldiers and the people of Virginia, grief found unchecked outlet. In camp, soldiers wept openly. Everywhere Jackson's body was taken, crowds gathered. Many people waited outside the small building at Guiney's Station while the embalmers from Richmond did their work. At each station along the R. F. & P., crowds met the special train carrying Stonewall's remains, his widow, members of his staff, Governor Letcher, and others. In Richmond the corpse was surrounded by people for two days—in its transit from the depot to the governor's house; then in a formal procession through the streets, led by President Davis and his cabinet, ending at the Capitol; and in the room of the Capitol where the body lay in state. Aboard a special train to Lynchburg on May 13, the corpse attracted more crowds to the depots. From Lynchburg, a James River canal boat took it upriver to be met by the corps of cadets of the Virginia Military Institute, who escorted it to lie in state in Jackson's old section room. A gun from the battery with which Jackson had taught artillery tactics fired every half hour until the next day, Friday, May 15. Then a procession of cadets, cavalrymen, wounded veterans, and weeping citizens followed the body to the grave, near that of Elinor Junkin Jackson, amid the sound of Lexington's church bells.

Everywhere, from Guiney's Station to Lexington, the metal coffin, covered with the newly authorized national flag of the Confederacy, was repeatedly smothered in flowers and surrounded by wreaths. During the train's pause at each depot, people handed in more flowers and wreaths through the car windows. Women were conspicuous among the mourners. Judith Brockenbrough McGuire noticed that almost every lady in Ashland visited the car containing the body while it stopped on the way to Richmond. Dr. William G. Shepardson described the scene at the Capitol for the *Mobile Advertiser and Register:* "Ladies especially wept profusely over the dead hero, and some pressed their lips upon the coffin." Men and women took their children to see the train—children in Gordonsville cried at the sight of the coffin—and to look at the face of the corpse lying in state. Charlotte Maria Wigfall told her brother: "He looked perfectly natural, more as if he were asleep than dead. . . . I expect you will think I am really blue, but you know Jackson has been my hero & favorite for a long time." Throughout the movements and ceremonies Mary Anna Jackson, dressed in mourning, followed the coffin with her infant daughter. "She was so evidently bearing all and doing all as she felt that her husband could have wished her to do," the Reverend William J. Hoge wrote after talking with her. "She was so patient amid all the pageantry—the oppressive pageantry."

Southerners in other states joined in mourning Jackson's death. In Columbia, South Carolina, a memorial service took place in the assembly chamber of the old state house on the morning of May 11. Among the speakers, the Reverend Benjamin M. Palmer of Louisiana and Colonel J. T. L. Preston "paid beautiful tributes to his memory." Many years later

John Witherspoon Ervin recalled the arrival of the news in a small town in South Carolina; the report was read aloud by the minister during worship service, after which everyone wept. Poets and publishers commemorated Jackson prolifically, enabling T. C. DeLeon to build a collection of forty-seven monodies and dirges. Variety theaters added laments for Stonewall to their programs, like the one recited to boisterous applause by Miss Ella Wren:

> He fell as a hero should fall;
>   'Mid the thunder of war he died.
> While the rifle cracked and the cannon roared,
> And the blood of the friend and foeman poured,
> He dropped from his nerveless grasp the sword
>   That erst was the nation's pride.
>
> Virginia, his mother, is bowed;
>   Her tread is heavy and slow.
> From all the South comes a wailing moan,
> And mountains and valleys reecho the groan,
> For the gallant chief of her clans has flown,
>   And a nation is filled with woe.

Another poem suggested that Jackson be buried near George Washington at Mount Vernon, where the twin graves would become a Mecca for pilgrims of freedom. For Robert L. Dabney the widespread public display of grief made Jackson unique: "No such homage was ever paid to an American."

Stonewall Jackson, until three days before receiving his wounds, had been in winter camp with the right wing of Lee's army along the south bank of the Rappahannock River, downstream from Fredericksburg. His last days of fighting began with General Joseph Hooker's effort to steal a march on Lee. As commander of the Army of the Potomac, Hooker, like his grievously mortified predecessor, Ambrose E. Burnside, had accepted the strategic proposition to which Lincoln had never fully converted McClellan: that his army's aim should be the steady weakening or the immediate destruction of the Army of Northern Virginia. To accomplish this, Hooker took the offensive in the last week of April, dividing his army into three unequal parts. He brought together his cavalry and sent it south to break Lee's supply line on the R. F. & P. He left General John Sedgwick in command of a force along the Rappahannock at Fredericksburg, intending to convince Lee that the whole Federal army was still there. At the same time, he sent the bulk of his army upriver to cross to the south bank behind the Confederates. If all had gone as

Hooker planned, his army would have lain across the roads behind Lee, while the Federal cavalry interrupted Lee's supplies. The Confederates, if they wanted to protect Richmond, would then have had no choice but to retreat or to make frontal assaults on the Federals' new positions.

On April 27, 28, and 29, three Federal corps, the 11th, 12th, and 5th, as well as part of the 2d—about 50,000 men—marched up the north bank of the Rappahannock, dividing among them the fords where they could cross, then also ford a tributary, the Rapidan River. On April 30 they converged along the Orange Plank Road, which ran westward from Fredericksburg toward Orange Court House, approximately parallel to and partly overlapping another road, the Turnpike. Coming south from the river down the Germanna Plank Road to intersect with the Orange Plank Road, the 12th and 11th Corps marched precisely, as if on parade. The long column went up and down over the rolling countryside; seen from a distance, with sunshine glinting off the shouldered arms, it looked like a giant serpent covered with shiny scales, gliding along the road. Experienced soldiers could see that when they had reached the crossroads known as Chancellorsville, where one large house stood, they were behind Lee's army and only ten miles from Fredericksburg. They expected to keep moving eastward toward the Confederates' rear. But Hooker had convinced himself that, once his forces achieved the crossing, Lee's ruin was certain. On the evening of April 28, he spoke "in the most extravagant vehement terms," saying "how he had got the rebels, how he was going to crush them annihilate them." After he reached Chancellorsville on the evening of April 30, he said: "The rebel army is now the legitimate property of the Army of the Potomac." This confidence led him to believe that he need only wait until Lee made suicidal attacks or retreated. Hooker planned for his army to assume favorable defensive positions on May 1 along roads three to five miles east of Chancellorsville.

Lee learned on the morning of April 29 that the Federals were crossing the Rappahannock upriver. After it became clear that they were moving in strength across the Rapidan to the Orange Plank Road, he decided to take most of his force—about 40,000 men—toward Chancellorsville. Jackson's corps led the way in the early morning hours of May 1. Colonel William Allan later wrote: "I well remember the elation of Jackson. He seemed full of life & joy. His whole demeanour was cheerful & lively compared with his usual quiet manner." Arriving about four miles east of Chancellorsville, where Confederate brigades that had fallen back from the Rappahannock fords were entrenching, Jackson decided to continue westward along the Turnpike and the Orange Plank Road, the same roads which guided the Federals' movement eastward. The exchange of fire between advance elements of the two armies began around 11:30.

Not long after noon, Hooker, who did not yet know that Lee's main force had left Fredericksburg, recalled the 5th and 12th corps to their earlier positions near the crossroads. Late in the afternoon, when he learned that the Confederates were pushing forward aggressively, in strength, Hooker ordered his army to entrench around Chancellorsville and along the Orange Plank Road to the west. He said: "I have got Lee just where I want him; he must fight me on my own ground." The same day, in Washington, President Lincoln reported "that Hooker had surrounded Lee, and that his army was bagged, prospectively."

Hooker was wrong. He did not know what was happening while he was speaking. In this condition he was not alone. Unfolding events made conflicting or indistinct impressions on the minds of many soldiers on both sides. Describing their actions afterward, they could not agree on what they had seen or done. They knew that every moment was full of significance, that their actions would live in history. As an enemy or as an ally everyone had been near Jackson and Chancellorsville at a critical juncture of the war, though they had not known exactly where they were. The countryside where the Federal army finally entrenched differed greatly from the open, rolling fields a few miles to the east—the terrain Hooker had intended to occupy. The Federals were in the Wilderness, a large tract of woods between the Rappahannock and Mattaponi rivers. The great hardwood trees once standing there had been felled long ago to provide wood for ore mines, to make charcoal for iron forges, and to open the land for settlement. But much of the area had since been abandoned; and, in place of the big old trees, a dense wood of scrub oaks and small loblolly pines had grown, with the closely massed trees further congested by hazel thickets and bound together by vines and matted briers. Within the Wilderness ran not only the Orange Plank Road and other through roads but also many narrow wagon roads used by woodchoppers and not fully known even by local people. The uncharted maze had no logic. General O. O. Howard, commander of the 11th Corps, later complained: "Such maps of the roads as we had we subsequently found to be wholly incorrect."

By the evening of May 1, Lee had brought up more than 47,000 men, most of them within a mile of Hooker's eastern lines, which formed an irregular semicircle around the Chancellorsville crossroads. Hooker's men, from the far left on the Rappahannock to the far right strung along the Turnpike through the Wilderness three miles west of Chancellorsville, numbered over 70,000. Lee first thought of trying to get between the Federals and their river fords but, after looking at the lines during the afternoon, decided against it. Jackson's reconnaissance convinced him that an attack on the center of Hooker's forces at Chancellorsville would be unwise. There remained only Hooker's right, the approximate position of which Lee learned that night.

The conference between Lee and Jackson late on May 1 subsequently became one of the memorable war tableaus that seemed to capture momentous, critical turns of events in a single image: Marse Robert and Stonewall, sitting on abandoned Yankee hardtack boxes, planning by firelight a flank attack to surprise the hapless Hooker. The picture became so vivid in retrospect that Hooker himself, touring the battlefield after the war, evoked it at one stop by saying: "It was under that tree that the mischief was devised which came near ruining my army." Some of Lee's and Jackson's staff officers disagreed in the conclusions they later drew from what they remembered of the generals' conversation. Dr. McGuire said that Jackson's staff all believed that he had first proposed the flanking march. Writing in 1866, Jedediah Hotchkiss, Jackson's cartographer, and William Allan, chief of ordnance in Jackson's corps, described Jackson explaining to Lee with the aid of a map the circuit of the Federals he had conceived. Lee was struck by "the audacity of this plan" but accepted it. In contrast, Colonel Charles Marshall, Lee's aide, recalled that Lee had shown Jackson on a map the route his corps should take through the Wilderness to strike the Federal right. In reply Jackson, far from originating the plan, had said that the Federals would withdraw back across the river in the night. Yet Captain Joseph G. Morrison, Jackson's brother-in-law, remembered hearing Jackson propose the flank attack and then convert a reluctant Lee to it, though Lee preferred a frontal assault.

In the first draft of his biography of Jackson, Dabney adopted Morrison's account and thereby irritated Lee, who wrote to Mary Anna Jackson to explain Dabney's errors. "I decided against" an assault, he recalled, "& stated to Genl. Jackson we must attack on our left as soon as practicable; & the necessary movement of the troops began immediately." In a postwar letter to Albert T. Bledsoe and in conversation with William Allan, Lee insisted that he had devised the plan and that Chaplain Beverly Tucker Lacy and a young cavalryman from Spotsylvania County knew the roads well enough to assure him that it was feasible. Nevertheless, Anna Jackson's biography of her husband described Stonewall first gathering information about the roads then outlining his proposed flank march on a map as he and Lee sat on the cracker boxes. All could agree on the power of genius to rule events. But whose genius had done so? The disagreements troubled the witnesses, clouding the triumph of mind intrinsic to great generalship. Giving a speech thirty years after the war, Colonel Marshall was reminded of a famous satirical attack on David Hume's principles of evidence, the critic showing that a rigorous application of them would oblige one to doubt that Napoleon existed. Marshall said that, after looking at the absolutely contradictory accounts of both Chancellorsville and Gettysburg, "a Bishop Whately might readily create historic doubts as to whether either was in fact fought."

Hearing of Jackson's death, Americans in the North and the South set a quantitative value on its military effect. How many soldiers was Jackson worth? Their estimates of his power, expressed in numbers of men as an equivalent, ranged from "thousands" in the *Savannah Republican* and "a brigade or a division" in the *Richmond Enquirer* to "a whole army" in the *Chattanooga Rebel.* Other figures ran from 20,000 up to 50,000. Henry Ward Beecher's periodical *The Independent* agreed: "Richmond papers scarcely exaggerate when they say that the Confederacy could better have lost fifty thousand men!" Jackson was not just Lee's executive officer; he was a force—one which could be measured in the units of war, units of the kind he brought to bear against Hooker's army on May 2. At the same time, the significance of Jackson's flank attack and of the ensuing battle was also weighed in other units, ones which tended to diminish Stonewall's power. Secretary Stanton used numbers to reassure Hooker on May 7, after the Federal retreat: "The result at Chancellorsville does not seem to have produced any panic. Gold has only risen six per cent in New York and at the close today had gone down four."

No one could afterward think of Jackson's parting from Lee on the morning of May 2 without dwelling on the knowledge that the two victorious generals would never meet again. Lee's secretary Colonel A. L. Long described in his memoirs "an indefinable superstition" he had felt at dawn when he saw Jackson's sword, left leaning against a tree, fall to the ground. It was "an omen of evil." Two hours after dawn, as the long column of almost 30,000 Confederates marched across the Orange Plank Road at the start of their circuitous route through the Wilderness, Lee and Jackson exchanged what E. Porter Alexander called "the last few words ever to pass between them." At a dinner party many years later, Colonel Marshall graphically described the scene, demonstrating Lee's posture and his forward wave of the hand as Jackson rode away. The moment became the subject of a painting by E. B. D. Fabrino Julio. An engraving executed soon after the painting was completed in 1869, as well as a chromolithograph in 1879, gave widespread fame to Julio's picture of the mounted generals taking leave of each other. Mark Twain studied the original in New Orleans and reflected on the importance of explicitly telling people the retrospectively defined meaning of what they see when one offers them a historical representation, so that they will not suffer uncertainty. Unless the painting were properly labeled, Twain said, it might as readily be taken to portray "Last Interview between Lee and Jackson" or "First Interview between Lee and Jackson" or "Jackson

Reporting a Great Victory" or "Jackson Apologizing for a Heavy Defeat" or "Jackson Asking Lee for a Match": "It tells *one* story and a sufficient one; for it says quite plainly and satisfactorily, 'Here are Lee and Jackson together.' The artist would have made it tell that this is Lee and Jackson's last interview if he could have done it. But he couldn't, for there wasn't any way to do it. A good legible label is usually worth, for information, a ton of significant attitude and expression in a historical picture."

Subsequently looking back at Jackson's actions on May 2, Southerners knew that he was doomed. They offset this thought by the hope that he lived on in spirit. Soldiers, ranging from General Lee to a Kentucky cavalryman with John Hunt Morgan, said that the memory of Jackson would survive and would move Confederates to fight harder. The influence that his spirit exerted on soldiers, according to a biographical pamphlet written just after his death, demonstrated the "invisible communication between the spiritual and material world. . . . some unappreciable, magnetic influence draws them on where the spirit of inspiration leads. Men, under such circumstances, become superhuman." Jackson's unique power, synonymous with victory, need not have died with him. It was obvious to the *Richmond Whig* that men who had felt the influence of Jackson's presence would "never yield to mortal foe." Thus he would, even in death, help to win Confederate independence.

Years after the Confederates surrendered, those who memorialized Stonewall Jackson found in the contemplation of his victories a temporary, imaginary Confederate autonomy. Discussing the commemorative exercises held on May 10, 1866, the *Richmond Examiner* invited its readers to respond to defeat with their hearts rather than to accept the outcome philosophically. In that event, they would not just "look upon the great civil war as a necessary stage in the development of a mighty nation" but would imagine what might have been if Jackson had lived. While thinking about him on the anniversary of his death, "the nationality which was denied to the valor of our arms and to the fervor of our petition, seems to be granted, if but for a little while, to the poignancy of our sorrow." The spirit of Jackson, vivid in the mind, would endure longer than mere political and military power, which were evanescent. Though the dreams and plans had vanished with the Confederacy, Jackson's fighting spirit must have been real.

The flanking march on May 2 stretched Jackson's corps along a sequence of narrow dirt roads through the Wilderness. The pace was fast despite the heat; many soldiers began to throw away things accumulated during winter encampment. Some fell by the way, exhausted. The soldiers did not know where they were going and had not eaten for more than a day but showed good spirits. The Confederate column kicked up clouds of dust, which Federal soldiers could see. At several points the column passed within plain view of the enemy; it took artillery fire from the 3d Corps. The Confederates saw a Federal observation balloon hovering above the trees, its aeronaut presumably looking down on them. As they passed within a mile and a half of the Turnpike, the noise of their rolling artillery wheels and their officers' commands reached Federal scouts and other soldiers.

At 9:30 Hooker sent an order, addressed to Generals Slocum and Howard, warning the 11th Corps to strengthen its defenses and to be prepared for an attack on its flank. Writing for *Century Magazine* in 1886, Howard said that the order had not reached him but that on his own initiative he had taken proper precautions. In a letter published in the same issue as Howard's account, Carl Schurz described the arrival of Hooker's order at Howard's headquarters: "I went in to General Howard at once and read it to him." Schurz recalled that no defensive measures were taken except putting a small rifle pit across the road. John Hay, working on his and John G. Nicolay's *Abraham Lincoln: A History,* complained on September 3, 1886: "I have just been reading Howard & Schurz in the Sep. Century. There is a flat contradiction—of the gravest character—between them. . . . These contradictions are very disconcerting to humble seekers after truth." Having recovered from the alarm that provoked his morning order, Hooker in his afternoon dispatches assumed that the Confederate movement was a retreat—the anticipated fruition of his original plan—and he prepared for pursuit. He urged Sedgwick to take Fredericksburg and advance to attack the rear of Lee's army from the east. "We know that the enemy is fleeing," he signaled at 4:10. After the war, veterans and defenders of the reputation of the 11th Corps censured their generals' carelessness on May 2. They gathered recollections of unheeded warnings repeatedly pressed in vain on division, corps, and army headquarters. The rebels' strength, direction, and intentions had been obvious to all but the willfully obtuse. Privates and regimental officers remembered in later years that during the afternoon they had easily detected the Wilderness's poorly kept secret. Yet General Hooker afterward explained that Jackson "had led his column by a long circuit, out of sight and hearing, through the dense forest." A Federal soldier, writing home when the battle was over, drew a curving black blob in his letter and wrote around it: "map of Gen Hooker's Plan of Operations on the Rappahannock." He told his family: "Subjoined you will find a plan of the battle, drawn in the dark—by a 'reliable gentleman' who was present. It is the plainest and most distinct of any we have had."

While Jackson's men were marching westward, the Federal 3d Corps, which had lain near the Turnpike, on the left of Howard's corps, was slowly moving southeastward. Its commander, General Daniel Sickles, wanted to reconnoiter and harass the Confederate column. Hooker authorized him to do so, cautiously, in the hope of cutting off part of the retreating enemy's artillery train. He ordered the 12th Corps and one of Howard's brigades to join this movement. The rest of the 11th Corps stayed where it was, as its friends drew farther away into the Wilderness and its enemies came closer. By the time Sickles's main force reached the route Jackson had followed, all but the tail of the Confederate column had passed to the west.

Early in the afternoon the hurrying Southern soldiers were forced to move to the side of the road to make room for a mounted man carrying a large yellow envelope and riding fast. Not long after they resumed the march, another courier rode by them from the rear, saying as he passed: "Gen. Jackson is coming but no cheering." Again they stepped to the side and saw Jackson riding forward on his sorrel. Holding his hat above his head in a continuous salute to acknowledge that all the men were raising their hats, he galloped by them in silence. When he reached the Orange Plank Road, three and one-half miles west of the point on it where he had left General Lee in the morning, he saw that the Federal soldiers, relaxing in their camps along the Turnpike, knew nothing of his army's approach. Fitzhugh Lee, who took Jackson to look at the enemy, watched his reaction: "Stonewall's face bore an expression of intense interest. . . . His eyes had a brilliant glow." His cheeks colored, and his lips moved—in prayer, Lee thought. But the Federals had extended their line farther west than Jackson had expected. The Confederate column had to continue its march more than a mile northwest of the Orange Plank Road to reach a position in which the divisions could span the Turnpike for a mile on either side, in preparation for their attack. Jackson waited for almost three hours while his men continued to arrive and take their places in long ranks perpendicular to the Turnpike. An aide, Captain W. F. Randolph, later wrote that he saw Jackson spending part of the time in prayer, kneeling beside a log. "I was profoundly impressed," Randolph recalled, "and a feeling of great security came over me."

Jackson's orders for the attack allowed no stopping. The lines were supposed to reinforce and support one another in pressing forward, without waiting for new dispositions to be dictated from headquarters. Late in the afternoon, at six o'clock or somewhat earlier, the Confederates charged in sweeping ranks through the Wilderness, driving ahead of them frightened rabbits, squirrels, quail, and other animals. Soldiers of the 11th Corps, when they saw screaming rebels running toward them just behind the scared game, were completely surprised, though most of them had time to turn from cooking supper to form lines. Their lines could not stand. While some units tried to hold the Confederates back, others broke and ran without firing a shot. Sergeant Luther B. Mesnard of the 55th Ohio Regiment afterward remembered how hard he had run: "As far as I could see, everything was fleeing in panic. . . . There was no one near whom I knew." General Howard rode among his troops, holding an American flag under the stump of his amputated right arm, working in vain, he wrote the following week, "to arrest the tide. . . . The most trying and dangerous position a commander can be in is when his troops have got a panic and are flying." After Howard's First Division gave way, some of its men, joining soldiers of the Third and Second divisions, briefly held a second, then a third temporary line of defense, both of which were flanked and overrun. The 25th Ohio Regiment, like the 55th, was in the First Division, receiving the initial assault. One of its soldiers described his regiment's reaction: "We soon became scattered to the four winds everyone for themselves. Darkness was now on us and Jackson was on us and fear was on us." Three miles to the east, on the other side of Hooker's army, General Lafayette McLaws, commander of one of the two Confederate divisions that had stayed with Lee, rode along his line, saying to the men who heard the distant gunfire: "Yell, men! Yell! Jackson is in their rear, make them think we are very strong here."

Afterward, rebels and Yankees described the surprise attack differently. With pleasure former Confederates recalled how the Federals had run and how the hungry Southerners chasing them had grabbed cooking beef and had drunk real coffee. But Confederates also knew that the suddenness of their attack and the sweep of their success had soon thrown Jackson's corps into disorder. General Raleigh E. Colston said in his report: "Owing to the very difficult and tangled nature of the ground over which the troops had advanced, and the mingling of the first and second lines of battle, the formation of the troops had become very much confused, and different regiments, brigades, and divisions were mixed up together." Although Jackson took twelve brigades on his march, he hit Howard's corps with only six of them. Two had been held back, without Jackson's permission, along the flanking route; two remained behind the assault; and two were deflected in the advance through the Wilderness by a false suspicion on the part of the forward brigade commander that Federals had unexpectedly appeared on his southern flank. Despite these reductions of Confederate strength, Federal writers remembered the attack as an irresistible phenomenon of nature—an avalanche, a hurricane, a flood, a cyclone, a western tornado. The regimental historian of the 107th Ohio described Jackson's corps, with "thirty to forty thousand men," covered by "the wilderness, so familiar to him," charging "in that solid and massed formation, for which he was so noted." Soldiers in other corps blamed the 11th Corps for failing to stand, attributing the panic to cowardice among German-Americans in the corps. Such critics agreed with Theodore A. Dodge that *"Americans* will make a stand even if outflanked and surprised." General Howard, in his letters describing the rout and in his recollections many years later, regretted his men's panic. Like Jackson, he was an evangelical Christian who wished that his soldiers would think about their immortal souls, not their earthly lives, and see that they were instruments of God's purposes. Two weeks after the battle he remarked: "If men were not afraid to die it would simplify matters very much. They are afraid & fear makes them run."

As his men charged, Jackson rode with them, leaning forward and stretching his hand beyond his horse's head. Every few minutes he repeated a variation of the order: "Press forward." Each time he heard soldiers ahead of him shout—a sign that the enemy again had fallen back—he raised his right hand for a few seconds. An officer rushed up to him and said: "General, they are running too fast for us; we can't come up with them." Jackson replied: "They never run too fast for me, sir." Riding with him, Captain Wilbourn watched Jackson halt beside dead Confederate soldiers and raise his hand, "as if," Wilbourn wrote, "to ask a blessing upon them and to pray God to save their souls." Several times Jackson broke into a gallop and caught up with men in the front. Captain Randolph recalled that, when soldiers saw the general, they broke ranks, rushed around his horse, and gave "the wildest cheers I ever heard from human throats."

The assault was the greatest of Jackson's military achievements; few dissented. Northerners' responses to news of his death almost always acknowledged his ability as a general. The standing they gave him varied from that of best fighting general in the Confederacy to that of greatest general and soldier of the war. The rebels owed their victories in Virginia largely or mainly to him. Beyond his essential attribute of courage, the quality in Jackson which struck Northerners most strongly was his energy. Speed, secrecy, zeal, dash, impetuosity, resoluteness—all manifested his primary power: force in motion. His energy won admiration for its own sake, even though it made him, in the words of an Iowa soldier, "the most dangerous foe the Union ever had." Northerners dwelt on Jackson's ability to instill his driving force into his soldiers, making them instruments and multiplications of his energy. Under his uniquely intense influence, men accomplished more than they otherwise could have done. *The Independent,* like other Northern editorializing, emphasized the cohesion and determination Jackson imposed on his army: "He had absolute control of his men, seeming almost to fascinate them. . . . His whole soul was in his work. He had no doubts nor parleyings within himself." Though friends of the union could rejoice that his death weakened the rebellion, they could also see his courage and energy as a credit to America, in which they shared. Charles Francis Adams, Jr., told his father in July 1863: "I am sure, as Americans, this army takes a pride in 'Stonewall' second only to that of the Virginians and confederates. To have fought against him is next to having fought under him." Effectiveness deserved Americans' respect, no matter what end it pursued.

Yet the kind of force that Jackson embodied in the minds of his enemies could be turned against him and his cause with a resoluteness like his own. Two weeks after Jackson's death, a soldier in the 7th New Jersey Regiment explained: "Mother you must Bear in mind that even those men that praise him and his daring would not hesitate a moment if they had the Chance to send a Ball through his *heart* a soldier praises Bravery not mater where found a soldier will shake hands with the enemy one moment and Shoot him the next." Jackson was vulnerable to the relentlessness he had made his special distinction. The union could prevail only if the North outlasted the South, killing Confederate energy by killing Confederates. An old woman from the western Virginia mountains told a Federal cavalry officer: "I have been praying every day for the death of Tom Jackson, for this war can't end while he lives."

In response to the Confederates' attack, brigades from the 3d, 12th, and 2d Corps of Hooker's army—which had been looking eastward and southeastward—turned westward to converge against Jackson's advance. When asked what orders to give a brigade he was sending, General Darius Couch, commander of the 2d Corps, replied: "Damn it! Go where the fighting is." But the brigade had already moved before its commander received these instructions. In obedience to orders he understood to have come from Hooker, General Alpheus Williams tried to push his division forward against the attacking Confederates. Men of the 11th Corps were running past him, in the opposite direction, and more Confederates were arriving in his front. Williams said two weeks afterward: "No one could tell friend from foe nor see a hidden enemy a rod away. . . . It was a conflict of great confusion." After several hundred of his men disappeared as prisoners or casualties, Williams gave up the advance. By eight o'clock the Federals had placed artillery along an elevation one-half mile west of Chancellorsville. In reply to Confederate artillery the double-shotted guns began to fire down the Orange Plank Road and into the woods on both sides, with infantry fire added. The disarrayed Confederate line was advancing through the Wilderness in the growing darkness when it was hit. A soldier of the 2d Louisiana Regiment told what happened: "The men seemed almost panic stricken, the groans & shrieks of the wounded was heart rending, artillery horses riderless, came thundering back with pieces & caissons horsemen dashing about, shells bursting in the ranks & grape shot tearing through the woods, all combined presented a most horrible spectacle." Jackson, moving to the front, was preoccupied with restoring the organization of his corps. He said: "This disorder must be corrected." He sent out his aides to speed the process and rode along, saying: "Men, get into line; Get into line. Whose command is this? Col. get yr. men instantly into line."

Dr. McGuire thought the fighting had ended when the artillery fell silent. He brought ambulances forward to collect the wounded. The Wilderness was on fire in many places, and he feared that disabled men would be burned alive. Jackson, however, meant to continue the advance. He ordered the mixed troops of the two lead divisions to restore their organization and fall back, in order to be replaced at the front by General A. P. Hill's division. It had followed the charge in the third line. According to Captain Wilbourn, Jackson showed "great impatience" to get Hill's troops into position spanning both sides of the Orange Plank Road. Jackson waited on horseback, just ahead of where his men were filing into the woods. General James H. Lane's brigade, which had stayed in column formation during the assault, took the lead in forming the new line closest to the enemy. Lane told his officers and men that they would soon be making a night attack. As Wilbourn later remembered, the Federals seemed to be gone, "and it was not known certainly whether they were still retreating or had made another stand and were trying to rally their discomforted columns. Gen. J. was very impatient to press forward." After Lane had placed two regiments south of the road—the 7th and 37th North Carolina—and two on the north side—the 18th and 28th North Carolina—and sent another ahead to cover the whole brigade's front as skirmishers, he met Jackson, his former instructor at the Virginia Military Institute. He later quoted Jackson's orders: "In an earnest tone, and with a pushing gesture of his right hand in the direction of the enemy he replied: 'Push right ahead Lane,' and then rode forward."

A bright moon shone on the Wilderness. Sounds alternated in the night: first the obliterating noise and the explosive hits of artillery fire; then abruptly contrasting silences, during which soldiers on both sides heard frogs, crickets, katydids, and the cry of whippoorwills. Six months later, John Esten Cooke noted in his diary that General J. E. B. Stuart said of the whippoorwills at Chancellorsville: "I suppose there were one thousand in sound of both armies." Cooke used the birds' distinctive call to set the scene for the narrative "Jackson's Death-Wound" in his popular book *Wearing of the Gray:* "From the gloomy thickets on each side of the turnpike, looking more weird and sombre in the half light, came the

Soldiers of the 7th Illinois Infantry Regiment, Third Brigade,
Fourth Division, 15th Army Corps, on top of Lookout Mountain,
Tennessee *(Courtesy of the Library of Congress)*

ABOVE. William Waud, Burning of McPhersonville, South
Carolina, February 1, 1865 *(Courtesy of the Library of Congress)*
BELOW. William Waud, Columbia, South Carolina, the morning
after the fire, February 18, 1865 *(Courtesy of the Library of Congress)*
OPPOSITE. Jackson's Mill, boyhood home of Thomas J. Jackson
*(Courtesy of the West Virginia and Regional History Collection,
West Virginia University Library)*

Columbia the morning after the fire

Cotton burning in foreground   Park of Columbia
                                      the Circle

Lt. Thomas J. Jackson in Mexico City
(Courtesy of the University of Virginia)

Laura Jackson Arnold
*(Courtesy of the West Virginia
and Regional History
Collection, West Virginia
University Library)*

"Where is Jackson?" "Here I am!" (Cartoon by a Federal officer)
(Courtesy of the William L. Clements Library)

Thomas J. (Stonewall) Jackson, April 1863
(Courtesy of the Library of Congress)

Mary Anna Jackson,
with her granddaughter
(Courtesy of Duke University)

BELOW.
Ellen Ewing Sherman
*(Courtesy of the Ohio
Historical Society)*

Main Street in Lancaster, Ohio, ca. 1862
(Courtesy of the Ohio Historical Society)

ABOVE RIGHT. Senator John Sherman
(Courtesy of the Library of Congress)
RIGHT. W. T. Sherman in May 1865.
Mathew Brady's lens was improperly
adjusted, but the camera made a
different and perhaps more
characteristic portrait than the more
familiar photographs.
(Courtesy of the Library of Congress)

Chromolithograph after E. B. D. Fabrino Julio,
The Last Meeting of Lee and Jackson
(Courtesy of the University of Virginia)

Douglas Southall Freeman lecturing on the battle of Chancellorsville
in Fredericksburg, Virginia, May 2, 1935 *(Courtesy of the Library of Congress)*

Sherman's men destroying
equipment in Atlanta,
November 1864
*(Courtesy of the
Library of Congress)*

Chromolithograph after G. P. A. Healy, *The Peace Makers* (W. T. Sherman, U. S. Grant, Abraham Lincoln, and David Dixon Porter aboard the *River Queen*, March 28, 1865) *(Courtesy of the Chicago Historical Society)*

W. T. Sherman in the 1870s,
while he was commanding general
of the U.S. Army
(Courtesy of the Library of Congress)

W. T. Sherman after his retirement
(Courtesy of the Library of Congress)

Saint-Gaudens's equestrian statue of Sherman,
on the occasion of its dedication, May 30, 1903
(*Courtesy of the New-York Historical Society*)

melancholy notes of the whippoorwill. 'I think there must have been ten thousand,' said General Stuart afterwards."

Jackson and a small party of horsemen rode beyond Lane's brigade, leaving A. P. Hill behind. Near that point, a road branched northeastward off the Orange Plank Road. Not far beyond, this branching road branched again, three ways: into Mountain Road—which ran parallel to and near the Orange Plank Road—and Bullock Road, which ran northeasterly toward the Rappahannock, and yet another road running west of north. Lieutenant Joseph G. Morrison later narrated his advance with Jackson on the Orange Plank Road. On the other hand, in 1896 David J. Kyle described his role in guiding Jackson forward along the Mountain Road. Captain Randolph, whose presence Morrison did not recall, gave his own subsequent narrative, in which Morrison was not present. No one except Kyle remembered Kyle. According to Randolph, Jackson was seeking the road leading to the Rappahannock. Captain Wilbourn accompanied Jackson with two signal officers and couriers; he afterward remained adamant in his belief that Jackson had not intended to go beyond the Confederate lines, but had inadvertently done so because Lane had failed to put skirmishers out. Wilbourn remembered that Jackson, before passing General Hill, had sent back his aide, Major Alexander Pendleton, with orders. But, in July, Pendleton told John Esten Cooke that he had ridden with Jackson beyond the skirmish line and had said: "Gen. don't you think this is the wrong place for you?" Jackson had replied: "The danger is all over. The enemy is routed. Go back and tell A P Hill to press right on." Dr. McGuire said later that Jackson had told him on May 3 "that he intended to renew the attack with Hills Div & throw his left between the Yankees & the river, & compell Hooker to attack him the next day or to surrender." It was a desperate plan, those who knew of it said afterward. A veteran of the Stonewall Brigade wrote that the soldiers "generally believed that if Jackson had succeeded in getting in the rear of the enemy, between Chancellorsville and the river . . . he would have been powerless to prevent Hooker's retreat across the Rappahannock at United States Ford; and that an attempt to hold the Ford would have been disastrous."

Jackson's aggressiveness, so much in evidence on the night of May 2, remained popular among Southerners after he died. The day following his death the *Savannah Republican* assured its readers that God still ordained Confederate independence, for which the fallen leader had fought so well; an editorial two days later joined the *Richmond Enquirer*'s call for an offensive drive into the North: "They never will cry peace until they see their cities blaze and their lands made desolate. We believe this as religiously as we believe in a God. . . . It surely must be plain at last that this is to be a war of extermination." General Stuart "should be this very moment destroying the railroads and bridges and burning the towns and cities of the Keystone State." Reflecting on the loss of Jackson, some of his admirers distinguished him from other Confederates as the preeminent advocate of victory by invasion, a triumph which only his fall in the Wilderness stopped him from attaining. His desire to take the war into the North was common knowledge, they said. As source material for Dabney's biography, G. D. Camden, who had known Jackson from youth, told a story about the march to Manassas in August 1862. He had overheard citizens of Salem, Virginia, talking about the Confederate army's destination as it passed. One person said that the generals planned an invasion of the North and that, when they had decided to march into Maryland and Pennsylvania, "Jackson laughed & it was the first time he was ever known to laugh, and he did not laugh then, but only went through the motions." Camden explained: "I mention this incident to prove that Gen J was in fact regarded by the masses at least as the great man of the war." His advocacy of invasion was part of his posthumous claim to greatness as a general. Anna Jackson was convinced that Jefferson Davis and some high-ranking Confederate officers had dismissed her husband as a fanatic because of his preference for aggressive war. They had wanted to prevent his promotion. In 1877 she asked former Governor Letcher to provide evidence of this for an article she was planning, and in her later book she included testimony that Jackson had urged invasion and had preferred combat with no prisoners left alive. Davis denied that his policy had been purely defensive. In 1889, commenting on one of the contentions that Jackson would have won the war had he not been held back from invasion, Davis said he wished Jackson's "memory might be defended from his friends."

More than thirty years after the battle of Chancellorsville, to imagine a different fate for the Confederacy was sometimes to put oneself in Jackson's mind on the night of May 2. A Birmingham newspaper said in May 1895: "He would have gone into Washington, and Gettysburg's fateful shaft would never have entered the soul of the South." Stonewall Jackson, with a few men, riding slowly along the moonlit road through the Wilderness, seemed thereafter to have been suspended in one of those moments of contingency out of which infinitely complex and remote consequences would multiply, varying according to the outcome of a single act. Even Americans who asserted their confidence in the fulfillment of God's providential design or in verifiable quantitative calculations of material forces were tempted to dwell on such moments when remembering the war. The course of history may have been ineluctable. It obviously could not be changed after it had unfolded. Yet the multiformity of the war's events and the capriciousness of its destruction invited imagination to defy systems of historical explanation and to change accomplished facts in retrospect—to conceive of a better story. Captain Randolph, one of the horsemen riding with Jackson, reflected on lost possibilities as he reminisced in 1901. He was sure that an unwounded Jackson would have taken the war to the Yankees. An advance along the Bullock Road would soon have tightened a net of steel around Hooker, whose immense army would have been forced to surrender. The Confederates would have occupied Washington and Baltimore, the whole North would have lain open to them, and the war would have ended with a clap of thunder. The Confederacy "would have taken its place high up among the family of nations. That blast in the wilderness put an end to the almost assured result, and the hope of a great southern empire became only a dream. Was it Providence, or fate? Who can tell?"

Despite his reputation as one of the union's most effective enemies, Jackson's death evoked from Northerners effusive praise of his character. Private letters, as well as editorials and other public comments, called him an admirable person. He had qualities that even his wartime opponents should respect. He was, according to various sources, quiet, modest, temperate, brave, noble, honorable, and pure. Beecher's periodical *The Independent* knew him to have been unselfish: "He fought neither for reputation now, nor for future personal advancement." O. O. Howard wished God would give the North "more men & more leaders than we now have, who possess the virtues of that man." Many people honored him for being conscientious—his sincere belief in the Confederate cause gave his mistaken actions integrity—and for being zealous on behalf of what he believed no matter how wrong he was. The *New York Post* and the *Boston Evening Transcript* called him a Puritan who brought a Yankee spirit to the Southern cause: "Profoundly imbued with religious sentiment, he became the fanatic of slavery and State rights." John W. Forney, editor of the *Washington Chronicle,* analyzed the paradoxical connection between conscientious energy and a wicked cause. The apparent moral and logical gap between admirable dedication and deplorable purposes was bridged by fanaticism, defined as enthusiasm combined with a "curious obliquity of reasoning powers." Readers as diverse as Sergeant John S. Cooper and President Lincoln praised Forney's editorial, which concluded: "Stonewall Jackson was a great general, a brave soldier, a noble Christian, and a pure man. May God throw these great virtues against the sins of the secessionist, the advocate of a great national crime." Conscientious enthusiasm in a good cause was patriotism; in a bad cause, fanaticism.

Jackson's Christian piety attracted more Northern comment than any other attribute. Almost everyone who discussed his death mentioned his faith, especially its consistency and its evangelical fervor. One report suggested that in the 1862 campaign he had known the topography of the Shenandoah Valley so well because he had traveled it repeatedly before the war for prayer meetings and temperance meetings. Another said he had held a prayer meeting with the wounded men of both armies after the second battle of Bull Run. Surely he must have been a holy man whose soul was saved, many Northern Christians hoped. None of them knew him so well as the relatives of his first wife did. Her uncle David Xavier Junkin wrote to George Junkin: "I loved him dearly—but now—he is with *dear, dear* Ellie." Another member of the Junkin family sent condolences to Anna Jackson, reminding her that in her bereavement, she had the precious consolation "that Jesus loved him, & that he loved Jesus. . . . He was the most consistent Christian, I think, I ever knew." The Junkin brothers had sided with the union. After hearing of Jackson's death, D. X. recalled his last meeting with Jackson, under the Maryland Heights at Harpers Ferry after the war had begun. Junkin had tried in vain for two hours to persuade Jackson that the rebellion was wrong. Then, in parting, they shook hands. "I said, 'Farewell, General; may we meet under happier circumstances; if not in this troubled world, may we meet in'—My voice failed me,—tears were upon the cheeks of both,—he raised his gloved hand, pointed upward, and finished my sentence with the words—'in heaven!' . . . and if we ever meet it will be 'in heaven!' " During the first two years of the war, D. X. had constantly remembered his brother's early, emphatic prediction. George Junkin had said of his son-in-law: "Jackson will perish in this war."

Augustus Choate Hamlin, historian of the 11th Corps, accepting David J. Kyle's story, concluded that Jackson had advanced with his escort along the Mountain Road; but Captain Wilbourn distinctly remembered that they had been on the Orange Plank Road, their horses' hooves clearly audible as they struck the boards that paved the road. Wilbourn did not know why Jackson had ridden forward, but in his narrative he suggested that Jackson had been looking for Confederate skirmishers to learn the enemy's intentions. Jackson's aides James Power Smith and Jedediah Hotchkiss, neither of whom rode forward with him, believed that the group found the enemy near and turned back. Yet Wilbourn and Morrison insisted that Jackson was still riding forward, away from the Confederate lines, when his party was fired on from their right, the south side of the road. Jackson afterward told Dr. McGuire that he thought one or two shots had come from the front, then a line of fire from the rear, but McGuire noted that the general was deaf in one ear and thus never good at telling the direction of sounds. Morrison wrote that the fire on the right came from Yankees; Wilbourn was as certain that the shooting had been done by Confederates. Two aides who had not been present took opposite views: Alexander Pendleton said the first fire came from the rear; Henry Kyd Douglas said the front.

The volley killed Captain Keith Boswell, mortally wounded Sergeant William E. Cunliffe, and wounded a courier, Joshua Johns. Several horses were hit; others bolted. Jackson rode off the road into the woods on the left, heading toward the Confederate lines; then the regiment on that side opened fire. The flash of their guns in the darkness showed Wilbourn that the soldiers were kneeling, in the proper stance to repel a cavalry charge. Three balls hit Jackson at once: in the left arm between his elbow and shoulder, in the left wrist, and in the right palm. The reins fell from Jackson's left hand at the same time that his sorrel frantically ran back toward the road, pulling him low under a branch. Frightened, riderless horses and others out of their riders' control ran in different directions. Getting the reins in his right hand, Jackson stopped his horse in the road and turned it back toward the Confederate lines, as Wilbourn and W. T. Wynn of the signal corps caught up with him.

In 1888 J. O. Kerbey, a Federal veteran, toured the Chancellorsville battlefield in the company of James Power Smith, Smith's father-in-law, Major Horace Lacy, and Vespasian Chancellor, owner of the land—all three of whom served on a committee to choose the location for a monument to commemorate the wounding of Jackson. Stopping along a road in the Wilderness, Lacy surprised Kerbey by saying: "This will do as well as any place near here to put our monument. No one can give us anything at all definite about the exact spot where he was wounded." Smith and Chancellor went to work with a tape measure, driving pegs to mark off a half-acre site. Kerbey afterward commented: "The object in placing the monument in this location is plainly stated to be:—because it is more convenient to tourists on the roadside than if it were placed in the rather dense wood where Jackson actually received his wound." He speculated that, in the future, the government might "reserve more of this battle-ground as a National park; hotels may spring up around its numerous springs. Here might appropriately be commemorated alike in a commingling of monuments the heroism of both sides." Memory and monuments would fix the essential meaning of the war—the conscientiousness, the unselfishness, the effectiveness of the combatants. Giving events their structure for the benefit of others would enable the participants to make their war and its significance accessible to those who could know it only at second hand.

General Lane was not with the regiment on the left side of the road, the 18th North Carolina, when it fired. He later worked to reconstruct what had happened. He was told that skirmishers had heard the voice of an unknown horseman calling in the dark for General Williams. A sergeant had shot at the man, then skirmishers had fired, then the whole line had fired. Lieutenant Colonel Forney George, commander of the 18th North Carolina, reported that he had been told that no one but the enemy was in his front. However, not only had Jackson and his party gone forward, but General A. P. Hill and his staff were also in front, closer to the Confederate line. George said that Hill and the staff officers, in order to escape the first fire, rushed the line, causing the men to think that Federal cavalry were charging them. The regiment fired several volleys. Captain Wilbourn remembered hearing Hill call at the top of his voice for his men to cease fire. Major John D. Barry, commanding on the regiment's left, told Lane that he had not known about the generals' going forward, that he had ordered the firing and then had told his men to keep shooting because the cry of "friends" was a lie. He said "that he could not tell friend from foe in such a woods."

Dr. McGuire never doubted that Jackson had been shot by men of the 18th North Carolina: "The ball that I cut out of his right hand was a smooth-bore—musket ball—such as the regiment in front of him, were armed with." Yet in subsequent years a diverse array of people took different views. Having published an article on the subject in 1866 and a letter in 1870, McGuire complained a few years later about the continuing contradictory stories of the wounding: "So many lies, by our own people and by the Yankees, have been told in regard to it, that I have almost concluded to stop reading any further reports." Still, other competing accounts appeared. Veterans of the 1st Massachusetts Regiment, the unit facing the Confederate lines just north of the Orange Plank Road, insisted that they had seen the Confederate horsemen in the moonlight, without knowing that Jackson was one, and had fired. A soldier of the regiment gave his version to the *Boston Evening Transcript* later in the month, and other versions of the claim to have shot Jackson remained part of the regimental lore into the twentieth century. William L. Hollis read Confederate accounts, including John Esten Cooke's, in the Boston Public Library and found them "not only contradictory but false." He remembered being a skirmisher and firing on Confederates at a distance of not more than ten feet from the road: "As I was standing alone in those dark Wilderness woods I could see the palid moon showing above the trees and could hear the whiporwills singing and everything was as still as death." Competing with the claims of the 1st Massachusetts, General Alfred Pleasonton, with the support of Colonel Clifford Thomson, contended that he had arrested the Confederate charge with canister from his artillery, which had felled Jackson. Unsympathetic Federal historians pointed out that Pleasonton had been more than half a mile south of the Orange Plank Road and had resorted in his subsequent writings to what one called "fabrication." The *Cincinnati Commercial* and the *Chicago Tribune* reported that Jackson had been picked off by a skirmisher or a sharpshooter, and General Alexander Hamilton wrote in 1904: "One of my sharp shooters of 52nd Regt. gave Genl. Stonewall Jackson at Chancellorsville the wound from which he died." Yankees' claims did not convince Southerners. In October 1865 the *Vicksburg Herald* rejected the pretensions of the 1st Massachusetts Regiment. Jackson "fell under the volley from his own men in returning within his lines," the *Herald* said. "No fact of the war can be better established."

Who was the lone horseman calling in the darkness for General Williams and, by some accounts, provoking the fire of Lane's brigade? Hamlin, in his history, decided that it was General J. F. Knipe, a brigade commander in General Alpheus Williams's division. But a Federal veteran, John Hays, suspected in 1910 that he had been the cause. Lost during the night of May 2, he had ridden across the Orange Plank Road, looking for his brigade, and had seen a small squad of mounted men just before a volley of musketry caused his horse to bolt. During his return to the battlefield on September 29, 1910, he pointed out the place where he remembered having seen the mounted men. As he did so, one of his traveling companions exclaimed: "Why! there is a monument." Hays found his memory of the famous night confirmed by the location of the monument, which "was not over twenty feet from the spot I had pointed out and it marked the place where General Jackson was mortally wounded."

Long after the night of May 2, people with diverse motives and irreconcilable stories put themselves in the scene. The Reverend Henry M. Field, celebrating reunion of the sections in his work *Blood Is Thicker Than Water,* narrated his visit to the South in the 1880s. He described Henry W. Grady in Atlanta, paying tribute to Sherman's gallantry, and Governor E. A. O'Neal of Alabama responding warmly to the sentiment "Liberty and Union forever!" This attitude was all the more significant because O'Neal was loyal to the memory of Stonewall Jackson, telling Field at dinner: "I was near him when he fell." To have been the cause of his wound, knowingly or not—even to have been close when the guns were fired—gave one an important part in events determining the outcome of the war. Once the outcome had been accomplished and was taken for granted, the actors' importance acquired in their minds a life of its own. To have known whom one was killing, to have acted purposefully, to have hurt or helped one's people by design or inadvertence, to be able to comprehend events in a manner consistent with others' comprehension of them sometimes seemed less important than to have been in the center of action doing something—anything. In the effort to reconcile results with the events apparently producing them and to define the importance of one's role in events, the story sometimes broke down, unable to sustain the structure of causation and moral lessons it was supposed to memorialize. Moments long in the past still had the power to confute and confuse, as they had done to the participants on the night of May 2.

Although many people in the North praised Jackson's earnestness, sincerity, and piety when they learned of his death, Northerners also denounced him as a traitor for turning his energy to the service of a malignant cause. The *New York Tribune* drew reassurance from the knowledge that he had "met death at the hands of fellow-traitors." This showed that "the Rebellion is devouring its authors." The most severe censure of the dead Jackson came from writers who hated the Confederacy for defending slavery. The *Chicago Tribune* likened his fighting and daring to that of pirates and captains of slave ships: "He prostituted his talents, and employed the acquirements his country bestowed on him, to compass the ruin of the best Government the world has known. And this he did in the behest of the most infamous and atrocious of all systems that ever blackened the page of civilization." *Harper's Weekly* denied that there was any necessary connection between effectiveness as a soldier and religious faith or purity of character. "The honesty of a man who tries to destroy the foundations of civil society because its peaceful progress enlarges human liberty, is not so striking as his monstrous crime." The popular lecturer James E. Murdoch, who traveled the North giving speeches and readings to promote the war effort and to help charities related to the war, refused to recite poetry that praised Southern heroism. He said: "I would not recognize a single virtue in them, even if it existed." Referring to Jackson as "the so-called Christian hero," Murdoch blamed the rebellion on the "injustice and evil" within the slaveholding states. Only by dying did Jackson cease to be an enemy. "As Christians we are called on to forgive our enemies; but we are not required to embalm their memories in praise or tears." In this rendering, Jackson's skill and enthusiasm looked not so much admirable as sinister. Strengths of character in such a man, the *Daily Illinois State Journal* commented, only "increase his power for evil when he is engaged in an evil cause." An opponent of moral truth and the nation's life, he deserved death. During May 1863 Captain A. F. Duncan of the 14th Pennsylvania Cavalry met Laura Jackson Arnold in Webster County, soon to be part of the new state of West Virginia. He wrote to his father that he had found Stonewall's sister to be "a very pleasant and intelligent lady, and as good a Union woman as I ever saw. . . . When she heard of her brother's death, she seemed very much depressed, but said she would rather know that he was dead than to have him a leader in the rebel army."

As soon as Jackson stopped his horse in the road and turned it back toward the Confederate line, he sat in the saddle, facing his men fifty yards away in the dark. He looked toward Lane's brigade with an astonished expression but said nothing to Wilbourn and Wynn. They saw nearby a mounted man whom they did not know. Wynn ordered the stranger to see what troops had fired, and the horseman rode away. John Esten Cooke, using Wilbourn's account in his biography of Jackson, gave the moment an air of mystery: "The turnpike was utterly deserted with the exception of himself, his companion and Jackson; but in the skirting of thicket on the left he observed some one sitting on his horse, by the side of the wood, and coolly looking on, motionless and silent. The unknown individual was clad in a dark dress which strongly resembled the Federal uniform; but it seemed impossible that he could have penetrated to that spot without being discovered, and what followed seemed to prove that he belonged to the Confederates. Captain Wilbourn directed him to 'ride up there and see what troops those were'—the men who had fired on Jackson—when the stranger slowly rode in the direction pointed out, but never returned with any answer. Who this silent personage was is left to conjecture." After the war a Federal general, Joseph W. Revere, published an account identifying himself as the lone rider, though he said that he had not known that the wounded man was Jackson until he had read Cooke's biography. In his memoirs Revere told a story of meeting Jackson in 1852 and later receiving a letter in which Jackson predicted that the two of them would be exposed to a common danger during the first days of May 1863. Former Confederates scoffed at the implausible story. Wilbourn recalled that "the solitary rider . . . did not know where he was & seemed too badly frightened to [know] which way to go & what to do." Wilbourn also objected to the way Cooke had narrated the incident: "The part in reference to the solitary rider was changed . . . so as to make it appear more like a romance than reality." Nevertheless, Cooke's narrative won praise from readers who had not been at the scene. In 1866 one of the principal literary entrepreneurs in New York, Evert Duyckinck, told him that his biography of the general was a success: "Your Stonewall reads well. . . . Your account of Jackson wounded on the field is an inexpressibly tragic passage of great power."

Still in the saddle, Jackson soon found that his left arm had been broken by a musket ball. Blood ran down his left arm and his right hand, filling his gauntlets; he said that he felt severe pain. Before he could be helped to dismount, he collapsed, a dead weight in Wilbourn's arms. The two young officers carried him to a pine tree just off the road, where they laid him down. To learn whether the general was conscious, Wilbourn said that it was most remarkable anyone had survived the firing. Jackson replied: "Yes it is Providential." Soon General A. P. Hill and other officers reached the spot. They said they were sorry he had been hurt; they tried to stop the bleeding and bind his wounds. While they worked, two Federal soldiers walked up to the small group. Hill ordered them taken into custody, and they surrendered without resistance, saying: "We were not aware that we were in your lines." A doctor arrived; Jackson was persuaded to drink some liquor. He remained quiet except when replying to others. Before going back to take command, Hill said: "I will keep it as secret as possible from the troops that you are wounded." Jackson answered: "If you please."

Through the writings of Cooke, Dabney, and many later authors, Hill's secret eventually became one of the most widely known and most often discussed episodes of the Civil War. At the first reunion of the United Confederate Veterans in July 1890 the ceremonies included a living tableau representing "The Wounding of Stonewall Jackson," displayed while a one-hundred-voice women's choir sang "Nearer, My God, to Thee." Yet the story that moved so many people was not quite an intelligible one. As he completed the last of his four narratives of the events, Wilbourn said that during the ten years since Jackson's fall many people had told him that in reading published accounts they could not clearly follow what had happened. "I sent Mr. Cooke & R. L. Dabney each at their request an acct of the wounding of Gen'l Jackson at the time as did other members of the staff & Maj Leigh . . . but both of them got the different accts so mixed that they give a somewhat confused idea of it." Wilbourn knew that, when he explained to confused people in person, his listeners understood the true course of events.

While the officers tried to help the wounded Jackson, Federals began to move artillery into the road nearby. By its fire Lane's brigade had revealed its position in the dark. Jackson had to be moved to the rear. He stood and walked a short way to the road. He was so weak that his aides decided to put him on a stretcher, and four soldiers were brought out of the line to carry it. The Federal artillery opened fire with canister. A hissing rush of iron pellets struck sparks from the rocks in the road and lit the night with glowing red tracks. Two stretcher bearers ran away. Jackson and his two aides lay down by the road as more shots passed over them into the Confederate ranks. Canister and shrapnel hit horses in the face and struck soldiers. Men and animals panicked and fell into tangled, screaming confusion along the Orange Plank Road. When the artillery let up, Jackson again walked toward the rear. His aides tried to conceal him from the soldiers, but one man saw him and exclaimed: "Great God that is old Gen. Jackson." General Dorsey Pender, working to keep his brigade of Hill's division in place, recognized Jackson. He said he was sorry to see the general wounded and told Jackson that disorder in his lines might force him to fall back. Jackson looked into his eyes and replied quietly: "Gen. Pender you must hold your ground."

Soon Jackson lay back down on the stretcher, and with the help of other soldiers the party moved out of the road to walk through the woods. The Federals kept firing volleys of small arms and artillery down both sides of the road. Many Confederate soldiers left their positions in the front lines and ran past Jackson to the rear. Watching the cannonade, men of the 33d Massachusetts Regiment could not believe "that any living thing could exist after it." They were told that some gunners were loading their pieces with trace chains. Jackson's aide Henry Kyd Douglas wrote in his memoirs: "Verily, in the language of General Sherman, 'war was hell' that night." One of the men carrying Jackson caught his foot in the tangle of vines and roots that wound through the Wilderness. He stumbled; Jackson rolled off the stretcher and fell on his broken arm. He groaned. He was badly bruised, and his wounds began to bleed again. Lying where he fell, he asked for whiskey. After a pause, the stretcher was raised again, and the party returned to the road. A half mile to the rear, they met Dr. McGuire coming forward with an ambulance. McGuire said: "I hope you are not badly hurt, General." Jackson replied calmly: "I am badly injured, Doctor; I fear I am dying."

Learning of Jackson's death, Southerners commonly said that the news stunned them, depressed them, or covered them with gloom. As soon as Catherine Edmonston saw black borders around the newspaper on May 11, she wrote that evening, "A chill went through my heart. . . . I care for nothing but him." People who had never seen Jackson, who knew him only through public report, still felt as if they had lost one whom they knew well—a close friend, a relative, a father. William M. Black-ford's diary and the *Charleston Courier*'s editorial used almost the same phrases: "Every one mourns his loss as a personal bereavement and a national calamity." He and his people and their nation all felt the blow. The words "love" and "beloved" recurred in the first reactions to his death. People thought of him as a good man to whom distant strangers could feel closely attached. And his admirers imagined themselves to be winning Confederate independence through his successes. In Richmond, on May 20, Joseph G. Dill wrote that "we all looked to him for victory," while on the same day a North Carolina soldier was writing: "I know that I shal look for him if I ever get into Another Battle. I knew that he could not save my life But I allways felt certain of victory when I cold see him About." The poet Sidney Lanier had good reason to call Jackson "thrice-beloved." In its most intense form, this identification with Jackson evoked the wish that one could save his life by taking his wounds or his death on oneself. The *Richmond Whig* and the *Savannah Republican* said that thousands of citizens and soldiers would have done so. Despite God's taking Jackson from them, Confederates could not readily accept the divine will and had to exclaim, the *Charleston Courier* said, with the lament of King David over his rebellious son Absalom: "Would God I had died for thee!"

Some Northerners rejoiced at news of Jackson's death. In occupied Winchester, Federal soldiers taunted Southern women by calling out: "We've killed Old Jack; Old Jack is dead." Federal prisoners of war shouted in the streets of Richmond: "Where's your Stonewall now?" The death of Jackson brought closer the day when the rebellion, too, would die. On May 24, Mary Caplinger wrote her husband, a soldier in the 31st Illinois Regiment, that it "makes me the gladest . . . to hear of them big Generals being killed." No commander was too powerful, no mind too masterful, to be exempt from soldiers' destruction, they boasted.

Before putting Jackson in the ambulance, Dr. McGuire gave him whiskey and morphine. Although his skin felt damp, his face looked pale, and his lips pressed back so tightly that they showed the outlines of his teeth, Jackson gave no utterance to his pain, except to say: "I feel sometimes as if I were dying." After reaching the hospital tent, McGuire let Jackson sleep until two o'clock in the morning. Then McGuire woke him and asked whether he wanted the arm to be amputated if that seemed necessary. Jackson told McGuire to do what he thought best. With the help of three other surgeons—one administering chloroform, one watching the pulse, and one taking up the arteries—McGuire executed a quick circular operation, cutting off Jackson's left arm two inches below the shoulder. As Jackson fell under the influence of the chloroform, he said: "What an infinite blessing" and repeated the word "blessing" until he passed out. He recovered consciousness not long after the operation, drank coffee, and talked about the wounding and the operation. He said that chloroform had given him the most delightful physical sensation he had ever enjoyed but that he would not wish to enter eternity in that condition. He told Joseph Morrison to go to Richmond and bring Anna Jackson to him. Later, at about 3:30 A.M., when Alexander Pendleton came to report that A. P. Hill had been wounded and that Stuart wanted orders, Jackson feebly replied, after an effort to concentrate: "I don't know—I can't tell, say to General Stuart he must do what he thinks best."

On the morning of May 3, Jackson lay listening to the sounds of battle around Chancellorsville, where the Confederates renewed their attack on

Hooker's lines. He received a penciled note from General Lee; it ended: "I congratulate you upon the victory which is due to your skill and energy." Jackson said: "Gen Lee is very kind; he should give the glory to God." He told Chaplain Lacy that the flank attack had been "the most successful military movement of my life" but that he had not planned it all out in advance. "I simply took advantage of circumstances, as they were presented to me in the providence of God. I feel that his hand led me." Jackson eagerly received reports of the fighting and was much affected when told that General Stuart had said to the Stonewall Brigade: "Charge & remember Jackson." He said that the name "Stonewall" belonged to the men, not to him. The news that the brigade's young commander, General E. F. Paxton, had been killed caused Jackson to turn his face away, close his eyes, and struggle to conceal his emotion. Lacy afterward described Jackson's confident assurance that God meant the loss of an arm to benefit one who loved Him. Jackson said that, after falling off the stretcher, he had thought that he would die on the field. At that moment, he had enjoyed the precious experience of possessing perfect peace as he gave himself into God's hands without fear. But he knew that, if he had not previously repented of his sins and believed on Christ, it would then have been too late to direct his mind to the way of salvation under such suffering and in such circumstances.

Jackson spent Monday, May 4, riding in an ambulance to the home of Thomas Chandler, near Guiney's Station on the R. F. & P. Lying on a mattress in the ambulance, he remained cheerful and talked about the fighting on Saturday. Teamsters and wounded soldiers along the road sadly made way when they learned who was passing. The Chandler house was full of wounded men, some of whom had erysipelas; so Jackson was placed in a smaller building nearby, where he slept that night.

The loss of Jackson elicited from Southerners rueful praise of his unique military genius. His death made his former victories appear even more magnificent, if possible, than they had seemed in his lifetime. Lee, referring to Jackson's "matchless energy and skill" at Chancellorsville, was only one of those who described the dead hero in superlatives, making him incomparable. Jackson's ability to command victory had known no limit. D. H. Hill wrote in general orders on May 26: "His genius and courage have been the chief elements in Southern success." To describe Confederates' conception of Jackson as a general at the time of his death the *Richmond Examiner* later used the word "invincible." His fall surprised Southerners all the more, the *Richmond Whig* said, because they had come "to regard him as one of those men who have a mission to fulfill, and who bear a charmed life." Providence had seemed to shield him, "and there was a sort of superstitious faith that he would pass unscathed through all dangers to the end." The introduction to Cooke's biography began: " 'Jackson is dead!' . . . The people of the Confederate States had begun to regard this immortal leader as above the reach of fate." The power his personality exerted over both Southerners and Northerners seemed in Confederates' memories to have surpassed that of others—"No name in these states was so electrical to troops as his"—and to have struck his enemies as supernatural: "ubiquitous, tireless, exhaustless in resources, the very magician of the field." One version of his generalship attributed his success partly to "a great intellect." General Humphrey Marshall said that Jackson's "mind was superior to all others engaged in the war, and that his loss would be greatly felt on that account." Writers likened him to Hannibal, Caesar, Frederick, and Napoleon. A longtime friend who had formerly thought Jackson's intellect unremarkable came to the conclusion that his was "the master mind of the war." Contemporary biographers emphasized that Jackson's successes did not depend on luck. Cooke quoted a newspaper editorial, published before Jackson's death, which gave Lee the central place in the war but also explained Jackson's crucial importance: for the South, Jackson was "the expression of its faith in God and in itself, its terrible energy, its enthusiasm and daring, its unconquerable will. . . . He came not by chance in this day and to this generation. He was born for a purpose."

Resting in the makeshift bedroom of the Chandlers' plain frame building, Jackson was cheerful on Tuesday, May 5. Dr. McGuire found the stump of the left arm healing properly. Jackson asked how long he would have to wait before returning to command. He assured Jedediah Hotchkiss that he hoped to be soon in the field, and he told Chaplain Lacy that he was perfectly willing to die, yet expected to recover. A cold rain fell on Wednesday. Jackson sought relief from discomfort with the same treatment he had induced McGuire to administer for nausea during the heat of May 4—cold wet towels applied to his stomach. Wednesday night nausea recurred.

As the report spread that Jackson had been shot by his own men, Southern newspapers and citizens consoled themselves with the thought that the Yankees could not exult in having killed him. Still, as Catherine Edmonston foresaw on May 7, Northerners "will say that his men did it purposely & that they were demoralized." Yankees would try to make the wounding of Jackson a sign of the Confederacy's weakness. Sure enough, after James Longstreet was hit by Confederate fire in the Wilderness a year later, the *New York Herald,* under the heading "SHOT FROM BEHIND," commented on both shootings: "No such accidents—if they were accidents—ever happened in our army. Robespierre was guillotined by the very men he had deluded into revolution. Let Jeff. Davis take care." In his newspaper writings after the war, Cooke deplored such innuendo: "It would be but a wild idea, if any one could conceive it, that these leaders were intentionally shot by their own men." Far better for Southerners to say with Dabney that the blow to Jackson came not from Federals but from God, not in His wrath but in His love: "It took God's favorite from the coming doom."

The morning of Thursday, May 7, found Jackson's condition worse. His breath came in gasps, with great difficulty, and his sunken cheeks were flushed with a high fever. He was restless and in pain. Dr. McGuire diagnosed "pleuro-pneumonia of the right side" and suspected that in falling from the stretcher Jackson had sustained contusion of the lung, with extravasation of blood in his chest. The doctor tried cupping, and he administered mercury with antimony and opium. During the day Anna Jackson arrived from Richmond. Though she tried to keep a cheerful demeanor in her husband's presence, his weakened condition shocked her. She later wrote: "He looked like a dying man." Yet she would not let herself believe that he was. The drug and his weakness left Jackson sometimes in a stupor, from which his mind occasionally emerged when he was directly addressed. As he always had done frequently, he told his wife that he loved her very much. At other times, in disturbed sleep or in waking imagination, he gave orders: "Maj. Pendleton, send in and see if there is higher ground back of Chancellors"; "Pass the infantry to the front"; "Tell Major Hawks to send forward provisions to the men"; "Order A. P. Hill to prepare for action." In 1891, after accounts of Jackson's dying had made the scene famous, admirers of Hill planned to put on a monument to him the words Jackson had spoken on his deathbed. But Jedediah Hotchkiss, who remembered Jackson's frequent censure of Hill for slowness and lateness, warned them that, if they did so, he would "come out in the papers" and reveal what Jackson had meant.

Jackson also prayed and occasionally conversed on religious subjects with members of his staff, his doctors, and his wife. He asked McGuire whether the people whom Jesus personally had healed had ever again suffered from the same disease. Jackson thought they had not. On May 8 he seemed to be resting more easily, and his wife thought him "more rational." He told her that she was much loved and that she should not look sad, but he spoke little. McGuire dressed the wounds, which were healing. Jackson found breathing difficult and felt great exhaustion. Still he expressed confidence in his recovery. When his wife told him that he probably would not survive, he replied: "I do not believe that I shall die at this time. I am persuaded the Almighty has yet a work for me to perform." He added that he was not afraid to die and would accept God's will. Before the end of the week, five doctors examined Jackson and consulted. Dr. Samuel B. Morrison agreed with McGuire's diagnosis at the time but later told Dabney that the general had died not of pneumonia but of *"prostration,* resulting from high excitement, fatigue, & lack of nourishment."

Southerners' praise of Jackson's skills as a general, swelling soon after his death, may still have been overshadowed by their commendation of his character as a Confederate patriot and sincere Christian. On the validity of the figure Stonewall, whom Jackson had created, these admirers staked their confidence in Southern devotion to the cause of independence. The Atlanta *Southern Confederacy* said: "He was one of the purest and best of men, the most unselfish and patriotic. His very name was a tower of strength and inspired more enthusiasm among our soldiers than any other General in the service." His service of principle and of duty would thus define the collective undertaking of which he was a part. This purity of intention was a sign, in the opinion of the Presbyterian minister James B. Ramsey, that God had given the Confederacy such a man and had answered his prayers in combat because God was preparing for Southerners "a glorious deliverance." The heart of Jackson's character and success was his Christian faith, which, more than any other quality, impressed those who mourned his death. The *Richmond Whig* attributed his power to "compulsion of conscience and a reverential conviction of obligation to his Maker." Stonewall Jackson had shown the world, Confederates said, that God favored those who served Him. The General Assembly of Southern Presbyterians in 1863 unanimously voted approval of the same editorial sentiment quoted in Cooke's biography: Jackson embodied "the expression of his country's confidence in God and in itself." The church of Christ looked on him as "the living exposition of those precious truths which it is her mission to testify to a dying world."

Ramsey, in his memorial sermon on May 24, wanted Southerners to learn from Jackson's career that the "secret source" of the general's fame was his love of God, which gave human will "a concentration of energy otherwise impossible." Chaplain Lacy, preaching in the Army of Northern Virginia on May 17, repeated to the soldiers Jackson's conviction "that a man was a better Genl or merchant or farmer or anything else for being a Christian." Within seventy-two hours of Jackson's death, Lacy wrote to R. L. Dabney, urging him to undertake a biography. The hero's life would be "seized upon by a host of scriblers," with the result that "its high Christian character will be marred." "For the sake of the cause of Christ," Dabney, as a Presbyterian minister and theologian, was fittest to perpetuate in print such an exemplification of faith. But, if necessary, Lacy was willing to undertake the task himself. Dabney preached a memorial sermon in June anticipating some of the themes in his biography of Jackson and echoing the lessons drawn by others. As Ramsey had said in May, if Confederates had possessed Jackson's godly spirit, the war would already have ended: "Trust in God and victory is ours." Dabney warned that Jackson's career was God's living sermon to show Confederates the qualities of character most essential to the times. He reinforced his admonition by quoting what Jackson once had said to him after a Sunday service in camp: "I do not mean to convey the impression that I have not as much to live for as any man, and that life is not as sweet. But I do not desire to survive the independence of my country." Dabney drew the wartime moral: "In his fall and that of the noble army of martyrs, every generous soul should read a new argument for defending the cause for which he died, with invincible tenacity."

Long after Lee's surrender, former Confederates recalled that Jackson's death had given Southerners a premonition of their coming defeat. It weakened their efforts in the last two years of the war. In the last paragraph of one of his narratives of Jackson's fall, published in September 1865, Cooke said: "With his disappearance from the scene, the fortunes of the South, like her banner, began to droop." Commemorating Jackson eleven months after the war, the *Richmond Examiner* interpreted the Confederacy's grief in May 1863 as "a true prophecy of final disaster." Veterans said the soldiers had known that "our star of destiny would fade, and that our cause would be lost without Jackson." A captain in the 13th Virginia Regiment later remembered: "Men who had fought without flinching up to this time became timid and fearful of success." G. F. R. Henderson, doing research for his biography *Stonewall Jackson and the American Civil War* in 1897, asked Hotchkiss to assess the effect of Jackson's death on the army and the Southern people. Hotchkiss remembered "that nearly all regarded it as the beginning of the end," an opinion confirmed by the battle of Gettysburg, after which "our army was steadily and constantly depleted by desertions and skulking." Only the greatest catastrophe could serve as an analogy for the loss of Jackson, Napier Bartlett suggested in 1874: "The melancholy news affected the Confederates in the same way that the fulfillment of the various omens predicted, before Troy could be captured, affected the city's defenders." Visiting Chancellorsville late in August 1911, David Gregg McIntosh, former colonel of Confederate artillery, was deeply affected by thoughts of the shooting of Jackson as a portent of the nation's doom. By far the most interesting place on the battlefield, he said, was "a little to the north side of the road, where a modest pedestal and block of stone mark the spot where Jackson fell. . . . No one can approach the spot without being awed by the consciousness that here the very genius of war fell a merciless victim to fate." Looking back on the war, McIntosh knew that, with the wounding of Jackson, the "nemesis of fate . . . threw its shadow over the fortunes of the Confederacy."

Dr. McGuire disagreed with Hotchkiss's recollection: "After Jackson's death the troops were always in fine humor, always sanguine of success." Many Southerners' private writings in May and June of 1863, like their public exhortations, took this view. They often asked how long the Confederacy could persevere in war; still, they expressed hope and confidence in God's favor. Alice Prioleau felt very dejected on June 30: "The bloody victories seem to have no effect on shortening the war—the future looks so gloomy . . . this long-continued suffering both bodily & mental pervading the whole country must be depressing in the extreme. . . . I fear I should have given in long ago." Nevertheless, she concluded: "I trust that Jackson's loss is not irreparable, that is, that others may be raised up to carry out Lee's plans." The expectation or the prayer that God would provide another Jackson ran through the thoughts of soldiers and civilians. Confederates usually said that God was teaching them not to idolize a man or to rely on human strength, but rather to trust Him for their victory. Judgments like those of the *Richmond Enquirer* and the *Richmond Whig* were widely repeated in the South. The *Enquirer* said that Jackson had "wrought out the mission for which he was ordered of Providence," while the *Whig* assured its readers that the Confederacy could defend itself: "The same Providence that gave us Jackson still rules the affairs of men."

Yet, as his life was an example, so his death was an admonition. They might prevail without Stonewall, but they could not hope to do so unless they emulated him. "General Jackson did not accumulate a fortune in this war. He did not speculate in sugar or molasses; in tobacco or in flour; he robbed no houses; stole no plate, nor jewels, nor pictures, nor wines; sold no passports, extorted no black mail." Selfless devotion like his was essential to Confederate independence. The *Savannah Republican* said: "If not the head, he was at least the heart of the revolution." Southerners dare not allow the soul of their hero to die, as his body had died. The Reverend Ramsey warned: "The spirit of Jackson, in our rulers, our military leaders, and our people can alone save us and perpetuate us as a nation." Fulfilling the expectations aroused by the name of Stonewall Jackson, T. J. Jackson was cut off in the midst of victory. The spirit of Stonewall gave Jackson fame, led him to his death, then still lived in the minds of others as an example commanding imitation. Jackson was supposed to have penetrated the important mysteries perhaps more fully than anyone else—the mysteries of making war, of directing events, of finding salvation, of seeing the next world. And he had never expressed a doubt of the justness or the success of the Confederacy.

On Saturday, May 9, Jackson opened his eyes as his wife bathed his head; he saw tears on her cheeks. He shook his head and said, in a low, authoritative tone: "Anna, none of that; none of that." His fever and restlessness had increased; his breathing grew more difficult; he was perceptibly weakening. Yet, despite attempts to dissuade him, he insisted on talking with Chaplain Lacy. They conversed about the most recent of Jackson's long-standing efforts to promote strict observance of the Sabbath. Lacy wanted to stay at Guiney's Station on Sunday, but Jackson told him to go preach to the troops, as usual. Saturday evening Anna Jackson suggested to her husband that she read him some Psalms. He said he was feeling too bad to attend to them but then added: "Yes; we must never refuse that; get the bible & read." Later he asked her to sing; she and her brother sang a few hymns, ending with one Jackson asked for—the 51st Psalm, asking God to cleanse of sin. That night Dr. Samuel Morrison gave Jackson his opinion that the illness was fatal. Jackson replied: "I think I shall be better by morning." James Power Smith sat by the bed until two o'clock Sunday morning, sponging Jackson's face as the general dozed restlessly in his fever.

Sunday morning brought warm, pleasant weather under a cloudless sky. Fifteen miles from Guiney's Station, General Raleigh E. Colston rode over the abandoned Chancellorsville battlefield, from which Hooker had earlier withdrawn his army to the north bank of the Rappahannock. He saw trees gunfire had split or cut off a few feet above the ground, as if a huge scythe had mown them, and bushes fractured in every branch by artillery and small arms fire. The air stank with a putrid odor rising from the corpses of hundreds of horses and from thousands of shallow graves eroded by rain. Skeletal hands and feet of the dead, black and fleshless, stuck out of the ground. Green carrion-flies hummed. Though the fighting had ended a week earlier, artillery shells occasionally exploded as they were overtaken by fires still moving through the Wilderness, turning to powder the bodies of wounded men caught by flames during the battle.

Jackson's mind wandered often Sunday morning. He was evidently suffering great pain and seemed disinclined to talk. Outside, many people waited under the trees on the Chandler place. Jackson appeared to be slipping into a state of semiconsciousness; the doctors told his wife that he was dying. She said to him: "Do you know that the doctors say, you must very soon be in heaven?" Under the influence of his sickness and of the opiate, Jackson did not seem to understand. She repeated the question in another form: "Do you know that in a very few hours, you will be with your Saviour?" He said nothing. Again she asked: "If God wills you to go today, do you not feel willing to acquiesce in his allotment?" Jackson said: "I prefer it," then repeated, with emphasis, "I prefer it." She told him he would soon see the Savior face to face; he replied: "I will be an infinite gainer to be translated." She asked where he wanted her to go with their child. He answered: "Back to your Father—You have a kind, good Father, but our Heavenly Father is better than all." She asked where he wanted to be buried. He said: "Charlotte," then "Charlottesville." She asked whether he did not wish to be buried in Lexington, and he answered: "Yes, Lexington, and in *my own plot.*" She wanted to know whether he had a message for his sister, Laura; he said: "I am too much exhausted," adding, "I have a great deal to say to you, but there is no occasion for it now." Their six-month-old daughter was brought to the bed. The general smiled and said: "Little darling, sweet one." He touched her with his bandaged right hand and closed his eyes.

Preaching to Confederate soldiers a week later, Chaplain Lacy said that General Jackson, when told he soon would die, replied: *"I am read[y]."* In subsequent months Lacy addressed several large audiences in North Carolina on the subject of Jackson's last hours. He told Peter W. Hairston that in Salisbury he had seen "200 persons in tears when he described the touching scene." Lacy complained that Dr. McGuire had restrained Jackson from talking. Lacy said he regretted that he had not conversed more with Jackson, "as he could have done without injury to his wound."

Before the war Jackson had thought about the importance of the moment of death while marking his copy of J. M. Mathews's *The Bible and Men of Learning.* He drew a line in the margin where Mathews said: "Like a man's last will and testament, his character is never irrevocably determined till he dies." Jackson marked the book's denunciation of Hume, Rousseau, and Voltaire as "lepers whose touch was defilement" and of Gibbon, who purveyed impiety and unbelief like an infectious disease. He noted the accounts of Christian believers' happy deaths, and he marked Mathews's version of the words of Sir Francis Newport, an unbeliever, on his deathbed: "Uttering a groan of inexpressible horror, he cried out, 'O the insufferable pangs of hell!'" Jackson often had said he knew that he was saved. Anticipating a happy eternity in heaven, where he would never part from his family, had long been his main escape from loneliness—the loneliness that had recurred since his boyhood and that the fame of Stonewall had both alleviated and deepened. In his last letter to Margaret Junkin Preston he wrote, she said in her diary, of his first wife, "our precious Ellie, and of the blessedness of being with her in heaven." Only with God could he escape isolation. In Lexington he once had confided to D. H. Hill that he thought of becoming a missionary. Jackson said: "I often think that I will die a stranger in a strange land."

In the early afternoon of May 10, Jackson spoke his last audible words. Anna Jackson told Dabney afterward that her husband had said them "in his dozing state." But in her biography of the general she wrote: "All at once he spoke out very cheerfully and distinctly the beautiful sentence which has become immortal as his last."

T. J. Jackson was dying and, James Power Smith recalled, "spoke no more." The last thing he saw was the tearful face of his wife. She cried to Dr. David Tucker: "Dr. cant you do something more?" He said: "No, Madam; human power can do no more." Then Jackson "looked up intelligently at his wife, & died."

CHAPTER 6

THE VICARIOUS WAR

IF AN all-hearing ear could have caught and a many-tongued voice retold the participants' history of the Civil War, the rendition would of course have contained as many stories as there were Americans, indeed many more, because few people could repeat their own stories consistently, and no two people could have lived or recalled the same one. Yet, for the most part, Americans of the war generation said that they knew "the" war. It had wrenched their lives away from other stories they had intended to create for themselves and their country. For a time, it had made many in both sections care about the war above all. Though they could not have had or have recalled identical experiences, they could share at least briefly a knowledge of the power that the war had wielded over them. In this dimension of the war's story, soldiers often found that their versions had much in common with one another, and many civilians tried to share the combat, though their knowledge depended on imagining deeds others had done. To invest the war with meaning and to make the resulting interpretation convincing to large numbers of people, the war had to be experienced vicariously. People had to live through not only their own war but that of others in order to comprehend what had happened to the country.

Many soldiers afterward spoke or wrote of the war in the same vein as Walt Whitman's comment: "No prepared picture, no elaborated poem, no after-narrative could be what the thing itself was." Yet the war and memories of it led large numbers of veterans to make prodigious, sometimes almost obsessive, efforts to convey their experiences to others. The impossibility of full success did not deter the attempt. In turn, civilians used a wide array of means to know more about the armies' violence. To create some common ground for knowing the war, to give the widest possible access to vicarious participation, gave people a common basis for sustaining the war with popular support and for explaining its course and its results. Whitman's subsequently famous assertion—"The real war will never get in the books"—has proven more popular with literary critics and historians, who quote it in their books about the war, than it was with the Civil War generation. Whitman himself did not write as if he believed that it applied to him. Only by incorporating the minds and lives of vast numbers of people in one great undertaking could the war attain the lasting effects Americans sought. They looked to it for spiritual betterment, for confirmation of political and constitutional beliefs, for communal security and progress. They felt it deeply, eager to do so. This many-sided effort to make war "real" to all was essential for the participants' willingness to embrace destruction with no certain limit. The vicarious war brought them together in justifying their complicity no matter what happened.

Two embodiments of the fighting—attracting the most eyes and representing widely shared attitudes—were generals and newspapers. Through praising or damning generals and by forming a notion of an ideal general, civilians took a hand in the war, proclaiming themselves fit to judge how it should be directed. Newspapers expressed, shaped, and sometimes manufactured impressions of popular opinion; in turn, civilians depended on newspapers for most of their immediate vicarious participation in the war. Despite intertwined rivalries among generals and among newspapermen, the armies' commanders and the press appeared to offer people their best hope of guiding the war.

In civilians' running comments on generals, commanders personified ways the war might be lost or won. To think of a great general meant, for many Americans North and South, to remember Andrew Jackson. Though dead for sixteen years when the war began, he remained the great American example of one who dominated history. He stood in contrast to the trimming, weak conduct of lesser men in later days. Jackson's firmness in opposing South Carolina's attempt to nullify federal law and his well-known hostility toward John C. Calhoun made him attractive to Northerners, especially because, though a slaveholder, he was determined to preserve the union. But Northerners stressed not so much his constitutional opinions as his relentless character, the same quality for which Southerners still honored him. In 1864 Jefferson Davis reminisced about meeting Jackson; Davis "thought him a *great* man, in *character* unsurpassed." People in both sections who believed that their government needed more stern energy spoke of a "military President" or a "dictatorship" with a ruler modeled on Andrew Jackson. Impatient with the Lincoln administration's slowness in acting against slavery, Thaddeus Stevens said in January 1862: "Oh, for six months' resurrection in the flesh of old Jackson! Give him power, and he would handle this rebellion with iron gloves." Wartime difficulties and surprises resulted not from the impossibility of making war serve one's purposes but from a shortage of men with Old Hickory's indomitable will. Jackson cut through legal quibbles, won complete victories, and killed or talked of killing men who crossed him. One of Stevens's constituents wrote that Federal generals should be ashamed of not having defeated the rebels in 1861: "Just grind us out another Jackson for this pressing occasion."

Andrew Jackson's contemporaries had likened him to Napoleon, and Americans during the Civil War also expected their generals to emulate Napoleon. For ambitious officers no career rivaled Bonaparte's in rapid advancement won by native genius, or in combining military success with fame and political power. Many Civil War commanders habitually struck what they imagined to be Napoleonic attitudes in writing and in demeanor. One inducement to do so was the frequency with which newspapers and citizens praised Napoleon-like generals. After the war Grant mocked those Federal generals who had been "always thinking about what Napoleon would do"; on the march into Pennsylvania in 1863 Lee told a British visitor that "he had forgotten all he had ever learned about Napoleon's campaigns." Nevertheless, the mystique of genius held sway. Grant and Lee were made Napoleonic whether they liked it or not. Sherman and Jackson did not shrink from the comparison. Hero-worshippers added to the list of American Napoleons not only McClellan and Beauregard but also such improbable candidates as John B. Floyd. The praise seldom dwelt on the details of Bonaparte's career, least of all his ultimate defeat, but instead conceived his life to have demonstrated that one man could mold battle to his will. Victory required that the people find the Napoleons in their armies and that generals find the Napoleonic qualities in themselves.

The ideal of a brilliant, daring, victorious commander loomed more vividly in the minds of many Americans than did the actual behavior and circumstances of the armies. People explained battles and campaigns by trying to fit events into their preconceived notions of how generals ought to act. Before the first battle of Bull Run, the *New York Herald* announced that George B. McClellan was "the Napoleon of the Present War"; thereafter the *Herald*'s publisher, James Gordon Bennett, assiduously promoted his favorite military Democrat for as long as he could, with the help of correspondents writing laudatory dispatches from the field. In puffing McClellan, Bennett had his own political purposes. He also appealed to a widely shared conception of generalship: "In every war it is a necessity that there be a leader whose deeds excite and whose successes concentrate the fervor of popular enthusiasm." For Napoleon-seekers this was their generals' duty. In hopes of a drastic and, thereby, a short war, the *Cincinnati Commercial* advocated "the Napoleonic policy of swift and decisive action." Stonewall Jackson, "like Napoleon," ruled the minds of his men, who "meet death for his sake and bless him when dying"; Sherman "demolished old established theories, and, like the First Napoleon, introduced new military maxims." The ideal commander, for Northerners and Southerners, had the power that one Confederate attributed to Lee: "He moves his agencies like a god—secret, complicated, vast, resistless, complete." The great general stood apart from ordinary men, who held him in awe.

The tie between generals and the populace was similar in both sections. The *Missouri Democrat,* like many Northerners early in the war, envied Confederates their aggressive commanders of the kind that "an impatient, tax paying people" in the North wanted. Although the general ought to be a genius, his strength, Americans assumed, came from them. A Confederate work entitled *The War and Its Heroes* said: "Each leader is not only a representative, but an impersonation. His heart is the heart of the Army." The public and the army demanded and helped to create their titans. Lincoln was impressed by Edmund Clarence Stedman's poem "Wanted—A Man," which described the ideal general:

> His to marshal us high and far;
> Ours to battle as patriots can.
> When a Hero leads the Holy War!
> Abraham Lincoln, give us a MAN!

No matter how deficient the men to whom Lincoln turned, they could count on grateful praise, for a while. "We have a true hero at last in Rosecrans," said the *Cincinnati Commercial*'s correspondent, "and are no longer forced to the worship of false gods." Joseph Hooker's courage, according to the *Boston Evening Transcript,* "is thoroughly pervaded by intellect . . . and his great fighting characteristic is his power of just and rapid thinking under fire." The general's orders led to deaths, but his mastery promised that his men served a cause destined to prevail through the power of genius.

Writing about Northerners' demand for a military hero, the radical Polish émigré Adam Gurowski complained that Thomas Carlyle had "denationalized some of the best American intellects." Americans ought to honor not individuals but "that collective hero—the people." But

Carlyle offered assurance that the extraordinary hero embodied and controlled the force moving history; people were not prisoners of a historical process more powerful than any human will. Carlyle's celebration of the hero had found receptive readers in America, where it was widely known by the end of the Mexican War. In both wars, Gurowski grumbled, Americans "gave incense to" a general; if he failed "they anxiously look around for another." The great general, in the eyes of most Americans, made his army what John W. Draper called "a mere centre of human force, capable of being directed with mathematical precision along any given line, and brought to bear irresistibly on any given point." In the copy of *Napoleon's Maxims of War* that J. E. B. Stuart gave to Stonewall Jackson, Stuart turned to Maxim IX—"The strength of an army, like the power in mechanics, is estimated by multiplying the mass by the rapidity"—and wrote in the margin: "(M.V.^{2})." Jackson's victories came from his intelligent direction of force. A general, if he had such power, stood as a cynosure of citizens' trust in the intelligibility of the war. The mind of their general was their guarantee against failure and futility.

In the course of the war, army generals felt the public's wrath for their inability to control men and events in the manner expected of them. Yet challenges to the prevailing definition of a great general were rare. Few supporters of the war would have agreed with Thomas Edwin Smith, a Federal officer, when he said: "I used to think war was a *science,* but its a mistake. . . . the great majority of battles are the result of axident. And the *results* are the results of axidents." By questioning belief in purposeful, controllable combat, Smith's conclusion would break the link between fighting and attaining spiritual and political benefits war was supposed to bring. If bloodshed and the outcome of battle were not under the control of a great mind, could beneficial results foretold by other leading minds have any guarantee better than chance? Would not accidental victory in accidental battle offer at best an ephemeral glory not only to generals but also to those who had believed in them? If the general ceased to be a figure of science, he might become a joke. Sketching, in *The Education of Henry Adams,* the multiple failures of nineteenth-century Americans to direct their nation's energies intelligently, Adams included a small tableau of compounded futility: John Hay, having published his and John G. Nicolay's generally unread *Abraham Lincoln: A History,* sometimes looked out the window of his Washington home onto Lafayette Square—dominated by Clark Mills's statue of Andrew Jackson—to see some retired former corps commander totter by; then Hay would remark, as Adams mischievously phrased it, "There is old Dash who broke the rebel lines at Blankburg! Think of his having been a thunderbolt of war!" Generals, unlike historians, once had "swayed the course of empire," as people who talked that way would have put it in wartime, but both had latterly come to the same condition of irrelevance, the name and victory of one general interchangeable with those of another and forgotten by all but Hay. The joke was on the person who remembered the hero.

A large part of newspaper reporting and editorializing on the war sought to show readers that events were conforming to the plans of those who directed the war or would do so as soon as the right men held power. Newspaper details gratified civilians' eagerness to participate in the war, while newspaper interpretations invited readers to believe that they could readily comprehend and manage the war. The standard for combat correspondents and for editorial influence had been set in the Crimean War by *The Times* of London and its foremost reporter, William Howard Russell. They had shown how a newspaper could make itself a principal actor in a nation's experience of war. Combining vivid narratives with comprehensive explanations, balancing inspirational episodes of heroism with pungent censure of commanders' and bureaucrats' incompetence—all expressed so authoritatively as to brook no questioning—*The Times* enabled its readers to visualize their army in the Crimea. Russell's dispatches made him better known than all but a few soldiers. The American newspapers that made fun of Russell's reporting from the United States in 1860 and 1861 paid him the tribute of envy. Before the war's first year ended, the *New York Herald* boasted that American correspondents had surpassed Russell's reporting from the Crimea "in point of truthfulness of statements, graphic power, and personal bravery on the part of the writers." Correspondents aspired to the fame of a Russell, and editors aspired to an influence and a preeminence like that of *The Times*.

Before the war James Gordon Bennett had made the *New York Herald* perhaps the most widely read newspaper in the country, and the *Herald* took fuller advantage of the war than any of its rivals did. Bennett claimed an increase in daily circulation from 100,000 to 123,000 in the first six months of 1862. He outstripped his competitors in number of reporters, copiousness of detail, and speed of news. The *Herald* eventually had sixty correspondents with the armies and spent more than half a million dollars on gathering news about the war. Neither Bennett nor his newspaper was respectable; yet they showed that they could sell the subjects of violence, sex, and race. The British traveler Edward Dicey found that every educated American with whom he spoke denied that the *Herald* "has any political influence whatever"; still, he said, "I find they all read it. . . . The *Herald* is a power in the country." Secretary of the Navy Gideon Welles noticed with displeasure that the New York papers, which the rest of the country imitated, took their "tone and direction" from the *Herald,* even when they were denying that they did so. Southern readers saw in the *Herald*'s call to crush the South "glimpses of the fires of hell."

The *Herald*'s wartime success simply drew the largest profit from a demand for news encountered by all papers. *Harper's Weekly* commented in June 1862: "News of the War! We all live on it. Few of us but would prefer our newspaper in these times to our breakfast." Editors often published several long accounts of a battle, reprinting other papers' dispatches. Soldiers were eager to read about themselves; citizens were impatient to know what the army was doing. During the fighting at Fair Oaks, Virginia, vendors of New York papers sold copies to men on the battlefield. Minnie Davis, recalling in later years her days as a slave, said that her mother "would steal the newspapers and read up about the war, and she kept the other slaves posted as to how the war was progressing." Although Southern papers had much smaller resources for gathering news and had lesser circulations, they fed a demand like that in the North. Papers in each section reprinted material from those in the other, most often editorials revealing how outrageously the enemy talked, but also battle narratives and officers' reports, all piling up details for an insatiable market. Editors tried to make the war a victory for their papers as well as their cause. The *Herald* bragged about its "illimitable circulation" and its great influence on many people's lives. The *Philadelphia Inquirer* boasted on April 11, 1865, that it had covered the city with an extra, reporting Lee's surrender, by midnight of April 9—the same day Lee and Grant had met—and that its edition of April 10 had sold almost 80,000 copies. This showed Philadelphia's enterprise and public spirit, as well as "the advantages THE INQUIRER possesses as an advertising medium." After his six-month visit to the United States, Edward Dicey concluded: "The American might be defined as a newspaper-reading animal."

Like Bennett, many Northern and Southern editors claimed to influence the minds of the people. John Swinton of the *New York Times*, outraged by Grant's restrictions on a reporter, wrote threateningly to Elihu B. Washburne: "A general is for a day—his power for an hour. The press is forever, and its power permanent and all-pervading." The newspapers' self-praise agreed with their critics that the press heeded public moods and demands, while also trying to stimulate readers' support for editors' views of the war. The papers professed to be authoritative in narratives, in political principles, and in judgments on the conduct of the war. They also intensified anxieties that could be relieved by authoritative answers. S. M. Johnson, who had written editorials for the *Herald* in the 1850s, concluded in May 1863 that a newspaper could no longer "capture the people" by force of ability and reasoning. Editors of the 1850s had envisioned newspapers as an influential force for cultural progress. But, during the Civil War, "we have an entirely different and *far less intelligent* public sentiment . . . a public sentiment feeding on excitement & passion." Though Johnson overstated the contrast between the decades, he had good grounds to conclude that the press during the war was doing less to educate than to excite. The papers with the largest circulations encouraged their readers' support for vigorous war-making. The *Chattanooga Rebel* claimed that the Southern press was "the inspiring power" behind the Confederate army's enthusiasm: "A united Press is synonymous with a united people."

The effort to link their readers with the war constrained newspapers even as it enhanced their importance. They reported selectively: to read about desertion, straggling, cowardice, or the breakdown of units in combat, except those of the enemy, was uncommon. Reporters encouraged readers to believe in decisive combat and the control of the battlefield by genius, helping them to this view by not describing all facets of the fighting. In March 1862, Lieutenant Stephen Minot Weld, a staff officer in the Army of the Potomac, helped a *Herald* reporter, Leonard A. Hendricks, copy his account of McClellan's advance into abandoned Confederate positions near Washington. Weld listened with amusement as Hendricks read out "the usual stereotyped phrases about the enthusiasm, alacrity, etc., of the soldiers," saying as an aside "big lie" after each phrase. When Weld suggested that there had been many Federal stragglers, not just a few, as the dispatch reported, Hendricks replied: "Oh, I know it, still I must write it so." Reporters' narratives grew less fantastic later in the war, but still strove for lurid effects, attracting a large audience. Editions of newspapers containing details of a major battle often sold five times the usual number of copies in Northern cities.

Though editors pushed forward their favorite generals and policies, the press also strove to give readers details to satisfy their curiosity or confirm their preconceptions. Newspapers led opinion only by hurrying to exaggerate it. Northerners and Southerners commented on the speed with which the papers shifted their imperturbable certitude to accommodate popular moods and unexpected outcomes on the battlefield. Southern papers early in 1864 praised Joseph E. Johnston's defensive position in northern Georgia, along Rocky Face Ridge, as the best possible. But Ben Pope, a Confederate soldier, predicted that, if Johnston failed there, "a host of writers will spring up, whose lucubrations will teem with severe criticisms upon the disadvantages &c of this, the selected line for receiving the enemy." After General William S. Rosecrans was defeated at Chickamauga and removed from command of the Army of the Cumberland, Mary A. Palmer wrote to her husband, a corps commander: "The papers are full of stories about Rosecrans *having fits* eating opium and a great many other things. how I should hate to have you picked to pieces as they do all that once get under the peoples displeasure." The oft-proclaimed power of the press could not be clearly distinguished from the power of the people—that is, from the publishing of widely held opinions and widely shared emotions. Newspapers supporting the war, though diverse, promoted in both North and South the belief in a great national public, Federal or Confederate, which felt the war as one person, which demanded success, and which no leader dared defy.

The communication between the press and the people, the blending of the minds of the two, was fullest in urging on and vicariously reliving the war's violence. In her diary entry of July 4, 1862, Ella Gertrude Clanton Thomas recorded her reactions while reading a Southern newspaper's account of the battle of Gaines' Mill. She was thrilled by the reporter's version of the storming of Federal artillery by Confederate troops. "I read *this* and my *heart beat loud* and strong but I felt my eye flash in admiration of such dauntless courage . . . I followed them in spirit and could understand the fixed determination of our men never to surrender." She wanted, as she had said a month before, " 'War to the knife and the knife to the hilt.' . . . I wish this war ended—the sooner we fight it out the better." She was the kind of reader, uniting anxiety and belligerence, for whom newspapermen in both sections wrote. Mary Hall, engaged to an officer in Sherman's army, told a friend: "They anticipate a dreadful battle at Atlanta and I can hardly wait for the arrival of the morning papers." Until the War Department stopped the practice, Northern newspapers published long lists of casualties, by name, specifying what part of the body each man had been wounded in or noting simply "killed." Southern newspapers continued such lists throughout the war. Some critics, especially in the armies, believed that the avidity with which civilians sought casualty lists and battle narratives went beyond concern for loved ones or for the nation's cause to become what the Boston minister John F. W. Ware called a "sickly craving." While Meade was being urged to keep the Army of the Potomac active in December 1863, Colonel Charles Wainwright commented that the newspapers did not want the army to settle into winter camp. "The public have got a taste for blood, and want more excitement. A week passed without reports of a battle with thousands killed and wounded—is very dull, rendering the papers hardly worth reading." No matter how large it grew, the war could not surfeit the public's "insatiable appetite for horrible news and rumors," in the words of the *Cincinnati Enquirer*.

When Mathew Brady exhibited in galleries his photographs of corpses lying on the battlefield, newspaper and magazine reviewers recognized a kindred purpose in his medium and in theirs: to bring the war to civilians vividly. The *Herald* said of the pictures: "Minute as are the features of the dead . . . you can, by bringing a magnifying glass to bear on them, identify not merely their general outline but actual expression. This, in many instances, is perfectly horrible, and shows through what tortures the poor victims must have passed before they were relieved from their sufferings." In a gallery the public could see part of the war. *Harper's Weekly* commented on another photographic exhibit: "The actuality of these views, the distinct detail, and the inflexible veracity, make them invaluable." Photographs, like reporters' prose, might sometimes be contrived, sentimental, deceptive; but both responded to a widespread desire to witness the dying. The urge to combat—sustained, encouraged, sometimes imagined where it did not exist—pervaded the most widely available descriptions of war. Despite editors' differences over politicians and generals, the common currency of newspaper language throughout America consisted of the words for fighting.

As so much attention to generals and newspapers suggests, civilians not only wanted to influence and to understand events, but also wanted to experience some of combat's intensity. They put themselves as close to soldiers as possible or, vicariously, in a soldier's place. Many people on both sides took combat to heart, not always with reluctance or distress, and found an emotional exaltation in doing so. If the nation's exertion of its power gave its citizens a fuller public identity, the process marked them lastingly, as combat marked soldiers. The quality of the experience varied widely, but those who committed themselves to the war found that they were in it as players and could not easily get out. The premises of the play—even its implausibilities of plot—became their reality yet were not under their control. Northerners and Southerners pursued clearly stated, intelligible goals in fighting each other, and they directed their resources toward their purposes more systematically than almost anyone would have thought possible at the start of 1861. At the same time, their experience of war was partly a flight into unreason: into visions of purgation and redemption, into anticipation and intuition and spiritual apotheosis, into bloodshed that was not only intentional pursuit of interests of state but was also sacramental, erotic, mystical, and strangely gratifying. This process of taking the war to heart, believing that it would change everyone, worked as strongly as any other influence toward making it more inclusive and more destructive.

Among Northerners, Abraham Lincoln made himself the preeminent example of the noncombatant united to the war, seeming to draw into himself the pain of its destructiveness. People said that he looked haggard and careworn, like a man "whose nights are sleepless, and whose days are comfortless." Some thought that his rising and falling spirits were attuned to the course of the war. Perhaps he reached his lowest point when Hooker withdrew the Army of the Potomac north of the Rappahannock after the battle of Chancellorsville. The journalist Noah Brooks later recalled: "Never, as long as I knew him, did he seem to be so broken, so dispirited, so ghostlike." His appearance invited psychological explanations. Some Republicans said that he was too sensitive, too kind to rebels, deserters, and cowards; he must be keenly aware of his own inadequacies, they thought. Peace-minded Democrats believed that he ought to be haunted by feelings of guilt. After Chancellorsville the *Dubuque Herald* commented: "No wonder the President looks wretched; no wonder he looks as if the ghosts of half a million of his slaughtered countrymen were pointing to their ghastly wounds, and accusing him of being their murderer!" Lincoln's admirers, too, suggested that he felt and embodied the war to an extraordinary degree. Early in 1863 Secretary Seward likened him to Jesus and his task as president to the Savior's.

As commander-in-chief, Lincoln had more responsibility for combat than any other civilian. He summoned men to the army; he chose their commanders; he repeatedly urged his generals to fight—to shorten the war by continual combat. Northerners and Southerners routinely spoke of the war as a personal undertaking of Lincoln's, as if he alone sustained and directed the Federal effort. Lincoln accepted the role figuratively, representing the North's resolve to crush rebellion by force. After making Grant lieutenant general in 1864, Lincoln, ready to leave military decisions to the generals, told Grant that earlier in the war he had given other commanders specific orders to fight because they procrastinated and because he felt "the pressure from the people at the North and Congress, *which was always with him.*" When those generals had obeyed him, then failed in battle, Lincoln had exclaimed: "What will the country say!"

Beyond his official function as agent of the North's war, Lincoln showed a strong interest in combat. He seemed fascinated by the skirmishing he saw at Fort Stevens during Jubal Early's raid into Maryland. Admiral David Dixon Porter found that Lincoln had a remarkable ability to visualize the localities where the fighting took place; he evidently devoted much effort to doing so. He said that he could have whipped Lee's army in Maryland before it got back across the Potomac after the battle of Gettysburg. And during Lincoln's last visit to the Army of the Potomac, Grant noticed that he "was really most anxious to see the army, and be with it in its final struggle." Like many people, Lincoln wanted to be a witness, at least in his mind's eye, to the fighting he helped bring about. His persuasiveness as president, his prospects for renomination and re-election, his stature in history—to which he devoted much care—turned in large part on the course of combat. If he were to be a great man, the war would make him one, as it made the union a nation.

Lincoln's carefully crafted public letters and addresses became the principal summaries of the justifications for the North's intent to fight. They won praise for expressing the war's meaning even before his death shed a glow on all his acts and words. Charles Sumner, vain about his own rhetorical skills, wrote: "We must all admit that he has said some things better than any body else could have said them." For his admirers Lincoln's gift lay in touching the feelings agitated by bloodshed. *Harper's Weekly* praised the words of the Gettysburg Address: "They can not be read, even, without kindling emotion." Defending him against the charge that he had prolonged slavery, his supporters argued that his words had done more than anyone else had done to convince the public that the war must end slavery. Yet Lincoln's prominence in that cause came only with intensifying war. Reading the proposals for gradual emancipation and colonization of slaves in Lincoln's message of December 1, 1862, Cyrus Clay Carpenter, later governor of Iowa, recognized the same arguments Henry Clay had used. Carpenter drew an unfavorable contrast between Clay's having developed these ideas as "cool thoughts of a great man in times of profound peace" and Lincoln's reaching them only by having them "driven into his head by the smell of burning Powder, the boom of Canon, the flame of burning towns, and the groans of dying men." Whether the war was needed to persuade Lincoln or only to enable him to persuade others, his blend of mystical images of consecration with rational arguments from self-interest reverted to the war as the great teacher whose spokesman he was. He achieved this power of expression seemingly because he experienced the war with singular intensity. He promoted the war's results through his words; his eloquence implied that he knew the suffering of all. Private Willie Scott, a black soldier, wrote of Lincoln: "if [he] had not went trough what he has where would the Colord man been he would been in slavery."

As a vicarious combatant, Lincoln achieved his fullest presence in the war through his popularity among Federal soldiers. Among them he had a reputation for kindliness and clemency. They gave him and the Republicans the overwhelming majority of their votes; as they knew better than anyone else, his victory meant persevering in the war. On the day of his second inauguration they celebrated in camp and made him one of them now that he, like many of them, had re-enlisted "in the veteran service." Private John Walter Lee wrote to his father about Lincoln: "He has proved a good and faithfull soldier." News of Lincoln's assassination brought out signs of soldiers' attachment to him. He was the representative of their purpose in fighting; they reacted to his death as if the rebellion had tried to nullify their work by killing their friend. Veterans of three or four years of combat—men who flinched at few sights of death—wept openly. One of them wrote: "No Wone hever node the Soldiers Love fore the Late President till Now." Despite Lincoln's reputation for forgiveness, the soldiers were not altogether false to his memory when they wanted to avenge his murder by leveling Southern cities, killing Confederate prisoners, and attacking civilians more severely than they had yet done. Severity had become their way of winning the war, with Lincoln's approval. If Sherman's men had destroyed Raleigh for revenge, as some spoke of doing, they would have been continuing a pattern of punishment Lincoln had sanctioned.

In death Lincoln joined the war's military casualties. A soldier's wife said: "When I think of the death of our President, it seems as if it was my own flesh and blood that had been called away." Lincoln's death was "a sacrifice upon the altar of Union and Liberty as certainly as that of any soldier who fell in battle." He had finally attained the full union with combat toward which his career as president had always tended. He had told of being with the army in his dreams. On the last night of 1862, after news of fighting at Murfreesboro, he dreamed of corpses on a battlefield in Tennessee, of gunfire in the night, of exhausted soldiers in the rain, and of crowds reading casualty lists posted at Willard's Hotel near the White House. At a cabinet meeting on April 14, 1865, Lincoln described a recurring dream in which he seemed to be on a singular vessel moving rapidly toward an indefinite shore. The dream, he said, had preceded almost every important military event, including the firing on Fort Sumter, the battles of Bull Run, Antietam, Stones River, and Gettysburg, as well as the fall of Vicksburg and of Wilmington. He had come to associate it with good news. Having dreamed it again on the night of April 13, he expected to hear soon from Sherman in North Carolina. Such ties to war put Lincoln into combat in ways beyond his preferring victory and his insisting that the army fight. His empathy, as his contemporaries imagined it, brought him closer to a state of mind wherein Federal victories belonged as much to him as to the soldiers, while the costs in wounds and death fell, as with combatants, on men he knew and finally, after the last dream, on him. Americans who revered Lincoln after his death found in his comprehensive spiritual experience of the war a fitting emblem of the passion and the sensibility of the nation's involvement in combat. By the same token, R. L. Dabney, William Preston Johnston, and other Southerners who said that General Lee died of a broken heart did not mean to offer a physiological diagnosis; they were making a figurative statement about the pain of Confederate defeat. For them, Lee's exceptionally sensitive character had absorbed and shared a larger portion of the feelings affecting Southerners, and his last years had acted out more intensely their shared reaction to the aftermath of the war.

In his memoirs Matthew H. Jamison, a veteran of Sherman's army, said: "No intelligent man questions the visions that crossed the disk of Abraham Lincoln's slumbers—that wonderful, startling portent of tremendous events." Jamison recalled his own portent: ten years before the war he had dreamed of a marching column of cavalry, infantry, artillery, and supply wagons, a sight he had never seen in life or in pictures but which grew familiar during the war. In retrospect he called that dream "the token of a coming day." Northerners and Southerners recorded dreams foretelling combat, sometimes casting the fate of one man in the fight, sometimes seeing the next battle or anticipating the coming of the war itself. In 1863 Elizabeth Oakes Smith, a Virginian, recalled a vision that had come to her in the summer of 1859: "I saw the immense camp of a vast soldiery—slaughter and demolition—sights to harrow up the soul—and then predicted—'there will be war—very soon will war come upon us—a terrible strife, which will last twenty years.' " Whatever predictive power dreams may have had—and it was not hard for civilians in wartime, especially Lincoln, to know that a battle was imminent—dreams of the war revealed some people's desire or compulsion to feel the battles more keenly. With S. B. Dunn, a teacher in Cambridge, Illinois, this feeling expressed itself in her wish to act. She dreamed that she visited Grant's army besieging Vicksburg to make sure that the city would fall. The next day she wrote: "I more than ever wish I was a man that I might fill one place left vacant by some brave soldier. At times when I first hear of the fearful loss of life in some engagements I can scarcely proceed with my duties in womans province."

Though the premonitory visions took the mind to the battlefield, they often, like Lincoln's, left the dreamer passively borne by the war, threatened or destroyed by it, as soldiers were. In Mississippi, Virginia, Ohio, and presumably elsewhere, variant versions of a supposedly predictive dream circulated in private and in the press. According to several accounts of it, a soldier dreamed that he would die the next day, that the greatest battle of the war would then be fought, and that peace would soon follow. The versions agreed that the soldier died. The dreamer's death seemed dramatically necessary to the story, lending a mysterious credibility to the rest of his prophecy. As with Lincoln's recurring dream, a battle ensued, auspicious because it seemed to promise peace, which nevertheless did not follow. More than a year before Lincoln said publicly that the war ruled him, not he the war, a Maryland politician gave the president a role that had the paradoxical logic of war dreams, wherein the actor was also a passive seer: "This new army will move down slowly like a glacier, but irresistibly. Mr. Lincoln will sit on it moving with it, possibly thinking he directs it, but really he will have as much to do with it as the bear on a glacier. After a while these people will be exhausted." Dreams gave civilians sensations akin to those of soldiers: fright, rage, awe, gruesome suffering, watching events unfold apparently beyond control. Premonitions and intuitions of war or of war's episodes were ruled by the violence, not by the mind to which the premonitions came. To imagine the end was not to fix the time of its coming. The last battle proved elusive; visions of death kept coming.

For some people's recollections of war experiences, the dream as a figure of speech most aptly expressed their sensation of having seen and done things that, upon reflection, could hardly have been real. A former delegate for the U. S. Christian Commission, who had spent a month with Sherman's army, wrote in 1866: "I look back upon the scenes there witnessed as upon a strange, terrible dream . . . indeed the whole experience of four dreadful years of war has a strange air of unreality almost in spite of its multiplied and sad evidences." Such a dream simile did not deny the reality of the experiences. They were the kinds of memories Walt Whitman had in mind when he said that the real war would not get in the books. They seemed dreamlike because they consisted of events remote from ordinary peacetime life, and their remoteness lay partly in their sabotaging the customary assumption that mind and will guided behavior. About ten days after Lee's surrender a Confederate veteran, Charles Woodward Hutson, said of the war: "The whole thing seems sometimes a fearful dream, too horrible to be real." Like the anticipatory dreams and visions in antebellum days and wartime, the war itself came as an unbidden, overpowering, inescapable series of events that refused to conform to conventional understanding. Everyone had dreams; no one thought they were literally true. But they remained in the memory. Similarly, the memory of waking deeds that defied rationalization could be consigned to the category of experience that could hardly be true. The problem of comprehension lay not so much in remembering what had happened as in understanding how it could have been allowed to happen among people who had set out to direct their own history.

Among citizens who felt the war's emotions strongly, the threat of powerlessness often took the form of anxiety about combat. They worried about soldiers whom they knew, the outcome of battles, the scale of casualties, and the management of the war. Sometimes distant civilians knew by telegraph, as New Yorkers and others did on December 13, 1862, that fighting was under way at the moment. Anna Shaw Curtis wrote to a friend: "You cannot imagine the feeling of knowing that there is a battle going on. It makes us so nervous." In other cases, people accustomed to hearing about an engagement only after it had ended would imagine what might be happening that had not yet been reported. They wrote diary entries like Samuel A. Wildman's: "Sunday is such a great day for battles. I wonder if fighting is not going on somewhere now. It is about time for another fight." Magazines and bookdealers provided maps on which one could chart the paths of the armies, moving pins day by day. Travelers in the North and in the South noticed a prevalent preoccupation with the war; events and rumors led civilians through cycles of suspense, fear, celebration, and gloom. A slave during the war, H. C. Bruce later recalled black people's conversations about the most recent word from the front: "When the news came that a battle was fought and won by Union troops, they rejoiced, and were correspondingly depressed when they saw their masters rejoicing, for they knew the cause thereof." People often said that such sustained apprehension exhausted them or threatened their mental balance. In 1863 a Virginia doctor estimated that "the anxiety brought on by the war" had so reduced natural resistance to disease that "the average of deaths is 30 per ct greater among the non-combatant population than before the war." Those who did not succumb to hopelessness most easily resolved tension by urging sustained, drastic fighting to end the war more quickly. Public officials felt this pressure. John Codman Ropes, later a historian of the war, suggested in 1863 that a record of the "fleeting impressions on the public mind" of despondency, exultation, hope, dissatisfaction, and the like would aid historians. Though the effect of such impressions could not easily be traced with precision and might be forgotten quickly once the war ended, they were, he thought, "very influential in shaping the course of the government, and of individuals in high places." Leaders on both sides knew the need to reassure their followers that fighting was making progress. The corrective for inconclusive, ill-managed combat was more combat.

Many noncombatants got closer to the war by traveling to the armies. Encampments of any duration attracted a stream of civilians. Women went long distances to be near husbands and relatives in the army. During the siege of Vicksburg in June 1863 a "great crowd" of them came down the Mississippi; though they were not allowed to come up the Yazoo River, some women reached the northernmost Federal lines. After hearing of a battle, large numbers of citizens headed for the scene, some to work as temporary nurses, others to find wounded relatives or the bodies of dead ones. At Gettysburg only Northerners could do so; during the summer of 1863 platforms at railroad stations in Harrisburg and Philadelphia were piled with coffins and India rubber sacks containing corpses in transit. Two weeks after the battle of Chancellorsville, Northern and Southern civilians met in the Wilderness on a common errand. Visiting Grant's army in the Mississippi Valley, one man said that if he could not find his son's body his wife would become insane. Day and night she cried: "Give me back my dead."

The armies' camps and battlefields fascinated many who had no personal or charitable mission. Though the civilians who took picnic lunches to eat while watching the first battle of Bull Run came in for ridicule after their quick retreat, combat never ceased to attract the curious. Richmonders climbed their city's hills to watch and listen to the exchange of artillery fire during the Seven Days battles; a minister later wrote that they were thinking about the hundreds of men "an hour before in joyous health now wounded and dying." Marylanders and Pennsylvanians gathered on the hills around Sharpsburg to watch the battle of Antietam, seeing more bloodshed than did spectators on any other day. As soon as battles ended, their sites became the tourist attractions they still are. As Southerners had done outside Manassas and Richmond, Northerners descended on Gettysburg. On July 5, 1863, nearby residents "came in Swarms to Sweep & plunder the battle grounds." They gathered spent lead to sell. Three weeks later, the field was still strewn with broken guns, clothing, knapsacks, cartridge boxes, ammunition, and some unburied Confederate corpses. The government forbade removal of anything by sightseers, but they concealed souvenirs in their clothes as they left. "All who come from a distance naturally desire to return home with some trophy of war." Dedication of the Federal cemetery in November brought another crowd. Reinterment of soldiers' remains continued during the winter, and citizens still came from all parts of the North to see the battlefield. By December 1865 the *Boston Evening Transcript* could report that the field had been almost stripped of "the more coveted relics." A person might hunt for hours without finding a Minié ball. Pieces of the battle of Gettysburg had been dispersed across the nation for which the winners had fought. Civilians traveling to the vicinity of the war—governors, soldiers' relatives, reporters, nurses, preachers, sutlers, photographers, embalmers, prostitutes of both sexes, and "greedy sight-seers . . . there to gratify their morbid curiosity"—represented in their actions the diversity of concerns that made the battlefield a cynosure of attention for Americans throughout the continent. In the process they blurred or overlapped the line between spectators and actors, bringing themselves more fully under the war's influence.

For some women their soldiers'-aid societies, sanitary fairs, and new organizations in support of the war did not suffice as a way to help the cause. They wanted to throw themselves into war as much in the manner of soldiers as possible. They recorded thoughts like those of Caroline Kean Davis, a Virginian: "I have the greatest desire to be active & useful now. I sometimes wish I was a *man* that I might take my place among the gallant defenders of our rights." Thousands of such women became nurses, touching combat by tending to its aftermath. A Southern woman in Massachusetts at the outbreak of war commented sardonically on the reaction of women there: "Some of the young Ladies are exceedingly anxious to imitate Florence Nightingale & distinguish themselves in the army." In the British hospitals of the Crimean War, Florence Nightingale had made herself famous for offsetting inefficiency in the army's administration and logistics, which had worsened disease and suffering among soldiers. Among Civil War nurses on both sides, "efficiency" was a word of highest praise. Mary A. Bickerdyke, who worked with Sherman's army, won praise as much for her "executive ability" as for her "all-embracing motherhood." A Confederate soldier described a nurse from Alabama as "a Napoleon of her department ... she possesses all the energy and independence of Stonewall Jackson."

A desire to emulate Florence Nightingale and to make women's aid to the American armies businesslike drew not just on nurses' wish for fame and power but also on their eagerness to sacrifice. They likened themselves to the soldiers or spoke of soldiers and nurses as "a band of Brothers and Sisters drawn together in one common cause." In this outlook the crucial distinction was no longer the old one between the man who in war "could assert his manhood, prove his courage, and win his laurels" and the woman who could only "follow her hero in thoughts and dreams." Rather, those who went to the war distinguished themselves from those who did not. Mary Bickerdyke told her young sons that she had to go with Sherman's men because soldiers—and, by implication, nurses—were protecting the homes of "the delicate gentlemen of our land." For women who strongly felt the difference between service and security, staying at home grew hard to bear. Evy Kell longed to "do *something*" and envied women who helped wounded Confederates in Atlanta; Emilie Quiner, a teacher in Madison, Wisconsin, reproached herself for not returning to a Federal hospital in Memphis where she had worked for several weeks after the fall of Vicksburg. "It seemed as though I had almost committed a crime in not going," she said.

Many women in the army hospitals died of communicable diseases or impaired their health. At least one-tenth of the nurses suffered a physical breakdown. Yet they often gloried in risks they ran. Warned that she would die if she continued to overwork herself, Margaret Elizabeth Breckinridge replied: "What if I do? Shall men come here and die by tens of thousands for us, and shall no woman be found to die for them?" In

July 1864 she died of erysipelas. A nurse in Annapolis, knowing she was dying, asked to be given a military burial among soldiers' graves. Her body was escorted by an honor guard, who fired a salute over her grave. Again and again women described their service in the hospitals as a duty, a compulsion, and a joy—"so sorry for the *necessity,* so *glad* for the *opportunity,*" in Clara Barton's words. They celebrated the efficacy of action, analogous to combat, as close to combat as they could get. Some of those most intensely devoted to war nursing knew that friends might think their enthusiasm odd or accuse them of indulging "morbid sympathy." But their aberration consisted of feeling dissatisfied with a civilian's more distant experience of war. The gap between citizens' support of fighting and soldiers' suffering troubled them. They wanted to cross to the soldiers' side or go near the war as representatives of civilians' empathy. Applying for a position as a nurse in Washington, a soldier's wife wrote: "I have thought so much of it of late that I have actually suffered myself." The most earnest nurses and the women wishing to join them tried to surrender themselves wholly to the conflict.

Of course, no one felt the capricious power of the war more fully than the young men it killed or wounded. Many civilians eager to be near the war in person or in imagination described these casualties, as did other soldiers. The sufferers' frailty held a strong fascination. From vigor and strength they suddenly had been transformed into the dead and the dying. For many people this commonplace fact of war never lost its thrill. As supporters and participants they made the war and took a keen interest in its effects, however sad but necessary. Recording their reactions to the sights and reports of the battlefield and the hospital, writers often dwelt on the physical beauty of the dying young men. The dying of beautiful youths made battles and hospitals more awful and yet more ennobling for survivors. Witnesses dwelt on blond hair, handsome features, lithe physiques, and the war's destruction of these. Counting the war's cost, Elizabeth Cady Stanton spoke of the dying of "our fair-haired boys," and Congressman Albert Gallatin Riddle imagined the casualties as "our broad-browed, open-eyed youths . . . pure as the mothers who bore them, and beautiful as their sisters in their homes." Sentimental songs and verse, such as "The Dying Soldier Boy" and "The Angel of the Hospital," gave civilians a chance to weep but hardly surpassed the effects for which reporters reached in describing corpses for the newspapers. "A remarkably sweet and youthful face was that of a rebel boy. Scarce eighteen, and as fair as a maiden, with quite small hands, long hair of the pale golden hue that auburn changes to when much in the sun, and curling at the ends," a *Cincinnati Gazette* correspondent wrote at Vicksburg. James Dinwiddie, a Virginian walking among the dead after the battle of Gaines' Mill, spent a long time gazing "in mute admiration" and "shedding a tear" over the body of a courageous Federal soldier "of splendid form face & figure." Preoccupation with young soldiers' beauty was partly erotic. Charles Benton, a Federal veteran, said in his memoirs that when he read Walt Whitman after the war he understood from his own experience working in hospitals, being hugged by "a beardless boy, with flaxen hair and sky-blue eyes," the close of Whitman's poem "The Wound-Dresser":

> I sit by the restless all the dark night, some are so
>   young,
> Some suffer so much, I recall the experience sweet and
>   sad,
> (Many a soldier's loving arms about this neck have
>   cross'd and rested,
> Many a soldier's kiss dwells on these bearded lips.)

Clara Barton, E. N. Harris, Phoebe Yates Pember, and other women had vivid memories of "spiritualized" youths they had helped or embraced, all of whom seem to have had "a graceful head of hair," "bewildered blue eyes," a "beautiful face and manly form."

The Civil War generation was familiar with the deaths of young people in peacetime. The sadness of youth and beauty cut off at their flowering was a staple of popular fiction and verse. These literary conventions easily assimilated the new scenes brought by the war. Yet combat was a destroyer different from the death that came in novels and verse—one with which the admirers of beautiful soldiers had an affinity that they did not have with peacetime illnesses and misfortunes, one which non-combatants encouraged despite mourning. The fascination with good-looking, dying soldiers partly expressed civilians' and soldiers' sense of the dread power of the growing war: it somehow looked greater when it struck down those who were stronger, more attractive than they. The scene almost always had some of the same elements: the youth was desperately wounded, sick, or dying; he reached a heightened emotional state full of passionate devotion to his family and his cause; he expressed heartfelt gratitude for the smallest kindnesses; despite his youth and his former strength, he had grown weaker than the civilian who aided him. The beautiful young men lay helpless, dependent on those who envied their glamor, pitied their fate, and admired their devotion. When a soldier nursed by Clara Barton reproved her later for not supporting an early peace in 1863, she reminded him that he had been "worn and exhausted . . . until *my* weak arm had greater strength than his, and could aid him." Civilians could triumph in the war by admiring yet outlasting soldiers' weak strength and dying youth. They had felt the effects of violence intensely and demonstratively without being destroyed by it. Mysteriously, soldiers' deaths could make civilians feel stronger. A minister who kissed a dying boy at Malvern Hill later recalled having prayed "that we who were spectators might be the truer and braver for what we had seen." The beautiful young men lived on in the survivors' memories. Long after the war, when asked about the price he had paid in impaired health as a result of his nursing work in Washington, Whitman summarized the compensations: "I got the boys, I got the Leaves." Beyond the erotic or sexual interest the boys held for Whitman or the women in the hospitals or others, the boys also embodied the war, as they appeared in poetry—including the "Drum-Taps" section of *Leaves of Grass*—in political speeches, in women's proud war work. The crucial part of Whitman's blunt phrasing, applicable to many people in the North and the South, was the expression "I got." Through their ties to soldiers, especially the casualties, they "got" the war. To make it theirs they used the boys they loved.

Conventions of popular literature shaped many Americans' expectations when war began. The glory of combat in a righteous cause, the grand figure heroes would cut as they strode through momentous events, appealed to fancy and to vanity. Veterans wryly recalled in later years their boyhood eagerness to become great soldiers like the ones they had read about. Stories of the Revolutionary War, the Napoleonic Wars, and the Mexican War fed their imagination, as did novels set in recent times or in a remote romantic past. In the 1850s teen-aged sons of abolitionists in Lima, Indiana, read *Uncle Tom's Cabin* and played a war game in which one group of boys were slaveholding Southerners inside a snow fort and another group attacked the fort to take the slaves and send them to Canada. Women, too, could win fame by rising to greatness in wartime. During the summer of 1864 a Virginian, James Madison Brannock, wrote to his wife about one of their acquaintances: "I presume Mollie Terry was glad that it fell to her lot to wait on those poor wounded Kentuckians. You know she used to say she would like to live during a revolution & be a Heroine." In the war stories the main characters dominated events, undergoing severe tests the better to show their strength, thereby winning the adulation of all. War was a setting for heroes, a straightforward narrative with conflict but not confusion, suspense but not doubt. At the center of the story were the leading figures, not violence itself.

After veterans had seen war, their earlier notions struck them as almost laughable; yet they testified to the pull those visions of imaginary glory had exerted on them. Their experience confirmed what Joseph Conrad later wrote: "We are the creatures of our light literature much more than is generally suspected in a world which prides itself on being scientific and practical, and in possession of incontrovertible theories." Reading and the youthful conceits it fostered did not cause the Civil War but did influence the expectations people took into war. Those expectations proved to be extraordinarily durable in the face of disillusionment, perhaps partly because they offset one main source of disillusionment: the vulnerability and insignificance of the self-imagined hero. Sharing the chance to demonstrate power and win glory was the heart of the communal experience of vicarious war. Without it the triumph would dissolve. The "light literature" of adventures and personal victories in war retained much of its popularity. Veterans added to it with their stories. Early in the twentieth century Douglas Southall Freeman found that former Confederates and those who wrote about them were giving their war "the glamour that makes the old man's tale thrilling to the youth and thereby stirs the military ardor of the new generation until it, in turn, is disillusioned by the hellish realities of war." The process Freeman described in 1939 elicited in 1880 General Sherman's best-known utterance. Speaking extemporaneously to veterans in Columbus, Ohio, he called them "boys," as usual, but he also used the word to refer to youngsters: "There is many a boy here to-day who looks on war as all glory, but, boys, it is all hell. You can bear this warning voice to generations yet to come." In its original setting Sherman's statement—afterward usually quoted as "war is hell"—was neither a prowar justification of atrocities nor an antiwar vision of chaos; it was an admonition to young people and, by extension, to all who expected war to resemble the popular descriptions of it.

Though the Civil War destroyed many fantasies of easy glamor, showing people that they had not known what they were committing themselves to, its supporters quickly adjusted to its growing violence. One could be appalled by inconclusive bloodshed, yet foresee worse to come and not shrink from it. In Washington, Texas, J. D. McAdoo anticipated resumption of the armies' active operations in the spring: "I think the campaign of 1863 will so far eclipse that of 1862, in its magnitude and slaughter that the latter will be comparatively forgotten. The mightiest contest of modern times, if not of all time, will occur in the Mississippi this spring and summer." One could almost take pride in realizing that Americans were capable of so stupendous a war. Notwithstanding their professed expectations of short, chivalrous war, it was possible that civilians had not been altogether surprised when bloodshed left few Americans untouched. They wanted war to consume the enemy's pride, to demonstrate who were the real Americans in a victory for one version of the nation and an abasement of the other. If the resolution required massive violence, it would be the more satisfactory because it had been catastrophic. How had the naive notions prevalent at the start given way so readily to killing on a scale supposedly unimaginable? Two veterans, John W. DeForest and Sidney Lanier, included set-piece passages on popular war enthusiasm in their respective Civil War novels, *Miss Ravenel's Conversion from Secession to Loyalty* and *Tiger-Lilies*, both published in 1867. They stressed the eagerness with which Americans had accepted war and had made it more terrible than that of other peoples. Writing an elaborate conceit about "the blood-red flower of war"— manured by human bones, sprinkled by tears, and growing only near a stream of human blood—Lanier referred to the Civil War, "grown in North America by two wealthy landed proprietors," as "the grandest specimen of modern horticulture." He described an "afflatus of war" sweeping through the South like a great wind, touching everyone. DeForest similarly dwelt on the unique vigor of Americans' zeal for destruction: "The excitement of Germany at the opening of the Thirty Years' War, of England previous to the Cromwellian struggle, was torpid and partial in comparison with this outburst of a modern, reading, and swiftly-informed free democracy. . . . from the St. Lawrence to the Gulf there was a spiritual preparedness for slaughter which was to end in such murderous contests as should make ensanguined Europe rise from its thousand battlefields to stare in wonder." The novelists used superlatives for the American war not because they wished to develop a systematic historical comparison with other wars but because they were dramatizing the effects of war that embraced the people, who could not make a nation without it. Americans, Lanier and DeForest implied, had somehow sensed that the war would be terrible and did not long hold back from making it so, perhaps exulted in it.

Throughout the war Americans persisted in expecting one climactic battle that would decide the outcome and end the fighting. In the act of trying to direct combat for the purpose of compelling an end to the war, they found that the violence refused to conform to their assumptions. In the last grand battle, they believed, the scale of effort would be so great, the killing so horrible, and the result so clear that the losers would concede defeat in the war, no matter what their remaining resources. In 1861 the *New York Herald* predicted a battle greater than Waterloo; in 1862 the *Richmond Enquirer* said: "We must have an Austerlitz before we can have peace." They assumed, as did the *Cincinnati Commercial,* that the "more blood there is shed at the start, the less there will be in the end. The more terrible and decisive the battles, the shorter the campaign." Long after the armies had fought battles far surpassing the expectations of 1861, newspapers continued to predict and citizens and soldiers to anticipate a single, final confrontation.

In the spring of 1862 the war was supposed to end in a dual encounter: between McClellan and Johnston in Virginia, Halleck and Beauregard at Corinth. That summer Lee and the Federal armies in Virginia were supposed to settle the war. At the end of the winter of 1862–1863, people anticipated what *Harper's Weekly* called "the *coup de grâce*" in the first great battle of the spring. The outcome at Vicksburg, George A. Mercer and other Southerners predicted in May, "must be *decisive*" because, though the Confederates had won at Chancellorsville, "we can see no results." The battle for Atlanta, to take place somewhere in northern Georgia in 1864, would be the great Armageddon, Northerners and Southerners foresaw. After John B. Hood replaced Joseph E. Johnston in command of the Army of Tennessee, the *Memphis Appeal,* published in Atlanta, said: "It is time, perhaps, that Stonewall Jacksonism had usurped the place of caution and strategy. . . . The war must end and the final battle be fought." As late as March 1865 the *Cleveland Plain Dealer* expected that "the grand decisive battle of this war" would occur when Sherman reached Virginia. "The loss of life will be appalling," but at the end "the sun of a second Austerlitz" would shine on Sherman and his army. Only after Lee had surrendered and the grand decisive battle, greater than all the others, had failed to occur did the *Cincinnati Commercial* comment on the long-standing mistaken anticipation. Its editor Murat Halstead had written to John Sherman in April 1863, urging a concentration against the Confederates in the west that would "end the war with a clap of thunder." Two years later the *Commercial* philosophically looked back at the public's impatience "for the decisive battle of the war—for the full exertion of our power in one grand master-stroke . . . that should end the war with a thunder-clap." Strangely, it had never come. "The peculiar feature of the engagements," the *Commercial* noted, "was their continuance for several days with hideous slaughter and indecisive results."

Confidence in the decisive battle's effect presupposed that the armies exemplified the fighting qualities of the societies from which they came. The great final combat would not kill so many men that the defeated side would be unable to replace them; nor would it win some strategic advantage hopelessly crippling the loser. Instead, it would demonstrate the greater fighting ability and resolve of one people, making the enemy's further resistance patently futile. An Indiana officer, Lieutenant Josiah C. Williams, said of the imminent fighting near Richmond in 1862: "I think if we whip them then, in one awful battle, they will certainly have their eyes opened and secumb." Hugh H. Honnoll, a Confederate soldier at Corinth, expressed a similar anticipation prevalent among Southerners: "The long looked for test will be decided between Northern and Southern Arms." In that battle one would see which society produced better men, avowed more just principles, had brighter prospects for future power, and possessed God's favor. In the words of the *New York Herald,* while all awaited the battles at Richmond and Corinth, "Society, government, politics, parties, everything, in fact, of the present and of the future, so far as this country is concerned, depends now upon the army of General McClellan and the army of General Halleck." One measure of strength would be willingness to sustain losses, not faltering no matter how many men fell on the way to victory. After the Confederate defeats at Gettysburg and Vicksburg, if not earlier, the war had all the marks of a contest of attrition, of resources, and of perseverance—not of preparation for the final stroke of a single battle. While supporting this struggle as it cumulatively grew more destructive than any conceivable last showdown, many people continued to see it in images little changed from those of the early days. The persistent imagining of one decisive test helped reconcile Americans to an accelerating war wherein such a test had no place.

Eager to triumph through inflicting and sustaining casualties so great as to overawe the enemy, Northerners and Southerners found that neither party could be shocked conclusively by bloodletting. The vicarious war, bringing together soldiers and civilians in a manifestation of their joint determination to make a successful society by force, became also the destructive war. This meant not only a war that destroyed, as all do, but also a war whose supporters and combatants, in numbers large enough to prolong it, saw no need to weigh the cost of violence in the balance against their purposes and interests. The notion of the climactic battle, derived in part from historians' capacity for clarifying bygone wars, presumed that wars were ruled by reason, at least in the matter of stopping them. A government judged its losses too great or its resources too thin or its original calculations erroneous or its regime's interests altered and, as the old books said, sued for peace. But a people who had made war their salvation, an epitome of their national pretensions, could not limit war by judging the implications of one battle or a series of battles. They were the nation; they were the war; they could not stop.

NONE OF the attempts by Northerners and Southerners to involve themselves in the war and to make it their creature surpassed their exercises in defining moral and spiritual benefits they would derive from their participation. It was to be a redemptive war, a transformation of society—a sacrifice, like Christ's, full of blessings and ordained by God. In these formulations Americans repeated many themes invoked by the British during the Crimean War. Apart from the supposed strategic importance of checking Russia, the proponents had said in 1854, war offered Britons an opportunity to redeem themselves from the selfishness and divisions of a commercial society. Tennyson expressed this view in his poem *Maud:*

> Let it go or stay, so I wake to the higher aims
> Of a land that has lost for a little her lust of gold,
> And love of peace that was full of wrongs and shames,
> Horrible, hateful, monstrous, not to be told;
> And hail once more to the banner of battle unroll'd!
> .   .   .   .
> Let it flame or fade, and the war roll down like a wind,
> We have proved we have hearts in a cause, we are noble still,
> And myself have awaked, as it seems, to the better mind;
> It is better to fight for the good, than to rail at the ill;
> I have felt with my native land, I am one with my kind,
> I embrace the purpose of God, and the doom assign'd.

By summoning a united people to patriotic sacrifice, nationalistic war reasserted communal strengths derived from devotion to transcendent ideals. Although Confederates often differentiated their new nation from the materialistic North, the South had many voices warning that its people, too, were endangered by their greed and worldliness. For them, as for their Northern counterparts, the Civil War had a moral dimension of the kind Britons had found in fighting selflessly.

The British portrayed themselves generously expending lives on behalf of weaker peoples threatened by the Russian autocrat. Americans claimed to be similarly altruistic in defense of self-government and national autonomy. What better proof could they give than throwing away lives in the cause? Tennyson's poem "The Charge of the Light Brigade" enjoyed wide popularity among both Northerners and Southerners. But they did not usually read it as a lament for men who had died unnecessarily. They did not usually mention—even to the extent that Tennyson did in the text of the poem—the confused, blundering orders that had launched the charge, or the futility of its casualties. As the British public had done when first reading the work, Americans made the suicidal cavalry assault an inspiring example of courage; Americans must emulate it in their war. Speaking of First Bull Run, Fredericksburg, Chancellorsville, Gettysburg, Vicksburg, Chickamauga, and other battles, people on both sides likened the bravery of their fallen troops to that of the Light Brigade at Balaklava. Like Carlyle, Tennyson not only detested Yankees but also thought the Civil War grotesque. Yet the writings of both men seemed to their American admirers to help make the Civil War intelligible. Tennyson's Crimean War poetry showed Americans how the British had found national salvation in combat. The *New York Herald* cited *Maud* as the record of war's correcting the social evils of a long peace by "infusing a healthy vitality into a nation."

Soldiers' bravery and death renewed their society's moral health. Earl Grey spoke sentiments many Britons shared when he said in the House of Lords: "I cannot but rejoice that, in the course of this contest, it has been proved to all the world that the British nation has not degenerated from its ancient courage." In 1854 and 1855 dramatic, detailed accounts of the fighting in the Crimea were widely read in Britain. Heroes of battle won sympathy through the work of sentimental writers and orators. The government created a new supreme decoration for valor, the Victoria Cross. The war had a popular following, a role for public opinion and emotion new to Britain's history. Its first important British historian, Alexander Kinglake, wrote in 1863: "Distinct from the martial ardor already kindled in England, there had sprung up amongst the people an almost romantic craving for warlike adventure." Notwithstanding Britain's dubious motives, muddled execution, and questionable accomplishments, the Crimean War ended with celebrations of national self-redemption more highly valued than the original purposes of state that ostensibly had mandated war.

In repeating the British experience by foreseeing improvement through war, Americans defined their war's promised effects according to the ills they saw in antebellum society, which they expected war to cure. Many people on both sides spoke of the danger to self-government arising from corruption and a dearth of civic-mindedness. To others the main danger exposed by the prewar years was an extreme of egalitarianism and majoritarianism. Defenders of slavery who thought that Confederate independence would reform the institution to make it more secure, like abolitionists who thought that war would make blacks fully free, trusted their hopes to the anticipated effect of irresistible demands that conflict would impose on society. The historian Benson J. Lossing wrote early in 1862: "I have felt profoundly impressed with the conviction that out of all this tribulation would come health, and strength, and purification for the nation." He unknowingly paralleled the words of a Georgia woman who had predicted in 1861: "The blood shed on Manassas Plains will yet bring *our* new government out of all its trials and tribulations, purified from its dross—and we shall yet be numbered among the great nations of the earth." Politics had grown partly rotten, and a cataclysm would attach voters and officials to the public good. The *Richmond Examiner* appealed to the example of the French Revolution; those among its leaders who failed to comprehend the crisis were executed, and the revolution succeeded through its excesses. The French "passed to the promised land through a red sea of blood." The Confederate revolution should similarly purge weaklings from its political leadership. War could vindicate democracy by proving that a self-governing people could withstand a crisis greater than the interests usually leading them to temporize. Unionists of course said that perpetuation of self-government depended on their triumph; they concluded that through fighting for it they attained a moral apotheosis guaranteeing the security of America's political system. In April 1865 the *Philadelphia Inquirer* described permanent benefits wrought by the war: "True democracy has reasserted its principles, after four years of bloody war, and from the ghastly memorials of the battle field and the ashes of burned towns, arises the genius of Liberty, purified and regenerated, no longer the Goddess of theory, but the vindicator of fact."

The egalitarianism, decentralization, selfishness, and disorder that seemed so ominous to some Southerners and Northerners had occupied their thoughts for years. The war had not created or first exposed these threats. Rather, the war came almost as a godsend to correct them, after the ordinary peacetime workings of politics apparently had sunk into irremediable corruption and demagoguery. With opposing concerns and interests, advocates of order, hierarchy, and governmental authority in both sections could agree that the 1850s had been an American nadir. They could greet war as a forcible demonstration that only discipline could save a republic. Critics of antebellum democracy expected to use war to serve ends that they had devised before seizing violence as their tool.

From its start the war looked like an opportunity to Northerners alarmed by the baseness of political life, by Americans' rush to what Frederic Henry Hedge called "civil dissolution." A Unitarian minister and a scholar of German philosophy and literature, Hedge believed that subordination was the fundamental principle of social order, as Americans at last would learn through war. Speaking three days after the first battle of Bull Run, Julian M. Sturtevant, president of Illinois College, predicted that war would correct the American tendency to object to all government. Even philosophers, he said, "cannot persistently see a political truth till it has been established by conflict and written in blood." The emblem of an orderly, stable society would be a national government with the power and the will to enforce law. Secessionists' confidence that they could defy the government with impunity was, for Northern conservatives, only one manifestation of an endemic American vice. Proving the Southerners wrong should also correct erroneous Northern exaggerations of democracy and freedom.

For secessionist critics of extreme democracy the great Southern anxieties—solidarity of the white population and security of slavery—had their solution not just in forming a new nation but in experiencing a war with its lesson, the strength of hierarchy and order. On Thomas Jefferson's birthday in 1864 Francis W. Gilmer called Jefferson "a great man, but sadly mistaken when he spoke of the great purity and intelligence" of the people. The South, like the North, was suffering from the "pestilence" of "election of judges, universal suffrage, all men born equal." As the Reverend C. H. Wiley and others acknowledged, the South once had helped to create and had embraced "the great American delusion of man's perfectibility by human agencies." But these critics usually portrayed democracy as a Yankee vice and said, with James H. Thornwell, "we are conservative." The war thus came as the South's salvation because it exposed the true tendencies of egalitarianism—radicalism, abolitionism, and atheism—which all Southerners must fight.

Among the expressions of confidence in war's benefits, offsetting an inability to control war, none was more wholehearted than that of Northerners who wanted to end slavery. This disparate group grew dramatically during the war; it included a smaller but still substantial and growing number who wanted to assure civil and political rights to former slaves; and it included a much smaller group that also wanted to redistribute property for the benefit of former slaves. Assessments of these Northerners by modern historians have passed through several phases, alternately commending efforts on behalf of black people's basic rights and deploring the narrow limits of whites' movement toward racial equality. Both the accomplishment of reforms—most notably, emancipation—and the circumscribing of those reforms owed much to antislavery people's reliance on the passions and exigencies of war to attain their ends. Longtime abolitionists, including some dedicated pacifists, embraced war partly because they had learned through experience that reason and moral suasion would not end slavery soon. In wartime, defenders of the Emancipation Proclamation newly converted to abolition tried to broaden its support mainly by appeals to the public's dedication to war and the nation. Campaigning for the governorship of Ohio, John Brough argued that the public should accept the Proclamation as an order from their commander-in-chief, to be obeyed whether they approved or not: "Like a soldier fighting in the ranks, I hold it to be my duty to obey him, my commanding officer, in all things, without questioning his policy in this great contest." Emancipation prevailed, James G. Blaine later explained, because Lincoln was able to link it in the minds of most Northerners with the war for the union, thus offering them a choice between union and slavery. "He would persuade them that both could not be saved and that they must choose the one which they regarded as the more worthy of preservation." The easiest, perhaps the only, way to achieve an adequate consensus for emancipation was to make it ancillary to winning the war.

To exploit war's persuasive effect most fully, building the greatest possible consensus, proponents of blacks' freedom and rights encouraged widely divergent expectations among Northerners, with the implied promise that winning the war would yield whatever societal solution one wished. Some people hoped for universal manhood suffrage and equality before the law. Frederick Douglass portrayed blacks' enlistment in the Federal army as their chance "to rise, in one bound, from social degradation to the plain of common equality with all varieties of men." On the other hand, many whites expected former slaves to become nothing more than industrious laborers, free but subordinate. Republican speakers often said that emancipation would keep black people in the South and induce Northern blacks to move to the South. Nor had the fantasy of all blacks' leaving America yet died among whites. The divided and obscure counsels with which the victors addressed the issues of postwar relations between the races had been crucial to promoting the war effort and to accomplishing those changes effected with war's help. Extravagant or incompatible expectations about the future of freed slaves could persist side by side, helping attract diverse groups to support of the war whether or not victory could give them what they expected. War was the best unifier but not the best guarantor.

The subsequent retreat from reconstruction, eroding or reversing many of the changes in blacks' status and power, was easier because of the connection between change and force. The constitutional doctrine legitimating Republican reconstruction consisted in the assertion that the defeated Southern states were still held in "the grasp of war" and so still subject to the victors' demands. Confronted with sustained resistance by Southern whites, these demands could prevail only as long as Northerners were willing to renew the use of force—that is, revert to wartime means of unity and persuasion. The dependence of the reconstruction settlement on force revealed that war and victory did not carry with them the finality, the all-sufficient resolution, so often promised. In 1865 the historian John Lothrop Motley anticipated a new era for the United States: "Thank God slavery is abolished and the accursed oligarchy based upon it . . . has gone to the nether regions along with it and we who believe in liberty and civilization and human progress can look forward through the immediate present to an almost unlimited future of prosperity and power for the great Republic." Not so much had been settled as Motley supposed. Although war facilitated profound changes in attitudes, political power, constitutions, and laws, it did not guarantee any part of reconstruction except what Northerners were willing to sustain continually by force or Southerners were willing to accept in the absence of renewed force. Of itself the war conclusively established only the success of Northern war-making. Nevertheless, some who deplored the pattern of Southern reaction against and Northern retreat from reconstruction looked back to the days of violence as a time when all could have been resolved by a sufficiently drastic stroke. George Washington Cable, writing on "The Negro Question" in 1888, regretted that enfranchisement of blacks had not come as emancipation had—"while the smoke of the war's last shot was still in the air, when force still ruled unquestioned, and civil order and system had not yet superseded martial law." He assumed that if black men's right to vote had been adopted as a war measure it would not have been subject to later erosion through politics and intimidation.

This faith in the rule of force as a dynamic agent of desirable change pervaded the wartime drive for emancipation. The most active opponents of slavery most vehemently urged harsher war against the would-be republic of slave states. In Congress, George W. Julian, eager to end slavery and transform the South, said that the government "should deal with rebels as having no rights under the Constitution, or by the laws of war, but the right to die. It should make war its special occupation and study, using every weapon in its terrible armory." In demanding more aggressive generals and more severity toward rebels, antislavery people took it for granted that mounting violence served their purposes. They thought that war was effecting through animosity a moral transformation that peaceable persuasion could not achieve. Hatred of slavery, in the words of Henry W. Bellows, "passed beyond a conviction of duty, or a moral and humane sentiment, into a passionate emotion, blind, unreasoning but terribly real & effective." Wendell Phillips said that each cannon lectured better than a thousand abolitionists; Theodore Dwight Weld said that events had become the only effective preacher: they reasoned and persuaded "with a logic, and rhetoric, invincible."

These men spoke and wrote metaphorically, as if violent coercion were an equivalent of preaching, as if an artillery barrage were a lecture. After all, the crucial result, an end to slavery, would be the same one for which they previously had used rhetoric and logic. This almost casual conflation neglected a distinction that Senator Benjamin F. Wade drew in the spring of 1862. He recalled the warning he had given Southern leaders during the secession winter. He had said of abolitionists like Garrison and Phillips: "They are theorists; they are right in theory, but they never will harm a hair of your head; but you attempt this secession, and the first blast of civil war is the death-warrant of your institution." Wade was dramatizing the difference between the effects of talking and the effects of war.

Abolitionists could not end slavery unless secessionists threatened the union, thereby shifting from talk to war and leaving the South open to an assault by more than abolitionists' words—by unionists' violence. If slavery were to end in this manner, it would do so, Wade implied, not because of a cosmically necessary, morally progressive confirmation of what was "right in theory," but because Southerners were too unwise or too unrestrained to avoid a war and thereby save their evil regime.

Drastic war brought emancipation and some of the other results that slavery's opponents sought. But violence did not bring to the citizenry a moral transformation of the kind that reformers had tried to produce by talking and then had assumed to be among the promised results of war. The people who undertook the destructive war that abolitionists wanted did not necessarily thereby become converts to or servants of the reformers' ethical system. In the spring of 1864 Senator Lazarus Whitehead Powell, a Democrat from Kentucky, tried on the floor of the Senate to discomfit Charles Sumner with a charge of inconsistency. He quoted from Sumner's oration "The Grandeur of Nations," given on July 4, 1845, in which Sumner had said: "War is utterly ineffectual to secure or advance the object at which it aims." The oration had denounced war categorically: "In our age there can be no peace that is not honorable; there can be no war that is not dishonorable." In response to Powell's charge that he was now contradicting himself, Sumner said: "At the time I made that remark I had very little idea of the barbarism of slavery." In anticipation of the nation's progress away from barbarism he recently had embraced, as he wrote to Francis Lieber, "War of subjugation with Emancipation." Newly convinced of its efficacy, Sumner had much to learn about war, the *Chicago Tribune* told him early in 1865. He thought war could be restrained by moral scruples. He did not want to retaliate against Confederate prisoners for Southerners' mistreatment of Federal prisoners. The *Tribune* accused him of "chicken-heartedness" and "Miss-nancy-ism." He had advocated policies in the 1850s that had led to war; now he needed to realize the drastic consequences of his acts: "Greek quotations must give place to Greek fire. . . . All war is retaliation—suffering—punishment of the innocent for the sins of the guilty. The question in relation to retaliation is not whether it is just to the individual who suffers. That question is never asked in war. But 'will it conduce to success?' "

The *Tribune*, a strongly antislavery paper, exemplified, as did Sumner, the inability of antislavery people or of anyone else to keep the course of war tied to and confined by the purposes they sought from it. This disparity between the effects of passionate violence and the goals of reformers also helped to vitiate the "grasp of war" doctrine during reconstruction because reconstruction was not war. It had neither the range of vehement support nor the extreme methods characteristic of war. Reconstruction measures, though not always clearly defined or consistently sustained, amounted to a political program, an undertaking mainly dependent on suasion. Its supporters could no longer rely on the momentum of destructive events to do their preaching for them, as in wartime; and, in the process of learning this, they found that the momentum of wartime events had not had so uniform an acceleration of progress or so assuredly progressive a direction as they had supposed. Of all the efforts among Northerners to make the vicarious war an inclusive experience, joining disparate people and opposing views, no group accomplished so great a change between 1861 and 1865 as those who advocated emancipation. Along with dissuading Southerners from belief in the military and economic power of their section, this was the most extensive change of minds effected by the war. It was a victory for the moral truths that abolitionists long had preached. More than the proponents of change acknowledged—or perhaps realized—they also had made morality a hostage of violence.

NO ASPECT of the story of the vicarious war mattered more to participants than their ability to show that they had acted correctly and could explain what they had done. From this need, in part, came the incalculably vast flow of writing about the war, most of which was private, intended only for the writer and a few others. Though seeking to clarify and justify wartime actions, this writing also contained many instances of participants' recalling episodes that horrified them or shamed them or confused them. Some actions they took or scenes they witnessed did not support the prevailing message of their story. In these accounts war had overwhelmed some people or many people for a while—moments or months—or, at least, had threatened to do so. Because the vicarious war incorporated much if not all of a society in its experiences, these deviations into an inexplicable, uncontrollable war confused the story for everyone, not just for a few soldiers immersed in bloodshed and destruction. Two elements of war writing—romanticizing war and fixing responsibility for war, especially for its unexpected excesses—sought to incorporate horrors and confusions into a narrative all could share. This effort entailed not so much systematic denial and omission as the integrating of recorded events into an explanatory scheme that deflected the shame of having participated, even vicariously, in war's worst scenes. These writings sought to sustain the war's intelligibility for those who had to live with the memory of its surprises.

Many people described combat as an agent of moral improvement for the whole society or for segments of it. The *New York Herald* signaled its conversion to a pro-war policy after fighting started by announcing that the country needed to have its "excessive prosperity" tempered by the demands of war: "Young America, North and South, was becoming almost spoiled for want of a fight." Activity, intensity, violence drew people out of their selfishness and passivity, improving them and society. A Virginian, Betty Kemp, wrote to Louisa B. Turner: "If the war works no other good I think it is developing the energies of the Southern Ladies." Sarah Grimké, an abolitionist from Charleston, had similar hopes for the war's effect on character: "How much that is grand & beautiful in human nature has been developed during this fearful struggle. How many hearts heretofore caged in the narrow circle of an enlarged selfishness have been drawn out of themselves & their loved ones, & lived & toiled & sacrificed for humanity."

A larger community—a nation, a sex, a race—derived moral benefits from the engagement of some of its members in the conflict. The Democratic party's state organ in New York, the *Albany Argus,* predicted: "A vigorous war would tone up the public mind, and impart to it qualities that would last after the calamities of the war had passed." In many people's eyes, combat proved the manhood of former slaves. George Washington Williams, a black veteran, wrote his *History of the Negro Troops in the War of the Rebellion* partly to show that those soldiers had stepped "from passive submission to the cruel curse of slavery to the brilliant aggressiveness of a free soldier . . . from the shame of degradation to the glory of military exaltation." Federal commanders' most stupid orders became black people's greatest glory because black soldiers made doomed assaults with unsurpassed courage. P. B. Randolph told the National Convention of Colored Men in 1864: "Wagner, Hudson, Petersburg, and all the other battles of this war have not been fought in vain; for the dead heroes of those and other bloody fields are the seeds of mighty harvests of human goodness and greatness, yet to be reaped by the nations and the world, and by Africa's sable descendants on the soil of this, our native land." Combat appeared transfigured, not just the clash of soldiers but the prowess of civilians. Serving the war made one powerful. Looking back at the war, Stella C. Coatsworth believed that it had changed women. "American women no longer follow in the dull, beaten track of examples, but striking out into new and untried paths, lay their plans and execute their purposes with self-poise and fearless of results. The late war has developed in woman new character, and enabled her to rise to a measure of usefulness that was hitherto, even by herself, undreamed of." No expression better summarized commitment to the war than her phrase "fearless of results." Enthusiasts of all kinds could throw themselves into war, confident that their exertions had a beneficial effect. Through war they became public figures, deriving a new stature—perhaps even a new character—from their newly active role.

To believe that an army's activities and casualties transformed the moral character of a group or of a society was to avow a mystical interpretation of the war. By what process did many people who did not bleed become purer as a result of the bleeding of others? How did those who bled improve their own moral state by bleeding? The people who said that soldiers' bloodshed was purifying society relied on some form of belief in atonement: "And almost all things are by the law purged with blood; and without shedding of blood is no remission." Many Northerners and Southerners, though they had said that there would be no war, or that a war would not last long or grow bloody, were ready at once to explain deaths and suffering as spiritual betterment their society long had needed. For many Christians the soldier's death fulfilled an almost Christ-like function, vicariously atoning for the sins of his people. In the best-known formulation of a mystical view of the war, Lincoln's second inaugural address, atonement sounded quantitative, an exact equivalency of recompense to God for past sins. In the South, as well as the North, cleansing achieved by bleeding had a strong appeal. It was a mysterious seizure, like the coming of grace, to which one surrendered. "I rejoice in this war. . . . It is a war of purification. You want war, fire, blood to purify you; and the Lord of Hosts has demanded that you should walk through fire and blood—You are called to the fiery baptism and I call you to come up to the altar. . . . Take a lesson from John Brown." These were the words not of an abolitionist but of Henry A. Wise, who had been governor of Virginia when the state hanged John Brown. Wise spoke to Virginians in an evangelical idiom familiar to most Americans—one which, in its wartime uses, assured them that the magnitude of the bloodshed was a sign of its spiritual efficacy. Believers could go on shedding blood, knowing that God was measuring it, that when He deemed His people cleansed the bloodletting would stop. It could not and should not stop sooner. Mystical faith in the moral benefits of combat sustained confidence that war would accomplish the intended political results. Purposes that depended on war—nationhood, honor, freedom, the societal ideal—thus relied for their anticipated fulfillment on unreason. They might seem self-evidently worthy, thereby justifying their adherents' violent measures. But, in the vicarious war, this worthiness had to be demonstrated or vindicated through a sacramental mystery, the central act of which was bloodshed. The great purposes became real only insofar as the flow of blood, whose volume no one could foresee, brought belief.

The war's paradox promised the triumph of purpose through the loss of control.

Confronting such a call for unlimited sacrifice in pursuit of transfiguration, how could participants know that war followed a plan to give them the expected blessings? What design would their story of the war have? T. J. Jackson and W. T. Sherman put forward the two most common answers: the providential and the naturalistic. Though both men came to represent the most drastic methods, neither thought that the violence overreached its purpose or became an end in itself. They took pains to integrate it into a coherent history. The appeal of both men's explanations crossed sectional lines. Jackson's providential outlook had much in common with that of Christian abolitionists, as well as other believers, while the supposedly scientific proposition that war was a natural process won adherents in the South and the North. God was the ultimate guarantor of the intelligibility of war for both Jackson and Sherman; but they saw God working in different ways.

For Stonewall Jackson, the course of combat was divinely ordered. Every incident came from the will of God. Apparent mistakes and confusion only seemed chaotic or disastrous; they were God's way of working out His beneficent intentions for those who loved Him. During the battles of the Seven Days, Jackson's forces were tardy in joining the attack at Gaines' Mill partly because guides put them on the wrong road, an error which threatened to throw his troops among other Confederates and which took more than an hour to correct, while the fighting was under way. R. L. Dabney, then Jackson's chief of staff, feared that the delay might do irreparable harm to the intended synchronized attack, but Jackson said: "No; let us trust that the providence of our God will so overrule it, that no mischief shall result." He took every opportunity to emphasize God's direction of events. Even some of his shortest, most urgent battlefield notes, let alone official reports, acknowledged his dependence on divine rule. In winter camp early in 1863 Charles J. Faulkner joined Jackson's staff to write the long-delayed reports of the battles fought during 1862. In one sentence of his account of the Valley Campaign he had Jackson say: "Leaving Winchester on the 31st of May I arrived that evening in the vicinity of Strasburg." Revising Faulkner's draft, Jackson changed it to read: "Having through the blessing of an ever kind Providence passed Strasburg before the Federal armies under Gens. Shields & Frémont effected the contemplated junction in my rear . . . I continued to move up the Valley Turnpike." Thus he dramatized the success of his risky march and ascribed it to God's favor. Confederates could make no greater mistake than to presume that they could win by human skill and strength alone. God humbled those who forgot Him. On the night of August 30, 1862, after Jackson's corps had undergone two days of intense combat near Manassas—in danger of being overwhelmed until Longstreet's corps joined Jackson's and the Confederates turned from defense to attack—Dr. Hunter McGuire said: "Our victory Gen. has been due only to hard downright fighting." Jackson replied: "No, Dr. it is due to the blessing of Divine Providence."

The greatest danger to the Confederate cause, Jackson believed, lay not in the Federal army's power but in sinfulness and irreligion among Southerners. He said that if Confederates were as Christian and God-fearing a people as they should be, peace would come very speedily. Like many Southern Presbyterians, he wanted the new nation's government to be explicitly Christian, conforming to God's laws revealed in the Bible. It "appears to me," he wrote, "that the old United States occupied an extreme position in the means it took to prevent the union of Church and State." He was making the same argument that the *North Carolina Presbyterian* had published in 1859. Two theologians whom Jackson respected, James H. Thornwell and R. L. Dabney, envisioned the regulating of all official acts by Christian doctrine. Thornwell said that the United States had failed as a union because it was a secular nation. Jackson worked to keep the Confederacy from pursuing the same irreligious course and thereby suffering the same doom. He did not advocate an established church; but he noted, evidently with approval, this sentence in the first volume of Bancroft's *History of the United States:* "Thus New Haven made the Bible its statute-book, and the elect its freemen." The main promise of Confederate independence consisted of an opportunity to infuse governmental policy with Christian conscience, making the state, like the churches, an inducement to piety and to salvation of souls. The most pious were of course the fittest to lead. Anticipating peace and independence soon, Colonel J. T. L. Preston wrote to Jackson in February 1863: "Christians too must be on the alert to invest into the origin of our new institutions the germ of a living religion. . . . no man will be in a position more influential in this regard than yourself, and I know that your heart will be in the work."

Jackson's evangelizing among his soldiers had a dual spiritual and military purpose. He had learned from Macaulay's *History of England* that Cromwell's victorious army combined rigid discipline with the fiercest religious enthusiasm: "That which chiefly distinguished the army of Cromwell from other armies was the austere morality and the fear of God which pervaded all ranks." Jackson knew that pious soldiers would prevail in combat. He told Chaplain Beverly Tucker Lacy that if he "commanded a *converted army,* he would feel confident." Ominously, the

Confederate army fell far short of his ideal. Fewer than half of Jackson's regiments had chaplains; the most glowing account of religious conversions among the troops claimed after the war only that one-third of the soldiers had been church members and praying men. Devout soldiers often complained that they were surrounded by the irreligious. Revivals in the Confederate army did not touch the great majority of men. And the spread of revivals, especially in the two years after Jackson's death, did not portend victory for the growing number of the righteous, as Jackson had hoped, but coincided with the Confederate army's reverses and impending defeat. Jackson, however, believed that revivals presaged and hastened victory. He tried to convert his army by urging that more ministers serve as chaplains. He encouraged and attended religious services in camp; he contributed money for the purchase of New Testaments and tracts to be distributed among the soldiers; he inquired anxiously about the progress of revivals in camp. In December 1862 he looked forward to "growing piety and many conversions in the army." The following month, to promote this trend, Jackson asked Lacy to take charge of organizing chaplains systematically, recruiting more ministers, and corresponding with others. Preachers, like generals, should meet and "devise successful plans for spiritual conquests." Jackson felt the urgency of this mission not only because he wanted sinners brought to Christ but also because successful evangelizing would lead directly to Confederate independence. God, seeing that Confederates built a republic devoted to Him, would direct the fighting to reward the faithful, as He had often done for Jackson. Events, then, followed an intelligible course. God guided them, and everyone who loved God influenced them by accepting His beneficence. Prayer shaped the war.

William Tecumseh Sherman did not believe that God was molding events in response to human petition, conduct, or spiritual state. In his mind the war did not obey the participants; they obeyed it. Recalling prewar conversations with Sherman in Louisiana, David F. Boyd wrote: "His only peculiarity about religion was, that he was such an advocate for *individual* religious *freedom,* that he thought it wrong ever to attempt to influence any one's religious convictions. I have often heard him about this: if I could I would *not* change the religion of a Hottentot or Feejee Islander, &c. &c." Married for almost forty years to a devout Roman Catholic, their children reared in the faith, Sherman joined no church. He regarded organized religion as a human invention and dismissed the doctrines of the Trinity and of transubstantiation as "mathematical impossibilities." He prefaced mention of the immortality of the soul with the word "if." Sherman did not oppose belief or the practice of Christianity. Chaplains accompanied his army, and revival meetings among soldiers went on during the Georgia and Carolina campaigns. At Goldsboro he sent three bottles of wine to the chaplain of the 33d Indiana Regiment for use in communion. But he did not think that evangelizing affected the course of combat or the outcome of the war.

As Sherman prepared for the Atlanta campaign early in 1864 he found that the supply trains from Nashville to Chattanooga and on to the army in northern Georgia barely met the army's daily needs. To build a reserve of food and ammunition he set out to double the volume that reached the army daily by appropriating boxcars as they arrived from the North and by excluding passengers from them to make room for more supplies. Ministers came to Nashville as delegates of the United States Christian Commission, then applied for passes to ride the railroad to the front lines. Sherman wrote on their applications: "Certainly not; crackers and oats are more necessary to my army than any moral or religious agency." When he confronted these clergymen in person he said: "Show me that your presence at the front is more valuable than 200 pounds of powder, bread or oats." They seldom did. To Sherman preachers were, for war's purposes, only "that weight of bottled piety." Sometimes religious emissaries came with passes from higher authority, which Sherman had to honor. In protest he lectured Assistant Secretary of War Charles A. Dana: "To make war we must & will harden our hearts. Therefore when preachers clamor, & the sanitaries wail don't join in, but know that war, like the thunderbolt follows its laws, and turns not aside even if the beautiful, the virtuous and charitable stand in its path."

To Sherman war was a natural phenomenon, guided by nature's laws, which God had created but which operated with the consistency of mathematics, not by God's "mere fiat." When humans, for example the rebels, willfully defied the movement of history—a movement like that of the universe toward order—their deviation would inevitably be corrected either by political persuasion or by violence. In the latter case, combat was as natural, as scientifically explicable, as the thunderstorm or the movement of planets; the ultimate result followed as ineluctably as did effects of the laws of physics. Though he took pride in military skill, Sherman did not think that leaders controlled the war or that generals necessarily dominated battle. He was willing to contemplate incalculable casualties, generations of war, if these proved to be the necessary means for inevitable progress. Outside Atlanta in August 1864 he wrote: "The war must go on. No human power not even the Copperheads or peace men, or Lincoln or Congress, or Jeff Davis can stop it. The causes all lie beyond their control." Sherman did not think that combat was orderly or that the outcome of battles was consistently predictable. War, like nature, was profligate with life. Part of his excitement in achieving planned results, such as the capture of Atlanta and Savannah or the cutting off of Augusta and Charleston, came from his knowledge that plans often failed and from his belief that he had decreased the cost war exacted for the accomplishment of its necessary object. Sherman did not stand aloof from violence in wartime or afterward. He never forgot the sensations of battle; he recalled Shiloh, where he had heard "the bones of the dead & living crunching under the artillery wheels" and had seen that "our wounded men, mingled with rebels, charred and blackened by the burning tents and grass, were crawling about begging for someone to end their misery." He reconciled himself to disorderly violence, costly blunders, unforeseeable numbers of casualties, and strategies that might fail. For him these were epiphenomena of cosmic law, which doomed Southerners' effort to escape their destined political orbit. "Wars are not all evil," he said late in life; "they are part of the grand machinery by which this world is governed."

No two generals enjoyed the successes of their strategic and tactical calculations more fully than Jackson and Sherman did. Even so, both of their definitions of combat qualified the commander's claim to rule the battlefield or guide the war. They could not know, except by faith, that the God of special providences or the God of impersonal universal laws governed the armies' conflict. But they did know that battle and its results could not be fully compassed by the minds of generals. Their versions of the superhuman forces guiding war had an undertone of desperation. They could prove the purposeful unfolding of history's design only by throwing themselves unreservedly into war.

Among the war generation's means of assimilating and explaining its experiences, scholars often have stressed the widespread penchant for sentimentalizing violence by representing combat as a source of moral inspiration. Throughout the war years and in the following decades, describing battles and death in laudatory, picturesque, figurative, or appealingly emotional language—now usually called romanticizing the war—was common. These methods of making havoc more tolerable to contemplate were practiced alongside extensive graphic, unblinking representations of the conduct and the effects of combat. Tales of viciousness and tales of glory were often complementary ways of describing the war. The worst violence, most bluntly represented and most deeply felt, did not necessarily lead veterans of it or their audience to disavow the war or the combatants' methods. As the war grew more terrible—as it apparently escaped control—its hold on many minds grew stronger. More important than the shock of killing, more desirable than peace, was the assurance that fighting the war would be proven right. With this assurance, derived in part from finding uplifting emotion in the violence, people could confront the worst scenes in person or at second hand.

Sentimental accounts of sad, sweet thoughts about war never died out. If the volume of them is a measure of the demand for them, it hardly had a limit. The popular press turned out a steady flow of stories, songs, and verses like "Mother, Can I Go?", "The Dying Soldier Boy," and "The Dead Drummer-Boy":

> He lived, he died; and so *memento mori.*
> Enough if on the page of War and Glory
> Some hand has writ his name.

Such works gratified civilians' expectation that combat should be a source of exalted feeling. Paul Hamilton Hayne made up for not serving in the Confederate army by writing poetry that celebrated its exploits and by lecturing to raise money for hospitals. "The subject was *'Heroism,'* " he said of a lecture in 1864, "a topic which permitted me to expatiate upon Confederate valor, self-sacrifice &c &c." Although combat grew ever more lethal, many people still found chivalry in it. By the time it got written, the war was in part a narrative of exciting, ennobling adventure. A reporter for the *New York Tribune* wrote to his managing editor in 1863: "Your suggestions about more of the Romance & picturesqueness of the war, & less of the common place will be of great service to me. I will endeavor to have them acted upon by all our correspondents." While the fighting was still under way some Northerners predicted that the memory of the courage and manhood demonstrated by both armies would form a bond between Northerners and Southerners in the reunited nation. The image of flowers growing on a battlefield recurred in war-time writing as a symbol of the love that could follow and arise from strife. The nobility of combat would sanctify the nation.

After the war, especially in the last two decades of the nineteenth century, this prediction about reunion came true. Hostility nourished by bitter memories did not vanish, but discussion of the war was increasingly dominated by popular writers, Memorial Day speakers, veterans, and politicians who dwelt on sentimental reconciliation and combatants' shared heroism and integrity of conscience. This development, serving postwar and especially post-reconstruction purposes, did not first arise in the 1870s and 1880s. It already had appeared in the wartime honoring of combat as an attainment of moral grandeur. Veterans of the war's worst scenes did not wholly abandon the language of nobility, even when violence was all around them. While the fighting was still fresh in his mind, General Joshua Lawrence Chamberlain, during the surrender cere-monies at Appomattox, anticipated the pattern of memory that prevailed in later decades. As the remnant of Lee's army, led by the Stonewall Brigade, marched past the First Division of the 5th Army Corps, Chamberlain gave his men the order for "carry arms," a salute to the Confederates. Few soldiers had seen more combat than he; he received the Congressional Medal of Honor for his actions at Gettysburg and was severely wounded at Petersburg. Yet Chamberlain had not given up the notion that fighting could be admirable. The day after the surrender he wrote of the Confederates: "I pitied them from the bottom of my heart. Those arms had been well handled & the flags bravely borne."

The honor of having fought well, rather than the reasons for having fought, set the prevailing tone for reminiscences emphasizing future sectional harmony. Southerners, after losing their antebellum campaign to get the North to recognize slaveholders' rights, then their wartime campaign to get the North to recognize the South's independence, mounted a new and finally successful campaign, with help from many Yankees, to get the North to recognize Confederate courage and sincerity in fighting. Romanticizing the war helped to promote consensus on the postwar settlement—discouraging Northern interference with the Southern racial order, accommodating Southerners to their economic subordination. Even the scale of conflict became a source of pride. Speaking of his fellow Confederates to a reunion of veterans from both the Army of Northern Virginia and the Army of the Potomac in 1895, William Roane Aylett said: "None but Anglo-Americans could have made such a fight, and none but our kindred could have whipped us."

Published war stories, most notably *Century Magazine*'s successful series in the 1880s, not only omitted what Robert Underwood Johnson called "political questions" but also stressed what Johnson's colleague at *Century*, C. C. Buel, called "the humanities of the War period." The *Century* articles were still "too military" for some readers; H. S. Brooks, publisher of the *Elmira Sunday Telegram* and the *Harrisburg Sunday Telegram*, asked Jedediah Hotchkiss to write a different kind of article about Stonewall Jackson: "Full of anecdotes—pathetic and heroic acts on the part of the soldiers of both armies." Many veterans obliged the public with colorful tales and bittersweet speeches, glorifying themselves and the men who had died, retelling the war as an exciting romance. The colors grew brighter, the heroes grander, the combat more vague, the winners and losers more alike as a theme for celebration of the war's magnificence. In 1890 David F. Boyd, who had served under Jackson, wrote to W. T. Sherman: "Around you & Stonewall Jackson will gather the *poetry* of our war. His *Valley Campaign* & his 'puritanism,' and your *March to the Sea*—the *Death-Knell* of the *Confederacy,* are the glittering points that will ever strike the popular mind, and inspire the poets imagination."

If Jackson's and Sherman's versions of the war could become the kind of poetry Boyd wanted, no aspect of the conflict could withstand transfiguration.

The recurrence of euphemisms and the frequency of heroic stories did not mean that a curtain had closed over the war, forever masking its scenes of viciousness and chaos. Romanticizing paralleled and often mixed with experiencing and remembering violence intensely. At no time did evasiveness, sentimentality, or hyperbole completely dominate the war generation's writing about combat. From the first battle of Bull Run through the first decade of the twentieth century many eyewitnesses told other people, in private and in print, about the appalling things they had seen and done on the battlefield. General Thomas W. Hyde, writing his memoirs in 1894, said: "I never expect to be fully believed when I tell what I saw of the horrors of Spottsylvania, because I would be loth to believe it myself, were the case reversed." Even so, he did tell. Soldiers said that no words could fully convey their experiences to a civilian, but they often tried to do so. Some men of both armies wrote home in the same tone that Private William Chunn of the 40th Georgia Regiment used in 1862: "I see no beauties in the preparation for the whole sale slaughter of the human race. I see no glory in numbering those on the battlefield slain. It is nothing but horror from beginning to end." Sixty years later a veteran of the 48th Virginia Regiment, Francis Smith Robertson, began his "Reminiscences," which included a graphic description of the "hell on earth" during the second day at Chancellorsville, by saying: "Nor can I feel justified in writing what might be termed, a lady-like history, of my most unladylike experiences."

Some of the most gruesome accounts of combat and its aftermath in hospitals and among corpses appeared in commemorative volumes devoted to celebration or to sectional reconciliation. Such works as Frank Moore's *Anecdotes, Poetry and Incidents of the War: North and South,* his *Women of the War; Their Heroism and Self-Sacrifice,* and George M. Vickers's *Under Both Flags: A Panorama of the Great Civil War*— published thirty years apart—contained not only the sentimental, noble war but also accounts of the terrifying war of violence that participants could not assimilate. The last of these books reprinted John A. Cockerill's "A Boy at Shiloh," which Sherman called the truest rendering of that combat. Cockerill, an associate of Joseph Pulitzer, was recalling his experiences on April 6, 1862, when he had been seventeen years old: "Everything looked weird and unnatural. The very leaves on the trees, though scarcely out of the bud, seemed greener than I had ever seen leaves, and larger. The faces of the men about me looked like no faces that I had ever seen on earth. Actions took on the grotesque form of nightmares. The roar and din of the battle in all its terror outstripped my most fanciful dreams of Pandemonium. The wounded and butchered men who came up out of the blue smoke in front of us, and were dragged or sent hobbling to the rear, seemed like bleeding messengers come to tell us of the fate that awaited us." Writing a history of the 58th Indiana Regiment in 1895, John J. Hight remembered the battle of Shiloh as "more like some opiatic fever dream than sober history" and described men "reckless of life beyond all reason, fighting with open wounds until death ensued by bleeding," while others, unhurt, fled to the river bluff.

Such narratives, though they of course could not fully re-create the experience, sought to show how combat had defied or destroyed the conventional workings of perception and thought. These writings offered instances of what looked like abrogation of laws that people had always trusted—the logical connection of cause and effect, the continuous existence of matter, the validity of consciousness. Veterans did not need to fill their writings with the vocabulary of chaos and nightmare in order to convey to a reader their exposure to unreason. Straightforward accounts of combat's effects on people sometimes hardly differed from an expressionist projection of the mind's inability to integrate what it encountered, as in William Preston Johnston's description of one battlefield after the armies had left it. "I saw on the battlefield a lost sheep straying among the dead. An old man—a farmer over whose place the storm of battle swept and left all a wreck, met us. He talked in a very excited way, his mind evidently shaken by the scenes he had passed thro'. He was mounted on a sorry pony, and he seemed to think that he was made whole by having secured 'a Yankee horse' of which he spoke with great glee. Little children played amid the vestiges of human wrath and horror." The Civil War generation did not lack for people willing to try to record the worst of the war, but such writers did not usually write about their experiences for the purpose of showing that their war or all war was morally wrong, meaningless, or mad. Some recent discussions of their sentimentalizing have implied that any other conclusion about war must partake of the most blatant romanticizing. Members of the war generation may have been inconsistent—confronting their disorienting experiences without questioning their earlier assumptions—but they did not remain naïve. Most people could not altogether avoid seeing or hearing about and remembering scenes like that on the ground in front of Battery Wagner after the failed assault led by Colonel Robert Gould Shaw and the 54th Massachusetts Infantry. "The ditch was literally choked up with dead bodies and it was possible to walk upon them for fifty yards without touching ground. One poor creature a yankee, had had his fore-head blown away, and his whole brain exposed; he still lived, and in his physical and mental blindness crawled upon hands and knees, like a beast, moaning and throwing sand over his body, face and into his skull." Eyewitnesses commonly settled for juxtaposition of memory and meaning. The scenes were terrible, but the war fulfilled a purpose. Soldiers and veterans did not want to keep to themselves an incommunicable knowledge of the disintegration of the war's moral structure. They wanted to share widely held notions of what their combat had accomplished. One of their ways of doing so was to tell others what they had done.

Romanticizing the war, insisting on its benefits and its place in a universal plan, exalting the great general who could sway battle—accounts in this mold kept the story from becoming one wherein destructiveness ruled all and destruction was the war's all-important object and result. At the same time, many soldiers fell under the influence of this tendency in the violence, and they experienced, in varying degrees, the feeling of having no purpose or identity other than that conferred by fighting the enemy. Soldiers said that they wanted to fight it out sooner, rather than later, and get the results at once. Some of the three-year men in the Federal army, after re-enlisting early in 1864, grew impatient at home during their thirty-day furloughs and returned to the army early. They felt "homesick for the field," impatient to share in the excitement of the final victory. The excitement, the accomplishment, sometimes lay in fighting—a release from anxiety and a distraction from adversity. Choices and plans, remote considerations and private intentions, seemed at times to disappear, as in Jackson's corps at the end of August 1862, when he decided to attack the Federals near Manassas before Longstreet had joined him. As soon as Jackson's waiting men saw the cluster of mounted officers break away from the general and start galloping toward their units, the soldiers "knew what it meant; and from the woods rose a hoarse roar like that from cages of wild beasts at the scent of blood." In his reminiscences a Federal officer used more genteel language to describe his own similar state of mind in battle; he said that he experienced "an elimination of all personality amidst the quickened activity and excitements of the action." Combat consumed him.

Soldiers on both sides expressed their eagerness for attacks, theirs or the enemy's, when they foresaw the opportunity to do a disproportionate amount of killing. Back in Virginia after their defeat at Gettysburg, the Confederates held a line south of the Rappahannock River that one of Colonel Alexander C. Haskell's couriers hoped the Yankees would assault. From his experience of battlefields, the young private could see, as readily as a general, the strength of his army's defensive position. "This boy had a feeling of positive pleasure, as much as Napoleon ever had in choosing his greatest battle fields, at the bare idea of an enemy making a bloody attack upon us in a position which his eye taught him was fatal to a foe. Such are the pleasures of war. Soldiers cannot always feel its horrors." When strongly moved, soldiers could enjoy its horrors, overcoming the enemy by throwing aside all restraints on violence. At Jonesboro, Georgia, south of Atlanta, during the Confederates' desperate attempt to prevent Sherman from cutting the last rail line into the city, soldiers of the Third Brigade of the Third Division of Sherman's 14th Corps took their revenge on Confederates who had shot down the first wave of the Federal assault: "Our boys scaled their re-doubts and then came our chance and then a slaughter commenced the like of which I never witnessed before and I pray I may never see again. A great many of the Rebels threw away their Arms and proposed to surrender but the next instant they were shot down or received a bayonett." Not until a bugle had sounded "Cease Fire" three times did the killing stop.

After months or years of fighting, a time came when veteran soldiers took war to be their inescapable reality—"the natural order of events," one man said. Combat seemed to pose the best test of character, distinguishing true men from false. During the Atlanta campaign John S. Casement wrote home from Sherman's army: "this is no place for Bombasts they are all Sneaking to the rear this is the place to try the mettle of men there is no such thing as passing Bogus on Intelligent men where the enemys Missels are flying pretty thick." In this outlook the man who could stand up to the fighting, the man who could be effective in it, especially the one who could lead in it served an ideal at least partially distinct from war's purposes of state. Alongside the religion of the rule of providence and the religion of the laws of the cosmos, there were signs of an atavistic religion in the armies and perhaps among the populace—a passionate, primitive one worshipping acts of violence.

In his postwar fiction J. W. DeForest suggested that the devout religious leader and the popular military commander shared a common temperament—a "passionate nature"—and worked a similar effect on their followers. The unbelieving fighter had in his character the makings of a religious zealot but adventitiously pursued a different path. His zeal lay in combat. In DeForest's story "The Brigade Commander" the main figure, a lapsed minister turned colonel, had become "the idol" of his brigade "because he had led them to victory and made them famous." One of the colonel's officers explained the commander's hold over his men: "Moses saw God in the burrnin' bussh, an' bowed down to it, an' worshippt it. It wasn't the bussh he worshippt; it was his God that was in it." The colonel, as his subordinate explained twice, was a human burning bush. And the god in him that the soldiers worshipped was "the God o' War," "the God o' Battles." Discerning in combat a god—a governing principle, a ruler of events, a rewarder of the faithful—veteran soldiers, DeForest suggested, devoted themselves to that god, even when their doing so overrode other systems of belief they may have avowed. "If a man will win battles and give his brigade a right to brag loudly of its doings, he may have its admiration and even its enthusiastic devotion though he be as pitiless and as wicked as Lucifer." According to conventional morality and institutional religion, the colonel was a bad man. But he was a good commander. DeForest implicitly denied that a Christian evangelist was superior to or essentially different from a successful commander. Commitment to combat became equivalent to, or a manifestation of, or a surrogate for religious belief. Without celebrating it, perhaps hinting at its futility, DeForest described the hold over men that fighting could seize.

Recalling occasions of surrender to violence—dwelling on scenes that ought to have been bad dreams—was unwise, a path to isolation from communal understanding of vicarious war. Sustained, unmediated recollection of the war would have entailed contemplating bloodshed that had no assured connection with rational plans or redeeming purposes. It would perhaps have disintegrated into fragments of remembered events, rumored events, imagined events, and remembered imaginings. It would not simply have debunked sentimental treacle written to obscure the "real" war; it would have dissolved the recorded history of the war, personal and national. Few veterans tried to take that path. Not even veterans' bitterest recollections usually led to repudiation of all prevailing modes of sharing the war. Ambrose Bierce, as a young Federal officer, drew clear, orderly maps of battlefields and won commendation for his skill and courage. Later, in his fiction and reminiscences, battlefields became confused scenes of aimlessness and brutality. He called combat "criminal insanity." Yet he also indulged a streak of romanticizing common to many veterans. He asked rhetorically: "Is it not strange . . . that I recall with difficulty the danger and death and horrors of the time, and without effort all that was gracious and picturesque?" Years after the war, John Esten Cooke, prolific writer of the picturesque, said in conversation: "There is nothing intellectual about fighting. It is the fit work of brutes and brutish men. And in modern war, where men are organized in masses and converted into insensate machines, there is really nothing heroic or romantic or in any way calculated to appeal to the imagination." Yet no one surpassed Cooke in celebrating individual courage and skillful mastery on the part of the war's Southern heroes. His readers, including his fellow veterans, preferred that version; and, he said, "I write for money." Cooke, too, preferred the heroes in his books to the brutal men he remembered. If veterans did not all write of the war as Bierce did at his most scathing or if Bierce, DeForest, and other critics of romanticizing failed to draw the darkest conclusions from their portraits of war, their restraint did not necessarily arise from self-deception or forgetfulness. They had to live with the war. Even Bierce, connoisseur of death, did so for fifty years.

Soldiers grew bitter, desperate, fatalistic—civilians grew distraught—but they clung to the proposition that their actions made a difference in a controversy that would direct their country's future into a more just or less just path. Robert G. Ingersoll, a Federal veteran, became in later years America's most celebrated agnostic, titillating his audiences with denunciations of a God who could delight in so cruel a world and follow it with a hell of perpetual torments as an afterlife. Perhaps he recalled his war experiences while describing "Nature" in 1893: "Life feeding on life with ravenous, merciless hunger—every leaf a battlefield—war everywhere." A sensitive, humane mind could hardly endure the vision, much less approve it. Ingersoll devoted himself to trying to shock others as he had been shocked by the thought of a divine plan that condoned malignity and suffering. Yet in leaving the army in 1863 he had not disavowed the war. He said: "I have seen enough of death & horror. . . . I have seen enough of bloodshed and mutilation." Still, he wanted rebellion to be defeated and slavery to be ended. He could leave the war, but he could not reject the nation created with the violence he was trying to escape. The completion of these tasks he left to others, who contrived ways to accomplish them other than by standing appalled at the universal battlefield.

Most of those who sustained the war did so by idealizing it. Those who abandoned visions of gallantry and moral exaltation in combat did not usually repudiate the fighting as pointless or merely bestial. In his *Incidents and Anecdotes of the War,* published in 1862, Orville J. Victor quoted a *New York Tribune* reporter's description of the battle of Shiloh: "Men lost their semblance of humanity, and the spirit of the demon shone in their faces. There was but one desire, and that was to destroy." Victor commented: "Men to contemplate it with serenity must be demons indeed, or else they must be mastered by emotions higher and nobler than love of life or self—the love of a cause which Heaven consecrates." Just as civilians found promises of national redemption in war, soldiers customarily thought of their fighting not as absurd, insane, or criminal but as effective. This belief was the minimal consolation for men who expected the war to accomplish worthy purposes. As Ingersoll may never have escaped it, even by repudiating God, men of less drastic outrage accommodated themselves to a life—one perhaps about to end abruptly and violently—in which effectiveness might be a virtue second to none, the best hope for survival, physical and mental. In his memoirs Joshua Lawrence Chamberlain listed strengths of character that emerged in combat and rejected the broadest implications of Sherman's remark that war was "all hell": "He did not mean to imply that its participants are demons." The veterans' reunions that were great municipal events, the handwritten unpublished war memoirs that began with justifications of secession or concluded with paeans to the union, the efforts to show how grotesque or inspiring or both the war had been—all reiterated the joint complicity of combatants and noncombatants in whatever the war had become.

If it were possible to write about the war in a way that would idealize the memory of combat, bring together soldiers' and civilians' experience of war, yet also portray an all-consuming war with no design, no cosmically sanctioned meaning, the text might be Oliver Wendell Holmes, Jr.'s Memorial Day address in 1895. Speaking to veterans and civilians, he tried to re-create the state of mind of a soldier in combat, but he deprived his audience of the reassurance offered by narrative and by the memory of purposeful action. In Sanders Theatre at Harvard College, President Charles W. Eliot introduced Holmes, then justice of the Massachusetts Supreme Judicial Court, by reminiscing about him as an undergraduate before he had gone to war: "He had no special athletic or martial tendencies. He loved literature and study." As a young officer in the 20th Massachusetts Regiment he had sustained three wounds, one of which left him with a long scar where a ball had hit him just above the heart, struck a rib, traveled around his chest under the skin, and had come out on his right side. Yet Holmes later wrote of his soldiering: "I was not born for it and did nothing remarkable in that way." He still loved literature and study; his main ambition before and after the war was to distinguish himself as an intellectual. Years after his Memorial Day address he said: "I always feel like explaining, if I refer to the war in a speech that I feel free to do so because that was not the sp[h]ere of my vocation and that my appreciations are for men of a different type."

Holmes began by likening his address to the music made by a blind man who played the flute as busy pedestrians passed him on Washington Street in Boston. Then he criticized his countrymen for their growing preoccupation with the material world. Businessmen seeking profits, rich people seeking pleasure, socialists seeking redistribution of property, humanitarians seeking to diminish suffering, moralists seeking perpetual peace, scientists seeking to explain all life as matter—all wanted a world of security from which they had excluded struggle, pain, or uncertainty. Holmes told his audience that they could not have it. Life would always consist of fighting and hardship, he said, and soldiers of the Civil War had shown how best to live. They set their honor ahead of their interests and their survival. Holmes called his address "The Soldier's Faith" and summarized it in these words: "I do not know what is true. I do not know the meaning of the universe. But in the midst of doubt, in the collapse of creeds, there is one thing I do not doubt, that no man who lives in the same world with most of us can doubt, and that is that the faith is true and adorable which leads a soldier to throw away his life in obedience to a blindly accepted duty, in a cause which he little understands, in a plan of campaign of which he has no notion, under tactics of which he does not see the use."

Soon after publication of "The Soldier's Faith" in December 1895, *The Nation* and the New York *Evening Post* censured Holmes for indulging in "sentimental jingoism" and for undermining reverence for human life, peace, and the rule of law. His address acknowledged that most of his contemporaries believed things that he did not believe. Holmes was accustomed to having people disagree with him. Like the blind flute player on Washington Street, he expected to be for the most part unheeded by the hurrying passers-by, who thought that they could see where they were going. He anticipated dissent; yet he asserted "that no man who lives in the same world with most of us"—that is, no one except people living in a mental world of privately defined reality—could doubt his view of the soldier's faith. Holmes was not exalting soldiers above civilians so much as he was using the soldier in combat as a metaphor, not only "a metaphor for the agnostic's plight," as the critic Cushing Strout has noted, but also a metaphor for human existence. He defined his contemporaries' situation as one of doubt and the collapse of creeds allaying doubt; no creed united them. Certainty about a cause was impossible; everyone "little understands" every cause. "Certitude is not the test of certainty," Holmes said in his essay "Natural Law." "We have been cock-sure of many things that were not so." No one could know what plan of campaign, if any, the directing force, if any, was following. And no one could see what effect his fighting, his living—the "tactics"—would have on the outcome. Soldiers in battle were assailed, Holmes said, by common sense, which he equated with the search for physical safety, pain-reduction, pleasure-seeking, and material well-being. Though some might put such a goal first, as Holmes saw his contemporaries doing in civilian life, their trying to avoid throwing away their lives could not evade uncertainty. Even the common-sense attempt to serve one's own interests did not assure that one's actions did so.

Frequently calling life a struggle, Holmes often referred to literal rivalries. He clung to Malthusian and pseudo-Darwinian economic views, conceiving economic life to be unalterably a contest over the division of a fixed total of resources. He thought that dangerous competitive sports strengthened participants because of the danger, producing "a race fit for headship and command." These opinions, Holmes knew, many people did not share. But in his metaphor, for which he claimed a general validity, the state of battle did not solely refer to people fighting one another. As he suggested in his Memorial Day address and as he elsewhere argued at greater length, all aspiration consisted of struggle, yet its future results or ultimate worth remained unknowable. For that reason, all struggle entailed risk—the risk that a person will have thrown away life in one or more meaningless undertakings. The worth of aspiration came not from assurance about the merits of its goal but from willingness to risk, which Holmes expressed in the figure of a soldier's duty. Figuratively, everyone was a soldier, confronting this duty blindly. One of the most noticeable patterns of selectivity in his discussions of the war was his emphasis on soldiers' being killed rather than on their killing. His versions of struggle were often sacrificial. In all spheres of life, he called men to be fighters—to defy their destiny, which was to be victims.

The Civil War, viewed in this light, did not consist of service to an ineluctably triumphant nation, whose existence vindicated its citizens' certitude; rather, the war consisted of myriad blind acts of faith. Its outcome reflected the preponderance of force one group of people with partially coinciding beliefs brought to bear against an opposing group with partially coinciding beliefs, both groups all the while holding many beliefs in common. Holmes's metaphor—an uncomprehending soldier acting blindly in the incomprehensible battle—was the antithesis of narrative, the negation of a clear story of events subject to comprehension and control. Holmes spoke not very differently than Lee's aide Colonel Charles Marshall when Marshall jokingly had complained in 1894 that the story of Chancellorsville depended on witnesses so contradictory that a subversive logician could call every occurrence into question, even the battle itself. What had happened in the Civil War? Holmes suggested that every answer depended not on a proven record, unimpeachable reasoning, or universal law but on belief that commanded assent by its adherents' power.

Long after the war, Holmes told Lewis Einstein "that he was not sure if, from a constitutional point of view, the South was not in the right." Such a concession held little importance for him because neither secession-ists' deductive reasoning nor unionists' definition of the republic nor abolitionists' assertions of human rights under natural law described anything substantive other than what their physical force could effect. To reason cogently from the Constitution's provisions to the act of secession and to conclude that one's reasoning was more in harmony with truth than was the outcome of the war struck Holmes as a vain exercise. Similarly, to conclude that the federal government's abolition of slavery brought the Northern cause into closer conformity with natural law was, he thought, to hypostatize the will of the powerful as the plan of the universe. Harold J. Laski summarized Holmes's view of natural law: "It means no more than the system which has become so fully a part of our intellectual climate that we cannot work our institutions successfully except upon its assumptions." Rights, Holmes argued, ultimately depended on "the fighting will of the subject to maintain them." Neither reason nor appeals to the moral order of the universe sufficed, since there would always be people who "will fight and die to make a different world," with different definitions of duties and rights: "When differences are sufficiently far reaching, we try to kill the other man rather than let him have his way." That was what the Federals had done to the Confederates. For Holmes law, rights—the United States—prevailed through the use of force. The Civil War was only the most overt demonstration of this fact. The crisis of 1861–1865 had not been a singular, atypical upheaval but only an extreme manifestation of the means by which the nation existed.

Holmes's avowal of the soldier's faith has attracted a diverse array of critics, especially since the publication of Edmund Wilson's book *Patriotic Gore* in 1962. Most have understood it to celebrate and encourage war. For some commentators Holmes was obsessed with memories of the Civil War and had become a militarist; for others he had so fully suppressed recollections of his disgust at violence that he had turned sentimental about combat. Critics have deplored Holmes's lack of humanitarian sympathies and his unprotesting acceptance of a world ruled by powerful men and aggressive nations in their own interest. He has been called an atheist, a mystic, a relativist, a nihilist, an existentialist. Refusing to denounce war as unjustifiable or irrational, while also refusing to see in war—the Civil War included—an assured moral sanction, Holmes has struck these readers as an empty man. They generally have assumed that his outlook was self-evidently wrong and have turned their attention to finding its supposed origins in his social class or his personal experience.

Holmes had a short reply to censure of "The Soldier's Faith." Edward Atkinson, a writer on economics, said to him after reading the published address: "I don't like it. It's bad morals and bad politics." Holmes reported his answer: "I civilly replied that I didn't care." His critics could not prove him wrong by disliking him or his conclusions. He refused to concede universal validity to the God of special providences or the God of mathematical laws of history's progress, and he doubted that human activities or existence had any cosmic significance. He repeatedly denied that he was advocating war or that he thought a soldier's life best. Even so, his metaphor has continued to repel readers, from his friend William James to the most recent writers. It implied that the powerful state, not ideas or principles, was the ultimate recourse in politics and that the man fighting blindly was the epitome of existence. Holmes's only faith seemed to be a belief in perpetual war. Holmes gave the vicarious war its greatest extent, placing all civilians at all times in the position of soldiers who had to act without certainty and who often fought without mercy. His "soldiers" did not master the struggle but were destroyed by it. Their cause, whether or not it prevailed, was ultimately ephemeral. Their nation had no more promise of perpetuity than did the systems of morality and politics that temporarily prevailed in it.

Several Confederate veterans praised Holmes's speeches for what they understood to be his celebrations of courage, but the full import of "The Soldier's Faith" bore little resemblance to Americans' writings about the war. Far from dismissing claims to possess certainty, far from replacing truths of right and wrong with desires imposed by force, people who wrote about the war often used the language of moral judgment. In doing so, they retrospectively sought to reclaim a measure of control over the war by demonstrating that it had not vitiated their ethical system. They fixed on some persons, groups, or section the moral burden of responsibility for causing the war and for making it so bloody, destructive, and vicious. Notwithstanding its supposed promise of redemptive results from bloodshed and sacrifice, the war also struck participants as the product of a great crime, waged and prolonged by conduct that was criminal. Even if the war generation had fallen far into violence, they had retained, they often said, the capacity to condemn the many wrongs of the war.

Who had committed the crime of causing the war? One explanation—probably the most common—blamed it on the other section, Northerners and Southerners each proclaiming their own side guiltless. Another often-repeated view attributed the war to extremists in both sections: abolitionists and fire-eaters, "political demagogues North and South," and "a few leading Blood thirsty leaders." Americans reiterated some version of Samuel Landes's comments: "It is not the peoples war at all, but [they] were led into it blindly till it is too late to remedy it." Such an outlook did not deter popular demands for vigorous war. It did reveal a widespread eagerness to be exonerated of the criminality attached to bloodshed. William E. Boggs, blaming the North, said: "There is a fearful responsibility in the sight of God, which rests *somewhere.*" Alfred Davenport, blaming the Confederates, asked about the numberless graves: "If nations and governments have moral responsibilities, where does the responsibility rest for these?" Many people were prepared to see war as a punishment for their society's sins; few would say that they had willed or had helped to bring on the bloodshed.

The most vehement censure focused on the moral responsibility of leaders who, had they acted otherwise, could have saved lives they instead threw away. Democratic critics of the Lincoln administration and of Lincoln's generals portrayed the growing destructiveness of the Federal war effort, especially the spring and summer offensives of 1864, as unforgivable atrocities. A few Democrats were ready to give up the union if that were a necessary consequence of stopping such a war. Most said that the union could be saved by restoring peace but that no nation could justly survive by the Republicans' methods. The antiwar press regularly referred to the combat as if it were devoid of moral meaning and intelligent direction. For the *Democrat* of Johnstown, Pennsylvania, conscription was "THE LOTTERY OF DEATH," and the battlefield was "THE SLAUGHTER PEN." Men who made such mindless war were guilty, according to Representative John D. Stiles, of "savage recklessness that appalls the Christian world and that for centuries to come will pollute our moral atmosphere with the sickening taint of blood." Republican warmongers were "covered from head to foot with the blood of their slaughtered fellow-citizens." Some Democrats who supported war nevertheless sought to distance themselves from the worst bloodshed and asked, as the *Detroit Free Press* did of Grant's last campaigns, "Could not all of this have been avoided, and a better result obtained?" These Democrats wanted the story of the war to show that, even if they had been unable to change it, they had identified the wrongdoing and had opposed it. The taint of war's evils would not be on them.

Leaders of the Confederacy faced moral judgment from some Southerners for their decisions about ending the fight for independence. The irreducible minimum of control over war lay in an ability and a willingness to stop it by giving up the struggle. At what point did further resistance to the Federals become unmistakably futile and every death in a doomed cause the fault of him who ordered it to no purpose? Joseph E. Johnston believed that "undertaking a war without the means of waging it successfully" would have been a "high crime." He wrote his memoirs partly to show that Southerners had not been guilty of such a crime in resorting to war; rather, Jefferson Davis and the Confederate government had squandered the available means. In his several accounts of discussions with Davis about surrender in April 1865, Johnston contrasted Davis's intransigence in the face of imminent defeat with his own determination "to avoid the crime of waging a hopeless war." For Lee the problem was still more intricate. His holding Richmond and Petersburg after Grant crossed to the south bank of the James River in June

1864 was strategically unsound. Grant later said that Lee could have prolonged the war into 1866 if he had taken his army out of the trenches defending those cities when he should have done so. Looking back, Grant speculated that Lee had known that the South would lose and had chosen a course designed to shorten the war, putting his duty as a citizen of the United States above his judgment as a soldier of the Confederacy. Passively, discreetly, Lee had curtailed the bloodletting. Writing about his years in the Confederate army, E. Porter Alexander argued that the Southern cause was doomed after Grant crossed the James; though Lee's influence, if exerted, could have stopped the war, the decision to do so belonged to Davis, who should have opened negotiations for peace. "The last chance of winning independence, if it ever existed, *had* now expired, & all rules must condemn the hopeless shedding of blood."

Other former Confederate officers said after the war that the inevitability of defeat had been clear in the winter of 1864–1865, but Davis, or "the politicians," could not face surrender. They knew, William J. Hardee recalled, that it was "only a question of the time it would take to use up the military force already organized." Yet "the politicians" preferred to "use up" those soldiers and wait until the generals surrendered, rather than take upon themselves the stopping of a hopeless war. Johnston's reiteration of the word "crime" obviously accused Davis; Lee, during the final winter, kept saying that the military situation was gloomy but that he relied on exertions by "the people." Though Lee's formulation was more subtle than Johnston's, both implied that civilians left the futile dying and the final defeat to the army. Having embraced war as a necessity, its supporters shrank from saying it had failed. Accepting responsibility for stopping it would imply that they could have stopped it earlier or perhaps have prevented it. If they claimed or exercised such power, they advertised their complicity in making war in vain.

In Atlanta, Sherman talked with Joshua Hill, a Georgia politician who had opposed secession and refused to take part in the war. Sherman made no secret of his intended march across the state and left Hill with the impression that Georgia could avoid such a fate by withdrawing from the Confederacy. But when Hill broached this choice to influential friends in Milledgeville and Augusta, he recalled afterward, many of them "thought I exaggerated the danger and overestimated his army, while others concluded, wisely perhaps, that it was too late to involve public opinion to give direction to such a crisis." In other words, Confederate leaders could not reverse the course of secession and thereby arrest its violent consequences; they must let the war unfold.

By 1864 many parts of the South had revealed, in elections and in other ways, the presence of large constituencies in favor of peace—which meant, tacitly or overtly, an immediate end to the Confederate war effort. But the men who controlled the government rejected this manner of ending Confederate history, and the men who stayed in the army were not prepared to repudiate or overthrow the Confederate government. Southerners criticizing their politicians, like Northern critics of the bloodshed ordered by Lincoln, Stanton, Grant, and Sherman, found in the last year or the last months of war the starkest example of inability to "give direction" to events. There remained only fatalistically pursuing attrition and destruction. To one looking back at the last part of the war, its leaders appeared to have foreseen how it would end but to have been unable to reach that ending except by drifting on through still more blood. This must have been wrong, and these leaders must have been to blame, their critics said. Faulting the leaders for letting the war go on was one way to believe that the war, even in its most destructive phase, need not have escaped intelligent direction and that it remained subject to moral standards. The needless deaths, few or many, betokened not the people's lapse of judgment but the weakness of the men who were responsible.

A few writers felt such intense outrage at deaths so numerous and profitless that they came close to indicting a whole generation for losing its moral sense in a carnival of slaughter. Recalling her visit to a Federal army hospital after the battle of Antietam, Ann R. L. Schaeffer wrote: "I could not help thinking how ridiculous our world must appear to superior intelligences—our incurring so much trouble, expense and suffering to maim and murder each other and after accomplishing this object, laying the poor creatures side by side—endeavoring to relieve their pain and save their lives." Perhaps the extraterrestrial mind, preserving its powers of reason while laughing at the folly of maddened human beings, had the one perspective—the one claim to clarity of vision—that a crazy war for worthy ends could not cloud. Most writers did not seek or attain so derisive a detachment; they had sympathies with one side or the other. But a few, like Schaeffer, could suggest that the participants had lost comprehension of their own violence. In denunciations of the excesses of the vicarious war, as in celebrations of its victories, William Tecumseh Sherman and Stonewall Jackson served as apt representatives of the extremes to which the war had gone.

Two of Sherman's severest critics, Henry Van Ness Boynton and Donn Piatt, built a case against his whole career. They were veterans who had taken up journalism in Washington after the war, specializing in revelations of official corruption. Sherman became one of Boynton's targets in 1875 after publishing his memoirs. Allied with defenders of the permanent bureaucracy of the army's staff departments, secretly paid by President

Grant's secretary Orville Babcock, and aided by War Department clerks, Boynton wrote a series of newspaper articles, subsequently published as a book, attacking Sherman's memoirs and his war record. He accused Sherman of stealing glory that rightfully belonged to other officers, as well as making many blunders that killed thousands of men at Shiloh, Vicksburg, Missionary Ridge, and in Georgia. In a typical passage, Boynton wrote that Sherman's men regarded the assault on Kennesaw Mountain as "an utterly needless move, and so an inexcusable slaughter." After the corruption of Babcock and Secretary of War W. W. Belknap had been exposed and Boynton had turned against them, too, he still attacked Sherman. In 1881 Boynton accused Sherman of having ordered the assault at Kennesaw Mountain in order to attract attention in the newspapers, which were devoting more space to Grant's Virginia campaign than to Sherman's in Georgia. Boynton said that the Kennesaw attack was "the most deliberate slaughter and cold blooded murder ever perpetrated."

Piatt's condemnations of Civil War generals and of the bloodshed over which they presided went far beyond those of Boynton, who still gave speeches about soldiers' pride and spoke of forging a nation through battles. Piatt had a political motive for attacking Sherman. Having served as a military aide to General Robert Schenck, he then helped Schenck try to take John Sherman's Senate seat in 1866, while General Sherman used his influence with veterans in the Ohio legislature to help re-elect his brother. In December, Piatt said that if he tried to get a federal job, "the Shermans, Dennisons Egglestons & Co. would bounce me in the most disgusting manner." Beyond this grudge, however, Piatt's strictures on the war had much wider scope than a personal vendetta against Sherman. "I had, instinctively, a horror of war," he wrote late in life. "The cruel brutality sickened me." He expressed his antipathy most fully in his book *General George H. Thomas: A Critical Biography,* which he did not live to complete. The last quarter of it was written by Boynton and James H. Wilson. Long stretches of the book had nothing to say about Thomas, instead berating the bloody crimes and blunders of other generals, especially Grant, Sherman, and Lee. Knowing that Piatt was at work on the book, A. F. Hough anticipated that he would use Thomas as a foil in order to discredit Grant; Hough advised Henry M. Cist to keep a check on Piatt lest the book lose credence by making false charges: "He is notoriously one of the most unreliable writers of the age." But the book's details were less important than its impassioned denunciation of men rising to rank and fame by ordering soldiers to their deaths.

Piatt presented himself as a friend of the suffering, sympathetic Jesus, whose spirit had been betrayed by both sides in the war. He scorned the populace and its leaders, calling the war "the darkest page in our country's history." Though he condemned slavery and secession, he could not reconcile himself to the agents or the means by which these evils had been defeated. He found fault with Federal generals who had spent so much blood in winning, and he praised generals who had been superseded as the war grew worse—Rosecrans, Buell, Pope, McClernand, Hooker, McClellan, and Wallace. Their main appeal in his eyes evidently lay in their having fallen out of favor with the butchers in charge of the war: Grant and Sherman, Lincoln and Stanton. Piatt's loyalties to his favorite generals did not run deep. Leaving aside Lee's vain victories, he wrote, "our military men on both sides seemed to be groping in the dark. They marched without a purpose and fought battles without other result than slaughter to their troops." He suggested that war monuments should be made not of bronze and marble but of the bones of the dead, memorials to stupidity and incompetence. In 1878 Piatt had called Sherman "the fool of luck," arguing that Grant and Sherman ought to have been court-martialed and shot for their conduct at Shiloh. But Grant and Sherman were only the most conspicuous, accessible objects for his more general indignation. Ostensibly writing within the celebratory tradition, praising some of the war's heroes and approving its outcome, he unsystematically but vehemently attacked belief in moral betterment and national progress through war, as well as generals' claims to have guided war intelligently. The Confederacy died of inanition, and the military leaders of the North were not so much triumphant victors as fools of luck who happened to be in command at the end.

Attributing accomplishments to a few generals the better to discredit others by contrast, Piatt tacitly subverted without directly repudiating belief in extraordinary men honored for their superior powers. He quoted one of Louis Napoleon Bonaparte's ministers to explain how a man of mediocre ability could remain a ruler: "See, I lay a narrow plank upon the ground, and any one can walk it. I lift that plank a hundred feet above the earth, and only one in a thousand has nerve enough to do so. The way to govern an empire is not to know that the plank is off the ground." Piatt faulted a political system that could succumb to such a gruesome war; he thought of American democracy as government by political parties in which capitalists bought control of the government by investing money to control the vote. His picture of the Civil War consisted largely of incompetent generals ignoring the momentousness of the disasters they perpetrated. Though they were admired by the deluded, their greatness amounted to little more than persevering in destruction while not seeing the chasm beneath them—the madness of their conduct. The public, he complained, mistook action for genius and hailed the "man-killer" as a hero. "The false yet fascinating glamour of war blinds the masses to the fact that a mere leader of men is such through an absence of the higher intellectual qualities. His self-reliance that makes him eminent is the result of ignorance." Piatt often mentioned private soldiers' heroism and patriotism; he did not argue that Civil War combat was futile or empty of glory. Yet his strictures on generals and on politicians who used them, newspapers that praised them, and a public that exalted them left little to celebrate in their soldiers' obedience. While crediting soldiers with winning the war despite generals' stupidity, Piatt hinted at a vision of crazy slaughter devoid of any just rationale. Indirectly, fitfully broaching an all-inclusive condemnation of the people who had made war, Piatt bestowed most of the obloquy attached to such slaughter on the men who had ordered it.

T. J. Jackson's severest critic wrote early in the twentieth century, and many readers mistook her for a Confederate apologist. In 1911 the novelist Mary Johnston published *The Long Roll,* with a fictional Stonewall Jackson as one of the main characters. Her vivid, detailed narratives of Confederate combat and battlefield triumph left the misleading impression that she was celebrating the South's war for independence. But her version of Jackson was not primarily heroic. Using Richard Taylor's memoirs and John Esten Cooke's works as sources for her description of Jackson, she gave their humorous exaggerations a sinister cast. The unprepossessing exterior of her Stonewall contained a fanatical war-maker. The book's frontispiece was a portrait of Jackson by N. C. Wyeth. Though it bore only a distant resemblance to photographs of Jackson, it fit the character in Johnston's novel, suggesting a dour, brutal man. Johnston, a pacifist during World War I, had written *The Long Roll* as an antiwar book, followed in 1912 by another Civil War novel significantly titled *Cease Firing.*

Anna Jackson, protesting that her husband had not resembled this fictional character, wrote to the newspapers, denying that the general had loved war, as Johnston's character did. However, the novelist made Stonewall a grim figure not mainly for the sake of sensationalizing her story but to show how people could be possessed by the demon of destruction. In her climactic battle narrative of Jackson's flank attack at Chancellorsville she turned the Wilderness, where the armies met, into a supernatural female figure. The personified Wilderness changed from her customary calm to an intoxicated, shrieking, blood-drinking fury—a maenad, a servant of Ares, a Valkyrie. "She chanted, she swayed, she cried aloud to the stars, and she shook her madness upon the troops, very impartially, on grey and on blue." Mary Johnston's version of the war portrayed people thinking themselves heroes while behaving like psychopaths. Though her soldiers were brave and devoted, their combat was savage and futile. Answering a letter from a reader in 1913, she said: "In writing these two books—*The Long Roll* and *Cease Firing*—the emphasis in my own mind shifted after a while from the tragedy of that war to the tragic absurdity and horror of all wars. . . . And war is altogether stupid as well as horrible."

Mary Johnston was a Virginian, and she dedicated *The Long Roll* to two Confederate officers, her father, John William Johnston, and his cousin Joseph E. Johnston. Her story dramatized Southern dedication but undercut her Stonewall Jackson's assertion that "we are righteously at war." In the course of the narrative Jackson fell victim to the combat he had so enthusiastically embraced. Johnston's description of the memorial ceremonies in Richmond after the general's death evoked the male figure of War whom the frantic female Wilderness had served: "There was lacking no pomp of War, War who must have gauds with which to hide his naked horror." While Jackson's admirers complained in 1911 that Mary Johnston's fictional general was vulgar, unlike the man himself, she had dealt with him more subversively than they realized. Her Stonewall was obsessed with and was killed by meaningless destruction. As one critic recognized in 1936, she had anticipated the war novels of a later generation. Her reader probably hears Johnston's own voice in her summary of the thoughts of one of her characters while he looked at Jackson: Major Cleave knew "that the immortals, if there were any, must be clamouring for the curtain to descend forever upon this shabby human stage, painful and sordid, with its strutting tragedians and its bellman's cry of *World Drama!*" She implicitly made Jackson condemn himself and indict his contemporaries. After Antietam, Ann Schaeffer had imagined superior intelligences watching the Civil War as a ridiculous farce; Mary Johnston imagined them thinking it a poorly performed tragedy whose actors overrated the play's importance.

The best-known summary of the war's meaning, Lincoln's second inaugural address, also suggested that the participants had battled in confusion. The generation had brought upon itself a quantity of bloodshed so great that reason could not explain the violence. If so much killing could be explained—and Lincoln did not go beyond saying "if"—it must be God's punishment of and white Americans' atonement for the offense of 250 years of slavery. This suggestion presupposed that God guided the war and that people neither controlled nor understood their actions. Like Donn Piatt, Mary Johnston, and other writers critical of the killing, which apparently had escaped limitation or guidance, Lincoln emphasized the participants' inability to account for what they were doing by connecting intent with result. He sketched a condition of bewilderment: "Neither party expected for the war, the magnitude, or the duration, which it has already attained. Neither anticipated that the *cause* of the conflict might cease with, or even before, the conflict itself should cease. Each looked for an easier triumph, and a result less fundamental and astounding. Both read the same Bible, and pray to the same God; and each invokes His aid against the other." This state of affairs hardly testified to Americans' insight into their own actions; it did not permit them the reassurance of knowing the causes or consequences of their own acts.

Lincoln had begun to think along these lines in 1862, as events defied his efforts; he had reached his view of the war by the early months of 1864, before Grant and Sherman had begun the Virginia and Georgia campaigns. Acknowledging that events had controlled him, he said of the war: "God alone can claim it." At about the same time, the *New York Tribune* reported that Confederate officials had plotted to capture or assassinate Lincoln. He said that if they did so they would gain nothing: "I am but a single individual, and it would not help their cause or make the least difference in the progress of the war. Everything would go right on just the same." If this were true of Lincoln, it was true of any individual or of the hundreds of thousands of individuals whom the war was killing. In the second inaugural address Lincoln explicitly declined to predict the progress of the war. It might not end soon, no matter how weak the Confederacy was. He expected Northern victory, but he suggested that the war might yet go on for the sole purpose of confounding and punishing the people of both sections. Obviously the war was defeating Southerners' assertions; Lincoln told Northerners that their minds, too, had not conformed to the movement of history. He thought that his address would endure but would not be immediately popular. "Men are not flattered by being shown that there has been a difference of purpose between the Almighty and them. To deny it, however, in this case, is to deny that there is a God governing the world." In this comment he implied, as he had done in the address, that the war, viewed solely as the work of human minds and deeds, had grown incomprehensible. Because the war had thwarted the designs, confuted the explanations, and absorbed rather than obeyed the efforts of those who had made it, to say that it acted out men's purposes alone was to say that human activity had no ultimate moral meaning, that there was no God, no cosmic design to events. If, instead, the course of the war were God's doing, He could reconcile its contradictions, explain its surprises, and validate its bloodshed in some cosmic logic or divinely weighed justice whose clarity and consistency were inaccessible to human minds. There was no other way to believe that what had happened made sense.

Lincoln correctly predicted that his summary of the war would not quickly win a following. Americans' effort to develop stories and interpretations on which large numbers of people could agree did not lend itself to the kind of paradoxes Lincoln posed. The vicarious war was least likely to unite its participants with an intelligible version of their experiences if it recorded primarily a loss of control, a war that ruled its creators. Yet this aspect of their experience was incipient in Americans' going to war in 1861. They accepted violence in the belief that a contest of physical force was the only way to resolve differences they had failed to resolve through the system of choices available in the mechanisms of self-government. If they lacked sufficient control over their political behavior—channeled, as it was, through long-standing institutions—to choose a national future and to win peaceful communal assent to the choice, how much less likely were they to manage violence judiciously and systematically? On the contrary, the coming of war was greeted by many people as an escape from selection and judgment and the rational connecting of actions with foreseeable consequences.

In December 1860 Senator James Dixon of Connecticut wrote to a constituent: "We are fast drifting into disunion & civil war. Meanwhile the master minds of the nation seem paralysed. Some talk of concessions—some of coercion—but all seem bewildered by the magnitude of the great event approaching. . . . Many of our friends say let the consequences be what they may, nothing can be done to prevent the evil." Political leaders could not avoid or direct the evil of war partly because so many people were prepared to accept it no matter what direction it took. The day after the election of Lincoln a newspaper report from Petersburg, Virginia, said: "Every man feels that something terrible is impending, but the issue no one undertakes to define, no one feels competent to define." By "issue" the reporter meant "outcome." Of course, many people in Virginia and elsewhere were making predictions about the outcome of the crisis. But if "issue" were understood to mean the coming course of events—that is, the impending terrible things that were about to happen—the reporter had good reason to say that no one could define it. Nor, he implied, could anyone avert it. Similarly, the many formulations designed to show how soldiers and civilians could direct the war, benefit from the war, and make the war a moral triumph for the nation were nevertheless also implicitly saying, as did the bewildered prophets of 1860, that the war must go on whether or not it fulfilled their apparently confident claims to have made it a force for good.

Striving for permanent, transcendent results and embracing as much of the populace as possible in that effort militated in favor of mounting violence and, ultimately, in favor of the excesses and evils that people had felt powerless to prevent. Again and again during the war, intimations of worse things yet to come were accompanied by resignation to the unavoidable. The day that Confederates fired on Fort Sumter, John Sherman wrote: "Civil war is actually upon us & strange to say it brings a feeling of relief—the suspense is over." Senator Sherman did not profess to know what the war would do. Two years later he speculated that, like the French Revolution, it might eventually destroy those who had made it; "still," he concluded, "there is no way but to go ahead." Thus the war's extremes had to be accepted as inevitable, even if the participants' actions defeated their intentions. Oliver P. Temple, a slaveholder who foresaw that secession and war would destroy slavery, afterward justified his decision to side with the Confederacy by recalling his helplessness in the face of the momentum of secession, which simultaneously had isolated him—forcing him to choose between Southerners and Yankees—and had provided him with plausible, though specious, reasons to escape that isolation by following the fire-eaters of whom he disapproved. Joining the war and pushing it to more drastic measures promised a lasting settlement of the long-vexed question of the citizen's relation to the nation. There would no longer be doubt and controversy about what country one belonged to or about whether one's country could survive. Whether they expected the union's conclusive triumph or the creation of a secure Southern Confederacy, supporters of the war would in victory finally escape the burden bequeathed to them by the Revolutionary founders: the burden of uncertainty over the republic's survival—the burden of trying to guide the polity without a promise of security, with a constant awareness that liberty or government or both might be destroyed by the people themselves at any time.

Not many Americans late in 1860 and early in 1861 said that they wanted a war. Even fewer foresaw a war so vast as the one that occupied the next four years. Most people in both sections approved of fighting, once it began over Fort Sumter. Eventually, more than three million men took part in it. The most common explanation for supporting the war said that actions by people on the other side left no alternative but choosing between war and degradation. Except in acknowledging sins for which war's miseries might be a punishment, few Americans attributed the war to themselves. Almost all of them would have said, as did the Democratic politician and Federal general Daniel Sickles: "I am not responsible." Speaking in Brooklyn at a patriotic rally in August 1862, he set no limits on what the belligerents might do, but the destruction would not be of his making. "I am not responsible for war, nor for the results that follow in the train of war. I am not responsible for history. No human power can control them. We must accept them as we find them." In this acceptance of whatever war might bring—as in the wide-spread expectation that war would produce a more secure and stable nation, a more competent government, a more public-spirited populace, a triumph for self-government—Americans turned to war to rescue them from the prospect of failure. Despite their differing aspirations, they often said in 1861 and afterward that they could not become the people they wanted to be except through war. The vicarious war thus was a civic necessity. Whoever was responsible for its coming fulfilled the avowed wartime wishes of many Americans who said that they had not wanted or started war.

CHAPTER 7

THE BATTLE OF KENNESAW MOUNTAIN

DESPITE the daily June rains, well-dressed Southern ladies went to the top of Kennesaw Mountain and looked through telescopes to see the war below. The twin hills of Little Kennesaw and Big Kennesaw, joined by a saddleback, rose about 800 feet above the surrounding countryside. Moving along the crest of Big Kennesaw, Confederate soldiers and their visitors had a panoramic view. More than nine miles to the northwest lay Allatoona Pass through which ran the tracks of the Western & Atlantic Railroad in its route from Chattanooga to Atlanta. The railroad came to the base of Kennesaw, then passed around it to the northeast, turning back southward to enter the town of Marietta two miles southeast of Kennesaw Mountain. Eleven miles beyond Marietta the tracks crossed the Chattahoochee River. From the top of Kennesaw one could see the church steeples and factory chimneys of Atlanta, six miles southeast of the Chattahoochee.

In the third week of June, the two armies which had been maneuvering and fighting since the first week of May were gathering around Kennesaw Mountain. Both armies—Johnston's 51,000 men and Sherman's 94,000—formed great irregular semicircles curving westward around Marietta from one flank two miles north of town to the other three miles south. On June 17 the ladies on the summit were watching one of Johnston's corps withdraw under fire from Lost Mountain four miles to the west. The corps was pulling back toward Kennesaw to complete a new Confederate line. The ladies saw smoke rising from artillery pieces, which were too far away to be heard. The white tops of thousands of U.S. Army wagons moved over the uneven landscape, passing among woods and cultivated fields. Federal soldiers advanced toward Kennesaw in four long columns. Near the base of the mountain, a house was burning. Looking through their telescopes at the distant skirmish, the ladies occasionally laughed.

General Johnston felt distressed by his army's situation. He wrote to his wife on June 18: "The Engineering system adopted by Sherman can not well be resisted by an inferior force. We can not get opportunity to fight on equal terms & may have to cross the Chattahoochee—burn this immediately." The river was the last—and Kennesaw Mountain was the next to the last—of a series of natural barriers that slaves and soldiers and engineers had fortified to keep Sherman's army away from Atlanta. From Rocky Face Ridge, just south of the Tennessee border, to these final defensible lines outside the entrenchments around Atlanta, Johnston had withdrawn his army. He had originally expected Sherman to use the much larger Federal force in direct assaults. Instead, the Federals had faced his lines with the Army of the Cumberland and the Army of the Ohio, while sending the Army of the Tennessee around his southern flank. Repeatedly, by large-scale movements, Sherman had threatened to reach the rear of the Confederate army and, by the movements of smaller units, had threatened to penetrate its defensive line and divide it. If Sherman could get a substantial force across the Western & Atlantic tracks behind Johnston's army, between it and Atlanta, the Confederates would have to assault entrenched positions rather than wait for Federal attacks. To prevent this, Johnston had protected his supply line and avoided heavy casualties by retreating. He said that he found it "humiliating, to see the apprehension of the people of a country abandoned to the enemy." But he believed that duty required him to conserve his army until it had the chance to fight with better prospects of success.

Although the two armies had not met in a single great battle during this campaign, elements of them were almost constantly shooting at each other. During one day of ordinary duty on the skirmish line the 200 men of the 92d Ohio Regiment fired 24,000 rounds of ammunition. Often dozens, sometimes hundreds of men were killed or wounded. Several battles between divisions yielded even more casualties. Before General Grant had gone to Virginia, Sherman had promised him, then repeated the promise in telegrams, that the western army would press Johnston hard enough to prevent any large transfer of Confederate troops from Georgia to Lee's army. In fact, Johnston was steadily losing men by desertion. At times, whole companies or every man posted on a picket line went over to the Yankees to get out of the war. The citizens' fear of the advancing Federal army, which pained Johnston, was well justified. For miles on both sides of the Western & Atlantic, Sherman's men and

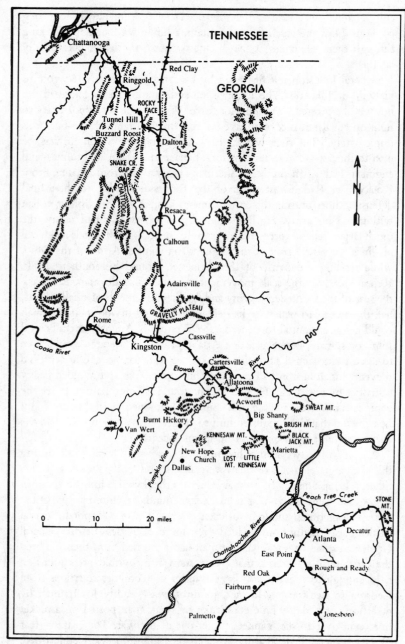

NORTHWEST GEORGIA

animals left almost nothing that could be consumed. Soldiers killed chickens, hogs, sheep, and cattle; army mules and horses ate the wheat, oats, grass, and corn. Men ransacked houses and burned many unoccupied buildings. Sherman wrote to his wife: "We have devoured the land. . . . All the people retire before us, and desolation is behind. To realize what war is one should follow our tracks."

Before withdrawing to the lines around Marietta, Johnston's army had occupied an elaborate system of breastworks along a ridge four miles west of Kennesaw Mountain—the watershed between the Etowah and Chattahoochee Rivers. In skirmishing before June 17, the Federal army's movements threatened to get between Kennesaw and the positions farther west, as well as to place artillery where it could command Johnston's most advanced fortifications. Already, on the 17th, Confederate engineers were planning new lines closer to Kennesaw Mountain. By the evening of the 18th, the left and right wings of Johnston's army had pulled back into a half circle eight miles long. A division commander, General T. C. Hindman, commented: "If Gen Johnston holds the Kennesaw we are well enough here. He can hold it if he will."

A Federal cavalryman, Silas C. Stevens, visited Sherman's headquarters in a patch of bushes and scrub oak. He found the general walking alone in front of a tent, smoking the short stump of a cigar. "His mind seemed to be occupied with distant thought, rather than the present surroundings." Stevens looked at Colonel Orlando M. Poe's maps, with their diagrams of the army's movements, and marveled at their intricacy. They showed how Sherman "could withdraw, and reform his various corps to a nicety, in all their various relations to the field of battle, and still keep the integrity of that formation, of the lines intact." Sherman did not have to rely solely on maps and reports for his understanding of the terrain. Twenty years earlier he had traveled through northwestern Georgia to record militiamen's claims for compensation from the federal government. Never content to be idle, he had made topographical sketches; during the Atlanta campaign, he surprised his soldiers with his seemingly miraculous foreknowledge of the hills, rivers, and roads that lay ahead. Looking up at the summit of Kennesaw Mountain through Poe's telescope, the general saw the place where he had stood on March 3, 1844, as a twenty-four-year-old lieutenant of artillery.

As General William J. Hardee's corps fell back to occupy the center of the new Confederate positions along the hills south of Kennesaw, Sherman thought that Johnston was about to abandon the whole line, including the mountain. On June 18 Sherman assumed that he could turn the Confederate defenses with another flanking movement. But he found that the Confederates intended to hold the long curving line, with its apex at the mountain, and that the position presented him a choice among difficulties. Lieutenant Matthew Jamison saw the general during the morning of the 19th, walking in the rain along trenches the Confederates had abandoned. Sherman was "gazing at the mountain." On June 22, Hood's corps, on the left end of the Confederate line south of Marietta, attacked the most advanced divisions of the 20th Corps and the Army of the Ohio. The Federals held their line, but Sherman learned from this fighting that Confederate defenses extended farther around Marietta than his own forces did. General John M. Schofield, commander of the Army of the Ohio, reported that the left wing of Hood's corps stretched a mile eastward beyond the end of the Federal right. Johnston's ring of entrenchments had the advantage of shorter distances between his units and of interior lines of movement, along which he could concentrate men more quickly than Sherman could. If Sherman were to detach a substantial force and send it still farther south and east toward the Western & Atlantic tracks behind Johnston, he would risk seeing those divisions cut off from his army and destroyed.

At the same time, Sherman did not want to remove the left wing of his army from the Western & Atlantic northwest of Marietta. To feed men and animals and to have enough ammunition, the Federal army needed about 65 boxcars full of supplies each day. Sherman was trying to get 130, to build a reserve. Having used up his surplus in temporarily leaving the rail line to get around Allatoona Pass, he depended on every shipment just to meet immediate daily demands. He worried that the Confederates would send into Tennessee a cavalry force strong enough to interrupt the flow of supplies from the North. Distribution of food from the rail head to an army spread along ten miles of entrenchments was made difficult by weeks of rain, which had turned every wagon road into mud. It was hard enough to keep men supplied while they stayed in one place; a rapid movement would be even more risky, if not impossible. As the two armies settled into their fortified positions, their firing from skirmish lines, incessant during periods of movement, slacked off. The artillery exchanged shots; the Federals were happy to do so because they learned where the Confederate guns were. But skirmishing no longer promised results, since neither side could advance without assaulting entrenchments. Sherman had extended his arc around Johnston as far as he thought prudent. To weaken his center in front of Kennesaw in order to lengthen one flank invited attack where his line was most vulnerable. Johnston might not attack, but it seemed unwise to give him a chance to divide the Federal force. General George H. Thomas, commander of the Army of the Cumberland, suggested trying to break Johnston's line by regular siege approaches with sapping tunnels. But experience had convinced Sherman that the Confederates would have new works ready to occupy by the time a sap weakened their position. Sherman saw only two alternatives: to stand still until the rains stopped, the roads dried, and a surplus of supplies accumulated; or to make a frontal assault. Private Stevens was right to suspect that the general's mind was occupied with distant thought.

A successful attack on the Confederate center could yield great results. To be defeated where a river impeded retreat was one of the worst fates an army could suffer. If Sherman could break up Johnston's army west of the Chattahoochee, he would avoid the risk of having to cross the river in the presence of an enemy, as well as the much greater cost in lives and time required to defeat Johnston in the fortifications of Atlanta. As soon as part of Thomas's army penetrated the center of the Confederate line, the Army of the Cumberland could advance in strength and either turn north to destroy Johnston's right wing with the help of the Army of the Tennessee or turn south to destroy Johnston's left wing with the help of the Army of the Ohio. Sherman imagined driving the Confederates "pell-mell into the Chattahoochee." Although he had consistently avoided making the frontal assaults Johnston had expected, Sherman had lately begun to think that his men, especially the Army of the Cumberland, took flanking too much for granted and lost opportunities by being too cautious. He believed that Thomas's men could have reached the Western & Atlantic tracks southeast of Marietta on June 18 if they had pressed forward at dawn as he had ordered. Instead, at 9:30 in the morning he had found two division commanders quarreling at a crossroads, each trying to get the other to take the lead. Sherman swore at them and got them started; but the result of the delay, he thought, was this impasse in the trenches around Kennesaw. During the following week Sherman decided that both his own men and the Confederates would learn a valuable lesson from a Federal assault, especially one with good prospects of success. He would shake them out of "the belief that flanking alone was my game," showing his men the advantages of boldness and teaching Johnston not to take anything for granted.

On June 24, Sherman ordered an assault on the center of the Confederate line along the ridge south of Little Kennesaw, to take place early on June 27. Two divisions of Thomas's army were to make the main attack, while part of the 15th Corps of the Army of the Tennessee charged at the base of Little Kennesaw. During the two days before the assault, the Army of the Ohio was to threaten the extreme left of Johnston's lines, in the hope of getting him to move men from the center to that flank and thereby, as Sherman said, "attenuate" the defenses. But, from the top of Kennesaw, Confederates could see that the bulk of the Federal army

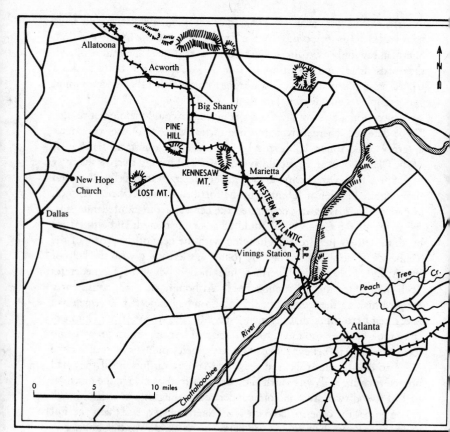

THE ROADS AROUND KENNESAW MOUNTAIN

still faced their center. Sherman later said that all three of his army commanders—Thomas, Schofield, and James B. McPherson—agreed with his decision to attack. Yet on the evening of June 26, after General John A. Logan, commander of the 15th Corps, complained to other generals in the Army of the Tennessee that the order would lead them to destruction the next day, McPherson, well known for his unfailing youthful good cheer, said to his generals: "So much the more reason that we should put our energies and hearts into carrying it out, so that it shall not fail on account of our disapproval." Logan wrote to his wife: "I can not say that I tho have strong hopes of success."

The rain had finally stopped, and both armies saw a beautiful sunset on the 26th. The last light turned the woods the color of fire. During the evening a correspondent of the *New York Herald* interviewed General Charles G. Harker, a twenty-seven-year-old regular army officer commanding one of the brigades that would lead the attack in the morning. Harker said: "They are powerful works; we can never take them; I will do my best, though." Late that night the captain of a company in one of Harker's regiments, John W. Tuttle of the 3d Kentucky, wrote in his diary: "received orders to be in readiness to march tomorrow morning at sunrise with sixty rounds of cartridges. (Hell expected)."

Though some of the tired Confederate soldiers, upon reaching the Kennesaw positions, had fallen down to rest instead of immediately going to work on entrenchments, the sound of approaching Federal artillery fire quickly roused them to start digging. One of their lieutenants said: "Boys, I'm going to get a cannon on my plantation when the war ends, there's nothing like it to make lazy people work." In the following days, the Confederates improved their interconnected earthworks along the rising and falling ridge which ran south for more than four miles from Kennesaw Mountain. On June 25, General Samuel G. French, commanding the division centered on Little Kennesaw, looked out over the lines of both armies. He wryly noted the difference between the numerous wagon trains, the tent cities, and the busy movements of the Federals spread out below him and the poverty and comparative quiet of the Confederate army, except along its front. There the soldiers had prepared the usual firing trenches by throwing up earth in front, leaving a step on which to kneel behind this cover, and topping the embankment with a log resting on blocks to protect their heads while they fired from between the dirt and the log. Transverse trenches went back at right angles from the main line. In front of the line soldiers felled trees and trimmed and sharpened the branches. In some places they implanted stakes pointing toward the enemy.

From the Confederate positions on the wooded side of Little Kennesaw, the hill sloped down to the entrenchments of the 15th Corps, 400 yards away and 300 feet below. Between the foot of the hill and the Federal lines a creek, swollen by recent rains, separated the two armies, its small valley running all along the base of the Kennesaw ridge. In front of Little Kennesaw the ground near the creek was swampy and thickly covered with brush, saplings, and matted vines. Because General French's line followed the hillside down to a point more than 200 feet lower, rose with the crest along another hill, and then dropped again where one of the roads to Marietta crossed it, the Confederates were able to use the hillsides for fortifications with crossing fields of fire for both artillery and infantry. Along an uneven line stretching more than a mile south of French, two Confederate divisions faced two Federal divisions. Still farther south, where the ground in front of the Confederates again dropped more steeply to the creek, lay the critical point, against which Sherman had ordered the main assault. It was the center and the western-most extension of Johnston's curving line; three miles behind it were Marietta and the Western & Atlantic tracks to Atlanta.

In a letter written on June 26, Sherman complained: "Johnston fights entirely behind earthworks, and they are so obscured by bushes & trees that we cannot see them till we receive a sudden and deadly fire." In their angles of the Confederate works, two of Hardee's division commanders, Generals Patrick Cleburne and Benjamin Franklin Cheatham, had pre-pared such a position across their narrow front. From the creek between the armies, the ground rose gradually toward the Confederates until, about eighty yards in front of them, it became a steeper wooded hillside. Cleburne's men had dug their trenches along the west side of one hill and across the crest of a connecting one, giving them a clear sweep in their front. Cheatham's line protruded in an angle manned by two brigades in a space of about 500 yards. The sites had been chosen in the dark, and Cheatham had seen the following day that they were "not accurately selected," because they were too far back from the crest where the hill began to level off. He had not tried to start new works but had made the existing ones as strong as possible. At the southern base of the salient was an eight-gun battery, with four Napoleon guns pointing toward the ground in front of the angle. At the northern base, two other guns pointed across the same ground. During the exchanges of artillery fire in recent days, Cheatham had kept these two guns silent and out of sight, covered with brush. Farther north a small fort held four guns. These pointed downhill toward the creek and were loaded with canisters full of iron pellets. On June 26, Cheatham and Hardee walked along the trench in the salient and talked to the men of the Tennessee regiments holding that part of the line. Cheatham, a rugged-looking man, wore a blue flannel shirt, gray pants, and a black slouch hat; "old Frank told us," a soldier later recalled, "we were going to be assaulted soon—that it was a weak place in the line—and that he didn't want a man to leave the ditches, that if they came so thick & fast we couldn't load & shoot, to catch them on our bayonetts & throw them to our rear—and, that if we were over powered & captured, that he would go with us to prison."

At three o'clock in the morning on June 27, three brigades of the 15th Corps began to file out from behind their entrenchments to form long double lines facing the base of Little Kennesaw and the adjacent hill. By four o'clock the men of Colonel Dan McCook's brigade, opposite Chea-tham's angle, were up for breakfast, with orders to be ready to march at six, leaving their knapsacks behind and carrying forty rounds in their cartridge boxes. At 5:30 A.M. the assistant adjutant general of O. O. Howard's 4th Corps watched the planning for the placement of Howard's divisions, especially that of General John Newton, two of whose brigades—under Harker and George D. Wagner—were to attack Cleburne's line. Making his first note of the day, the adjutant wrote: "The country is so thickly wooded, and the topography is such that it is almost impossible to tell anything about the enemy's works. . . . We are about to make an assault upon works we know little about." Dawn revealed that the day would be clear and hot. Soon after sunrise, General Jefferson C. Davis, whose division of the 14th Corps was to attack with Newton's, took his brigade commanders—McCook, Colonel John G. Mitchell, and General James D. Morgan—out to look at the enemy's lines. They chose the points on Cheatham's angle that McCook and Mitchell would try to penetrate. The Confederate line was 300 yards uphill from the creek and 100 feet above it, obscured by trees.

The brigades began to move into position just behind the Federal trenches at seven o'clock. McCook called his five regimental commanders together and told them that they were going to charge the rebel works. The 85th Illinois was to lead the way as skirmishers, then rejoin the column after driving back the rebel skirmishers; the 125th Illinois was to go over the enemy line first; the 86th Illinois was to turn left and occupy the Confederate works. A quarter of a mile to the north, General Harker talked to his eight regimental commanders, telling them that, as soon as they broke the Confederate line, other brigades would come forward and take up the fight.

Harker did not like the formation General Howard had prescribed for the assault—a compact column with a narrow front, of the Napoleonic kind taught by manuals copied from the French. The brigade would have a front of about thirty-five men, each regiment consisting of eight successive lines of that length, with ten yards separating each of the regiments in the column. Harker's brigade would thus present almost two thousand men, massed together in a rectangle 75 yards wide and 150 yards long. Wagner received the same orders for his brigade, 100 yards to Harker's right, and General Nathan Kimball was to support their assault in the same formation. When Harker and Kimball learned these plans at division headquarters on the night of June 26, they condemned the formation. Their commander, General Newton, told them that such were the orders; "and of course," Kimball later wrote, "we obeyed and did the best we could."

Such a compact charge was supposed to overwhelm the enemy with superior numbers at the point of attack. The impetus of so many men moving against a short stretch of works could, in theory, breach the line before the defenders' fire could stop the column. Since men massed together would not fire as they advanced, their success depended on reaching the enemy quickly, before many of them were shot. In case of delay or failure to reach their goal, their dense formation would become a source of vulnerability rather than strength. Newton pointedly noted in his report that the formation had been "prescribed by General Howard." Howard afterward commented: "But for the slashings, abatis, and other entanglements, all proving to be greater obstacles than they appeared to our glasses, the little column would have lost but a few men before arriving at the barricades."

As attacking brigades lined up just behind the Federal earthworks, other brigades replaced them in the trenches, and others formed behind them to follow and to widen the planned gap in the Confederate defenses. The process was not complete by eight o'clock, the hour Sherman had specified for the charge, and Harker's and Wagner's men had to stand in ranks, facing the creek and the rising ground beyond, until McCook's and Mitchell's men off to the right were ready to advance at the same time. They waited silently. One man carefully relaced his shoes, tucking away the ends of his shoestrings so that they would not catch on any obstacle. Others tore up letters they had received and threw the pieces away. Around them the Federal artillery opened fire, concentrating its explosives on the hillside above and shaking the earth for miles around. McCook's brigade formed on the downward slope toward the creek—fewer than 1,800 men but with a wider front, making a shorter, broader column. Just before moving into the open, they were told what they were expected to do. Through the trees on the hillside, they could see part of the Confederate line of head logs and thrown-up dirt. Most men were silent; some looked up at the sun above the Kennesaw ridge; a few were talkative and restless. The colonel of the 52d Ohio Regiment heard a veteran soldier say to a friend in a low voice: "Aye! God, Jim, that hill's going to be worse'n Pea Ridge. We'll ketch hell over'n them woods." Shots from the Confederate skirmish line at the base of the hill and from a sharpshooter in a tree hit some men. One man, on the left end of the rear regiment, writhed on the ground. Colonel Dan McCook walked along his brigade. Five years before, at the age of twenty-five, he had shared a failing Kansas law firm with Sherman and had given the July 4th oration in Leavenworth. Awaiting the signal to advance, after the artillery had fallen silent, he recited lines from Macaulay to his men in a clear, shrill voice:

> Then out spake bold Horatius
> The Captain of the Gate,

> "To every man upon this earth
> Death cometh soon or late.
> And how can man die better
> Than facing fearful odds
> For the ashes of his fathers
> And the temples of his Gods?"

Twenty-one years afterward, Sherman wrote: "McCook was my law partner, and *I* caused his death."

Between 8:30 and 9:00 the signal shot came from a piece at Thomas's headquarters. Artillery fire reopened along the ten-mile front and continued incessantly from more than 200 guns. Soldiers from six Federal corps moved toward the Confederate lines, and the men of yet another corps, the 23d, were already pressing the extreme left of Johnston's army. General French, on Little Kennesaw, and Captain Thomas Edwin Smith of the 79th Ohio Regiment—more than four miles apart, in each other's line of sight—looked out from their respective vantage points on the same scene along the base of the Kennesaw ridge. They saw flashes and billows of smoke from Federal artillery well before the boom of the discharge reached their ears. Clouds of dust seemed to leap up from the Confederate works where shells hit. Confederate artillery on the mountain and along the ridge replied to the fire but tended to overshoot the enemy's gun emplacements, throwing up dirt in the rear and blasting a cornfield. Lines of men in blue uniforms appeared to rise from the earth and rush down the slope toward the creek bed. Blue smoke from muskets marked the line of the skirmishers' advance; white smoke from artillery rose over the field and partially obscured the view until breezes broke it up, revealing a converging charge toward Cleburne and toward Cheatham's salient. "It was the greatest *war* spectacle I have ever seen," Smith wrote the next day. "A newspaper correspondent would doubtless describe the scene as 'Grand in the Extreme' But it was all *sickening* to me."

At opposite ends of the main attack, skirmishers from two divisions of the 20th Corps southeast of the ridge and from divisions of the 16th and 17th corps north of Kennesaw Mountain moved forward simultaneously, trying to make it look like a general assault all along the line. The 20th Corps men advanced their skirmish line a short way. At the base of Kennesaw, skirmishers of the 17th Corps—one regiment from each brigade—had been ordered by General McPherson to "press forward." Only the five companies of the 16th Iowa on picket duty did so. In their five minutes of running toward the Confederate skirmish line, more than one-third of them were hit. In Company C, Corporal Bair's brains were blown out as he took his first step; Private McLaughlin lost his right leg;

Private Davidson took two balls in the shoulder blade; Private Kughn was hit in the neck; Private Brown was shot through the side; Private Mullen continually yelled to keep up the charge until his lower jaw was shattered by a Minié ball and left hanging by a strip of skin; the company commander, Captain Sam Duffin, was mortally wounded. Within seventy-five yards of the Confederate skirmishers, the line of Iowans stopped, fired a volley, and ran back toward their trenches. Several men lay caught in the open behind partial cover. In Company C, Private Frank McDuff was shot through the left lung. Private Marcel Auge, trying to fire at the rebels, saw his right hand torn apart. He threw away his rifle, jumped up to run for the trenches, and was felled with multiple hits before he could go five steps. Having watched from the Federal line, Lieutenant Martin Gebbart of the 15th Iowa said: "It was done in gallant style, but sadening to see them repulsed and shot down like dogs." Private Henry Clinton Parkhurst survived the skirmish and later recalled: "After the fighting was over, we learned that the battle of Kennesaw Mountain had been fought and lost, and that our charge had been a mere demonstration to alarm the enemy."

Sherman stayed with the 15th Corps, watching the assault near Little Kennesaw and communicating with Thomas by messages. Three brigades of the corps, in two lines almost half a mile long, headed for the base of the ridge at a run. They charged the Confederate skirmish line and overran it in hand-to-hand fighting with bayonets and rifle butts. One Confederate regiment lost 128 of its 265 men, killed or captured. When the skirmish line broke, the attackers followed the retreating pickets toward the ridge. They were further slowed and their alignment was disrupted by the marshy ground and thick growths of trees, brush, and vines along the creek. Wading through the mud and thrashing through the undergrowth, they came under artillery fire from the northeast, east, and southeast at several elevations in the hills.

The men who reached the open ground felt tired from their exertion in the morning heat. They had come to this point without a clear visual image of the Confederate entrenchments ahead. At last they saw what they faced. The northernmost brigades looked up a steep rise studded with boulders and gnarled oaks. Below the crest, one of French's brigades manned a trench line of dirt, stone, and logs, with stripped and sharpened trees lying before it. To the Federals' left, on the even higher incline up Little Kennesaw, another Confederate brigade had a clear field of cross-fire. Seeing this, some men turned and headed back the way they had come. Others started to climb toward the Confederates. They no longer moved in cohesive companies or regiments but were a swarm of men, each acting on his own. The ridge would have been hard to scale even if artillery shells from both armies had not been passing over their heads and if rifle fire had not been hitting them from several angles. In some places the attackers came up to the base of perpendicular surfaces. Major Thomas T. Taylor saw that "they had not the moral support of 'the touch' of elbows—the organizations had been broken."

General French reinforced the Confederate line by moving two regiments from Little Kennesaw to help repulse the assault. Where the steepness or the contours of the ridge denied the Confederates a clear shot, they threw rocks, clubs, tools, and other heavy objects down on the Yankees. Captain Jacob Augustine, commander of the 55th Illinois Regiment, climbed slightly ahead of his men, carrying his sword. Shouting, "Forward, men!" he stood erect and was knocked flat by a bullet in the chest. Three of his men were shot through the head; fourteen in all were killed; two men lost one of their legs, two lost one of their arms, and twenty-eight others were hit.

Not much of the uphill charge was needed to convince men all along the line of the three divisions that their effort was doomed. Though some of them got close to the Confederates and Lieutenant Colonel Rigdon S. Barnhill was killed within ten yards of the enemy's trench, the rush up the ridge by Logan's men did not last long. A Confederate soldier in the Missouri brigade told his sister: "We mowed them down like hay." The men who survived the move forward had to turn their minds to the dangerous work of getting back to a safer place. Their withdrawal was not a sudden turnaround of the whole 15th Corps line from attack to retreat but an accelerating shift of numbers from men going toward the enemy to men going toward the rear, until every man who could move headed downhill. Some clung to temporary shelter while others dug new trench lines closer to the base of the ridge. Moving back from the steeper ground, Federal soldiers came more directly into the field of Confederate artillery fire, and gunners had their range. Private Joseph Grecian of the 83d Indiana Regiment later wrote: "Shells would strike and plow up the ground, covering us with dirt and bursting in the earth would kill or wound some and hoist others from a chosen position. These things, mingled with the cries of the wounded and dying of both armies, made the scene terrible." Most men reached the new, quickly dug line of entrenchments safely, but they could see those who did not: "Heads, arms &c were blown off & scattered over the earth."

In the Federal charge against Kennesaw ridge the largest mass of men moved forward at the signal about a mile and a half south of the 15th Corps assault. The brigades of Wagner, Harker, McCook, and Mitchell headed for that stretch of Confederate trench the generals on both sides had spotted as one of the weakest points in Johnston's long line. Wagner and Harker were supposed to hit north of the salient while McCook and Mitchell were to go directly against it. Harker had protested to his division commander in vain; he had given a packet of papers to a friend, saying as he did so: "I shall be killed." At General Thomas's signal, Wagner's and Harker's brigades went forward.

Though the columns' formation was designed to break the enemy's line with many men in a narrow space, Harker's soldiers had to climb over their own entrenchments before running down to the creek and up toward the Confederates. Once exposed in front of their works, they wanted to move rather than stand still. So they rushed ahead, line by line, rather than in a compact column. Their struggle through thickets, vines, and bushes near the creek broke their lines and their momentum. The leading regiment, the 51st Illinois, was ready to go up the ridge while most of the other regiments were still behind the Federal works. To their left, Wagner's brigade moved forward in better order but was more exposed to artillery and small-arms fire as soon as it came into the open.

In front of Wagner's men, the ridge sloped more evenly and gradually upward, in a broad hollow, between higher elevations on either side. They ran into a clear field of fire. Harker's brigade had the cover of a steeper rise, which, once the men crossed the creek, kept them out of sight of the Confederate line in front of them until they ran up over the crest of the ridge. Confederate artillery facing both brigades and a battery looking down on Harker from his right fired grapeshot and explosive shells into the regiments, killing or wounding several men with each hit. In the heat, soldiers were sweating even before they began to move. Excitement and the exertion of working through the underbrush and running uphill made their hearts beat faster; men who were hit bled more.

The last time General Wagner saw Captain Kirkpatrick of the 40th Indiana Regiment, which led his column, Kirkpatrick was waving men forward with his sword; he asked Wagner in passing: "Where shall I strike the enemy's lines?" More than 200 yards short of the Confederates, the captain's regiment was hit by a volley of rifle fire, but the survivors pushed on while the Confederates reloaded. Within 100 yards of the trench, a second volley and the artillery's blast of grapeshot and canister broke up the 40th Indiana, cutting some men in half. Dense fumes of gunpowder smoke clouded the hillside in front of the Confederates. Wagner's column lost its order as men in the front veered away to escape the artillery's field of fire, and the rear regiments jammed up in confusion. Some men kept going uphill, but most lay down, exhausted, and tried to use the ground as cover.

The forward regiments of Harker's brigade ran up the steeper slope nearby with bayonets fixed and no caps in their rifles. As the 51st Illinois

Regiment topped the crest and came within sight of the Confederate trench about thirty yards ahead, the Confederates fired a volley which hit many men and caused the others to drop to the ground. The regiment's adjutant, Henry W. Hall, took eleven balls in his body. The front of Harker's column stopped before the regiments in the rear had left the Federal entrenchments. As more men ran up from the creek, they clustered in a dense crowd lying on the hillside below the crest.

A few men in both brigades pushed on, climbed over the felled trees and sharpened branches, and reached the outer face of the Confederate entrenchments. In Wagner's brigade, the regimental colors of the 100th Illinois were put on the enemy's works. In Harker's brigade, the color bearer of the 3d Kentucky was killed in a similar attempt. Color Sergeant Michael Delaney of the 27th Illinois got a bayonet thrust in the arm as he put his regiment's flag on the works. He held on and was shot in the mouth. The colors fell into the Confederate lines. Confederate soldiers killed men in the dirt in front of them, one by one, or dragged them over into the trench. Federal soldiers farther back lay flat, returning the enemy's fire but ignoring officers' attempts to get them to stand up again. The commander of Harker's skirmishers said afterward: "There was no concerted action."

While running up the ridge, Harker's men could see their young general, on horseback, urging their charge forward. He sent back a report, which reached Howard at 9:25, saying that the enemy's works were formidable and that artillery was sweeping down his front ranks. When Harker saw that the charge had stopped short of the Confederate line, he rode around the right flank of his brigade, up to the crest of the ridge, and into the center, between his men and the enemy. He raised his hat and called out: "Forward, men, and take those works." The men who stood up were all shot down. Harker was hit by a ball which broke his right arm, penetrated his body, and went through his spine. Colonel Luther P. Bradley, commander of the 51st Illinois, sent word to General Howard that Harker had been mortally wounded, that the brigade could not move any farther, and that the head of the column was "all smashed up and disorganized."

At 9:30, Thomas sent a message to Sherman: "General Howard reports that he has advanced and is doing well." Sherman replied at 9:50: "All well. Keep things moving." At 9:40 Colonel Emerson Opdycke, in charge of the skirmish line for Newton's division, reported that, although the assault had been broken up, Wagner's brigade lay close to the enemy and a new column could go through it and break the Confederate line. Newton ordered General Nathan Kimball to move his brigade into the same route Wagner had taken and to "rush it right through." Howard reported to Thomas at 9:50 that the first assault had failed to take the entrenchments on the ridge. At 10:07, Thomas's order came back: "Make another attack."

Kimball's brigade—1,041 men—moved forward in the same formation, on Wagner's left. The lead regiments—the 74th, 88th, and 44th Illinois—were under constant artillery fire as they went through the brush and woods. Moving into the open on the ridge to assault the works, the 74th Illinois was, Kimball said, "swept away" by balls and pellets from the Confederate rifles and batteries. Of the 207 men who went forward, 56 were hit, 27 of them fatally. Wagner tried to start his brigade up the ridge again at the same time that Kimball attacked but soon fell back under the heavy fire. Before Kimball could send the 88th Illinois against the works he received General Newton's order to stop the assault.

Some with orders and some without, the men of the three brigades turned back toward Federal lines. Harker's brigade broke first; the men rushed down the slope "like an immense herd of infuriated buffaloes running over and trampling each other under foot." Seeing this, Confederate soldiers gave up the cover of their head logs and stood to take better aim at the racing, stumbling men. General Wagner noticed more fire from the enemy on his right; the rebels who had been shooting at Harker's men were turning toward him. When Wagner's brigade started to go back, many of Cleburne's Alabamians and Mississippians got so excited that they climbed out of their trench and started to chase the Yankees, giving out what a newspaper reporter called "infernal yells." Fire from the Federal line quickly ended this countercharge. Kimball's brigade withdrew in better order. Some of the wounded, including General Harker, were carried off the ridge, but many still lay where they had fallen, scattered with the dead from the front of the Confederate entrenchments down to the base of the ridge. Confederates kept shooting at wounded officers, hitting them again and again where they lay. During ninety minutes of fighting, 654 men of Newton's division had been killed or wounded.

Against the point of the angle in Cheatham's line, General Jefferson C. Davis sent Dan McCook's brigade, with the brigade of Colonel John G. Mitchell on their right. At the sound of Thomas's signal gun McCook's skirmishers took the lead in moving down toward the creek, followed by four regiments marching evenly under their battle flags at the regular pace of sixty steps per minute. Cheatham's main battery of Napoleon guns began to fire at the advancing column but did not at first do much harm because the range was continually changing. The two hidden guns remained covered with brush, waiting for the Yankees to get so close that Federal artillery would have to stop firing at the Confederate line.

In crossing the creek and pushing through the brush, the brigade lost some of its order, but the men restored their alignment as they went across a broad yellow meadow at the base of the ridge. They increased their pace from quick time to double quick time. In the rear regiment, the 52d Ohio, Sergeant John T. Fowler was hit, his tongue sticking out as he fell. Major J. T. Holmes, once a professor at Richmond College, saw one of his former students whom he had enlisted, Corporal Isaac Newton Wycoff, fall face forward with arms stretched out, rifle still in the right hand. A man near Holmes whirled around, showing a white face and a clear intent to run back. Holmes lifted his sword and said: "Stop, Joe." The soldier turned and moved on with the regiment.

Some of the Tennesseeans in Cheatham's line stood up in the trench and craned their necks above the head log to see the blue mass of men running toward them. The Confederates took special aim at color bearers; the flag of the 52d Ohio was carried briefly by four men in quick succession. One was killed, one was mortally wounded, one was hit in the arm, and one lost an arm. A fifth man again raised the colors. When the brigade reached the woods, where the ground rose more steeply, the men began to run uphill among the trees. The Confederate infantrymen held their fire while the Federals were climbing to the crest of the ridge. The 1st and 27th Tennessee Regiments held the tip of the salient; Cheatham had arranged to support them with artillery from both bases of the angle. The bends in the Confederate trench line as it followed the ridge enabled him to converge the fire of two brigades on the point of McCook's attack. While the infantry waited, Lieutenant William Vaught finally removed the camouflage from his two hidden guns, which were loaded with double charges of grapeshot.

When McCook's lead regiment, the 125th Illinois, topped the crest of the ridge and came within sixty yards of the 1st and 27th Tennessee, Cheatham's men opened fire. Almost all the men at the front of the column were hit. At close range, from both sides, the artillery began to fire into the lines of men farther back. In the 125th Illinois, fifty-three men were killed and sixty-three wounded. Confederate soldiers shouted "Chickamauga" and "Come on." Although the head of the column lost its order as soldiers fell or moved confusedly in different directions, the other regiments still advanced into the fire behind the 125th Illinois. The next regiment, the 86th Illinois, lost ninety-eight men. Some men ran up to the outer face of the Confederate trench and planted the staffs of regimental colors in the loose dirt. Soldiers exhausted by the steep climb fell to the ground. Wounded and panicked men turned to run back down. The last regiment in the column, the 52d Ohio, still climbed to the crest, meeting crowds of bleeding men who were breathing hard as they pushed their way through and rushed to the rear.

Dan McCook accompanied the assault at the right of his brigade, in front with the 125th Illinois. He reached the entrenchments and shouted: "Come on boys, the day is won." A ball went through his right lung, and he fell a few feet from the earthworks. Seeing McCook hit, Colonel Oscar F. Harmon, commander of the 125th Illinois, left his position to lead the brigade. One of McCook's staff officers, Captain Charles Fellows, who was engaged to Harmon's daughter, was urging the men to keep up the attack. As he called, "Come on boys—we'll take—" he was hit and fell dead near McCook. Within a few minutes, in the act of commanding "Forward," Colonel Harmon was shot through the heart; he fell back into the arms of some of his men. While the rear regiments continued to move up the hill into the Confederate crossfire, soldiers carried the bodies of Fellows and Harmon, and the fatally wounded McCook, back toward the Federal lines. Colonel Caleb Dilworth took command of the brigade. The regiments' successive attempts to breach the works met repeated volleys from the Confederates in the angle and along the ridge to the north.

The barrels of the Tennesseeans' weapons grew hot from constant firing; little pellets of melted lead fell out of the muzzles after each shot. Powder smoke blackened men's faces; their dry tongues swelled in the heat. Federal soldiers lying on the ridge fired into the trench lines, hitting many Confederates. About 250 of Cheatham's men were killed or wounded. Inside the trench the blood of nearby men spurted over others who kept shooting. In the constant concussion of gunfire, soldiers bled from the nose and ears. A captain of the 1st Tennessee was killed as he tried to take one of the stands of colors implanted in front of him in the dirt of the angle. Federal soldiers were shot in saving colors and Confederates in seizing them. Sergeant W. J. Wolty of the 27th Tennessee jumped out of the works to grab a flag; the Yankee who chased him fell; Wolty waved the colors as he went back over the top of the trench, and the rebel yell rose along the line.

The greatest confusion in McCook's brigade developed on its right flank, where men were exposed to the worst crossfire. The 52d Ohio Regiment in the rear kept its lines intact despite the enemy fire that broke the formation of the regiments ahead of it. Within twenty minutes of leaving the Federal lines the soldiers saw that they could not break through the Confederate entrenchments. Instead of retreating, most of them stayed on the ridge. Flat on the ground, they found whatever protection from Confederate fire that they could, including rocks, stumps, tree trunks, and the bodies of other men of the brigade, lying dead where they had fallen. With good aim they fired into the enemy line, forcing the Confederates to slacken their fire. The Federal soldiers soon found that, below the crest of the ridge along a line thirty to sixty yards in front of the entrenchments, men could lie slightly below the Confederates' sight and fire. Under this cover many of them unfixed their bayonets, began to break up the dirt, and used tin cups and plates as shovels to throw up crude earthworks. They pushed sticks, rocks, brush, and pieces of wood forward to shield themselves as they dug, while others kept firing at the enemy's trench.

Between this new line and the Confederate trench, many unwounded men still pressed themselves to the dirt while constant shooting from both sides continued inches above them. Some wounded men who rose and tried to run down the slope were killed by the fire they were trying to escape, shot in the back. Most soldiers lying above the crest worked their way downhill to get behind the dirt their friends were piling up. Sergeant Nixon B. Stewart of the 52d Ohio waited on the exposed ground for his chance. One man lay dead nearby on his right. Another, within reach on his left, was wounded in the head but alive. A soldier of the 22d Indiana Regiment got up to start back and fell dead across Stewart's feet. The man with the head wound sat up and began to talk deliriously. Confederates threw rocks, bayonets, tools, and fuse grenades over their head logs, and Federal soldiers threw similar weapons up into the trench. Men in the open who were so close to the trench that they felt sure they would be killed took the Confederates' invitation to come over and surrendered. Sergeant Stewart decided instead to take his chances and managed to get below the crest.

By the time that Federals began to dig in, men of the 1st Tennessee were running short of ammunition; Federal soldiers noticed that the heaviest fire came from the right rather than from the front. The commander of the 1st and 27th Tennessee, Colonel Hume R. Field, shot Yankees alongside his men until a ball hit his head and paralyzed one side of his body for a while. As the fire slackened, many Confederate soldiers, sweating and wet with the blood of other men, gave way to exhaustion and vomited in their trench. They had killed or wounded 410 men in twenty minutes. Many of these, or what was left of them, lay in plain view not many yards away. Captain James Iredell Hall of the 9th Tennessee Regiment called it "a frightful and disgusting scene of death and destruction." He later wrote: "During all the four years of the war I do not remember ever to have seen the ground so completely strewn with dead bodies."

General Thomas concluded his 10:45 dispatch to Sherman: "McCook's brigade was also very severely handled. . . . Colonel McCook wounded. It is compelled to fall back and reorganize. The troops are all too much exhausted to advance, but we hold all we have gained." Thomas sent word up the ridge to McCook's men and to Mitchell's, who were throwing up dirt along the crest farther south, that he would get entrenching tools and other supplies to them as soon as night came.

Sherman still hoped, at 11:45, that Thomas's men could renew the assault and in the afternoon break the Confederate line. Jefferson C. Davis thought for a while that his brigades might still be able to do it; at Thomas's request, Howard asked his division commanders whether they could break through. By 3:30 all the generals had agreed that no further assault should be made. Sherman's message to Thomas at 4:10 said: "You may order all ground of value gained to-day to be secured." Soldiers who had survived the charge and were back in their own camps had no wish to try again. Men of the 15th Corps said that Little Kennesaw was worse than the steep ground at Vicksburg. A newspaper reporter heard one of Wagner's men say: "Damn these assaults in column; they make a man more afraid of being trampled to death by the rear lines than he is of the enemy. They might do on a marble floor." Private Henry G. Shedd, who was in Wagner's brigade, wrote in his diary: "I don't care how much the rebels charge our works, but this thing of having to charge theirs I don't like & I don't know who would." Yet the assault looked "feeble" to a Massachusetts officer, Captain Charles F. Morse; he believed that the Easterners of the 20th Corps would have done better. He said: "I would like to see a little of the Army of the Potomac spirit infused into these Westerners; they do very well for skirmishing but for heavy work they are decidedly not the troops."

The medical corps hurriedly began to take the wounded Federals away from the camps around Kennesaw. Because the army might move at any time, the doctors were ordered to get the men to the rear within twenty-four hours. Every available vehicle—ambulances and wagons—loaded with wounded men, jolted over the muddy, rutted roads for six or more miles to reach the tracks of the Western & Atlantic. Each arriving train of boxcars, emptied of food and ammunition, was filled with disabled soldiers. Long lines of cars marked "Pittsburgh & Fort Wayne" or "Delaware & Lackawanna" or "Baltimore & Ohio" or with the names of other roads, carrying almost 2,000 injured men lying on the floors, headed slowly northward toward Chattanooga.

Late in the day Sherman wrote to Thomas: "I regret beyond measure the loss of two such young and dashing officers as Harker and Dan. McCook. . . . Had we broken the line to-day it would have been most decisive, but as it is our loss is small, compared with some of those East.

It should not in the least discourage us. At times assaults are necessary and inevitable. At Arkansas Post we succeeded; at Vicksburg we failed." Yet Sherman was already considering another large-scale flanking movement. He tried to reassure his men that he would not needlessly risk their lives in useless assaults. "All the soldiers knew," one of Thomas's cavalrymen later recalled; "the word was given out that night." After sunset the army's brass bands struck up a series of lively patriotic tunes.

The music did not drown out the sound of gunshots near Cheatham's salient. Both the Federals and the Confederates feared a sudden night attack across the short distance between the lines. They kept firing at one another in the dark. Men on both sides were digging to improve their entrenchments. With the help of tools, the Federal soldiers soon had three lines of breastworks under the crest of the ridge, confronting the angle they had attacked. Throughout the hot afternoon and into the night the soldiers in both sets of works listened to the moans and calls for help from wounded men still lying among corpses in front of the trenches. Federal soldiers rescued some; others managed to roll downhill to safety; others died where they lay, and the cries diminished. Cheatham's men, to make sure that they could see any movements of the enemy in the dark, threw out burning balls of cotton soaked in turpentine. These threw flickering light on the narrow stretch of ground covered with bodies. The fire spread to leaves and brush, charred the corpses, and caught wounded men, whose screams showed that they were still alive as they burned.

While McCook's men fortified their position, their officers regrouped the mixed units and straightened out the line. Their trenches angled downhill to connect with the new line dug by Harker's men and extended to Mitchell's brigade on the right. Three of McCook's regiments stayed in front and two stayed in reserve, the regiments taking turns facing the Confederates. General Davis offered to remove them from the ridge and put another brigade in their place, but the soldiers refused. The Confederates rolled out chevaux-de-frise—logs bristling with long spikes—to obstruct the approach to their trench. In daytime men on both sides took such constant pains in shooting that anyone who could be seen by the enemy was sure to be hit.

On the morning of June 28, the armies still faced each other in two great semicircles around Marietta. Their commanders were uncertain about what to do next. Sherman wrote: "We have constant fighting along lines for ten miles, and either party that attacks gets the worst of it. I will persevere, and think I can find a soft place. At all events, we can stand it as long as they. Johnston will not come out of his parapets, and it is difficult to turn his position without abandoning our railroad." The same day Johnston wrote: "We had quite a stirring day yesterday. The enemy approached our lines every where—& attacked at four or five points—at all of which they were repulsed with loss." He warned Louis T. Wigfall: "You expose your children to risk by leaving them in Atlanta while its fate is uncertain." But Johnston's note to his wife on the 29th said: "It is by no means certain that you will be compelled to leave Atlanta. The enemy may not attempt to cross the Chattahoochee at present."

June 28 was another hot day. The hundreds of corpses between the armies swelled and turned black. They were covered with flies and emitted a stench that nauseated men in the trenches. On the morning of June 29 the commanders along the angle agreed to cease fire so that Federal soldiers could bury their dead. Unarmed soldiers of both armies were supposed to keep away everyone except burial details, but crowds of men gathered atop the trenches to watch the work and to see each other. Shallow graves were dug where the dead had fallen. Some bodies were carried downhill to Federal lines, while others were pulled into the graves from a distance, with hooks made from bent bayonets.

Confederate generals came out to look at what their men had done in the battle. General George Maney, whose name was still attached to the brigade that held the angle, was elegantly dressed; Cheatham looked like a farmer. Cleburne and Hindman joined the group. Federal officers shared their whiskey with the Confederate generals, and the Southerners asked officers of the 14th Michigan Regiment about friends and relatives in Tennessee whom the Yankees had seen recently. While the officers talked and drank, soldiers swapped canteens, exchanged newspapers, and traded coffee for tobacco. Federal soldiers gathered around Cheatham and Hindman to get autographs. Two large men, a Northerner and a Southerner, held a wrestling match, which the Yankee won. The mounds of the hasty cemetery, extending about 100 yards across the front, were finished in the afternoon. The soldiers went back behind their entrenchments, and a signal shot was fired, ending the truce. The strange silence lasted a few minutes longer. Then the familiar sound of steady small-arms fire broke out all along the line.

Johnston already had Georgia militiamen and slaves working on fortifications near the Chattahoochee. Sherman's men at the extreme southern end of his lines could hear the continuous sound of trains moving supplies eastward, away from Marietta. On July 1, Johnston wrote to his wife: "I have been in constant expectation of an attack—or some movement that might compel us to quit this position—thinking this calm must be that which is said to precede a storm." Sherman was planning such a movement. He intended to return to his practice of flanking. He wrote to Ellen Sherman: "It is enough to make the whole world start at the awful amount of death & destruction that now stalks abroad, daily for the past two months has the work progressed and I see no signs of a remission till one or both and all the armies are destroyed when I suppose the balance of the people will tear each other up. . . . I begin to regard the death & mangling of a couple thousand men as a small affair, a kind of moving dash—and it may be well that we become so hardened. . . . I suppose the people are impatient why I dont push on more rapidly to Atlanta but those who are here are satisfied with the progress." Sherman was waiting for the roads to dry and for arriving trains to give him a surplus of supplies large enough to enable his army to leave the railroad for a few days. When all was ready, he ordered McPherson to move the Army of the Tennessee away from the base of Kennesaw and go around behind the rest of the army, heading south of Marietta for the Chattahoochee. Sherman did not believe that Johnston would attack Thomas at the base of Kennesaw ridge or would risk the breaking of the rail line in his rear and a campaign in the open countryside.

McPherson's army began to move on the night of July 2; in the dark Johnston's army abandoned the ridge, the mountain, and all the lines around Marietta. At dawn on July 3, Sherman looked through the telescope turned toward Kennesaw Mountain. He watched Federal skirmishers crawling cautiously up the hill. When they reached the top, they began to run along the crest; then he knew that the Confederates were gone. At 8:30 in the morning he rode into Marietta.

Sherman had hoped to catch the Confederate army outside of fortifications during its retreat, but Johnston had prepared his route of withdrawal well and had built strong fortifications on the west bank of the Chattahoochee. The Federals did not assault them. General Grant had telegraphed to Washington on June 28: "Please telegraph Sherman that he can move his army independent of the desire which he has expressed of detaining all of Johnston's force where it is." Sherman planned another flanking movement to cross the Chattahoochee and force Johnston to abandon the defense of Atlanta and risk battle or to withdraw into the city's trenches.

On July 5, the Third Division of the 14th Corps was in the advance as the Army of the Cumberland headed for the river north of the Confederate positions. Sherman, Thomas, and General John M. Palmer, the corps commander, rode with them. They passed a frame house, on the side of which was written: "You cant wip Johnson's army you yankey dogs; if you dont believe it try us in an open field fight." The division's skirmishers climbed a hill near Vining's Station on the Western & Atlantic. From it they could see the valley of the Chattahoochee and, nine miles away, the city of Atlanta. Confederate camps lay scattered over the land; men worked on multiple lines of fortifications; long trains of covered supply wagons were moving. In the distance, Atlanta's tall white spires, commercial buildings, and houses were visible among the factories emitting dense clouds of smoke from black chimneys.

A few minutes after the skirmishers reached the hill, Sherman, Thomas, and other officers arrived. For a moment the two commanders, friends since their days at West Point, stood looking at the city in silence. Thomas, a stout, slow-moving man, seemed impassive as usual—betraying no emotion on his calm, bearded face. Sherman walked around nervously, his dark eyes sparkling and his wrinkled face lit up. He glanced at Atlanta; he glanced at the Chattahoochee; and he glanced at many points in the valley, looking for the best place to cross the river.

CHAPTER 8

THE DESTRUCTIVE WAR

PART I *The Last Year*

IN THE LAST YEAR of the war, not even the bloodiest repulses turned back the Federal army's pressure on the shrinking Confederate forces. The momentum of destroying the rebellion, though slowed, was not reversed. The battle of Kennesaw Mountain was a comparatively minor action in the fighting that spread over Virginia and Georgia. It was an almost negligible interruption in the movement of Sherman's army, one part of which eventually destroyed the Army of Tennessee and another part of which ranged over Georgia, South Carolina, and North Carolina. Federal armies' way of grinding Confederate resistance into the ground was often messy and wasteful. Still, most Northerners sustained the government in these costly means of winning. With disparate motives and purposes Northerners could agree that increasingly destructive war was necessary, punitive, and patriotic.

Sherman's campaigns in the last year did only part of winning the war, perhaps not the most important part. The fall of Southern cities, the dismantling of Southern railroads, the army's depredations among Southern civilians had as their ultimate object weakening and eventually destroying the Army of Northern Virginia. Though Sherman's activities were subordinate, his successes most fully dramatized the extent and thoroughness of the North's beating down resistance. His name stood for the war's momentum. Thereafter Sherman remained in the public eye for twenty-five years, probably the most widely and enduringly publicized

321

American of his day. In his career the worst of the war and the best of the nation were supposed to find their link, their ultimate complementary relation. Sherman believed that killing and wounding so many soldiers on both sides, as well as violently intimidating and punishing so many Southern civilians, were parts of the process by which Americans attached themselves to their nation. This crucial union, of citizens, not just of states, made possible the prosperous, powerful country Sherman endlessly extolled. The power of wartime destruction to assure America's happiness and safety did not end in 1865. For Sherman the public's memory of the government's ability to attract devotion and to compel obedience remained latent in the postwar nation and its still comparatively weak federal government. Never again could anyone doubt the existence of that power, as people often had done before the war. Yet this postwar reliance on the capacity to revive coercion like that used during the war's last year also implied a vulnerability in the nation, a still insufficient union of citizens. Troubled by the thought of such a vulnerability, Sherman used his position as public representative of the nation's triumph to urge Americans toward union and security. In his own life and in his reputation he exemplified one dimension of the destructive war's legacy.

A few weeks before the 1864 spring campaign began, Sherman wrote to Grant: "That we are now all to act on a common plan, converging on a common center looks like enlightened war." For the first time, two generals who knew and trusted each other would be cooperating, commanding the two largest armies. The idea of using war in Georgia to hurt the Confederate cause in Virginia was not new or hard to understand. In August 1863, while the Confederates still held Chattanooga, the *Cincinnati Commercial* had published an article by a unionist from Georgia. He argued that Federal strategy in the west should focus on taking Chattanooga, followed by winning control of the Western & Atlantic Railroad, taking Atlanta, then holding the Georgia Railroad and Augusta. Such a campaign would seize much of the Confederacy's manufacturing, especially munitions. More important, it would cut off Georgia as a principal supplier of food and clothing to the Confederate army. "Without her the rebellion can not exist." Thus Atlanta should be the campaign's "cardinal point; it is the core of the whole South." The difficulty lay not in perceiving these strategic propositions but in acting on them. As the Confederates withdrew into northwest Georgia at the end of November 1863, after their defeat at Missionary Ridge, a Federal campaign of this kind began to look feasible. Sherman's imagination ran ahead: he told his brother in December 1863 that, if Lee held out in Virginia, "you must needs wait till we reenlist & recruit our Army of the Mississippi and swing round by Georgia & the Carolinas."

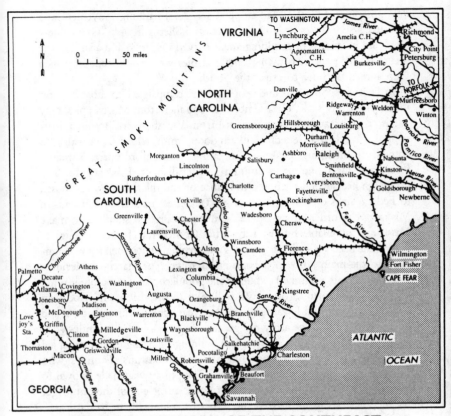

THE RAIL NETWORK OF THE SOUTHEAST

After Grant went east to assume supreme command, execution of the Georgia campaign fell to Sherman, who still depended on his friend. Sherman found in Grant's generalship a larger guarantee of victory: in Sherman's eyes Grant never doubted, never hesitated, never imagined disaster. Victory went to the man who grasped the critical juncture of a campaign or a battle, then struck with full force. With some exaggeration Sherman said after the war that Grant "never failed to divine and seize" the supreme moment when he ought to risk everything. Thanks to his insight and equanimity, "results follow in natural course." From his collaboration with Grant, Sherman derived his assurance that the war would continue inexorably until the Confederacy was destroyed. Sherman had many ideas about the means by which the war could accomplish its purpose; he needed faith that those means would work. Later recalling how Joseph E. Johnston had stopped a Federal flanking movement and inflicted heavy losses near Dallas, Georgia, Sherman said: "Grant knew of it, and his words of encouragement nerved my brain and arm." In the spring of 1864 the two main Federal armies were commanded by men who agreed on how to crush the South.

In February, Sherman undertook a brief campaign like those he later made on a larger scale. He assembled 25,000 men from Mississippi Valley garrisons and marched them eastward from Vicksburg to Meridian, Mississippi. He ordered General William Sooy Smith, with 7,000 cavalry, to come from Memphis, break up General Nathan Bedford Forrest's smaller force, and meet Sherman's column at Meridian on February 10. The campaign had several purposes: to reduce or end the threat Forrest posed to Federal lines of communication in Tennessee; to destroy railroads in Mississippi in order to cut off the state as a source of supplies; to make Mississippi untenable by any substantial Confederate force, thereby reducing the need for Federal garrisons and freeing 20,000 men for reassignment to the main army in the spring offensive. The march to Meridian and back was also designed to punish the populace. A week before leaving Vicksburg, Sherman wrote: "We will take all provisions and God help the starving families. I warned them last year against this visitation, and now it is at hand." The army did great damage in a path fifty miles wide along the 125-mile route, leaving few buildings standing except occupied houses, seizing or destroying livestock and foodstuffs. Families who stayed in their houses were plundered. "The policy was made known to the troops before leaving," one soldier wrote at the end of the campaign, "& the Generals made little or no effort to restrain them in the least." One object of the march, soldiers understood, was "to create a moral impression on the citizens of Mississippi."

Confederate forces under General Leonidas Polk withdrew before Sherman, removing most of the military stores eastward into Alabama. The Federals took Meridian on February 14, but the cavalry from Memphis did not appear. Smith delayed the start of his march, advanced slowly, then turned back in the face of attacks by Forrest. Sherman said at the end of February that he could have destroyed Polk's army if Smith had carried out his orders. During the five days he spent in Meridian, Sherman put his troops to the destruction of the tracks, bridges, and rolling stock of the railroads converging there. Though Confederates regained use of these rail lines in April and May, Sherman always insisted that the damage had been irreparable, helping to cause John B. Hood's three-week delay in Alabama in November—a delay contributing to Hood's subsequent defeat in Tennessee. Sherman did not like to hear the Meridian campaign called a "raid." He stressed its strategic benefits:

securing the Mississippi Valley and strengthening the Federals for the 1864 campaign in Georgia. Nevertheless, as a punitive assault on civilians' spirit, the march across Mississippi was also a raid, almost a rehearsal for the more extensive marches through Georgia and the Carolinas. Northerners, praising the campaign, understood it to be an example of the means for defeating the rebellion. The *Chicago Tribune*'s reporter wrote: "Nothing in the whole war has shown the rebel weakness, the inside rottenness of the Confederacy as plainly as this expedition." He and others noted the spread of despondency and defeatism, even among Mississippians whose bitterness toward the Yankees grew stronger. Sherman saw continued determination among Southerners: "No amount of poverty or adversity seems to shake their faith. . . . plenty tired of war, but the masses determined to fight it out." The Meridian campaign, he boasted, took Mississippi out of the war for most purposes. That result, accomplished by a new extent and severity of ruin, was only a prologue, foreshadowing the main theme of the war's last year.

The Atlanta campaign in northwestern Georgia has often been praised—not least by its two opposing commanders—as an example of consummate strategic skill. It nevertheless contained many surprises for both commanders, and their orders included much improvisation and guesswork. The only fixed plan was for the Federals to keep advancing. As they began their contest Sherman and Johnston expected their armies to meet in one decisive battle. Yet neither man wanted to order a general assault under disadvantageous conditions, especially not against an entrenched enemy. Johnston thought that the Federals, who outnumbered his army by a ratio of five to three, would attack his positions near Dalton. A Federal victory could be more sweeping or a Federal defeat less disastrous there than farther south because the Federals' base, Chattanooga, was near, while the Confederates' base, Atlanta, was too far away to be a refuge. Conversely, the closer to Atlanta the armies fought their crucial battle, the more risk the Federals ran that in case of defeat they would be destroyed far from refuge. Sherman understood this reasoning and did not welcome the prospect of the Confederates' falling back toward Atlanta. He, too, wanted a conclusive battle in northwestern Georgia, but he did not intend to attack Johnston's fortifications en masse. Instead, beginning on May 7, he sent McPherson and the Army of the Tennessee south of Johnston's position to threaten the Confederates' rail line and force them out of their defenses. This movement induced Johnston to withdraw southward to new positions around Resaca, but McPherson did not try to prevent a Confederate retreat by holding the rail line in the Confederates' rear before Johnston moved. Sherman believed that if McPherson had done so, the Confederates would have been forced to fight "the decisive battle" in the valley of the Oostanaula River between Dalton and Resaca or to retreat eastward, losing artillery and supplies.

For the next two months the armies continued almost constant skirmishing and maneuvering, with heavy fighting between some units. Sherman later explained that his method of maneuvering his large army—almost 100,000 men—was "to leave one part exposed inviting an attack by the enemy, aiming to inflict on him a superior loss while the rest of the army is moving to some exposed and vital object or line of retreat to the enemy. The whole movement from Chattanooga to Atlanta was composed of different phases of this 'Game.'" Johnston prepared and repeatedly withdrew to new entrenchments closer to Atlanta, waiting, he said, for an occasion to attack part of Sherman's army where Confederates would have an advantage. He complained: "My antagonist is the most cautious that ever commanded troops—fortifies, whenever he halts, before our cavalry learns his position." Sherman's first resort to flanking rather than to an assault on the Confederates near Dalton disoriented Johnston. The Confederate commander never fully recovered. On May 16 he wrote: "The necessity of falling back from Dalton & Resaca for the same reason—that the enemy, from the formation of the Country could prevent our retreat in case of disaster, has interrupted every thing that was systematic with us."

In many ways the two commanders waged an aleatory campaign. They often had an imperfect idea of each other's location; by separating his columns to invite a Confederate attack Sherman gambled that he would be able to concentrate his superior numbers for a general engagement before Johnston could destroy one segment of the Federal army with a sudden assault. Except for an aborted intent to attack at Cassville, Johnston did not try. By slowly withdrawing he gambled that Sherman eventually would make a mistake big enough to enable the Confederates to destroy or disperse part or all of the Federal army. Each general contended that the hills and rivers of northwestern Georgia helped the other. Sherman said that the obstructing mountains, streams, and forests offset his numerical advantage; Johnston said that the terrain and the rivers protected Sherman's flanking movements, while Sherman's superior numbers made those movements free of risk. Johnston explained the absence of a general battle by saying on May 20: "We have been pressed back . . . by mere weight." Sherman explained that, ever since his initial failure to cut off Johnston's retreat, "I have had no alternative but to press his rear." Until late in June, Sherman expected a major battle north of the Chattahoochee River, believing that Johnston must contest the Federals' crossing to the outskirts of Atlanta. Sherman regarded his crossing the

Chattahoochee without the loss of a man as one of his greatest tactical accomplishments. Yet Johnston did not oppose the crossing on the north bank and did not try to take advantage of it on the south bank while the Federal force was divided by the river. He was relieved of command on July 17. The conclusive battle had not come.

Later that summer and in subsequent years Johnston wrote and talked about what he would have done if he had retained command. He said that he had planned to attack the Federals as they crossed Peach Tree Creek north of Atlanta's defenses. His successor, John B. Hood, carried out this plan on July 20 and was repulsed by the Army of the Cumberland. Johnston also thought of bringing Georgia state troops to hold the city's fortifications while his three corps hit the flank of Sherman's army, hoping to crush them against the Chattahoochee. Hood sent Hardee's corps to attack Sherman's left, east of Atlanta, on July 22. Despite achieving surprise—Sherman had assumed that Hood was leaving the city after the fighting on the 20th—the Confederates suffered heavily without breaking up the Army of the Tennessee. Though Johnston, in retrospect, emphasized his aggressive intentions while in command, his later self-justifications spoke mostly of defense, of trying to hold Atlanta indefinitely. He said that he would have kept open at least one of the rail lines into the city by stockpiling enough supplies to outlast any foray that Sherman might make away from his own supply line to cut the Macon & Western south of the city. Even with the leisure to devise a plan of action against Sherman after the fact, Johnston could not find more than the hope for a stalemate, which, he contended, would have forced Sherman to attack the city's fortifications and at last meet his doom. Johnston argued that Hood need not have evacuated Atlanta on September 1, after the Confederates had failed to prevent the cutting of the Macon railroad. Apart from these strategies he had been denied the chance to try, Johnston's memory dwelt most often on Sherman's unaccountable failure to launch a general assault at any time in the campaign. By cataloguing Confederate successes in evading flanking movements and repelling partial assaults he tried to show how fully he would have succeeded if Sherman had cooperated. "I know I should have beaten him," Johnston told William Swinton of the *New York Times,* "had he made such assaults on me as General Grant did on Lee."

WITHIN A WEEK of taking Atlanta, Sherman made plans for further incursions into Georgia. Hood's army had been expelled, not destroyed, but Sherman showed less interest in forcing battle with it than in marching eastward. He said that if the Confederates stayed in Georgia and threatened the Western & Atlantic rail line, the Federals would have to go after Hood. But if Hood went into northern Alabama, where Confederate supplies were being gathered, Sherman did not want to pursue, once Hood was well away from the Western & Atlantic. Jefferson Davis intended that Hood's army should interfere with Sherman by moving against the rail line and provoking a conclusive battle or, if Sherman headed east, by obstructing the Federals' movements. After agreeing to this plan, Hood decided instead to move northward into Tennessee, and Davis assented to what he formerly had disapproved. Hood's attacks along the Western & Atlantic in September and October brought Sherman out of Atlanta but did not induce him to follow Hood farther west than Gaylesville, Alabama. Counting on the damage he had done to the railroads in Mississippi with his Meridian raid, Sherman reasoned that Hood would be delayed in Alabama, awaiting supplies, long enough for the Federals under Thomas to assemble an adequate force to confront him in Tennessee. On October 21 Thomas told Grant that he could hold the line in Tennessee. On November 2 Grant authorized the march across Georgia that Sherman had repeatedly urged.

The main purpose of this campaign was not mayhem, though destruction accompanied Sherman's army everywhere it went. For Sherman the long marches achieved important effects simply by being unstoppable. They could go on indefinitely; they could become harsher; they represented dramatically the sure coming of the South's defeat. During the first week of October, at the same time that Sherman began to persuade Grant and the men in Washington to let him make the march, Johnston, too, saw advantages for the Federals in such a campaign. In Macon he learned from visiting Confederate officers that Hood had abandoned central Georgia to attack the Federal supply line northwest of Atlanta. "This movement," he wrote to his brother, "has uncovered the route (thro' Macon) by which the army of Va. is supplied, & the shops at which ammunition is prepared & arms repaired for the army of Tennessee. If Sherman understands that either Charleston, Savannah, Pensacola or Mobile is as good a point for him as Chattanooga, he will not regard Hood's move." He told General Dabney H. Maury: "In Georgia, at present, we are at Sherman's mercy. . . . it is in his power to ruin us at once." Confederate officials in Virginia stressed the importance of their rail link to Georgia. Davis cited it as one of his reasons for superseding Johnston, whose retreats, Davis believed, would have continued and would have lost the crucial tie. Lee, hoping in July that Hood had won his battles at Atlanta, anticipated that the Confederates could reopen a flow of supplies from Alabama and eastern Mississippi. For the latter part of 1864 he was counting on stockpiles in eastern Georgia, as well as sources in the Carolinas. A month after Sherman's army had crossed Georgia to the sea, General D. H. Hill wrote from Augusta: "Letters and dispatches from Richmond are very urgent in regard to forwarding supplies to that point." Commanders on both sides understood that cutting the line between Georgia and Virginia would force Lee out of Richmond and Petersburg.

After the war, Southern critics of Sherman scoffed at his overrated march to the sea, recalling that he had faced little armed resistance and had covered hundreds of miles easily through a rich countryside that fed his army well. This was the same vast extent of territory and wealth of resources that once was to have made conquest of the Confederacy by invasion an absurd notion. Sherman knew more about Southern wealth than did many of the people who relied on its power. He had obtained from Joseph C. G. Kennedy, superintending clerk of the census of 1860, a volume describing the population, livestock, and agricultural produce of Georgia, county by county. From its quantitative details he saw how he could subsist his army in the process of disproving the Southern claim to impregnability which those resources supposedly vindicated. In 1865 he testified to "the value of these statistical tables and facts, for there is a reasonable probability that, without them, I would not have undertaken what was done." His successful campaign had the inevitability of a design supported by science. He told Thomas Ewing: "No military expedition was ever based on sounder or surer data." The more one knew about the Confederacy the more confidently it could be destroyed.

Though Sherman's 62,000 men greatly outnumbered the Confederate forces in Georgia, he eased his march by encouraging the enemy to avoid him. In October, Sherman had spoken of taking Macon, Milledgeville, Augusta, and Savannah. But he did not attempt so many conquests. As the Federals left Atlanta on November 15 and 16, their left column moved along the Georgia Railroad toward Augusta, destroying track, and their right column pushed toward Macon along the Macon & Western. Confederate forces continued to cover both cities while Sherman's columns, as planned, turned away from them to converge on the capital, Milledgeville. Well before Sherman reached Savannah, observant people in Richmond could see that he had directed the march so as "to induce the collection of troops at points at which he seemed to be aiming & then he has passed them by, leaving the troops useless and unavailable." Even a short siege of Augusta would have been impractical because Sherman could feed his army only by moving it. And he intended to work again on Confederates' anxiety about Augusta during a second march yet to come.

Both Grant and Beauregard afterward said that, once Hood and Sherman started to march in opposite directions, Hood could have mounted an invasion to the Ohio or beyond by ignoring Nashville. Hood instead was still seeking victory over the Federal armies. His defeats at Franklin and Nashville destroyed his army, though Grant and Sherman privately complained that Thomas had let the Confederates push so far north of the Alabama line. Thomas's success at Nashville, almost simultaneous with Sherman's taking Savannah, left the Federal commanders free to plan the complete crushing of the Confederacy in the east during 1865. Before his appointment to supreme command Grant had expected to lead the western army in the capture of Atlanta and then, still holding the city, to occupy the Georgia railroads, much as the Georgia unionist had recommended in the *Cincinnati Commercial.* After taking Atlanta, Sherman saw disadvantages in trying to hold the city and keep the army's supply line intact. His plan to leave Atlanta and march eastward still shared Grant's original assumption that the western army's operations should promote victory in Virginia. Before leaving Atlanta for Savannah, Sherman envisioned a second movement northward from Savannah, through the Carolinas, which would conclusively disrupt the rail network at its bottleneck in Columbia. By the time Sherman's army reached the outskirts of Savannah, early in December, Grant was anticipating the defeat of Lee within a few months. He wanted to move most of Sherman's army to Virginia by sea and "wipe out Lee." Learning that the available vessels could not accomplish this in less than two months, Grant approved Sherman's plan to march overland. Sherman's cutting off foodstuffs and munitions from Georgia would ruin any Confederate hope of eking out another summer's campaign in defense of Richmond. But Grant could see that Lee had no such prospects, no matter what Sherman did.

A movement through South Carolina posed greater risks than one through Georgia. The rivers and their bordering swamps, widened and deepened by winter rains, presented obstacles along which Sherman could be delayed by a force much smaller than his. The army could not afford delay; as a precaution, Sherman told the navy what points on the coast he would use as a base if he had to withdraw to get supplies by sea. He need not have worried. The Confederates did little to impede his march northward. Again he used the two wings of his army to feint in directions he did not intend to go—one toward Branchville and Charleston, the other toward Augusta. The flooded Savannah River had delayed his advance into South Carolina until February 1. The next day the Confederate cavalry commander, General Joseph Wheeler, reported to D. H. Hill: "Enemy's movements now look as though Branchville rather than

Augusta is their destination though it is impossible yet to determine."

While Wheeler wrote, the Confederate generals Beauregard, Hardee, Hill, and G. W. Smith held a conference and decided not to try to unite their forces—soon numbering about 40,000—to oppose Sherman. They gave as a reason for staying in Charleston and Augusta the need to hold those cities during negotiations for peace, which they professed to expect soon. They also argued that ordering a concentration of forces at any place Sherman might reach first would be "in violation of all maxims of the military Art," a phrase with the sound of Beauregard in it. The generals settled for vague, improvisatory plans, envisioning a belated concentration at Columbia if Sherman headed that way. Of course, by the time his direction became unmistakable, uniting to confront him would be impossible. Sherman and his generals expected to have to fight a battle for the South Carolina Railroad at Midway, sole link between Virginia and Georgia, but Beauregard had decided not to defend it a week before Sherman reached it. People in Richmond and Confederate soldiers in South Carolina could see the folly of holding back from risk, and they criticized their generals. "The necessity of concentration and the abandonment of all secondary points was patent, and among subordinates freely discussed at the time," Johnson Hagood later wrote, "but the paralysis of approaching death seemed to be upon the direction of our affairs."

At a banquet in St. Louis in July 1865 Sherman said: "Years ago I thought Columbia would be the scene of the great and final struggle of the war. I thought our western army would go eastward and our eastern army southward to Columbia, and that we would fight it out there." Although no such battle occurred, Sherman's estimate of the importance of Columbia did not diminish. The city became his ultimate objective as soon as Hood headed north and west in Georgia and Alabama. In later years Sherman often claimed that his capture of Columbia gave the rebellion its final blow. "I deliberately put myself and army where if not absolutely destroyed and overwhelmed, the existence of a Southern Independent Confederacy was an impossibility—From the moment my army passed Columbia S. C. the war was ended." The material support for a nation—the coalescence of armed force on its behalf, the movement of supplies from the place of production to the point of use—would then no longer exist on a scale comporting with pretensions to be a nation.

General Lee understood Sherman's Carolina campaign in much the same way. Two days after Beauregard had decided not to make a stand farther south than Columbia, Lee urged a concentration of troops "at Branchville or some more advanced point." As soon as Sherman took Columbia, Lee began to speak of evacuating the defenses of Richmond and Petersburg; he expected Grant to attack during the last week of

February. Grant, however, did not want Lee to leave the trenches until Sherman was near or the Army of the Potomac could prevent Lee's escape southward. Given the opportunity, Lee placed Johnston in command of the forces in North Carolina. The last Confederate chance, if any, lay in uniting Lee's and Johnston's armies to fight Sherman or Grant before the other could arrive to help. Sherman predicted that Lee would start the movement when the Federals reached the Neuse River in North Carolina. Lee instead chose the Roanoke River, which crossed his last supply line and the Virginia border, as the point where Sherman's arrival would force the Confederates out of their trenches.

Frequently urging that Sherman's advance be obstructed, that supplies be removed from the Federals' path, that troops and civilians unite to stop Sherman, that all remember "the vital importance of . . . preserving our railroad communications as far as practicable," Lee remained in his fortified lines, waiting. He wrote after the war: "As regards the movements of General Sherman it was easy to see that unless they were interrupted I should be compelled to abandon the defense of Richmond." Grant's final offensive began after the conference between Grant, Sherman, and Lincoln in the last week of March, while Sherman's army was still at Goldsboro, North Carolina. Sherman's marches had not starved Lee out; in fact, during its last months the Army of Northern Virginia had been fed in large part with food from the North, smuggled in along the coasts of North Carolina and southern Virginia with the connivance of Benjamin F. Butler. Sherman had shown that Lee would have to come out eventually, and Lee had waited until the last hour to do so. John Esten Cooke said after the war that Lee's February preparations to join Johnston had been "stopped by the Richd people," and Jefferson Davis acknowledged on April 4 that "the necessity of keeping constant watch over the approaches to the capital" had forced Lee to forgo "more than one opportunity for promising enterprises." As Sherman put it in later years, "Lee clung to his intrenchments for political reasons, and waited for the inevitable."

AT THE START of his Virginia campaign, Grant did not foresee that the Army of the Potomac's work in ending the war would differ so markedly from that of the western army. In the ensuing months he gave the eastern soldiers much hard combat and prolonged trench warfare. Though the easterners made less dramatic movements than those in the west, Grant still saw the two Federal armies engaged in the same inexorable process of destroying Southern resistance, the accomplishments of one army impossible without the work of the other. He expressed Sherman's dependence on the Army of the Potomac bluntly, saying in August that withdrawing pressure on Lee or exchanging all Confederate prisoners "would insure the defeat of Sherman." Grant's offensive in Virginia decimated both his army and Lee's. The cost in his men's blood that Grant paid for confining and pushing and weakening Lee was high. Grant gave orders to General Meade before the campaign began: "Lee's Army will be your objective point. Wherever Lee goes there you will go also." To make sure, Grant went, too—in effect commanding the Army of the Potomac through Meade.

During the spring of 1864 the most intense, prolonged, bloody fighting of the war took place from the Rappahannock to the James River. Between May 3 and June 3 the Federals lost at least 50,000 men killed, wounded, captured, or missing, while the Confederates lost about 32,000. The disparity arose mainly from Federals' assaults, in which they were more exposed to fire. The battles' names—the Wilderness, Spotsylvania Court House, Cold Harbor—thereafter brought back to the mind the shock of masses of men thrown against other masses. The place names were familiar from earlier years of the war; the images of battle were not new: attacks, repulses, combatants' rage, woods afire, living and dead ground together into the mud, wounded dying slowly between the lines. Yet soldiers in both armies and civilians following events at a distance felt themselves in a different kind of war. Combat on a scale that once would have been thought a single great climax of the war went on for weeks, and nothing seemed to change, except the armies' positions and the length of the casualty lists. Grant said "that this fighting throws in the shade everything he ever saw, and that he looked for no such resistance." He was surprised but not deterred.

First some of his own troops in May 1864, and then subsequent writers, harshly criticized Grant for throwing away men's lives in the Virginia campaign. The critics attributed the losses to Grant's lack of skill and, by extension, his lack of feeling. They used expressions such as "brute masses," "blind attacks," "a bloody butcher," and, especially important to Southerners, "the momentum of numbers." So many casualties with such unsatisfactory results showed that Grant lacked higher generalship, had no strategy, no spark of military genius. How could he keep ordering men to their deaths unless he were as callous and mentally torpid as the words "rude," "brute," "blind," and "butcher" implied? When Whitelaw Reid wrote of the soldiers who refused to renew the attack at Cold Harbor, "There were brains in those ranks," he clearly implied where brains were lacking. By August, after the disastrous assault through the mine crater at Petersburg, Secretary of the Navy Gideon Welles, though wishing Grant success, feared that the general was not equal to his responsibilities. Welles thought of "the slaughtered thousands of my countrymen who poured out their rich blood for three months on the soil of Virginia from the Wilderness to Petersburg under his generalship"; if Grant succeeded he would be vindicated, but if he failed there could be no adequate atonement. The nation's destiny had been committed to Grant; "if it is an improper committal where are we?" The bloodshed was so vast that Welles could hardly account for it with the rationale that had prevailed before the spring of 1864. Earlier in the war, Federal generals' hesitancy had raised doubts about their strength of mind and character, their devotion to national unity and universal freedom. In the rush of deaths and wounds in 1864, Grant's lack of hesitancy provoked many to deny his competence and his humanity.

The notion that Grant knew or tried no kind of war but attrition through massed assaults has often been discredited. His Vicksburg campaign had divided and defeated large Confederate forces with comparatively small loss to either side, using an innovative strategy until the enemy lay surrounded and besieged. Grant thought about trying an even bolder stroke for the Virginia campaign: abandoning his base of supplies and marching southwest to cut Lee's supply line along the Richmond & Danville Railroad and the South Side Railroad. Lee presumably would then have to attack the Federals on ground of their choosing or abandon Richmond. Not knowing the Army of the Potomac well enough to judge its ability to carry out such a plan, Grant decided not to take the risk, lest failure turn too many Northerners against the Federal war effort. A Shenandoah Valley expedition under Franz Sigel and, later, David Hunter failed to reach Lee's western communications. Grant fought along the roads to Richmond and Petersburg. He knew that the Army of Northern Virginia could not stay behind entrenchments or defend Richmond if its supply lines were cut nearby. A Federal army south of the James River, across Lee's rail lines, would make Lee's defensive positions in northern Virginia untenable. Benjamin F. Butler and his Army of the James failed to attain that goal in May, but the country south of the James remained Grant's ultimate objective while he tried, north of Richmond, to exhaust the Confederates by combat or to preempt their line of defense. Grant did not draw so sharp a distinction between maneuver and attrition as some later critics did. Lee also saw that the two went together. After the war he "spoke of Grant's gradual whirl and change of base from Fredericksburg to Port Royal, then to York River and then to James River, as a thing which, though foreseen, it was impossible to prevent." The Federals had decided, Lee said, that if they could not outmaneuver his army they must crush it. Grant found that Lee would take no great risks of the kind he formerly had taken against McClellan and Hooker.

Both armies narrowly lost opportunities for greater successes during May and June, but neither gave the other scope for dramatic departures from the close contact of the armies' lines.

Lee knew that Grant's methods, if sustained, would work. Lee had said in June 1863 that he wanted to draw the Army of the Potomac out where it could be assailed, rather than give it time to renew an advance on Richmond; for the Confederates to be forced back into the city's entrenchments would be "a catastrophe." Planning the spring campaign in 1864, before Grant took command, Lee again thought of forcing the Army of the Potomac back to Washington, thereby alarming the enemy enough to forestall a Federal advance. "If we could take the initiative and fall upon them unexpectedly we might derange their plans and embarrass them the whole summer." Lee's comparative weakness in numbers and Grant's continuous offensive—the pressure back toward Richmond that Lee had long feared and repeatedly avoided—thwarted Lee's visions of audacity. Even so, the fruits of the offensive came more slowly than Grant had hoped. Federals' heavy attacks, which failed to break the Confederate line or to yield any clear victory, sapped many veteran soldiers' trust in him. By the time the army reached Cold Harbor, where Grant ordered belated and poorly conceived assaults that cost 7,000 casualties to no purpose, soldiers complained bitterly. Some talked of mutiny and of refusing to fight. After crossing the James River but failing to take Petersburg, Grant gave up frontal attacks.

Except for regretting the assaults at Cold Harbor, Grant made no apologies for the way he had conducted the campaign. Its toll on the rebels was great and irreparable. Confederate soldiers knew, as Lee did, that constant combat or prolonged siege worked against them. Private Creed Thomas Davis of the 1st Virginia Artillery Regiment said that he and others were demoralized by the fighting at Spotsylvania Court House. He wrote in his diary a week later: "Genl Grant seems to be no nearer whipped than before the battles, what an old bull dog." The men foresaw, one Confederate veteran recalled, "that this kind of war would wear them out eventually." They could only hope that the Northern army and populace would refuse to continue or that General Lee would somehow contrive another of his diversions. "The last man in the Confederacy is now in the Army," Grant wrote; Lee was steadily losing men by desertion, sickness, capture, and Federal attacks. Grant argued that the battles in May crippled the Army of Northern Virginia enough to break it of its penchant for the offensive. Though not Federal victories, they "inflicted upon the enemy severe losses, which tended in the end to the complete overthrow of the rebellion." He said that he did not see how the Confederacy would be defeated except by fighting, "and fighting means that men must be killed." His aide Horace Porter later offered the corollary to that conclusion: "Grant could have effectually stopped the carnage at any time by withholding from battle. He could have avoided all bloodshed by remaining north of the Rapidan, intrenching, and not moving against his enemy."

President Lincoln, in his first meeting with Grant and often thereafter, dwelt on the expense of the war, rising toward $4,000,000 per day, and the danger that the government would lose its public support and its ability to sell bonds and finance the war before the Confederates were defeated. A few days before the fall of Atlanta, Secretary of the Treasury William Pitt Fessenden wrote: "Oh, for a great victory. What a financial operation it would be. If General Grant doesn't help me out of this scrape, I am a lost man." As it happened, his helper was Sherman, but Grant understood that doing too little, allowing the war to drag on, posed more danger to him, to Lincoln, and to the Federal cause than did maintaining the offensive. If increasing the casualties could hasten the end of the war, reducing its cost in dollars, more deaths would be the price of showing the public that the nation could win the war and pay for it. For years Lincoln had urged generals to wear down the Confederate army by using the North's superior numbers aggressively. After Republican reverses in the 1862 elections he had told Senator Lyman Trumbull that he "supposed they grew out of the inaction of our armies." Grant's assignment was to end inaction. Subsequently defending his intent to overcome the Confederate army "by mere attrition, if in no other way," he invoked the balance between lives and dollars that preoccupied Lincoln. He said of his plans: "Whether they might have been better in conception and execution is for the people, who mourn the loss of friends fallen, and who have to pay the pecuniary cost, to say." Grant thus implicitly asked whether those who faulted him for losing so many men would have supported a longer war fought on another plan at greater expense.

Notwithstanding heavy bloodshed, Grant's spring campaign won much praise. Republican newspapers cheered the army on, as did the *New York Herald*. Joseph Medill of the *Chicago Tribune* recalled in May that he had told Lincoln early in the year "that until we crushed in pitched battles the two great rebel armies no headway need be expected—no permanent advantage could be achieved." As long as Grant's combat promised ultimate success his methods were not generally repudiated. Grant's determination to keep fighting pleased Lincoln. After the battle of the Wilderness, Grant said to a young *New York Tribune* correspondent carrying dispatches to Washington: "If you see the President, tell him from me that, whatever happens, there will be no turning back." The message so delighted the president that he embraced the reporter and kissed him on the forehead. A few days later Lincoln said to a crowd: "I believe I know (and am especially grateful to know) that Gen. Grant has not been jostled in his purposes." Speaking in Philadelphia in June he approvingly paraphrased and won cheers for Grant's dispatch from Spotsylvania Court House, promising to fight it out on that line if it took all summer. Even after Grant had been stopped at Petersburg and Lincoln's expectations of continued public support had fallen to their lowest point, he urged Grant on. "I have seen your dispatch expressing your unwillingness to break your hold where you are. Neither am I willing. Hold on with a bull-dog gripe, and chew & choke, as much as possible." When 55 percent of the Northern electorate voted for Lincoln, including 71 percent of the voters in the Army of the Potomac, hardly any of them could have failed to know that he intended to continue the war, using the pressure and attrition practiced by Grant and Sherman. If Grant was a butcher, he was a hired man. His employers were the government of the United States and the people who sustained the government, and he kept his job.

Sherman always defended Grant's sustained assault on the Army of Northern Virginia. Having predicted a much longer war, Sherman was less concerned with the need to hasten the end than with finding and using the means for overcoming the rebellion. He often said in later years that Grant's methods had been necessary. In February 1888, General William F. Smith published a short article in *The North American Review,* in which he contrasted Grant with "great captains." He quoted Thiers's *History of the French Revolution*— "When war is conducted as a purely mechanical routine, and consists in pushing and killing the enemy in front, it is hardly worthy of history"—then commented: "War 'conducted as a mechanical routine' was perfectly exhibited in the 'Campaign of Attrition,' inaugurated by General Grant on the 5th of May, 1864." Allen Thorndike Rice, editor of the *Review,* wrote a rebuttal of Smith's article for the March issue, relying heavily on suggestions he received from Sherman. Sherman argued, as have Grant's twentieth-century defenders, that the Virginia campaign was sound, "scientific" war-making. By unrelieved pressure, Grant had held Lee's army "as it were in a vice" while other Federal armies destroyed Lee's resources. When that process was nearly complete and Sherman had come within supporting distance, Grant had disposed of Lee.

Sherman approved of Grant's campaign for another reason, apart from his belief that it conformed to the principles of the "highest authorities" among military thinkers. He, too, published an article in February 1888: "The Grand Strategy of the War of the Rebellion" in *Century Magazine.* It argued that McClellan ought to have taken in 1862 the course Grant finally took two years later. McClellan should have moved southward from Fredericksburg and "fought steadily and persistently." When Grant took command he, unlike McClellan, "knew that a certain amount of fighting, 'killing,' had to be done to accomplish his end." Attrition was not a mistake but a necessity. Some critics said that Grant could have reached the outskirts of Richmond and Petersburg by water, as McClellan had done in 1862, sparing his army the bloodletting of the campaign from the Wilderness overland. Sherman replied that the location of the killing did not matter. The bloodshed still would have been necessary on the banks of the James and the Appomattox if it had not occurred on those of the Rapidan and the Mattaponi. Sherman had concluded during the war that "the South would never give up as long as it had an army of any size worth mentioning." The South contained a certain number of men—he twice mentioned the figure 300,000—who would not stop fighting. If the North wanted to reunite the nation under the federal government, these men would have to be killed. Killing them would unavoidably entail the deaths of many Northerners. The war consisted of this "awful fact," as Sherman called it. The people who believed that the war could have been won differently were trying to escape this fact, which Grant had faced.

Opening his book on the Virginia campaign, General Andrew A. Humphreys reviewed possible alternative advances into Virginia in 1864 different from Grant's method of moving against Lee, then suggested that these other approaches would not have avoided the difficulties and casualties experienced on the road from Fredericksburg. Lee could have stymied an advance up the James or could have met the Federals west of Richmond, where the Army of the Potomac would "have fought battles corresponding to those it fought on the route to Richmond." With this brief foray into counterfactual argument, Humphreys prepared his readers for a narrative of the Virginia campaign by depriving them of the consoling speculation that great bloodshed had been militarily unnecessary: "Move as we might, long-continued, hard fighting under great difficulties was before us, and whatever might be the line of operations adopted, the successful execution of the task of the Army of the Potomac could only be accomplished by the vigorous and untiring efforts of all belonging to that army, and by suffering heavy losses in killed and wounded, and that the whole army well understood." The Army of the Potomac's task was destruction of the Army of Northern Virginia. If Grant, by consummate generalship, could have reversed the ratio of casualties between the two armies, losing three to Lee's five rather than five to Lee's three, the campaign, for all that greater skill, would yet have been one of attrition—acting out Sherman's "awful fact" at a somewhat lower cost in Northerners' lives. Since the Federals had to destroy Lee's army, rather than he having to destroy theirs, the burden of the offensive lay on them, as did their suffering a preponderance of the casualties. After criticizing Grant's failure to minimize losses, General Joshua Lawrence Chamberlain's memoirs concluded: "Grant was necessary to bring that war to a close, whether by triumph of force or exhaustion of resources. . . . What other men could not do, he did." The question was not whether there would be attrition. The question was which Federal commander would persevere in it. Private Frank Wilkeson, a new volunteer in 1864, asked veteran soldiers of the Army of the Potomac what McClellan would have done with the army if he, rather than Grant, had taken command in the spring; "they shrugged their shoulders and said dryly: 'Well, he would have ended the war in the Wilderness—by establishing the Confederacy.'"

Sherman, Grant, and Lincoln agreed that Confederate resistance continued partly because many Southerners still assumed that the North would not reduce them to the last extremity, that they knew the limits of what the North would do to win the war. These Southerners still failed to grasp Northerners' insistence on the reality of the nation, embodied in its adherents' power and resolve. Grant portrayed his 1864 campaign as more than a calculable trading of lives; it was an assault on a state of mind, "a morale" arising from Confederates' belief that the Army of Northern Virginia could win independence by a skillful, courageous defense. Sherman, too, saw a need to destroy that morale: "Immense slaughter is necessary to prove that our northern armies can & will fight. That once impressed will be an immense moral power." Drastic action would force Southerners to rethink their assumptions about Federal intent. Lincoln often alluded to the persistence of Southerners' assumption that the nation could not overcome them. He warned that, instead of complaining about what the Federal army was doing to civilians, they ought to think about what worse things it might do if the war went on. They could not, as they seemed to expect to do, spend ten years trying to break up the union and count on remaining inviolate in the attempt. Lincoln liked to use metaphors—asking whether the war should be fought with squirts of rosewater from elder stalks, saying of the Federal armies' concerted 1864 offensive that those not skinning could hold a leg, warning that he would not give up the game leaving any available card unplayed, biblically commenting that Sherman's march to the sea and Hood's defeats would bring those who sat in darkness to see a great light. These were euphemisms. He was saying that the Federal army would change Southerners' minds by shedding more blood, destroying more property, and inflicting more suffering than their illusions of independence could withstand.

Sherman's marches across the South were an exercise in reshaping people's perception of the United States by demonstrating what those who believed in the country's permanence could do to confirm their belief. The path of Sherman's army—sometimes more than fifty miles wide, sometimes less than thirty—missed the great majority of people in the states through which it passed. Comparatively few white people saw him or his men. When he said that he could "make Georgia howl," he meant that many people besides those hurt by his army would make "a great howl against the brute Sherman." They would do so because his army scared them and because they saw in the marches proof of how weak they and the Confederacy were. As late as December 1864 some Southerners besides politicians and editors still talked like Lieutenant Edward Barnwell Heyward in South Carolina, saying that Sherman would come to a disastrous end: "He can hardly cross the Savannah river alive. . . . Sherman's army is on a retreat and will be badly beaten soon." Sherman devised his campaigns to help "break the pride of the South." In its Confederate manifestation, Southern pride consisted of reliance on the ability of the army and the government to protect the people; it consisted of Southerners' promise to die fighting rather than submit; it consisted of the Confederacy's future glory based on what Sherman called "that political nonsense of slave rights, States' rights, freedom of conscience, freedom of the press, and such other trash as have deluded the southern people." In place of these expectations that Southerners held about the war, Sherman said, "I propose to demonstrate the vulnerability of the south and make its inhabitants feel that war & individual ruin are synonimous terms."

Taking a large army through the Confederacy would prove to distant Southerners, as well as to those in Sherman's path, that the North had the power to conquer the South. Lincoln's re-election showed that the North would use that power. "This may not be war, but rather statesmanship," Sherman wrote to Grant. By this distinction he evidently referred to using military means to achieve political results in the minds and in the behavior of civilians. Such "statesmanship" was, in fact, "a hard species of warfare," he said after reaching Savannah; "but it brings the sad realities of war home to those who have been directly or indirectly instrumental in involving us in its attendant calamities." Sherman thus asserted that ruin at the hands of the stronger power was one of the "realities" of war and that anyone "directly or indirectly" implicated in waging war was subject to the effects of these realities. The wasting of the countryside in the army's track was a form of education, juxtaposing Southerners' abject state, stripped of their goods and left hungry, with their imaginings of inviolable grandeur. "The lesson has been well taught and by many has been thoroughly learned," Henry Hitchcock wrote from Savannah, echoing Sherman. "No other teaching *can* enlighten those who have been drugged & stupefied with the lies & brag of Jeff. Davis and his organs." Sherman used his marches as an empirical argument against the existence of the Confederate States of America. He went far to supplant Southerners' deductive proofs of the Confederacy's autonomy with his inductive proofs of the Confederacy's collapse. Southerners could see that they were not a corporate people standing against an enemy; they were desperate individual Americans confronted by the power of the government that they had tried to define away.

Although the army represented federal authority, Sherman used his soldiers to give Southerners a taste of life without government. He often had said that secession amounted to the abrogation of government, inviting anarchy. Southern planters arrogantly imagined that they had made the South, creating their own prosperity "by virtue alone of their personal industry and skill," and that they therefore could do as they pleased with their own. Yet their wealth and security depended more than they had admitted on "the protection and impetus to prosperity given by our hitherto moderate and magnanimous Government." They had not created the land; they were a tiny, weak, ephemeral proportion of the earth's population. Their only title to the "use and usufruct" of the land was "the deed of the United States." If they preferred to base their claim on their strength in war, "they hold their all by a very insecure tenure." When Southerners protested against destruction of their property, Sherman lectured them: "You must first make a government before you can have property. There is no such thing as property without a government." By secession and war, Southerners had abjured government and thus cast themselves adrift in a world of power through violence. All that they had was forfeit to anyone stronger than they. The soldiers' depredations put this doctrine into practice, face to face. Southerners could not secure their property by an appeal to the Confederate government; nor could they secure their property by a claim of rights under the United States government, which they had disavowed. In practice they had no property, as the soldiers demonstrated. If the federal government stopped short of expropriation or wholesale deportation, it did so, Sherman warned, not for lack of right or power but on the supposition that Southerners could become useful citizens once they learned that they depended on the United States, not on their own "vainglory & boasting." He expected Southerners and their descendants to remember the experiment in throwing off a government and to refrain from repeating it. His army's marches would help accomplish what the Constitution and generations of politicians had failed to secure: permanent national unity.

THE STORY of Sherman's Georgia and Carolina campaigns, with their myriad vivid incidents as soldiers encountered civilians, has been told often. The marches are among the few episodes of the Civil War that still live in popular speech. The picture of a swath of devastation sometimes takes on a lurid fascination, with overblown images of a blasted landscape not found in the surviving record. In 1959 Colonel Allen Julian, director of the Atlanta Historical Society, told an interviewer from the *Atlanta Constitution* about his visit to Marietta, where he met a lady who assured him that in the fire after Sherman followed Johnston east from Kennesaw Mountain the town had been completely leveled. "Then," Julian recalled, "after tea we went out to see the fine ante-bellum homes." A substantial number of antebellum structures survive along the army's route from Atlanta to Savannah. Fewer escaped the torch in South Carolina. Soldiers did their greatest damage to cotton, cotton gins, barns, government and railroad buildings, livestock, food, and all manner of portable property. Inhabited houses were seldom destroyed, but they usually were looted and defaced, and the occupants were subjected to taunts, insults, threats, and sometimes violence. Soldiers took from rich and poor, black and white. Most men spent most of their time marching or in camp, not accosting civilians. But foragers assigned to gather food, not to mention bummers and stragglers—men who left their units to lead a freer, more violent, and more dangerous life along the outskirts of the army's progress—missed little in their path. Some black women were raped; some victims of robbery were killed or severely injured—atrocities that none of the Federal armies in the South fully suppressed. Georgians and Carolinians, white and black, also suffered at the hands of the Confederate cavalry shadowing Sherman's movements.

By elaborate though unsuccessful efforts to conceal food and valuables, Southerners showed that they knew the soldiers were interested mainly in these, not in physical violence. And the soldiers did thorough work. In Goldsboro, North Carolina, where the long campaign from Atlanta ended, Private Edmund J. Cleveland, whose corps had rejoined Sherman from Tennessee, noticed that "on almost every corner were boys of Sherman's army selling tobacco, watches, silver, etc., captured in the late march." On such a strenuous march, men could carry only a fraction of the loot. The greatest part of the material harm done to civilians consisted, as Sherman said, of "simple waste and destruction." To him the civilians' most common distresses—fear, humiliation, the shock of losses, the need to beg and scramble for a small supply of coarse food—looked like minor evils when set against the great evil of the war, for which he held them responsible. He often denied that the damage done by his soldiers was new to war. The soldiers' conduct did not differ in principle from that of other countries' soldiers in other wars; nor did the system of foraging violate precedent and internationally recognized practice. Sherman habitually treated the losses of private citizens as matters of petty significance to the campaign.

Sherman's men were veterans of two or three years in the army. They had known combat from Shiloh to the battles around Atlanta. In Mississippi, in the march to Chattanooga and to Knoxville, and in the Atlanta campaign they had grown accustomed to covering long distances. Their march to Savannah was comparatively easy. The weather was good, most of the route yielded ample food with plenty left over to waste, the rivers were efficiently bridged, and Confederates put up slight resistance. From Savannah to North Carolina the way was much harder. Yet the columns continued to average about ten miles a day while doing a thorough job of pillage and destruction. Among these young men Sherman had an almost unquestioned prestige and popularity. He gave his army the best of soldiering: continual triumphs with few casualties. Cities, towns, and rich plantations fell into their hands; many black people praised them; every day brought new scenes and new adventures. The rate of sickness in regiments wading through swamps during winter was lower than the usual rate in stationary camps. For all of this the soldiers gave credit to their commander. Sergeant Young J. Powell said they thought "that there never was such a man as Sherman or as they call him (Crazy Bill) and he has got his men to believe that they cant be whiped." Since Sherman, at the age of forty-five, commanded men mostly in their early twenties, it is not surprising that they said when they saw him: "There stands the daddy of this army"; "There's our old dad." The nickname "Crazy Bill"—as in the words for heated, twisted rails along the track of the Georgia Railroad: "Crazy Bill's Cast-Iron dough-nuts"—recalled the bygone newspaper reports that Sherman was insane. It was a joke for the soldiers because his insanity had consisted of saying that a vast army would be needed to conquer the South. Now they were it.

A week out of Atlanta, General Jefferson C. Davis, commander of the 14th Corps, told one of Sherman's aides that he condemned the soldiers' straggling and burning, but he had found that "the belief in the army is that Genl. S. favors & desires it, & one man when arrested told his officer so." Sherman's general orders for the march had instructed the army to "forage liberally on the country." A soldier who saw Sherman watching him carry away irregularly seized food called out to the general: "Forage liberally!" while other men laughed. Sherman kept a straight face, but he knew, as in the case of one woman for whose house he refused to post a guard, "The soldiers will take all she has." Just by giving his men the opportunity to do damage Sherman had provided adequate encouragement. Furthermore, many men agreed, in Samuel K. Harryman's words, that "Shermans policy for South Carolina is understood to be destruction as we go." They believed that his purpose in the campaign was "to do just what we want him to do, that is to crush the last particle of wind out of the Confederacy, in the shortest possible time, and at the least possible expense." Even those who deplored damage to property could also reason that it was "better thus than to des[t]roy life" to win the war. If the rebellion were to be crushed, Chaplain G. S. Bradley said, somebody had to suffer; making Confederate soldiers' families destitute would cause men to desert and thereby take the enemy out of the field by means other than killing. The marauders among Sherman's men acted on and sometimes avowed the conclusion he had presented in his public warnings to Southerners. Private William Bluffton Miller of the 14th Corps said that the army would "devastate their land entirely" unless the Confederates ended the war: "They have forfeited all their rights."

Many black people welcomed the destructive war waged by Sherman's men. Though former slaves did not pursue reprisal against their masters by widespread violence and desolation, they were often eager to see the Yankees punish Southern whites. Both the smooth progress of the marches and the extent of damage owed much to blacks who lived along the route. Sherman sought out knowledgeable people who could tell him about roads, bridges, the locations of plantations, and distances. They gave word of the Confederate cavalry's movements. Blacks' stories of some masters' extraordinary cruelty encouraged soldiers to use "the torch." At the ornate new house of a Georgia state legislator, near Herndon, a domestic servant named Louisa said: "It *ought* to be burned." When an officer asked her why, she replied: " 'Cause there has been so much devilment here, whipping niggers 'most to death to make 'em work to pay for it." Much to the surprise or, at least, distress of white residents, blacks showed soldiers where food, valuables, and livestock had been hidden. They did so under duress, they often said, but they were remarkably helpful. Describing the burning of factories near Milledgeville, a reporter mentioned "the delight of the negroes at the destruction of places known only to them as task-houses, where they had groaned under the lash." As soldiers tore up the Georgia Railroad, an old black man said: "Many a dark population has worked on dat R. Rd—contractor for dis section *whipped some of 'em to death*—buried one in dose woods." Sherman's men often robbed and destroyed among the blacks' dwellings as well. The army's main blow to the Confederacy and to slavery depended not on soldiers' benevolence but on their capacity to break down the South's resistance. Black people understood Sherman to be doing that. In old age Alfred Sligh recalled: "Durin' de war I see much of de soldiers who say they not quit fightin' 'til all de damn-Yankees am dead. Dis was so, durin' de first two years. After dat I see more and more of de damn-Yankees, as they pass through 'flictin' punishment on 'most every-body. . . . We work on, 'til Sherman come and burn and slash his way through de state in de spring of 1865. I just reckon I 'member dat freedom to de end of my life." The burning, slashing, and punishment were inseparable from the freedom—a single memory.

Despite insults and violence that black people suffered from part of the army, most welcomed its arrival with jubilation, and thousands set out to follow the columns. More often than any other greeting, soldiers heard that newly freed slaves had been patiently waiting for Northerners to come. Sherman's march was the inevitable working out of God's will. In the last week of December 1864, during Christian witnessing at a Savannah church service, one old man "said he had been praying for the deliverance of his people from bondage for 40 years, but he knew the time would come." At the same service a young man said: "I have wanted to preach the gospel to my people for a long time, but the law would not let me, but Sherman and his army, as instruments in the hands of God, had divided the Red sea of slavery, and the people were passing over." Sherman's march was God's answer to the people's prayers. They had been sure He would answer, and they had waited. It had been only a matter of time until the Northern whites did to the Southern whites what the slaves always had known must be done.

Many times during the marches, as well as in Savannah, hundreds of blacks sought out Sherman. They were the first celebrators of his fame, the earliest in a series of crowds and audiences and hand-shakings that lasted for the rest of his life. He heard shoutings and hosannas; he had many long conversations. As word spread in Savannah that he would receive visitors, a steady flow of black people came to his office, a dozen or twenty at a time, to meet him and to make comments such as: "Been prayin' for you all long time, sir, prayin' day & night for you, and now, bless God, you is come." Sherman counseled hard work and orderly behavior in their new state of freedom. However, his importance to ex-slaves at the time of emancipation lay not in his opinions about future race relations but in his standing as God's agent for the violently destructive overthrow of the slaveholders. Fugitives from slavery in South Carolina told him that white people were frightened just by his name.

He replied that the fleeing whites feared his soldiers, not the name of the general. But the black men demurred: "Oh no, it's de name ob Sherman, su'; and we hab wanted to see you so long while you trabbel all roun' jis whar you like to go. . . . you keep cumin' and a cumin', an dey allers git out." The name of Sherman was no longer bounded by the acts, words, and intentions of the man. It had become a talisman, a folk word standing for the means by which the Southern cause had died. Twisted rails were "Sherman's corkscrews"; chimneys left standing after houses burned were "Sherman's monuments" and "Sherman's Sentinels"; the men who did the damage were "Sherman's bummers"; the ruins of Columbia, South Carolina, were "Sherman's Brick yard"; the objects of Boston charity drives were "Sherman's Freedmen." Sam Aleckson found that, like other slaves freed by the war, he was looked down upon by some blacks who had been free before the war; they called him a "Sherman Cutloose." He wrote late in life: "I am persuaded however that all the Negroes in the slave belt, and some of the white men too, were 'Cutloose' by General Sherman." For the defeat of the Confederacy, for the belief that the South could be forced to change, for proof that the permanence of the old order was not divinely decreed, for signs that Northern unionists wanted a nation and black people wanted freedom more than their enemies had imagined—for all these the words "Sherman's march" evoked the limitless possibilities attainable through mayhem.

Sherman's calculations of the effect that his marches would have on the minds of Southern civilians and soldiers came true. Many Confederates had grown pessimistic or defeatist before his successes in the autumn of 1864. The scope and severity of Sherman's subsequent movements broke down much of the remaining faith in the rhetoric of Southern inviolability. Eliza Andrews wrote in her diary on January 11, 1865: "I used to feel very brave about Yankees, but since I have passed over Sherman's track and seen what devastation they made, I am so afraid of them that I believe I should drop down dead if one of the wretches should come into my presence." Though she lived in southwestern Georgia and Sherman was headed away from her, she assumed that the Yankees eventually would come to her region, too, sparing nothing and no one. Expecting such a fate became common among Southerners. Before the Federals began to move northward from Savannah, South Carolinians knew that "it is here their malice will rage fiercest." Governor Andrew G. Magrath called on citizens to leave a scorched earth in the path of the oncoming Sherman and to "fight him at every road." Privately Magrath reported to Jefferson Davis: "It is not an unwillingness to oppose the enemy, but a chilling apprehension of the futility of doing so, which affects the people." The

Federals met no substantial resistance in South Carolina, and retreating Confederate forces lost more and more men by desertion. According to Private Arthur P. Ford, the "most influential cause of desertion was the news that reached the men of the great suffering of their wives and children at home, caused by the devastations of Sherman's army." In the Army of Northern Virginia the problem grew so great that Longstreet's corps had a stronger picket guard posted in its rear, to stop deserters, than in its front. Almost 8 percent of Lee's army deserted between February 15 and March 18. Among soldiers from other states, the failure of South Carolinians to fulfill in adversity the pretensions they had flaunted in seceding offered a bitter satisfaction. Joseph C. Haskell, a South Carolina artilleryman serving in Virginia, had to put up with taunts; "many seem to regard it almost as a triumph that South Carolinians, when put to the test are no better than any body else." Sherman was administering "the test," and the whole South was failing it. S. H. Boineau, a South Carolinian, summarized what the march to the sea meant: "Unmistakeable facts present themselves before us." Substituting the facts of Sherman's march for faith in the Confederate ideal, Southerners reached the conclusion Governor Magrath had foretold: "the desire for Peace will outgrow the desire for Freedom."

The marches' effectiveness in ending defiance convinced Sherman that a quick return to peacetime government would pose no difficulties. Politically, he remained an antebellum Whig unionist. The United States was his idol: in its cause he was willing to use destruction so extensive that he was taken aback by his own creation and assumed that its victims were lastingly impressed by their own violent subjugation. Though he knew that the war, if prolonged, could destroy any aspect of Southern society, he did not think of destruction as an instrument of reform; nor did he think that the Northern war effort included any necessary transformations of Southern society beyond returning rebels to political loyalty. The South, without the distractions of defending slavery or claiming to be separate from the North, could quickly prosper by emulating and complementing the Northern economy.

When Sherman met Joseph E. Johnston outside Durham, North Carolina, eight days after Lee's surrender to Grant, Sherman intended to offer the same terms of surrender that Lee had accepted: disbandment of Confederate troops under a parole exempting them from punishment. But Johnston, with approval from Jefferson Davis and the cabinet of the fleeing Confederate government, urged on Sherman a more comprehensive peace agreement. In exchange for a general surrender throughout the South, Confederates wanted to commit the United States government to the status quo ante bellum, entailing recognition of existing state governments and of citizens' political and property rights, implicitly establishing a basis for future legal claims for recompense of former slaveholders and holders of the Confederate debt. In the days after Lincoln's assassination, Sherman thought that an agreement with Johnston, ratified by the new president, would help quickly restore order to the South. He believed that Lincoln had intended a prompt return to local home rule in the South and that he could accomplish Lincoln's design in a single stroke. Sherman also feared guerrilla disorders among Southerners unable to accept defeat, and he assumed that these could best be prevented or suppressed by leaving local power in the hands of former Confederate leaders. All these expectations Sherman embodied in a peace agreement he sent to Washington. It extended "a general amnesty"—which Sherman evidently meant only for Confederate soldiers but did not limit in his written wording—and it committed the executive branch of the federal government to the recognition of Southern state governments and officials, to the restoration of political, personal, and property rights as defined by federal and state constitutions, to the re-establishment of federal courts and the submission of rival state governments' claims to the United States Supreme Court.

Sherman argued that war had left the South abject, that the North's control of the federal government and of the nation's future was unquestioned. The quickest way to unite the South with the nation would be to trust its leaders' acceptance of the war's result and to appeal to their self-interest to lead Southerners in cooperative subordination as they formerly had led in resistance. After Sherman's peace agreement was rejected by President Johnson, publicly denounced as a sell-out by Secretary of War Stanton, and criticized all over the North as a betrayal of the war's goals, he still said that time would prove him right. In the following years he watched for vindication. He had predicted that the Northern public would not long support the expense of keeping troops in the South for political purposes or the exclusion of large segments of the white population from political power. As Republicans legislated the new rules of Southern politics, he had warned that Congressional reconstruction, by basing Republican power in Southern states primarily on black voters, would intensify the hostility of white opponents. Withdrawal of the army from a political role by 1877 and the return to power of Democrats, Redeemers, and ex-Confederates struck Sherman as a belated acceptance of his aborted agreement with Johnston in 1865. Republicans finally had come around to his position by force of necessity.

All the while, Sherman urged Southerners to busy themselves with economic improvement. For him the greatest threat posed by secession— the greatest heresy of the rebels—was not their goal of perpetuating the antebellum South, which had prospered in the union, but their attack on optimism, on faith in national progress, an attack implicit in their attempt to fortify provincially rather than prosper continentally. They tried to hoard their wealth and consign the North to ruin. Sherman hoped that Southerners after the war would quickly regain their confidence in a union that would grow richer than any section could do alone. He told delegates at a convention in Little Rock, Arkansas, in December 1865 to turn their energies away from protesting exclusion of ex-Confederates from politics and to turn toward developing their state's resources. Though he deplored Republicans' reliance on Northern-born politicians in Southern state governments, he wanted Southerners to welcome Northern emigrants as developers of the land and as entrepreneurs. Sherman traveled across the South in 1879 and "noticed closely every sign of commercial, manufacturing and industrial progress." Evan P. Howell of the *Atlanta Constitution* got him to write a public letter commending the potential for development in Atlanta, northern Georgia, northern Alabama, and eastern Tennessee. He visited Atlanta again in 1881 for the First International Cotton Exposition and called it "the best step yet made for the 'New South.'" Long after he had seen much evidence that he had misplaced his trust, Sherman kept hoping that the war's severity had cured Southerners of sectional politics. He clung to the expectation underlying his proposed peace terms in 1865: "Time and renewed industry . . . will finally bring all parties of the South into general harmony of interest and consequent opinion with the rest of the country."

The outcry in the North against Sherman's leniency in his peace agreement died down quickly in the spring of 1865. Grant went to North Carolina but left Sherman in command to receive Johnston's surrender on terms like those given to Lee. Jefferson Davis was soon caught and imprisoned. Stanton's exaggerated public suggestions of betrayal and insubordination lost credence. Most censure of Sherman faded in May. Within a week of Stanton's bulletin explaining the administration's initial rejection of the terms, newspapers began to change their line. On April 24 the *Philadelphia Inquirer* said: "General Sherman has sealed his fate." Five days later the *Inquirer* repealed Sherman's doom and said that no one had done more than he to suppress the rebellion: "Let us forget this little episode in a grand career, and let us resolve to discharge the duty of gratitude which is due to General Sherman." The survival of Sherman's popularity after his presumptuous intrusion into complex and controversial political matters seems, in retrospect, an early demonstration of the limits on Northerners' interest in sustaining the use or the threat of force in peacetime to change the South and to protect the rights of blacks.

Sherman's agreement with the Confederates would have precluded voting by blacks unless Southern whites extended the franchise, and he contemplated little change in former slaves' economic role. He assured Johnston: "Negros would remain in the South and afford you abundance of cheap labor." Sherman would have preferred a geographical separation of the races. His Special Field Order Number 15, issued at Savannah on January 16, 1865, after consultation with Stanton, reserved a thirty-mile-wide strip of abandoned land along the coast for blacks, granting those who settled there whatever "possessory title" the federal government could convey. This was primarily a wartime measure to provide means of subsistence for former slaves who had taken over plantations or had come to the coast as refugees. Sherman privately thought it might also begin "a system of segregation" gradually parting the two races, who would "acquire separate property." By the summer of 1865 he doubted that such a scheme was feasible, but his peace terms still would have provided for the lasting political and economic subordination of blacks to whites. Despite Sherman's well-known disapproval of "radical" reconstruction measures and his attempt to forestall them, his success in destroying the rebellion outweighed in most Northerners' minds his disapproval of assuring blacks the full status of citizens or his skepticism about trying to give the South a new set of political leaders. Though the strongest antislavery Republican papers, such as the *Cincinnati Gazette* and the *Chicago Tribune,* were the harshest in denouncing his concessions to the rebels—and Thaddeus Stevens tried to prevent his promotion to lieutenant general in 1866—there was no concerted effort by "radicals" to end his military career. John M. Corse's account of opinion in the northwest in August 1865 might serve for other parts of the North as well. He wrote to Sherman: "The conservative republicans & Democrats are enthusiastically your admirers while the Radicals even are not disposed to say severe things against you."

Sherman's effectiveness in war had won him many admirers among Northerners whose political views did not jibe well with his plan of reconstruction. According to Thomas Ewing, Jr., "he has a deep hold on the hearts and sympathies of the Republicans to none of whom were the propositions acceptable." Republicans described Sherman's disinclination to reform the South as a moral and political blindness. John C. Gray, Jr., conversed with him in May and found that Sherman had clung to the outlook prevalent in the North in 1861: the war's sole purpose was to maintain the union. Gray, like some Republican editors, believed that Sherman did not understand the war's larger meaning for Northerners. In 1867 the Worcester *Spy* concluded: "Sherman is organically wrong. He is a race-hater, and oligarchic by instinct. Though his brain may accept the issues of the war, his temperament will fight against their logical conclusions." Sherman treated the war as a solely military undertaking, failing to comprehend the political question on which it turned and showing "no special sympathy with the moral sentiment which animated the patriotism of the Northern States." By his willingness to concede so much to the rebels, stopping or even reversing the war's promised revolution as soon as fighting ended, Sherman revealed, *Harper's Weekly* said, that "he utterly misunderstands the scope of the war." Even so, if radical violence gave impetus to war's transforming effects on society, its supporters could hardly repudiate Sherman in the same way they had repudiated McClellan, who neither understood the destined scope of the war's changes nor furthered moral and social revolution by using radical military means. Sherman had waged the kind of war Republicans wanted. While his popularity in 1865 helped to vindicate their methods, its survival despite his conservatism was one sign of weakness in public support for radical reform through war. Emergency war powers, passionate nationalism, the energy of Sherman's war-making might hasten the coming of a new republic, purged of antebellum evils and backwardness. However, if Sherman failed to see or to sustain the war's regenerative mission and nevertheless held his place in public esteem, his moral blindness might yet prove to be widely shared when regeneration did not quickly and easily follow victory.

Sherman deplored Republicans' use of the army to support state administrations in the South. He said that such garrisons were "obnoxious to our ideas of self government," and he thought it "beneath a soldiers vocation" to be "hauled about, under the orders of, and control of Treasury agents & marshals & sheriffs, at the bidding of Senators, members of Congress &c &c." He contended that the Republican approach, cutting the army's size while using troops in politics, was self-defeating because it left the army too small to intimidate completely the white populace of the South but intrusive enough to provoke resentment. Republicans' opponents in the South were restrained from more violent action only by "the memory of our war power." Obviously, the federal government would not maintain garrisons indefinitely for political purposes. Most soldiers had been withdrawn from reconstruction politics by 1875, when Sherman repeated his ten-year-old prediction about the role of "the rebel element" in Southern state government: "They have the votes, the will, and will in the end prevail."

In the end, the Southerners whom he had wanted the North to trust in 1865 disappointed him. Widespread killing and violent intimidation of blacks and of white Republicans, as well as juries' frequent refusal to indict or to convict the perpetrators, "embarrassed" Sherman in his efforts to convince Northerners that onetime rebels had become good citizens.

And Southerners revived sectional politics, restoring an alliance with Northern Democrats, returning to power in Congress, and renewing constitutional challenges to federal authority. Having at last won most of the concessions Sherman had offered them in 1865, Southerners talked as if they had learned nothing from the war, as if they had not done wrong in waging it, almost as if they had not lost it. Belatedly, in the 1880s, Sherman became an advocate of black men's right to vote. He saw that the ending of slavery had increased Southern power in Congress and in the electoral college by counting blacks fully in apportionment of seats in the House of Representatives while the increasing curtailment of blacks' voting enabled Democrats to strengthen their control. Even for "the new young men" whom Sherman admired, such as Henry W. Grady, permanent dominance by the white race mattered more than constitutions and laws. Seeing defiance of law always made Sherman think of anarchy and war. The next fight, he said, would come from blacks who would use force to win their rights. For twenty years Sherman had overstated the transformation wrought among rebels by the ruin that war had inflicted. In 1884 he conceded, with regret, that Southerners still clung to "the absurd idea that the slave and free states of 1860 have diverse and opposing interests." He had mistaken the collapse of Southern aspirations to nationhood for a full integration of the union, the goal with which he had justified his severity in war and his forbearance in peace. He wanted to believe that the nation had been conclusively vindicated in the minds of all by its wartime strength. The erosion not only of Republicans' plans for reconstruction but also of his own hopes distressed him, adding to his postwar fears that the nation was weaker than anyone in 1865 could have anticipated.

THOUGH Sherman confessed that he had erred in some of his predictions about peacetime, he never wavered from his definitions of the nature of war. He had shown their validity in action, conclusively; such a demonstration remained for him the nation's chief source of security. Nevertheless, far from settling disputed questions about the conduct of war and the power of the nation-state, Sherman's pronouncements and actions aroused controversy, which still continues. His version of the destructive war disturbed many people long after resolution of the sectional conflict. As a theorist or casuist on the subject of war, Sherman did not develop extended formal arguments; he made brief pronouncements in letters and speeches. These generalizations, though unsystematic, set forth a consistent view. He saw peace as the realm of law, reason, predictable governance, and shared rules of politics. Peacetime was in the hands of politicians. Though law ultimately depended on the government's power to maintain its authority, the presence of force in the rule of law ordinarily remained subtle and benign, mediated through politicians' ability to win the people's consent. War was an essentially different, almost an opposite, condition. The conduct of war did not conform to politicians' purposes so much as it negated their customary methods and signalized their failure. Though presidents and congresses continued to rule during war, they did not rule war. Especially in the zone where armies operated, but also, ultimately, in war's outcome and in the fate of nations, war obeyed its own law. For Sherman that law consisted of the use of force until one side submitted to the other.

In war the power of some people over others was no longer confined by precedent, compromises, and documents. Instead, it consisted of direct violence in many forms, ranging from killing thousands of men to taking some food—violence cumulatively demonstrating the subjugation of the weaker to the stronger. Some of Sherman's most widely quoted statements were simply aphoristic summaries of this qualitative distinction between the workings of peace and those of war: "war is war, and not popularity-seeking"; "War is cruelty and you cannot refine it"; "war is simply power unrestrained by constitution or compact." In these and other kindred remarks, Sherman did not contend that war necessarily would or should grow as violent as the participants could make it. Rather, he meant that in war one side could not rely on peacetime methods and rules—appeals to public opinion, to humanitarianism, to the fundamental law of civil government—as a binding restraint on the other side's use of force. The belligerents might not do all the harm within their power, usually did not, but they had no guarantee against the possible use of the maximum extremity of violence.

Some of Sherman's generalizations about war resembled those of Carl von Clausewitz, though neither Sherman nor other Civil War generals had read *On War*. Like Clausewitz, Sherman imagined the theoretical possibility of an absolute state of war wherein violent conflict absorbed all endeavor. Mounting violence ever more closely approximated the all-encompassing belligerence incipient in war. Sherman would have agreed that war was "an act of force to compel our enemy to do our will," and he shared Clausewitz's emphasis on war's objective: influencing the mind or spirit or morale of the enemy. On the other hand, in Sherman's categorical separation of war from law, of politicians from generals, he diverged sharply from Clausewitz's assumption that fighting could be subordinated to the political purposes of governments. Like Clausewitz, Sherman saw military force as a means of political persuasion. But Clausewitz had more confidence in politicians' capacity to control that force. "War, therefore, is an act of policy," he wrote. "Were it a complete, untrammeled, absolute manifestation of violence (as the pure concept would require), war would of its own independent will usurp the place of policy the moment policy had brought it into being; it would then drive policy out of office and rule by the laws of its own nature." Clausewitz thus rejected the proposition that war must follow a dynamic of violence until one belligerent succumbed, whereupon peace and political designs, characteristic of peace but not of war, regained their sway. For him the concept of absolute violence was an abstraction, a fiction useful for defining the extent to which belligerents committed themselves to war. Their conduct would never be altogether devoid of political calculations. Sherman, by contrast, and notwithstanding his talk of "statesmanship," hardly allowed a suggestion that politicians might measure or restrain destruction. He put the dichotomy between violence and governance to the Savannah Chamber of Commerce in these words: "It is reduced to a simple question of war. . . . When war is done we can soon bring order out of chaos, and prosperity out of ruin & destruction."

Sherman accepted civilian supremacy over the military and the subordination of army officers to statute law. But he kept trying to construe war as a unique condition distinct from the activities of the civil authorities, a condition in which soldiers had only one goal—defeating resistance—and used whatever violence they needed: "When the Congress has declared war, has provided the ways and means, and the President, as constitutional commander-in-chief, has indicated the measures, then the soldier goes in with confidence to restore *peace*. Of these measures the commanding officer on the spot must often be the sole judge. The law then becomes the law of war, and not of peace." By "law of war" he meant not international rules of conduct but the supplanting of civil government by violence. Insofar as governmental policy in wartime entailed more complex, discrete purposes than simply forcing the enemy to stop fighting, Sherman's view of war tended to make it "usurp the place of policy" by leaving soldiers free to move war toward "a complete, untrammeled, absolute manifestation of violence"—indeed, by denying that war could be otherwise.

Sherman's definition made war a realm where anything was conceivable—seizing property, deporting the enemy, exterminating a resisting populace. "Many, many peoples with less pertinacity," he warned Southerners, "have been wiped out of national existence." While he argued on the one hand that war's limits consisted only in the victor's discretion, on the other he ascribed the violence that did occur not to governments' choices but to war's imperative. His entity "war" took on the attributes of a process of nature controlling all the participants, using them, as lightning or earthquakes used matter, to establish a new equilibrium through upheaval. Once Northerners accepted war by deciding that they must preserve the union, they could say, as Sherman did, "We had no choice and we have no choice yet. We must go on, even to the end of time, even if it result in sinking a million of lives and desolating the whole land, leaving a desert behind." Such an extent of violence, if it occurred, would flow from a state of war the belligerents had entered. This approach made Federal war measures not the choice and the responsibility of men who ordered them but inescapable phenomena of an altered state of being known as "war." "Reason is silent & impotent and men in arms listen to nothing but force." Force followed its own laws of acceleration.

Whether marveling at his ruthless effectiveness or deploring his ruthless lack of scruples, writers often have mentioned Sherman's relentless logic, a characterization that would have gratified him. But his exercise in definitions amounted to a repudiation of reason—or, more precisely, an assertion that his enemies had repudiated reason and by doing so had freed him from its constraints. Sherman was not offering arguments about the Civil War or the nature of war; he supposed himself to be stating unarguable truths. His definitions left no place for the peace-minded Northerners who reasoned that the union was not worth the bloodshed and suffering undertaken to secure it. His version of ineluctable war gave no credence to Confederates who reasoned that the war's cost and length would convince Northerners to forgo further effort notwithstanding the North's superior strength. Sherman denied the validity of these arguments by asserting that war could not stop—need not even be moderated—until the test of force established the victor's supremacy conclusively. He knew that these rival reasonings had widespread influence. He did not undertake to refute them but instead swept them away. He intended to eliminate from the minds of those who clung to the efficacy of reason any hope that Northerners could choose to forgo war and to give up the union. He would do so by showing those who thought war had limits a universe of violence that might destroy them at any moment without compunction, a universe in which the actions of his army amounted only to a beginning. If one treated Sherman's definitions of war and his wartime actions as logic, one could not refute him; one could only acquiesce or try to stop him.

Sherman's assertions have seemed so readily applicable to the conduct of war in the twentieth century that his campaigns and writings have struck many people as precedents for "modern" warfare. The connection has necessarily been more figurative than literal. If Sherman had a direct influence on military men's thinking about war in the nineteenth century, it consisted not in his attacks on civilian society but in his innovations in the use of railroads—both his system for supplying his own army and his exploitation of his enemy's vulnerability to the breaking of lines of communication. He liked to hear that his campaigns won respect from professional officers for these successes. He did not think of himself as a prophet of a fundamentally transformed, "modern" war. The chapter of his memoirs devoted to the Civil War's military lessons dwelt on organizational, technological, and tactical changes in conventional combat.

The notion that twentieth-century war-makers have consciously imitated the methods of Sherman's marches has been put forward most earnestly by B. H. Liddell Hart. He found in Sherman's conduct an alternative to the appalling attrition on the western front in World War I, a concentration instead on "the economic target" and "the moral target"—that is, the spirit of the civilian population. After World War II Liddell Hart often said that German officers professed their indebtedness to him in making their plans but that they were really indebted to Sherman, from whose campaigns he had learned the techniques of strategy, especially penetration of the enemy's country, that the Germans supposedly had studied. However, his writings on Sherman did not foreshadow the blitzkrieg or tank warfare, and recent scrutiny by John J. Mearsheimer leads to the conclusion that Liddell Hart's influence on the conduct of World War II existed mainly in Liddell Hart's mind. Sherman's purpose was not Liddell Hart's goal of avoiding a war of attrition. Sherman accepted such a war as a necessary means for the union's victory. His modern reputation has been for the most part very different from the soldier of carefully calculated, economical war whom Liddell Hart portrayed.

In the twentieth century the name of Sherman has taken on an incantatory quality; speak it, and all the demons of destruction appear. Sherman the creator of modern war has been largely a rhetorical rather than a historical figure. His words have remained vivid, but it would be difficult, if not impossible, to demonstrate his direct influence on belligerents' conduct in the twentieth century. Trying to understand why modern war has brought violence to civilian populations, most writers have traced belligerents' lack of restraint to its origins in broad changes in society, changes in political and economic organization and in accompanying attitudes. For example, in one version, an industrial, materialistic civilization dominated by the machine wreaks violence indiscriminately, justifying any means of war by the demands of the machine, which the society exists in order to serve. Or the waging of war by democracies and other societies basing their war effort on mass appeals to patriotism and on mass conscript armies erodes the distinction between combatants and noncombatants, holding out to each belligerent the prospect that damage inflicted

on the enemy's economy and civilian population will win a war at lower
cost. Or a racist, imperialist society, assuming its cultural superiority,
dismisses the idea of restraints on the violence with which it seeks dominion. Conceptions of what is modern in war thus tend toward the total,
the unlimited, the massively destructive, because modern warmaking is
by definition beyond individuals' control and sweeps them into a vortex
of events allowing no fixed standards of scale and momentum and morality in the actions of masses of people. James Truslow Adams wrote in
1934: "What the horrors of the next war are to be, no one dares envisage."
It went without saying that the next war would be more modern than
its predecessor.

Modernity, then, comprises a state of mind, an outlook conducive to
the worst in war. As Bruce Catton has summarized: "The thing that
makes modern war so appallingly frightful is not so much the hideous
things which in our sublime innocence we call 'weapons' as it is the
development of an attitude which makes the unlimited use of these
weapons something that is taken for granted." This erosion of ethical
constraints in the modern mind's view of war was the focus of Robert
Penn Warren's indignation when he called total war "the concept that
we now accept as normal." For the origin or the epitome of these
definitions, some twentieth-century writers have regularly returned to
Sherman. Though they treated the societal, political, and cultural attributes of modernity as an epochal transformation—obviously not originating in one man, one war, or one country—they gave Sherman a unique
prominence.

Kitchener's devastations in the Transvaal, the German policy of
Schrecklichkeit or "frightfulness," the bombing of Coventry and London,
the fire-bombing of Dresden and Tokyo, the atomic-bombing of Hiro-
shima and Nagasaki—all went back, along "a straight line of logic," to
Sherman. In some way not very precisely defined by these later writers
he had launched the history of war on a course threatening to destroy
the world. Catton suggested that the "agonizing uncertainty" of living
under the threat of nuclear war has been part of Americans' atonement
for beginning the development of modern war in the 1860s. Finding
Sherman guilty has been one method of reasserting that war can be
regulated, that moral standards can apply to belligerents' behavior and
wrongful actions can be condemned, punished, or avoided. If Sherman
had written and behaved similarly in the twentieth century but had served
on a losing side, Otto Eisenschiml argued in 1963, he probably would
have been tried and executed as "a war criminal."

Writers not especially concerned with the Civil War also have found
in Sherman the father of later American misdeeds. Condemning the most

destructive American actions during the war in Vietnam, Michael Herr used bitter irony to contrast the war's stated goal of freedom for Vietnamese with Americans' methods of waging it: "It was axiomatic that it was about ideological space, we were there to bring them choice, bringing it to them like Sherman bringing the Jubilee through Georgia, clean through it, wall to wall with pacified indigenous and scorched earth." More bluntly, Mary McCarthy, writing about one of the court-martials that followed the killing of Vietnamese civilians at My Lai, called Sherman's march "an earlier war crime." The common purpose in these formulations of Sherman's responsibility was not so much to offer a historical argument about causation as to condemn war in which destruction lost contact with its rationale. For this moral argument Sherman served as an evocative symbol—a sinister genius, a Machiavelli, a Napoleon, whose reputation took on a life of its own.

The actions of Sherman's men bore little resemblance to the mass killings of civilians in twentieth-century war. Few if any writers have contended that Sherman made those mass killings possible or necessary, that twentieth-century war would have taken a different course without Sherman's example, or even that Sherman alone brought modernity to the Civil War. Instead, his marches and his statements have provided a satisfyingly specific example of a change in warfare, a change toward a now-familiar vocabulary of the drastic which can also serve for the far more massive violence of the twentieth century. By emphasizing the "logic" of Sherman and the "memory" of Sherman in his bearing on later wars, writers have found his role in modern war less in his army's deeds than in his words, particularly his accepting the idea of limitless violence and his writing about making war on civilians as if such conduct were inevitable. Mention of Sherman as the progenitor of modernity usually dwells on his terrible words. Once set forth, the words fixed themselves in the minds of others long after Sherman's death—who does not know that war is hell?—and made it impossible to think about war without also thinking that the words might be true, that war had no certain limits. Even in disputing or deploring his view one could not recapture the confident assertion that laws of civilization governed nations' conduct to make the world progressively more humane. The more that twentieth-century wars fit Sherman's words, the closer seemed the link between his having written them and their having come true, between learning to conceive of total war and embracing it.

The Civil War, as practiced by the belligerents and characterized by Sherman, implemented two propositions which later wars took much further: that the nation and the nation's professed ideals admit no necessary limit in their fight to prevail; that the methods of waging war do not differ categorically if at all between the belligerent whose cause is labeled just and the belligerent whose cause is labeled unjust. Neither of these propositions commands universal assent, yet modern belligerents have acted as if they were true. Sherman did not discover them or create a "logic" for them but treated them as obvious truths. He had come to his view of war not primarily by reasoning but by intensely emotional experience, especially in 1861 and 1862 when his alarms and his old-fashioned prescriptions for armies fighting armies had been called insanity by people eager to take devastation to the rebels. To reason from the proposition that hurting and intimidating civilians would more quickly win a war to the conclusion that attacking civilians was inevitable in war could be accomplished by logic of a sort. But the origins of waging war in that manner lay mainly in "the dramatic 'logic' of a sequence of events"—the narrative of war that Sherman and other war-makers constructed for themselves in order to dramatize the necessity of their actions. Expansion of the violence came less from belligerents' rational calculation than from their passion, which convinced them of the inevitability and the moral validity of the course of events. The line that went back from recent times to Sherman was not so much a chain of reasoning as a shared story of destined national triumph. Sherman did not make anyone in the twentieth century do destructive things. He only made some people think about what belligerents were doing. They looked at their wars and saw him.

FOR NORTHERNERS who applauded the harshness of Sherman's campaigns and read his letters defining war, his words rang true, and his deeds matched them. "You gave us victory," John Mason Loomis wrote to him from Chicago; "you instructed Burbridge, you answered Hood by pen and fire. . . . You struck the chord, that throughout this land vibrates in hearty true response when you told the Mayor of Atlanta the saving truth." Sherman's letter to General Stephen G. Burbridge had authorized deportation of Kentuckians who harbored guerrillas. His exchanges with Hood and with Atlanta's civilian authorities were perhaps Sherman's most widely known war writings. *Harper's Weekly* quoted and praised them before and after the march to the sea: "General Sherman does not play at war. 'War is cruelty,' he says, 'and you can not refine it,' and he believes that they who have brought war upon the country will justly feel its sharpest edge." His letter, according to *Harper's*, expressed the nature of war not only for Atlantans but for the nation: "General Sherman says to the Mayor of Atlanta what every true heart in the land confirms and approves." The *New York Herald* printed Sherman's letter and predicted that everyone in the country would see or hear every syllable of it and that all would endorse it except "the snivellers and peace men."

Northerners had many sources of copious information about devastations wrought by Sherman's soldiers, even leaving aside the thousands of private letters from Sherman's men and the boxes shipped from camp, full of things taken from Southern homes. Newspapers created bigger headlines to fit the momentousness of the great marches, which remained at the top of the front page even when information was fragmentary. The *Herald* and the *Philadelphia Inquirer* printed maps across which the swath of Sherman's progress lengthened.

"SHERMAN MAKING A CLEAN SWEEP IN GEORGIA,"

"SHERMAN'S TRIUMPHANT MARCH,"

"SHERMAN, COLUMBIA OURS!"

GOOD NEWS

WM. TECUMSEH SHERMAN.

Another Splendid Triumph.

SOUTH CAROLINA'S CAPITAL OURS

or, in a punning vein at the expense of Confederate bluster, "General Sherman Firing the Heart of South Carolina"—headlines followed the campaigns with glee. By the time that Sherman had reached North Carolina, *Harper's Weekly* was publishing engravings of foragers returning to camp with fancy clothes, watches, and other loot; a full-page engraving depicted the burning of Columbia, with soldiers drinking, dancing, breaking open chests, and carrying plunder as women and children fled the scene. Reporters and editors did not stint enthusiasm for what a *Cincinnati Commercial* correspondent called "a new principle in our warfare"—showing Southerners that none of them were safe anywhere.

The many accounts of destroyed property and scared civilians most often evoked, in print and in private, the comment that Georgians and Carolinians deserved what they were getting. Some popular war books published in later years drew a veil over the actions of Sherman's men, but others dwelt on scenes of flame and desolation with the same kind of approval Northerners had shown in 1865. The prolific writer Joel T. Headley praised the march and told his readers that the army "moved over the fertile country like the locusts of Egypt. A garden was before them, a desert behind them." Writing in 1868, Whitelaw Reid condemned

Sherman for the army's attacks on civilians but acknowledged that the Northern public had enjoyed reports of the marches. After the Carolina campaign, the "popularity of Sherman rose even higher than when he reached Savannah." Jubilation over Sherman's successes grew louder in the streets, bigger in newspapers' typeface, and more frequent in Northerners' letters as details of destruction came north. In a war whose often surprising course and scale had sometimes called into question the supposition that masterful hands guided events in conformity with history's grand design, such sweeping success gratified Northerners. Grant's circumscribing and reducing the Army of Northern Virginia was crucial to defeat of the Confederacy. Thomas's defeat of Hood's Army of Tennessee was an essential part of Sherman's claim to have calculated his strategy correctly. But the unstoppable momentum of Sherman's marches had a dramatic appeal even greater than their role in ending the war. The marches conspicuously, unmistakably gave victory two attributes that unionists long had deemed most fitting as symbols of Northern triumph. Sherman's army dramatized both progress and nemesis. The applause for it contained little if any hint that Northerners saw paradox or irony in uniting the two.

The idea of war that hurt civilians did not shock Sherman's many admirers. In 1861, while he had still been punishing soldiers for trespassing on private property, *Harper's Weekly* had posed a choice between attacking the enemy at a disadvantage with assaults on fortified positions or hitting the rebels where they were vulnerable. "To molest their homes and jeopard their 'personal property' is to attack them where they are weak." That was "common sense," *Harper's* said in its editorial titled "The Way to Put Down the Rebellion." More than three years later, in the last year of the war, this argument from efficacy seemed irrefutable as Sherman proved that Southerners would yield to such methods. In Fort Dodge, Iowa, R. E. Carpenter said of the march to the sea: "It has struck more terror, I am sure, into the hearts of Traitors in the South than any campaign of the war." The word "campaign" could as readily apply to bringing terror among civilians as to defeating enemy armies. The campaign was against traitors. The Union League Club of New York greeted Sherman in June 1865: "When you visited upon the absurd and truculent vanity of South Carolina the just vengeance she had provoked we *here* rejoiced at your wide array sweeping across the country of that ridiculous chivalry. . . . We talked of you, we praised you, we loved you, for the directness and patriotic singleness of duty, with which you made war." Northerners recognized in Sherman's marches a form of triumph they long had wanted, a fulfillment of demands they had made since secession began.

Sherman's view of war was no more in advance of his compatriots' than was his treatment of rebels. His famous letters did not so much give Northerners new ideas as restate the premises on which the war effort rested. Samuel Powel, a member of a prominent Philadelphia family, wrote in January 1863: "War is simply despotism, tyranny, brute force of the worst kind; & both sides must be under its full ban while it lasts. For the time it must virtually overthrow all other rule. Let us theorize as we like, it must be so." The inadequacy of theory, law, or reason for controlling war's practices was almost a truism. Northerners and Southerners blamed the other side for abrogating the laws of war first, but then joined in saying that their own side must wage the same kind of war the enemy did. Stonewall Jackson's admirers believed that, given the chance, he could have been the agent of Confederate victory by taking a war of destruction and intimidation to the enemy's territory. Praising Jubal Early's burning of Chambersburg, Pennsylvania, Sergeant J. Adger Smyth of the 25th South Carolina Regiment said in August 1864 that "the universal belief" among Southerners was that "our burning & destroying in Yankee Land" would best speed the coming of peace and take revenge for Federals' abuse of civilians: "The golden rule does not apply to Governments at war." Powel and Smyth were as thoroughgoing as Sherman in their representations of war hurtling along its career, blind to moral dicta.

If Sherman read the May 31, 1862, issue of *Harper's Weekly* he saw these words: "When the rebels invoked war they invoked despotism. War is the appeal to brute force. War reaches and maintains its ends by violence." By the time that Sherman began to write in this vein and to be published throughout the North and the South, Americans were familiar with the case he made. He went beyond restating it to show how it worked. Few people suggested that there was any other way for either side to win the war. The hypothetical narrative ending in Confederate independence posited Southern methods much like those Grant and Sherman used in the last year of the war. What if, by frontal assaults with heavy casualties—more successful than those at Shiloh, the Seven Days, Second Manassas, Chancellorsville, Gettysburg, Chickamauga—Confederates could have wiped out a Federal army in the way Grant wanted to wipe out Lee's army? What if Confederates could have killed enough Federal soldiers to convince most Northerners that peace Democrats were right to say that Republicans' war was futile? What if Confederates had mounted more devastating raids across the Northern countryside, and had thereby succeeded in demoralizing Northern civilians? The even remotely plausible imaginings of Confederate success subscribed to the view of war which Federals followed to win and which many people in both North and South had espoused before Yankees pursued it successfully.

The vocabulary of religious and moral purpose in the North's waging war, like the naturalistic vocabulary of physical force and national survival, included words that drew no line between civilians and soldiers in the just punishing of transgressors. For many Northerners these words of righteousness applied to Sherman's work, even though he did not use them. Images of fire as an agent of moral purgation through destruction—rhetorical figures used in the sectional conflict long before Sherman's marches—became attached to his name. People accustomed to propounding their moral judgments through biblical metaphors used words suited to scenes of a rain of fire descending on an entire population as a collective chastisement for the community's sins. Preaching in New Haven, Connecticut, O. T. Lanphear warned against showing pity or mercy to incorrigible secessionists; with measures like Grant's order for the devastation of the Shenandoah Valley and Sherman's expulsion of civilians from Atlanta the armies were finally becoming equal to their task. "Let it be shown that when a state insults the law of the land, by deliberate secession, it is like a withered branch cast forth from the national tree, to be gathered, cast into the fire and burned." A figure of speech originally dealing with belief in Christ had become a political metaphor; Sherman and Sheridan, by their marches, could further transform it from the figurative to the literal. Like the momentum of devastation in Sherman's track, which could grow beyond the text of Sherman's orders to become as awful as secessionists' crime, hyperbole about God's purging flames could take on a wider meaning than the words' ostensible intent, a meaning that called for real fire.

At the end of *Uncle Tom's Cabin* Harriet Beecher Stowe addressed white Americans of both sections, reminding them that they shared complicity in the evil of slavery. This injustice invited upon America the earthquake to be produced by the spreading of Christ's spirit. His kingdom was coming, she warned. To portray the consequences that Christ's return would have for wrongdoers she wove together passages from the prophet Malachi, foretelling judgment against "those that oppress the hireling in his wages, the widow and the fatherless"—that is, slaveholders and their supporters—and those "that turn aside the stranger in his right"—obviously, Northerners who did not help slaves escape bondage. For a vision of the fate of such people after the Second Coming she combined and emended Malachi and the 72nd Psalm: "Who may abide the day of his appearing? 'for that day shall burn as an oven . . . and he shall break in pieces the oppressor.'" Readers familiar with their Bibles would recall verses accompanying those that Stowe used: "He is like a refiner's fire"; "all the proud, yea, and all that do wickedly, shall be stubble; and the day that cometh shall burn them up"; "ye shall tread down the wicked; for they shall be ashes under the soles of your feet in the day that I shall do this, saith the Lord of hosts." Stowe's appeal to white Americans to confront their guilt and do justice to the oppressed in conformity with Christ's spirit became a sweeping incendiary threat through the visionary language of the Old Testament. She conveyed her warning in words that pointed toward the ending of slavery in a punitive fire.

Sixteen years later Stowe wrote about Sherman and his march. "Sherman knew war, almost intuitively," she said, calling him the "war-prophet." She praised the skill of his campaigns that had pierced the heart of the rebellion and coursed through the vitals of the Confederacy. She was especially impressed by his careful study of census statistics, which had shown him where his army could live off the land. In her new book Stowe was still advocating Christian humility for the North, urging Wendell Phillips to become less vindictive toward Southerners, who had now been humbled. But in retrospect she could see that God's flaming purgation of slavery from the land had taken the form of Sherman's march. In her postwar vocabulary the "oppressor" was clearly the Southerners, whom God had spoken against "in the voice of famine and battle, of fire and sword." The "guilty land" was now the Confederacy, which Northerners had rightly "riven and torn." For scriptural words applicable to its fate she turned back to the Old Testament and borrowed the words "astonishment" and "desolation" from the prophet Jeremiah, who said: "The Lord could no longer bear, because of the evil of your doings, and because of the abominations which ye have committed; therefore is your land a desolation, and an astonishment, and a curse, without an inhabitant, as at this day." Counseling Phillips and her readers to be charitable, Stowe invoked the spirit of Calvary in preference to that of Sinai as a guide for dealing with the defeated South; yet her words for the accomplishing of that defeat, like her warning in *Uncle Tom's Cabin* about the imminent coming of Christ's kingdom, again equated righteousness with burning, smashing, and laying waste. In the years between her two books, the metaphors of destruction had come to life as the millennial promise had not. Christ had not come, but Sherman had done His work.

As long as the war generation lived, Sherman's campaigns were part of the nation's glory. For twenty-five years, in orchestra halls, at reunions, and at hundreds—perhaps thousands—of civic and patriotic festivities, Sherman never for long escaped the sound of musicians playing "Marching Through Georgia." He once said: "I wish I had a dollar for every time I have had to listen to that blasted tune." During a reunion of the Grand Army of the Republic in Boston, he stood for seven hours, reviewing a parade that included 250 bands and 100 drum corps, each of which struck up "Marching Through Georgia" as it approached the reviewing stand. A veteran saw him turn his head away to hide an expression of disgust as the tune started yet again. For decades the song remained part of the standard music of patriotism, like "The Battle Hymn of the Republic." The march to the sea as a festive, triumphant climax to the war took a place among the staples of popular culture. A ten-cent biography of Sherman issued by Street & Smith, publishers of dime novels, said: "No man save Grant did so much to bring the fratricidal strife to a speedy close as he. But for the tactics employed by these comrades in arms, the sanguinary struggle might have been dragged on for many years longer." The marches did not stand out in Northerners' minds as deviations from other means used to win the war. Sherman and Grant and their armies were partners in victory.

In the last year of the war supporters of Sherman's campaigns claimed his army as their representatives; the soldiers were agents of the people's will. After the fall of Atlanta the *New York Herald* said of Grant's and Sherman's armies: "Those great assemblages of men are the American people under arms. . . . those armies are the essence, the heart, the brain, the hand of the American people." Colonel Absalom H. Markland met Sherman's army on the Georgia coast with fifteen tons of mail from the North and with a personal message for the commander. He shook hands, saying: "General Sherman—Before leaving Washington I was directed by the President to take you by the hand, wherever I met you, and say from him, 'God bless you and the army under your command.'" Like Lincoln's letter to Sherman thanking him for the Christmas gift of Savannah and describing the march as "an important new service," the mail was full of enthusiasm. An Illinois newspaper editor wrote to one soldier in January: "I am so lost in wonder and admiration of that great march through Ga. & its glorious termination in Gen. Sherman's 'Christmas Present,' that even to be known & remembered by one of the participators in it is a very valuable thing to me." While the army waited in Georgia, Northerners anticipated its next march, which would punish South Carolina and end the war. Though he had painstakingly planned the march to the sea and knew why it went smoothly, Sherman still marveled at the volume of praise he received for his skill. He wrote to his wife: "I can hardly realize it for really it was easy, but like one who has walked a narrow plank I look back and wonder if I really did it." The march was bigger than its commander. Sherman, nemesis of rebels and righteous besom of destruction, acquired in civilians' minds an aura of inevitability surpassing his own confidence in his campaigns' success. As the marches unfolded, many people saw that the union had to triumph in just such a manner, that the war had always pointed toward the marches. Sherman, in the words of the Reverend Edward Payson Powell, "has been called out from among our thirty millions," the one man who could accomplish the destined work as an instrument of his country.

The means by which Sherman carried out the popular will—"making war sustain war," one reporter said—established him in many minds as "the great military light of the nineteenth century." To his admirers he looked modern, and Americans were nothing if not modern. His successes came from decisiveness, speed, efficiency, statistics, sophisticated logistics, long-range planning, large-scale operations, and thorough results. By the time he reached North Carolina he was more than "one of the great men of the time"; his name could stand for the spirit of the times. A *Cincinnati Commercial* correspondent, mentioning a recent two-week trip, remarked in passing: "A fortnight is an age in these fast days—the days of railway, telegraph, and Sherman." Though his energetic measures to subdue the South ended one career for him as a representative of his culture, he soon entered another, much longer career promoting national consolidation and rapid economic development. For him time was "coursing along with railroad speed," and the United States must move with it. Southerners had been foolish to think otherwise. After the fall of Atlanta he outlined to a South Carolinian, Catharine Joyner, some of his grandiose plans for his next move. She thought that he overestimated what the federal government would support him in doing. When she expressed her reservations, "he drew himself up very stately & replied quite in a lordly manner, 'Madam I am the man of the 19th century at the North, can get whatever I ask for.'" He liked to shock rebels with outrageous statements. All the same, he had aptly brought together in one phrase his war-making, Northerners' eagerness for victory, and the coming era that he welcomed.

PART II *The War and the Future of the Nation*

IN MARCH 1891, a month after Sherman died, the New York Chamber of Commerce gave America's foremost sculptor, Augustus Saint-Gaudens, a commission to execute a statue of him. Saint-Gaudens had been fascinated by the general ever since he had followed news of the great marches as a boy of seventeen. In 1887, with the help of Whitelaw Reid, he had persuaded the impatient old man to sit for a portrait bust. Saint-Gaudens had no commission for the bust and, his son later wrote, felt "a deep-rooted horror of the futility of war." He wanted to do the bust because of his intense interest in Sherman's personality: "He always set so high a premium on virility and nervous energy that the personification of this in the General stirred his enthusiasm as few things outside his art had ever inspired it." As usual, Saint-Gaudens took a long time to complete the work commissioned by the Chamber of Commerce. After much labor and many subtle modifications, he had the bronze group cast, and it was unveiled on Memorial Day, 1903, at Fifth Avenue and Fifty-ninth Street in New York City, where it still stands. A military parade of veterans, speeches, and subsequent comments, like the work itself, made clear that Saint-Gaudens strove to embody in his work the connections among—perhaps even the unity of—Sherman, Northern victory, and America.

The group consists of an equestrian statue of Sherman, approximately twice life size, with the general and his horse closely following an allegorical winged female figure, representing Victory. Though the horse's gait is a walk, the animal conveys a high degree of forward-moving tension, pushing slightly uphill, closely reined in by the rider. Saint-Gaudens took great pains, with many inquiries to Sherman's daughter Elizabeth and to veterans who had seen the general often, in order to portray Sherman as he would have looked during the war. A cape of the kind in which he was photographed at the end of the war billows out behind his shoulders in the statue. Though Saint-Gaudens used his bust of the sixty-eight-year-old retired general as the basis for his head of Sherman in the statue, the portrait was in many respects the likeness of Sherman with which Americans were most familiar—unruly hair, wrinkled, bearded face, and firmly set jaw. In pressing forward, horse and rider have trod across a broken bough of Georgia pine. The figure of Victory, clad in flowing wind-blown robes, extends her right arm in the direction of their joint movement and holds up a palm branch in her left hand. She wears a laurel wreath in her hair, and the breast of her robe bears the figure of the American eagle as it appears on the Great Seal of the United States. The eagle also appears on the horse's saddle and on Sherman's uniform's belt buckle. Careful observers, from Kenyon Cox in 1903 to Kathryn Greenthal in 1985, have noticed the ways in which Saint-Gaudens stressed the unity of his group. Greenthal has written: "Every element in the Victory figure reflects one in the statue: her outstretched right arm, the arch of the horse's head; her skirt, his tail; her wings, the general's cloak. The horse follows her obediently, keeping pace with her as he bears the general onward."

Early commentators saw in the group a depiction of distinctively American qualities. Recalling his work on the bust, Saint-Gaudens wrote: "This task was also a labor of love, for the General had remained in my eye as the typical American soldier ever since I had formed that idea of him during the Civil War." By portraying, in highly individualized detail, a unique personality, Saint-Gaudens made Sherman the representative American. The Civil War had been fought not by a few extraordinary heroes or by generic unknown soldiers but by known soldiers, like this one. President Theodore Roosevelt understood the risk Saint-Gaudens had taken in putting together an allegorical figure and "grim, homely, old Sherman, the type and the ideal of a democratic general." The result could have been a ludicrous failure but was, Roosevelt believed, "the very highest note of the sculptor's art." Saint-Gaudens's friend Kenyon Cox emphasized for readers of *The Nation:* "She is an American Victory, as this is an American man on an American horse." Cox probably knew that the model for Victory's head had been Sherman's niece, Elizabeth Cameron.

Some who found fault with the sculpture agreed that it was American, but attributed its defects to that quality. Though Henry Adams admired Saint-Gaudens and commissioned one of the artist's greatest works, in *The Education of Henry Adams* he used Saint-Gaudens and especially the Sherman monument as examples of the blighted American spirit. He saw the work in progress in Paris and studied a full-sized plaster model of the group at the Exposition of 1900. In *The Education* he wrote: "For a symbol of power, St. Gaudens instinctively preferred the horse, as was plain in his horse and Victory of the Sherman monument. Doubtless Sherman also felt it so. The attitude was so American, that, for at least forty years, Adams had never realized that any other could be in sound taste." Though Saint-Gaudens had the spirit of Cellini and of the *cinquecento,* he was, for the purposes of Adams's book, a lost soul in the twentieth century, incapacitated by his American upbringing for comprehending greater expressions of power, such as sex and the Virgin. Saint-Gaudens could only conceive a goddess as human expression, beauty, purity, taste.

On a trip to New York in 1914, the artist J. B. Yeats somewhat similarly contrasted America with the Renaissance and found the Sherman monument emblematic of Americans' deficiencies. For love, for dreams, for meaning in life Americans substituted admiration and action. Saint-Gaudens's group was "art characteristic of a race living on the surface." Sherman and the horse seemed to Yeats to be vividly rendered, while Victory looked like a young American Gibson girl, her wings an excrescence. The allegorical and supernatural elements of human life were lost in the mundane. Michelangelo would have made Victory every-thing—an immortal with strong shoulders to support her wings—with the general and the horse clearly subsidiary. Americans, Yeats implied, could not represent the meaning of the war in art because they were fit only to act, to observe, and to admire—not to love or to understand.

Henry James, studying Saint-Gaudens's group in New York not long after its unveiling, also questioned the heterogeneity of its elements or, as he called it, the figures' "ambiguity." He saw in them the overwhelm-ing military advance of "the Destroyer" and the idea that the Destroyer is a messenger of peace, "with the olive branch too waved in the blast and with embodied grace, in the form of a beautiful American girl, attending his business." James would have preferred not the "perversity" of Saint-Gaudens's scheme but "a Sherman of the terrible march," signify-ing "the misery, the ruin and the vengeance of his track," since these were the reasons for memorializing Sherman. Saint-Gaudens seemed to James to be confounding a destroyer with a benefactor. To stress this unwel-come ambiguity in Saint-Gaudens's conception, James gave the figure of Victory an olive branch, symbolizing peace, though in fact she carries a palm branch to signify victory. The only olive branch in the sculpture appears, along with arrows, in the talons of the American eagle depicted on the apparel of Victory, Sherman, and the horse. That ambiguity, however, did not provoke James's comment. By emphasizing the sculp-tor's refinement and taste, and by calling the Victory figure an American girl, James suggested that Saint-Gaudens's striving for an allegorical dimension served only to put a glittering veneer on Sherman's horrors. The general is not following winged Victory but is having his destruc-tiveness graced with beauty. Similarly, James dramatized the energy of urban activity and the vulgarity of design in the monument's immediate surroundings at Fifth Avenue and Fifty-ninth Street. By competing with movement, noise, electric streetcar cables, and a towering jumble of buildings—and by still attracting attention to its own refinement—Saint-Gaudens's group succeeds, James hinted, through being beautifully irrelevant. It is a triumph of the sculptor's art in defiance of both its setting and the true significance of its subject.

The monument's admirers and detractors agreed from different per-spectives that it was somehow American and that it aroused, by its muscular tension and its image of relentless wind-blown advance, a sense of power. Kenyon Cox wrote: "One of the most remarkable things about the group is the extraordinary sense of movement and of irresistible force conveyed by it. The gait of the horse is only a quick walk, but horse and rider and striding Victory move onward with a rush, and one feels that nothing can arrest their progress." Whether or not an observer finds

Saint-Gaudens's group to be unified and consistent, the sculptor evidently meant it to be, and he used this shared energetic momentum to join the figures. In that respect, at least, the figures harmonized with the "vehemence" and "dauntless power" James discerned in the life of New York City. Saint-Gaudens portrayed Sherman's individuality but did not give him a heroic posture. The uplifted arm so common among generals' equestrian statues belongs, in this group, to Victory. The force of war embodied in Sherman's movement follows the path set by destiny, allegorized as the angel of Victory. The bronze angel is, of course, invisible to the bronze general, but his confident advance has its way cleared by her. The emblems associated with her show that destiny decrees the triumph of the United States.

In the eyes of an observer for whom the figure of Sherman overpowers that of Victory, Saint-Gaudens's group must fail to have its intended effect. Sherman appears as an important individual contributor to the momentum of war and of America, yet also as a part of that momentum, which is greater than he. The general wins victories by following Victory. To see him as the all-powerful hero or the all-terrible destroyer would be to give him a dominant role, defeating the balanced tension between the figures for which the sculptor strove.

Secretary of War Elihu Root, in his speech at the unveiling on Memorial Day, 1903, did not try to interpret Saint-Gaudens's work; but Root's description of Sherman expressed a similar tension. Root wanted his audience to know that Sherman had been an extraordinary man—no one could confidently say that the union would have prevailed without him. Sherman's perpetual fame inhered in his crucial wartime actions and did not depend on posthumous monuments. At the same time that Root, like Saint-Gaudens, made Sherman a conquering figure, Root also, like Saint-Gaudens, intended to celebrate the victory of America as a nation. Sherman's successes thus seemed both contingent and necessary, both his own acts and history's plan. In 1903 the world was beginning to realize the consequences of American nationality—"immeasurable possibilities for good or evil in hundreds of millions of people, free, independent, self-governing, with limitless resources, with vital force and energy never surpassed." Perhaps, without Sherman, it might never have happened. But Root linked the wartime Sherman with the march to America's future taking shape while Saint-Gaudens worked and Root spoke. Sherman had been an instrument in creating the America familiar to viewers of the monument. "In peace he was constantly solicitous for the adoption of measures for the future welfare and greatness of his country. He urged on to success the building of the Pacific roads which he foresaw would pacify and civilize the plains and bind together our widely separated seaboards." Even while portraying Sherman's role in the war as "essentially decisive" Root could not avoid seeing Sherman as an agent of what had to come. By perpetuating this tension, his dedicatory speech comported well with Saint-Gaudens's monument.

If the surging stride of the mounted Sherman and American Victory looking down Fifth Avenue signified anything beyond the wartime march through the South, that significance could hardly be simply Sherman's vivid personality or Victory's benevolent promise of peace or Saint-Gaudens's aestheticism. Although, as Henry James suggested, the group artistically defies its environment—a painstakingly accurate rendering of a Civil War general and an anachronistically allegorical angel thrust among modern urban energy—it might also express the prevailing spirit of its surroundings. Root and Saint-Gaudens and the members of the Chamber of Commerce knew that Sherman had enjoyed being a New Yorker in his last years and had welcomed the national power and industry and commerce of which New York was the epitome. Whether or not Saint-Gaudens embodied an intuition of Sherman's outlook in his work, Sherman certainly believed that the momentum of wartime victory was continuous with the momentum of national development. For Henry Adams and Henry James, such an idea could not be conveyed in good taste; and, if a sculpture manifested refinement, it could not convey a worthwhile idea about America. Hence, Saint-Gaudens's work must be beautiful but anachronistic or powerful but superficial.

Insofar as Saint-Gaudens's work effectively combined representations of Sherman, the North's triumph, movement, power, and the nation's destiny—and insofar as these representations belonged at the heart of New York City—the Sherman monument and its setting carried forward the main message Sherman took to Americans after the war. Consolidation of nationality, rapid changes in expanding industry and commerce, growth of American power: all were ineluctable and beneficial. One should move with them as with destiny. This was the world that financed Saint-Gaudens's commissions, that he lived in while he worked on the Sherman group during the 1890s, and that encircled the gilded bronze after its unveiling. Saint-Gaudens's monument, faithful to the spirit of Sherman, came nearer to celebrating that world than to ignoring it.

P. D. STEPHENSON, an old Confederate veteran writing his autobiography, remained bitter about Sherman's destructive marches. If anything could increase his anger, it was the popularity Sherman had enjoyed since the war. "I saw him, close, soon after the war, in a theatre in St. Louis Mo. when the audience recognizing him sent up a deafening din! Popular idol he was, then; but poor material for popular idol! He stood up in his box and stared back at them with a sneer and grin upon his face, as if to say, 'well—here I am; now look at me'!!" In almost constant travel throughout the northern and western United States, combined with speech-making everywhere he went—including several trips in the South, where crowds of blacks and whites met him at the depots—Sherman became perhaps the most widely known, most durably famous, most often applauded American of his time. His repertoire extended far beyond war-related functions such as veterans' reunions and memorial days. Commencement addresses, whistle-stop remarks from train platforms, speeches at dedications of public works, historical commemorations of colonial and Revolutionary days, talks to schoolchildren, responses to after-dinner toasts at conventions of carriage-builders, cattlemen, and the like: Sherman's public speaking ranged from carefully prepared and revised formal addresses to brief extemporaneous comments, and it seldom abated.

J. B. Pond, a theatrical manager and agent, invited Sherman to go on the lecture circuit after his retirement from the army, predicting that he would do better at the box office than Mark Twain, who made $30,000 in one season. Sherman declined, but he spent between $400 and $500 a year complying with requests for his portrait or his autograph. In 1888 he made an engraved portrait available in major cities for 50 cents a copy to spare himself this growing expense. One of his friends wrote: "No face was so familiar to almost everybody as the face of 'Uncle Billy Sherman.'" He often appeared among other dignitaries at large civic functions; yet the crowd singled him out. At the 1880 celebration of the two-hundredth anniversary of the discovery of St. Anthony Falls in Minnesota, the audience ignored the order of speakers on the program to "set up a loud cry for 'Sherman, Sherman,' and accompanied their cries with clapping of the hands." When his turn came to speak, "his appearance was greeted with loud and enthusiastic applause." A writer in Donn Piatt's Washington *Capital* said that Sherman's public utterances had "a healthy, democratic sort of flavor" Americans liked: "He talks a great deal, and with a freedom from conventional restraints which is refreshing, if not always instructive." Other, more friendly, commentators often called him the characteristic American: "His personality has been as deeply impressed upon the nation as his great deeds." To explain people's admiration for Sherman, his contemporaries turned most often to his outspoken talk, his frankness that won him the respect of many who disagreed with him on public questions. Smith P. Galt thought that Sherman's rhetorical skill consisted especially of bluntness free from temporizing: "He was neither a humorous or eloquent orator, but yet was one of the most popular public speakers of his time. The audience loved the independent spirit, that cared nothing for place or party." When Sherman spoke fearlessly and pungently his audiences and the newspaper readers could see how like him they were, or wished they were. On his retirement one of many editorials called him "the fitting representative of a land so vast, a people so diversified, and a civilization so energetic."

Paradoxically, the press, which Sherman despised, was a leading promoter of his fame. Sherman's hostility to newspapers was well known. He had, he said, "conceived a terrible mistrust of the Press in California," where he had seen irresponsible editors producing "villainous sheets, reviling private character, insulting common decency, exciting . . . Vigilance committees mobs and treason." In wartime he denounced editors and reporters for causing soldiers' deaths by eagerly publishing military secrets. Nevertheless, Sherman's relations with the press were more complex than his denunciation and his wartime threats to "clip the wings of this public enemy" suggested. He won growing popularity among correspondents accompanying his army. From a reporter's point of view, Sherman had the supreme virtue of being good copy—vigorous, vivid, and graphic. He knew that these qualities put him in the newspapers: "They are simply crazy for any thing spicy," he wrote to Sheridan after the war. W. F. G. Shanks, a *Herald* reporter, suspected that Sherman's famous contempt for reporters "was in a great measure affected" and that Sherman wanted publicity. Not long after the war James Gordon Bennett, recalling the *Herald*'s conflicts with Sherman, said in conversation: "Sherman threatened to hang me, and I tried to hang him—neither succeeded." The cynical old publisher laughed and added: "There is something good about the fellow and I like him." Sherman won over the *Herald*, as he had won over the *Cincinnati Commercial.* Even papers that denounced him in later years, such as the *Cincinnati Gazette* and the *New York Sun,* always found him newsworthy. One of his friends recalled: "He hated the newspapers, yet through necessity, almost, he read them every morning, making running comments on what they said." He stayed in the news for thirty years. He talked amiably with reporters, commented on almost any subject, and proved so useful to the papers that, he complained, "I constantly read interviews with me, manufactured out of whole cloth." Far from curbing the press, Sherman became one of its fixtures. He won popularity partly by professing to scorn it.

Sherman often complained in private about demands on his time made by people who seemed to assume that he belonged to them, that his life should be an entirely public one devoted to helping Americans praise themselves. Much of his life was consumed by the idea of the nation because he undertook to embody it for people who wanted to believe in it. He sometimes made light of his comprehensive, protean American-ism: "I am become a sort of 'show-man' and must appear one day as a Scots-man—next an Irish-man—then a simon pure descendant of the religion of New England." By turns he spoke as a sometime Southerner, a California pioneer, an adopted citizen of St. Louis, a native son of Ohio, a familial representative of New England, a longtime resident of Wash-ington, D. C., and an enthusiastic New Yorker. He occasionally joked about the lack of substance in his public statements. He called his remarks "a few generalities," telling one audience: "I have just made my appear-ance merely to gratify your curiosity." A skeptical witness, like Judge Matthew P. Deady in 1883, might conclude that Sherman's popularity owed much to his gift for empty flattery of his listeners. Deady attended a reception in Vancouver, Washington, where 2,000 people welcomed the general: "They were very enthusiastic over Sherman who made them a rather telling speech with nothing in it."

Sherman kept appearing at all kinds of gatherings. He was perpetually campaigning to influence the minds of those who heard and saw him or read what he said. He knew that his "frank and outspoken sentiments" won him "the respect of a great mass of people"; he believed that his tour of the South in 1879 encouraged national sentiment there, and he sought the same result in other parts of the country. As he neared retirement he took gratification from having used his power of persuasion to foster the nation's development. "Every day I am reminded of little things done, or words spoken which have borne fruit. I honestly believe in this way I have done more good for our country and for the human race, than I did in the Civil War." Sherman's public statements almost always had a message. His blandest appeals to patriotism, like his flattery of his audiences, ended in a call for unity in support of Sherman's vision of America. "His sentences were almost epigrams," Smith P. Galt said. "Each was loaded with an idea, and it was felt where it hit." Sherman wanted to encourage Americans in the belief that history was moving in the direction he was pointing. He used his unique stature to didactic effect.

Two perennial reminders of Sherman's fame were veterans' reunions and public talk of electing him to the presidency. In both cases he turned a conventional form of discussion partly away from its customary chan-nels. He did not become simply another old general who celebrated bygone victories or helped the Republicans hold power for four or eight more years. If people wanted to see Sherman at reunions or to demand that he seek the presidency, he would use the occasion to preach to them. Sherman was president of the Society of the Army of the Tennessee for twenty-one years. He attended its annual meetings and those of other large veterans' organizations, including the Society of the Army of the

Potomac and the Grand Army of the Republic. He also appeared often at lesser reunions, as small as a picnic of the Irish-American river and waterfront workers who had served in the 8th Missouri Regiment. He still traveled extensively at the age of seventy, responding to pleas like the one that took him to Boston: "There will be fifty thousand of your old boys in line and you are their living idol! . . . your absence will cause a *riot.*" The larger reunions attracted crowds of spectators outnumbering the veterans. A gathering in Columbus in 1888 brought 40,000 veterans and 60,000 others. Supporting these reunions, he kept in mind a wider audience, in the galleries of the convention halls and in the country at large. The assembled veterans, he said, tangibly represented their nation's unity and stability. He spoke to both veterans and spectators in Des Moines in 1875: "The eyes of the country are upon us, and . . . we wield an influence and power to-day for which we will be held accountable." Sherman saw in each meeting a further dissemination of what he called "the old army feeling of unity."

Though Sherman had close ties to Republicans, especially his brother the senator, he avoided party affiliation, never voted after 1856, and criticized some policies of both parties. In turn, Democratic and Republican politicians and newspapers both censured and praised him. His reputation for political independence helped make his popularity possible. Perversely, many people wanted to capitalize on so much nonpartisan esteem by electing Sherman to the presidency. Some Democrats talked of nominating him in 1868 and 1872, mentioning his dislike of Republican policies for reconstruction. Many Republicans spoke of nominating him in 1876, 1880, and 1884. He may have come closest to nomination in 1884. John Sherman, James G. Blaine, and others assumed that the convention would turn to the retired general if Blaine failed to gain a majority of delegates on an early ballot. The Republicans thus could use Sherman to keep themselves in power. Senator James R. Doolittle explained to Sherman that Republican politicians did not relish the idea of Sherman as president, "but they may fear defeat, more than they fear you." Blaine won the nomination, then lost the election.

Perhaps no American so likely to be elected has rejected the prospect of the presidency so often and so bluntly as Sherman did. During the 1884 convention he sent telegrams from St. Louis to a friend among the delegates. The first, on June 3, read: "Please decline any nomination for me in language strong but courteous." The second, two days later, said: "I will not accept if nominated, and will not serve if elected." Six months earlier, he had written: "If nominated or elected by an unanimous vote I should decline." Sherman believed that the presidency destroyed those who held it. If it did not kill the incumbent it tortured him with greedy opportunists' demands, made him the tool rather than the master of others, and gave him "a mere office of four years with a scanty maintainance, and then a life of absolute void." Presidents did not reform politics but lost their dignity and integrity complying with the wishes of the factions that put them in office. "I am not in harmony with either party," Sherman wrote in 1875, "and would not sacrifice my individuality for all their blandishments or curses." He knew that, if he were a candidate, he and his family would come under attack because of his wife's and his children's Roman Catholic faith. And he argued that in the 1880s it made little difference to the country's well-being who became president. Thomas T. Gantt, often critical of Sherman, credited him with sincerity and good sense on this score: "He talks on political subjects like a magpie—but he has more than once, steadily repudiated all political aspirations: has refused to be *manipulated.*" For Sherman in the 1880s the presidency would have been a demotion. He called the office an "empty honor."

Sherman's message to Americans varied little for twenty-five years. Few of his speeches, no matter what the occasion, left out an appeal on behalf of continued national development along the lines of the last third of the nineteenth century. Proponents of extended interlocking transportation networks, expanding market agriculture, tariff-protected growth of manufacturing, and the gold standard had no more enthusiastic supporter. However, Sherman's speeches and writings did not dwell on governmental policy and economics so much as they celebrated accomplishments and evoked images of an ever-improving future. Chauncey Depew, who had often shared a speakers' platform with Sherman, recalled in 1892: "He was building railroads across the continent on paper, and peopling those vast regions with prosperous settlements, long before they had any roads but the paths of the buffalo, and any inhabitants but roving tribes of wild Indians." In Sherman's appeals, work toward the national destiny he described became synonymous with patriotism. The war alone had not sufficed to make nationhood permanently secure. Sherman strove to do so by narrating the country's future before it occurred. If he could persuade or reassure Americans that their history would follow the plot he so often described, he could help make his narrative come true. He could also restore his own sometimes faltering belief that Americans would lead progress rather than divide and drift into futility.

On May 20, 1869, in the War Department office in Washington, Sherman and others heard three rings of an electric bell, activated by the telegraph signaling the driving of the last spike in the transcontinental railroad. Sherman remarked that "his feeling was that 'the Lord might come for him now if He saw fit'!" Telegraph offices across the country were receiving the same signal. The moment dramatized for Sherman the national ties embodied in railroads. As commander of the Department of the Missouri for the previous four years, he had treated railroad construction as the army's most important concern. He held the same view during his fifteen years as commanding general. He praised financiers for risking their capital; he admired engineers and laborers, many of them veterans, for their ingenuity and speed. In the war years Sherman had done more to destroy railroads than any other American. He and his staff officers had devised new ways to make railroads contribute more to destruction of life and property in the South. For the same goal—national consolidation—he saw his veterans in 1867 building railroads and planning more. "Instead of the great art of destruction, they are now practicing the better art of *construction.*" He rode the length of all the transcontinental lines several times and went out of his way to ride the new Canadian Pacific in 1886.

As in the Mississippi River and its tributaries, Sherman saw in railroads a mystical influence no less than a practical utility. He sounded almost like Walt Whitman, imagining San Francisco as "a necessary link between Europe, America, Japan, China" and the railroad connecting San Francisco to the eastern United States as "a link in the chain which binds all mankind together." Sherman received free passes from some companies but owned no railroad stock. He defended the companies against their growing number of critics in the 1870s and 1880s. He had no sympathy with strikes in 1877 and in 1886. His speeches in the Midwest scolded farmers for state laws and political campaigns hostile to railroad corporations. For Sherman the builders of western railroads were public benefactors, visionaries fulfilling their dreams. He wrote to one of them in 1888: "I honor the men who did the work of building up our great inland empire." He thus paid tribute to those who had met the challenge he had given to the same man twenty-three years earlier, when Sherman had promised to help the railroads while he commanded in the west: "I trust that such advantage will be taken, that the ravages of war will soon be forgotten, and the efforts of all men be again devoted to the farms, mines, roads and machines that go to make up national wealth."

Sherman had little patience with unemployed or underpaid workers or with Southerners who complained about the impoverishment of their section. He told them to join the development of the continent. Unhappy workers should go west and take a homestead. Southerners should welcome migration from the North and should try to attract immigrants arriving from Europe. He did his part by recommending the South to Northerners interested in moving. To one who did relocate he wrote: "I know my opinion has turned many an emigrant to Montana & Oregon—

it may result the same to your region. Increased population means increased consumption and consequent prosperity." Sherman enjoyed studying census tables charting the growth of population and the swelling production of staple crops and manufactured goods. Economic depression, drought, the world commodities market, details of railroads' capitalization and rates and operating methods, farmers' indebtedness, workers' conditions did not temper his promises for the future. The momentum of national growth promised to overcome all hindrances.

Changing the west through an influx of ranchers, farmers, and miners struck Sherman as "the grandest conquest of any army of civilization over nature." He spoke of land not yet occupied by emigrants from the east as "wild and desolate," "waste places," and "absolute desert." For its transformation he used the word "redeemed." Killing bison made room for cattle. Before addressing a convention of western cattlemen he did some research to confirm that a domestic cow impregnated by a bison bull would die in trying to deliver the calf because of its hump. Clearly the two could not live together, and elimination of the buffalo was part of progress. The spreading cultivation of wheat, corn, and other foodstuffs made wild wastelands "blossom as the rose, fit habitations for civilized men and women." Sherman's imaginings of western agriculture sometimes outstripped his computations. At a banquet in honor of James B. Eads in 1875 he praised the engineer for bridging the Mississippi at St. Louis and for planning to clear the bars at the river's mouth, opening it to vessels of deeper draft. More wheat, produced by a multiplying population, could float down the river: "The surplus of food for shipment abroad will be simply infinite." Civilization's victory over the continent transformed not only animals and crops but also minerals. Sherman told a New York audience in 1884: "Every mountain and hillside in the great West has been tapped and bored, and every rock has been tested by hammer and chisel and acid, so that silver, gold, copper, and zinc are found to abound everywhere; and recently tin has been discovered."

Sherman finally made peace with California, which had betrayed his youthful optimism. He recalled in his memoirs the days when the sudden peopling of California by the gold rush had made the state's name, in his mind, a synonym for risk, fraud, and ruin. But in the saga of subsequent progress that he narrated to his many postwar audiences, the taking of California was the essential basis for and the beginning of Americans' prosperity in the west. No place had brought Sherman's vision more fully to life. To the New York branch of the Society of California Pioneers he said in 1880: "California has almost realized the Grecian fable of Aphrodite, the goddess of love and beauty, who came forth the perfect woman from the foam of the sea. With her majestic harbors and cities;

with her gold glittering in the western sunlight, her luxury and extravagance rivalling the oldest cities of the earth; with her fruits and flowers gladdening the eye of the most refined; and with railroads and telegraph everywhere, California stands to-day the envy of mankind." Most important, this almost mythical, yet factual, story of success happened through "American energy, which has worked out this grand transformation." Sherman wanted to push all Americans to exert this national energy and reap such a reward from the whole continent.

America's cities fascinated Sherman. He visited almost all of them again and again, congratulating their citizens on growth since his previous stay. Cities were centers of commerce; and, he assured the Chicago Board of Trade, commerce ruled the world. Sherman had no more scathing comment about any place than to call it an "old played out town" or a "city of the past." Santa Fe, New Mexico, was more than 300 years old but had been surpassed by hundreds of towns not ten years old because they had "railroads & modern enterprise." For decades he hoped that St. Louis would become the greatest metropolis of the Mississippi Valley and of the United States, but he finally had to concede the one distinction to Chicago and the other to New York. When he moved from St. Louis to New York in 1886 he gave a number of reasons for doing so but omitted one that an acquaintance in St. Louis understood: "In N. Y. he will be amused. Here he is bored." St. Louis was no longer growing, multiplying its activities, extending its economic power. After his move Sherman wrote: "New York is unquestionably the great city of America, and will be the arbiter of the world." A city established its power by its commercial spirit, its openness to any man and any transaction. Let the man buy, Sherman urged the Chicago Board of Trade. "Let him come and make a contract for all the wheat on earth, if he will pay for it. . . . you are yet but plunging your feet in the ocean of progress." A month before celebrating his sixty-ninth birthday in New York he wrote: "One feels almost rejuvenated by the hum of commerce." He often told young people that, if he could, he would trade his fame and stature for their youth—not just to prolong his life but because the United States was only beginning to attain its destined wealth, power, and scope for enterprise. He wished to share the even more energetic times to come. He advised one woman: "Impress on your son the great truth, the fact that the best part of our national life is in the future." This expectation underlay Sherman's enthusiasm for growing, busy cities, foci of the productivity of the regions they dominated. Speaking to citizens of Portland, Maine, in 1890, he described Portland, Oregon, predicting that the eastern city would be overshadowed by its western namesake. Though he reminisced about the war, as he was expected to do in public appearances, he urged his audiences to look forward, confident of "the transcendant future open to the young and ambitious of our favored land." Activity appealed to Sherman more than retrospection did. Activity promised that his prophecy was coming true.

Sherman had seen the country at first hand to an extent hardly anyone else matched. He had read its history, and in his later years he seemed to have lived much of that history. As he traveled and spoke and shook hands—so often that he almost lost the nail on the little finger of his right hand—he figuratively brought to the scene of his public appearances word from the rest of the country and lessons from its past. He did not profess to agree with all his audiences or to represent all their opinions; rather, he embodied the nation to which he tried to secure their allegiance. Eight months after his death, one of the many memorial speakers said: "General Sherman was the most interesting man of his day. For years he wrote and spoke incessantly, but the people never had enough and always wanted to hear and read more. The people wanted to hear him because he was American to the core. Whatever he said and did smacked of American soil. The Tiber and the Mediterranean were nothing to him compared with the Mississippi and Lake Michigan. To him the river Jordan didn't begin to be as sacred as the Tennessee." For at least a few minutes, with a few "generalities," as he called them, he offered visible, audible proof of the survival of the nation, that entity of many definitions, an entity of whose existence Americans could never get enough reassurance.

Sherman's speeches often placed the story of America within the larger drama of human history and the workings of the cosmos. Some of his most lyrical passages summarized his view of the governance of the universe by knowable, internally consistent, all-embracing laws. He enthusiastically joined those who believed that the lives of polities conformed to laws of behavior as rigorous as the laws of physics governing matter. Ultimately, physics and history were components of a single system that moved the universe. His confidence in a nation's progress could have no surer guarantee than a vision encompassing the progress of all things. Sherman befriended colleges and universities and encouraged the work of scholars. He helped the paleontologist Othniel C. Marsh make research trips for dinosaur fossils in the west. He served as a regent of the Smithsonian Institution for nine years and eulogized its secretary, the physicist Joseph Henry. He praised the life of scholarship in commencement addresses; he received honorary degrees from Yale, Princeton, and Dartmouth. Sherman envied scientists, who were, he thought, confirming by their research the existence of an orderly, comprehensible universe. Citing Franklin's work on electricity, Henry's work on electromagnetism, and Louis Agassiz's discovery in the Amazon of the living fish he had articulated from fossil vertebrae, Sherman asked his audience at Princeton: "What earthly enjoyment can compare with that which attends the discovery of some new principle of natural law or some new application of an old principle?" All additions to knowledge, by finding further evidence of underlying unity, confirmed the rule of law. In an address at Washington University in St. Louis, Sherman described the work of the Smithsonian Institution, "keeping pace with all *new knowledge*" and making it available to all professors and students. "In like manner the contributions of this country are supplied to other countries thus bringing all scientific men into harmonious relations, which ultimately must establish an universal republic, wherein the knowledge of nature's laws will form a bond of union that must contribute to the peace of the world."

Education consisted of showing people how their lives were part of a system in motion. Americans, Sherman said, had "intense energy of thought and action which impels our people onward." That energy should be guided. He told professors that they, like Joseph Henry at his telescope, should "look away beyond the dusts and clouds of the hour into that vast space where nature has hung up, as it were, her model of truth and of beautiful order. Point your students to it as the chief object of all education, purifying the soul, exalting the understanding and imparting the delights which ever attend the acquisition of true knowledge." As education directs thought and action toward conformity with the design of the universe, "we cannot fail to carry our beloved country to a plane of civilization worthy its grandeur of extent, and the great and varied advantages with which it has been endowed by a beneficent Creator." Sherman promised that any kind of study—artistic creation, research into the physical world, analysis of "the slow development of races of men and animals or the progress of human laws and customs"— would contribute to the great object all existence served.

Among contemporary thinkers, Sherman owed most to John William Draper. A chemist and medical professor at the University of the City of New York—later New York University—Draper did important work in diverse fields: radiant energy, human physiology, and the development of photography and the electric telegraph. He was also an influential intellectual historian. Soon after the war Sherman read Draper's *History of the Intellectual Development of Europe* and his *Thoughts on the Future Civil Policy of America*. He found in them a welcome elaboration of the unity of all nature, an assurance of the ineluctable advance of knowledge and the power of the human mind, and the promise of Americans' "inevitable march to imperial greatness." He wrote to the publisher: "I confess that I have derived much instruction from Dr Drapers works, and shall read all that comes from the same source." In 1867 the first volume of Draper's *History of the American Civil War* was published. Sherman already had begun a correspondence with Draper and offered to help him with the project. Sherman's papers, written reminiscences, and comments on drafts became important source material for the second and third volumes.

Draper purported to explain history by integrating human activities with their natural environment, which in turn conformed to cosmic law. He provided for Sherman, as for himself, a faith, ostensibly scientifically verifiable fact, that the organized society, the people consolidated in the state, was a necessary phenomenon of nature. Within the seeming chaos of human behavior a system was at work, and order was articulating itself; indeed, this process constituted the movement of history. Most satisfyingly for Sherman, Draper would show in the story of the Civil War that nature's laws decreed and guided the violence. Before reading the first volume Sherman wrote: "I . . . infer that you will find in the events of the recent war a series of facts that will illustrate the great principles that regulate the affairs of men grouped together as a community." After completing the volume, Sherman delighted in the prospect of scholars' discovering the law that governed history. "To find out the law, & apply it to the varying phases of the worlds progress is surely the most captivating study that the human mind can conceive of." Draper and Sherman complemented each other: the scholar and the soldier, each regarding the activities of the other as a confirmation and an extension of his own. Sherman's deeds in war exemplified Draper's conclusions; Draper's writings validated their shared faith in a purposeful universe, in the accessibility of everything to science, and in the benefits of the Civil War.

If the war had been an element of progress, it followed that destruction was intrinsic to progress. History's unfolding plan demanded the war's violence. Sherman made this case in some of his speeches, and Draper supported it in his history. "Though half a million of precious lives were sacrificed," Sherman said in 1883, "though thousands of millions of dollars were wasted; though devastation and ruin marked the land from Pennsylvania to the Gulf, great and lasting good has resulted." The good accrued not in spite of killing and destroying but because of them. Northerners should not apologize for the way they had conducted the war. They could not have brought about the much-improved America of the 1880s in any other way. Nineteen years after the march across Georgia and the Carolinas, Sherman called it "a bold enterprise which largely contributed to our national success: a success which inured to the advantage of the whole human race, and must therefore have been acceptible to a good God."

Draper treated the fall of Columbia, South Carolina, as the climax of his history. There Sherman and the army came as a nemesis upon all that South Carolina represented: delusory neglect of the role of physical power in pretensions to sovereignty, exaltation of individuals' ambitions at the expense of government, the anachronism of slavery, and the inveigling process of secession. Draper interpreted the chastisement of South Carolina as a necessary foundation for the new order that Northern victory would bring. "It was the painful but profound conviction of many persons who were versed in the political affairs of the nation that no durable peace could be hoped for, no security against future assaults on the government provided, no guarantee against the disturbance of the tranquillity of the country obtained, unless this march were made." Here Draper was concerned not with cutting off Lee's supplies or hastening war's end but with national progress the war was destined to promote, for which only Sherman's destructive intimidation of the Carolinians sufficed. In his conclusion Draper reminded his readers that peace had been secured not by one crushing victory in battle "but by a total exhaustion of the war-power of the South"; that is, by sustained violence and devastation. The war had left Americans one nation wherein all were free under a single unchallenged government—beneficial results neither side had fully planned or foreseen. "To thoughtful men it furnishes another proof that the progress of nations is not the result of the devices of individuals, but is determined by immutable law." Sherman agreed. Rather than make the Civil War the centerpiece of American history, he subsumed it within a more important story: "The Civil War in America was but a single step in the progress of the world to a newer and higher civilization." Sherman embraced scientists, historians, and popularizers like John Fiske as guarantors of the nation, ultimately of the world order, because they laid out irrefutably the path along which he and all persons immersed in worldly affairs were advancing, knowingly or not. The men who looked into telescopes or microscopes or machinery or law and found symmetry were his ideal Americans, promising happiness for all on the principle that ultimately nothing was unknowable or out of control.

Sherman repeated in the 1880s what he had said in the 1860s: he still thought the Civil War had been "one of the most causeless, foolish wars ever devised by the brain of man." It was causeless and foolish in its origins and in its conduct, both of which arose from ignorance. The ambitious Southerners who started the war were ignorant of the extent of Northerners' power and attachment to the union. Southerners ignorantly following secessionist leaders did not know that their hopes were based on lies. Northerners were ignorant of the scale of the Confederate threat and were correspondingly slow to make war with sufficient force. Sherman himself had been ignorant of the methods the North would have to use; he had learned by experience. These were partial manifestations of a larger ignorance, he suggested. Before the war "we remained to ourselves a mystery. We could handle foreign countries, but there came that dreadest of all—the contest with ourselves." Americans of both sections had not understood their own relation to what they called the United States. Not only did they conflict with each other along sectional lines and in many other ways tending toward dissolution of the bonds connecting them, but they also failed to perceive that their identity as citizens depended on the nation, which could exist only through their active loyalty to the government. Supposing that they could at once be Americans and yet stand aloof from the fate of the American government, by seceding from it or failing to defend its existence energetically or ignoring it to pursue selfish interests, they lived an inconsistent life as citizens, one of unresolved internal conflict. Sherman's strictures against mobs, vigilance committees, irresponsible newspapers, abolitionists, secessionists, and other portents of anarchy in antebellum America arose from his belief that Americans before the war did not understand themselves as civic actors. Looking back from the 1880s, he saw that they had not known how fully their personal destinies were united with the survival and progress of the nation. They learned the direction of their history only through war, which was a foolish way to gain knowledge but an effective one: "The Civil War demonstrated that we, its citizens, could defend the Government against the greatest of all enemies—OURSELVES." If Americans had possessed enough insight not to be the enemies of their civic selves they would not have fought their "causeless" war.

The war, then, had started in a flight from self-knowledge. It had slowly, painfully corrected deficient knowledge of the opposing section and of the true course of history. In his public statements Sherman often made the war his text for sermons on the importance of education. At a Princeton commencement Sherman referred to himself as "I, the mere soldier," paying tribute to scholars. Despite this show of humility, he believed that soldiers, too, had advanced Americans' insight. The Civil War had made Americans learn that they were living out a collective destiny they could not defy or shirk without bringing disaster upon themselves. They must study to know the nation's direction and to conform to it. This had been the point of Sherman's sarcastic reply to the request that he not burn the college library in Columbia: "If there had been a few more books in this part of the world there would not have been all this difficulty." If Southerners had learned more about the North, about the rest of the world, and about history, they would not have succumbed to the delusions that had brought them to ruin. However, the presence of plenty of books in the North had not sufficed to teach Northerners their duty fully. They had underestimated the dedication the nation would exact from them. Only through violence did all come to know. Draper, a professor, used the metaphor of a school to explain the war's function. Americans at last were beginning to understand progress and development. "How true it is that, for a nation to be great, it must aim at something above its animal nature! We are in the act of transition from the animal to the intellectual. War, civil war, with its dread punishments, is not without its uses. In no other school than that of war can society learn subordination, in no other can it be made to appreciate order." In this path to knowledge, Sherman was the Joseph Henry, the Louis Agassiz, of war. He supplanted ignorance of power with irrefutable facts. Learning one's relation to the United States through violence was, in his view, continuous with learning the earth's place in the cosmos through research.

Sherman's encomiums on education called for colleges to do peacefully what war had done violently and wastefully. Recommending support for Benjamin S. Ewell's efforts to reopen the College of William and Mary after the war, Sherman wrote: "A proper system of education, will sooner accomplish what we all want in our country, than any other single course of action. It will reach the judgment of the rising generation and convince them that to share in the honors and progress of our country, they must conform to natural laws which are world wide and not local." It was Americans', especially Southerners', affliction that, without a civil war, they had been incapable of comprehending their own relation to their country's role in history—a relation that the College of William and Mary, not long ago the home of secessionist and proslavery thought, was, Sherman assumed, now capable of teaching. Notwithstanding Sherman's habitual praise of Northerners' wartime courage and patriotism, despite his justifications of the North's waging of war, his message had as its ulterior theme the folly of the war. When he said Americans were better for having learned from it, he usually left unsaid the corollary: they were the worse for having needed it to learn.

On the ultimate end toward which American history was moving, as on the reason for history to happen at all or the question of an afterlife, Sherman remained an agnostic. He mistrusted metaphysics, philosophy, and religious or ethical systems that tried to change what he took to be human nature. He thought of himself as dealing with realities, with immediate, tangible activities: work, material well-being, the security of life and property. If there were harmony in the universe it was physical, in the movement of inanimate things and the behavior of living creatures. The orderliness of speculative thought, represented in prescriptive definitions of the purpose of existence and in elaboration of comprehensive, internally consistent systems of morality, he regarded as an exercise in imagination and introspection, not an advance in understanding human activity. A search for ultimate moral truth struck Sherman as a dangerously abstracted state of mind. He chose to explain his life—and staked its worth on his choice—by saying that the proper concern of living consisted of accessible, concrete details. At the same time, he did not believe that the societal order had a secure grounding or a guarantee of continuity. All the supposedly solid bases—government, property, law—people could destroy as readily as construct. But, without these, they would live in a world where nothing stood between one person and the material wants and physical force of another. The primal concerns did not change; only the manner of addressing them did. To suppose that these concerns could be reconciled in practice by philosophy, religion, or ethics was to live in a fool's paradise.

While still in his thirties, Sherman had written: "The philosopher or morallist who simply seeks happiness, might most readily attain it by directing the energies of his mind toward his inner self and there find repose & contentment, but while so engaged a ruder world outside goes clamorously on, and soon carries the philosopher spite of himself towards a gulf of ruin. Whilst gliding along the smooth channels of fancy, and poetry, of truth and honor, sincerity and charity, his bark is crushed and utterly annihilated by contact with some rude piratical hulk." Before the Civil War, Sherman had entered the course of conduct he followed for the rest of his life: living "outside" in the rude clamorous world, trying to avoid the gulf, fighting pirates. His explanations of how Federals had won the war, like his celebrations of economic growth after the war, continually returned to his claim to have grasped realities. He had brought Southern theorists and visionaries out of their delusions by confronting them with facts. He could subdue the lawless by demonstrating the power of an organized society to defend its interests. No one more consciously and consistently represented the rationale on which defenders of the prevailing order acted. No one worked harder to prolong and justify their predominance. Uniting history, biology, physics, and technology as sources of a prescriptive system for guiding society, Sherman and his allies found truth in institutions whose force could be felt physically, irrespective of the vagaries of opinion on morality or equity.

Sherman occupied his intensely active, wide-ranging, retentive mind primarily with data and stories. With them he guarded himself against the solipsism that he shunned in philosophers and ethicists of all kinds, as well as from the ruin awaiting a mind devoted to the illusory rather than to the record of events and to information about tangible things. But his security could not be solely personal. If the world of public affairs and practical activities did not conform to Sherman's understanding of it, he would be lost. He had no alternative vision of order and harmony and justice—no other world, ethical or millennial or supernal—to assure him an ultimate justification different from the history of his own times. Twice he had experienced dangerous disjunction between his perceptions and public events: once in the financial panics of the 1850s, once in Kentucky in 1861. The first time he had retreated into obscurity. The second time he had devoted himself to making his reality the nation's, an endeavor that continued until his death.

IN CONTRAST with Sherman's public optimism and enjoyment of success, his private view of his own career and of his times contained many elements of disappointment, doubt, and foreboding. Except for taking inspection trips in the west made possible by his official position, he disliked serving as commanding general of the army. Republicans and Democrats seemed to him equally willing to attack the army demagogically. He devoted much effort to preserving professional military knowledge and the army's institutional memory and spirit, pending the inevitable future day when the country again would need the army in a new war. Sherman also shared with many conservatives a scorn for the ordinary workings of partisan politics and for the mode of governance in Washington produced by that system. The outcome of the Civil War had strengthened his confidence in the government's survival but had not increased his enthusiasm for democracy. Economic depression, unemployment, and workers' strikes caused Sherman more concern than he usually admitted in public. At his gloomiest, he joined other alarmist elitists in anticipating war between the propertied and the propertyless. If prosperity failed, self-government would fail; if government failed, the United States would not lead the history of progress but would decline into oblivion. The inquiring, energetic, peripatetic, talkative, public Sherman was always working to forestall the consequences of dangers in American life. Studying census reports to find evidence of economic growth, advocating westward migration, promoting railroad construction, preaching patriotism, always moving in search of signs of progress: the self-proclaimed man of the nineteenth century contained a man who feared the worst.

As commanding general from 1869 until 1883 Sherman had little to do but make inspection trips, write letters and reports, and urge Congress not to cut the army's appropriation. The peacetime army was managed by the secretary of war and by officers of the permanent staff bureaucracy, who preserved the independence of their operations from the authority of officers commanding line troops. Grant's secretary of war, William Worth Belknap, used his office for personal gain. Sutlers to whom he gave the lucrative trade at army posts paid kickbacks to his family. Belknap's successors during the last seven years of Sherman's service, though more honest and more considerate toward Sherman, continued to run the army from the office of the secretary of war. Establishing army posts, distributing resources, and moving troops were in large part political decisions, affecting expenditure of federal money and allocation of patronage. Politicians would not leave such decisions in the hands of a general. Whichever party had a majority in Congress, Sherman found the Military Affairs Committee of the House of Representatives unsympathetic to professional officers and eager to reduce the army's size. In 1870 he privately spoke of the committee as "volunteer sore heads"—that is, men who had been volunteer officers during the war and who still envied the greater fame won by regulars. In 1878 he complained that Speaker Samuel J. Randall put "the smallest men" on the committee. Sherman thought of them as "small fry, who failed as soldiers, but who possessed the qualities deemed necessary for members of Congress," then took out their envy on the army. Thus Sherman found himself not so much commanding troops as resisting attacks on the military academy and on the army's appropriation in a city where "officers are treated as fungi on the body politic." Not surprisingly he enjoyed his travels and his personal fame more than his work in Washington, which consisted mainly of lobbying on behalf of the army.

Though Sherman could not derive much gratification from his official position and though he got many reminders that the army was peripheral in American society, he still believed that the country needed the army. By representing and defending the institution, as in his other propagandizing, he saw himself promoting the nation's security. The purposes Sherman foresaw for the army implied a troubled national future. At a low point in his dealings with Belknap, Sherman wrote to Sheridan: "Whilst I possess no military status, I will endeavor to help Dept & Division commanders, in the maintenance of discipline; and in preserving the semblance of an army." Sherman had known in 1866 that the military establishment would be cut back to "a skeleton or mere farce of an army," as it had been before the war. Nevertheless, it could, he thought, sustain its distinctive spirit, which he traced back to Baron Friedrich Wilhelm von Steuben and the training of the Continental Army at Valley Forge during the winter and spring of 1777–1778. The baron's manual of discipline, the Blue Book, had embodied the army's newfound respect for professional skill, obedience to superiors, dedication to the government, and soldiers' loyalty to one another. The United States Military Academy continually renewed, with each graduating class, the army's knowledge of the importance of discipline and training to America's victories, beginning with the Revolutionary War. The academy meant more to Sherman as a repository of military memory and a source of military ambition than as a school for technical instruction in engineering.

The Steuben tradition entered a new era in the work of Lieutenant Colonel Emory Upton, whose early writings analyzed changes in infantry tactics developed during the war. In 1875 Sherman sent Upton on a two-year tour of inspection to study foreign armies. The resulting book, *The Armies of Asia and Europe,* held up professional armies, especially that of Prussia, as the best models for the United States to emulate. Upton wrote a history of American military policy to show the drawbacks of relying on militia and short-term volunteers. A regular army ready for war would save lives, save money, and fight more effectively when war came. Upton's almost obsessive ambition to create a modern American army took him beyond the bounds of the politically feasible, as Sherman told him. Yet Upton summarized the military lesson of America's wars and the message of recent wars in Europe with a theme Sherman could endorse: the value of preparing soldiers for war while the nation was at peace. In 1881 Sherman ordered the establishment of the School of Application at Fort Leavenworth. The school did not have a well-defined function in its early years, but he intended it as an embodiment of the current state of knowledge about active campaigning, in a camp where such knowledge could be imparted through experience, as well as study. He feared that West Point's critics might eventually get Congress to abolish the academy. Then, "for good fighting men, we will have to depend on Leavenworth." A year before he retired, Sherman spoke at the School of Application, defending the regular army as an essential part of the government and advising officers on their professional responsibilities. He thought of the printed text of his address as "my legacy, my last will and testament."

Since the army would remain small, Sherman knew that any substantial use of military force would require mustering state militias and volunteers. He anticipated that these civilians could more quickly learn soldiers' ways by imitating regulars, who had never abandoned those ways. "An army . . . is not to be measured in importance by its numbers, or its muster-rolls, but by the animus, the soul, which inspires it. Be it ever so small, provided it be true to its destiny, true to its country, it becomes in time of danger the Promethean spark which gives life and energy to the whole." Sherman hoped that regulars' influence could emanate even in peacetime through state militias organized, armed, and trained at federal expense, a plan he steadily advocated. He argued that the army, just by retaining its discipline, its "soul," instilled organization in a volatile society. Respect for soldiers carried with it a restraining effect on civilians. Defending the disciplinary practices of the academy, Sherman wrote in 1879: "The regularity of the military system now become habitual at West Point has begotten habits of order, obedience and respect to authority, which enter directly into the army, and thence go to the country, and have borne fruits of infinite value to this democratic country, if it has not been its actual salvation."

The political ideas of republicanism, embodied in governmental institutions, could not alone sustain a nation, Sherman concluded. For Americans to remain attached to their country they also needed a material bond: the prosperity it offered them. His calls to patriotism promised wealth. His speeches stressed the abundance of the nation's resources and the prospect of widening benefits from them because he thought that without prosperity or the expectation of it the United States would have no adequate basis for cohesion. No matter how much poverty he saw in the depression of the 1870s, in the South after the war, or in the cities of the North, Sherman kept seeking signs of well-being to reassure him while he told others how much richer the future would be. Still, success in such a campaign did not guarantee security; Southerners had defied the government and tried to leave the union while their section enjoyed prosperity. Just a fear of future limitations on their main source of wealth, slavery, had sufficed to alienate large numbers of people from the United States. In defeating secession, the government had resorted to its other means of securing loyalty through the influence of material motives: when the fact or the hope of prosperity failed to compensate for the insufficiency of republican principles as a basis for unity, the government used force. He thought it probably would have to do so again, eventually.

Sherman reminded some of his audiences that the United States Army was older than the institutions created by the Constitution—older than the Declaration of Independence. George Washington had made the army "the right hand of his administration of law and justice in the face of clamoring theorists." The army, then, was not extraneous to the nationhood defined by "theorists" but was intrinsic to the existence of an independent United States and to the purposes the country's government served. Sherman agreed with defenders of order whom historians have called genteel reformers. He shared their distress in seeing that the Civil

War had not produced a stable society presided over by an efficient, unchallenged government. Like them he conflated peace, law, the dominant order, and the nation. With them he worked to concentrate more coercive power in the hands of government, to build a secure state supported by more than opinion. Augmenting militias and improving their discipline looked not toward the next international war but toward suppression of anticipated domestic threats to order. The strikes of 1877 gave the greatest impetus to building militias. Partly because Congress would not strengthen the army or take the lead in centralizing governmental power, Sherman more anxiously supported state and local measures to create a military or protomilitary core of discipline in American society.

Sherman quoted the Declaration of Independence to remind people that the new government in 1776 had justified itself by claiming to promote citizens' right to "safety and happiness." He underlined "safety." No matter how often he said that America's progress entailed a hope of happiness for all, he could not expect the nation to subsist on that faith alone: "Though peace has ever been the controlling genius of our laws and institutions, we are forced to admit that what ministers to the happiness of one class or race often works to the misery of another; and that with Indians, Mexicans, foreign nations, and our own people we have had four great wars and innumerable small ones, so that to accomplish 'safety' in the past, every generation of men since the settlement of this continent has been compelled to take up arms for defense or offense, and it would be foolish to conclude that the future will be different from the past." The beneficiaries of progress and of the nation's existence might be fewer than Sherman optimistically promised, he had to concede. But the government that served those beneficiaries, though it met resistance, must not quail on account of this uneven dispensation of happiness. Alongside his customary effusive accounts of America's destiny ran his warnings against overconfidence: "The day of the millennium has not yet dawned, and the world is full of demagogues, dynamite fiends, fools, hypocrites, and mischief-makers. The greatest security to life and property, the largest measure of human happiness, are possible only where the government is a fair representative of the mass of the people, with power sufficient to protect the quiet, industrious family as against the profligate reckless disturber of the public peace." Such peace depended on government's "physical power." Since "the Army must be that force, active or passive," one could see that, even when the army was not violently suppressing resistance, it defended civic order by its "passive" threat of force.

Thus Sherman saw as essential to the nation's survival a readiness for violent conflict. Long after defeat of secession, other versions of the destructive war might appear at any time. The nation had no lasting, certain security. Ostensible confidence in the Civil War's enduring disciplinary effect on society expressed a hopeful assertion, not an accomplished fact. The alternative to its success was, in John W. Draper's words, "the hideous contemplation of a disorganization of the Republic, each state, and county, and town setting up for itself, and the continent swarming with the maggots bred from the dead body politic." Draper's political fever dream of 1865 became a more general social nightmare for Sherman and for many others preoccupied with order after the onset of economic depression in 1873 and after the strikes of 1877. Sherman was traveling in the west when President Hayes ordered federal troops to help suppress labor organizations and strikers' resistance to state authorities. He did not return to Washington during the strike, and he had little to do with the army's actions, but he approved of Hayes's decision. Like his fellow alarmists, Sherman hardly differentiated among American labor unions, the Paris Commune, the International Workingmen's Association, and anarchists. He saw no important distinction between striking against employers and violently attacking property and propertyholders. However, in his public statements he did not summon doomsday fantasies of rabid urban masses and crumbling institutions. Rather, he showed confidence. Commenting afterward on the strikes, Sherman told a Memorial Day audience in New York: "The armies that were disbanded in 1865 still live in the spirit, and these will never, in my judgment permit this Government to drift into anarchy." His critics, such as the editor of the *Labor Enquirer* in Denver, who called him a "puffed up military aristocrat," could only carp about the elaborate public receptions he received. Sherman had made himself Americans' best example of how their nation dealt with disorder. "I am not afraid of the red flag," he said in 1887; "if any disturbing element comes in from abroad or within, we will squelch it quicker than we did the civil war."

Sherman published his memoirs—he was among the first of the leading generals to do so—in large part to help give lasting life to the war's teachings. With plenty of free time while Belknap ran the army from the War Department, Sherman wrote a two-volume work in 1873 and 1874. Having helped Draper with his history, Sherman also wanted to influence George Bancroft and others who were writing "durable history," works that would shape future Americans' understanding. Sherman's message came out clearly in his remarks on the first battle: "We had good organization, good men, but no cohesion, no real discipline, no respect for authority, no real knowledge of war. . . . the lesson of that battle should not be lost on a people like ours." From the descriptions of upheaval in gold rush California, through the account of the folly of secessionists and the working out of their dire punishment, to the last chapter full of instructions on making a good army, Sherman's pages reverted to his favorite themes: the value of order and strong government, the disasters that arose in their absence, and the influence of the regular army in sustaining government and forestalling disaster. On behalf of maintaining continuity in professional military expertise he wrote: "In times of peace we should pursue the 'habits and usages of war,' so that, when war does come, we may not again be compelled to suffer the disgrace, confusion, and disorder of 1861."

To this end Sherman's memoirs were more a venture than a certain triumph. Rather than restating truths everyone accepted, he was reminding people of things he feared they might forget. Soon after his memoirs were published he said: "The danger was that much special knowledge & experience gained by the war would be lost, and I endeavored to secure & perpetuate it." For Sherman the Civil War's technical military legacy—new uses for railroad and telegraph, new weapons, new open-order tactics, and the like—blended indistinguishably with the war's political guidance for the safety of the state. If only he could make the war as vividly monitory for later generations as he and others had made it for doubters in the South, Americans' memory of the experience, or his readers' and his audiences' memory of his version of the experience, would leave the army and thereby the nation secure against the chaos always incipient in such dubious, nebulous notions as equality and self-government.

A WAR more terrible than the Georgia and Carolina campaigns, which Sherman sometimes conjured up to shock recalcitrant Southerners after 1865, did come to many Indians west of the Mississippi while Sherman commanded the Department of the Missouri and while he served as commanding general. In the conflicts of those twenty years, Sherman's view of war as an instrument of progress found its fullest application. Sherman's certitude about the government's use of violence in this case was not tempered by friendship and empathy, of the kind he said he felt for Southerners. He often said that the way of life of defiant Indians was doomed and that those who clung to it were doomed. Occasionally he admired the courage of men who would fight rather than submit; but he showed no compunction in hurrying their ruin. He validated conquest partly by pointing to its magnitude—so awesome a change, he argued, must have been a necessary one. However, Sherman's conclusive answers, derived from his stressing, indeed greatly overstating, the fall of Indian civilizations, did not serve to quiet the anxiety that intruded into all phases of his public life. For the Indians' defeat represented to him the most troubling of human fates, one he had spent much of his life trying to deflect from his own society: the spectacle of a people being destroyed by the ineluctable movement of history.

For the job of waging war in the west Sherman felt distaste. Having commanded 100,000 combat troops in one great army, he found himself with fewer than 12,000, widely scattered in small detachments. To one interested in advancing military knowledge or demonstrating skill in winning war, campaigns against Indians were, Sherman thought, mostly meaningless. He called it "dirty work" and "inglorious war." The government used the regular army not because the threat was so great but because westerners called for federal protection and wanted the benefit of federal expenditures. At some places the army's policing did not so much protect settlers as obviate volunteer or militia attacks on Indians. Westerners denounced Sherman for not doing enough to circumscribe and destroy Indians. When residents of Pueblo, Colorado, petitioned for protection in 1866 Sherman sarcastically replied that there were more signatures on the petition than soldiers in any nearby garrison. Who was protecting whom?

Soon after taking command in the west during the summer of 1865 Sherman read a report by General John Pope. It accurately predicted the process of dispossession impending for western tribes, and it blamed present and future violence on white people—both settlers and the government, which fostered westward migration. Pope wrote: "What the white man does to the Indian is never known. It is only what the Indian does to the white man, (nine times out of ten, in the way of retaliation,) which reaches the public. The Indian in truth, has no longer a country. His lands are every where pervaded by white men, his means of subsistence destroyed, and the homes of his tribe violently taken from him. Himself and his family reduced to starvation, or to the necessity of warring to the death upon the white man whose inevitable and destructive progress threatens the total extermination of his race." Sherman did not join officers like Pope and John M. Corse in calling whites' conduct morally wrong. However, he did explain the origins of western Indian wars in much the same way, tracing them to defects in the federal government's policies, misconduct by its agents, and aggression by westerners.

His awareness of whites' provocations that contributed to Indians' violence did not sway Sherman's reaction to hostilities. He treated outbreaks as inevitable and defended his officers' most drastic actions. To the commander at Fort Phil Kearny on the Bozeman Trail, construction of which had aroused steady resistance by the Sioux, he wrote: "We must try and distinguish friendly from hostile & kill the latter, but if you or any other commanding officer strike a blow I will approve, for it seems impossible to tell the true from the false." Four months later the decoying and killing of eighty-one soldiers outside the fort provoked Sherman to write: "We must act with vindictive earnestness against the Sioux, even to their extermination, men, women, and children. Nothing else will reach the root of this case." No such radical policy ensued. But Indians' attacks on whites always made him ready for severity. He explained to Sheridan in 1869: "I always approve any thing done by troops, as on the spot the officer is a better judge than we are here."

The Peace Policy of the Grant administration, like the earlier establishing of the Taylor Peace Commission of 1867, supposedly offered an alternative to the military offensives intermittently advocated by Sherman and others. Even so, Sherman's definition of Indians at peace had much in common with that of the Peace Policy's benevolent-minded proponents. Serving on the Taylor Commission, he told those Sioux who came to a council at North Platte, Nebraska: "You can own herds of cattle and horses like the Cherokees and Choctaws. You can have cornfields like the Poncas, Yanktons, and Pottawatomies.... We want you to cultivate your land, build houses, and raise cattle. We propose to help you there as long as you need help. We will also teach your children to read and write like the whites.... We now offer you this, choose your own homes, and live like white men, and we will help you all you want." Sherman said belligerently what many civilians critical of the army's belligerence said benevolently: Indians must accept territorial restrictions and must acculturate themselves to the civilization of the whites sufficiently to give up all forcible resistance.

Sherman's view of acculturation differed from that of the Peace Policy's advocates mainly in his skepticism about the prospects for success. He doubted that those Indians still in resistance would accept the system voluntarily or could conform to whites' expectations. And he thought that the process of civilizing was for some tribes only a slower form of destruction. Sherman supported abrogation of treaties, relocation of tribes, and other measures tending to undermine tribal identity as a basis for resistance. He defined the goal of the 1869 winter campaign against the Cheyennes, Arapahos, and Kiowas as killing and punishing the hostile, after which the government should "mark out the spots where they must stay, and then systematize the whole (friendly and hostile) into camps with a view to economical support, until we can try and get them to be self-supporting, like the Cherokees and Choctaws." Transforming the resisting Indians into contented, self-supporting, "civilized" settlers seemed unlikely to Sherman, while the prospect of whole tribes withering away as distinct entities through the effects of relocation and confinement meant simply that civilizing did not work. In saying that he hoped the Sioux would "cluster" along the Missouri River in 1869 "till they become civilized or demoralized," he was not drawing a sharp distinction between the two fates.

Though Sherman several times mentioned the possibility that all members of defiant tribes might be killed, he resented the recurrent accusation that he and the army aggressively sought to exterminate Indians. He denounced Wendell Phillips for making this charge after the battle of Little Big Horn and wrote to Phillips's friend Samuel Foster Tappan: "I have never advocated the killing of anybody, white or Indian, except as punishment for crime, or to save the lives and property of our people." Overstating his past self-restraint, he meant to disassociate himself from causing hostilities. Throughout the western conflicts Sherman presented extermination as a possible result of some Indians' failure to adapt to white people's transformation of the west. Opposition to the course of history amounted to a sentence of death. In 1865, when Confederate armies were surrendering, he had believed that 100,000 more Southern rebels would have to be killed or banished because they could not "adapt themselves to the new order of things." They had a "wild nature" like Indians, and peace would require their removal. Any show of enmity toward the progress he served brought out Sherman's most lethal threats, just as any sign of inability to join that progress awoke his contempt. With his writs of extermination, Sherman condemned people to extinction from history. The vast majority of those so condemned did not die violent deaths at the hands of his troops. But for him they had vanished, even while alive, into the oblivion that overtook obsolete ways of thinking and living.

Sherman replied to easterners' criticisms of the army's Indian wars by connecting the fighting in the west with the displacement and destruction of Indians since the start of European colonization. It was hypocritical of white people who lived in safety and prosperity on lands once the habitat of Indians—often wrested from the original possessors by force— to condemn a process in the west from which they benefited in the east. Sherman told an audience in Connecticut that the extermination of the Pequots in 1637 had been right because it had made possible the Connecticut of 1881. He admonished the crowd to "remember above all things when you criticise sharply and flippantly the Indian policy of the nation, and condemn the army that it was you who first set the example for the Indian policy now pursued, when you drove the Pequots from these very lands almost 250 years ago." Thus he made his listeners the destroyers of the Pequots. By conflating early colonists and modern residents Sherman meant to link people in the east with western settlers for whom other tribes were being driven aside and decimated. There were only two sides—civilization and barbarism: "The process begun in Massachusetts Pennsylvania and Virginia remains in operation today, and it needs no prophet to foretell the end."

As Sherman marshaled his argument, reaching even to the workings of the cosmos, to show the mandate for the Indian's doom, he intensified the terror of succumbing to such a fate. No worse disaster could befall a people than for them to be unfit to identify themselves with the future. If destructive war proved that the victors were staying abreast of the future's demands, war therein found its best justification. Sherman's expressions of hostility, pity, or scorn for Indians had in common his detachment from people whose experiences showed him the fatal consequences of trying to maintain stasis. After the Taylor Peace Commission had disbanded and Grant had won the presidential election, Samuel Foster Tappan wrote to Sherman, his fellow commissioner, warning him that commanding the army during the wars against Indians would damage the reputation he had won in the Civil War. Though Sherman and his allies had outvoted Tappan on the commission, Sherman ultimately would be the loser. "We make the Indian an outlaw for no crime," Tappan said, "and then compel our army to enforce that atrocious decree of outlawry—which posterity will of course condemn. Upon my honor I do not envy you—better be the victim than the instrument of oppression." Hardly any remarks could have grated on Sherman more. Tappan was saying that future generations would not thank the army for its role in opening the west to settlement—the accomplishment in which Sherman took most pride. And Tappan was proclaiming the moral superiority of victims, a notion wholly at odds with the understanding of history and the vision of the future Sherman preached. To Sherman victims were not admirable. They were weak or deluded or obsolete and therefore about to be crushed. Sherman had feared this fate for America during the early part of the Civil War. Not until he had begun to see that the North could learn how to subjugate the rebels had he gained confidence. If the North meant to win, he had written in August 1862, "we must begin at Kentucky and reconquer the country from them as we did from the Indians. It was this conviction then as plainly as now that made men think I was insane." The proposition that subjugation was necessary did not strike him as eccentric or immoral; it was self-evident. Sherman did not see how one could honor a rebel or prefer to be in the place of a defeated Indian. Twenty-two years after the Taylor Peace Commission had ended its work, Sherman still remembered Samuel Foster Tappan incredulously. In one of his last speeches he said that Tappan "was simply an Indian lover. I think he loved an Indian better than himself." As a matter of military action, of facilitating whites' settlement of the west, Indian resistance seemed to Sherman an almost negligible irritant. The conflict grew portentous in his rhetoric when he was using defeat of the Indians to confirm his faith, which he never freed from doubt, that the United States must be the nation of the future. Sanity lay in success.

Annually General O. O. Howard sent a New Year's greeting to Sherman, who had picked him to command the Army of the Tennessee in the marches across Georgia and the Carolinas, then had encouraged him to stay in the army during the Indian wars. At the end of 1883, not long after Sherman had retired to St. Louis, Howard wrote to him: "I thought I caught a little sprinkling of sadness in some publications of remarks imputed to you since your retirement." Trying to cheer him up, Howard said that Sherman would soon be active again. Sherman was not sorry to be retiring; nor did he give any sign of fearing that he would be inactive. A hint of sadness, an undercurrent of pessimism, long had run through some of his public and many of his private statements about the future. Sometimes he conveyed his doubts in the manner of his friend Samuel Clemens, partially disguising them in humor. At a convention banquet of the National Wholesale Drug Association he spoke, as he often did, in response to a toast to the army. The drug wholesalers cheered his joke, evidently not perceiving how bitterly he mocked the vicarious war and parodied his accustomed peacetime role—inspirational speaker representing the heroic Civil War and the nation's bright prospects. He said to them: "I suppose the words of the English toast, given at all their gatherings: 'Here's to a bloody war and a sickly season,' will be in favor here. A bloody war to make plenty of dead and wounded and dying for you people to sell your drugs to, for the doctors to finish up, for the clergy to say a final prayer for, and for the lawyers to divide up their raiment." In this fleeting image war was nothing but death and suffering; peace was nothing but greed and ambitious futility. Perhaps no one dwelt on such thoughts amid the laughter, but they touched Sherman's worries, which he could not dispel with jokes. During his traveling and writing and speaking he did not escape the persistent fear that his efforts might prove vain and his vision might be mistaken.

Living in Manhattan, at 75 West Seventy-first Street, in his last years, Sherman recalled his earlier notion of retiring to Coeur d'Alene, Idaho. By 1888 the thought no longer appealed to him. "Gold was discovered there, a railroad is built, and the beautiful forests are being swept away, and the virgin lakes & streams robbed of their trout and I am forced to choose this great city, for the final act of my drama of life. I feel like apologizing but on the whole it is the best I can do." Few people saw more than Sherman did of the changes in the trans-Mississippi west between 1848 and 1890. Few people promoted those changes more fervently. Of course, it had to happen, he said, and only a fool defied what had to happen. But occasionally the vision of progress appeared to him inverted, a reversal of his expectations reminiscent of the shock he had undergone in gold rush San Francisco, where the search for prosperity had turned out to be the antithesis of order and happiness. During 1888 Sherman wrote to an old California friend: "Nature in her wild majesty has more charms for me than mans most cultured work and I sometimes deplore the early discovery of gold at Coloma, which has revolutionized the Great West, defaced and deformed the Sierra Nevadas, stript the forests from the Rockies, and swept out of existence the millions of buffalo, elk, deer & antelope which only thirty years ago made the plains the paradise of the hunter and Indian." The two Californias, the pastoral and the lucrative—the two Americas in radically foreshortened perspective—could not be so readily reconciled as Sherman had promised his many audiences. If the nation did not attain a harmony aptly symbolized by the Mississippi River and its tributaries, the alternative epitome of American life might be the Sacramento River and its tributaries—teeming with miners whose stay was brief, whose destination was not fixed, whose labor mostly enriched someone else. A reverie of nostalgia for unspoiled nature, like an outburst of sarcasm, did not change Sherman's predominant public message. Rather, his second thoughts hinted to him, in troubled, aberrant moments, that he might be launched on a crazy career with Americans who had no secure ties to each other or to America.

Sherman felt the urgency of moving his audiences toward patriotism and of sending easterners to settle the west partly because he thought that propertyless people were dangerous. He never approved of universal manhood suffrage, though he accepted it as a political fact. Seeing partisan politics as an exercise in opportunism, he expected an electorate with a shrinking proportion of propertyholders to choose officials who would increase taxes on property to confiscatory levels; politicians would use government and the proceeds of taxation for their own advantage while demagogically deluding the majority of voters, who had nothing to lose and imagined themselves to have everything to gain. Eventually propertyholders would have to defend themselves, and the conflict probably would be violent. Agitation of public passions during presidential campaigns seemed to Sherman a near approach to indiscriminate violence. Political parties, he thought, did not channel fervor and discontent into lawful outlets through mock revolutions; instead, they created and intensified discontent, arousing for the benefit of party irresponsible hostilities that might overwhelm the country. "We are liable to smash into a thousand pieces every time we have an election," Sherman said.

While talking, even during the depression following the Panic of 1873, about the nation's wealth and promise, Sherman met poverty constantly, in the persons of veterans who turned to him for help. Between his wife's extensive activities in Catholic charities and his own hand-outs to veterans, he spent thousands of dollars a year on the poor. He often complained about doing so. The unending line of out-of-work veterans, pension-seekers requesting testimonials of their service, widows and orphans looking for government work wore on his patience and jarred his notion of the war's legacy. With the armies' disbandment in 1865 and long afterward, the wandering, begging veteran—often also a crippled veteran—appeared on streets and roads throughout America. The growing number of rootless, unemployed men during the depression of the 1870s made the tramp a menacing figure in the eyes of many Americans, who routinely associated the tramp with the veteran. Was it conceivable that Sherman's own men could be a source of alarm? In 1884 he wrote: "Too many of our old soldiers are drifting about the country aimless and helpless, so that I am always relieved when any of them are prosperous." He did not like to see veterans, guarantors of the nation's defeat of anarchy, sunk in the poverty that most threatened America's stability.

Sherman felt the greatest concern about large cities, where mobs—that is, the propertyless—might "by taxation or force appropriate the property and acquired wealth of their more industrious neighbors." He advised his friends in St. Louis, after the general strike there, to plan for suppression of mobs, to strengthen their police and militia, and to "watch the embryo communists and break them up before they acquire too much head." The strikes of 1877, with the accompanying workers' organizations, violence between militiamen and strikers, and destruction of property, especially that of railroads, disturbed Sherman more than his confident public statements revealed. Coming so soon after threats of civil war during the winter dispute over resolving the presidential election, the two crises revealed in a single year the related threats of volatile partisanship and concerted attack on property. He said that the "labor riots" would be the model for the coming climactic fight against the mob, perhaps "with arms and in blood." Sherman had that prospect in mind when he wrote of "breakers which are steadily rising round about us, threatening to engulf ship, passengers and all in utter ruin. We have passed the ordeal of civil war safely, but in our very midst are forming societies who hate property, who hate men of refinement, of honor, integrity and all the qualities which adorn human society and life. These men must be met openly and valorously." He had more trouble coping with his anticipation of inevitable class war than the propertied classes had in avoiding the great confrontation he predicted. The strikes had not come near the radical goals or all-encompassing violence so loosely attributed to them, and they were followed by forcible suppression of strikers and unions. Sherman's alarm over intestine enemies and the possible ruin of the country went beyond the known threats. His anxieties and his scenarios of conflict, shared by many of his contemporaries, amounted to an oblique confession that his faith in America's assured progress was not whole. This uncertainty pervaded Sherman's world more fully than the activities of propertyless voters, strikers, and "embryo communists" could explain. Sherman had anarchic doubts about the certainty of progress, and these posed more subversive threats to his promises for the future than radicals posed to his society.

Sherman and his mentor John W. Draper detected the rule of cosmic law in human affairs by the light of faith. Viewed in a different light, Americans' behavior did not readily disclose the steady movement of history according to laws that Sherman expected to be mathematically calculable. He cautioned Draper in 1867: "If you be right that we are under the influence of a law, urging us as a nation toward a higher and better destiny, you must make wide allowances for perturbations and aberrations as violent as those that guide the comet, or bring home the wandering aeriolytes." To demonstrate America's progress would require sophisticated computation, so deviant were the phenomena to be accommodated. Sherman trusted that upheavals—civil war, conquest of the west, the growth of cities—followed an orderly plan. Yet the guiding force reconciling so many drastic and apparently chaotic actions was amorphous in Sherman's mind, much vaguer than the disparate concrete results it purported to direct. Sherman used the language of astronomy and geometry without finding in history the precision his metaphors implied. He said in 1883: "It does look to me as though the events of this world were moving as it were in little epicycloids, each generation repeating the same follies and the same wisdom with the regularity of the seasons, whilst the greater directing ellipse reaches out higher and higher up into the infinite domain of the unknown."

Reassurance offered by history's supposedly immutable laws seemed questionable as events of the 1870s and 1880s showed that the Civil War had not guaranteed a fully unified, pacified nation or an unchallenged governmental and social order. Perhaps the pattern of infinite progress, no less than the pattern of nations' cycles of triumph and ruin familiar to eighteenth-century Americans, would reveal that the United States had too soon fallen from its conspicuous place in history by discarding the fruits of victory. Among proponents of a newly solidified nationality and an expanding industrialism, Sherman was not alone in fearing that a failure of prosperity would entail a failure of self-government. Leaving his doubts implicit when he spoke publicly, Sherman urged Americans to identify themselves with progress because he believed that the country had no special exemption from the cycles or aberrations whereby peoples were destroyed for their failure to comprehend the direction of history's movement. The subjugation of once-triumphant civilizations such as China and India, the collapse of once-proud empires like Spain's and Rome's, "which claimed to be eternal," held a warning for Americans: their role in progress was not assured, not perpetual; they could throw it away, whereupon "others more hardy, more virtuous, will come after and displace us as we have displaced the Indian."

The spectacle of extinct empires and dispossessed peoples sometimes suggested to Sherman that the United States might postpone but could not escape following them into oblivion. In his more fatalistic moments he doubted the efficacy of trying to put off the day by stimulating people to patriotism and economic endeavor. When their epicycloid of history had traced its course their usefulness to progress, or their ephemeral triumph, would end. "As long as our country is in the ascendent scale," he wrote in 1881, "men will occur equal to the occasion; but when the time comes for a decline then no personal efforts will avail or succeed." Sherman entertained but resisted the thought that the epicycloids and ellipses curved pointlessly, going nowhere. Near the end of his travels through Europe in 1872 he wrote to Joseph Henry: "In treading upon the ashes of dead men in Italy, Egypt—on the banks of the Bosphorus, one almost despairs to think how idle are the dreams and toils of this life, and were it not for the intellectual pleasure of knowing & learning, one would almost be damaged by travel in these historic lands." Americans could most readily sustain their confidence in the future by staying on their own continent, where they extended and improved their civilization without encountering mocking ruins. Yet there they had the 300-year-long admonitory memory of the supplanting of the Indians. That conquest, too, would fade away, Sherman thought but seldom said. Praising the transformation of the west in conformity with "the laws of nature and civilization," he nevertheless concluded: "This drama must end. Days, years and centuries follow fast. Even the drama of civilization must have an end."

After Sherman's death his former aide, John E. Tourtellotte, wrote: "I saw him cast down but twice—once after the publication of his Memoirs, when some persons insisted he had been unjust; and once, when he thought Tom had deceived him in choosing a profession." These episodes had in common their defeat of Sherman's plans to leave public life. He put his oldest surviving son, Thomas, through law school, expecting that the family could move to St. Louis and support itself by the son's law practice, the father's pension, and their real estate investments. But in May 1878 Thomas, at the age of twenty-one, revealed his long-standing intention to become a Jesuit priest. Sherman took the news as a blow hardly less severe than the death of his favorite child, Willie, who had contracted typhoid fever during a visit to the army in the summer of 1863. He felt bitter disappointment over Thomas's turning to a life in the church—"a defunct institution"—and to thoughts of the soul's eternal salvation rather than to a leading role in America's growth. Though Thomas aspired to an active life as a missionary, his father saw the priesthood as the inward-looking, otherworldly life of the moralist seeking to escape reality. Thomas was repudiating the principle on which his father had built his life, Sherman thought, and, in doing so, was leaving him with the burden of practical material responsibilities, especially that of supporting the rest of the family alone. Sherman further regretted that his plans for escaping Washington and the government were ruined. "By force of circumstances I must stick by the army, pitied by some, and scorned by others."

The other shock—critics' attacks on his memoirs after their publication in 1875—troubled Sherman more briefly but also struck him as a repudiation despite his having acted on the best motives. He had written the volumes as testimony for history and as a valedictory summary of political and military lessons. Instead he found himself defending his wartime accomplishments in order to rebut his critics. The memoirs, sealing the union's victory in history and exposing defects in the War Department's structure, showed why it was time for him to retire, but Thomas Sherman's departure for seminary broke up the plan for family operations in St. Louis. General Sherman remained on active duty for another five years and, as soon as he retired, began work on a second edition of his memoirs.

Tourtellotte saw his hero "cast down" partly because Sherman felt some distaste for his public role as national hero and propagandist. Lamenting his son's decision, he wrote to an old friend in St. Louis: "The dream of my life was to settle down near you without the public obligations now forced on me. When I could be as it were myself—not driven to desperation all the time by the demands and claims of others." Those obligations included not only his official duties and his help to veterans and their relatives, but also his nationwide campaigning. Though he told Americans to identify themselves with the nation, as he had done, Sherman did not want to lose his version of "myself" in his fellow Americans' eagerness for him to represent their own and their nation's greatness. His traveling and speech-making fulfilled only a fraction of the public appearances he was invited to make. He often complained that veterans and other groups expected him to spend all his time with them. His darker view of the role of national hero came out in his sardonic response to a proposed national mausoleum for the remains of distinguished Americans. He wrote: "I have neither the time, inclination nor ability to discuss the proposition of an American Westminster. I once visited the catacombs under ancient Syracuse. Our guide said there were a million interments, but the contents of every chamber had been sold for manure. I asked him if a single grave had been spared; not one. As it was in the beginning, is now, and ever will be. Amen!" Was it worthwhile to devote so much of his life to a public identity whose attempt at influence might be even more vain than an effort to make heroes' interments—and, by extension, their nation's life—everlasting? Yet, after retiring to St. Louis at last, he found that "spite of all I may do, I cannot cease to be General Sherman, pulled & hauled about." The two Shermans—"General Sherman" and "myself"—had not become one. But beginning, perhaps, with his finding a way to conquer the Confederacy, "General Sherman" had become essential for the continued confidence of "myself" in purposeful existence, personal and national. Late in life, looking back to the days "when we were soldiers battling for the life of a nation," Sherman wrote to an old friend: "I sometimes doubt if that nation be worthy the sacrifices then made, but good or bad I must cling to her fortunes."

CHAPTER 9

THE GRAND REVIEW

FOR the last time four corps of Sherman's army lay camped along heights that overlooked a river separating the army and the city toward which it marched. The river was the Potomac, and the city was Washington. Upon the army's arrival at Alexandria, after a fast march through Virginia, Sherman had received the War Department's order to prepare for a grand review in the capital, to take place on Wednesday, May 24. While General Meade and his Army of the Potomac passed in review along Pennsylvania Avenue on Tuesday, Sherman's men took positions on and near the Arlington heights, awaiting their turn. In the evening the First Division of the 15th Army Corps marched across the Long Bridge into Washington and camped for the night in vacant lots and streets. The Second Division stayed on the south bank of the river, but its men had to get up at two o'clock Wednesday morning to eat breakfast and cross the bridge in the dark. As the sun rose, long columns of the 17th, 20th, and 14th Corps wound among the hills of Alexandria and Arlington; a steady flow of more than 55,000 soldiers kept the Long Bridge full.

For several days Sherman's men had been getting ready. They drew some new uniforms from government stores; they used large amounts of blacking to polish shoes, cartridge boxes, and belts; they cleaned rifles and bayonets to a bright shine. General John W. Geary bought white gloves for all the men of his division and issued them just before the 20th Corps crossed the Potomac. Of Sherman's 186 infantry regiments all but 30 came from western states. Many of these westerners believed that they had done far more than the Army of the Potomac to defeat the rebellion. Yet eastern civilians and soldiers, they thought, looked on them as wild

406 THE DESTRUCTIVE WAR

skirmishers and undisciplined raiders, not a real army. The review would give them a chance to show that they were veterans who surpassed the paper-collar soldiers of the east in every way. Tuesday evening, after watching Meade's army perform, Sherman met with some of his generals to plan for the next day. They decided to include in their column exhibits of their great marches—wagons, ambulances, pontoons, captured live-stock, pets, and a few of the black people who had come out of the South with them. At the same time, Sherman wanted his army to march better than their rivals. He sent word to the officers: "Be careful about your intervals and your tactics. Don't let your men be looking back over their shoulders. I will give you plenty of time to go to the capitol and see everything afterward, but let them keep their eyes fifteen paces to the front and march by in the old, customary way." By the time this message reached the soldiers, it had been simplified: "Boys remember its 'Sherman' against the 'Potomac'—the west against the east today."

Meade's army had passed in review before a large crowd lining Penn-sylvania Avenue—a *New York Herald* reporter set the number of specta-tors at 75,000—and even more people awaited Sherman. Both regularly scheduled and special trains brought citizens from all parts of the North; more arrived on May 23. Boats from Alexandria unloaded all day, and the roads in Maryland filled with travelers headed for Washington. Governors and other politicians came to take conspicuous places in cheer-ing men from their home states. Hotels and boarding houses were full; many people slept outdoors or stayed up all night. Fathers and mothers brought their children to see a pageant of patriotism which would never again be equaled. In response to a telegram from her husband, Ellen Sherman came from Lancaster with her father and her son. Seven hours of watching and cheering the 84,000 men of the Army of the Potomac on Tuesday did not wear out the spectators. They crowded Pennsylvania Avenue again Wednesday morning, hours before nine o'clock.

The avenue from the Capitol to the Treasury building was lined with trees on both sides and with low buildings—Willard's Hotel, five stories high, was taller than most. Many structures flew American flags from poles on the roof or had flags hung across their facades. Public buildings were still striped with large black crepe ribbons of mourning for Abra-ham Lincoln, and their flags were at half staff. Bunting, colorful streamers, and floral displays decorated poles and windows. All along the avenue banners and signs were tied to the front of buildings or suspended across intersecting streets where passing soldiers could read the messages: "The Public Schools of Washington Welcome the Heroes of the Republic. Honor to the Brave." "We Welcome Our Western Boys. Shiloh, Vicksburg, Atlanta, Stone River, Savannah, and Raleigh." "Welcome, 15th and 17th Army Corps." "The West is proud of her gallant sons." "Ohio welcomes her brave boys home." "The Pride of the Nation." "The Nation Welcomes Her Brave Defenders." A banner hanging from the Treasury building, where Pennsylvania Avenue met Fifteenth Street, said: "The Only National Debt We Can Never Pay is the Debt We Owe to the Victorious Union Soldiers."

At the expense of the federal government, the district government, various states, and individuals, temporary stands with tiers of benches for spectators had been erected at several places along the route of march, especially on both sides of Pennsylvania Avenue between Fifteenth and Seventeenth streets. Employees of the Quartermaster General's department had their own stand in front of Corcoran's Art Museum; other special sections were reserved for disabled veterans and for students from Edward M. Gallaudet's school for the deaf. Government clerks sat on the roof of the Treasury building; people gathered on roofs along the avenue, and boys climbed into trees. Privileged people occupied balconies and windows overlooking the avenue. Some enterprising landlords rented window positions for $5.00, which was 30 percent of the monthly pay of the privates who would be marching past. Pennsylvania Avenue had a firm surface of compact, rounded cobblestones, through which ran two sets of streetcar tracks. The District of Columbia Fire Department had cleaned and watered the street, and guards were posted along the avenue and at intersections to keep people and vehicles out of the line of march. For a distance of more than a mile the broad avenue lay empty of traffic, waiting for the files of soldiers forming behind the Capitol on East Capitol Street.

The crowd stood eight, ten, or more deep all along the route. Men and women, blacks and whites, adults and children pressed together, intent on seeing the military spectacle. Most people came in their best clothes. Men wore suits or jackets, white shirts, various kinds of bow ties, and a wide range of hats—from flat straw to high silk stovepipe—or no hat at all. Women parted their hair in the middle, covered it with a bonnet, and tied a huge bow under the chin, below which they combined tight bodices with full skirts. Many raised open umbrellas to shade themselves. A mixed, confused array of colors met the eye, both from diverse clothing and from flowers, bouquets, wreaths, and small flags that women carried. Photographers set up large glass-plate-negative view cameras on tripods. Black women held up their babies. Hawkers moved through the crowd selling purple lemonade. Wednesday, the 24th, was another refreshing spring day, with clear blue skies, some light white clouds, and a cooling breeze from the northeast. Along Maryland Avenue citizens put out barrels of ice water for soldiers passing from the Long Bridge to Capitol Hill.

In wooden stands rising from both sides of Pennsylvania Avenue along the two blocks in front of the White House, dignitaries took their reserved seats. Governors, senators, representatives, justices of the Supreme Court, family members, guests, and newspaper reporters occupied the places in Lafayette Square, across from the White House. The roofed presidential stand in front of the White House—decorated with bunting, flags, three big stars shaped from evergreen, and banners naming battles won by the Federal armies—held President Johnson, his cabinet, generals and staff officers, some family members, and the diplomatic corps in a bright display of formal dress and full uniform. In a line at the front sat Attorney General Speed, Secretary Stanton, the President, General Grant, Secretary Welles, Postmaster General Dennison, General Meade, and Quartermaster General Meigs, who had first proposed holding a review of both armies. Except for Andrew Johnson's clean-shaven face, they formed a row of blue uniforms, dark suits, and full beards. Below them, at street level, stood a small honor guard. Stretching in both directions from the two central stands, rising rows of seats held other generals, naval officers, and officials of the executive branch. A system of yellow and red tickets, numbered and unnumbered, was supposed to control access to the seats and to standing room on the curbs between the Treasury building and Corcoran's Art Museum. But, by the second day of the review, the controls had partly broken down, and twice as many pedestrians massed in front of the reviewing stands to watch Sherman's army.

Shortly before nine o'clock the men of the First Division of the 15th Army Corps stood waiting in a column with its front at the west base of Capitol Hill and the rest of it wrapping around the south end of the Capitol and extending out East Capitol Street, where the other divisions waited on side streets, as did the 17th Corps. Divisions of the other corps were still approaching Capitol Hill and crossing the Long Bridge. The width of the column was made uniform by giving all regiments a company front of twenty files and a depth of fifteen to twenty ranks, the men closed in mass. Musicians were consolidated to give each brigade a single band. Drummers stayed with their regiments. As General Sherman, General Howard, and Sherman's staff officers rode to take their places at the head of the column, people in the large crowds on Capitol Hill tried to reach Sherman and shake hands with him.

At nine o'clock Adjutant General Edward Townsend fired an artillery piece as the signal for the review to begin. Along the column, regimental commanders shouted the order for right shoulder arms, followed by

"Forward! March!" The first of the brigade bands struck up a march; the drum corps set a steady beat, and the column started to move up Pennsylvania Avenue.

The men of the 15th Corps marched with a long, rhythmically swinging stride, causing thousands of fixed bayonets to sway back and forth in unison and gleam in the sun. The ranks stayed as straight as a tight cord while advancing steadily and evenly. Again and again, without noticeable deviation, thousands of feet came down firmly on the cobblestones at the same instant, the tread resounding in a precise, ceaseless beat. A soldier wrote home afterward: "The marching was hard on our feet." But, another explained, "The march had to bea in stile." Despite their earlier cleaning efforts, not many of Sherman's men had obtained new uniforms in recent days. Their blues looked dingy—"as if," one witness said, "the smoke of numberless battle-fields had dyed their garments, and the soil of insurrectionary states had adhered to them." They wore large slouch hats made of felt rather than the tight caps worn by the Army of the Potomac. The western men were, in the aggregate, taller than easterners, more muscular and more deeply tanned. They kept their eyes steadily to the front, the only way to maintain exact alignment. They showed a grim, determined facial expression. Spectators described it variously as a businesslike scowl, as nonchalance, and as *sang froid*. One soldier said that the men "marched right along as if no one was present."

In advance of the moving column rode several separated ranks of horsemen. First appeared the 9th Illinois Mounted Infantry. Behind this ceremonial guard came Sherman and Howard. At Sherman's request, Howard had relinquished his place as commander of the Army of the Tennessee for the review. His empty right sleeve pinned to the blouse of his uniform, he accompanied Sherman. A contingent of staff officers followed. At a short interval, General John A. Logan rode at the head of the Army of the Tennessee, with his staff, including Mary Ann "Mother" Bickerdyke. After them, General William B. Hazen led the 15th Corps. General Charles R. Woods, commander of the First Division, followed by his brother General William B. Woods, commander of the First Brigade, brought up the rear of the sequence of mounted officers. Their horses, Hazen later recalled, "were magnificent, owing to our frequent opportunities for capture." Behind them brass bands played, and a steadily lengthening column of infantry tramped in even cadence onto the avenue.

From the crowds on both sides of the street rose a loud roar of cheering, clapping, and shouting. The sound swelled as it rolled up Pennsylvania Avenue, pushed forward by the approach of Sherman and the 15th Corps. Women waved handkerchiefs and small American flags;

they threw bouquets and flowers into the ranks; they sent boys running to give wreaths to passing officers. Sherman soon had two large wreaths, one around his horse's neck and one on his own shoulders. To some soldiers the combination of bands playing, drums beating, the regiments' regular tread, and the yelling and applauding seemed almost to shake the buildings. People on the curb cried out: "Sherman, Sherman, that's he; the tall man." Groups of ladies on balconies called to him, begging him to look in their direction. A reporter for the *Cleveland Plain Dealer* listened to Sherman being "vociferously cheered all along the line," then wired a dispatch, saying: "The greeting of this hero was in the highest degree enthusiastic." People wept and laughed and showed, in one witness's opinion, "the joy of being the end of a long and wearisome and terrible war." An old man grew so excited at the passing of the 15th Corps that he jumped out of the crowd into the street and shouted: "I have lived to see the Grand Army of the Union, I, God."

Riding a powerful, spirited thoroughbred, Sherman wore a complete uniform, very different from his usual careless dress on the march. Like his men, he was trim and deeply tanned. To his brother he "looked the picture of health and strength." He sat erect in the saddle and did not glance right or left, hardly acknowledging cheers and calls except, perhaps, by a slight nod. Among those watching him was Walt Whitman, clerk in the Indian Bureau and volunteer nurse in Washington's military hospitals. As usual, the poet carried folded pieces of paper stitched to make small booklets for taking notes. On one of them he wrote with a pencil:

2d day
May 24, 1865

15th & 17th Corps
First the broad capacious open waiting
    avenue—then singly
Gen. Sherman, passing rapidly
by—the sudden shouts,
quite tumultuous,—but
he pays no more attention
to it, than if ~~he~~ it
was the wind blowing —
— the large magnificent bouquet—he
turns, one of his generals
from behind
rides up & takes it from
him—~~a~~ & still the
shouting crowd, & still

the perfect deafness &
immobility of the great
soldier—with I think
a shade of scornfulness & haughty ~~iness~~
~~& scornful p~~ passion
on his nervous face.
Haughty here to this ephemeral popular
hurrahing, but, as I know
from many a soldier of
his army

Here, with an unfinished, canceled word, Whitman stopped writing.

For almost thirty minutes Sherman led the steadily growing column of the Army of the Tennessee in a straight line, extending the wave of applause. When he reached the Treasury building, where he turned right to head north on Fifteenth Street, he looked back along Pennsylvania Avenue. "It was a magnificent sight," he said afterward, "the bayonets forming a perfect compact mass, swaying easily with the marching step." A crowd of men and women in front of Willard's Hotel had pressed out from the curb to the streetcar tracks in order to look toward the Capitol and see the same sight. For a mile the avenue was filled with men of the 15th Corps. Yet Sherman and the citizens were looking at only one-third of one of his four corps. On a temporary scaffolding above Fifteenth Street, facing down the avenue, and at other points along the line of march, "Brady and Gardner, the enterprising photographers," worked busily to take many pictures with the help of their assistants.

At the north end of the Treasury building Sherman turned left onto the two-block stretch of Pennsylvania Avenue that ran past the White House. The brick house serving as headquarters of General C. C. Augur, military commander of the District of Columbia, stood on his right, next to the lower corner of Lafayette Square. Inside, Secretary of State William Henry Seward, still recovering from the injuries of a carriage accident and from the wounds of an attempted assassination, sat near a second-story window to watch the review. Seeing him, Sherman rode near the building, took off his hat, and bowed low from the saddle. Seward returned the salute.

As Sherman turned the corner of the Treasury building and came in sight of the tiers of benches—filled with governors, generals, members of Congress, diplomats, disabled soldiers, deaf students, civil servants, family members, and guests—everyone stood up at once and shouted in a blended roar. One of them later recalled: "There was something almost fierce in the fever of enthusiasm aroused by the sight of Sherman."

Although John Sherman, Ellen Sherman, Thomas Ewing, and Ulysses S. Grant had known the man whom they stood to salute since his youth, most in the crowd had only followed news of his army's exploits from a distance, without having seen its commander. Though they did not know him as a familiar figure, they approved of what he had done, and this was their chance to show that they did. A reporter's dispatch said: "The enthusiasm, as he first appeared, is almost indescribable." The 4th Minnesota Regiment's band began to play "Marching Through Georgia." With his hat in his hand and his eyes turned left toward President Johnson and General Grant, Sherman rode past the reviewing stand. General Howard saluted with his left hand and guided his horse with the reins under the stump of his right arm. The President, General Grant, members of the cabinet, and the others took off their hats to return Sherman's and Howard's salute, while people in the stands continued to cheer and wave American flags. As the front of the 15th Corps approached, Sherman and Howard rode onto the grounds of the White House, behind the reviewing stand, and left their horses with orderlies. The brass band and the drummers wheeled out of the line of march to stand in front of the dignitaries, providing music for the First Brigade as it passed in review; and the first of a long approaching line of regimental colors were dipped in salute as General William B. Woods's brigade marched by.

Entering the reviewing stand, General Sherman first greeted Ellen Sherman, their eight-year-old son Tom, and Thomas Ewing. He then shook hands with President Johnson. Secretary Stanton, whose denunciation of Sherman's peace terms had been published a month earlier, began to offer his hand to the general, but Sherman did not take it. He passed Stanton with a slight bow and moved on to shake hands with Grant and members of the cabinet, finally taking his place near the west end of the main stand. John Sherman noticed that "everyone within sight could perceive the intended insult" to Stanton. Describing his rebuff of the secretary, General Sherman wrote four days later: "No man I don't care who he is shall insult me publicly or arraign my motives."

General Hazen, General Charles Woods, and, successively, other corps and division commanders left the column after saluting the president and joined the reviewing party while their men passed. Men of the 15th Corps, one witness said, evoked from the crowd "unstinted admiration" of "their free, swinging stride, their boldness of bearing, and their powerful physique." Their corps badge—a cartridge box with the label "40 rounds"—advertised their combative spirit. The reporter D. P. Conyngham had accompanied the army through the South; he told readers of the *New York Herald* that the men of Woods's division, as they passed in review, were "fine, tall, long limbed, strapping fellows," in whom the west could take pride. A series of bands, including an exceptionally good one which led the Second Division, kept up the music with tunes such as "Yankee Doodle," "Dixie," "John Brown's Body," and "The Girl I Left Behind Me." Drummers sounded ruffles as the passing regimental colors were dipped before the reviewing stand. Most regiments had gone through several sets of colors during the war. Some had comparatively new flags, while many had clung to their stained, ripped, and ragged silks, on which were sewn the names of the regiment's battles—"Shiloh," "Vicksburg," "Atlanta," and others. The 29th Ohio Regiment's new flag had thirteen battles on it. From every staff and every company guidon hung long black streamers of mourning for the death of Lincoln. The dirtiest, most tattered and bullet-ripped colors produced the loudest cheers. On the Army of the Potomac's day, people in the crowd had exhausted their supply of flowers before the review ended. For Sherman's army, there were not only many more onlookers but they also came better prepared. The regiments turned the corner of the Treasury building and marched westward in exact alignment and regular cadence. At the order, the soldiers brought their rifles to carry arms smoothly and in unison. Mounted officers saluted with their swords; color bearers lowered the combat-worn colors; and the crowd again and again shouted, clapped, and threw flowers, wreaths, and bouquets. General Sherman returned each salute; General Grant "lifted his hat with reverence and deep feeling"; President Johnson held the brim of his hat in his right hand, waved it from left to right, and occasionally rested it on his left shoulder with his arm crossing his chest. Beyond the reviewing stand, the men returned precisely to right shoulder arms; the colors came back up; and the regiments marched on to Seventeenth Street.

Preceding each of Sherman's divisions, its pioneers—construction laborers—marched like the soldiers. Conspicuously tall, muscular black men, they carried axes, picks, and spades at the position of right shoulder arms and moved forward in double ranks, keeping perfect alignment and step. "Significant frontispiece," an eastern officer commented. D. P. Conyngham, having seen them at work in the preceding months, said of their proud marching: "They knew well that they represented many thousands of dollars lost to the confederacy." For an hour and fifteen minutes the three divisions of the 15th Army Corps passed the reviewing stand. By the time that the artillery of the corps appeared, Pennsylvania Avenue from the Capitol to the Treasury was filled with the 17th Army Corps, while the 20th and the 14th corps took their preparatory places on Capitol Hill. The 15th Corps artillery included Captain Francis DeGress and his twenty-pounder Parrott guns, which had fired the first shells into Atlanta and Columbia. His pieces were "in capital condition," an officer wrote, "and it did me great good to point them out and speak of his fine shooting and most excellent discipline." Between the rear of the 15th Corps and the front of the 17th marched the 1st Michigan Engineers. They had demolished arsenals, factories, and railroad facilities from Atlanta to Fayetteville. The rumbling of the artillery wheels moved away westward while, from the vicinity of the Treasury building, bugle calls and the music of another band announced General Frank Blair at the head of the 17th Corps. As soon as the crowd recognized Blair, who was stouter and more tanned than in his days as a member of Congress, they cheered loudly.

In the rear of each division came six covered ambulance wagons three abreast. Their well-used stretchers, stained with the blood of many men, hung strapped to the sides. Interspersed at various places in the column were moving tableaus designed to represent the march through Georgia and the Carolinas. Black men serving as cooks led mules and jacks of all sizes and shades. The animals were burdened with large packs, from which hung kettles, pans, gridirons, hams, and sides of bacon. On top of the packs rode pets belonging to soldiers—dogs, raccoons, squirrels, game cocks, and at least one monkey. Cows, sheep, and goats were forage on the hoof. A soldier leading a jackass with a white goat riding on its back heard from someone in the crowd the question: "Where did you get your goat, Mister?" He replied: "In Atlanta." Whole families of black people—old men, women with children, youngsters sitting on mules, and former field hands leading animals laden with forage—walked up the middle of Pennsylvania Avenue, as the soldiers had told them to do. As bummers and refugees passed, the onlookers' patriotic cheering for marching regiments gave way to laughter and applause at the varied show.

Often, while the constant rhythmic footfall and the beat of the drums continued, the people in front of the White House, like those elsewhere along the avenue, could hear several bands at once, near and far, playing different tunes. Echoes from the buildings mixed with competing bands and created what one soldier called "a perfect carnival of music." Spectators joined in shouting the choruses of the most familiar songs—"When this cruel war is over," "When Johnny comes marching home," and "Tramp, tramp, tramp! the boys are marching." As one of Blair's divisions passed the reviewing stand, the densely packed crowd sang the best known of all the war songs:

> John Brown's body lies a-mouldering in the grave
> But his soul goes marching on.

Among those who heard this chorus was Murat Halstead, editor of the *Cincinnati Commercial,* who had first reported, late in 1861, that Sherman was insane. Halstead rested his notepaper on his knee as he produced a dispatch, working in the midst of the crowd while soldiers marched by. He wrote: "It is the army of the desolation of the South, that has made its mark of blood and ashes for two thousand miles, littering the whole line of its tremendous march with graves and the ruins of the habitations of its enemies. These are the men who brought the war home to the South, and brought the first wail of despair from the enemies of American nationality; and you can read something of this grand and terrible history in the dark faces of the heroes."

Not until shortly after noon did the 20th Army Corps begin to march from East Capitol Street, around the Capitol, and onto Pennsylvania Avenue. The 14th Corps still had about ninety minutes to wait before its column started to move. Pennsylvania Avenue remained full of passing regiments and cheering, clapping citizens. Although some soldiers found the review a tiresome bore, most of those who recorded their comments said that they enjoyed the applause for their service to the nation. Captain Frank L. Ferguson, an officer commissioned from the ranks, later recalled: "There never was a beardless country boy any prouder than I was at the age of 22 years as I marched up thru the citty of Washington and went past the reviewing stand." Frederick Marion, a soldier in the 31st Ohio Regiment, wrote to his sister about the review three days afterward: "We was proud that we belonged to Sherman army and it paid us for all the hard marches that we have endured and the dangers we have passed through. Who would not be one of Shermans bummers?" With few exceptions the men kept their eyes to the front and maintained their impassive expressions—their look of "don't care a damnativeness," Halstead called it—apparently indifferent to the public enthusiasm. "All the same," Private Robert Hale Strong said, "we took it in." Sometimes their composure faltered when delegations from their home states gave special cheers for them. As the white-gloved 5th Ohio Regiment—in Geary's division of the 20th Corps—passed the reviewing stand, the soldiers heard a voice in the crowd call out: "How are you Cincinnati boys?" Smiles appeared on all the faces, across a twenty-man front. Soldiers from the Army of the Potomac joined the crowd and pressed out into the avenue especially to greet their former comrades in the 20th Corps, serving in the west since late in 1863. With General Joseph A. Mower at its head, the corps marched even better, its men believed, than Sherman's other corps. The Army of the Potomac's men shouted themselves hoarse. New Yorkers at hotels along the avenue yelled for the Empire State's boys in the 20th Corps.

With the help of a newspaper containing the order of march, Sherman closely watched each unit of his army. He caught the eye of every commanding officer and returned every salute. To the people near him in the presidential stand he kept up a steady flow of pithy, graphic talk, describing incidents of the campaigns involving soldiers passing at the moment. One witness said of him: "I never saw Gen'l Sherman looking prouder in my life." When the 31st Ohio Regiment approached, a young woman in the stand gave the general a wreath for the regimental colors, and Sherman threw it to the color bearer while the crowd applauded. D. P. Conyngham wrote: "Those who saw Sherman blandly smile and bow to the admiring multitude could not realize that he was the same nervous, restless spirit that followed Johnston and swept through the confederacy like an avenging Nemesis."

When the column had to mark time due to a delay beyond the reviewing stand, the regiment temporarily on display went through the manual of arms. At the command "Order Arms," all the rifle butts hit the paving stones in one stroke. One regiment's execution of the drill "so astonished and pleased the crowd, that the appreciation was simply tremendous." In the afternoon the 20th and 14th Corps opened larger intervals between their brigades and between the rear of one division and the front of the next. This left Pennsylvania Avenue empty in front of the reviewing stand for several minutes at a time. During these breaks, people on the curbs surged forward in a crowd to see the politicians and the generals up close. In response to the united calling of his name, Johnson or Grant or Sherman or Howard or Logan stood up to bow. When the music of another approaching band proclaimed the advance of the next brigade, guards in front of the president's stand pushed the crowd back out of the middle of the avenue. As the afternoon wore on, more people ignored the guards and rushed to the White House side of the street, even while regiments were passing in review.

Though the last regiment of the 14th Army Corps left Capitol Hill six hours after Sherman had led the way, the crowd along Pennsylvania Avenue did not noticeably diminish in size or in the volume of its enthusiasm. The public's demonstrativeness struck men in all four corps. They heard people say: "This is the Grand Union Army that put down the rebellion," and "Do not they look like Soldiers; they have seen Service." Some onlookers raised their hands above their heads in what looked like prayer; mothers held up little children; old men wept. The soldiers whom they welcomed came in triumph but showed some of its cost. Conyngham described them as "thin, embrowned and war worn," while Mary Clemmer Ames noticed "the bronzed and haggard, and aged-in-youth faces of the boys before us," which made her think of the dead ones left behind in the South.

On the day of the review, the editorial writer for the *New York Herald* praised "Sherman's legions, who passed like a sword through the vitals of the rebellion." The veterans of the Civil War might never fight again; but it was certain that "their souls and those of their slain comrades will be marching on. On—till thrones shake and crumble at the sound of their coming, and are crushed beneath their steady tramp. On—till the people everywhere rise and demand their liberties with invincible voices. On—till no despot tyrannizes over his fellow men, and no aristocracy lords it over the down-trodden masses. On—till every nation is a republic, and every man a freeman. On—till the soldiers of Grant, Sherman and Sheridan have saved the world as they have saved the Union." Lincoln's secretaries John G. Nicolay and John Hay later summarized the significance of the grand review: "The whole country claimed these heroes as a part of themselves, an infinite gratification forever to the national self-love; and the thoughtful diplomatists who looked on the scene from the reviewing stand could not help seeing that there was a conservative force in an intelligent democracy which the world had never before known."

Throughout the morning and the early afternoon, the lengthening column of Sherman's army, after passing the reviewing stand, followed the upper streets of Washington to new camps northwest of the city. The train of supply wagons paralleled the soldiers' route on side streets. By 3:30 the review was over, the music of the last brass band moving off to the west. For a while the president, members of his cabinet, and the generals stood talking in the reviewing stand, Sherman with his arm around Grant's waist. Again the spectators filled the avenue in front of them to see the famous men as they went their separate ways. Trying to leave the stand, Sherman met a crush of people who wanted to shake his hand and give him flowers. In one hand and under his arm he put as many flowers as he could hold and, for a while, patiently shook hand after hand. But he grew less affable as he pushed down toward the street, step by step. He began to refuse the proffered hands. Finally he forced his way through the crowd, brushing men aside, and said angrily: "Damn you, get out of the way! Get out of the way!" The crowd parted; he reached his horse, mounted it, and rode away alone.

NOTES

IN THE FOLLOWING NOTES I have listed the sources for the narratives in Chapters 1, 7, and 9, as well as the sources of quotations in the other chapters. I have added citations of secondary works and some additional original sources where they seemed likely to be helpful. In the text I have reproduced the spelling and punctuation of manuscript sources without adding [*sic*]. I have made one large exception by regularizing W. T. Sherman's capitalization of the first letters of words. Sherman wrote rapidly and capitalized erratically. With his way of forming some letters of the alphabet it is impossible to tell whether he intended to write a capital letter. When publishing selections from his correspondence in his memoirs, Sherman regularized his capitalization in accordance with standard usage, and I have followed his example.

Collections of documents, manuscript repositories, books, and articles are cited in full the first time they appear in each chapter, then in shorter form thereafter. More specific citations of manuscript numbers, box numbers, and the like are included when the location of the cited document is not apparent from the arrangement of the collection.

I have dispensed with superscript numerals in the text to indicate notes and have instead used page numbers and key words to identify the relevant citations.

CHAPTER ONE

Notes for Pages 3–33

For a careful study of the origins and extent of the fire in Columbia see Marion Brunson Lucas, *Sherman and the Burning of Columbia* (College Station, Tex., 1976). For the strategic context see John G. Barrett, *Sherman's March Through the Carolinas* (Chapel Hill, N.C., 1956). My narrative is based on the following sources: A. A. Abbott, *Prison Life in the South* (New York, 1865), 124–177; J. Cutler Andrews, *The South Reports the Civil War* (Princeton, N.J., 1970), 488–495; Matthew Page Andrews, *The Women of the South in War Times* (Baltimore, Md., 1920), 247, 254; Sidney Andrews, *The South Since the War: As Shown by Fourteen Weeks of Travel and Observation in Georgia and the Carolinas* (Boston, 1866), 31–35;

Henry J. Aten, *History of the Eighty-Fifth Regiment, Illinois Volunteer Infantry* (Hiawatha, Kan., 1901), 274–275; J. P. Austin, *The Blue and the Gray: Sketches of a Portion of the Unwritten History of the Great American Civil War* (Atlanta, 1899), 158–163; Daniel B. Baker, *A Soldier's Experiences in the Civil War* (Long Beach, Calif., 1914), 46–47; *Boston Evening Transcript*, March 22, 1865; G. S. Bradley, *The Star Corps; or, Notes of an Army Chaplain, During Sherman's Famous 'March to the Sea'* (Milwaukee, Wis., 1865), 264; Alonzo L. Brown, *History of the Fourth Regiment of Minnesota Infantry Volunteers During the Great Rebellion 1861–1865* (St. Paul, Minn., 1892), 372–379; entries of Feb. 16–22, 1865, *Diary of E. P. Burton, Surgeon of the 7th Reg. Ill.* (Des Moines, Iowa, 1939), 62–64; S. H. M. Byers, "The Burning of Columbia," *Lippincott's Magazine*, XXIX (1882), 255–261; S. H. M. Byers, "Some Personal Recollections of General Sherman," *McClure's Magazine*, III (1894), 212–213; S. H. M. Byers, *With Fire and Sword* (New York, 1911), 153–173; Mrs. Campbell Bryce, *Reminiscences of the Hospitals of Columbia, S.C. During the Four Years of the Civil War* (Philadelphia, 1897), 27; Mrs. Campbell Bryce, *The Personal Experiences of Mrs. Campbell Bryce During the Burning of Columbia, South Carolina by General W. T. Sherman's Army, February 17, 1865* (Philadelphia, 1899); J. R. Boyles, *Reminiscences of the Civil War* (Columbia, S.C., 1890), 58–59; C. Vann Woodward, ed., *Mary Chesnut's Civil War* (New Haven, Conn., 1981), 568, 695, 710–722, 741, 753, 783; *Cincinnati Commercial*, Feb. 20–23, March 3, 8, 11, 17, 18, 31, 1865; *Daily Illinois State Journal* (Springfield), Feb. 20, 1865; *Daily Missouri Democrat* (St. Louis), March 24, 1865; Charles [Laforest] Dunham to Mr. and Mrs. Simeon H. Dunham, March 30, 1865, in Arthur H. DeRosier, Jr., ed., *Through the South with a Union Soldier* (Johnson City, Tenn., 1969), 168; entries of Feb. 15, 18, 20, 1865, Alexander G. Downing, *Downing's Civil War Diary*, ed. Olynthus B. Clark (Des Moines, Iowa, 1916), 253, 255; John K. Duke, *History of the Fifty-Third Regiment Ohio Volunteer Infantry During the War of the Rebellion: 1861 to 1865* (Portsmouth, Ohio, 1900), 176–181; John Smith Dye, *History of the Plots and Crimes of the Great Conspiracy to Overthrow Liberty in America* (New York, 1866), 228–230; William Andrew Fletcher, *Rebel Private Front and Rear*, ed. Bell Irvin Wiley (Austin, Tex., 1954 [orig. publ. Beaumont, Tex., 1908]), 141–144; J[oseph] Grecian, *History of the Eighty-Third Regiment, Indiana Volunteer Infantry* (Cincinnati, Ohio, 1865), 69–71, 75–76; *Harper's Weekly*, IV (1860), 757, IX (1865), 193, 200–201, 209, 217; W. B. Hazen, *A Narrative of Military Service* (Boston, 1885), 337, 346–355; J. P. Carroll, *The Burning of Columbia* (Charleston, S.C., 1888); William Wyndham Malet, *An Errand to the South in the Summer of 1862* (London, 1863), 87–88, 92; Joseph LeConte, *The Autobiography of Joseph LeConte*, ed. William Dallam Armes (New York, 1903), 141–142, 184; Joseph LeConte, *'Ware Sherman: A Journal of Three Months' Personal Experience in the Last Days of the Confederacy* (Berkeley, Calif., 1937), 80–91, 140–143; *Louisville Democrat*, March 21, 1865; Charles R. Woods to M. F. Force, June 17, 1870, in M. F. Force, *Marching Across Carolina: Read Before the Ohio Commandery of the Loyal Legion, May 2d, 1883* (Cincinnati, Ohio, 1883), 17; Alfred Lamb, *My March With Sherman to the Sea* (n.p., 1951), [7]; *News and Courier* (Charleston, S.C.), June 15, 1881; entry of Feb. 13, 1865, Edmund Newsome, *Experience in the War of the Great Rebellion* (Carbondale, Ill., 1880), 115; *New York Herald*, Feb. 19, March 2, 3, 11, 15, 18, 20, June 28, 1865; George Ward Nichols, *The Story of the Great March* (New York, 1865), 152–176; W. T. Sherman to H. W. Halleck, Dec. 24, 1864, *The War of the Rebellion: A Compilation of the Official Records of the Union and Confederate Armies* (Washington, D.C., 1880–1901), Series I, Vol. XLIV, 798–800; W. T. Sherman to H. W. Halleck, April 4, 1865, *ibid.*, Vol. XLVII, Part I, 20–23; O. M. Poe to [?], Oct. 8, 1865, *ibid.*, 170–171; Jno. Moore to W. T. Sherman, April 9, 1865, *ibid.*, 189; O. O. Howard to L. M. Dayton, April 1, 1865, *ibid.*, 196–199; John A. Logan to A. M. Van Dyke, March 31, 1865, *ibid.*, 224–229; Cha[rle]s R. Woods to Max Woodhull, Feb. 21, 1865, *ibid.*, 242–244; W. B. Woods to F. H. Wilson, March 26, 1865, *ibid.*, 252; Geo[rge] A. Stone to Fred. H. Wilson, Feb. 19, 1865, *ibid.*, 264–265; John M. Oliver to G. Lofland, March 30, 1865, *ibid.*, 310; J[udson] Kilpatrick to E. B. Beaumont, April 5, 1865, *ibid.*, 860–861; W. T. Sherman, Special Field Orders, No. 26, Feb. 16, 1865, *ibid.*, Vol. XLVII, Part II, 444–445; W. T. Sherman to [O. O.] Howard, Feb. 16, 1865, *ibid.*, 445; W. T. Sherman to [H. W.] Slocum, Feb. 16, 1865, *ibid.*, 445; John A. Logan to C. R. Woods, Feb. 16, 1865, *ibid.*, 447; C. R. Woods to Max Woodhull, Feb. 16, 1865, *ibid.*, 447; Max Woodhull to C. R. Woods, Feb. 16, 1865, *ibid.*, 447–448; W. B. Hazen to Max Woodhull, Feb. 16, 1865, *ibid.*, 448; J[udson] Kilpatrick to [W. T.] Sherman, Feb. 16, 1865, *ibid.*, 449–450; Fred. H. Wilson to Max Woodhull, Feb. 17, 1865, *ibid.*, 456–457; C. R. Woods to Max Woodhull, Feb. 17, 1865, *ibid.*, 457–458; Jno. E. Smith to M[ax] Woodhull, Feb. 17, 1865, *ibid.*, 459–460; J[ohn] M. Corse to Max Woodhull, Feb. 17, 1865, *ibid.*, 460; F[rank]

P. Blair, Special Orders, No. 44, Feb. 17, 1865, *ibid.*, 460–461; L. E. Yorke to John A. Logan, Feb. 20, 1865, *ibid.*, 502–503; A. G. Magrath to [Jefferson] Davis, Jan. 22, 1865, *ibid.*, 1035–1036; George W. Pepper, *Personal Recollections of Sherman's Campaigns in Georgia and the Carolinas* (Zanesville, Ohio, 1866), 306–318; *Philadelphia Inquirer*, Jan. 21, Feb. 23, March 11, 1865; A. Toomer Porter, *The History of a Work of Faith and Love in Charleston, South Carolina*, 4th ed. (New York, 1882), 108–121; W. T. Sherman, *Memoirs of General William T. Sherman*, 2d ed. (New York, 1886), II, 252–288; *Anderson Record* (S.C.), Feb. 17, 1937; *The Portfolio* (Columbia, S.C.), Feb. 15, 1865 [a copy of this issue is in the Henry Hitchcock Papers, Library of Congress]; [Sallie E.] Taylor *et al.*, eds., *South Carolina Women in the Confederacy*, [I] (Columbia, S.C., 1903), 200, 217–225, 243–338; Mrs. James Conner *et al.*, eds., *South Carolina Women in the Confederacy*, II (Columbia, S.C., 1907), 147–149, 178–183; James G. Gibbes, "The Burning of Columbia," *The State* (Columbia, S.C.), Feb. 23, 1908; Nixon B. Stewart, *Dan. McCook's Regiment, 52nd O. V. I. A History of the Regiment, Its Campaigns and Battles* (Alliance, Ohio, 1900), 154–156; *The Story of the Fifty-Fifth Regiment Illinois Volunteer Infantry in the Civil War, 1861–1865* (Clinton, Mass., 1887), 410; Samuel Toombs, *Reminiscences of the War, Comprising a Detailed Account of the Experiences of the Thirteenth Regiment New Jersey Volunteers* (Orange, N. J., 1878), 204; "From the Diary of a Private," *New York Times*, May 13, 1894; *Columbia Phoenix*, March 23–April 20, 1865; William A. Nicholson, *The Burning of Columbia* (Columbia, S.C., 1895); Anna Tillman Swindell, *The Burning of Columbia* (n.p., 1924); Mary S. Whilden, *Recollections of the War 1861–1865* (Columbia, S.C., 1911); Theodore F. Upson, *With Sherman to the Sea: The Civil War Letters, Diaries & Reminiscences of Theodore F. Upson*, ed. Oscar Osburn Winther (Baton Rouge, La., 1943), 150–154; entries of Feb. 13–20, 1865, Charles W. Wills, *Army Life of an Illinois Soldier Including a Day by Day Record of Sherman's March to the Sea: Letters and Diary of the Late Charles W. Wills* (Washington, D.C., 1906), 345–351; George P. Rawick, ed., *The American Slave: A Composite Autobiography* (Westport, Conn., 1972), Series I, Vol. II, South Carolina Narratives, Part Two, Narrative of John Franklin, pp. 84–86; Whitelaw Reid, *Ohio in the War: Her Statesmen, Her Generals, and Soldiers* (Cincinnati, Ohio, 1868), I, 476; Edwin J. Scott, *Random Recollections of a Long Life, 1806 to 1876* (Columbia, S.C., 1884), 59–86, 168–210; Mrs. D. Giraud Wright, *A Southern Girl in '61: The War-Time Memories of a Confederate Senator's Daughter* (New York, 1905), 228–229; D. Leib Ambrose, *History of the Seventh Regiment Illinois Volunteer Infantry* (Springfield, Ill., 1868), 296–298; August Conrad, *The Destruction of Columbia, S.C.*, trans. W[illia]m H. Pleasants (Roanoke, Va., 1902 [orig. publ. Hanover, 1879]); David P. Conyngham, *Sherman's March Through the South. With Sketches and Incidents of the Campaign* (New York, 1865), 324–339; James Wood Davidson, "Who Burned Columbia?" *The World* (New York), June 17, 1875; John William Draper, *History of the American Civil War* (New York, 1870), III, 546–551; Michael C. Garber, Jr., "Reminiscences of the Burning of Columbia, South Carolina," *Indiana Magazine of History*, XI (1915), 285–300; George W. Nichols, "The Burning of Columbia," *Harper's New Monthly Magazine*, XXXIII (1866), 363–366; James McCarter, "The Burning of Columbia Again," *ibid.*, 642–647; F. Y. Hedley, *Marching Through Georgia* (Chicago, 1890), 365–391; James D. Hill, "The Burning of Columbia Reconsidered," *South Atlantic Quarterly*, XXV (1926), 269–282; Oliver Otis Howard, *Autobiography of Oliver Otis Howard* (New York, 1908), II, 118–128; entries of Feb. 17–20, 1865, Oscar L. Jackson, *The Colonel's Diary*, ed. David P. Jackson [Sharon, Pa., 1922], 182–185; Matthew H. Jamison, *Recollections of Pioneer and Army Life* (Kansas City, Mo., 1911), 308–311; William Benjamin Johnson, *"Union to the Hub and Twice Around the Tire": Reminiscences of the Civil War* (n.p., 1950), 85–87 [pagination from typescript, Library of Congress]; Henry W. Slocum, "Sherman's March from Savannah to Bentonville," Robert Underwood Johnson and Clarence Clough Buel, eds., *Battles and Leaders of the Civil War* (New York, 1888), IV, 686; Henry S. Nourse, "The Burning of Columbia, S.C., February 17, 1865," *Papers of the Military Historical Society of Massachusetts*, IX (1912), 419–447; Edward Sill, "Who Is Responsible for the Destruction of the City of Columbia, S.C., on the Night of 17th February, 1865?" *The Land We Love*, IV (1868), 361–369; Francis Butler Simkins and James Welch Patton, *The Women of the Confederacy* (Richmond, Va., 1936), 271, n. 80; T. H. Ellis, "Columbia—As Seen by a Rebel Scouting Party the Day After Sherman's Evacuation," *The Southern Bivouac*, I (1882), 74–78; E. L. Welles, "Who Burnt Columbia? Testimony of a Confederate Cavalryman," *Southern Historical Society Papers*, X (1882), 109–119; "Who Burned Columbia?—General Sherman's Latest Story Examined," *ibid.*, XIII (1885), 448–453; [Hosea Whitford Rood], *Story of the Service of Company E, and of the Twelfth Wisconsin Regiment, Veteran Volunteer Infantry, in the War of the Rebellion* (Milwaukee, Wis., 1893), 407–409; H. G. McArthur, *Personal Experiences and Recollections of Major H. G. McArthur* (n.p., n.d.); [William Gilmore Simms], *Sack and Destruction of the City of Columbia, S.C.* (Columbia, S.C., 1865); Hallie Boyles, "Octavia Chaires Manuscript," *Tallahassee Democrat,* June 2, 1963; *Mixed Commission on British and American Claims, Appendix—Testimony* (Washington, D.C., 1873), XXIII; J. T. Trowbridge, *The South: A Tour of Its Battle-Fields and Ruined Cities* (Hartford, Conn., 1866), chap. 77; Clinton [?] to wife, Feb. 18, 1865, James Porter Crane Letters, Atlanta Historical Society, Atlanta, Georgia; entries of Feb. 12–20, 1865, Diary of Major T. W. Osborn, Bowdoin College, Brunswick, Maine; [Oliver] Otis [Howard] to [Elizabeth Howard], [ca. March 6], 1865, O. O. Howard Papers, *ibid.;* entry of Feb. 17, 1865, John W. Bates, Diary, Civil War Miscellaneous Collection, United States Army Military History Institute, Carlisle Barracks, Pennsylvania; entries of Feb. 15–18, 1865, Ensign H. King, Diary, *ibid.;* Frank L. Ferguson, [Reminiscences], *Civil War Times Illustrated* Collection, *ibid.;* entries of Jan. 13–Feb. 14, 1865, Jacob Heffelfinger, Diary, *ibid.;* entry of Feb. 17, 1865, Henry Hurter, Diary, *ibid.;* entries of Feb. 12–19, 1865, Edward E. Schweitzer, Diary, *ibid.;* entries of Feb. 12–18, 1865, J[ames] R. M. Gaskill, Memoranda, Chicago Historical Society, Chicago, Illinois; [Thomas] Edwin Smith to [Maria Smith], January [i.e., March] 14, [1865], Thomas E. Smith Letters, Box 2, Cincinnati Historical Society, Cincinnati, Ohio; Andrew Hickenlooper, Personal Reminiscences, I, 301–325, 330–331, Andrew Hickenlooper Collection, Box 1, *ibid.;* Andrew Hickenlooper to Maria Smith, March 28, 1865, Box 9, *ibid.;* Hiram Calkins to James G. Bennett, Feb. 23, 1865, James Gordon Bennett Papers, Perkins Library, Duke University, Durham, North Carolina; R[achel] S[usan] C[heves] to [J. R. Cheves], March 2, 18, 1865, Rachel Susan Cheves Papers, *ibid;* [Rachel Susan Cheves], [Statement, ca. 1866], *ibid.;* R[achel] S[usan] C[heves] to Dr. Reynolds, [ca. 1866], *ibid.;* H[arriott] H[orry] Ravenel to R. N. Gourdin, January 21, 1865, Robert Newman Gourdin Papers, *ibid.;* J[ane] M[urphy] Cronly, "Some Incidents of the War as Personally Experienced," 18, Cronly Family Papers, *ibid.;* Paul H. Hayne to [Eugene Lemoine] Didier, May 3, 1877, and Paul H. Hayne to [Elizabeth Oakes Prince Smith], June 19, 1882, Paul Hamilton Hayne Papers, *ibid.;* R. B. Hoadley to Cousin Em, April 8, 1865, Robert Bruce Hoadley Papers, *ibid.;* Sam. W. Snow to parents, March 28, 1865, Snow Family Papers, *ibid.;* Ellen Kerrison, "Reminiscences of the Burning of Columbia," United Daughters of the Confederacy, South Carolina Division, Edgefield Chapter, Papers, *ibid.;* entries of Feb. 13, 18–20, 1865, Anthony J. Baurdick, Diary, Woodruff Library, Emory University, Atlanta, Georgia; W[illiam] Baugh to father, n.d., and William Baugh to parents, March 14, 27, 1865, William G. Baugh Letters, *ibid.;* Augustine [Smythe] to mother, Feb. 9, 1865, Daniel McCord Wright Papers, Box 42, Georgia Historical Society, Savannah; Louisa Cheves Smythe, [*re* Burning of Columbia], *ibid.;* R. W. Gibbes to [Samuel Jackson], June 14, 1865, Dr. Samuel Jackson Folder, Society Miscellaneous Collection, Historical Society of Pennsylvania, Philadelphia; [?] to W. T. Sherman, Dec. 30, 1872, John Wanamaker Scrap Book, *ibid.;* Wade Hampton to John P. Nicholson, July 28, 1875, John P. Nicholson Collection, Henry E. Huntington Library, San Marino, California; John P. Nicholson, Scrapbook on the Burning of Columbia, *ibid.;* W. T. Sherman to [Willard] Warner, Aug. 3, 1881, William Tecumseh Sherman Letters, Illinois State Historical Library, Springfield; Benjamin H. Grierson, "The Lights and Shadows of Life: Including Experiences and Remembrances of the War of the Rebellion," 734–736, Benjamin H. Grierson Papers, Box 21, *ibid.;* entry of Feb. 17, 1865, Charles H. Brush, Diary, Brush Family Papers, Box 1, *ibid.;* entries of Feb. 17–19, 1865, George L. Childress, Diary, *ibid.;* entries of Feb. 13–18, 1865, William E. Strong, "Extracts from Journal," 229–253, William E. Strong Papers, *ibid.;* entries of Feb. 10, 14, 16–18, 1865, George N. Compton, Diary, *ibid.;* entries of Feb. 13, 18, 1865, Charles Gottlieb Michael, Diary, Indiana Historical Society, Indianapolis; entries of Feb. 17, 18, 20, 1865, Eli J. Sherlock, Diary, *ibid.;* John J. Hardin to father and mother, March 29, 1865, John J. Hardin Papers, Indiana State Library, Indianapolis; entries of Feb. 12–15, 1865, James Edwin Catlin, Diary, Iowa State Historical Society, Iowa City; entries of Feb. 13, 15–17, 20, 1865, R. J. McQuilkin, Diary, *ibid.;* entries of Feb. 17–18, 1865, John Gay, Diary, *ibid.;* [Jacob Ritner] to [Emeline Ritner], n.d. [March 1865] and March 14–15, 1865, Jacob Ritner Letters, *ibid.;* Geo[rge] W. Keckler to Clint Parkhurst, Feb. 17, 1915, Henry Clinton Parkhurst Collection, Box 1, *ibid.;* Emma [Niernsee] Atkinson, "Granny's Recollections for Her Grandchildren," Oct. 31, 1927, 1–17, March 12, 1934, 5–6, Niernsee Family Papers, Maryland Historical Society, Baltimore; entries of Feb. 17, 20, 1865, E. P. Failing, Diary, Failing-Knight Papers, Massachusetts Historical Society, Boston; entries of Feb. 16–17, 1865, Samuel Storrow, Diary, *ibid.;* James E. Love to [E. M.

Wilson], Jan. 29, Feb. 4–16, 1865, James E. Love Papers, Missouri Historical Society, St. Louis; John J. Safely to Mary McEwen, Dec. 22, 1864, and April 9, 1865, McEwen Papers, *ibid.;* Petition of Amelia Feaster to United States Senate and House of Representatives, June 26, 1866, 39th Congress, Senate 39A-H1-H2, Box 33, Petitions and Memorials, Claims, A–L, National Archives, Washington, D.C.; Exhibits H, J, X, in support of H. R. 14529, Records of the United States House of Representatives, 63rd Congress, HR 63A–F 38.1, Record Group 233, *ibid.;* W. T. Sherman to [O. O.] Howard, Feb. 15, 1865, T. J. Goodwyn, Certificate, Feb. 19, 1865, and O. O. Howard to W. T. Sherman, Feb. 20, 1865, Military Division of the Mississippi, Letters Received, Box 3, Record Group 393, Part 1, No. 2484, *ibid.;* A. R. Chisolm, "Life and War Experience of a Confederate Aide-de-camp serving under Generals Beauregard, Lee and Johnston," chap. 17, 10–11, and A. R. Chisolm, "Notes personal of Lieut Col Alex Robt. Chisolm relative to the War of Secession," 75–79, A. R. Chisolm Papers, New-York Historical Society, New York, New York; J. G. Burr to D. L. Swain, June 18, 1866, Walter Clark Papers, Volume 4, North Carolina Division of Archives and History, Raleigh; W. T. Sherman to [Henry S.] Turner, June 18, 1881, W. T. Sherman Papers, Ohio Historical Society, Columbus; W. T. Sherman, [Autobiography], [1868], 47–48, *ibid.;* C. Irvine Walker to W. T. Hewett, March 5, 1914, W. T. Hewett Papers, Princeton University, Princeton, New Jersey; W. T. Hewett, Notebooks 1–6, *ibid.;* W. T. Sherman, Notes on Special Field Order No. 26, Feb. 16, 1865, W. T. Sherman Papers, Library of Congress, Washington, D.C.; Jno. W. G. to sister, March 1, 1865, *ibid.;* Ezra D. Carpenter to W. T. Sherman, March 8 and April 2, 1866, *ibid.;* Charles R. Woods to W. T. Sherman, April 7, 1866, *ibid.;* W. T. Sherman, "Abstract of the Georgia & Carolina Campaigns of 1864–5," [Feb. 17, 1867], *ibid.;* C. P. Kingsbury to W. T. Sherman, July 4, 1868, *ibid.;* W. T. S[herman], [Answers to Interrogatories], Testimony of Genl W. T. Sherman in the case of A. Barclay vs. the U.S., March 26, 1872, *ibid.;* A. P. Wood to W. T. Sherman, June 19, 1873, *ibid.;* H. W. Benham to W. T. Sherman, June 28, 1873, *ibid.;* John A. Lynch to W. T. Sherman, July 10, 1873, *ibid.;* Herman Bader to J. Holt, Sept. 15, 1873, *ibid.;* B. F. Potts to W. T. Sherman, Sept. 19, 1873, *ibid.;* J. L. Dunn to W. T. Sherman, Sept. 19, 1873, *ibid.;* H. L. Clark to W. T. Sherman, June 28 and July 12, 1875, *ibid.;* Carlos J. Stolbrand to W. T. Sherman, June 19, 1881, *ibid.;* W. P. Chapman to W. T. Sherman, June 22, 1881, *ibid.;* M. C. Osborn to W. T. Sherman, July 29, 1881, *ibid.;* S. C. Logan to W. T. Sherman, Oct. 18, 1886, *ibid.;* A. E. Wood to W. T. Sherman, Feb. 13, 1888, *ibid.;* W. T. Sherman to Editor, [Washington] *Chronicle,* Sept. 12, 1873, Letterbooks, Volume 90, *ibid.;* W. T. Sherman to William Martin, March 20, 1874, *ibid.;* W. T. Sherman to Joseph G. Breckinridge, June 27, 1887, Volume 98, *ibid.;* entry of Feb. 17, 1865, Diary of a Private in the 66th Illinois Volunteers, W. T. Sherman Scrapbooks, Volume 109, *ibid.;* Harriette C. Keatinge, [Narrative of the Burning of Columbia, S.C.], Harriette C. Keatinge Papers, Library of Congress; W. T. Sherman to William Carson, March 11, 1888, and W. T. Sherman to Caroline Carson, April 5, 1888, James L. Petigru Papers, *ibid.;* entry of Dec. 13, 1864, Diary of Henry Hitchcock, Henry Hitchcock Papers, *ibid.;* H[enry Hitchcock] to [Mary Hitchcock], March 12, 1865, *ibid.;* Wade Hampton to L. J. Cist, Aug. 11, 1867, Wade Hampton Personal Miscellany, *ibid.;* entry of Feb. 17, 1865, W. C. Johnson, "Through the Carolinas to Goldsboro, N.C.," W. C. Johnson Personal Miscellany, *ibid.;* entries of Feb. 15–17, 1865, John N. Ferguson, Diary, John N. Ferguson Personal Miscellany, *ibid.;* [Louise Clack], "My Experience of the Civil War of 1861–1865 by a New Orleans Woman," 6–7, Robert L. Nicholson Collection, *ibid.;* W[illia]m C. P. Breckinridge to Issa D. Breckinridge, Feb. 17, 18, 1865, Breckinridge Family Papers, Volume 240, *ibid.;* U. S. Grant to W. T. Sherman, Dec. 19, 1864, Orlando M. Poe Papers, *ibid.;* O. M. Poe to Col. Yates, Feb. 16, 18, 1865, and O. M. Poe to R. Delafield, April 1, 1865, Poe Letterbooks, *ibid.;* L[ydia] M. J[ohnston] to [Louise Sophia Wigfall], Feb. 19, 1865, Wigfall Family Papers, Box 1, *ibid.;* [James] McCarter, Mr. McCarter's Journal, chaps. 24–26, McCarter Personal Miscellany, *ibid.;* W. T. Sherman to Ellen [Sherman], March 12, 1865, William Tecumseh Sherman Papers, University of Notre Dame, Notre Dame, Indiana; entries of Feb. 16–18, 1865, W. T. Sherman, Diary, *ibid.;* unidentified newspaper clipping, [ca. April 1, 1872], Thomas Ewing Sherman Scrapbook, *ibid.;* entry of March 22, 1865, Annie DeVeaux, Diary, South Carolina Historical Society, Charleston; A. G. Magrath to J. C. Breckinridge, Feb. 28, 1865, Andrew Gordon Magrath Letterbooks, *ibid.;* A. G. Magrath, Message to Senate and House of Representatives, April 26, 1865, Orders, Messages, etc., *ibid.;* Notes from Rose Ravenel's Account, Mrs. St. Julien Ravenel Papers, Box 11–333, *ibid.;* T. Pinckney Lowndes to Aunt Becky, July 17, 1865, Box 11–334, *ibid.;* Entry of Sept. 4, 1864, Adele Allston Vanderhorst,

Diary, *ibid.;* [Harriott Middleton] to Susan [Middleton], Feb. 28, March 2, 10, 21, 29, April 5, 1865, Cheves-Middleton Papers, Box 12-167, *ibid.;* Harriet Poyas Walker to W. T. Sherman, Feb. 27, 1888, enclosed in W. T. Sherman to W. F. Vilas, March 4, 1888, William F. Vilas Papers, State Historical Society of Wisconsin, Madison; M[ichael] Griffin to [Samuel] Glyde [Swain], April 1, 1865, Samuel Glyde Swain Papers, Box 1, *ibid.;* Mrs. John Dimitry, "Memminger's Canaries," 5, Louisiana Historical Association Collection, Series 65-B, Box 24, Howard-Tilton Library, Tulane University, New Orleans, Louisiana; Frank Schaller to W[illia]m Preston Johnston, Jan. 21, 1866, Albert Sidney Johnston and William Preston Johnston Papers, Box 13, *ibid.;* entries of Feb. 16–18, 1865, C. C. Platter, Diary, University of Georgia, Athens; [Henry G. Noble] to [Ruth], March 14, 1865, Henry G. Noble Letters, Michigan Historical Collection, Bentley Library, University of Michigan, Ann Arbor; entries of Feb. 14, 17, 1865, John Wesley Daniels, Diary, *ibid.;* William Baird, [Reminiscences], 88–100, *ibid.;* entries of Feb. 11–20, 1865, Jesse S. Bean, Diary, Southern Historical Collection, University of North Carolina, Chapel Hill; J[ulia] E. Lee to Sallie, n.d. [ca. Sept. 26, 1900], Mrs. J. Hardy Lee Papers, *ibid.;* James Achille de Caradeuc, "The War," 11–12, de Caradeuc Papers, *ibid.;* Lawrence W. Taylor, "Boy Soldiers of the Confederacy," 4–7, Franklin Harper Elmore Papers, *ibid.;* Mrs. Sally Elmore Taylor, "Memoir of Mrs. Sally Elmore Taylor written by Herself, 1908–1910," 108–112, *ibid.;* entries of Feb. 11, 16, 1865, William W. Gordon, Diary, *ibid.;* E. W. Nims to Millie, Oct. 30, 1865, Elizabeth White Nims Papers, *ibid.;* [R. S. Finley] to M. A. C[abeen], March 30, 1865, Robert Stuart Finley Papers, *ibid.;* A. G. Magrath to R. E. Lee, Jan. 16, 1865, A. G. Magrath to [Jefferson] Davis, Jan. 21, 22, 1865, R. E. Lee to A. G. Magrath, Jan. 27, 1865, W. J. Hardee to R. E. Lee, Feb. 6, 1865, W. Porcher Miles to A. G. Magrath, Feb. 8, 1865, Andrew Gordon Magrath Papers, South Caroliniana Library, University of South Carolina, Columbia; John R. Niernsee, Special Report of the Acting Commissioner and Architect of the New State House, April 20, 1865, *ibid.;* E. V. Ravenel to [Allan Macfarlan], March 21, 1865, Allan Macfarlan Papers, *ibid.;* Daniel Heyward Trezevant, "Burning of Columbia," *ibid.;* Mrs. H. H. Simons, "The Burning of Columbia," *ibid.;* Mary Leverette to Caroline, March 18, 1865, *ibid.;* Peter J. Shand to Mrs. Howard Kennedy, March 9, 1868, *ibid.;* Harriott H. Ravenel, "Burning of Columbia, 1865," *ibid.;* S. Sosnowski, "Burning of Columbia," Sosnowski-Schaller Family Papers, *ibid.;* R. W. Gibbes to [A. G. Magrath], Feb. 28, 1865, R. W. G[ibbes] to Allston, March 14, [1865], Robert Wilson Gibbes Papers, Box 2, *ibid.;* Mrs. W. K. Bachman to Kate Bachman, March 27, 1865, *ibid.;* Kate Bachman, "Read Before the Daughters of the Confederacy on the Birthday of Jefferson Davis June 1898," 17–24, *ibid.;* T. J. Goodwyn to [Colin Campbell] Murchison, June 8, 1866, *ibid.;* Yates Snowden, "Sherman—Burning of Columbia," Scrapbook, *ibid.;* Wade Hampton to *New York Day Book,* June 15, 1865, Wade Hampton to [James Parsons] Carroll, May 25, 1866, Wade Hampton to [P. G. T.] Beauregard, April 22, 1866, [Wade Hampton] to [Mary H. Hampton], June 8, 1866, Wade Hampton to [Daniel Heyward] Trezevant, Dec. 27, 1872, Hampton Family Papers, Box 5, *ibid.;* John A. Palmer to Joseph A. Woodward, March 1, 1866, *ibid.;* L. Blanch Johnston, "Sherman's March to the Sea," *ibid.;* Julia [Gott] to [Ann], Feb. 27, 1865, Julia Gott Papers, *ibid.;* Anonymous, [MS Account of the Burning of Columbia], *ibid.;* Sister Charles to Bettie Ridley, July 9, 1866, Anna and Bettie Ridley Collection, *ibid.;* Louisa McCord, "Recollections of Louisa Rebecca Hayne McCord," 54–66, *ibid.;* Emily Geiger Goodlett, "The Burning of Columbia by Sherman," *ibid.;* Ella R. Glass, [Reminiscences of the Burning of Columbia], Glass Family Papers, *ibid.;* Chloe A. Carwile, "Recollections of the Burning of Columbia," *ibid.;* entries of Feb. 17–19, 1865, C. G. Ward, Diary, *ibid.;* Mary to Mrs. Smythe-Flynn Papers, Box 1, *ibid.;* Scrapbook, Volume 1, Girls of the Sixties Collection, *ibid.;* entries of Feb. 11–17, 1865, Emily Caroline Ellis, Diary, *ibid.;* R[obert] W[ilson] to Robert [Shand], Dec. 31, 1913, Shand Family Papers, *ibid.;* Sallie Coles Heyward, [Reminiscences], *ibid.;* W[illia]m Stokes to wife, Feb. 12, 15, March 2, 3, 1865, William Stokes Papers, *ibid.;* Robert Wallace Shand, "Incidents in the Life of a Private Soldier," 128–130, *ibid.;* [Robert Wilson] to Robert [Shand], March 1, 1865, *ibid.;* entries of Dec. 31, 1864–Feb. 28, 1865, Emma Florence LeConte, Journal, *ibid.;* entries of Feb. 13–21, 1865, Grace Elmore, Diary, *ibid.;* [Augustus Robert Taft], [Diary of Events in Winnsboro, S.C.], *ibid.;* L[eroy] F[ranklin] Y[oumans] to Mary, March 11, 1865, *ibid.;* Yates Snowden, "The Burning of Columbia," Yates Snowden Papers, Box 38, *ibid.;* entries of Feb. 13–20, 1865, Edward Abijah Rowley, Diary, *ibid.;* John McKenzie, "Who Pillaged and Burnt Columbia?" Thomas Legare Papers, *ibid.;* J[oseph] Wheeler to D. H. Hill, Feb. 2, 1865, Narrative of W. E. Johnson, March 15, 1866, John LeConte to D. H. Hill, April

30, 1866, Wade Hampton to D. H. Hill, Dec. 4, 1865, Wade Hampton to Editors of the *Day Book,* June 19, 1865, Deposition of Orlando Z. Bates, June 16, 1865, Deposition of John McKenzie, June 19, 1865, Deposition of Robert W. Gibbes, June 1865, Statement of John Stork, April 27, 1866, Statement of T. J. Goodwyn, April 9, 1866, Statement of J. W. Parker, March 15, 1866, Statement of John McKenzie, March 18, 1866, Statement of C. Bruce Walker, March 19, 1866, Statement of Orlando Z. Bates, March 19, 1866, Statement of John R. Niernsee, March 25, 1866, Statement of James G. Gibbes, March 30, 1866, D. H. Hill Papers, Box 9, Virginia State Library, Richmond; Statement of W[illia]m H. Orchard, May 1, 1866, Box 10, *ibid.;* entries of Feb. 15–19, 1865, William David Evans Diary, Western Reserve Historical Society, Cleveland, Ohio; W. T. Sherman to [Carlos Johan] Stolbrand, June 20, 1881, W. T. Sherman Collection, Bancroft Library, University of California, Berkeley; Ira B. Sampson, "My Second Escape from a Southern Military Prison," Schoff Collection, Soldiers' Diaries, Box 6, Clements Library, University of Michigan, Ann Arbor.

CHAPTER TWO

Notes for Pages 34–78

34 "I believe . . . country"]   H[arriott] H[orry] Ravenel to mother, [Sept. 1862], Mrs. St. Julien Ravenel Papers, Box 11–333, South Carolina Historical Society, Charleston.

"The torch . . . policy"]   Senate, Jan. 10, 1861, *Congressional Globe,* 36th Congress, 2d Session, 310.

35 "I only pray . . . utterly"]   Annie R. Maney to Bettie Kimberly, May 12, 1861, quoted in Stephen V. Ash, *Middle Tennessee Society Transformed, 1860–1870: War and Peace in the Upper South* (Baton Rouge, La., 1987), 78.

"The bombardment . . . senses"]   *Memphis Avalanche,* reprinted in Frank Moore, ed., *The Rebellion Record: A Diary of American Events* (New York, 1861–1868), II, 75.

"desolations . . . Rio Grande"]   *Norfolk Day Book,* Feb. 28, 1862, reprinted in *New York Herald,* March 4, 1862. See also John Letcher to Francis W. Pickens, April 28, 1862, James S. Schoff Civil War Collection, Letters and Documents, Box 5, Clements Library, University of Michigan, Ann Arbor; [J. D. B.] DeBow to [Charles] Gayarré, June 22, 1862, Charles E. A. Gayarré Papers, Louisiana State University, Baton Rouge.

37 "make . . . war"]   House of Representatives, Sept. 11–12, 1862, Proceedings of First Confederate Congress, Second Session, *Southern Historical Society Papers,* XLVI (1928), 107, 125. See also *Memphis Appeal* (Grenada, Miss.), Sept. 15, 1862. On Lee's calculations in 1862 and 1863 see Louis H. Manarin, "Lee in Command: Strategical and Tactical Policies" (Ph.D. diss., Duke University, 1964), 339–358, 421–422, 453–454, 466.

"We . . . Virginia"]   *Richmond Dispatch,* Sept. 17, 1862.

"were . . . public"]   Edward A. Pollard, *The Lost Cause; A New Southern History of the War of the Confederates* (New York, 1866), 310.

"make . . . destroyed"]   Elise Bragg to [Braxton Bragg], Aug. 13, 1862, Braxton Bragg Papers, Box 3, Western Reserve Historical Society, Cleveland, Ohio. See also Braxton [Bragg] to [Elise Bragg], Sept. 18, 1862, Braxton Bragg Papers, Missouri Historical Society, St. Louis; Braxton Bragg to [Elise Bragg], Nov. 9, 1862, 63M336, University of Kentucky, Lexington; Grady McWhiney, *Braxton Bragg and Confederate Defeat* (New York, 1969), I, 199–200; *Memphis Appeal* (Grenada, Miss.), Sept. 10, 1862.

"The only . . . begin it"]   [A. S. Pendleton] to [Kate Corbin], June 28, 1863, William Nelson Pendleton Papers, Southern Historical Collection, University of North Carolina, Chapel Hill.

"One feels . . . army"]   Halsey [Wigfall] to [Louis T. Wigfall], Aug. 4, 1864, Wigfall Family Papers, Box 3, Manuscript Division, Library of Congress, Washington, D.C.

37–8 "Let . . . waste"]   *Savannah Republican,* June 23, 26, 1863.

38 "and let . . . two years"]   John S. Foster to Jennie Ralston, May 12, 1863, James Foster Correspondence, Louisiana State University.

38 "cut . . . go"]   E. P. Petty to [Margaret Petty], [May 1863], Norman D. Brown, ed., *Journey to Pleasant Hill: The Civil War Letters of Captain Elijah P. Petty, Walker's Texas Division CSA* (San Antonio, Tex., 1982), 213.

"mistaken philanthropy"]   *Mobile Tribune*, March 6, 1864. See also *Richmond Whig*, June 20, 1864.

"It . . . flames"]   Howell Cobb, Jr., to [Mary McKinley], Dec. 19, 1864, Cobb-Erwin-Lamar Collection, University of Georgia, Athens.

"In retaliation . . . train"]   Kennedy quoted in Martin Burke to [John A.] Dix, March 25, 1865, *The War of the Rebellion: A Compilation of the Official Records of the Union and Confederate Armies* (Washington, D.C., 1880–1901), Series II, Vol. VIII, 429.

"Reliance . . . work"]   Jacob Thompson to Judah P. Benjamin, Dec. 3, 1864, quoted in John G. Nicolay and John Hay, *Abraham Lincoln: A History* (New York, 1890), VIII, 22. See Nat Brandt, *The Man Who Tried to Burn New York* (Syracuse, N.Y., 1986); Frank L. Klement, *Dark Lanterns: Secret Political Societies, Conspiracies, and Treason Trials in the Civil War* (Baton Rouge, La., 1984), 189–191.

39 "There were . . . destruction"]   Entry of July 30, 1864, J. Kelly Bennette, Diary, University of North Carolina.

"We . . . country"]   Fielder C. Slingluff, "The Burning of Chambersburg," *Southern Historical Society Papers*, XXXVII (1909), 155.

"he . . . negroes"]   B. S. Schneck, *The Burning of Chambersburg, Pennsylvania* (Philadelphia, 1864), 53.

"burning . . . satisfaction"]   Entry of Aug. 6, 1864, Frank E. Vandiver, ed., *The Civil War Diary of General Josiah Gorgas* (University, Ala., 1947), 131. See also J. A. Early to B. T. Johnson, April 16, 1881, Bradley T. Johnson Papers, Swem Library, College of William and Mary, Williamsburg, Virginia; Jubal Anderson Early, *Autobiographical Sketch and Narrative of the War Between the States* (Philadelphia, 1912), 404; *Richmond Whig*, Aug. 5, 1864.

40 "defend . . . prisoners"]   T. J. Jackson to [Thomas Jackson Arnold], Jan. 26, 1861. This letter is printed in Thomas Jackson Arnold, *Early Life and Letters of General Thomas J. Jackson "Stonewall Jackson"* (New York, 1916), 293–294. The printed version substitutes ellipses for the words "even to taking no prisoners," which appear in a copy of the letter owned by the Virginia Military Institute, Lexington. For further confirmation of Jackson's preference for such a policy, see R. L. Dabney, *Life and Campaigns of Lieut.-Gen. Thomas J. Jackson (Stonewall Jackson)* (New York, 1866), 192, and R. L. Dabney to *The Sun* (Baltimore), June 15, 1889.

"proposing . . . himself"]   *Daily South Carolinian* (Columbia), Feb. 6, 1864.

"In one . . . service to us"]   T. J. Jackson to [A. R. Boteler], [Feb. 1862], Thomas J. Jackson Personal Miscellany, New-York Historical Society, New York, New York.

"Let us . . . earnest"]   T. J. Jackson to A. R. Boteler, March 3, 1862, *ibid.*

"invade . . . time"]   James R. Graham, "Reminiscences of Gen. T. J. ('Stonewall') Jackson," in Mary Anna Jackson, *Memoirs of Stonewall Jackson* (Louisville, Ky., 1895), 494.

"It would . . . Penn."]   R. E. Lee to [Jefferson] Davis, June 5, 1862, Douglas Southall Freeman, ed., *Lee's Dispatches: Unpublished Letters of General Robert E. Lee* (New York, 1913), 5–6. See also [R. L. Dabney, Notes], "Hon. A. R. Boteler states . . ." Charles William Dabney Papers, Box 32, University of North Carolina.

"I am . . . Potomac"]   T. J. Jackson to A. R. Boteler, March 7, 1863, Thomas J. Jackson Papers, Washington and Lee University, Lexington, Virginia.

41 "he desired . . . bitter" and "replied . . . rears"]   J[ohn] Chamblin to D. H. Hill, May 25, 1885, D. H. Hill Papers, Box 10, Virginia State Library, Richmond.

"destroy . . . point"]   G. F. R. Henderson, *Stonewall Jackson and the American Civil War* (New York, 1961 [orig. pub. London, 1898]), 133. See also Mary Anna Jackson, *Life and Letters of General Thomas J. Jackson (Stonewall Jackson)* (New York, 1891), 313–315; A. R. Boteler, "Stonewall Jackson in the Campaign of 1862," *Southern Historical Society Papers*, XL (1915), 165, 172–173; Dabney, *Life and Campaigns of Jackson*, 486.

41 "I shall . . . beasts"]   John D. Imboden to Jefferson Davis, March 2, 1861 [1862], John D. Imboden to T. J. Jackson, April 29, 1862, Letters Received by Confederate Secretary of War, 1861–1865, Microcopy No. 437, Reel No. 54, National Archives, Washington, D.C.

"The difficulty . . . service"]   T. J. Jackson to R. L. Dabney, March 29, 1862, Robert L. Dabney Papers, Union Theological Seminary in Virginia, Richmond.

"black revolution"]   *New York Herald*, Oct. 30, 1860.

"for our people . . . first" and "that when . . . country"]   R. L. Dabney to *The Sun* (Baltimore), June 15, 1889.

42 "what Stonewall . . . short"]   S. H. M. Byers, "Some Personal Recollections of General Sherman," *McClure's Magazine*, III (1894), 218.

Sumner]   Charles Sumner to [Richard Henry] Dana, [May 31, 1862], Dana Family Papers, Box 16, Massachusetts Historical Society, Boston.

"genuine general"]   Adam Gurowski, *Diary, From March 4, 1861, to November 12, 1862* (Boston, 1862), 213.

"Jackson . . . feared"]   Alfred Brundage to Fannie, June 14, 1862, *Kenneth W. Rendell Catalogue 96* (1974), Item 34.

43 "Running . . . Jackson"]   Entry of June 26, 1862, Journal of Eliza Woolsey Howland, in Georgeanna Woolsey Bacon, ed., *Letters of a Family During the War for the Union, 1861–1865* (n.p., 1899), II, 428.

"Stonewall . . . *guerre*"]   *New York Times*, July 4, 1862.

"sudden . . . armies"]   *Harper's Weekly*, VI (July 19, 1862), 450.

audacity]   *New York Times*, July 11, 1862; *Cincinnati Commercial*, July 15, 1862.

"He has . . . either side"]   [Henry W. Bellows] to [Thomas Starr] King, July 4, 1862, Henry W. Bellows Papers, Massachusetts Historical Society.

"ubiquitous . . . flanks"]   Wilbur Fisk Letters, Letter No. 13, Sept. 6, 1862, *Northern Virginia Daily* (Strasburg), June 17, 1965.

"swearing . . . men"]   Andrew [Duncan] to sister, Sept. 3, 1862, William McKinley Collection, Box 2, Western Reserve Historical Society.

"Look out . . . Philadelphia"]   Samuel E. Radcliffe to father, Sept. 9, 1862, Schoff Civil War Collection, Letters and Documents, Box 10, Clements Library.

44 "the greatest . . . demon"]   George E. Farmer to father, Sept. 10, 1862, George E. Farmer Papers, Washington University, St. Louis, Mo.

"drop . . . them"]   *New York Herald*, Sept. 9, 1862.

"Escape . . . rascal"]   John W. Geary to Mary [Geary], Nov. 16, 1862, John W. Geary Collection, Atlanta Historical Society, Atlanta, Georgia. See also Michael C. C. Adams, *Our Masters the Rebels: A Speculation on Union Military Failure in the East, 1861–1865* (Cambridge, Mass., 1978), 129.

black people]   R. Mead, Jr., to folks at home, May 28, 1862, Rufus Mead, Jr., Papers, Library of Congress; entry of May 24, 1862, Laura Lee, Diary, College of William and Mary; entry of May 25, 1862, Cecil D. Eby, Jr., ed., *A Virginia Yankee in the Civil War: The Diaries of David Hunter Strother* (Chapel Hill, N.C., 1961), 43.

"No man . . . freedom"]   *New York Herald*, Jan. 22, 1863; entry of Jan. 24, 1863, Diary of Jedediah Hotchkiss, Jedediah Hotchkiss Papers, Library of Congress. See also James B. Stewart, *Wendell Phillips: Liberty's Hero* (Baton Rouge, La., 1986), 219–228.

"God of vengeance"]   Donn Piatt and Henry V. Boynton, *General George H. Thomas: A Critical Biography* (Cincinnati, Ohio, 1893), 94.

44 "unique and irresistible"]   William Swinton, *Campaigns of the Army of the Potomac* (New York, 1866), 289–290.

"the bluest . . . Presbyterian"]   Entry of July 5, 1862, William Owner, Diary, Library of Congress.

45 "pride . . . birth"]   [Catherine Cooper Hopley], *"Stonewall" Jackson, Late General of the Confederate States Army* (London, 1863), 174.

"an honorable . . . man"]   *Harper's Weekly,* VI (Aug. 30, 1862), 556.

"Stonewall"]   Entry of Sept. 21, 1862, David Lane, *A Soldier's Diary: The Story of a Volunteer, 1862–1865* (n.p., 1905), 12; entry of Dec. 13, 1862, Napoleon Radcliff, Journal of the War of the Rebellion, Henry E. Huntington Library, San Marino, California.

"a man . . . character"]   T. C. H. Smith, [Manuscript on John Pope's Virginia Campaign], chap. 1, 19–22, chap. 5, 1–6, Thomas C. H. Smith Papers, Box 3, Ohio Historical Society, Columbus.

Whittier]   John Greenleaf Whittier, *The Complete Poetical Works of John Greenleaf Whittier* (Boston, 1894), 342–343; J. G. Whittier to Francis F. Browne, Nov. 15, 1885, in Francis F. Browne, ed., *Bugle-Echoes: A Collection of the Poetry of the Civil War, Northern and Southern* (New York, 1886), 124; Lenoir Chambers, *Stonewall Jackson* (New York, 1959), II, 193–194n.

46–7 "in the event . . . opposite"]   Thomas [J. Jackson] to [Laura Jackson Arnold], Oct. 6, 1855, Thomas J. Jackson Papers, Library of Congress.

47 "He regretted . . . brief"]   G. D. Camden to R. L. Dabney, Nov. 25, 1863, Charles William Dabney Papers, Box 31, University of North Carolina. See also A. R. H. Ranson, "New Stories of Lee and Jackson," *South Atlantic Quarterly,* XII (1913), 297–299.

"unremitting attention"]   *Cincinnati Commercial,* Sept. 28, 1861.

"Almost alone . . . act"]   Frank S. Reader, *History of the Fifth West Virginia Cavalry* (New Brighton, Pa., 1890), 136. See also Edward D. Neill, "Reminiscences of the Last Year of President Lincoln's Life," in *Glimpses of the Nation's Struggle: A Series of Papers Read Before the Minnesota Commandery of the Military Order of the Loyal Legion of the United States* (St. Paul, Minn., 1887), 44.

"she was . . . left"]   [Samuel Wilson Compton], Reminiscences, Vol. 14, 78–79, Vol. 12, 49, Samuel Wilson Compton Papers, Perkins Library, Duke University, Durham, North Carolina.

"except . . . country"]   William Douglas Hamilton, *Recollections of the Civil War After Fifty Years, 1861–1865* (Columbus, Ohio, 1915), 30.

"union patriot" . . . "Stonewall" . . . examination]   John M. Burson to Roy Bird Cook, Jan. 1948, Roy Bird Cook Collection, Box 3, West Virginia and Regional History Collection, West Virginia University, Morgantown; John M. Burson, "Some Unwritten History in the Life of Stonewall Jackson," unidentified newspaper clipping, Nov. 17, 1930, Charles William Dabney Papers, Box 32, University of North Carolina. See also *Buckhannon Record,* June 4, 1937.

"The biographer . . . enemies"]   [D. H. Hill], Address, Daniel Harvey Hill Papers, North Carolina Division of Archives and History, Raleigh. The main biographical studies of Jackson are Henderson, *Stonewall Jackson;* Chambers, *Stonewall Jackson;* Frank E. Vandiver, *Mighty Stonewall* (New York, 1957); Roy Bird Cook, *The Family and Early Life of Stonewall Jackson,* 3d ed. (Charleston, W.Va., 1948); Arnold, *Early Life and Letters of Jackson.*

48 "to Come . . . bound out" and "to make drudges of them"]   Thomas Neale to Lewis Maxwell, June 6, 1833, Neale Family Papers, West Virginia University. On Jonathan Jackson see Stephen W. Brown, *Voice of the New West: John G. Jackson, His Life and Times* ([Macon, Ga.], 1985), 124.

49 "a land . . . mortality"]   Thomas [J. Jackson] to [Laura Jackson Arnold], Feb. 28, 1848, Library of Congress.

49 "the impersonation . . . beauty"]   Dabney, *Life of Jackson*, 11–12.

"My mother . . . now"]   M. A. Jackson, *Life and Letters of Jackson*, 19. See also Blake
B. Woodson to William [Woodson], Dec. 6, 1831, Cook Collection, Series VI, Box
1, West Virginia University; T. J. Jackson to [Laura Jackson Arnold], April 6, 1861, T.
J. Jackson Manuscripts, Virginia Military Institute.

"my . . . home"]   T. J. Jackson to Laura Jackson Arnold, Aug. 2, 1845, in Arnold,
Early Life and Letters of Jackson, 71.

"This is news . . . me"]   Thomas [J. Jackson] to [Laura Jackson Arnold], July 6, 1850,
Jackson Papers, Library of Congress.

"he could . . . dyspepsia"]   Henry Kyd Douglas, *I Rode With Stonewall* (Chapel Hill,
N.C., 1940), 122.

50 "No, rice . . . 92"]   Entry of April 18, 1863, Diary of Jedediah Hotchkiss, Hotchkiss
Papers, Library of Congress.

"violent character"]   Thomas [J. Jackson] to [Laura Jackson Arnold], April 1, 1850,
Jackson Papers, *ibid*.

"This water . . . waters"]   Thomas [J. Jackson] to [Laura Jackson Arnold], July 11,
1852, *ibid*.

"He had . . . pain" and "he would . . . old"]   Margaret J. Preston, "Personal Reminis-
cences of Stonewall Jackson," *Century Magazine*, XXXII (Oct. 1886), 932–933. See also
T. J. Jackson to Laura J. Arnold, Oct. 26, 1847, Cook Collection, Series VI, Box 1, West
Virginia University.

"raw boned . . . suffering"]   D. M. Frost, Memoirs, Richard Graham Papers, Missouri
Historical Society.

51 "It is . . . acquaintance"]   Thomas [J. Jackson] to [Laura Jackson Arnold], Aug. 10, 1850,
Jackson Papers, Library of Congress.

"traced . . . impression"]   Dabney, *Life of Jackson*, 10.

"before . . . own"]   Thomas [J. Jackson] to [Laura Jackson Arnold], March 8, 1850,
Jackson Papers, Library of Congress.

rumors of a child]   [Ezra Ayres Carman], Note in folder marked "Report of Brig. Gen.
Jno. R. Jones, comdg Jackson's Division, Artillery of Jackson's Division," Studies,
Antietam, Record Group 94, National Archives; [R. L. Dabney, Notes], "Statement of
Dr. Bland," Charles William Dabney Papers, Box 32, University of North Carolina;
"A Brief Interview with Edward Jackson, First Cousin to General Stonewall Jackson,"
Cook Collection, Box 1, West Virginia University. The Carman note is printed in
Holmes Alexander, *The Hidden Years of Stonewall Jackson* (Richwood, W. Va., 1981),
187.

52 "Whilst I . . . misery"]   Thomas [J. Jackson] to [Laura Jackson Arnold], June 6, 1853,
Jackson Papers, Library of Congress.

"punishment . . . Laws" and "from the path . . . life"]   T. J. Jackson to L. J. Arnold,
March 8, 1850, *ibid*.

"His views . . . Arminianism"]   [William S. White], "My acquaintance with Lieut.
Gen. T. J. Jackson," Charles William Dabney Papers, Box 32, University of North
Carolina.

"His repugnance . . . determined"]   D. H. Hill, "The Real Stonewall Jackson," *Century
Magazine*, XLVII (Nov. 1893–Apr. 1894), 625.

"turn . . . perdition"]   T. J. Jackson to Mary Anna Jackson, Oct. 13, 1862, Charles
William Dabney Papers, Box 32, University of North Carolina.

"Jackson's . . . life"]   [White], "My acquaintance with Jackson," *ibid*.

"had his . . . pulpit"]   M. A. Jackson, *Life and Letters of Jackson*, 60.

53 *"wholly* . . . plaintive"]   [R. L. Dabney, Notes], "Rev. B. T. Lacy's Narrative," Charles
William Dabney Papers, Box 32, University of North Carolina.

53 "And God . . . away"]   T. J. Jackson's Bible, Virginia Historical Society, Richmond.

"I have . . . here"]   [R. L. Dabney, Notes], "Dr. McGuire's Narrative," Charles William Dabney Papers, Box 31, University of North Carolina.

"had almost" . . . "had followed"]   Henry Brown to R. L. Dabney, Aug. 5, 1863, *ibid.*

"Jesus . . . unbelief"]   Mark 9:23–24, Jackson's Bible, Virginia Historical Society.

54 "God . . . faith"]   [T. J. Jackson] to [Laura Jackson Arnold], April 6, 1861, Jackson Manuscripts, Virginia Military Institute.

"I have . . . moment"]   T. J. Jackson to Mary Anna Jackson, Oct. 5, 1859, Charles William Dabney Papers, Box 32, University of North Carolina.

"an intellectual . . . lady"]   T. J. Jackson to Lowry Barney, Aug. 18, 1853, in Cook, *Family and Early Life of Jackson,* 118.

"vivacity and beauty"]   Elizabeth Randolph Preston Allan, *A March Past: Reminiscences of Elizabeth Randolph Preston Allan,* ed. Janet Allan Bryan (Richmond, Va., 1938), 120.

"I deserved . . . him"]   Maggie [Margaret Junkin] to Ellie [Elinor Junkin], n. d., Charles William Dabney Papers, University of North Carolina. See also [Margaret Junkin], "To My Sister," [erroneously attributed to T. J. Jackson], Cook Collection, Box 1, West Virginia University.

"such . . . person"]   Allan, *March Past,* 61.

"Duty . . . worship"]   Preston, "Personal Reminiscences," *Century Magazine,* XXXII (Oct. 1886), 930.

"The weather . . . happiness"]   Thomas [J. Jackson] to [Laura Jackson Arnold], Oct. 19, 1853, Jackson Papers, Library of Congress.

"joyous . . . afflictive"]   Thomas [J. Jackson] to [Margaret Junkin], March 1, 1855, Margaret Junkin Preston Papers, University of North Carolina.

"troubled . . . love"]   T. J. Jackson to Mrs. Neale, Feb. 16, 1855, M. A. Jackson, *Life and Letters of Jackson,* 84–85.

55 "I look . . . *her*"]   Thomas [J. Jackson] to [Laura Jackson Arnold], Nov. 14, 1854, Jackson Papers, Library of Congress.

"from that . . . feared"]   T. J. Jackson to [Laura Jackson Arnold], July 18, 1856, *ibid.*

"with . . . spared"]   M. A. Jackson, *Life and Letters of Jackson,* 169–170.

"more . . . fascinating"]   D. H. Hill to R. L. Dabney, July 11, 1864, Dabney Papers, Union Theological Seminary in Virginia.

"startling caress" and "luxuriated . . . dignity"]   M. A. Jackson, *Life and Letters of Jackson,* 121, 108. See also Mary Anna Jackson, [Introduction to Extracts from Letters], Charles William Dabney Papers, University of North Carolina.

"I can . . . tenderness"]   Mary Anna Jackson to Mrs. Brown, Jan. 2, 1863, Jackson Manuscripts, Virginia Military Institute.

"deep . . . *piety*" and "my . . . heart"]   M. A. J[ackson] to [Fanny B. Graham?], July 20, 1863, Charles William Dabney Papers, University of North Carolina.

"as confiding as possible"]   M. A. Jackson, [Introduction to Extracts], *ibid.*

56 "I am in . . . while"]   T. J. Jackson to M. A. Jackson, Oct. 20, 1862, M. A. Jackson, *Life and Letters of Jackson,* 365.

"he rarely . . . think of"]   *Ibid.,* 423.

"Objects . . . humility"]   [T. J. Jackson], [Book of Maxims], Thomas Jonathan Jackson Papers, George H. and Katherine M. Davis Collection, Howard-Tilton Library, Tulane University, New Orleans, Louisiana.

"his natural . . . grace"]   [R. L. Dabney, Notes], "Dr. McGuire's Narrative," Charles William Dabney Papers, Box 31, University of North Carolina.

57   "The manner . . . alarm"]   [D. H. Hill], Address, Hill Papers, North Carolina Archives.

"loathed . . . flesh"]   Richard Taylor, *Destruction and Reconstruction: Personal Experiences of the Late War* (New York, 1879), 80.

"scion . . . elite"]   John Alexander Williams, *West Virginia and the Captains of Industry* (Morgantown, W. Va., 1976), 255. See also John A. Williams, "The New Dominion and the Old: Ante-Bellum and Statehood Politics as the Background of West Virginia's 'Bourbon Democracy,' " *West Virginia History,* XXXIII (July 1972), 330, 335–336.

"very . . . influential"]   G. D. Camden to R. L. Dabney, Nov. 25, 1863, Charles William Dabney Papers, Box 31, University of North Carolina.

"I consider . . . desirable" and "Indeed . . . revived"]   Thomas [J. Jackson] to [Laura Jackson Arnold], April 2, 1851, Jackson Papers, Library of Congress. See also Thomas [J. Jackson] to [Laura Jackson Arnold], Nov. 2, 1857, *Charles Hamilton Catalogs, Auction No. 14* (Sept. 22, 1966), Item 203.

"I am . . . him"]   T. J. Jackson to J. M. Bennett, April 17, 1860, Harvey Mitchell Rice, *The Life of Jonathan M. Bennett: A Study of the Virginias in Transition* (Chapel Hill, N.C., 1943), 260–261, n. 27.

"from a family . . . life"]   Lewis Maxwell *et al.* to John C. Spencer, June 14, 1842, Thomas J. Jackson Papers, University of North Carolina.

58   Samuel Hays]   [R. L. Dabney, Notes], "Statement of Dr. Bland," Charles William Dabney Papers, Box 32, University of North Carolina.

"my . . . *friend"*]   T. J. Jackson to Samuel L. Hays, Feb. 2, 1849, Cook Collection, Box 1, West Virginia University.

"I am . . . success"]   T. J. Jackson to John E. Hays, Jan. 22, 1857, Cook, *Early Life of Jackson,* 144.

"Brig. . . . Army"]   Flyleaf of T. J. Jackson's copy of Charles Davies, *A Treatise on Shades and Shadows, and Linear Perspective* (Philadelphia, 1840), Virginia Historical Society.

"by . . . teeth"]   Rufus R. Wilson, "Stonewall Jackson," *Southern Historical Society Papers,* XXII (1894), 160. See also W. H. C. Whiting to R. L. Dabney, Nov. 30, 1863, Charles William Dabney Papers, Box 31, University of North Carolina.

"means . . . desire"]   Thomas [J. Jackson] to [Laura Jackson Arnold], May 25, 1847, Jackson Papers, Library of Congress.

"Afraid . . . myself"]   Hunter McGuire, *Address by Dr. Hunter McGuire . . . Delivered on 23d day of June, 1897* (Lynchburg, Va., 1897), 15.

58–9   "within . . . you" and "I sent . . . brigade"]   T. J. Jackson to Laura J. Arnold, Oct. 26, 1847, Cook Collection, Series VI, Box 1, West Virginia University.

59   "At the time . . . myself"]   [T. J. Jackson] to J. P. Benjamin, Oct. 10, 1861, Charles William Dabney Papers, Box 31, University of North Carolina. Jackson's draft of this letter is in Jackson Papers, Davis Collection, Tulane University.

Harrison Republican]   *Harrison Republican* (Clarksburg, Va.), Dec. 10, 1847, quoted in Cook, *Early Life of Jackson,* 105.

"should . . . war" and "glory . . . Castile"]   [T. J. Jackson] to [Laura Jackson Arnold], Aug. 3, 1849, *Charles Hamilton Catalogs, Auction No. 14* (Sept. 22, 1966), Item 202.

"I say . . . life"]   Thomas [J. Jackson] to [Laura Jackson Arnold], March 1, 1851, Jackson Papers, Library of Congress.

59–60   "cultivate his mind" and "It will . . . for it"]   [R. L. Dabney, Notes], "Col. Preston's Narrative," Charles William Dabney Papers, Box 32, University of North Carolina.

60   "You may . . . be" and "My friends . . . eminence"]   [T. J. Jackson], [Book of Maxims], Jackson Papers, Davis Collection, Tulane University; Joel Hawes, *Lectures to Young Men, on the Formation of Character &c* (Hartford, Conn., 1851), 74.

fond of teaching]   Entry of April 14, 1863, Diary of Jedediah Hotchkiss, Hotchkiss Papers, Library of Congress.

60–1 "In order . . . forces"]   Notes on Physical Constitution of Bodies, Jackson Papers, Davis Collection, Tulane University.

61 "Discussions . . . found it"]   J. C. Hiden, "Stonewall Jackson," *Southern Historical Society Papers,* XX (1892), 308.

"trying ordeal"]   Thomas [J. Jackson] to [Laura Jackson Arnold], Jan. 10, 1852, Jackson Papers, Library of Congress.

adjutant]   Thomas T. Munford, "How I Came to Know Major Thomas Jonathan Jackson," Munford-Ellis Papers, Thomas T. Munford Division, V.M.I. Papers, Duke University. See also Bertram Wyatt-Brown, *Southern Honor: Ethics and Behavior in the Old South* (New York, 1982), chap. 6.

"he was . . . cracked"]   E. A. W. letter, May 23, 1863, *Cincinnati Commercial,* June 5, 1863. See also John S. Wise, "Stonewall Jackson As I Knew Him," *The Circle,* III (1908), 143.

"Major . . . corner"]   Hiden, "Stonewall Jackson," *Southern Historical Society Papers,* XX (1892), 309.

"Major . . . disgusted"]   Thomas T. Munford to Jed[ediah] Hotchkiss, Aug. 11, 1897, Hotchkiss Papers, Box 21, Library of Congress.

62 "They . . . vain"]   Hill, "The Real Stonewall Jackson," *Century Magazine,* XLVII (Nov. 1893–Apr. 1894), 627.

"no small . . . chair"]   James L. Kemper, *Address of Gov. James L. Kemper . . . July 3, 1877* (n.p., n.d.), 14–15; William Couper, *One Hundred Years at V.M.I.* (Richmond, Va., 1939), I, 313–314.

"never appreciated"]   M. Anna Jackson to W. N. Pendleton, Dec. 30, 1872, Pendleton Papers, University of North Carolina; Couper, *One Hundred Years,* I, 263.

Wise]   John S. Wise, *The End of an Era* (Boston, 1899), 238–243.

"in our . . . five"]   [D. H. Hill], Address, Hill Papers, North Carolina Archives.

63 Amazing Grace]   William S. White, *Rev. William S. White, and His Times: An Autobiography,* ed. H. M. White (Richmond, Va., 1891), 158. See also Anne C. Loveland, *Southern Evangelicals and the Social Order, 1800–1860* (Baton Rouge, La., 1980), 226.

"Oh . . . catechism"]   James Power Smith, "With Stonewall Jackson in the Army of Northern Virginia," *Southern Historical Society Papers,* XLIII (1920), 60. See also T. J. Jackson to J. L. Campbell, June 7, 1858, J. L. Campbell Letters, University of North Carolina.

"In my . . . faithfully"]   M. A. Jackson, *Life and Letters of Jackson,* 182.

"Whilst . . . myself"]   T. J. Jackson to Mary Anna Jackson, July 21, 1861, Charles William Dabney Papers, Box 32, University of North Carolina.

niece]   T. J. Jackson to niece, Feb. 25, 1860, Jackson Papers, Library of Congress.

"Without . . . occupy"]   Thomas [J. Jackson] to [Laura Jackson Arnold], Dec. 12, 1859, *ibid.*

64 reading Shakespeare]   M. A. Jackson, *Life and Letters of Jackson,* 113. Jackson's copy of Shakespeare's works is at the Virginia Historical Society. See also Thomas [J. Jackson] to [Laura Jackson Arnold], March 23, 1848, Jackson Papers, Library of Congress.

"endeavors . . . all"]   George Winfred Hervey, *The Principles of Courtesy* (New York, 1856), 27.

64–5 Europe]   Notebooks and "Journal of T. J. Jackson from 4th July . . . 1856," Jackson Papers, Davis Collection, Tulane University; Thomas [J. Jackson] to [Laura Jackson Arnold], July 18, Oct. 25, Dec. 6, 1856, Jackson Papers, Library of Congress; Hunter McGuire to Jedediah Hotchkiss, July 17, 1897, Jedediah Hotchkiss Papers, #2822, Alderman Library, University of Virginia, Charlottesville; Bradley T. Johnson, "Personal Recollections of 'Stonewall' Jackson," in M. A. Jackson, *Memoirs of Jackson,* 530–531; *The Times* (London), June 11, 1863.

65 "where . . . her"] T. J. Jackson to Maggie [Margaret Junkin Preston], Nov. 16, 1861, General Manuscripts Miscellaneous, Princeton University, Princeton, New Jersey. Printed, in altered form, in Elizabeth Preston Allan, *The Life and Letters of Margaret Junkin Preston* (Boston, 1903), 130–131.

"that . . . Creator"] M. A. Jackson, *Life and Letters of Jackson*, 143. See also Donald G. Mathews, *Religion in the Old South* (Chicago, 1977), chap. 4.

65–6 "I have . . . goods"] Thomas [J. Jackson] to [Laura Jackson Arnold], July 18, 1856, Jackson Papers, Library of Congress. On investments see also T. J. Jackson to uncle, Jan. 28, 1854, Cook Collection, Box 1, West Virginia University; M. J. Preston, "Personal Reminiscences," *Century Magazine*, XXXII (Oct. 1886), 931; Mary Anna Jackson to Mrs. Brown, March 17, 1864, Jackson Manuscripts, Virginia Military Institute; Thomas [J. Jackson] to [Laura Jackson Arnold], Oct. 1855 and June 6, 1856, Jackson Papers, Library of Congress; Appraisals of T. J. Jackson's Estate, June 2, 1863, Jackson Papers, Davis Collection, Tulane University, and June 5, 1863, Cook Collection, Series VI, Box 1, West Virginia University. Jackson's investment plans and holdings are summarized in Katharine L. Brown, *Stonewall Jackson in Lexington: The Christian Soldier* (Lexington, Va., 1984), 10–12.

66 "a dissolution of the union"] Thomas [J. Jackson] to [Laura Jackson Arnold], June 6, 1856, Jackson Papers, Library of Congress.

"the dangers . . . stand"] G. H. M., "Stonewall Jackson in Lexington, Va.," *Southern Historical Society Papers*, IX (1881), 42–43. See also Rufus R. Wilson, "Stonewall Jackson," *ibid.*, XXII (1894), 163; George H. Moffett to J. G. Paxton, May 16, 1908, Elisha F. Paxton Letters, University of Virginia. Jackson's vote for the Breckinridge-Lane ticket is recorded in "Poll of an Election," Nov. 6, 1860, Jackson Manuscripts, Virginia Military Institute.

"I feel . . . slavery"] T. J. Jackson to [Thomas Jackson Arnold], Jan. 26, 1861, Arnold, *Early Life and Letters of Jackson*, 294.

67 "I am . . . secession"] Thomas [J. Jackson] to [Laura Jackson Arnold], Feb. 2, 1861, *The Rendells, Catalogue 131* (1977), Item 10. Also printed in Cook, *Family and Early Life of Jackson*, 154.

"Why . . . good"] James B. Ramsey, *True Eminence Founded on Holiness* (Lynchburg, Va., 1863), 16. See also Haskell Monroe, "Southern Presbyterians and the Secession Crisis," *Civil War History*, VI (Dec. 1960), 351–360; C. C. Goen, *Broken Churches, Broken Nation: Denominational Schisms and the Coming of the American Civil War* (Macon, Ga., 1985), 171–179.

"that if Virginia . . . rescue"] John T. Harris to Tho[ma]s J. Jackson, Feb. 6, 1862, Jackson Papers, Davis Collection, Tulane University. On Jackson's secessionist views see also [White], "My acquaintance with Jackson," Charles William Dabney Papers, Box 32, University of North Carolina.

"were those . . . son"] D. X. Junkin, *The Reverend George Junkin, D.D., LL.D.: A Historical Biography* (Philadelphia, 1871), 504.

Calhoun] J. C. Calhoun to George Junkin, Sept. 17, 1846, Margaret Junkin Preston Papers, University of North Carolina.

"The traitor . . . traitor"] W[illia]m S. White to [R. L. Dabney], Aug. 25, 1862, Dabney Papers, Union Theological Seminary in Virginia.

"The pseudo . . . wrong"] D. X. Junkin, *George Junkin*, 519.

"I am . . . the rest"] Graham, "Reminiscences of Jackson," in M. A. Jackson, *Memoirs of Jackson*, 487.

"the false . . . moral truth"] D. X. Junkin, *George Junkin*, 524. See also Geo[rge] Junkin to L. J. Cist, March 22, 1862, Simon Gratz Autograph Collection, Historical Society of Pennsylvania, Philadelphia.

"The Lord . . . come"] George Junkin, *Political Fallacies* (New York, 1863), 9. See also *New York Herald*, Nov. 24, 1862; George Junkin to Francis McFarland, Jan. 18, 1861,

Francis McFarland Collection, Washington and Lee University; Jed[ediah] Hotchkiss to [Sara Hotchkiss], March 27, 1863, Hotchkiss Papers, Library of Congress.

68 "this intrepid general"] *Richmond Examiner,* Jan. 23, 1862, reprinted in *New York Herald,* Jan. 26, 1862; *New Orleans Crescent,* Feb. 15, 1862.

"His object . . . Stonewall is"] *Richmond Whig,* reprinted in Moore, ed., *Rebellion Record,* IV, 342.

"He is . . . day"] P. W. Alexander, "Confederate Chieftains," *Southern Literary Messenger,* XXXVII (1863), 37.

"He is . . . no rest"] Entry of June 11, 1862, Catherine Ann Devereux Edmonston, *Journal of a Secesh Lady,* ed. Beth G. Crabtree and James W. Patton (Raleigh, N.C., 1979), 191–192.

"Hurrah . . . think about"] W. Henry Sullivan to friend, June 29, 1862, Lalla Pelot Papers, Duke University.

"Bless his . . . expected"] Entry of Jan. 28, 1863, Diary of Mary Cornelia Wright, Louisiana State University.

"Their souls . . . the same"] *Close Up the Ranks* (Richmond, Va., 1864), 4.

69 "panders . . . existed"] L[afayette] McLaws to Elizabeth Ewell, Feb. 18, 1863, Richard S. Ewell Papers, Library of Congress. See also A. P. Hill to [J. E. B.] Stuart, Nov. 14, [1862], J. E. B. Stuart Papers, Virginia Historical Society.

"These things . . . Redeemer"] T. J. Jackson to M. A. Jackson, Oct. 20, 1862, M. A. Jackson, *Life and Letters of Jackson,* 363–364.

"an explanation . . . invincibility"] *Knoxville Register,* Sept. 20, 1862, reprinted in *New York Herald,* Oct. 27, 1862.

"Gen. Jackson . . . patriot"] Quoted in [John Esten Cooke], *The Life of Stonewall Jackson* (Richmond, Va., 1863), 85.

"he can . . . victory"] "The Religious Element in War," Aug. 10, 1862, Graves Scrapbook, Volume I, Manuscripts Division, Maryland Historical Society Library, Baltimore.

"He is . . . piety"] Alexander, "Confederate Chieftains," *Southern Literary Messenger,* XXXVII (1863), 37.

"He was . . . annoyed him"] Douglas, *I Rode With Stonewall,* 35.

70 "You must . . . His purpose"] T. J. Jackson to Mrs. Osburn, Sept. 29, 1862, *Kenneth W. Rendell Catalogue 102* (1974), Item 61.

Anna Castleman] T. J. Jackson to Anna Castleman, April 22, 1862, Jackson Papers, Davis Collection, Tulane University.

Mary Matilda Hademan] T. J. Jackson to [Mary Matilda] Hademan, April 15, 1863, Scrapbook *re* Thomas Jonathan ("Stonewall") Jackson, Montrose Jonas Moses Collection, Duke University.

"soon bless . . . peace"] T. J. Jackson to W. G. Paine, April 9, 1863, Schoff Civil War Collection, Letters and Documents, Box 4, Clements Library.

"I feel . . . admire them"] T. J. Jackson to Mary [Tucker Magill], Nov. 14, 1862, in Mary Tucker Magill, *Women, or Chronicles of the Late War* (Baltimore, Md., 1871), viii–x.

"so quiet . . . new uniform"] Entry of Nov. 16, 1862, Cornelia McDonald, *A Diary With Reminiscences of the War and Refugee Life in the Shenandoah Valley, 1860–1865* (Nashville, Tenn., 1935), 105.

D. H. Hill] Robert Stiles, *Four Years Under Marse Robert* (New York, 1904), 72.

A. R. Boteler] Douglas, *I Rode with Stonewall,* 34. See also Peregrine Hays to Mary Hays, July 17, 1862, Cook Collection, Box 2, West Virginia University.

71 "never did . . . citizen"] Entry of May 11, 1863, William Kauffman, ed., *The Diary of Edmund Ruffin: The Years of Hope* (Baton Rouge, La., 1976), II, 647–648.

71 "magnificent . . . Stonewall"]   Quoted in Markinfield Addey, *The Life and Military Career of Thomas Jonathan Jackson* (New York, 1863), 236.

"You . . . Confederacy"]   Edward A. Pollard, "Stonewall Jackson—An Historical Study," *Putnam's Magazine*, new series, II (1868), 738. See also J. Cutler Andrews, *The South Reports the Civil War* (Princeton, N.J., 1970), 31.

"My prayer . . . heart"]   T. J. Jackson to M. A. Jackson, Oct. 20, 1862, M. A. Jackson, *Life and Letters of Jackson*, 360–364.

"All admire . . . not"]   Charles M. Blackford to Susan Leigh Blackford, Aug. 19–26, 1862, in Susan Leigh Blackford, comp., *Memoirs of Life In and Out of the Army in Virginia During the War Between the States* (Lynchburg, Va., 1894), I, 211.

72 "No thought . . . great cause"]   Robert L. Dabney, "True Courage: A Discourse Commemorative of Lieut.-General Thomas J. Jackson," *Discussions by Robert L. Dabney* (Mexico, Mo., 1897), IV, 448.

"the very . . . hero"]   James A. Seddon to Jefferson Davis, Nov. 26, 1863, *Official Records,* Series IV, Vol. II, 994.

73 "I hope . . . City"]   Mary E. Boddie to Carrie, June 21, 1862, Fred J. Herring Collection, Small Manuscript Collections, Box 9, Arkansas History Commission, Little Rock.

"The fact . . . the war"]   *Richmond Dispatch*, May 29, 1862, quoted in *American and Commercial Advertiser* (Baltimore), June 14, 1862.

no prisoners]   C. Vann Woodward, ed., *Mary Chesnut's Civil War* (New Haven, Conn., 1981), 361, 501–502; [J.] Adger [Smyth] to Janey, Aug. 7, 1864, Adger-Smyth[e] Collection, Box 11-408, South Carolina Historical Society.

"By their . . . extermination"]   Entry of July 4, 1862, J. B. Jones, *A Rebel War Clerk's Diary at the Confederate States Capital,* ed. Howard Swiggett (New York, 1935), I, 142.

"Let . . . lick"]   *Richmond Whig*, Aug. 23, 1862.

"give . . . army"]   House of Representatives, Sept. 12, 1862, Proceedings of the First Confederate Congress, Second Session, *Southern Historical Society Papers*, XLVI (1928), 122.

74 "The ground . . . Yankees"]   *Richmond Whig*, Aug. 15, 1862.

"The people . . . river"]   William H. Burnley to mother, Sept. 6, 1862, Burnley Family Papers, Box 7, University of Virginia. See also *Memphis Appeal* (Grenada, Miss.), July 26, 1862.

R. E. Lee]   Entry of Feb. 19, 1870, "Conversations with Gen. R. E. Lee," MS Volume 3, William Allan Papers, University of North Carolina; J. William Jones, "A Chaplain's Recollections of 'Stonewall' Jackson," in M. A. Jackson, *Memoirs of Jackson*, 477; W. G. Bean, ed., "Memoranda of Conversations Between General Robert E. Lee and William Preston Johnston," *Virginia Magazine of History and Biography*, LXXIII (Oct. 1965), 478.

Fitzhugh Lee]   Fitzhugh Lee, "General Jackson One of the World's Greatest Soldiers," in M. A. Jackson, *Memoirs of Jackson*, 611.

J. William Jones]   Jones, "Chaplain's Recollections," *ibid*., 477; J. William Jones, "Stonewall Jackson," *Southern Historical Society Papers*, XIX (1891), 156.

P. G. T. Beauregard]   G. T. Beauregard to Cha[rle]s C. Jones, [Jr.], April 1, 1875, William K. Bixby Collection, Missouri Historical Society.

74–5 "I never . . . opponents"]   Jed[ediah] Hotchkiss, Answers to G. F. R. Henderson's Queries, Query 7, enclosed in [Jedediah Hotchkiss] to William Chase, March 28, 1892, Hotchkiss. Papers, Library of Congress.

75 "one . . . campaign"]   *Chattanooga Rebel* (Atlanta, Ga.), Oct. 9, 1863, reprinted in *Cincinnati Commercial,* Oct. 21, 1863.

"in whose . . . exist"]   Cha[rle]s E. Fenner, *Ceremonies Connected With the Unveiling of the Statue of General Robert E. Lee* (New Orleans, 1884), 31.

75 "Probably . . . differently"]   John S. Mosby, "General Stuart at Gettysburg," *Weekly Times* (Philadelphia), Dec. 15, 1877.

"his taking . . . have been"]   W. T. Sherman to G. T. Lanegan, June 18, 1881, W. T. Sherman Papers, Library of Congress.

76 Hood on Jackson]   J. B. Hood, *Advance and Retreat: Personal Experiences in the United States and Confederate States Armies* (New Orleans, 1880), 191–192, 283. See also Richard M. McMurry, *John Bell Hood and the War for Southern Independence* (Lexington, Ky., 1982), 150–151; Steven E. Woodworth, *Jefferson Davis and His Generals: The Failure of Confederate Command in the West* (Lawrence, Kan., 1990), chap. 14.

77 "Hood . . . entered"]   A. R. Chisolm, "Life and War Experience of a Confederate Aide-de-Camp," XIV–10, Alexander Robert Chisolm Papers, New-York Historical Society.

"had gotten . . . each other"]   Entry of Dec. 17, 1868, "Conversations with Lee," Allan Papers, University of North Carolina.

"He certainly . . . errors"]   John Cheves Haskell, "Reminiscences of the Confederate War," 38, Virginia Historical Society. On Jackson's shortcomings see Douglas Southall Freeman, *Lee's Lieutenants: A Study in Command* (New York, 1942–1944), I, xxv, 479–481, 576–579, II, xxiii, 3, 43–47; Robert G. Tanner, *Stonewall in the Valley: Thomas J. "Stonewall" Jackson's Shenandoah Valley Campaign Spring 1862* (Garden City, N.Y., 1976), 252–258, 307–309; Robert K. Krick, *Stonewall Jackson at Cedar Mountain* (Chapel Hill, N.C., 1990), chaps. 7–9.

Johnston letter]   J. E. Johnston to T. J. Jackson, May 27, 1862, printed in *New York Herald,* June 16, 1862. See also Campbell Brown, "My Confederate Experience," I, 35–36, University of North Carolina.

resign]   D. H. Hill to R. L. Dabney, July 21, 1864, Dabney Papers, Union Theological Seminary in Virginia.

"one very . . . him"]   H. E. G[ourdin] to R. N. Gourdin, Sept. 15, 1862, Robert Newman Gourdin Papers, Duke University. See also Grady McWhiney, "Who Whipped Whom? Confederate Defeat Reexamined," *Civil War History,* XI (March 1965), 11–12.

CHAPTER THREE
Notes for Pages 79–143

79 *"making . . . desert"*]   James Dixon to Leonard Bacon, Dec. 26, 1860, Bacon Family Correspondence, Series I, Box 7, Sterling Library, Yale University, New Haven, Connecticut. See also Hans L. Trefousse, *Benjamin Franklin Wade: Radical Republican from Ohio* (New York, 1963), 139.

"We propose . . . *rebels*"]   Sam E. Brown to John Sherman, April 14, 1861, John Sherman Papers, Manuscript Division, Library of Congress, Washington, D.C.

79–80 "restore . . . traitors"]   W[illia]m DeLoss Love, *Wisconsin in the War of the Rebellion* (Chicago, 1866), 156.

80 "General . . . Manassas"]   *New York Herald,* Aug. 11, 1861.

"The keys . . . done"]   *Harper's Weekly,* VI (April 19, 1862), 242.

"firmly . . . Indians"]   [Catherine C. Hopley], *Life in the South; From the Commencement of the War* (London, 1863), II, 396. See also Edward Dicey, *Six Months in the Federal States* (London, 1863), II, 141–142.

"War . . . against him"]   *Cincinnati Commercial,* July 25, 1862. See also A. G. Curtin to E. M. Stanton, May 28, 1862, Edwin M. Stanton Papers, Library of Congress.

81 "I say . . . consume"]   *New York Herald,* July 16, 1862.

"From the . . . extermination"]   [John Esten Cooke], "Introductory," 15, John Esten Cooke Papers, #38-599-A, Alderman Library, University of Virginia, Charlottesville.

81   "Oh for . . . only way"]   J. W. Davenport to [Henry Smith], Sept. 14, 1862, John W.
Davenport Letters, Ohio Historical Society, Columbus.

"The necessities . . . necessary"]   [Thaddeus Stevens], [Draft of speech], [1863], Thaddeus Stevens Papers, Vol. 2, Library of Congress.

"You cannot . . . history"]   Senate, July 9, 1862, *Congressional Globe,* 37th Congress,
2d Session, 3200.

82   "would banish . . . citizens"]   S. M. Stevens to [E. M.] Stanton, March 18, 1862, Letters
Received by the Secretary of War, Main Series, Microcopy No. 221, Roll No. 207,
National Archives, Washington, D.C.

"the neat . . . civilization"]   Carl Schurz, *"For the Great Empire of Liberty, Forward!"
Speech . . . on Friday Evening, September 16, 1864* (New York, [1864]), 13.

"that a new . . . world"]   M. Goldsmith to James Edward Calhoun, July 23, 1865, James
Edward Calhoun Papers, Box 3, South Caroliniana Library, University of South Carolina, Columbia. See also Hans L. Trefousse, *Carl Schurz: A Biography* (Knoxville, Tenn.,
1982), 154–155.

82   "What matters . . . upon it"]   Horace Binney Sargent to Charles Sumner, Sept. 1, 1863,
Letters Received by the Secretary of War, Main Series, Microcopy No. 221, Roll No.
240, National Archives.

"Does . . . Nation"]   T[homas] S[tarr] K[ing] to [H. W.] Bellows, Jan. 20, 1863, Henry
W. Bellows Papers, Massachusetts Historical Society, Boston. See also Chester Forrester
Dunham, *The Attitude of the Northern Clergy Toward the South, 1860–1865* (Toledo, Ohio,
1942), esp. chap. 6.

82–3   "This war . . . Massachusetts"]   Auguste Laugel, *The United States During the War*
(New York, 1866), 175. See also Joel H. Silbey, "The Surge of Republican Power:
Partisan Antipathy, American Social Conflict and the Coming of the Civil War," in
Stephen E. Maizlish and John J. Kushma, eds., *Essays on American Antebellum Politics,
1840–1860* (College Station, Tex., 1982), 199–229; Lewis P. Simpson, *Mind and the
American Civil War: A Meditation on Lost Causes* (Baton Rouge, La., 1989).

83   "good old . . . tranquility"]   *New York Herald,* Aug. 11, 1864. On Democrats see Jean
H. Baker, *Affairs of Party: The Political Culture of Northern Democrats in the Mid-Nineteenth
Century* (Ithaca, N.Y., 1983); Joel H. Silbey, *A Respectable Minority: The Democratic Party
in the Civil War Era, 1860–1868* (New York, 1977); Frank L. Klement, *The Copperheads
in the Middle West* (Chicago, 1960); Hubert H. Wubben, *Civil War Iowa and the
Copperhead Movement* (Ames, Iowa, 1980); Kenneth M. Stampp, *Indiana Politics During
the Civil War* (Indianapolis, Ind., 1949); William Frank Zornow, *Lincoln and the Party
Divided* (Norman, Okla., 1954); Edward L. Gambill, *Conservative Ordeal: Northern
Democrats and Reconstruction, 1865–1868* (Ames, Iowa, 1981); Robert W. Johannsen,
Stephen A. Douglas (New York, 1973), chap. 31.

"military proclamation" and "political . . . candidate"]   F. P. Blair, [Sr.], to [Mrs. E.
T. Throop Martin], Sept. 11, 1864, Throop and Martin Family Papers, Box 6, Princeton
University, Princeton, New Jersey. On McClellan, see Stephen W. Sears, *George B.
McClellan: The Young Napoleon* (New York, 1988), 227–229 and chap. 15.

"Will you compromise . . . besom of war"]   House of Representatives, Dec. 15, 1862,
Congressional Globe, 37th Congress, 3d Session, 97.

84–5   "Beware . . . years"]   *Cincinnati Commercial,* June 12, 1863. On Seward see John Hay's
diary, Nov. 8, 1864, quoted in John G. Nicolay and John Hay, *Abraham Lincoln: A
History* (New York, 1890), VII, 388.

85   "The nation's . . . man"]   F. P. Blair, [Sr.], to [Mrs. E. T. Throop Martin], Sept. 11,
1864, Throop and Martin Family Papers, Princeton University. See also H. G. Stebbins
to [S. L. M.] Barlow, Jan. 20, 1864, S. L. M. Barlow Papers, Henry E. Huntington
Library, San Marino, California.

"I feel . . . war"]   Harvey Reid, *The View from Headquarters: Civil War Letters of Harvey
Reid,* ed. Frank L. Byrne (Madison, Wis., 1965), 86.

85 "They have . . . intentions"]   *Newark Journal* quoted in entry of Jan. 3, 1863, William Owner, Diary, Library of Congress. Also quoted in *Savannah Republican*, April 20, 1863. See also Victor Hicken, *Illinois in the Civil War* (Urbana, Ill., 1966), 80–81; Reid Mitchell, *Civil War Soldiers* (New York, 1988), chap. 4.

Pope's order]   George E. Farmer to Maggie, July 27, 1862, George E. Farmer Papers, Washington University, St. Louis, Missouri; [J. W. Sligh] to [Eliza W. Sligh], July 27, 1862, Sligh Family Correspondence, Michigan History Collection, Bentley Library, University of Michigan, Ann Arbor; John Beatty, *The Citizen-Soldier; or, Memoirs of a Volunteer* (Cincinnati, Ohio, 1879), 153.

"complete conquest" and "consume . . . armies"]   Ulysses S. Grant, "The Battle of Shiloh," in Robert Underwood Johnson and Clarence Clough Buel, eds., *Battles and Leaders of the Civil War* (New York, 1887), I, 486.

an officer]   James Goodnow to Nancy Goodnow, Dec. 1, 1862, James H. Goodnow Papers, Library of Congress.

86 "the ideas . . . procession"]   Wilbur F. Hinman, *The Story of the Sherman Brigade* (Alliance, Ohio, 1897), 121.

"completely . . . war"]   Will[iam Lusk] to mother, Nov. 22, 1862, William Thompson Lusk, *War Letters of William Thompson Lusk* (New York, 1911), 231.

"We have . . . they are"]   R. Mead, Jr., to folks at home, May 28, 1862, Rufus Mead, Jr., Papers, Library of Congress.

"a desert . . . may"]   C. C. C[arpenter] to [Susan C. Burkholder], Aug. 4, 1862, and C. C. Carpenter to brother, Aug. 6, 1862, Cyrus Clay Carpenter Papers, State Historical Society of Iowa, Iowa City.

"I did not . . . north"]   Entry of Nov. 19, 1864, Horatio Dana Chapman, *Civil War Diary. Diary of a Forty-Niner* (Hartford, Conn., 1929), 100.

"I say no"]   S. M. Stevens to [E. M.] Stanton, March 18, 1862, Letters Received by the Secretary of War, Main Series, Microcopy No. 221, Roll No. 207, National Archives.

"Southern . . . Soldiers"]   *Harper's Weekly*, VII (Feb. 7, 1863), 88–89.

"mere . . . class"]   Women's Loyal National League, *Proceedings of the Meeting of the Loyal Women of the Republic, Held in New York, May 14, 1863* (New York, 1863), 6.

87 "unsexed . . . Yankees"]   Orville J. Victor, ed., *Incidents and Anecdotes of the War* (New York, 1862), 395.

"The ladies . . . the town"]   S. J. F. Miller to father and mother, July 24, 1862, Kemper Family Papers, Cincinnati Historical Society, Cincinnati, Ohio.

"their poor . . . suffered"]   George H. Cadman to wife, Nov. 23, 1863, George Hovey Cadman Papers, Southern Historical Collection, University of North Carolina, Chapel Hill.

sexual intercourse]   Bell Irvin Wiley, *Confederate Women* (Westport, Conn., 1975), 162–163; [Nugens?] to Joseph B. B[oyd], April 2, 1864, Joseph B. Boyd Papers, Cincinnati Historical Society.

"We shall . . . fighting *you*"]   Virginia [Wade] to husband, Feb. 26, 1864 [1865], Mrs. Albert Rhett Heyward Papers, University of North Carolina. See also George C. Rable, *Civil Wars: Women and the Crisis of Southern Nationalism* (Urbana, Ill., 1989), 171–180; Francis Butler Simkins and James Welch Patton, *The Women of the Confederacy* (Richmond, Va., 1936), 235–240.

James H. Hammond]   Senate, March 4, 1858, *Congressional Globe*, 35th Congress, 1st Session, 961–962; Drew Gilpin Faust, *James Henry Hammond and the Old South: A Design for Mastery* (Baton Rouge, La., 1982), 347.

88 "The ignorant . . . they enjoyed"]   *New York Herald*, Aug. 30, 1862.

"the inevitable . . . society"]   *Richmond Enquirer*, July 18, 1863.

88   "The Southern . . . North"]   C. L. Burn to brother, Nov. 11, 1860, Burn Family Papers, University of South Carolina.

"In their . . . inferiors"]   *Daily Missouri Democrat* (St. Louis), Feb. 22, 1865.

"It just . . . other people"]   M[ichael] Gapen to sister, Dec. 17, 1862, Michael Gapen Collection, Chicago Historical Society, Chicago, Illinois.

"The chivalry . . . respect them"]   Entry of Sept. 14, 1863, David Lane, *A Soldier's Diary: The Story of a Volunteer, 1862–1865* (n.p., 1905), 92.

"The people . . . freemen"]   Albert [S. Hall] to Cybelia Hall, Jan. 8, 1863, Vertical File, Albert S. Hall Papers, Western Reserve Historical Society, Cleveland, Ohio.

89   "count . . . capital"]   *New York Herald,* Feb. 23, 1862.

"capitalist slaveholder" and "that capital . . . labor"]   *Harper's Weekly,* VI (Sept. 6, 1862), 562.

"rebel . . . mud-sills"]   *Newark Advertiser* reprinted in *Cincinnati Commercial,* Feb. 23, 1865. See also James L. Huston, *The Panic of 1857 and the Coming of the Civil War* (Baton Rouge, La., 1987), chap. 8.

90   "civil . . . kind"]   W. T. Sherman to Ellen [Sherman], Dec. 12, 1859, William Tecumseh Sherman Papers (consolidated microfilm collection), University of Notre Dame, Notre Dame, Indiana. Sherman is now attracting biographers. Since its publication Lloyd Lewis, *Sherman: Fighting Prophet* (New York, 1932) has been the standard life. A classic of American biography, it nevertheless has grave defects. Other biographical works include B. H. Liddell Hart, *Sherman: Soldier, Realist, American* (New York, 1929); Earl Schenck Miers, *The General Who Marched to Hell: William Tecumseh Sherman and His March to Fame and Infamy* (New York, 1951); James M. Merrill, *William Tecumseh Sherman* (Chicago, 1971).

"any one . . . first step"]   W. T. Sherman to John Sherman, June 18, 1860, W. T. Sherman Papers, Library of Congress.

"Many gentlemen . . . so soon"]   W. T. Sherman to Ellen [Sherman], Nov. 23, 1860, Sherman Papers, University of Notre Dame.

"burst out . . . will end"]   D. F. Boyd to P. T. Sherman, Dec. 7, 1891, *ibid.* See also D. F. Boyd to W. T. Sherman, July 17, 1875, W. T. Sherman Papers, Library of Congress.

91   "the cruel . . . Ohio"]   W. T. Sherman to Ellen [Sherman], Dec. 16, 1860, Sherman Papers, University of Notre Dame.

"hearing . . . current"]   W. T. Sherman to John Sherman, Dec. 1, 1860, W. T. Sherman Papers, Library of Congress.

"a terrible . . . war"]   William M. Levy to *Shreveport Times,* June 22, 1875.

"would be . . . *in time"*]   Braxton Bragg to [P. G. T. Beauregard], Feb. 6, 1866, A. Conger Goodyear Collection, Box 2, Sterling Library, Yale University.

"The wounds . . . prescience"]   M. C. Manning to W. T. Sherman, July 28, 1865, W. T. Sherman Papers, Library of Congress.

"I was amazed . . . peace"]   W. T. Sherman, [Autobiography], [1868], 215, W. T. Sherman Papers, Box 12, Ohio Historical Society.

"that the country . . . minute"]   W. T. Sherman, *Memoirs of General William T. Sherman,* 2d ed. (New York, 1886), I, 196.

"I see . . . therein"]   W. T. Sherman to Ellen [Sherman], Jan. 8, 1861, Sherman Papers, University of Notre Dame.

92   "an absurd impossibility"]   W. T. Sherman to Ellen [Sherman], Jan. 20, 1861, *ibid.* See also W. T. Sherman to Rob[er]t C. Winthrop, Oct. 13, 1886, Winthrop Papers, Massachusetts Historical Society.

"would enable . . . service"]   W. T. Sherman to S. Cameron, May 8, 1861, CW 398, Huntington Library.

92 "The men . . . rear"]   W. T. Sherman to Thomas Ewing, Sept. 15, 1861, Thomas Ewing and Family Papers, Library of Congress.

"They cleaned . . . haste"]   C. Wheeler to father, July 23, 1861, Cornelius Wheeler Papers, State Historical Society of Wisconsin, Madison.

"an armed mob"]   W. T. Sherman to Ellen [Sherman], July 24, 1861, Sherman Papers, University of Notre Dame.

"No goths . . . Virginia"]   W. T. Sherman to Ellen [Sherman], July 28, [1861], *ibid.*

93 "I was severe . . . invasion"]   W. T. Sherman to Thomas Ewing, Sept. 15, 1861, Ewing Family Papers, Library of Congress. See also Sherman, *Memoirs,* 2d ed., I, 216–219; John DuBois Barnes, "My Army Life," 97–174, HM 28916(a), Huntington Library; William T. Lusk to [Elizabeth Freeman Lusk], Aug. 15, 1861, *War Letters of Lusk,* 67.

"the best . . . money"]   W. T. Sherman to Henry Coppée, June 13, 1864, Simon Gratz Autograph Collection, Historical Society of Pennsylvania.

Sherman's doubts]   W. T. Sherman to Ellen [Sherman], [Aug. 1861], Sherman Papers, University of Notre Dame.

Morton and Yates]   W. T. Sherman to Ellen [Sherman], Sept. 18, 1861, *ibid.;* O. P. Morton to Simon Cameron, Sept. 12, 1861, and O. P. Morton to John C. Frémont, Sept. 22, 1861, *The War of the Rebellion: A Compilation of the Official Records of the Union and Confederate Armies* (Washington, D.C., 1880–1901), Series I, Vol. IV, 257, 266.

94 "No enthusiasm . . . Kentucky" and "aid . . . small"]   A. S. Johnston to [Jefferson Davis], March 18, 1862, and William Preston to William Preston Johnston, April 18, 1862, Albert Sidney Johnston and William Preston Johnston Papers, Box 10, Howard-Tilton Library, Tulane University, New Orleans, Louisiana. See also [J. F. Gilmer] to [Louisa Gilmer], Oct. 17, 23, 25, Nov. 14, 1861, Jeremy Francis Gilmer Papers, University of North Carolina; T. C. Reynolds to W. T. Sherman, Nov. 7, 1877, Thomas C. Reynolds Papers, Missouri Historical Society; Thomas Lawrence Connelly, *Army of the Heartland: The Army of Tennessee, 1861–1862* (Baton Rouge, La., 1967), 67, 87.

"all . . . destroy us"]   W. T. Sherman to Oliver D. Greene, Sept. 27, 1861, *Official Records,* Series I, Vol. IV, 279. See also W. T. Sherman to John Sherman, Oct. 5, 1861, W. T. Sherman Papers, Library of Congress; W. T. Sherman to Thomas Ewing, Sept. 30, 1861, in Joseph H. Ewing, "The New Sherman Letters," *American Heritage,* XXXVIII (July–Aug. 1987), 26.

"All . . . command"]   W. T. Sherman to Ellen [Sherman], Oct. 6, 1861, Sherman Papers, University of Notre Dame.

"committing . . . cause" and "the whole . . . way"]   W. T. Sherman to Robert Anderson, Sept. 29, 1861, University of Kentucky, Lexington.

"Make . . . stubs"]   B. F. Scribner, *How Soldiers Were Made; or the War As I Saw It Under Buell, Rosecrans, Thomas, Grant and Sherman* (New Albany, Ind., 1887), 28.

95 slaves returned]   W. T. Sherman to [John Basil] Turchin, Oct. 15, 1861, and W. T. Sherman to [A. McD.] McCook, Nov. 8, 1861, *Official Records,* Series I, Vol. IV, 307, 347.

"His mind . . . resolute"]   *Louisville Journal,* Oct. 8, 1861, reprinted in *Cincinnati Commercial,* Oct. 9, 1861.

"the superior . . . headed"]   *Cincinnati Commercial,* Oct. 25, 1861.

"He performs . . . dispatch"]   *New York Times,* Oct. 16, 1861.

"a brilliant . . . Green"]   *Ibid.,* Oct. 6, 1861.

"The least . . . soil"]   *Ibid.,* Oct. 5, 1861.

"will not . . . Tennessee"]   Garrett Davis to W. T. Sherman, Oct. 12, 1861, James F. Aldrich Collection, Chicago Historical Society.

"The force . . . inadequate"]   W. T. Sherman to [A.] Lincoln, Oct. 10, 1861, *Official Records,* Series I, Vol. IV, 300.

95 60,000 men] W. T. Sherman to Lorenzo Thomas, Oct. 8, 1861, W. T. Sherman Papers, Library of Congress.

96 East Tennessee and George H. Thomas] [Abraham Lincoln], [Views of a plan of campaign—1861], *Official Records,* Series I, Vol. LII, Part I, 191–192; entry of Dec. 11, 1861, Diary, Salmon P. Chase Papers, Library of Congress; W. T. Sherman to Geo[rge] H. Thomas, Nov. 8, 11, 12, 1861, de Coppett Collection, Princeton University; W. T. Sherman to S. P. Chase, Oct. 14, 1861, Chase Papers, Library of Congress.

Sherman harried] *New York Herald,* Aug. 5, 1864; W. T. Sherman to John Sherman, Jan 8, 1862, W. T. Sherman Papers, Library of Congress; W. T. Sherman to Ellen [Sherman], Jan. 29, 1862, Sherman Papers, University of Notre Dame.

"I then said . . . space"] W. T. Sherman's annotations in *Memoirs of General William T. Sherman* (New York, 1875), I, 41, Jared W. Young's Sherman Collection, Special Collections, Northwestern University, Evanston, Illinois.

96–7 "was tired . . . enemy"] Lorenzo Thomas to Simon Cameron, Oct. 21, 1861, *Official Records,* Series I, Vol. IV, 314. See also Sherman, *Memoirs,* 2d ed., I, 229–231, 238–242; W. T. Sherman to Thomas Ewing, Dec. 12, 1861, W. T. Sherman Papers, Library of Congress.

97 "bring . . . confusion"] O. M. Mitchel to "Judge," Oct. 12, 1861, Clinton H. Haskell Collection, Clements Library, University of Michigan, Ann Arbor.

"Sherman . . . extraordinary amts"] M[ontgomery] Blair to [Benjamin F.] Butler, Oct. 22, 1861, Benjamin F. Butler Papers, Library of Congress.

"I again . . . nation"] W. T. Sherman to L. Thomas, Oct. 22, 1861, *Official Records,* Series I, Vol. IV, 316.

Lorenzo Thomas's report] *New York Tribune,* Oct. 30, 1861; Henry Villard, *Memoirs of Henry Villard, Journalist and Financier, 1835–1900* (Boston, 1904), I, 209–213; Murat Halstead, "Recollections and Letters of General Sherman," *The Independent,* LI (June 15–22, 1899), 1610–1613.

"whose force . . . future"] W. T. Sherman to L. Thomas, Nov. 4, 1861, *Official Records,* Series I, Vol. IV, 332–333.

"desponding . . . insubordinate"] John Sherman to Ellen [Sherman], Dec. 14, 1861, Sherman Papers, University of Notre Dame.

"with some ridicule . . . crazy"] John B. Haskin to W. T. Sherman, Feb. 8, 1890, W. T. Sherman Papers, Library of Congress.

98 "at the signal"] [W. T. Sherman] to Ellen [Sherman], Oct. 25, 1861, Sherman Papers, University of Notre Dame.

"shoot . . . dogs"] Ellen Sherman to Maria Ewing, Nov. 11, 1861, Ewing Family Papers, Library of Congress.

"The idea . . . now"] W. T. S[herman] to Ellen [Sherman], Nov. 1, 1861, Sherman Papers, University of Notre Dame.

wagons] T[homas] L[eonidas] Crittenden to W. T. Sherman, Nov. 5, 1861, War 1861–5 Papers, New-York Historical Society; W. T. Sherman to George H. Thomas, Nov. 3, 11, 12, 1861, de Coppett Collection, Princeton University.

"determined . . . disaster" and "too strong . . . prudent"] [J. F. Gilmer] to [Louisa Gilmer], Oct. 25 and Nov. 14, 1861, Gilmer Papers, University of North Carolina.

"I magnified . . . enemy"] A. S. Johnston to [Jefferson Davis], March 18, 1862, Johnston Papers, Tulane University. See also Steven E. Woodworth, *Jefferson Davis and His Generals: The Failure of Confederate Command in the West* (Lawrence, Kan., 1990), 52–56.

"Our forces . . . sacrifice"] W. T. Sherman to George McClellan, Nov. 3, 1861, W. T. Sherman Papers, Library of Congress.

"You should . . . emergency"] W. T. Sherman to [William] Dennison, Nov. 6, 1861, William Coffey Papers, Ohio Historical Society.

98 "has been . . . responsible for it"]   W. T. Sherman to John Sherman, Jan. 8, 1862, W.
T. Sherman Papers, Library of Congress. See also Ellen Sherman to Thomas Ewing, Jr.,
March 20, 1862, Ewing Family Papers, *ibid.*

99 "insanity" . . . "to heart"]   Ellen Sherman to Maria Ewing, Nov. 11, 1861, Ewing
Family Papers, *ibid.;* Ellen Sherman to John Sherman, Nov. 10 and Dec. 17, 1861, W.
T. Sherman Papers, *ibid.* On Sherman's condition in Louisville see also J. F. Speed *et
al.* to W. T. Sherman, Nov. 12, 1861, in Victor L. Jacobs, "Was Uncle Billy Off His
Rocker?" *Manuscripts,* XVII, No. 3 (1965), 21–27.

"vast force" . . . "whole line"]   W. T. Sherman to Geo[rge] H. Thomas, Nov. 11, 1861,
de Coppett Collection, Princeton University. See also Michael C. C. Adams, *Our Masters
the Rebels: A Speculation on Union Military Failure in the East, 1861–1865* (Cambridge,
Mass., 1978), 86.

"has the *go* . . . men" and "seems to lack . . . commanders"]   *Cincinnati Commercial,*
Nov. 12, 1861.

"Forward"]   *Ibid.,* Nov. 16, 1861.

"Sherman's . . . head"]   A. K. McClure, *Abraham Lincoln and Men of War-Times*
(Philadelphia, 1892), 212.

"took . . . head"]   Entry of Nov. 26, 1861, Diary, William E. Smith and Ophia D.
Smith, eds., *Colonel A. W. Gilbert: Citizen-Soldier of Cincinnati* (Cincinnati, Ohio, 1934),
71.

99–100 "stampeded" . . . "unfit for duty"]   H. W. Halleck to George B. McClellan, Dec.
2, 1861, *Official Records,* Series I, Vol. LII, Part I, 198; Henry W. Halleck to W. T.
Sherman, Dec. 18, 1861, *ibid.,* Vol. VIII, 445–446. See also H. W. H[alleck] to wife,
Dec. 14, 1861, James S. Schoff Civil War Collection, Letters and Documents, Box 4,
Clements Library.

100 origins of *Commercial* report]   M[urat] Halstead to [W. T.] Sherman, March 16, 1876,
W. T. Sherman Papers, Library of Congress; Donald W. Curl, *Murat Halstead and the
Cincinnati Commercial* (Boca Raton, Fla., 1980), 27; Villard, *Memoirs,* I, 209–213; John
F. Marszalek, *Sherman's Other War: The General and the Civil War Press* (Memphis,
Tenn., 1981), chap. 3.

"foul hovels" and "a sea of mud"]   Anthony Trollope, *North America,* ed. Donald
Smalley and Bradford Allan Booth (New York, 1951 [orig. publ. London, 1862]),
392–393.

"a very morose . . . man"]   Henry [Spaulding] to uncle, April 16, 1862, Henry
Spaulding Papers, Duke University. See also entries of Jan. 5, 6, 20, 1862, Henry Dysart,
Diary, State Historical Society of Iowa; Henry [S. Wadsworth] to aunt, June 23, [1862],
Henry S. Wadsworth Letters, Civil War Papers, Missouri Historical Society; [Henry
M. Hempstead] to wife, Sept. 23, 1864, Henry M. Hempstead Papers, Bentley Library,
University of Michigan.

"sadly . . . enemy"]   [W. T. Sherman] to Ellen [Sherman], Jan. 19, 1862, Sherman
Papers, University of Notre Dame. See also W. T. Sherman to Phil[emon B. Ewing],
Jan. 20, 1862, in Ewing, "New Sherman Letters," *American Heritage,* XXXVIII (July–
Aug. 1987), 26.

"I feel . . . Mississippi"]   W. T. Sherman to Ellen [Sherman], Jan. 11, 1862, Sherman
Papers, University of Notre Dame. See also W. T. Sherman to John Sherman, Jan. 4,
1862, W. T. Sherman Papers, Library of Congress.

101 "It will . . . war"]   *New York Times,* Dec. 9, 1861.

"overlook . . . crime" and "They will . . . Death"]   John Sherman to [W. T. Sherman],
Nov. 17, 1861, Sherman Papers, University of Notre Dame.

"What has kept . . . *consequences"*]   J. H. Jordan to John Sherman, Dec. 22, 1861, Jan.
1, 1861 [1862], John Sherman Papers, Library of Congress.

"We should . . . sword"]   Edwin M. Stanton to Charles A. Dana, Feb. 2, 1862, quoted
in Benjamin P. Thomas and Harold M. Hyman, *Stanton: The Life and Times of Lincoln's
Secretary of War* (New York, 1962), 146.

101 "riding . . . storm"]   W. T. S[herman] to Ellen [Sherman], Nov. 1, 1861, Sherman
Papers, University of Notre Dame.

"I was convinced . . . success"]   W. T. Sherman to Thomas Ewing, Dec. 24, 1861,
Ewing Family Papers, Library of Congress.

102 "rise . . . armies" and "acts . . . violence"]   W. T. Sherman to John Sherman, Jan. 8,
1862, W. T. Sherman Papers, *ibid.*

"the people . . . settlement"]   W. T. Sherman to John Sherman, Jan. 9, 1862, *ibid.*

"In these . . . insane"]   W. T. Sherman to Thomas Ewing, Dec. 12, 1861, Ewing Family
Papers, *ibid.*

103 "disappeared . . . rear"]   W. T. Sherman to John A. Rawlins, April 10, 1862, *Official
Records,* Series I, Vol. X, Part I, 249.

"I was not . . . man"]   Crafts J. Wright to John Sherman, April 30, 1862, John Sherman
Papers, Library of Congress. See also W. T. Sherman to Ellen [Sherman], April 11, 1862,
Sherman Papers, University of Notre Dame; A. W. McCormick to Thomas Ewing, Dec.
5, 1862, Ewing Family Papers, Library of Congress; Edwin D. Judd to Gideon Welles,
May 28, 1862, Gideon Welles Papers, Vol. 50, Library of Congress; Thomas Kilby Smith
to wife, May 8, 1862, Walter George Smith, *Life and Letters of Thomas Kilby Smith* (New
York, 1898), 202. On McClernand see W. T. Sherman to Ellen [Sherman], April 23,
1863, Sherman Papers, University of Notre Dame.

104 "disorganized . . . exhausted"]   B[raxton] B[ragg] to [Elise Bragg], April 8, [1862],
Braxton Bragg Papers, Missouri Historical Society.

"fought . . . ground"]   L[eonidas] Polk to S. Cooper, Sept. 1862, *Official Records,* Series
I, Vol. X, Part I, 408.

"It is . . . victory on the 7th"]   H. W. Halleck to E. M. Stanton, April 13, 1862, *ibid.,*
98. See also U. S. Grant to N. H. McLean, April 9, 1862, *ibid.,* 110.

"at last . . . paper"]   W. T. Sherman to Ellen [Sherman], April 14, 1862, Sherman
Papers, University of Notre Dame.

"performed . . . October"]   W. T. Sherman to John Sherman, May 12, 1862, W. T.
Sherman Papers, Library of Congress.

"I suppose . . . enemy"]   W. T. Sherman to John Sherman, May 26, 1862, *ibid.*

"for a . . . time"]   W. T. Sherman to Ellen [Sherman], April 11, 1862, Sherman Papers,
University of Notre Dame. See also Benjamin H. Grierson, "The Lights and Shadows
of Life: Including Experiences and Remembrances of the War of the Rebellion," 194,
Benjamin H. Grierson Papers, Box 17, Illinois State Historical Library, Springfield.

105 Whitelaw Reid]   Bingham Duncan, *Whitelaw Reid: Journalist, Politician, Diplomat*
(Athens, Ga., 1975), 18–19.

"Of course . . . sentiment"]   *Cincinnati Commercial,* June 23, 1863. See also J. Cutler
Andrews, *The North Reports the Civil War* (Pittsburgh, Pa., 1955), 179–181.

"spurious reputation"]   *Cincinnati Gazette,* May 6, 1862. Compare *Cincinnati Commercial,* April 18, 29, May 7, 1862.

"Who ever . . . under"]   E. Hempstead to [Elihu B. Washburne], April 15, 1862, Elihu
B. Washburne Papers, Vol. 24, Library of Congress. See also J. M[edill] to Elihu B.
[Washburne], May 24, 1862, *ibid.,* Vol. 25; W. T. Sherman to Ellen [Sherman], Oct.
14, 1863, Sherman Papers, University of Notre Dame; McClure, *Abraham Lincoln,* 177;
U. S. Grant to E. B. Washburn[e], May 14, 1862, John Y. Simon, ed., *The Papers of
Ulysses S. Grant* (Carbondale, Ill., 1967–), V, 119–120.

"carry . . . countrymen"]   Senate, May 9, 1862, *Congressional Globe,* 37th Congress, 2d
Session, 2037.

105–6 "Our . . . fault"]   W. T. Sherman to Alfred T. Goodman, May 1, 1862, HM 21698,
Huntington Library. See also Sherman, *Memoirs,* 2d ed., I, 274–275; W. T. Sherman to
[Benjamin Stanton], [June 1, 1862], and W. T. Sherman to Benjamin Stanton, July 12,
1862, W. T. Sherman Papers, Library of Congress; John Sherman to W. T. Sherman,

Aug. 29, 1863, *ibid.;* Thomas Ewing, *Letter of Hon. Thomas Ewing to His Excellency Benj. Stanton* (Columbus, Ohio, 1862); Thomas Ewing to [Hugh Ewing], Feb. 25, 1863, Hugh Boyle Ewing Papers, Ohio Historical Society.

106 "constant . . . rash"]   W. T. Sherman to Ellen Sherman, May 23, 1862, Charles Ewing Papers, Library of Congress.

"The political . . . belongs"]   W. T. Sherman to Ellen [Sherman], April 24, 1862, Sherman Papers, University of Notre Dame.

"like vultures . . . creation"]   W. T. Sherman to Ellen [Sherman], May 6, 1862, *ibid.*

"So greedy . . . not before"]   W. T. Sherman to Ellen Sherman, May 23, 1862, Charles Ewing Papers, Library of Congress. See also W. T. Sherman to [Philemon Ewing], May 16, 1862, Ewing Family Papers, *ibid.*

"Figures . . . standard"]   W. T. Sherman to Ellen [Sherman], April 11, 1862, Sherman Papers, University of Notre Dame.

"We must . . . begin"]   W. T. Sherman to Charles Ewing, April 25, 1862, Charles Ewing Papers, Library of Congress.

107 "the country . . . beasts"]   W. T. Sherman, General Orders, No. 49, July 7, 1862, *Official Records,* Series I, Vol. XVII, Part II, 81.

"didn't come . . . war"]   *Cincinnati Commercial,* July 28, 1862.

"I cannot . . . friends"]   W. T. Sherman to [Maria Ewing Sherman], Aug. 6, 1862, W. T. Sherman Papers, Ohio Historical Society.

"with . . . hand"]   *New York Herald,* Aug. 4, 1862.

"The only . . . conciliation"]   John Sherman to W. T. Sherman, Aug. 24, 1862, W. T. Sherman Papers, Library of Congress.

"to hold . . . parties"]   W. T. Sherman to [H. W.] Halleck, July 14, 1862, *Official Records,* Series I, Vol. XVII, Part I, 23.

Randolph and expulsion from Memphis]   W. T. Sherman to Ellen [Sherman], Sept. 25, 1862, Sherman Papers, University of Notre Dame; W. T. Sherman, Special Orders, No. 254, Sept. 27, 1862, *Official Records,* Series I, Vol. XVII, Part II, 240; W. T. Sherman to C. C. Walcutt, Sept. 24, 1862, *ibid.,* 235–236; W. T. Sherman to U. S. Grant, Oct. 4, 9, 1862, *ibid.,* 260–262, 273; W. T. Sherman to John A. Rawlins, Oct. 18, 1862, *ibid.,* 280; W. T. Sherman to P. A. Fraser, Oct. 22, 1862, *ibid.,* 288; W. T. Sherman to T. C. Hindman, Oct. 17, 1862, *ibid.,* Series II, Vol. IV, 631–632; W. T. Sherman to Samuel R. Curtis, Oct. 18, 1862, *ibid.,* 633; entry of Jan. 17, 1863, W[illiam] W[illiston] Heartsill, *Fourteen Hundred and 91 Days in the Confederate Army* [Marshall, Tex., 1876], 101. Sherman suspended his order of expulsion, but some families were sent out of the city. See W. T. Sherman to E. M. Stanton, Dec. 16, 1862, War 1861–5 Papers, New-York Historical Society. On the effectiveness of punitive military action to suppress guerrillas see Stephen V. Ash, *Middle Tennessee Society Transformed, 1860–1870: War and Peace in the Upper South* (Baton Rouge, La., 1987), 154–157.

"great atrocities" and "burned . . . citizens"]   W. T. Sherman to Ellen [Sherman], [Sept. 1862], Sherman Papers, University of Notre Dame.

107 "energetic . . . zeal"]   W. T. Sherman to John A. Rawlins, Sept. 4, 1862, *Official Records,* Series I, Vol. XVII, Part II, 201.

107–8 "He is . . . rest"]   Quoted in Grierson, "Lights and Shadows," 276, Grierson Papers, Illinois State Historical Library.

108 "We cannot . . . people"]   W. T. Sherman to Charles Ewing, July 8, 1862, Charles Ewing Papers, Library of Congress.

"burn . . . destroy"]   Thomas Kilby Smith to mother, July 23, 1862, Walter Smith, *Life and Letters of Smith,* 232.

"no life . . . power"]   W. T. Sherman to T. C. Hindman, Oct. 17, 1862, *Official Records,* Series II, Vol. IV, 632.

108 "who made war" and "generally . . . else"]   W. T. Sherman to Editor, *Bulletin,* Sept. 21, 1862, in Sherman, *Memoirs,* 2d ed., I, 304–306.

"land . . . interior"]   W. T. Sherman to Samuel R. Curtis, Oct. 18, 1862, *Official Records,* Series II, Vol. IV, 633.

"brutal wretch" and "Hundreds . . . perdition"]   W. T. Sherman to [Maria Ewing Sherman], Aug. 6, 1862, Sherman Papers, Ohio Historical Society.

"I feel . . . people"]   W. T. Sherman to [Maria Ewing Sherman], Oct. 4, 1862, *ibid.*

"make . . . revenge"]   *Chattanooga Rebel,* Oct. 7, 1862.

109 Buell]   D. C. Buell to [?], July 10, 1864, Henry Boynton Correspondence, Ezra Ayres Carman Papers, Box 2, New York Public Library, New York, New York.

"extermination"]   [W. T. Sherman] to Ellen [Sherman], July 31, 1862, Sherman Papers, University of Notre Dame.

"universal . . . colonization"]   W. T. Sherman to [U. S.] Grant, Aug. 17, 1862, *Official Records,* Series I, Vol. XVII, Part II, 178.

"Enemies . . . country"]   W. T. Sherman to [John Sherman], Aug. 13, 1862, HM 25547, Huntington Library.

"Three . . . lives"]   W. T. Sherman to R. M. Sawyer, Jan. 31, 1864, *Official Records,* Series I, Vol. XXXII, Part II, 280–281.

Southern social order]   W. T. Sherman to H. W. Halleck, Sept. 17, 1863, *ibid.,* Vol. XXX, Part III, 695–696.

"may take . . . strength upon"]   W. T. Sherman to H. W. Hill, Sept. 7, 1863, *ibid.,* 403. See also W. T. Sherman to Jesse Read and W. B. Anderson, Aug. 3, 1863, Palmer Collection, Box 1, Western Reserve Historical Society.

110 "as Belligerents . . . people" and "We are . . . property"]   W. T. Sherman to Thomas Hunton, Aug. 24, 1862, Ira Berlin *et al.,* eds., *Freedom: A Documentary History of Emancipation, 1861–1867* (Cambridge, 1985), Series I, Vol. I, 293–294. See also W. T. Sherman to D. D. Porter, Nov. 12, 1862, HM 23303, Huntington Library; Edward Hagerman, *The American Civil War and the Origins of Modern Warfare: Ideas, Organization, and Field Command* (Bloomington, Ind., 1988), 207–209.

"Don't . . . century"]   W. T. Sherman to [John Sherman], Aug. 13, 1862, HM 25547, Huntington Library. See also W. T. Sherman to W. K. Strong, Nov. 1, 1862, Schoff Collection, Letters and Documents, Box 7, Clements Library.

"I want . . . concentrate"]   W. T. Sherman to [D. D.] Porter, Dec. 20, 1862, Palmer Collection, Box 1, Western Reserve Historical Society.

"into Vicksburg . . . possibility"]   W. T. Sherman to D. D. Porter, Dec. 28, 1862, HM 23299, Huntington Library.

112 "There is . . . yards"]   S. D. Lee to E. P. Alexander, Nov. 30, 1862, Edward Porter Alexander Papers, Box 1, University of North Carolina. See also Dabney H. Maury, "Grant's Campaign in North Mississippi in 1862," *Southern Magazine,* XIII (Oct. 1873), 414–415.

Morgan]   Sherman, *Memoirs,* 2d ed., I, 319–323.

Grant]   U. S. Grant to A. Lincoln, July 22, 1863, Simon, ed., *Papers of Grant,* IX, 97.

"This was . . . unhinged"]   David Dixon Porter, Private Journal No. 1, "Journal of Occurrences during the War of the Rebellion," 465, David Dixon Porter Papers, Box 19, Library of Congress.

"The only . . . approach"]   W. T. Sherman to John Sherman, April 3, 1863, W. T. Sherman Papers, Library of Congress.

"A stupid . . . government"]   Reprinted in Moore, ed., *Rebellion Record,* VI, 310.

"cannot . . . falsehood"]   W. T. Sherman to F. P. Blair, [Jr.], Feb. 2, 1863, W. T. Sherman Papers, Library of Congress. On Knox and other reporters see also Thomas

Wallace Knox, *Camp-fire and Cotton-field* (New York, 1865), 253–259; Thomas W. Knox to W. T. Sherman, Feb. 1, 1863, W. T. Sherman Papers, Library of Congress; Porter, Private Journal No. 1, "Journal of Occurrences," 478–479, Porter Papers, *ibid.;* W. T. Sherman to Frank P. Blair, Jr., Feb. 1, 2, 3, 1863, and Frank P. Blair, Jr., to W. T. Sherman, Feb. 1, 1863, Blair Family Papers, *ibid.;* Tho[ma]s Kilby Smith to [Eliza Bicker Walter Smith], Feb. 4, 22, 1863, Thomas Kilby Smith Papers, Huntington Library; *New York Herald,* Jan. 9, 15, 18, 1863; Sylvanus Cadwallader, *Three Years With Grant As Recalled by War Correspondent Sylvanus Cadwallader,* ed. Benjamin P. Thomas (New York, 1955), 45; Andrews, *North Reports the War,* 378–383; Marszalek, *Sherman's Other War,* chap. 5.

113 "full . . . retraction"] Henry L. Patterson to Thomas Ewing, March 16, 1863, Ewing Family Papers, Library of Congress. The *Missouri Republican* report was reprinted in the *Cincinnati Commercial,* Jan. 15, 17, 1863.

Fort Hindman] U. S. Grant to A. Lincoln, July 22, 1863, Simon, ed., *Papers of Grant,* IX, 97–98; W. T. Sherman to John Sherman, Jan. 17, 1863, W. T. Sherman Papers, Library of Congress; Porter, Private Journal No. 1, "Journal of Occurrences," 482–490, Porter Papers, *ibid.;* [Absalom Hanks Markland], "A Chapter in War History," Markland Papers, Manuscript Department, The Filson Club, Louisville, Kentucky.

"The one . . . success"] *New York Herald,* Jan. 21, 1863. See also John A. McClernand to A. Lincoln, Jan. 16, 1863, John A. McClernand Papers, Illinois State Historical Library.

"Say Vicksburg . . . so on"] [W. T.] Sherman to Ellen [Sherman], Jan. 28, 1863, Sherman Papers, University of Notre Dame.

"Discussion . . . begin"] W. T. Sherman to [Murat] Halstead, April 8, 1863, *Official Records,* Series I, Vol. XVII, Part II, 896.

"their ability . . . indefinitely"] W. T. Sherman to John Sherman, Jan. 6, 1862 [1863], W. T. Sherman Papers, Vol. 10, Library of Congress.

113–14 "to subdue . . . determination"] W. T. Sherman to John Sherman, Jan. 25, 1863, *ibid.,* Vol. 11.

114 "an axiom in war"] U. S. Grant, *Personal Memoirs of U. S. Grant* (New York, 1885), I, 542–543n.

"quoted . . . concentration"] James Harrison Wilson, *Under the Old Flag* (New York, 1912), I, 160.

"I feel . . . war"] W. T. Sherman to John Sherman, April 26, 1863, W. T. Sherman Papers, Library of Congress.

115 "universal . . . destruction" and "not . . . war"] W. T. Sherman to Ellen [Sherman], May 6, 1863, Sherman Papers, University of Notre Dame.

"exclamations of joy"] John Russell Young, *Around the World with General Grant* (New York, 1879), II, 624.

"was the . . . history"] Grant, *Personal Memoirs,* I, 528.

"The fall . . . time"] U. S. Grant to H. W. Halleck, May 24, 1863, *Official Records,* Series I, Vol. XXIV, Part I, 37.

"The only . . . hope"] J. E. Johnston to William Mackall, June 7, 1863, William W. Mackall Papers, University of North Carolina.

"I see . . . other"] Young, *Around the World,* II, 626.

115–16 "The capture . . . war" and "could also . . . war"] W. T. Sherman to Ellen [Sherman], July 5, 1863, Sherman Papers, University of Notre Dame.

116 "It settles . . . make it"] [W. T.] Sherman to [W. D.] Sanger, July 29, 1863, W. T. Sherman Papers, Louisiana State University.

"should have . . . war"] Sherman, *Memoirs,* 2d ed., I, 362.

"civil compromises . . . thick and fast"] W. T. Sherman to J. A. Rawlins, Sept. 17, 1863, *ibid.,* 370–371.

116 "you . . . blush"]   W. T. Sherman to John A. Rawlins, Aug. 4, 1863, *Official Records,* Series I, Vol. XXIV, Part III, 574.

116–17 "I, poor . . . rail"]   W. T. Sherman to Leslie Coombs, Aug. 11, 1864, Letterbook, Vol. 3/5, Military Division of the Mississippi, Record Group 393, Part 1, No. 2484, National Archives.

117 "If the Vicksburg . . . people"]   Young, *Around the World,* II, 625.

117–18 "The government . . . North"]   W. T. Sherman to S. P. Chase, Aug. 11, 1862, Salmon P. Chase Papers, Historical Society of Pennsylvania.

118 "It is none . . . consequences"]   W. T. Sherman to [Stephen A.] Hurlbut, Nov. 18, 1863, *Official Records,* Series I, Vol. XXXI, Part III, 187.

"If it is true . . . yours"]   *Cincinnati Commercial,* Dec. 26, 1864.

"I attribute . . . disunion"]   W. T. Sherman to S. L. Fremont, July 18, 1865, Dorothy Fremont Grant Collection, North Carolina Division of Archives and History, Raleigh.

119 "a few . . . desolation"]   W. T. Sherman to James M. Calhoun *et al.,* Sept. 12, 1864, *Official Records,* Series I, Vol. XXXIX, Part II, 419.

"almost alone . . . vain"]   W. T. Sherman to Caroline Carson, Jan. 20, 1865, James L. Petigru Papers, Library of Congress.

"the senseless . . . crowd"]   W. T. Sherman to S. L. Fremont, July 18, 1865, Grant Collection, North Carolina Archives. On Southerners' collective responsibility see also W. T. Sherman, [Memorandum], Jan. 15, 1865, Hitchcock Family Papers, Box 3, Missouri Historical Society; W. T. Sherman, Special Orders, No. 285, Oct. 22, 1862, *Official Records,* Series I, Vol. XVII, Part II, 289–290; W. T. Sherman to H. W. Halleck, Sept. 17, 1863, *ibid.,* Vol. XXX, Part III, 696; W. T. Sherman to R. M. Sawyer, Jan. 31, 1864, *ibid.,* Vol. XXXII, Part II, 278–281; W. T. Sherman to T. Turner, March 25, 1865, Society Miscellaneous Collection, Historical Society of Pennsylvania.

120 "Firmness . . . temper"]   *Western Star,* June 27, 1829, quoted in unidentified newspaper clipping, Charles R. Sherman Papers, W. T. Sherman Papers (consolidated microfilm collection), University of Notre Dame.

"I gladly . . . father"]   John Sherman, *Recollections of Forty Years in the House, Senate and Cabinet: An Autobiography* (Chicago, 1895), I, 20.

"approached . . . ability"]   W. T. Sherman to William Henry Smith, July 8, 1885, W. T. Sherman Papers, Ohio Historical Society. See also B. M. Atherton to W. T. Sherman, Aug. 30, 1864, W. T. Sherman Papers, Library of Congress; Charles S. Parrish to W. T. Sherman, Oct. 22, 1866, *ibid.;* C. K. Smith to John Sherman, May 22, 1864, John Sherman Papers, *ibid.;* John Sherman to Mary Sherman, Sept. 9, 1838, *ibid.,* W[illiam] J. R[eese], *Sketch of the Life of Judge Charles R. Sherman* (n.p., [1872]); Carrington T. Marshall, ed., *A History of the Courts and Lawyers of Ohio* (New York, 1934), I, chaps. 13–16.

"the greatest . . . leaders"]   Alvin M. Josephy, Jr., *The Patriot Chiefs: A Chronicle of American Indian Resistance* (New York, 1969), 173.

"savage" . . . "warrior"]   R[eese], *Sketch of Sherman,* 14. See also W. T. Sherman to W[illia]m Stanley Hatch, Nov. 22, 1872, William Tecumseh Sherman Letters, Illinois State Historical Library.

121 "Cumpy King"]   W. T. Sherman, [Autobiography], [1868], 3–4, W. T. Sherman Papers, Ohio Historical Society.

Elizabeth Stoddard Sherman]   W. T. Sherman to [T. DeWitt Talmage], Dec. 12, 1886 [1888], in Edward Bok, *The Americanization of Edward Bok: The Autobiography of a Dutch Boy Fifty Years After* (New York, 1921), 216–218; John Sherman, *Recollections,* I, 89–90.

122 "I have . . . Ewing"]   Murat Halstead, "Recollections of Sherman," *The Independent,* LI (June 15–22, 1899), 1610.

army or navy]   T. Ewing to [Lewis] Cass, Aug. 1, 1835, General Correspondence, Sherman Papers, University of Notre Dame; Sherman, *Memoirs,* 2d ed., I, 14.

122 "falling . . . dependency"]   W. T. Sherman to John Sherman, June 11, 1843, W. T. Sherman Papers, Library of Congress.

"I think . . . weaned"]   W. T. Sherman to Thomas Ewing, Jr., Sept. 17, 1852, Ewing Family Papers, *ibid.*

"Of course . . . you"]   W. T. Sherman to Thomas Ewing, June 21, 1866, *ibid.*

"she would . . . Lancaster"]   Eleanor Sherman Fitch, Note, Sherman Papers, University of Notre Dame. See also W. T. Sherman to Thomas Ewing, Jr., Aug. 30, 1852, Ewing Family Papers, Library of Congress.

123 "travelling demagogues"]   W. T. Sherman to John Sherman, Oct. 24, 1844, W. T. Sherman Papers, Library of Congress.

"the new . . . party" and "to follow . . . respect"]   W. T. Sherman to [Henry S.] Turner, May 4, 1856, Sherman Papers, Ohio Historical Society.

"Mr Ewings . . . change it"]   John Sherman to W. T. Sherman, Dec. 18, 1864, W. T. Sherman Papers, Library of Congress. See also W. T. Sherman to Hugh Ewing, July 2, 1873, Sherman Papers, University of Notre Dame; W. T. Sherman to Ellen B. Ewing, Nov. 28, 1842, Sept. 17, 1844, Feb. 3, 1848, and [W. T.] Sherman to Ellen [Sherman], June 6, 1852, *ibid.; Cleveland Plain Dealer,* May 31, 1865. Views shared by Sherman are summarized in Daniel Walker Howe, *The Political Culture of the American Whigs* (Chicago, 1979); Robert W. Johannsen, "Lincoln, Liberty, and Equality," in *The Frontier, the Union and Stephen A. Douglas* (Urbana, Ill., 1989), 249–266.

124 "humbuggery"]   W. T. Sherman to Philemon B. Ewing, April 13, 1840, Philemon B. Ewing Papers, Ohio Historical Society.

"are easily . . . Hero"]   W. T. Sherman to Thomas Ewing, Jan. 20, 1844, Ewing Family Papers, Library of Congress. On instruction in the academy see James L. Morrison, Jr., *"The Best School in the World": West Point, The Pre-Civil War Years, 1833–1866* (Kent, Ohio, 1986), chap. 6.

"aristocratic and anti-republican"]   "The Military Academy," *North American Review,* LVII (Oct. 1843), 287.

"An officer . . . industrious"]   W. T. Sherman to [Willard] Warner, Jan. 20, 1866, Sherman Letters, Illinois State Historical Library. See also Edward M. Coffman, *The Old Army: A Portrait of the American Army in Peacetime, 1784–1898* (New York, 1986), chap. 2.

"that intense . . . bred"]   W. T. Sherman to [James A.] Garfield, Aug. 4, 1870, W. T. Sherman Papers, Library of Congress.

125 "firm & independent"]   W. T. Sherman to John Sherman, Aug. 3, 1856, *ibid.*

House of Representatives]   W. T. Sherman to P. B. Ewing, July 23, 1841, Philemon B. Ewing Papers, Ohio Historical Society.

"that our . . . anarchy"]   [W. T.] Sherman to Ellen [Sherman], June 6, 1862, Sherman Papers, University of Notre Dame.

"calculated . . . governments" and "real trouble . . . law"]   W. T. Sherman to G. M. Graham, Jan. 5, [1861?], W. T. Sherman Letter-book, 1859–1862, State Historical Society of Wisconsin.

"Together . . . this war"]   Gouverneur Kemble Warren to Emily Forbes Chase, May 1863, in Emerson Gifford Taylor, *Gouverneur Kemble Warren: The Life and Letters of an American Soldier, 1830–1882* (Boston, 1932), 112.

"Civil war . . . people"]   House of Representatives, April 20, 1864, *Congressional Globe,* 38th Congress, 1st Session, 1767.

126 "has been . . . shame"]   Daniel S. Dickinson, "The Union: It Must and Shall Be Preserved. An Address . . . July 10th, 1861," Moore, ed., *Rebellion Record,* II, 265–266.

"jarring . . . states"]   J. Holt to J. F. Speed, May 31, 1861, *Cincinnati Commercial,* June 11, 1861.

126 "a race . . . Mexico"]   J. Holt to [John Cadwalader?], Nov. 30, 1860, Cadwalader Collection, John Cadwalader, Jr., Section, Historical Society of Pennsylvania. See also *Cincinnati Commercial*, Aug. 6, 1862; *New York Herald*, Jan. 21, April 11 and 25, Aug. 11, Sept. 29, 1861; *Harper's Weekly*, V (May 18, 1861), 306, (Aug. 3, 1861), 482; [Governor Kirkwood's First Meeting with President Lincoln], Samuel Kirkwood Papers, Box 1, State Historical Society of Iowa; Speech by Levi Hubbell, ca. April 25, 1861, in Love, *Wisconsin in the War*, 155; Robert W. Johannsen, *To the Halls of the Montezumas: The Mexican War in the American Imagination* (New York, 1985), esp. 156–158, 266; Richard Slotkin, *The Fatal Environment: The Myth of the Frontier in the Age of Industrialization, 1800–1890* (New York, 1985), 174–190.

"the fate . . . war"]   W. T. Sherman to James M. Calhoun *et al.*, Sept. 12, 1864, *Official Records*, Series I, Vol. XXXIX, Part II, 418. See also W. T. Sherman to John Sherman, Jan. 6, 1858, W. T. Sherman Papers, Library of Congress; W. T. Sherman to S. P. Chase, Jan. 11, 1865, Chase Papers, Historical Society of Pennsylvania; W. T. Sherman to [Willard] Warner, Feb. 16, 1867, Sherman Letters, Illinois State Historical Library; W. T. Sherman to [W. C. Church], July 28, 1865, William C. Church Papers, Library of Congress.

"I would not . . . slave"]   W. T. Sherman to [Thomas Ewing, Jr.], Dec. 23, 1859, Ewing Family Papers, Library of Congress.

126–7 "refractory . . . negroes"]   Yates Snowden, [Reminiscences], Yates Snowden Papers, Box 38, University of South Carolina.

127 "necessary . . . world"]   W. T. Sherman to John Sherman, Dec. 9, 1860, W. T. Sherman Papers, Library of Congress.

"this state . . . reality"]   W. T. Sherman to John Sherman, May 23, 1843, *ibid.*

"I would . . . delusion"]   W. T. Sherman to John Sherman, April 30–May 1, 1859, *ibid.* See also W. T. Sherman to John Sherman, Nov. 30, 1854, March 20, 1856, March 12 and May 8, 1860, *ibid.*

"it will . . . the end"]   W. T. Sherman to John Sherman, Dec. 9, 1860, *ibid.*

"the sweet . . . picnic"]   W. T. Sherman to [Mrs. Hamilton Hawkins Draper], Jan. 15, 1865, in Andrew Sparks, "Old 'War Is Hell' Dreamed of Picking Magnolias," *Atlanta Journal and Constitution Magazine* (Nov. 23, 1958), 14. See also Sherman, *Memoirs*, 2d ed., I, 29; W. T. Sherman to Annie Gilman Bowen, June 30, 1864, W. T. Sherman Papers, University of South Carolina; W. T. Sherman to W. F. Vilas, March 4, 1888, William F. Vilas Papers, State Historical Society of Wisconsin.

"would have resisted . . . rights"]   W. T. Sherman to Daniel M. Martin, Aug. 10, 1864, in Grenville M. Dodge, *Personal Recollections of President Abraham Lincoln, General Ulysses S. Grant, and General William T. Sherman* (Council Bluffs, Iowa, 1914), 171.

128 "crisis . . . come"]   W. T. Sherman to John Sherman, May 8, 1860, W. T. Sherman Papers, Library of Congress.

"mere . . . mad"]   W. T. Sherman to [Thomas Ewing, Jr.], Dec. 23, 1859, Ewing Family Papers, *ibid.*

"South . . . pretext"]   W. T. Sherman to Annie Gilman Bowen, June 30, 1864, Sherman Papers, University of South Carolina.

"A more quiet . . . exist"]   W. T. Sherman to John Sherman, April 18, 1848, W. T. Sherman Papers, Library of Congress.

"pastoral land"]   W. T. Sherman, [Autobiography], [1868], 103, Sherman Papers, Ohio Historical Society.

129 "palaces . . . years"]   W. T. Sherman to Geo[rge] Gibson, April 17, 1848, Sherman Collection, Bancroft Library, University of California, Berkeley.

"the chaos of 1849–50"]   W. T. Sherman to Stephen J. Field, Nov. 28, 1880, HM 31037, Huntington Library.

"the wild . . . mountains"]   W. T. Sherman to [H. B. Ewing], June 15, 1852, Sherman Papers, Ohio Historical Society.

129 "The aged . . . idol"] W. T. Sherman to Geo[rge] Gibson, Aug. 5, 1848, Sherman Collection, Bancroft Library.

"look . . . vortex"] W. T. Sherman to E. O. C. Ord, Oct. 28, 1848, in W. T. Sherman, *The California Gold Fields in 1848: Two Letters from Lt. W. T. Sherman, U.S.A.* (n.p., [1964]). On the gold rush see esp. J. S. Holliday, *The World Rushed In: The California Gold Rush Experience* (New York, 1981).

"The fabulous . . . contract"] W. T. Sherman, [Autobiography], [1868], 119, Sherman Papers, Ohio Historical Society.

"there . . . here" . . . "the Democracy" and "every . . . other"] W. T. Sherman to [?], Aug. 25, 1848, W. T. Sherman Papers, Library of Congress. See also Sherman, *Memoirs,* 2d ed., I, 50–110; W. T. Sherman, "Old Times in California," *North American Review,* CXLVIII (March 1889), 273–275.

129–30 "splendid . . . partnership"] Sherman, *Memoirs,* 2d ed., I, 91. See also W. T. Sherman to Alphonse Sutter, Oct. 16, 1855, W. T. Sherman Papers, Library of Congress; W. T. Sherman to [R.] Jones, March 15, 1850, *ibid;* W. T. Sherman to Thomas Ewing, April 28, 1849, Ewing Family Papers, *ibid.*

130 "I believe . . . fortunes"] W. T. Sherman to Geo[rge] Gibson, April 29, 1849, Sherman Collection, Bancroft Library.

"There is . . . cities"] W. T. Sherman to John Sherman, July 14, 1841, W. T. Sherman Papers, Library of Congress. On Ewing see Abby L. Gilbert, "Thomas Ewing, Sr.: Ohio's Advocate for a National Bank," *Ohio History,* LXXXII (1973), 5–24. On antebellum banking see esp. James Roger Sharp, *The Jacksonians Versus the Banks: Politics in the States After 1837* (New York, 1970); William Gerald Shade, *Banks or No Banks: The Money Issue in Western Politics, 1832–1865* (Detroit, 1972); Larry Schweikart, *Banking in the American South from the Age of Jackson to Reconstruction* (Baton Rouge, La., 1987).

131 "He will . . . business"] Ellen Ewing to P. B. Ewing, March 5, 1850, Philemon B. Ewing Papers, Ohio Historical Society.

"with the prospect . . . years"] Ellen Sherman to Maria Ewing, Dec. 4–12, 1853, Ewing Family Papers, Library of Congress.

"This . . . village"] W. T. Sherman to John Sherman, June 3, 1853, W. T. Sherman Papers, *ibid.*

"too cautious . . . California"] W. T. Sherman to Ellen [Sherman], April 12–15, 1853, Sherman Papers, University of Notre Dame.

"leave me . . . success"] W. T. Sherman to Ellen [Sherman], May 11, 1853, *ibid.*

"we stand . . . fast"] W. T. Sherman to Ellen [Sherman], April 12–15, 1853, *ibid.*

"Neither . . . Earth"] [W. T.] Sherman to [Henry S.] Turner, April 12, 1854, Sherman Papers, Ohio Historical Society.

"the Battle of 23 Feby"] W. T. Sherman to [Henry S.] Turner, Feb. 25 and 28, 1855, *ibid.*

132 "Look . . . you"] W. T. Sherman to Ellen [Sherman], June 16, 1855, Sherman Papers, University of Notre Dame.

"where men . . . open"] Louis McLane, Jr., to Sophie [McLane], Oct. 2–15, 1853, McLane-Fisher Family Papers, MS 2403, Manuscripts Division, Maryland Historical Society Library, Baltimore.

"Without . . . *scale*"] W. T. Sherman to Thomas Ewing, Jr., Aug. 9, 1858, W. T. Sherman Papers, Library of Congress.

"All parties . . . me"] W. T. Sherman to John Sherman, June 15, 1854, *ibid.*

133 "At that . . . dream"] W. T. Sherman to B. R. Alden, July 16, 1858, *ibid.*

"In a strict . . . offers"] W. T. Sherman to [Henry S.] Turner, April 2, 1857, Sherman Papers, Ohio Historical Society. On banking in San Francisco, see Roger W. Lotchin, *San Francisco, 1846–1856: From Hamlet to City* (New York, 1974), 57–63.

133 "magnificent"] W. T. Sherman to [Ethan Allen Hitchcock], Oct. 18, 1856, Ethan Allen Hitchcock Papers, Library of Congress.

"debilitating medicines"] W. T. Sherman to [Ethan Allen Hitchcock], March 4–8, 1855, *ibid.* On the experience and treatment of asthma in the nineteenth century, see David McCullough, *Mornings on Horseback* (New York, 1981), chap. 4.

"quite . . . times"] Ellen Sherman to Maria Ewing, Aug. 12, 1854, Ewing Family Papers, Library of Congress.

insanity] Ellen Sherman to John Sherman, Nov. 10, 1861, W. T. Sherman Papers, *ibid.*

"I trust . . . San Francisco"] Ellen [Sherman] to [W. T. Sherman], Aug. 10, 1857, Sherman Papers, University of Notre Dame.

"I . . . have . . . reach"] W. T. Sherman to John T. Doyle, July 7, 1878, John T. Doyle Papers, California Historical Society, San Francisco.

"cursed land"] W. T. Sherman to [Henry S.] Turner, Feb. 18–19, 1858, Sherman Papers, Ohio Historical Society.

"There seems . . . here"] W. T. Sherman to James H. Lucas, June 4, 1858, Lucas and Hunt Papers, Missouri Historical Society.

133–4 "I shall . . . better"] W. T. S[herman] to [S. M.] Bowman, Aug. 14, 1857, W. T. Sherman Papers, Library of Congress.

134 "I can . . . San Francisco"] W. T. Sherman to [Eugene] Casserly, [ca. Sept. 1864], de Coppett Collection, Princeton University.

"I suppose . . . empire"] W. T. Sherman to Ellen [Sherman], Feb. 13, 1860, Sherman Papers, University of Notre Dame.

"compelled . . . cabin"] C. M. Hitchcock to [Ethan Allen Hitchcock], May 10, 1858, Ethan Allen Hitchcock Papers, Library of Congress. On Sherman's California career see Dwight L. Clarke, *William Tecumseh Sherman: Gold Rush Banker* (San Francisco, 1969).

"mad rush" and "a flock of sheep"] W. T. Sherman to E. A. Hitchcock, June 18, 1858, Ethan Allen Hitchcock Papers, Library of Congress.

"a shabby place"] W. T. Sherman, [Autobiography], [1868], 202, Sherman Papers, Ohio Historical Society.

"I have . . . always"] W. T. Sherman to Thomas Ewing, Sept. 18, 1858, Ewing Family Papers, Library of Congress.

135 "It is California all over"] W. T. Sherman to Ellen [Sherman], Sept. 25, 1858, Sherman Papers, University of Notre Dame.

"Financial . . . here"] W. T. Sherman to Alexander Perry, April 21, [1860], Sherman Letter-book, State Historical Society of Wisconsin.

Vigilance Committee] See esp. Robert M. Senkewicz, *Vigilantes in Gold Rush San Francisco* (Stanford, Calif., 1985). For Sherman's accounts see W. T. Sherman to [Henry S.] Turner, May 18–20, 1856, William T. Sherman Papers, Missouri Historical Society; W. T. Sherman to E. A. Hitchcock, June 19, 1856, Ethan Allen Hitchcock Papers, Library of Congress; W. T. Sherman to [Thomas Ewing], May 21, 1856, March 22, 1857, Ewing Family Papers, *ibid.;* W. T. Sherman to [Henry S.] Turner, July 2, Aug. 18, Sept. 4–5, Oct. 19, Nov. 4, 1856, Sherman Papers, Ohio Historical Society; W. T. Sherman to John Sherman, July 7, Aug. 3, 19, 1856, W. T. Sherman Papers, Library of Congress; W. T. Sherman to Stephen J. Field, Feb. 25, 1868, Huntington Library; Sherman, *Memoirs,* 2d ed., I, 146–160. See also Lotchin, *San Francisco,* chap. 9.

136 "moderate ideas"] W. T. Sherman to [J. Neely] Johnson, June 9, 1856, John Neely Johnson Papers, Bancroft Library.

"sweep . . . bay"] W. T. Sherman, [Autobiography], [1868], 167, Sherman Papers, Ohio Historical Society.

"the mob in broadcloth"] John T. Doyle to P. Tecumseh Sherman, Dec. 22, 1891, Sherman Papers, University of Notre Dame.

136–7 "have regarded . . . men"]   W. T. Sherman to Thomas Ewing, June 16, 1856, in Herbert G. Florcken, "The Law and Order View of the San Francisco Vigilance Committee of 1856," *California Historical Society Quarterly*, XIV (1935), 369.

137 "Being in a business . . . me"]   W. T. Sherman to John Sherman, July 7, 1856, W. T. Sherman Papers, Library of Congress. See also W. T. Sherman to [W. A.] Scott, Nov. 17, 1856, W. A. Scott Papers, Bancroft Library; J. Neely Johnson to W. T. Sherman, June 10, 1856, Johnson Papers, *ibid.*

"had a right . . . moment" and "the Vigilance War"]   W. T. Sherman to Thomas Ewing, March 22, 1857, Ewing Family Papers, Library of Congress.

"I am . . . rebellion"]   W. T. Sherman to [Thomas Ewing, Jr.], April 6, 1861, *ibid.*

"the republican theory" . . . "fulfill them"]   Thomas G. Cary, "San Francisco Vigilance Committee, 1856," [Oct. 1, 1885], 70–72, Beinecke Library, Yale University. See also Tho[ma]s G. Cary to [William T.] Coleman, Jan. 7, 1878, San Francisco Committee of Vigilance, 1856, Papers, Bancroft Library.

"while . . . law" and "one of . . . self-government"]   William T. Coleman, "San Francisco Vigilance Committees," *Century Magazine*, XLIII (Dec. 1891), 142, 150. See also Harold M. Hyman and William M. Wiecek, *Equal Justice Under Law: Constitutional Development, 1835–1875* (New York, 1982), 5–6.

138 "cautious" . . . "tendencies"]   Josiah Royce, *California From the Conquest in 1846 to the Second Vigilance Committee in San Francisco: A Study in American Character* (Boston, 1886), 438–461. On Royce, see esp. R. Jackson Wilson, *In Quest of Community: Social Philosophy in the United States, 1860–1920* (New York, 1968), chap. 6.

Bancroft]   Hubert Howe Bancroft, *The Works of Hubert Howe Bancroft*, XXXVII: *Popular Tribunals* (San Francisco, 1887), II. For Bancroft's criticisms of Sherman's memoirs see pp. 284–289. For a critique of the Vigilance Committee as an agency of social control see David A. Johnson, "Vigilance and the Law: The Moral Authority of Popular Justice in the Far West," *American Quarterly*, XXXIII (1981), 558–586.

"Johnsons . . . San Francisco"]   W. T. Sherman to Hugh [Ewing], Dec. 18, 1860, Sherman Papers, Ohio Historical Society.

"California . . . affair"]   W. T. Sherman to [Henry S.] Turner, Aug. 28, 1881, *ibid.*

Ku Klux Klan]   W. T. Sherman to [John Sherman], March 21, 1871, W. T. Sherman Papers, Library of Congress.

Knights of Labor]   W. T. Sherman to John T. Doyle, March 22, 1888, John T. Doyle Papers, California Historical Society.

"The influence . . . *sham*"]   W. T. Sherman to John T. Doyle, Jan. 4, 1884, *ibid.*

139 "This universal . . . courts"]   W. T. Sherman to John Sherman, Dec. 18, 1860, W. T. Sherman Papers, Library of Congress.

"that it is . . . Mississippi"]   W. T. Sherman to [H. B. Ewing], June 15, 1852, Sherman Papers, Ohio Historical Society.

"the mutual . . . fact"]   W. T. Sherman to G. Mason Graham, Aug. 12, 1860, Sherman Papers, Louisiana State University.

140 "Unless . . . cannon"]   Frank P. Blair, Jr., to [Montgomery Blair], [Oct. 11, 1862], Blair Family Papers, Library of Congress. See also Wubben, *Civil War Iowa and the Copperhead Movement*, 14–17.

"Even . . . river"]   O. P. Morton to Abraham Lincoln, Oct. 27, 1862, Stanton Papers, Library of Congress. See also Stampp, *Indiana Politics*, 12, 160–161; Johannsen, *Stephen A. Douglas*, 796–797, 864.

"We stand . . . traitors"]   *New York Herald*, Oct. 30, 1863. See also John [Grierson] to Benj[amin Grierson], March 26, 1861, Benjamin H. Grierson Papers, Illinois State Historical Library; Love, *Wisconsin in the War*, 187; Trollope, *North America*, ed. Smalley and Booth, 21; *Chicago Tribune*, Jan. 12, 1863; John A. Logan to I. N. Haynie, Jan. 1, 1861, John A. Logan Papers, Library of Congress; House of Representatives, July

4, 1861, *Congressional Globe,* 37th Congress, 1st Session, 5; *Cincinnati Commercial,* Aug. 1, 1862, March 28, 1863.

140 "the grand artery of America"]   W. T. Sherman to Ellen [Sherman], March 10, 1864, Sherman Papers, University of Notre Dame.

"the spinal column of America"]   W. T. Sherman to [H. W.] Slocum, July 24, 1864, *Official Records,* Series I, Vol. XXXVIII, Part V, 246.

"the valley . . . America"]   W. T. Sherman to [H. W.] Halleck, Sept. 17, 1863, *ibid.,* Vol. XXX, Part III, 694.

"It is a beautiful . . . Louisiana"]   W. T. Sherman to [Willard] Warner, Jan. 22, 1866, Sherman Letters, Illinois State Historical Library.

141 "but the task . . . cost"]   W. T. Sherman to Thomas Ewing, Jr., April 4, 1862, Sherman Papers, University of Notre Dame.

"You took . . . pause"]   W. T. Sherman to [H. W.] Halleck, July 16, 1862, *Official Records,* Series I, Vol. XVII, Part II, 100.

"cutting . . . sea"]   Sherman, *Memoirs,* 2d ed., I, 324. See also John A. McClernand to Edwin M. Stanton, Nov. 10, 1862, Stanton Papers, Library of Congress.

"dead sure" . . . "a Savior"]   W. T. Sherman to [U. S.] Grant, March 10, 1864, *Official Records,* Series I, Vol. XXXII, Part III, 49.

"The man . . . the man"]   W. T. Sherman to [H. W.] Halleck, July 16, 1862, *ibid.,* Vol. XVII, Part II, 100.

"Here . . . empire"]   W. T. Sherman to [U.S.] Grant, March 10, 1864, *ibid.,* Vol. XXXII, Part III, 49.

"I represent . . . Valley"]   W. T. Sherman to [H. W.] Slocum, July 24, 1864, *ibid.,* Vol. XXXVIII, Part V, 246.

"the nature of our people"]   W. T. Sherman to John Sherman, Aug. 18, 1865, W. T. Sherman Papers, Library of Congress.

142 "On two . . . America"]   J. W. Draper to W. T. Sherman, July 8, 1867, *ibid.*

"You like . . . Death"]   W. T. Sherman to Thomas Hunton, Aug. 24, 1862, Berlin *et al.,* eds., *Freedom,* Series I, Vol. I, 293.

"To secure . . . mad"]   W. T. Sherman to John A. Logan, Dec. 21, 1863, John A. Logan Papers, Sterling Library, Yale University. Printed, with slightly different wording, in *Official Records,* Series I, Vol. XXXI, Part III, 459.

"the new men" . . . "Rocky Mountains"]   W. T. Sherman to Geo[rge] H. Braughn, May 9, 1879, W. T. Sherman Papers, Library of Congress. Published in *Daily Picayune* (New Orleans), May 26, 1879.

143 "History . . . immortal"]   T. M. Post, *Palingenesy. National Regeneration. An Address* (St. Louis, 1864), 6.

"As soon . . . muddy waters"]   W. T. Sherman to Ellen [Sherman], March 10, 1864, Sherman Papers, University of Notre Dame.

CHAPTER FOUR

Notes for Pages 144–192

144 "The world" . . . "contests"]   [John Esten Cooke], "Introductory," 1, 3, 10–11, John Esten Cooke Papers, #38-599-A, Alderman Library, University of Virginia, Charlottesville.

145 "the most . . . Revolution"]   *New York Herald,* Aug. 30, 1861.

radicals]   Samuel T. Spear, *Radicalism and the National Crisis, A Sermon . . . October 19th 1862* (Brooklyn, N.Y., 1862), 1–10.

146 "The ider . . . at all"]   Terah W. Sampson to Jerome T. Sampson, April 26, 1863, Terah W. Sampson Letters, Manuscript Department, The Filson Club, Louisville, Kentucky.

"I dare . . . nations"]   James D. Richardson, ed., *A Compilation of the Messages and Papers of the Presidents* (New York, 1897), I, 215. See also Stow Persons, "The Cyclical Theory of History in Eighteenth Century America," *American Quarterly*, VI (1954), 147–163; Drew R. McCoy, *The Last of the Fathers: James Madison and the Republican Legacy* (Cambridge, 1989).

Bancroft]   *New York Herald*, Feb. 23, 1862. See also Paul C. Nagel, *One Nation Indivisible: The Union in American Thought, 1776–1861* (New York, 1964), chap. 1; Paul C. Nagel, *This Sacred Trust: American Nationality, 1798–1898* (New York, 1971), chaps. 1–2; Kenneth M. Stampp, "The Concept of a Perpetual Union," in *The Imperiled Union: Essays on the Background of the Civil War* (New York, 1980), 3–36; Garry Wills, *Inventing America: Jefferson's Declaration of Independence* (Garden City, N.Y., 1978), prologue.

147 "the progress . . . World"]   *New York Herald*, Aug. 30, 1861.

"the unity . . . nation"]   Frank Moore, comp., *Memorial Ceremonies at the Graves of Our Soldiers* (Washington, D.C., 1869), 103.

"its schoolboy . . . demi-gods"]   *Harper's New Monthly Magazine*, XXXV (July 1867), 210.

"our constitutions . . . power"]   *New York Herald*, Dec. 17, 1860.

Continental Army]   W[illia]m H. Spencer to E. M. Stanton, March 29, 1866, Military Order of the Loyal Legion of the United States, Massachusetts Commandery, Autograph Collection, Document 318, United States Army Military History Institute, Carlisle Barracks, Pennsylvania.

"My father . . . country"]   Clara Barton to E. M. Stanton, April 29, 1864, Clara Barton Papers, Box 6, Manuscript Division, Library of Congress, Washington, D.C. See also "War Lectures," [1868], *ibid.*, Box 9.

"our Revolutionary sires"]   *Detroit Free Press*, July 15, 1862. See also The Ladies' National Covenant, "Address to the Women of America," May 2, 1864, in Frank Moore, ed., *The Rebellion Record: A Diary of American Events* (New York, 1861–1868), XI, 20–21.

148 "The chief . . . Government"]   *New York Tribune*, April 17, 1861.

"one question . . . differences"]   *New York Herald*, May 9, 1861.

"You ask . . . Country"]   F. M. Niven to [R. L.] Dabney, May 7, 1861, Robert L. Dabney Papers, Union Theological Seminary in Virginia, Richmond.

149 "Damn . . . again"]   Edward Everett Hale, *The Man Without a Country* (Boston, 1926), 7.

"to throw . . . country" and "all . . . country"]   *Ibid.*, 48, 43. See also Morton Keller, *Affairs of State: Public Life in Late Nineteenth-Century America* (Cambridge, Mass., 1977), 4; Thomas J. Pressly, *Americans Interpret Their Civil War* (New York, 1965 [orig. publ. Princeton, N. J., 1954]), 41.

"I am in . . . rong"]   J. Curl to William Coffey, Jan. 24, 1864 [1865], William Coffey Papers, Ohio Historical Society, Columbus.

150 "Is it nothing . . . ancestry"]   Joseph Holt, *Speech of Hon. Joseph Holt of Kentucky . . . September 3, 1861* (New York, 1861), 7. See also William L. Barney, *Flawed Victory: A New Perspective on the Civil War* (New York, 1975), 28.

"I want . . . raised you"]   William and Mahaly Atwood to [Evan Atwood], July 27, 1863, in Evan Atwood, "A Short History of My Life," Small Manuscript Collections, Box 4, Arkansas History Commission, Little Rock.

"The essential . . . else"]   Murat Halstead to Salmon P. Chase, Aug. 24, 1863, quoted in V. Jacque Voegeli, *Free But Not Equal: The Midwest and the Negro During the Civil War* (Chicago, 1967), 129.

"What though . . . prevail"]   Henry [Spaulding] to wife, Feb. 10, 1863, Henry S. Spaulding Papers, #844, University of Virginia. Within the extensive literature on nationalism see esp. Benedict Anderson, *Imagined Communities: Reflections on the Origin and Spread of Nationalism* (London, 1983); Boyd C. Shafer, *Nationalism: Its Nature and Interpreters* (Washington, D.C., 1976); Anthony D. Smith, *Theories of Nationalism* (New York, 1971); Yehoshua Arieli, *Individualism and Nationalism in American Ideology* (Cambridge, Mass., 1964); David M. Potter, "The Historian's Use of Nationalism and Vice Versa," in *The South and the Sectional Conflict* (Baton Rouge, La., 1968), 34–83; Frederick Hertz, *Nationality in History and Politics: A Psychology and Sociology of National Sentiment and Nationalism* (London, 1944).

150 "It has . . . eternal"]   *New York Herald,* Jan. 7, 1861.

151 "both a prayer . . . ages"]   Alexander H. Vinton, *A Sermon Preached on the National Thanksgiving Day, November 26th, 1863* (New York, 1863), 11.

"must be . . . immortal"]   John G. Nicolay and John Hay, *Abraham Lincoln: A History* (New York, 1890), VIII, 191. See also Major L. Wilson, *Space, Time, and Freedom: The Quest for Nationality and the Irrepressible Conflict, 1815–1861* (Westport, Conn., 1974), 206–210.

"must . . . at all"]   James McKaye, "Birth and Death of Nations: A Thought for the Crisis," Moore, ed., *Rebellion Record . . . Supplement,* [XII], 56.

"the proposition . . . equal"]   Roy P. Basler *et al.,* eds., *The Collected Works of Abraham Lincoln* (New Brunswick, N.J., 1953), VII, 23.

"a great . . . being"]   *New York Herald,* Oct. 18, 1863.

"commanding presence" . . . "self-directed"]   James Freeman Clarke, *Discourse on the Aspects of the War Delivered . . . April 2, 1863* (Boston, 1863), 5–8.

152 "the period . . . began"]   Francis Lieber to [Richard Henry Dana, Jr.], Oct. 26, 1864, Dana Family Papers, Massachusetts Historical Society, Boston. See also Francis Lieber to Rob[er]t J. Breckinridge, Dec. 5, 1863, Breckinridge Family Papers, Vol. 231, Library of Congress; Nagel, *This Sacred Trust,* 145–147; Frank Freidel, *Francis Lieber: Nineteenth-Century Liberal* (Baton Rouge, La., 1947), chaps. 8, 15.

"convenient . . . fictions" and "the Idea of Nationality"]   John William Draper, *History of the American Civil War* (New York, 1867–1870), III, 640.

"We have heard . . . States"]   *New York Herald,* Oct. 10, 1861. See also Lilian Handlin, *George Bancroft: The Intellectual as Democrat* (New York, 1984), 150–153, 271.

"In the nineteenth . . . unification"]   Entry of March 5, 1862, Louis Moreau Gottschalk, *Notes of a Pianist,* ed. Jeanne Behrend (New York, 1964), 56.

153 "An Israelite . . . nation"]   *Philadelphia Inquirer,* May 2, 1863.

"would be . . . Constitution"]   [Henry Bellows], [Memorandum, ca. Jan.–Feb. 1863], Henry W. Bellows Papers, Massachusetts Historical Society. See also Henry W. Bellows to wife, April 23, 1863, *ibid.* Compare Nagel, *One Nation Indivisible,* 105–108, and Phillip Paludan, *A Covenant With Death: The Constitution, Law and Equality in the Civil War Era* (Urbana, Ill., 1975), 45–47, 61–108.

"The Constitution . . . life"]   House of Representatives, Dec. 17, 1862, *Congressional Globe,* 37th Congress, 3d Session, 114. See also *Cincinnati Commerical,* Aug. 1, 1862, April 20, 1863.

154 "It is a severe . . . bloodshed"]   *The Army Reunion: with Reports of the Meetings . . . December 15 and 16, 1868* (Chicago, 1869), 169.

E. L. Godkin]   Harold M. Hyman, *A More Perfect Union: The Impact of the Civil War and Reconstruction on the Constitution* (New York, 1973), 285.

154–5 "consolidation . . . nation" and "From . . . existence"]   *Harper's Weekly,* V (May 18, 1861), 306.

155 "forces . . . volcano"]   E. Porter Alexander, *The Confederate Veteran: Address of Gen. E. Porter Alexander, Delivered . . . June 9, '02* (Cedar Rapids, Iowa, [1902]), 6–7. See also Charles Francis Adams, *The Constitutional Ethics of Secession and "War Is Hell": Two Speeches* (Boston, 1903), 19–22.

155 "has proved ... earth"] Jacob Behm to Jacob and Matilda Seidler, Feb. 1, 1864, Jacob Behm Letters, *Civil War Times Illustrated* Collection, U. S. Army Military History Institute.

"our rapid ... people"] *American and Commercial Advertiser* (Baltimore), May 18, 1863.

"They are vain ... times"] [James Dawson Burn], *Three Years Among the Working-Classes in the United States During the War* (London, 1865), 225. On workers' nationalism and support for the Northern war effort see David Montgomery, *Beyond Equality: Labor and the Radical Republicans, 1862–1872* (New York, 1967), 92–96; Iver Bernstein, *The New York City Draft Riots: Their Significance for American Society and Politics in the Age of the Civil War* (New York, 1990), 197–198; J. Matthew Gallman, *Mastering Wartime: A Social History of Philadelphia During the Civil War* (Cambridge, 1990), chap. 9.

155–6 "imperial future" ... "this war"] Draper, *History of the Civil War*, III, 675–676.

156 "war ... Americans"] *Daily Missouri Democrat* (St. Louis), March 2, 1865.

"the meaning ... forgetting it"] "Address on Robert E. Lee ... Jan. 19, 1921," Edwin L. Stephens Papers, Louisiana State University, Baton Rouge. See also Susan Speare Durant, "The Gently Furled Banner: The Development of the Myth of the Lost Cause, 1865–1900" (Ph.D. diss., University of North Carolina at Chapel Hill, 1972), 371. For a different view see David Herbert Donald, "A Generation of Defeat," in Walter J. Fraser, Jr., and Winfred B. Moore, Jr., eds., *From the Old South to the New: Essays on the Transitional South* (Westport, Conn., 1981), 3–20.

"Southern schoolboy ... fields"] Stanhope Sams, *The Study and Teaching of Southern History. An Address ... July 5, 1894* (Atlanta, 1894), 5.

157 "before ... subsides"] Margaret J. Preston to [C. C.] Buel, May 17, 1886, Century Company Papers, Letters, Box 17, New York Public Library, New York, New York.

"on the *great* question" ... "separate govt"] E. P. Alexander to G. E. Pickett, June 16, 1866, Confederate Miscellany, Ic, James Longstreet Papers, Woodruff Library, Emory University, Atlanta, Georgia.

158 "that if he ... refuge"] John Paris, *A Sermon: Preached ... on the 28th of February, 1864* (Greensborough, N.C., 1864), 11.

159 "pure ... deaths"] E. B. Treat & Co., Circular for *Wearing of the Gray*, John Esten Cooke Papers, University of Virginia.

"sacred trust" and "Rebels ... belong"] Mary Tucker Magill, *History of Virginia for the Use of Schools* (Lynchburg, Va., 1890), 269–270, 274.

"injury and oppression"] *Dedication of Tomb of Army of Northern Virginia, Louisiana Division* (New Orleans, 1881), 30.

"blind with prejudice"] William C. Chase, *Story of Stonewall Jackson* (Atlanta, 1901), 193.

"innocent in conscience"] Daniel Bedinger Lucas, "On the Death of Stonewall Jackson," *South Atlantic Quarterly*, XVI (1917), 231.

"When they ... representatives"] George William Peterkin, *An Address by Bishop Peterkin ... January twentieth 1905* (n.p., [1905]), 12.

160 "knew ... leaders"] Hunter McGuire, *Address ... Delivered on the 23d day of June, 1897* (Lynchburg, Va., 1897), 14.

"A country ... itself"] John Warwick Daniel, *Character of Stonewall Jackson* (Lynchburg, Va., 1868), 22.

"In fact ... left"] *South Branch Intelligencer* (Romney, W. Va.), Sept. 9, 1892.

161 "Jackson ... with them"] Reprinted in *Cincinnati Commercial*, May 15, 1863. See also John Newton Lyle, "Sketches Found in a Confederate Veteran's Desk," Washington and Lee University, Lexington, Virginia; Hunter McGuire to Jedediah Hotchkiss, July 17, 1897, Jedediah Hotchkiss Papers, University of Virginia; Mary C. Stribling, "Lee and Jackson Contrasted," James Mercer Garnett Papers, Box 1, *ibid.*; Susan Leigh Blackford, comp., *Memoirs of Life In and Out of the Army In Virginia During the War Between the*

States (Lynchburg, Va., 1894), I, 211–212; Allen C. Redwood, "With Stonewall Jackson," *Scribner's Magazine*, XVIII (June 1879), 223; J. M. Brown, "My Recollections of General (Stonewall) Jackson," 12, John M. Brown Papers, Barker Texas History Center, University of Texas, Austin.

161 "constantly . . . pulpit"]   [D. H. Hill], Address, Daniel Harvey Hill Papers, North Carolina Division of Archives and History, Raleigh. On Jackson's relations with his men see James I. Robertson, Jr., *The Stonewall Brigade* (Baton Rouge, La., 1963), 24–25.

162 "all . . . country" and "ambitious . . . youths"]   R. P. Chew, *Stonewall Jackson: Address of Colonel R. P. Chew . . . Delivered . . . June 19, 1912* (Lexington, Va., 1912), 64.

"what earnestness . . . made"]   Randolph Barton to William A. Anderson, July 23, 1915, Anderson Family Papers, #38-96, University of Virginia.

"a strong . . . appeal"]   James Power Smith, *Quit You Like Men: Sermon Preached at the Virginia Military Institute June 24th, 1906* (Lynchburg, Va., n. d.), 9. See also W[illiam] H[enry] T[appey] Squires, *The Land of Decision* (Portsmouth, Va., 1931), 323. Compare Dixon Wecter, *The Hero in America: A Chronicle of Hero-Worship* (Ann Arbor, Mich., 1963 [orig. publ. New York, 1941]), 288.

"Thy hand . . . faith"]   William McLaughlin, *Ceremonies Connected With the Unveiling of the Bronze Statue of Gen. Thomas J. (Stonewall) Jackson* (Baltimore, Md., 1891), 27.

163 "To the South . . . religion"]   J. J. Clopton, *The True Stonewall Jackson* (Baltimore, Md., 1913), 22. See also Henry Alexander White, *Southern Presbyterian Leaders* (New York, 1911), 448–449; Charles Reagan Wilson, *Baptized in Blood: The Religion of the Lost Cause, 1865–1920* (Athens, Ga., 1980), 127.

"subjugation" . . . "glory"]   Virginia, *Inauguration of the Jackson Statue, Tuesday, October 26, 1875* [Richmond, Va., 1875], 14–15.

164 "the first . . . States" and "The conditions . . . example"]   Chase, *Stonewall Jackson*, Introduction, 412, 438. See also, for example, Daniel, *Character of Jackson*, 63; James H. Wood, *The War: "Stonewall" Jackson, His Campaigns and Battles, the Regiment As I Saw Them* (Cumberland, Md., [1910]), 181; B. Howell Griswold, Jr., *The Spirit of Lee and Jackson* (Baltimore, Md., 1927), 9–10.

"alien . . . speculation"]   John B. Gordon and Charles C. Jones, Jr., *The Old South: Addresses Delivered Before the Confederate Survivors' Association in Augusta, Georgia . . . April 26th, 1887* (Augusta, Ga., 1887), 17.

"civilization of industrialism"]   Bradley T. Johnson, *The Constitution of the Confederate States* (Baltimore, Md., 1891), 16.

Berkeley Minor]   Berkeley Minor, "The South and the Union," *Southern Historical Society Papers*, XXX (1902–1903), 332–338.

"a 'stone wall' . . . irreverence"]   McLaughlin, *Ceremonies Connected With the Statue*, 27.

164–5 "Herbert Spencer . . . influences"]   Unidentified newspaper clipping, [May 10, 1883], Robert Alexander Lancaster Scrapbook, 1883, Virginia Historical Society, Richmond.

165 "I don't think . . . money"]   R. L. Dabney to Jubal A. Early, June 19, 1889, Jubal Early Papers, Library of Congress.

"Why has . . . ascendancy"]   D. H. Hill to Jubal Early, July 29, 1885, Early Family Papers, Virginia Historical Society.

"to preserve . . . soldiers"]   D. H. Hill to Daniel P. Smith, Jan. 20, 1867, Daniel Pratt Smith Papers, #1319-A, University of Virginia, courtesy of Mrs. Edmund Berkeley. See also Ray M. Atchison, "*The Land We Love*: A Southern Postbellum Magazine of Agriculture, Literature, and Military History," *North Carolina Historical Review*, XXXVII (Oct. 1960), 506–515.

166 "we old Confederates"]   R. L. Dabney to Jubal A. Early, June 19, 1889, Early Papers, Library of Congress.

"It is not . . . one of them"]   J. A. Early to [Henry B. Dawson], July 15, 1871, War 1861–5 Papers, Box 3, New-York Historical Society, New York, New York.

166 "omit . . . country"]   R. E. Lee to J. A. Early, Oct. 15, 1866, Early Papers, Library of Congress.

166–7 "I a 'submissionist' . . . dreamed of it"]   J. A. Early to [James L.] Kemper, Feb. 9, 1862, James L. Kemper Papers, Virginia State Library, Richmond. See also Jubal Anderson Early, *Autobiographical Sketch and Narrative of the War Between the States* (Philadelphia, 1912).

167 "I shall . . . despair"]   Jubal Early to Thomas Lafayette Rosser, May 10, 1866, Thomas Lafayette Rosser Papers, #1171, University of Virginia.

"It would afford . . . century"]   J. A. Early to D. H. Hill, March 27, 1867, D. H. Hill Papers, Box 10, Virginia State Library.

"unprofitable life"]   J. A. Early to S. H. Early, July 15, 1867, Early Papers, Library of Congress.

"care to live"]   J. A. Early to [D. H. Hill], Dec. 4, 1886, Hill Papers, Box 10, Virginia State Library.

"take up . . . exterminated"]   J. A. Early to D. H. Hill, March 27, 1867, *ibid.*

"did desert . . . Confederacy"]   J. A. Early to D. H. Hill, Oct. 17, 1885, Hill Papers, North Carolina Archives.

"fossils" . . . "enemies"]   Jubal A. Early, *The Campaigns of Gen. Robert E. Lee. An Address . . . January 19th, 1872* (Baltimore, Md., 1872), 52.

168 "rid . . . misrule"]   Fitzhugh Lee to Jubal Early, May 9, 1875, Early Papers, Library of Congress.

"recrimination . . . reminiscences"]   R. E. Withers to [Jubal Early], April 24, 1876, *ibid.* See also J. L. Kemper to J. A. Early, Oct. 22 and 23, 1875, and J. R. Tucker to [Jubal Early], May 18, 1876, *ibid.*

"a social . . . Ishmaelite"]   John S. Wise, *The End of an Era* (Boston, 1899), 228.

"renegades" and "Let . . . you"]   J. A. Early to Jed[ediah] Hotchkiss, Aug. 22, 1884, Early Papers, Library of Congress. See also Gaines M. Foster, *Ghosts of the Confederacy: Defeat, the Lost Cause, and the Emergence of the New South, 1865–1913* (New York, 1987), chap. 4.

"the development . . . resources"]   R. M. T. Hunter to R. L. Dabney, Nov. 4, 1866, Dabney Papers, Union Theological Seminary in Virginia.

Intelligencer]   *Cincinnati Commercial*, June 3, 1865. See also James Michael Russell, *Atlanta, 1847–1890: City Building in the Old South and the New* (Baton Rouge, La., 1988), chaps. 5, 6.

"When . . . extent" and "The nationality . . . questioned"]   *Columbia, S.C., The Future Manufacturing and Commercial Centre of the South* (Columbia, S.C., 1871), 49–50, 61. See also Howard J. Marshall, "Gentlemen Without a Country: A Social and Intellectual History of South Carolina, 1860–1900" (Ph.D. diss., University of North Carolina at Chapel Hill, 1979), 44.

"To be sure . . . land, etc."]   Tho[ma]s L. Broun to Edwin Broun, Aug. 2, 1865, Roy Bird Cook Collection, Series V, Box 1, West Virginia and Regional History Collection, West Virginia University, Morgantown.

169 "the Greater South"]   Clement A. Evans, *Contributions of the South to the Greatness of the American Union* (Richmond, Va., 1895), 21. See also M. C. Butler, "Southern Genius: How War Developed It in an Industrial and Military Way," *Southern Historical Society Papers,* XVI (1888), 281–295; William C. P. Breckinridge, "The Ex-Confederate, and What He Has Done in Peace," *ibid.,* XX (1892), 235; John Randolph Tucker, *The Old and the New South* (Columbia, S.C., 1887), and, in general, Paul M. Gaston, *The New South Creed: A Study in Southern Mythmaking* (New York, 1970).

"I have endeavoured . . . right"]   R. L. Dabney to T. J. Jackson, March 5, 1863, R. L. Dabney Papers, University of Virginia. On Dabney see David Henry Overy, "Robert Lewis Dabney: Apostle of the Old South" (Ph.D. diss., University of Wisconsin, 1967).

169 "hireling proletariat"]   Robert L. Dabney, "The New South," *Discussions by Robert L. Dabney* (Mexico, Mo., 1897), IV, 1–24, quoted at p. 8.

"the radicalism of the age"]   R. L. Dabney to R. H. Fleming, March 15, 1883, Dabney Papers, University of Virginia.

"unconquerable and free"]   R. L. Dabney, "Stonewall Jackson," *Southern Historical Society Papers*, XI (1883), 156. See also "General T. J. Jackson, An Elegy, 1887," *Discussions by Dabney*, IV, 588–593.

170 "In no event . . . subjugation" . . . "We hope not"]   Dabney, "Stonewall Jackson," *Southern Historical Society Papers*, XI (1883), 153, 125–126.

171 North and South]   Allen Tate, *Stonewall Jackson, The Good Soldier: A Narrative* (New York, 1928), 11–12, 17, 39–40. See also Daniel Joseph Singal, *The War Within: From Victorian to Modernist Thought in the South, 1919–1945* (Chapel Hill, N.C., 1982), chap. 8, esp. 240–241.

172 "Beyond this . . . limit"]   Tate, *Stonewall Jackson*, 286. See also Allen Tate to Roy Bird Cook, May 8, 1928, Cook Collection, Box 3, West Virginia University.

"never . . . stranger"]   Sarah Ann Tillinghast, [Reminiscences], 50–51, Tillinghast Family Papers, Perkins Library, Duke University, Durham, North Carolina.

173 "The social . . . being"]   Senate, Jan. 11, 1861, *Congressional Globe*, 36th Congress, 2d Session, 328.

"It is no . . . gone"]   Anthony Trollope, *North America*, ed. Donald Smalley and Bradford Allan Booth (New York, 1951 [orig. publ. London, 1862]), 357.

"The North . . . province"]   J. H. Thornwell, *The State of Our Country* (Columbia, S.C., 1861), 23.

174 "The people . . . North"]   Senate, Dec. 4, 1860, *Congressional Globe*, 36th Congress, 2d Session, 4.

"she would . . . slaves"]   Entry of Nov. 8, 1860, Diary of John B. Floyd, Historical Society of Pennsylvania.

"were literally . . . secede"]   Reprinted in *New York Herald*, Nov. 28, 1864.

"the hissing . . . earth"]   *"Stonewall Jackson's Way." A Sketch of the Life and Services of Maj. John A. Harman* (Staunton, Va., 1876), 43.

"Those who . . . States"]   Senate, Dec. 13, 1860, *Congressional Globe*, 36th Congress, 2d Session, 87. See also William J. Cooper, Jr., *Liberty and Slavery: Southern Politics to 1860* (New York, 1983), esp. 220, 257, 267–268.

175 "What a humbug . . . time"]   Benjamin S. Ewell to Thomas Tasker Gantt, Aug. 6, 1865, Benjamin S. Ewell Papers, Swem Library, College of William and Mary, Williamsburg, Virginia.

"I could . . . manner"]   Wade Hampton to [J. William] Jones, Jan. 2, 1871, Hampton Family Papers, Box 5, South Caroliniana Library, University of South Carolina, Columbia. See also Bertram Wyatt-Brown, *Southern Honor: Ethics and Behavior in the Old South* (New York, 1982), 105–111.

"I think . . . companions"]   Jonathan Worth to D. G. Worth, May 15, 1861, J. G. deRoulhac Hamilton, ed., *The Correspondence of Jonathan Worth* (Raleigh, N.C., 1909), I, 144.

176 "every community" . . . "a priori"]   Senate, Jan. 10, 1861, *Congressional Globe*, 36th Congress, 2d Session, 309.

"They had never . . . logic"]   George Cary Eggleston, "Notes on Cold Harbor," Robert Underwood Johnson and Clarence Clough Buel, eds., *Battles and Leaders of the Civil War* (New York, 1888), IV, 231.

"the freedom . . . sires"]   Jefferson Davis to soldiers [of the Army of Tennessee], Oct. 14, 1863, *The War of the Rebellion: A Compilation of the Official Records of the Union and Confederate Armies* (Washington, D.C., 1880–1901), Series I, Vol. XXX, Part IV, 744.

176 "Now alone . . . hope"] Speech in Augusta, Georgia, Oct. 5, 1864, Dunbar Rowland, ed., *Jefferson Davis, Constitutionalist: His Letters, Papers and Speeches* (Jackson, Miss., 1923), VI, 357.

177 "It is but . . . within it"] W. C. Oates to [E. P. Alexander], Aug. 25, 1868, Edward Porter Alexander Papers, Southern Historical Collection, University of North Carolina, Chapel Hill. See also Walter L. Buenger, "Secession Revisited: The Texas Experience," *Civil War History,* XXX (Dec. 1984), 305; Richard E. Beringer, Herman Hattaway, Archer Jones, William N. Still, Jr., *Why the South Lost the Civil War* (Athens, Ga., 1986), chap. 4; James L. Roark, *Masters Without Slaves: Southern Planters in the Civil War and Reconstruction* (New York, 1977); J. Mills Thornton, III, *Politics and Power in a Slave Society: Alabama, 1800–1860* (Baton Rouge, La., 1978), esp. chap. 6; David M. Potter, *The Impending Crisis, 1848–1861,* completed and edited by Don E. Fehrenbacher (New York, 1976), chap. 17.

"the conquest . . . forward"] I. V. Duzanse to Louis P. Griffith, Aug. 8, 1861, Civil War Papers, MS 1860, Manuscripts Division, Maryland Historical Society Library, Baltimore.

177–8 "To speak . . . them"] Jefferson Davis to Confederate Congress, July 20, 1861, Rowland, ed., *Letters, Papers and Speeches,* V, 118. See also James W. Silver, *Confederate Morale and Church Propaganda* (Tuscaloosa, Ala., 1957), 26–27.

178 "Where freemen . . . development"] Reprinted in *Mobile Advertiser and Register,* May 2, 1863.

"the South . . . world"] A. Battle to G. W. Randolph, April 29, 1862, *Official Records,* Series IV, Vol. I, 1102. On the South's economic dependence see James Oakes, *Slavery and Freedom: An Interpretation of the Old South* (New York, 1990).

179 "know they . . . penetrated"] House of Representatives, Feb. 15, 1861, *Congressional Globe,* 36th Congress, 2d Session, 942.

"Men who . . . secured"] Braxton Bragg to [Harvey Washington Walter], April 8, 1866, Harvey Washington Walter Papers, University of North Carolina.

"has been . . . made it"] Jan. 11, 1864, quoted in Thomas H. Baker, "Refugee Newspaper: The Memphis *Daily Appeal,* 1862–1865," *Journal of Southern History,* XXIX (Aug. 1963), 344.

"the South . . . liberty"] *Richmond Dispatch,* Jan. 30, 1862.

180 "they tell . . . comprehension"] Sally [Grattan] to [Alexander Brown], Feb. 11, 1862, Alexander Brown Papers, Duke University. See also Drew Gilpin Faust, "Altars of Sacrifice: Confederate Women and the Narrative of War," *Journal of American History,* LXXVI (March 1990), 1220–1228; George C. Rable, *Civil Wars: Women and the Crisis of Southern Nationalism* (Urbana, Ill., 1989), chaps. 4, 10.

"It has become" . . . "the phrases . . . wanted"] *Richmond Enquirer,* Aug. 6, 1863.

"our name . . . horror"] *Ibid.,* Feb. 10, 1863.

181 "appalling desolation" and "ravages . . . Rhine"] J. H. Thornwell, *Our Danger and Our Duty* (Columbia, S.C., 1862), 3.

"vilest passions"] Jefferson Davis, Proclamation to the Soldiers of the Confederate States, Aug. 1, 1863, *Official Records,* Series IV, Vol. II, 687.

"southern white . . . overseers"] James Madison Brannock to Sarah [Caroline Gwin Brannock], April 16, 1862, James Madison Brannock Papers, Virginia Historical Society. See also entry of Jan. 13, 1861, Susan Cornwall, Journal, University of North Carolina; [Lafayette McLaws] to wife, Nov. 16, 1862, Lafayette McLaws Papers, *ibid.; Richmond Sentinel* reprinted in *Cincinnati Commercial,* Aug. 17, 1864; House of Representatives, Feb. 18, 1861 [1862], Proceedings of the First Confederate Congress, First Session, *Southern Historical Society Papers,* XLIV (1923), 14.

"subordinate to their own negroes"] *Richmond Whig,* Dec. 28, 1864.

181 "the sufferings . . . Hungarians"] G. T. Beauregard to R. L. Dabney, Aug. 6, 1861, Dabney Papers, Union Theological Seminary in Virginia. See also *Richmond Whig*, Feb. 23, 1864.

"the criminals . . . rebellion"] *Chattanooga Rebel*, Nov. 2, 1862.

John Copeland] John T. to John Copeland, Jan. 26, 1865, filed by date in W. T. Sherman Papers, Library of Congress.

"What we . . . last"] *Atlanta Intelligencer* (Macon, Ga.), Nov. 18, 1864, reprinted in *New York Herald*, Nov. 26, 1864. See also the interview with Jefferson Davis in [James R. Gilmore], *Down in Tennessee, and Back By Way of Richmond* (New York, 1864), 272, 279; Mary Elizabeth Massey, *Refugee Life in the Confederacy* (Baton Rouge, La., 1964), 17.

"white slaves"] *State Gazette* (Austin), Oct. 13, 1860, reprinted in *New York Herald*, Oct. 25, 1860.

182 "for the . . . continent" and "a supreme . . . democracy"] Thornwell, *Our Danger*, 4–5. See also Jack P. Maddex, Jr., "Proslavery Millennialism: Social Eschatology in Antebellum Southern Calvinism," *American Quarterly*, XXXI (1979), 46–62; James Oscar Farmer, Jr., *The Metaphysical Confederacy: James Henley Thornwell and the Synthesis of Southern Values* (Macon, Ga., 1986), chap. 8; Mitchell Snay, "Gospel of Disunion: Religion and the Rise of Southern Separatism, 1830–1861" (Ph.D. diss., Brandeis University, 1984), 59–70, 91–98.

"We are not dependent . . . Labor"] James D. Greenlee to [James D.] Davidson, Sept. 24, 1861, James D. Davidson Papers, University of Texas.

"the poorest . . . world"] J. H. Hammond to Mrs. F. H. Pratt, Feb. 5, 1861, in *New York Herald*, March 11, 1861.

"the North . . . power" . . . "among . . . earth"] *Christian Index* reprinted in Moore, ed., *Rebellion Record*, I, 183; *Memphis Appeal*, Dec. 26, 1861. On Americans and England see William Brock, "The Image of England and American Nationalism," *Journal of American Studies*, V (Dec. 1971), 225–245. See also Kenneth S. Greenberg, *Masters and Statesmen: The Political Culture of American Slavery* (Baltimore, Md., 1985), chap. 4; John Brawner Robbins, "Confederate Nationalism: Politics and Government in the Confederate South, 1861–1865" (Ph.D. diss., Rice University, 1964), 48.

"We must rule . . . earth"] *Richmond Whig*, Aug. 20, 1861.

"The lines . . . people"] *Richmond Dispatch*, Feb. 10, 1863.

183 "No two . . . Lincolnites"] John Izard Middleton to [Mrs. J. Francis Fisher], July 22, 1861, Cadwalader Collection, J. Francis Fisher Section, Box 7, Historical Society of Pennsylvania. See also William R. Taylor, *Cavalier and Yankee: The Old South and American National Character* (Cambridge, Mass., 1979 [orig. publ. 1961]); Drew Gilpin Faust, *A Sacred Circle: The Dilemma of the Intellectual in the Old South, 1840–1860* (Baltimore, Md., 1977); John M. McCardell, Jr., *The Idea of a Southern Nation: Southern Nationalists and Southern Nationalism, 1830–1860* (New York, 1979); Sharon Elaine Hannum, "Confederate Cavaliers: The Myth in War and Defeat" (Ph.D. diss., Rice University, 1965).

"Talk . . . ruin"] Senate, Dec. 30, 1863, Proceedings of the First Confederate Congress, Fourth Session, *Southern Historical Society Papers*, L (1953), 154–155.

183 "All classes . . . contagion"] William W. Bennett, *A Narrative of the Great Revival Which Prevailed in the Southern Armies* (Philadelphia, 1877), 41–42. See also, for example, Rob[er]t S. Hudson to Jefferson Davis, Oct. 5, 1863, *Official Records*, Series IV, Vol. II, 856–857; W. H. Whiting to [D. H.] Hill, June 15, 1863, D. H. Hill Papers, Box 6, Virginia State Library; A. J. Neal to mother, July 23, 1864, Andrew J. Neal Papers, Emory University; Willi[am Chunn] to Lila [Land Chunn], Jan. 17, 1863, William Chunn Letters, *ibid.;* entry of April 23, 1863, George A. Mercer, Diary, University of North Carolina.

184 Howell Cobb's speech] *Atlanta Intelligencer*, Jan. 30, 1864, reprinted in *Cincinnati Commercial*, Feb. 13, 1864. See also David Donald, "The Proslavery Argument Recon-

sidered," *Journal of Southern History,* XXXVII (Feb. 1971), 16–18; Lewis P. Simpson, *The Dispossessed Garden: Pastoral and History in Southern Literature* (Athens, Ga., 1975), 62–64, 80–82; Drew Gilpin Faust, *The Creation of Confederate Nationalism: Ideology and Identity in the Civil War South* (Baton Rouge, La., 1988), chap. 3; Kenneth Moore Startup, "Strangers in the Land: The Southern Clergy and the Economic Mind of the Old South" (Ph.D. diss., Louisiana State University, 1983); James L. Huston, *The Panic of 1857 and the Coming of the Civil War* (Baton Rouge, La., 1987), chap. 4; Dan T. Carter, *When the War Was Over: The Failure of Self-Reconstruction in the South, 1865–1867* (Baton Rouge, La., 1985), 104–111; David Bertelson, *The Lazy South* (New York, 1967), 221–228.

184 "Two . . . union"] *Richmond Enquirer,* Feb. 16, 1863.

184–5 "The breach . . . people"] John S. Foster to Sinah, June 20, 1862, James Foster Correspondence, Louisiana State University.

185 "revolutions" . . . "oppression"] *Mississippi Baptist,* reprinted in Moore, ed., *Rebellion Record,* I, 182.

"a readiness . . . Union"] E[thelbert] Barksdale to Jefferson Davis, July 29, 1863, Rowland, ed., *Letters, Papers and Speeches,* V, 581.

"The day . . . *power*"] James Phelan to Jefferson Davis, July 29, 1863, James S. Schoff Civil War Collection, Letters and Documents, Box 10, Clements Library, University of Michigan, Ann Arbor. On Mississippi see also R[ichard] I[rvine] M[anning] to mother, July 19, 1863, Williams-Chesnut-Manning Papers, Box 8, University of South Carolina; Daniel Ruggles to B. S. Ewell, Aug. 10, 1863, *Official Records,* Series I, Vol. XXIV, Part III, 1053; R. S. Hudson to Jefferson Davis, March 14, 1864, *ibid.,* Vol. XXXII, Part III, 625–626; E. S. Dargan to [James A.] Seddon, July 24, 1863, *ibid.,* Series IV, Vol. II, 664; John K. Bettersworth, *Confederate Mississippi: The People and Policies of a Cotton State in Wartime* (Baton Rouge, La., 1943), chaps. 3, 10, 11; William C. Harris, *Presidential Reconstruction in Mississippi* (Baton Rouge, La., 1967), chap. 1.

"that we . . . system"] Entry of May 24, 1863, George A. Mercer, Diary, University of North Carolina. On the breakdown of Confederate cohesion see, for example, Stephen V. Ash, *Middle Tennessee Society Transformed, 1860–1870: War and Peace in the Upper South* (Baton Rouge, La., 1987), 162–166; Stanley Lebergott, "Why the South Lost: Commercial Purpose in the Confederacy, 1861–1865," *Journal of American History,* LXX (June 1983), 62–70; Lawrence N. Powell and Michael S. Wayne, "Self-Interest and the Decline of Confederate Nationalism," in Harry P. Owens and James J. Cooke, eds., *The Old South in the Crucible of War* (Jackson, Miss., 1983), 29–45; Paul Escott, "Southern Yeomen and the Confederacy," *South Atlantic Quarterly,* LXXVII (1978), 146–158.

"serious endurance"] J. W. M[iles] to Mrs. T. J. Young, July 7, [1865], James Warley Miles Papers, Duke University.

"And now we . . . independanc"] J. W. Yale to daughter, May 17, 1865, Civil War Miscellany, Civil War Biographical File, University of Texas. For a review of the scholarly literature on the contention that the Confederacy was weakened by Southerners' feelings of guilt see Gaines M. Foster, "Guilt Over Slavery: A Historiographical Analysis," *Journal of Southern History,* LVI (Nov. 1990), 665–694.

186 "the absence . . . people"] R. E. Lee to M. F. Maury, Sept. 8, 1865, Robert E. Lee Letterbook, Virginia Historical Society.

"The South . . . war"] *New York Herald,* April 29, 1865.

"many men . . . to us"] Jonathan Worth to [W. A.] Graham, Feb. 15, 1865, William Alexander Graham Papers, North Carolina Archives.

"Richmond . . . Washington"] Edward A. Pollard, *The Lost Cause Regained* (New York, 1868), 27. On Pollard see Jack P. Maddex, Jr., "Pollard's *The Lost Cause Regained:* A Mask for Southern Accommodation," *Journal of Southern History,* XL (Nov. 1974), 595–612.

"We were not . . . Wigfall"] W. P. J[ohnston] to [Rosa Johnston], July 5–10, 1865, Albert Sidney Johnston and William Preston Johnston Papers, Howard-Tilton Library,

Tulane University, New Orleans, Louisiana. On the Confederate government's innovations and failure see Frank E. Vandiver, "The Confederacy and the American Tradition," *Journal of Southern History*, XXVIII (Aug. 1962), 277–286; Frank E. Vandiver, "The Civil War as an Institutionalizing Force," in William F. Holmes and Harold M. Hollingsworth, eds., *Essays on the American Civil War* (Austin, Tex., 1968), 73–87; Emory M. Thomas, *The Confederacy as a Revolutionary Experience* (Englewood Cliffs, N.J., 1971); Emory M. Thomas, *The Confederate Nation, 1861–1865* (New York, 1979), esp. chaps. 9, 12; Paul David Escott, *After Secession: Jefferson Davis and the Failure of Confederate Nationalism* (Baton Rouge, La., 1978); David Donald, "Died of Democracy," and David M. Potter, "Jefferson Davis and the Political Factors in Confederate Defeat," in David Donald, ed., *Why the North Won the Civil War* (Baton Rouge, La., 1960), 77–114; Charles Edward Cauthen, *South Carolina Goes to War, 1860–1865: The James Sprunt Studies in History and Political Science*, XXXII (Chapel Hill, N.C., 1950), 165, 171–177, 217; Ella Lonn, *Desertion During the Civil War* (New York, 1928), esp. chap. 4.

187 "I am not . . . obtaining it"]   Thomas D. Spear to A. H. Stephens, Sept. 24, 1864, Alexander H. Stephens Papers, Library of Congress.

"are our . . . destinies"]   *Richmond Enquirer*, Sept. 27, 1864.

"The people . . . unconquerable"]   W[illia]m C. P. Breckinridge to Issa D. Breckinridge, Jan. 25, 1865, Breckinridge Family Papers, Library of Congress.

"Many . . . gun"]   James T. Odem to Eleanor Odem, July 27, 1863, James T. Odem Collection, #7093-M, University of Virginia.

188 "Our hearts . . . failure" and "we had . . . end"]   George Cary Eggleston, *A Rebel's Recollections* (Bloomington, Ind., 1959 [orig. publ. New York, 1875]), 172, 175.

"My motto . . . them"]   J. P. Kendall to parents, April 16, 1864, William Deveraux Kendall Collection, Henry E. Huntington Library, San Marino, California.

"What would . . . that" and "There is . . . there is"]   John S. Wise, "Robert E. Lee," 42, John Sergeant Wise Papers, Box 17, Wise Family Papers, Virginia Historical Society. For another version see Wise, *End of an Era*, 434–435.

"moral atrophy" and "We can . . . Union"]   A. G. Magrath to [Jefferson Davis], Sept. 15, 1864, *Official Records*, Series IV, Vol. III, 652.

189 "Break in . . . join"]   *Richmond Sentinel*, Nov. 25, 1864, reprinted in *New York Herald*, Nov. 28, 1864. See also *Chattanooga Rebel* (Selma, Ala.), Nov. 21, 1864; *Richmond Whig*, Nov. 19, 1864.

"our own . . . enemy" and "utter annihilation"]   *Augusta Constitutionalist*, Nov. 22, 1864, and *Savannah News*, Nov. 22, 1864, reprinted in *New York Herald*, Nov. 29, 1864.

Howell Cobb and Robert Toombs]   Howell Cobb *et al.*, Address to the People of Georgia, Feb. 1862, in Moore, ed., *Rebellion Record*, IV, 193. See also Massey, *Refugee Life*, 229–230.

Richmond Examiner]   Nov. 24, 1864, reprinted in *New York Herald*, Nov. 27, 1864. See also *Montgomery Mail*, Sept. 18, 25, 1864; *Richmond Whig*, Oct. 19 and Nov. 24, 1864; *Daily South Carolinian* (Columbia), Oct. 11, 1864; *Reporter* (Selma, Ala.), reprinted in *Richmond Enquirer*, Nov. 4, 1864.

Zebulon Vance]   *Richmond Whig*, Feb. 23, 1865. See also Z. B. Vance, "By the Governor: A Proclamation to the People of North Carolina," Feb. 14, 1865, *Official Records*, Series I, Vol. XLVII, Part II, 1188–1191.

"Sherman's . . . sealed"]   *Richmond Whig*, Feb. 24, 1865. See also *Christian Index* (Macon, Ga.), Jan. 26, 1865.

"His expeditions . . . subjugating"]   *Richmond Examiner*, Feb. 22, 1865, reprinted in *New York Herald*, Feb. 25, 1865. See also *Daily Clarion* (Meridian, Miss.), Feb. 5, 1865.

"His track . . . ever"]   *Richmond Sentinel*, Feb. 7, 1865, reprinted in *New York Herald*, Feb. 10, 1865. See also the account of an interview with the owner of the *Richmond Sentinel* in Charles A. Page, *Letters of a War Correspondent*, ed. James R. Gilmore (Boston, 1899), 337.

189 "Notwithstanding . . . independence"]   *Daily South Carolinian* (Chester), April 12, 1865.

190 "a new phase" and "Nothing . . . free"]   Jefferson Davis to the People of the Confederate States of America, April 4, 1865, Rowland, ed., *Letters, Papers and Speeches,* VI, 530.

"It is marvelous . . . behind it"]   Entry of May 4, 1865, Josiah Gorgas, Diary, William C. Gorgas Papers, Library of Congress.

190–2 antebellum society and the Civil War]   See esp. Roy Franklin Nichols, *The Disruption of American Democracy* (New York, 1948), esp. chap. 27; Michael F. Holt, *The Political Crisis of the 1850s* (New York, 1978); C. C. Goen, *Broken Churches, Broken Nation: Denominational Schisms and the Coming of the American Civil War* (Macon, Ga., 1985); Robert H. Wiebe, *The Opening of American Society: From the Adoption of the Constitution to the Eve of Disunion* (New York, 1984), part 3; Thornton, *Politics and Power,* esp. xxi, 460–461; Robert W. Johannsen, "America's Golden Midcentury," in *The Frontier, the Union, and Stephen A. Douglas* (Urbana, Ill., 1989), 287–306; David Donald, "An Excess of Democracy: The American Civil War and the Social Process," *Centennial Review of Arts and Science,* V (1961), 21–39; Thomas B. Alexander, "The Civil War as Institutional Fulfillment," *Journal of Southern History,* XLVII (Feb. 1981), 3–32; Rowland Berthoff, *An Unsettled People: Social Order and Disorder in American History* (New York, 1971), esp. 293–296. For a criticism of this view see Phillip S. Paludan, "The American Civil War as a Crisis in Law and Order," *American Historical Review,* LXXVII (1972), 1013–1034.

CHAPTER FIVE

Notes for Pages 193–231

193 "Let us pass . . . trees"]   [R. L. Dabney, Notes], "Last days" [Mrs. Jackson's narrative], Charles William Dabney Papers, Box 32, Southern Historical Collection, University of North Carolina, Chapel Hill; R. L. Dabney, *Life and Campaigns of Lieut.-Gen. Thomas J. Jackson (Stonewall Jackson)* (New York, 1866), 723.

"Let us cross . . . trees" and "the beautiful . . . immortal"]   Hunter McGuire, "Account of the Wounding and Death of Stonewall Jackson," in Hunter McGuire and George L. Christian, *The Confederate Cause and Conduct in the War Between the States* (Richmond, Va., 1907), 229; Mary Anna Jackson, *Life and Letters of General Thomas J. Jackson (Stonewall Jackson)* (New York, 1891), 471.

"Was his . . . valley"]   Margaret J. Preston, "Stonewall Jackson's Dying Words," in Mary Anna Jackson, *Memoirs of Stonewall Jackson* (Louisville, Ky., 1895), 647; Dabney, *Life of Jackson,* 724.

"His face . . . nature"]   R. T. Bennett, "An Address before the Ladies' Memorial Association," *Southern Historical Society Papers,* XXXIV (1906), 55.

194 "a gleam . . . eye"]   H. M. F[ield], "Stonewall Jackson, Soldier and Saint," *New York Evangelist,* LX, Number 30 (July 25, 1889).

"Victory . . . triumphs"]   William A. Swank, *In Memory of Thomas J. Jackson, of Virginia* (Norfolk, Va., 1879).

"a vision" . . . "no more"]   Henry M. Field, "Stonewall Jackson," *Harper's New Monthly Magazine,* LXXXIII (1891), 918.

"as if of relief" and "a land . . . feared"]   McGuire, "Account of Wounding and Death," in McGuire and Christian, *Confederate Cause and Conduct,* 229; James Power Smith, "Stonewall Jackson's Last Battle," Robert Underwood Johnson and Clarence Clough Buel, eds., *Battles and Leaders of the Civil War* (New York, 1888), III, 214.

Pollard, Peterkin, and Benét]   Edward A. Pollard, "Stonewall Jackson—An Historical Study," *Putnam's Magazine,* new series, II (1868), 740; George William Peterkin, *An Address by Bishop Peterkin . . . January twentieth 1905* (n.p., [1905]), 12; Stephen Vincent Benét, *John Brown's Body* (New York, 1928), 277–278.

194 "peaceful as a lamb" and "calmly . . . trees"]   Jefferson Davis, "An Address made by Jefferson Davis in behalf of the Southern Historical Society," Dunbar Rowland, ed., *Jefferson Davis, Constitutionalist: His Letters, Papers and Speeches* (Jackson, Miss., 1923), IX, 167.

194–5 "The man . . . trees"]   Reprinted in *Southern Historical Society Papers*, X (1882), 334–335.

195 "across . . . battle"]   Dabney, *Life of Jackson*, 724.

"Those conflicts . . . trees"]   S. C. N., "Last Words of Stonewall Jackson," Aug. 20, 1866, *Louisville Courier* clipping in Roy Bird Cook Collection, West Virginia and Regional History Collection, West Virginia University, Morgantown.

" 'Neath . . . river" and "Our . . . overblown"]   Paul Hamilton Hayne, *Poems of Paul Hamilton Hayne* (Boston, 1882), 74, 83.

196 "without hesitation" and "that he did . . . do so"]   J. B. Hood, *Advance and Retreat: Personal Experiences in the United States and Confederate States Armies* (New Orleans, 1880), 49.

"And it was . . . the other"]   Ezekiel 47: 5–7, 13.

"Ah! Capt. . . . to grief"]   [R. E. Wilbourn] to [John Esten Cooke], Dec. 12, 1863, John Esten Cooke Scrapbook, #5295-E, John Esten Cooke Papers, Alderman Library, University of Virginia, Charlottesville; R. E. Wilbourn to J. A. Early, Feb. 19, 1873, Jubal A. Early Papers, Manuscripts Division, Library of Congress, Washington, D.C.

"No man . . . Jackson"]   Entry of May 8, 1863, Cornelia McDonald, *A Diary With Reminiscences of the War and Refugee Life in the Shenandoah Valley, 1860–1865* (Nashville, Tenn., 1935), 161.

"Every heart . . . country"]   *Savannah Republican*, May 5, 1863.

Charleston Courier]   May 8, 1863.

197 "My prayers . . . Jackson"]   Entry of May 6, 1863, Diary of D. Coleman, University of North Carolina.

"lighten . . . joy" and "with the . . . ears"]   *Savannah Republican*, May 11, 1863.

"noble . . . services" and "struggle . . . humanity"]   W. C. Rives to T. J. Jackson, May 10, 1863, Scrapbook *re* Thomas Jonathan ("Stonewall") Jackson, Montrose Jonas Moses Collection, Perkins Library, Duke University, Durham, North Carolina.

"We all . . . victories"]   R. E. Colston, "Address . . . Before the Ladies' Memorial Association," *Southern Historical Society Papers*, XXI (1893), 45.

"he could not . . . die"]   William Allan, [Memoirs], 182, William Allan Papers, MS Volume 8, University of North Carolina.

"God . . . much"]   [R. L. Dabney, Notes], "Rev. B. T. Lacy's Narrative," Charles William Dabney Papers, Box 32, *ibid.*

"We cannot . . . republic"]   *Richmond Examiner*, May 5, 1863.

"seemed . . . responsibility"]   William Allan, [Memoirs], 182, Allan Papers, MS Volume 8, University of North Carolina.

"The announcement . . . suddenness"]   Jefferson Davis to R. E. Lee, May 11, 1863, *The War of the Rebellion: A Compilation of the Official Records of the Union and Confederate Armies* (Washington, D.C., 1880–1901), Series I, Vol. XXV, Part II, 791.

198 Judith Brockenbrough McGuire]   Entry of May 12, 1863, Diary of Judith Brockenbrough McGuire, in Matthew Page Andrews, *The Women of the South in War Times* (Baltimore, Md., 1920), 180.

"Ladies . . . coffin"]   *Mobile Advertiser and Register*, May 20, 1863.

"He looked . . . time"]   C[harlotte] M[aria] W[igfall] to [Halsey Wigfall], May 12, 1863, Wigfall Family Papers, Library of Congress.

198 "She was . . . to do" and "She was . . . pageantry"] W[illiam] J. H[oge] to wife, May 13, 1863, in Peyton Harrison Hoge, *Moses Drury Hoge: Life and Letters* (Richmond, Va., 1899), 184–185.

"paid . . . memory"] Entry of May 11, 1863, Journal of Thomas Hart Law, South Caroliniana Library, University of South Carolina, Columbia.

199 John Witherspoon Ervin] *The Observer* (Charlotte, N.C.), clipping in Jackson Scrapbook, Moses Collection, Duke University.

"He fell . . . woe"] Frank Moore, ed., *The Rebellion Record: A Diary of American Events* (New York, 1861–1868), VII, Poetry and Incidents, 11; *Richmond Examiner*, May 15, 1863.

Mount Vernon] "Jackson is Dead," Confederate Songs from the Library of E. Annie Smith, Civil War Papers, Manuscripts Division, Maryland Historical Society Library, Baltimore.

"No such . . . American"] Dabney, *Life of Jackson*, 731.

200 "in the most . . . them"] Charle[s F. Morse] to Robert [M. Morse, Jr.], May 7, 1863, Charles F. Morse Papers, Massachusetts Historical Society, Boston.

"The rebel . . . Potomac"] William Swinton, *Campaigns of the Army of the Potomac* (New York, 1866), 275.

"I well . . . manner"] Allan, [Memoirs], 175, Allan Papers, University of North Carolina.

201 "I have . . . ground"] John Bigelow, Jr., *The Campaign of Chancellorsville: A Strategic and Tactical Study* (New Haven, Conn., 1910), 259.

"that Hooker . . . prospectively"] T. J. Barnett to [S. L. M.] Barlow, May 2, 1863, S. L. M. Barlow Papers, Henry E. Huntington Library, San Marino, California.

"Such maps . . . incorrect"] Oliver Otis Howard, *Autobiography of Oliver Otis Howard* (New York, 1908), I, 362.

202 "It was under . . . army"] Samuel P. Bates, "Hooker's Comments on Chancellorsville," Johnson and Buel, eds., *Battles and Leaders,* III, 218.

Dr. McGuire] Hunter McGuire to Jedediah Hotchkiss, May 19, 1896, Jedediah Hotchkiss Papers, Box 3, University of Virginia.

"the audacity of this plan"] Jed[ediah] Hotchkiss and William Allan, *The Battle-fields of Virginia. Chancellorsville* (New York, 1867), 42.

Charles Marshall] David Gregg McIntosh, Notes concerning a dinner party, Feb. 24, 1887, David Gregg McIntosh Papers, Virginia Historical Society, Richmond.

Joseph G. Morrison] D. H. Hill to R. L. Dabney, July 21, 1864, R. L. Dabney Papers, Union Theological Seminary in Virginia, Richmond; J. G. Morrison to R. L. Dabney, Oct. 29, 1863, Charles William Dabney Papers, Box 31, University of North Carolina.

"I decided . . . immediately"] R. E. Lee to [Mary Anna] Jackson, Jan. 25, 1866, Thomas Jonathan Jackson Papers, George H. and Katherine M. Davis Collection, Howard-Tilton Library, Tulane University, New Orleans, Louisiana.

Bledsoe and Allan] R. E. Lee to A. T. Bledsoe, Oct. 28, 1867, Letter Book of Gen. R. E. Lee, Nov. 29, 1866–Sept. 12, 1870, Lee Family Papers, Virginia Historical Society; William Allan, "Conversations with Gen. R. E. Lee," 4, Allan Papers, MS Volume 3, University of North Carolina.

Mary Anna Jackson] M. A. Jackson, *Life and Letters of Jackson,* 435; Mary Anna Jackson to Giles B. Cooke, 1895, Faculty/Staff File, Thomas J. Jackson, Virginia Military Institute, Lexington.

203 "a Bishop Whately . . . fought"] Charles Marshall, *Appomattox: An Address Delivered Before the Society of the Army and Navy of the Confederate States in the State of Maryland* (Baltimore, Md., 1894), 4. See Richard Whately, *Historic Doubts Relative to Napoleon Buonaparte* (Cambridge, 1832 [orig. publ. 1819]).

203 "thousands" . . . "a whole army"] *Savannah Republican,* May 12, 1863; *Richmond Enquirer,* May 7, 1863; *Chattanooga Rebel,* May 13, 1863.

"Richmond . . . men"] *The Independent,* XV (May 14, 1863); *Richmond Examiner,* May 5, 1863.

"The result . . . four"] Edwin M. Stanton to [Joseph] Hooker, May 7, 1863, Joseph Hooker Papers, Box XIV, Folder J, Huntington Library.

"an indefinable superstition" and "an omen of evil"] A. L. Long, *Memoirs of Robert E. Lee* (Richmond, Va., 1886), 258.

"the last . . . them"] E. P. Alexander, *Military Memoirs of a Confederate: A Critical Narrative* (New York, 1908), 333.

Colonel Marshall] McIntosh, Notes . . . 1887, McIntosh Papers, Virginia Historical Society.

203–4 Mark Twain] Mark Twain, *Life on the Mississippi* (New York, 1911 [orig. publ. 1883]), 332. On Julio's painting see Mark E. Neely, Jr., Harold Holzer, and Gabor S. Boritt, *The Confederate Image: Prints of the Lost Cause* (Chapel Hill, N.C., 1987), 133 and Plate 11.

204 Lee; cavalryman] R. E. Lee, General Orders, No. 61, May 11, 1863, *Official Records,* Series I, Vol. XXV, Part II, 793; entry of May 14, 1863, Diary of J. D. Sprake, Manuscript Department, The Filson Club, Louisville, Kentucky.

"invisible . . . superhuman"] [Charles Hallock], *A Complete Biographical Sketch of "Stonewall" Jackson* (Augusta, Ga., 1863), 19–20.

"never . . . foe"] *Richmond Whig,* May 12, 1863.

"look . . . nation" and "the nationality . . . sorrow"] *Richmond Examiner,* May 10, 1866, reprinted in *Saint Louis Dispatch,* May 15, 1866.

spirit of Jackson] [James Dabney McCabe], *The Life of Lieut. Gen. T. J. Jackson* (Richmond, Va., 1863), 124; Colston, "Address . . . Before the Ladies' Memorial Association," *Southern Historical Society Papers,* XXI (1893), 47.

205 Howard; Schurz] O. O. Howard, "Jackson's Attack Upon the Eleventh Corps," *Century Magazine,* XXXII (Sept. 1886), 766; C[arl] Schurz to [Joseph] Hooker, April 22, 1876, in Samuel P. Bates, "Chancellorsville Revisited by General Hooker," *ibid.,* 780–781; Johnson and Buel, eds., *Battles and Leaders,* III, 196, 220.

"I have just . . . truth"] John Hay to [Richard Watson] Gilder, Sept. 3, 1886, HM 8484, John Hay Letters, Huntington Library.

"We know . . . fleeing"] Bigelow, *Campaign of Chancellorsville,* 290.

"had led . . . forest"] Bates, "Hooker's Comments on Chancellorsville," Johnson and Buel, eds., *Battles and Leaders,* III, 219.

"map . . . Rappahannock" and "Subjoined . . . had"] H. S. Curtiss to [family], May 12, 1863, Bernhard Knollenberg Collection, Box 10, Sterling Library, Yale University, New Haven, Connecticut.

206 "Gen. Jackson . . . cheering"] B. B. Carr, "Sketch of the battle of Chancellorsville as seen by B. B. Carr Co E 20th N.C. Regt.," Military Collection, Civil War, Box 70, North Carolina Division of Archives and History, Raleigh.

"Stonewall's . . . glow"] Fitzhugh Lee, *General Lee* (New York, 1894), 247–248.

"I was . . . over me"] W. F. Randolph, "Chancellorsville," *Southern Historical Society Papers,* XXIX (1901), 331.

207 "As far . . . I knew"] Luther B. Mesnard, [Reminiscences], 30, *Civil War Times Illustrated* Collection, United States Army Military History Institute, Carlisle Barracks, Pennsylvania.

"to arrest . . . flying"] [Oliver] Otis [Howard] to [Elizabeth Howard], May 9, 1963, O. O. Howard Papers, Bowdoin College, Brunswick, Maine.

207 "We soon . . . on us"]   Thomas Evans, [Memoir], 14, Library of Congress.

"Yell . . . here"]   Lewis E. Warren, "Recollections of the War Between the States," 15, Confederate Miscellany, Box 1, Woodruff Library, Emory University, Atlanta, Georgia.

"Owing . . . together"]   R. E. Colston to A. S. Pendleton, May 9, 1863, *Official Records,* Series I, Vol. XXV, Part I, 1004–1005.

207–8 "thirty to forty thousand men" . . . "in that . . . noted"]   Jacob Smith, *Camps and Campaigns of the 107th Regiment Ohio Volunteer Infantry* (n.p., [1910?]), 73.

208 "Americans . . . surprised"]   Entry of May 11, 1863, Journal of Theodore A. Dodge, Library of Congress.

"If men . . . run"]   [Oliver] Otis [Howard] to [Eliza Gilman], May 17, 1863, Howard Papers, Bowdoin College.

"Press forward"]   R. E. Wilbourn to R. L. Dabney, Dec. 12, 1863, Charles William Dabney Papers, University of North Carolina.

"General . . . sir"]   Randolph, "Chancellorsville," *Southern Historical Society Papers,* XXIX (1901), 332.

"as if . . . souls"]   R. E. Wilbourn to R. L. Dabney, Dec. 12, 1863, Charles William Dabney Papers, University of North Carolina.

"the wildest . . . throats"]   Randolph, "Chancellorsville," *Southern Historical Society Papers,* XXIX (1901), 333.

"the most . . . ever had"]   Jerome [B. Satterlee] to parents, brother, and sister, May 23, 1863, Jerome B. Satterlee Letters, State Historical Society of Iowa, Iowa City.

208–9 "He had . . . himself"]   *The Independent,* XV (May 14, 1863).

209 "I am sure . . . under him"]   Charles Francis Adams, Jr., to Charles Francis Adams, July 22–23, 1863, Worthington Chauncey Ford, ed., *A Cycle of Adams Letters, 1861–1865* (Boston, 1920), II, 57.

"Mother . . . next"]   Hugh Roden to family, May 24, 1863, Roden Papers, James S. Schoff Civil War Collection, Soldiers' Letters, Box 12, Clements Library, University of Michigan, Ann Arbor.

"I have been . . . lives"]   Account of Thomas Frelinghuysen McKinley McLean, Cook Collection, Series VI, Box 2, West Virginia University.

"Damn it . . . fighting is"]   John Hays to *Carlisle Herald,* Oct. 1, 1910, in *Carlisle Herald,* Oct. 8, 1910.

"No one . . . confusion"]   A. S. W[illiams] to daughter, May 18, 1863, in Milo M. Quaife, ed., *From the Cannon's Mouth: The Civil War Letters of General Alpheus S. Williams* (Detroit, Mich., 1959), 192.

209–10 "The men . . . spectacle"]   Will[iam] Clegg to cousin, May 8, 1863, Rowley-Gifford-Clegg Papers, Filson Club.

210 "This disorder . . . corrected" and "Men . . . line"]   [R. L. Dabney, Notes], "Maj. Cobb's memorandum," Charles William Dabney Papers, Box 31, University of North Carolina.

"great impatience"]   R. E. Wilbourn to J. A. Early, Feb. 19, 1873, Early Papers, Library of Congress.

"and it was . . . forward"]   R. E. Wilbourn to John Esten Cooke, Dec. 12, 1863, John Esten Cooke Papers, University of Virginia.

"In an earnest . . . forward"]   James H. Lane, "History of Lane's North Carolina Brigade," *Southern Historical Society Papers,* VIII (1880), 494.

whippoorwills]   Entry of Nov. 5, 1863, John Esten Cooke, Diary, John Esten Cooke Papers, University of Virginia; John Esten Cooke, *Wearing of the Gray; Being Personal Portraits, Scenes and Adventures of the War* (New York, 1867), 300.

211 Joseph G. Morrison]   J[oseph] G[raham] Morrison to Spier Whitaker, Jan. 27, 1900, Virginia Historical Society; J. G. Morrison to R. L. Dabney, Oct. 29, 1863, Charles William Dabney Papers, Box 31, University of North Carolina.

David J. Kyle]   David J. Kyle, "Jackson's Guide When Shot," *Confederate Veteran*, IV (1896), 308.

Captain Randolph]   Randolph, "Chancellorsville," *Southern Historical Society Papers*, XXIX (1901), 333–334.

Wilbourn on Pendleton]   R. E. Wilbourn to [?], May 1863, Charles J. Faulkner Papers, Virginia Historical Society.

"Gen. don't you . . . you" and "The danger . . . on"]   [Rough notes of an account of the battle at Chancellorsville as related by Maj. Pendleton], John Esten Cooke Papers, University of Virginia.

"that he intended . . . surrender"]   Hunter McGuire to J. A. Early, March 6, 1873, Early Papers, Library of Congress.

"generally believed . . . disastrous"]   John O. Casler, *Four Years in the Stonewall Brigade* (Dayton, Ohio, 1971 [orig. publ. Guthrie, Okla., 1893]), 149. See also Edward Porter Alexander, *Fighting for the Confederacy: The Personal Recollections of General Edward Porter Alexander,* ed. Gary W. Gallagher (Chapel Hill, N.C., 1989), 214–215.

211–12 "They never . . . extermination" and "should be . . . State"]   *Savannah Republican*, May 13, 1863.

212 "Jackson . . . motions" and "I mention . . . war"]   G. D. Camden to R. L. Dabney, Nov. 25, 1863, Charles William Dabney Papers, University of North Carolina.

Mary Anna Jackson]   Mary Anna Jackson to John Letcher, March 17, 1877, Thomas Jonathan Jackson Manuscripts, Virginia Military Institute; M. A. Jackson, *Life and Letters of Jackson*, 308–321.

"memory . . . friends"]   Jefferson Davis to J. T. Scharf, June 10, 1889, J. Thomas Scharf Collection, MS 1999, Maryland Historical Society Library.

"He would have . . . South"]   *The Great South* (Birmingham, Ala.), May 22, 1895. For a recent example of the enduring appeal of such speculation see Iver Bernstein, *The New York City Draft Riots: Their Significance for American Society and Politics in the Age of the Civil War* (New York, 1990), 3.

213 "would have . . . tell"]   Randolph, "Chancellorsville," *Southern Historical Society Papers*, XXIX (1901), 336–337.

"He fought . . . advancement"]   *The Independent*, XV (May 14, 1863).

"more men . . . man"]   [Oliver] Otis [Howard] to [Roland B. Howard], May 16, 1863, Howard Papers, Bowdoin College.

"Profoundly . . . rights"]   *New York Post*, May 13, 1863; *Boston Evening Transcript*, May 13, 1863.

"curious . . . powers" and "Stonewall . . . crime"]   *Washington Chronicle*, May 13, 1863. See also entry of May 13, 1863, John S. Cooper, Diary, Duke University; A. Lincoln to John W. Forney, May 13, 1863, Roy P. Basler *et al.*, eds., *The Collected Works of Abraham Lincoln* (New Brunswick, N.J., 1953), VI, 214.

214 prayer meetings and temperance meetings]   *The Independent*, XV (May 14, 1863).

prayer meeting with the wounded]   *Cincinnati Commercial*, May 14, 1863.

"I loved . . . Ellie"]   D. X. Junkin to G. Junkin, May 18, 1863, in D. X. Junkin, *The Reverend George Junkin, D. D., LL. D.: A Historical Biography* (Philadelphia, 1871), 551–553.

"that Jesus . . . knew"]   E. Junkin to Mary Anna Jackson, Aug. 3, 1863, Jackson Manuscripts, Virginia Military Institute.

"I said . . . in heaven" and "Jackson . . . war"]   D. X. Junkin to G. Junkin, May 18, 1863, D. X. Junkin, *George Junkin*, 551–553.

214 Hamlin, Wilbourn, and the road]   Augustus Choate Hamlin, *The Battle of Chancellorsville* (Bangor, Me., 1896), 107–109; R. E. Wilbourn to J. A. Early, Feb. 19 and March 3, 1873, Early Papers, Library of Congress.

Smith, Hotchkiss, and Jackson turning back]   [R. L. Dabney, Notes], "Lt. Smith's Narrative," Charles William Dabney Papers, Box 32, University of North Carolina; [Jedediah Hotchkiss] to Hunter McGuire, Oct. 8, 1898, Jedediah Hotchkiss Papers, Box 23, Library of Congress.

Wilbourn, Morrison, and Jackson riding forward]   J. G. Morrison to R. L. Dabney, Oct. 29, 1863, Charles William Dabney Papers, Box 31, University of North Carolina; R. E. Wilbourn to R. L. Dabney, Dec. 12, 1863, *ibid.;* R. E. Wilbourn to John Esten Cooke, Dec. 12, 1863, John Esten Cooke Papers, University of Virginia; R. E. Wilbourn to J. A. Early, March 3, 1873, Early Papers, Library of Congress.

McGuire]   Hunter McGuire to J. A. Early, March 6, 1873, Early Papers, Library of Congress.

214–15 Morrison, Wilbourn, and direction of fire]   J. G. Morrison to R. L. Dabney, Oct. 29, 1863, Charles William Dabney Papers, Box 31, University of North Carolina; R. E. Wilbourn to R. L. Dabney, Dec. 12, 1863, *ibid.;* J. G. Morrison to Spier Whitaker, Jan. 27, 1900, Virginia Historical Society; R. E. Wilbourn to [?], May 1863, Charles J. Faulkner Papers, *ibid.;* R. E. Wilbourn to John Esten Cooke, Dec. 12, 1863, John Esten Cooke Papers, University of Virginia; R. E. Wilbourn to J. A. Early, Feb. 19 and March 3, 1873, Early Papers, Library of Congress.

215 Pendleton; Douglas]   [Rough notes of an account by Pendleton], John Esten Cooke Papers, University of Virginia; Henry Kyd Douglas, *I Rode With Stonewall* (Chapel Hill, N.C., 1940), 222.

"This will do" . . . "reserve . . . sides"]   J. O. Kerbey, *On the War Path: A Journey Over the Historic Grounds of the Late Civil War* (Chicago, 1890), 172, 171, 168.

216 Forney George]   F. George to James H. Lane, May 9, 1863, *Official Records,* Series I, Vol. XXV, Part I, 920.

Wilbourn on cease-fire]   R. E. Wilbourn to J. A. Early, Feb. 19, 1873, Early Papers, Library of Congress.

"friends" and "that he . . . woods"]   Lane, "History of Lane's Brigade," *Southern Historical Society Papers,* VIII (1880), 495; "Wounding of Lieutenant-General T. J. Jackson," *The Land We Love,* I (July 1866), 181.

"The ball . . . with" and "So many . . . reports"]   Hunter McGuire to J. A. Early, March 2, 1873, Early Papers, Library of Congress.

1st Massachusetts Regiment]   *Boston Evening Transcript,* May 22, 1863; Robert G. Carter, "The Wounding of Stonewall Jackson," Robert G. Carter Papers, Virginia Historical Society.

"not only . . . false" and "As I . . . death"]   William L. Hollis to Hunter McGuire, May 16, 1896, Hotchkiss Papers, University of Virginia.

Pleasonton]   Alfred Pleasonton, "The Successes and Failures of Chancellorsville," Johnson and Buel, eds., *Battles and Leaders,* III, 180–182; "Death of General Jackson," *The Old Dominion,* IV (1870), 162; A. Pleasonton, [Indorsement], May 29, 1866, on Pennock Huey to A. Pleasonton, May 18, 1866, *Official Records,* Series I, Vol. XXV, Part I, 785.

217 "fabrication"]   Hamlin, *Chancellorsville,* 90.

sharpshooter]   *Cincinnati Commercial,* May 14, 1863; *Chicago Tribune,* May 15, 1863; Alexander Hamilton to W. M. Shaw, Nov. 4, 1904, *Cohasco, Inc., Catalogue No. 24* (1982), Item 77.

"fell under . . . established"]   Reprinted in *Daily Clarion* (Meridian, Miss.), Oct. 8, 1865.

J. F. Knipe]   Hamlin, *Chancellorsville,* 106.

217 "Why . . . monument" and "was not . . . wounded"]   *Carlisle Herald*, Oct. 8, 1910.

"Liberty . . . forever" and "I was . . . fell"]   Henry M. Field, *Blood Is Thicker Than Water: A Few Days Among Our Southern Brethren* (New York, 1886), 33, 65–68.

218 "met" . . . "authors"]   *New York Tribune*, May 14, 1863.

"He prostituted . . . civilization"]   *Chicago Tribune*, May 16, 1863.

"The honesty . . . crime"]   *Harper's Weekly*, VII (May 30, 1863), 338.

James E. Murdoch]   James E. Murdoch, *Patriotism in Poetry and Prose: Being Selected Passages from Lectures and Patriotic Readings by James E. Murdoch* (Philadelphia, 1864), 93–97.

"increase . . . cause"]   *Daily Illinois State Journal* (Springfield), May 14, 1863.

218–19 "a very pleasant . . . army"]   *Wheeling Intelligencer*, June 8, 1863.

219 "The turnpike . . . conjecture"]   [John Esten Cooke], "Stonewall Jackson's Death," Sept. 1865, clipping in Scrapbook, William E. Brooks Papers, Box 1, West Virginia University.

Joseph W. Revere]   Joseph W. Revere to *New York Herald*, Dec. 16, 1869, reprinted in *Richmond Dispatch*, Dec. 22, 1869; Joseph W. Revere, *Keel and Saddle: A Retrospect of Forty Years of Military and Naval Service* (Boston, 1872), 254–257, 276–278.

"The solitary . . . do" and "The part . . . reality"]   R. E. Wilbourn to J. A. Early, Feb. 18 and 19, 1873, Early Papers, Library of Congress.

"Your Stonewall . . . power"]   Evert Duyckinck to John Esten Cooke, March 23, 1866, John Esten Cooke Papers, Library of Congress.

220 "Yes it is Providential" and "We were . . . lines"]   R. E. Wilbourn to [?], May 1863, Charles J. Faulkner Papers, Virginia Historical Society.

"I will keep . . . wounded" and "If you please"]   R. E. Wilbourn to R. L. Dabney, Dec. 12, 1863, Charles William Dabney Papers, University of North Carolina.

"I sent . . . of it"]   R. E. Wilbourn to J. A. Early, Feb. 18 and March 3, 1873, Early Papers, Library of Congress.

221 "Great . . . Jackson"]   R. E. Wilbourn to [?], May 1863, Charles J. Faulkner Papers, Virginia Historical Society.

"Gen. Pender . . . ground"]   J. G. Morrison to E. P. Alexander, July 2, 1869, Edward Porter Alexander Papers, University of North Carolina.

"that any . . . after it"]   Adin B. Underwood, *The Three Years' Service of the Thirty-Third Mass. Infantry Regiment 1862–1865* (Boston, 1881), 67.

"Verily . . . night"]   Douglas, *I Rode With Stonewall*, 223.

"I hope . . . General" and "I am . . . dying"]   McGuire, "Account of Wounding and Death," in McGuire and Christian, *Confederate Cause and Conduct*, 220.

"A chill . . . him"]   Entry of May 11, 1863, Catherine Ann Devereux Edmonston, *Journal of a Secesh Lady*, ed. Beth G. Crabtree and James W. Patton (Raleigh, N.C., 1979), 392.

"Every one . . . calamity"]   Entry of May 11, 1863, Diary of William M. Blackford, in Susan Leigh Blackford, comp., *Memoirs of Life In and Out of the Army In Virginia During the War Between the States* (Lynchburg, Va., 1894), II, 82; *Charleston Courier*, May 12, 1863.

221–2 "we all looked . . . victory" and "I know . . . About"]   [Joseph G. Dill] to [D. C. E.] Brady, May 20, 1863, William Weaver Papers, Duke University; F. M. Nixon to uncle, May 20, 1863, Thomas Nixon Papers, *ibid.*

222 "thrice-beloved"]   Sidney Lanier, "The Dying Words of Stonewall Jackson," in *Poems of Sidney Lanier* (New York, 1884), 230–231.

identifying with Jackson]   *Richmond Whig*, May 12, 1863; *Savannah Republican*, May 11, 1863.

222 "Would God . . . thee"]   *Charleston Courier,* May 12, 1863.

"We've killed . . . dead"]   Entry of May 9, 1863, McDonald, *Diary With Reminiscences,* 161.

"Where's your Stonewall now?"]   John R. Thompson, Correspondence with *The Index,* May 12, 1863, John R. Thompson Collection, #38-705, University of Virginia.

"makes me . . . killed"]   Mary Caplinger to Leonard Caplinger, May 24, 1863, Leonard J. Caplinger Collection, Huntington Library.

"I feel . . . dying"]   McGuire, "Account of Wounding and Death," in McGuire and Christian, *Confederate Cause and Conduct,* 220; [R. L. Dabney, Notes], "Dr. McGuire's Narrative," Charles William Dabney Papers, Box 31, University of North Carolina.

"What an infinite blessing" and "I don't . . . best"]   McGuire, "Account of Wounding and Death," in McGuire and Christian, *Confederate Cause and Conduct,* 222–223.

eternity]   [R. L. Dabney, Notes], "Lt. Smith's Narrative," Charles William Dabney Papers, Box 32, University of North Carolina.

223 "I congratulate . . . energy"]   R. E. Lee to T. J. Jackson, May 2, [1863], Jackson Papers, Davis Collection, Tulane University.

"Gen. Lee . . . God"]   [R. L. Dabney, Notes], "Lt. Smith's Narrative," Charles William Dabney Papers, Box 32, University of North Carolina.

"the most . . . my life" and "I simply . . . led me"]   [R. L. Dabney, Notes], "Rev. B. T. Lacy's Narrative," *ibid.*

"Charge . . . Jackson"]   [R. L. Dabney, Notes], "Lt. Smith's Narrative," *ibid.*

"Stonewall"]   McGuire, "Account of Wounding and Death," in McGuire and Christian, *Confederate Cause and Conduct,* 224.

Jackson and God]   [R. L. Dabney, Notes], "Rev. B. T. Lacy's Narrative," Charles William Dabney Papers, Box 32, University of North Carolina; W. N. Pendleton to [A. E. Pendleton], May 14, 1863, William Nelson Pendleton Papers, *ibid.;* entry of Nov. 18, 1863, Diary of Peter W. Hairston, *ibid.*

"matchless energy and skill"]   R. E. Lee to S. Cooper, Sept. 21, 1863, *Official Records,* Series I, Vol. XXV, Part I, 803.

"His genius . . . success"]   D. H. Hill, General Orders, No. 20, May 26, 1863, D. H. Hill Papers, Box 6, Virginia State Library, Richmond.

"invincible"]   *Richmond Examiner,* May 10, 1866, reprinted in *Saint Louis Dispatch,* May 15, 1866.

223–4 "to regard . . . life" and "and there . . . end"]   *Richmond Whig,* May 12, 1863.

224 "Jackson . . . fate"]   [John Esten Cooke], *The Life of Stonewall Jackson* (New York, 1863), 7.

"No name . . . as his" and "ubiquitous . . . field"]   Entry of May 11, 1863, Journal of Robert G. H. Kean, University of Virginia; *Richmond Examiner,* May 10, 1866, reprinted in *Saint Louis Dispatch,* May 15, 1866.

"a great intellect"]   *Richmond Whig,* May 12, 1863.

"mind . . . account" and "the master mind of the war"]   G. D. Camden to R. L. Dabney, Nov. 25, 1863, Charles William Dabney Papers, Box 31, University of North Carolina.

"the expression . . . purpose"]   [Cooke], *Life of Jackson,* 7–8.

McGuire; Hotchkiss; Lacy]   McGuire, "Account of Wounding and Death," in McGuire and Christian, *Confederate Cause and Conduct,* 226; entry of May 5, 1863, Diary of Jedediah Hotchkiss, Jedediah Hotchkiss Papers, Library of Congress; [R. L. Dabney, Notes], "Rev. B. T. Lacy's Narrative," Charles William Dabney Papers, Box 32, University of North Carolina.

"will say . . . demoralized"]   Entry of May 7, 1863, Edmonston, *Journal of a Secesh Lady,* ed. Crabtree and Patton, 389.

224–5 "No such . . . care"] *New York Herald,* June 4, 1864.

225 "It would be . . . men"] J. Esten Cooke, "The Fall of Ashby," Scrapbook, John Esten Cooke Papers, Box 1, Library of Congress.

"It took . . . doom"] R. L. Dabney, "General T. J. Jackson. An Elegy, 1887," in *Discussions by Robert L. Dabney* (Mexico, Mo., 1897), IV, 592.

"pleuro-pneumonia . . . side"] McGuire, "Account of Wounding and Death," in McGuire and Christian, *Confederate Cause and Conduct,* 226.

"He looked . . . man"] Mary Anna Jackson to [Laura Jackson Arnold], Sept. 12, 1864, Jackson Manuscripts, Virginia Military Institute.

Jackson's orders] [R. L. Dabney, Notes], "Rev. B. T. Lacy's Narrative," and "Last days" [Mrs. Jackson's narrative], Charles William Dabney Papers, Box 32, University of North Carolina; M. A. Jackson, *Life and Letters of Jackson,* 466.

"come out in the papers"] Jed[ediah] Hotchkiss to Hunter McGuire, June 8, 1896, Hotchkiss Papers, Library of Congress. On Hill see James I. Robertson, Jr., *General A. P. Hill: The Story of a Confederate Warrior* (New York, 1987).

Jesus healed] [R. L. Dabney, Notes], "Rev. B. T. Lacy's Narrative," Charles William Dabney Papers, Box 32, University of North Carolina.

"more rational"] Mary Anna Jackson to [Laura Jackson Arnold], Sept. 12, 1864, Jackson Manuscripts, Virginia Military Institute.

225–6 "I do not . . . perform" and *"prostration . . . nourishment"*] [R. L. Dabney, Notes], [Narrative of Dr. Morrison], Charles William Dabney Papers, Box 32, University of North Carolina; Sam B. Morrison to uncle, May 13, 1863, Florida Atlantic University, Boca Raton, printed in *Miami Herald,* Feb. 9, 1988.

226 "He was . . . service"] *Southern Confederacy* (Atlanta), May 12, 1863.

"a glorious deliverance"] James B. Ramsey, *True Eminence Founded on Holiness. A Discourse Occasioned by the Death of Lieut. Gen. T. J. Jackson* (Lynchburg, Va., 1863), 18.

"compulsion . . . Maker"] *Richmond Whig,* May 12, 1863.

"the expression . . . itself" and "the living . . . world"] W. A. Alexander, comp., *A Digest of the Acts and Proceedings of the General Assembly of the Presbyterian Church in the United States* (Richmond, Va., 1888), 398.

"the secret source" and "a concentration . . . impossible"] Ramsey, *True Eminence,* 12.

"that a man . . . Christian"] [Henry C. Burn] to mother, May 18, 1863, Burn Family Papers, University of South Carolina.

Lacy on biography] B. T. Lacy to R. L. Dabney, May 13, 1863, Jackson Papers, Davis Collection, Tulane University.

227 "Trust . . . ours"] Ramsey, *True Eminence,* 21.

"I do not . . . country" and "In his . . . tenacity"] Robert L. Dabney, "True Courage. A Discourse Commemorative of Lieut.-General Thomas J. Jackson," in *Discussions by Dabney,* IV, 449, 451.

"With his . . . droop"] [John Esten Cooke], "Stonewall Jackson's Death," Scrapbook, Brooks Papers, West Virginia University.

"a true . . . disaster"] *Richmond Examiner,* May 10, 1866, reprinted in *Saint Louis Dispatch,* May 15, 1866.

"our star . . . Jackson"] Casler, *Four Years in the Stonewall Brigade,* 153.

"Men . . . success"] Samuel D. Buck, *With the Old Confeds: Actual Experiences of a Captain in the Line* (Baltimore, Md., 1925), 83.

"that nearly . . . end" and "our army . . . skulking"] [Jedediah Hotchkiss] to Tho[ma]s L. Rosser, Dec. 28, 1897, Hotchkiss Papers, Library of Congress.

227 "The melancholy . . . defenders"] [Napier Bartlett], *A Soldier's Story of the War; Including the Marches and Battles of the Washington Artillery, and of Other Louisiana Troops* (New Orleans, 1874), 177.

227–8 "a little . . . fate" and "nemesis . . . Confederacy"] David Gregg McIntosh, "The Campaign of Chancellorsville," *Southern Historical Society Papers,* XL (1915), 59, 82.

228 "After . . . success"] Hunter McGuire to Jed[ediah] Hotchkiss, Dec. 23, 1897, Hotchkiss Papers, Library of Congress.

"The bloody . . . ago" and "I trust . . . plans"] Alice Prioleau to Harriott [Middleton], June 30, [1863], Cheves-Middleton Papers, Box 12-164, South Carolina Historical Society, Charleston.

"wrought . . . Providence" and "The same . . . men"] *Richmond Enquirer,* May 13, 1863; *Richmond Whig,* May 12, 1863.

"General . . . black mail"] *Richmond Enquirer,* reprinted in *Charleston Courier,* May 23, 1863.

"If not . . . revolution"] *Savannah Republican,* May 11, 1863.

"The spirit . . . nation"] Ramsey, *True Eminence,* 20.

229 "Anna . . . that"] [R. L. Dabney, Notes], [Narrative of Dr. Morrison], Charles William Dabney Papers, Box 32, University of North Carolina.

"Yes . . . read"] [R. L. Dabney, Notes], "Last days" [Mrs. Jackson's narrative], *ibid.*

"I think . . . morning"] [R. L. Dabney, Notes], [Narrative of Dr. Morrison], *ibid.*

Chancellorsville battlefield] Colston, "Address . . . Before the Ladies' Memorial Association," *Southern Historical Society Papers,* XXI (1893), 44–45.

229–30 "Do you" . . . "I prefer it"] [R. L. Dabney, Notes], "Last days" [Mrs. Jackson's narrative], Charles William Dabney Papers, Box 32, University of North Carolina.

230 "I will . . . translated" and "Back . . . all"] Mary Anna Jackson to [Laura Jackson Arnold], Sept. 12, 1864, Jackson Manuscripts, Virginia Military Institute.

"Charlotte" . . . *"plot"*] M. A. Jackson, *Life and Letters of Jackson,* 470.

"I am too . . . now"] Mary Anna Jackson to [Laura Jackson Arnold], Sept. 12, 1864, Jackson Manuscripts, Virginia Military Institute.

"Little . . . one"] M[ary] A[nna] J[ackson] to [Fanny B. Graham?], July 20, 1863, Cook Collection, West Virginia University.

"I am ready"] [Henry C. Burn] to mother, May 18, 1863, Burn Papers, University of South Carolina.

"200 persons . . . scene" and "as he . . . wound"] Entry of Nov. 18, 1863, Diary of Peter W. Hairston, University of North Carolina.

J. M. Mathews] J. M. Mathews, *The Bible and Men of Learning; in a Course of Lectures* (New York, 1855), 164, 31, 39, 186. Jackson's copy is at the Virginia Historical Society.

"our precious . . . heaven"] Entry of May 12, 1863, Journal of Margaret Junkin Preston, in Elizabeth Preston Allan, *The Life and Letters of Margaret Junkin Preston* (Boston, 1903), 165.

231 "I often . . . land"] D. H. Hill to R. L. Dabney, July 11, 1864, Dabney Papers, Union Theological Seminary in Virginia.

"in his dozing state"] [R. L. Dabney, Notes], "Last days" [Mrs. Jackson's narrative], Charles William Dabney Papers, Box 32, University of North Carolina.

"All . . . last"] M. A. Jackson, *Life and Letters of Jackson,* 471.

"spoke no more" . . . "died"] [R. L. Dabney, Notes], "Lt. Smith's Narrative," Charles William Dabney Papers, Box 32, University of North Carolina.

CHAPTER SIX

Notes for Pages 232–295

232 "No prepared . . . was"] Walter Lowenfels, ed., *Walt Whitman's Civil War* (New York, 1971), 14.

233 "The real . . . books"] *Ibid.,* 293.

"thought him . . . unsurpassed"] [William Preston Johnston], "Memoranda of the President," July 10, 1864, Albert Sidney Johnston and William Preston Johnston Papers, Howard-Tilton Library, Tulane University, New Orleans, Louisiana.

"military President"] Harvey Reid to father, Aug. 26, 1864, Frank L. Byrne, ed., *The View from Headquarters: Civil War Letters of Harvey Reid* (Madison, Wis., 1965), 181.

233–4 "dictatorship"] Entry of March 3, 1862, Charles Campbell, Diary, Charles Campbell Papers, Box 18, Swem Library, College of William and Mary, Williamsburg, Virginia.

234 "Oh . . . gloves"] House of Representatives, Jan. 22, 1862, *Congressional Globe,* 37th Congress, 2d Session, 440.

"Just grind . . . occasion"] A. H. Hood to [Thaddeus Stevens], Jan. 8, 1862, Thaddeus Stevens Papers, Manuscript Division, Library of Congress, Washington, D.C. See also John William Ward, *Andrew Jackson: Symbol for an Age* (New York, 1955).

"always . . . do"] John Russell Young, *Around the World With General Grant* (New York, 1879), II, 352.

"he had . . . campaigns"] Francis Lawley to Jubal A. Early, May 14, 1872, Jubal Early Papers, Library of Congress.

Napoleon] See, for example, *New York Herald,* Jan. 9, 1863; *Cincinnati Commercial,* Dec. 24, 1864; Micajah Woods to [John R. Woods], Aug. 19, 1861, Micajah Woods Papers, Alderman Library, University of Virginia, Charlottesville; [John Esten Cooke], *The Life of Stonewall Jackson* (Richmond, 1863), 102; W. J. Underwood to L. B. and M. L. Underwood, April 15, 1861, Underwood/Key Family Papers, Atlanta Historical Society, Atlanta, Georgia.

234–5 "the Napoleon . . . War" and "In every . . . enthusiasm"] *New York Herald,* July 16, 1861.

235 "the Napoleonic . . . action"] *Cincinnati Commercial,* April 29, 1861.

"like Napoleon" and "meet . . . dying"] Newspaper clipping, George William Bagby Scrapbook, Virginia Historical Society, Richmond.

"demolished . . . maxims"] J. T. Headley, *Grant and Sherman: Their Campaigns and Generals* (New York, 1866), 132.

"He moves . . . complete"] "Narrative of a Rebel Lieutenant," Sept. 6, 1862, in Frank Moore, ed., *The Rebellion Record: A Diary of American Events* (New York, 1861–1868), V, 404.

"an impatient, tax paying people"] *Missouri Democrat,* reprinted in *Chattanooga Rebel,* Dec. 2, 1862.

"Each . . . Army"] *The War and Its Heroes* (Richmond, Va., 1864), iv.

"Wanted—A Man"] Francis F. Browne, ed., *Bugle-Echoes: A Collection of the Poetry of the Civil War, Northern and Southern* (New York, 1886), 120–121.

"We have . . . gods"] *Cincinnati Commercial,* Jan. 13, 1863.

"is thoroughly . . . fire"] *Boston Evening Transcript,* reprinted in *Cincinnati Commercial,* Nov. 27, 1862.

235–6 Gurowski] Entry of March 5, 1864, Adam Gurowski, *Diary: 1863–'64–'65* (Washington, D.C., 1866), 128. On Carlyle see Walter E. Houghton, *The Victorian Frame of Mind, 1830–1870* (New Haven, Conn., 1957), chap. 12; Leo Marx, *The Machine in the Garden: Technology and the Pastoral Ideal in America* (New York, 1964), 170–179; Michael Timko, *Carlyle and Tennyson* (Iowa City, Iowa, 1988), 43–54.

236 "a mere . . . point"]   John William Draper, *History of the American Civil War* (New York, 1867–1870), II, 187.

"(M.V.?)"]   *The Officer's Manual. Napoleon's Maxims of War* (Richmond, Va., 1862). Jackson's copy is in the Thomas Jonathan Jackson Papers, George H. and Katherine M. Davis Collection, Tulane University.

"I used . . . axidents"]   T. E. Smith to Will, Jan. 28, [1863], Thomas E. Smith Letters, Cincinnati Historical Society, Cincinnati, Ohio.

Henry Adams]   [Henry Adams], *The Education of Henry Adams: An Autobiography* (Boston, 1961 [orig. publ. 1918]), 325–326.

237 "in point . . . writers"]   *New York Herald*, March 20, 1862. On *The Times* see *The History of The Times: The Tradition Established* (London, 1939), 167, 183–186; Martin Crawford, "William Howard Russell and the Confederacy," *Journal of American Studies*, XV (Aug. 1981), 191–210.

circulation]   *New York Herald*, Nov. 8, 1860, June 18, 1862.

"has any . . . country"]   Edward Dicey, *Six Months in the Federal States* (London, 1863), I, 32–33.

"tone and direction"]   Entry of Aug. 13, 1864, Howard K. Beale, ed., *Diary of Gideon Welles* (New York, 1960), II, 103. On Bennett see Don C. Seitz, *The James Gordon Bennetts, Father and Son: Proprietors of the New York Herald* (Indianapolis, Ind., 1928); Oliver Carlson, *The Man Who Made News: James Gordon Bennett* (New York, 1942); Joseph J. Mathews, *Reporting the Wars* (Minneapolis, Minn., 1957); Bernard A. Weisberger, *Reporters for the Union* (Boston, 1953); J. Cutler Andrews, *The North Reports the Civil War* (Pittsburgh, 1955); James L. Crouthamel, "James Gordon Bennett, the *New York Herald*, and the Development of Newspaper Sensationalism," *New York History*, LIV (July 1973), 294–316; Michael Schudson, *Discovering the News: A Social History of American Newspapers* (New York, 1978), 23–31, 50–57.

238 "glimpses . . . hell"]   B. Lewis Blackford to mother, Dec. 10, 1861, Blackford Family Papers, #6403, University of Virginia.

"News . . . breakfast"]   *Harper's Weekly*, VI (June 14, 1862), 378.

"would steal . . . progressing"]   George P. Rawick, ed., *The American Slave: A Composite Autobiography* (Westport, Conn., 1972), Series II, Vol. XII, Georgia Narratives, Part I, 257.

"illimitable circulation"]   *New York Herald*, Sept. 9, 1863.

"The American . . . animal"]   Dicey, *Six Months in the Federal States*, I, 43.

"A general . . . all-pervading"]   J[ohn] Swinton to [Elihu B. Washburne], July 13, [1864; filed as 1863], Elihu B. Washburne Papers, Volume 31, Library of Congress. See U. S. Grant, *Personal Memoirs of U. S. Grant* (New York, 1885), II, 143–145.

238–9 "capture the people" and "we have . . . passion"]   S. M. Johnson to S. [L. M.] Barlow, May 30, 1863, S. L. M. Barlow Papers, Henry E. Huntington Library, San Marino, California. See also Michael G. McGerr, *The Decline of Popular Politics: The American North, 1865–1928* (New York, 1986), chap. 5.

239 "the inspiring power" and "A united . . . people"]   *Chattanooga Rebel*, Sept. 27, 1862.

Leonard A. Hendricks]   Stephen Minot Weld, [Jr.], to [Stephen Minot Weld], March 10, 1862, *War Diary and Letters of Stephen Minot Weld, 1861–1865* (Boston, 1979 [orig. publ. 1912]), 71.

"a host . . . enemy"]   Ben [H. Pope] to Franklin, May 9, 1864, Civil War Correspondence, Box 2, University of Georgia, Athens.

239–40 "The papers . . . displeasure"]   M. A. P[almer] to [John M. Palmer], Oct. 29, 1863, John M. Palmer Papers, Illinois State Historical Library, Springfield.

240 Ella Gertrude Clanton Thomas]   Entries of June 9 and July 4, 1862, Ella Gertrude Clanton Thomas, Journal, Duke University, Durham, North Carolina.

240 "They anticipate . . . papers"]   Mary [Hall] to friend, May 16, 1864, Mary Cheney Hall Correspondence, Chicago Historical Society, Chicago, Illinois.

"sickly craving"]   John F. Ware, *Manhood, The Want of the Day* (Boston, 1863), 15.

"The public . . . reading"]   Entry of Dec. 16, 1863, Allan Nevins, ed., *A Diary of Battle: The Personal Journals of Colonel Charles S. Wainwright, 1861–1865* (New York, 1962), 309.

"insatiable . . . rumors"]   Quoted in Andrews, *North Reports the War*, 647.

241 "Minute . . . sufferings"]   *New York Herald*, Oct. 5, 1862.

"The actuality . . . invaluable"]   *Harper's Weekly*, VIII (Aug. 6, 1864), 499. See also W. Fletcher Thompson, Jr., *The Image of War: The Pictorial Reporting of the American Civil War* (New York, 1959), 57, 147–150; Alan Trachtenberg, *Reading American Photographs: Images as History, Mathew Brady to Walker Evans* ([New York], 1989), 72–77; Timothy Sweet, *Traces of War: Poetry, Photography, and the Crisis of the Union* (Baltimore, Md., 1990), chaps. 3–5.

"whose nights . . . comfortless"]   Entry of June 5, 1863, Adam Gurowski, *Diary, from November 18, 1862 to October 18, 1863* (New York, 1864), 241–242.

242 "Never . . . ghostlike"]   Noah Brooks, *Washington in Lincoln's Time*, ed. Herbert Mitgang (New York, 1958), 61.

"No wonder . . . murderer"]   Reprinted in *Cincinnati Commercial*, June 6, 1863.

Seward]   [Henry Bellows], [Memorandum, ca. Jan.–Feb. 1863], Henry W. Bellows Papers, Massachusetts Historical Society, Boston. See also John Hay to [William H.] Herndon, Sept. 5, 1866, Manuscript of William H. Herndon's Life of Lincoln, Volume II, 463, Ward Hill Lamon Papers, Huntington Library.

"the pressure . . . with him"]   Grant, *Personal Memoirs*, II, 122.

"What will the country say"]   Brooks, *Washington in Lincoln's Time*, ed. Mitgang, 61.

"was really . . . struggle"]   Young, *Around the World*, II, 354, 358.

243 "We must . . . said them"]   C[harles] S[umner] to [Salmon P.] Chase, April 12, 1865, Salmon P. Chase Papers, Library of Congress. See also James G. Blaine, *Twenty Years of Congress: From Lincoln to Garfield* (Norwich, Conn., 1884), I, 492; House of Representatives, Jan. 6, 1864, *Congressional Globe*, 38th Congress, 1st Session, 117.

"They can not . . . emotion"]   *Harper's Weekly*, VII (Dec 5, 1863), 770.

"cool thoughts" . . . "dying men"]   C. C. C[arpenter] to [Susan C. Burkholder], Dec. 12, 1862, Cyrus Clay Carpenter Papers, State Historical Society of Iowa, Iowa City.

"if he . . . slavery"]   Willie Scott to [John G. Hudson], April 16, [1865], John G. Hudson Collection, Small Manuscript Collections, Box 4, Arkansas History Commission, Little Rock.

"in the veteran service" and "He has . . . soldier"]   J. W. Lee to father, March 5, 1865, John Walter Lee Letters, State Historical Society of Iowa.

244 "No Wone . . . Now"]   R. Rey to Lizzie, April 29, 1865, Rudolphe Rey Personal Miscellany, New-York Historical Society, New York, New York.

"When I . . . away"]   Addie to [John A. Griffin], April 27, 1865, John A. Griffin Papers, Illinois State Historical Library.

"a sacrifice . . . battle"]   Bella DeLoss Dudley, "A Personal Narrative of the Civil War," 184, William Henry Dudley Papers, Box 2, State Historical Society of Wisconsin, Madison.

Dabney and Johnston on Lee]   R. L. Dabney, "Stonewall Jackson," *Southern Historical Society Papers*, XI (1883), 153; Henry M. Field, *Blood Is Thicker Than Water: A Few Days Among Our Southern Brethren* (New York, 1886), 96–97.

245 "No intelligent . . . events" and "the token . . . day"]   Matthew H. Jamison, *Recollections of Pioneer and Army Life* (Kansas City, Mo., 1911), 43.

"I saw . . . years"]   Entry of June 27, 1863, Diary, Elizabeth Oakes Smith Papers, #38-707, University of Virginia.

245 "I more . . . province"]   S. B. D[unn] to John [Griffin], June 7, 1863, John A. Griffin Papers, Illinois State Historical Library. See also Eliza W. Sligh to [J. W. Sligh], Dec. 11, 1861, Sligh Family Correspondence, Michigan History Collection, Bentley Library, University of Michigan, Ann Arbor; entry of July 31, 1864, Ella Gertrude Clanton Thomas, Diary, Duke University; entry of July 5, 1864, Diary of [Miss Abby], University of Georgia; Ira Blanchard, [Memoir], 2, Illinois State Historical Library.

soldier's dream]   Entry of July 30, 1862, Matella Page Harrison, Diary, University of Virginia; entries of April 4 and 27, 1862, Samuel A. Wildman, Diary, Wildman Family Papers, Box 1, Ohio Historical Society, Columbus; John Forman to [Robert A.] Newelle, April 28, 1862, Robert A. Newell Papers, Louisiana State University, Baton Rouge.

246 "This new . . . exhausted"]   Lew [?] to Kate [Bond], Sept. 16, 1862, Bond-McCulloch Family Papers, MS 1159, Manuscripts Division, Maryland Historical Society Library, Baltimore.

"I look . . . evidences"]   J. E. Chapin to Mrs. W[illia]m A. Ross, June 20, 1866, James Osgood Andrew Clark Papers, Woodruff Library, Emory University, Atlanta, Georgia.

"The whole . . . real"]   [Charles Woodward Hutson] to [?], April 18–20, 1865, Charles Woodward Hutson Papers, Southern Historical Collection, University of North Carolina, Chapel Hill. See also John N. Opie, *A Rebel Cavalryman with Lee, Stuart, and Jackson* (Chicago, 1899), 12.

246–7 "You cannot . . . nervous"]   Anna [Shaw Curtis] to [Elizabeth Russell Lyman], Dec. 14, 1862, Theodore Lyman Papers, Box 13, Massachusetts Historical Society.

247 "Sunday . . . fight"]   Entry of July 20, 1862, Samuel A. Wildman, Diary, Wildman Family Papers, Ohio Historical Society.

"When the news . . . thereof"]   H. C. Bruce, *The New Man. Twenty-nine Years a Slave. Twenty-nine Years a Free Man* (New York, 1969 [orig. publ. York, Pa., 1895]), 99–100.

"the anxiety . . . war" and "the average . . . war"]   Entry of Sept. 16, 1863, Charles Campbell, Diary, Charles Campbell Papers, College of William and Mary.

"fleeting . . . mind" and "very influential . . . places"]   John C. Ropes to John C. Gray, Jr., Sept. 18, 1863, John Chipman Gray and John Codman Ropes, *War Letters, 1862–1865,* ed. Worthington Chauncey Ford (Boston, 1927), 208. On connections between the public and the war see Randall C. Jimerson, *The Private Civil War: Popular Thought During the Sectional Conflict* (Baton Rouge, La., 1988); Eric L. McKitrick, *Andrew Johnson and Reconstruction* (Chicago, 1960), 24–28; George C. Rable, *Civil Wars: Women and the Crisis of Southern Nationalism* (Urbana, Ill., 1989), chap. 10; Earl J. Hess, *Liberty, Virtue, and Progress: Northerners and Their War for the Union* (New York, 1988).

"great crowd"]   W. T. Sherman to Ellen [Sherman], June 2, 1863, William Tecumseh Sherman Papers (consolidated microfilm collection), University of Notre Dame, Notre Dame, Indiana. See also Mary C. Hall to friend, June 6, 1863, Hall Correspondence, Chicago Historical Society. See, in general, Mary Elizabeth Massey, *Bonnet Brigades* (New York, 1966), chap. 4.

248 "Give me back my dead"]   Mrs. A. H. [Jane C.] Hoge, *The Boys in Blue; or Heroes of the "Rank and File"* (New York, 1867), 187.

"an hour . . . dying"]   William W. Bennett, *A Narrative of the Great Revival Which Prevailed in the Southern Armies During the Late Civil War* (Philadelphia, 1877), 158.

"came in . . . grounds"]   Entry of July 6, 1863, David S. Sparks, ed., *Inside Lincoln's Army: The Diary of Marsena Rudolph Patrick* (New York, 1964), 268; J. T. Trowbridge, *The South: A Tour of Its Battle-Fields and Ruined Cities* (Hartford, Conn., 1866), 33.

"All who . . . war"]   Letter from S. J. K., July 28, 1863, *Cincinnati Commercial,* Aug. 4, 1863.

"the more coveted relics"]   *Boston Evening Transcript* quoted in *Saint Louis Dispatch,* Dec. 20, 1865.

248 "greedy . . . curiosity"]   Sylvanus Cadwallader, *Three Years With Grant As Recalled by War Correspondent Sylvanus Cadwallader,* ed. Benjamin P. Thomas (New York, 1955), 231.

249 "I have . . . rights"]   Entry of Feb. 14, 1865, Caroline Kean (Hill) Davis, Diary, Virginia Historical Society, Richmond.

"Some . . . army"]   [Charlotte Wigfall] to [Charlotte Maria Wigfall], May 13, [1861], Wigfall Family Papers, Box 2, Library of Congress. See also "The Influence of Woman," *Harper's Weekly,* VI (Sept. 6, 1862), 570; Nina Bennett Smith, "The Women Who Went to War: The Union Army Nurse in the Civil War" (Ph.D. diss., Northwestern University, 1981), 5–7.

"efficiency"]   Phoebe Yates Pember, *A Southern Woman's Story* (New York, 1879), 192; [Clara Barton], [War Lectures, 1866–1868], Clara Barton Papers, Series 1, Box 9, Library of Congress.

"executive ability" and "all-embracing motherhood"]   Florence Shaw Kellogg, *Mother Bickerdyke As I Knew Her* (Chicago, 1907), 124–125. See also Hoge, *Boys in Blue,* 117–128; Ann Douglas, *The Feminization of American Culture* (New York, 1977), 75–76.

"a Napoleon . . . Jackson"]   Bennett, *Narrative of the Great Revival,* 59.

"a band . . . cause"]   Sarah Grimes to Mrs. William Coffey, May 28, 1864, William Coffey Papers, Ohio Historical Society.

"could assert . . . laurels" and "follow . . . dreams"]   Frank Moore, *Women of the War; Their Heroism and Self-Sacrifice* (Hartford, Conn., 1867), 245. See also Kathleen L. Endres, "The Women's Press in the Civil War: A Portrait of Patriotism, Propaganda, and Prodding," *Civil War History,* XXX (March 1984), 31–53; Rable, *Civil Wars,* chaps. 6, 7.

"the delicate gentlemen of our land"]   Mary A. Bickerdyke to James and Hiram [Bickerdyke], Sept. 9, [1864], Mary Ann Ball Bickerdyke Correspondence, Library of Congress.

"do *something*"]   Evy [Kell] to [Julia Blanche Munroe Kell], July 5, 1864, John McIntosh Kell Papers, Duke University.

"It seemed . . . going"]   Entry of Sept. 27, 1863, Emilie Quiner, Diary, State Historical Society of Wisconsin.

nurses' health]   Massey, *Bonnet Brigades,* 63.

"What if . . . them"]   Hoge, *Boys in Blue,* 231–234. See also entry of Dec. 30, 1863, Nicolas B. Wainwright, ed., *A Philadelphia Perspective: The Diary of Sidney George Fisher Covering the Years 1834–1871* (Philadelphia, 1967), 464; Moore, *Women of the War,* 38–52, 75–90, 345–346; entry of July 5, 1865, N. L. Parmater, Diary, Ohio Historical Society.

250 "so sorry . . . *opportunity*" and "morbid sympathy"]   Clara Barton to T. W. Meighan, June 24, 1863, Barton Papers, Box 6, Library of Congress. See also Carrie McNair to Mrs. Adams, Feb. 17, [1862], Ephraim Adams Papers, Box 4, State Historical Society of Iowa.

"I have thought . . . myself"]   Mrs. Nathan A. Tinkham to [W. E. Boardman], Nov. 28, 1864, United States Christian Commission, Communications Received, Box 6, Record Group 94, Number 740, National Archives, Washington, D.C. See also M. A. Ball to [George H.] Stuart, Aug. 11, 1864, *ibid.,* Box 4. On civilians' concern see Robert H. Bremner, *The Public Good: Philanthropy and Welfare in the Civil War Era* (New York, 1980), chaps. 2, 3.

"our fair-haired boys"]   Women's Loyal National League, *Proceedings of the Meeting of the Loyal Women of the Republic, Held in New York, May 14, 1863* (New York, 1863), 5.

"our broad-browed . . . homes"]   House of Representatives, Dec. 11, 1861, *Congressional Globe,* 37th Congress, 2d Session, 67. See also entry of Dec. 31, 1861, Lucy Buck, Diary, University of Virginia; Robert Stiles, *Four Years Under Marse Robert* (New York, 1904), 299–300.

250 songs and verse]   Moore, *Women of the War,* 98–99; Moore, ed., *Rebellion Record,* IV, Poetry and Incidents, 95.

"A remarkably . . . ends"]   Moore, ed., *Rebellion Record,* VII, Poetry and Incidents, 52.

251 "in mute" . . . "figure"]   James D[inwiddie] to Bettie [Carrington Dinwiddie], June 29, 1862, James and Bettie Carrington Dinwiddie Papers, University of Virginia.

"a beardless . . . eyes"]   Charles E. Benton, *As Seen from the Ranks: A Boy in the Civil War* (New York, 1902), 193–196.

Barton; Harris; Pember]   [Clara Barton], [War Lectures, 1866–1868], Barton Papers, Box 9, Library of Congress; E. N. H[arris] to [Mrs. Joel Jones], June 19, [1862], in E. N. Harris, "Extracts from the Third Report of the Ladies' Aid Society," Society Miscellaneous Collection, Historical Society of Pennsylvania, Philadelphia; Pember, *Southern Woman's Story,* 43–44. See also Smith, "Women Who Went to War," 88–90, 127.

"worn . . . him"]   Clara Barton to T. W. Meighan, June 24, 1863, Barton Papers, Box 6, Library of Congress. See also entry of Jan. 12, 1862, Lucy Buck, Diary, University of Virginia. On Barton see Ellen Langenheim Henle, "Clara Barton, Soldier or Pacifist?" *Civil War History,* XXIV (June 1978), 152–160. On antebellum deathbed scenes see Lewis Saum, *The Popular Mood of Pre–Civil War America* (Westport, Conn., 1980), 94–103.

252 "that we . . . seen"]   E. W. Locke, *Three Years in Camp and Hospital* (Boston, 1872), 136–137.

"I got . . . Leaves"]   Quoted in Daniel Aaron, *The Unwritten War: American Writers and the Civil War* (New York, 1973), 74.

Uncle Tom's Cabin]   Theodore F. Upson, *With Sherman to the Sea: The Civil War Letters, Diaries & Reminiscences of Theodore F. Upson,* ed. Oscar Osburn Winther (Baton Rouge, La., 1943), 1–3. On the effects of prewar reading see also entry of June 29, 1864, Ella Gertrude Clanton Thomas, Journal, Duke University; V. L. Pendleton, Reminiscences of V. L. Pendleton, 87, Kate Clark Pendleton Arrington Papers, University of North Carolina; Tho[ma]s Kilby Smith to [Eliza Bicker Walter Smith], Feb. 4, 1863, Thomas Kilby Smith Papers, Huntington Library; Charles Woodward Hutson, "My Reminiscences," 65, Hutson Papers, University of North Carolina; James A. Connolly to Mary Dunn Connolly, Aug. 11, 1864, Paul M. Angle, ed., *Three Years in the Army of the Cumberland: The Letters and Diary of Major James A. Connolly* (Bloomington, Ind., 1959), 253; [David Wyatt Aiken] to [Virginia Smith Aiken], Aug. 29, 1864, David Wyatt Aiken Papers, South Caroliniana Library, University of South Carolina, Columbia; Thomas W. Hyde, *Following the Greek Cross or, Memories of the Sixth Army Corps* (Boston, 1894), 48; A. B. Carpenter to parents, Sept. 29, 1861, Arthur B. Carpenter Collection, Civil War Manuscript Collection, Series I, Box 7, Sterling Library, Yale University, New Haven, Connecticut; entry of Oct. 12, 1862, Robert B. Taylor, Diary, University of Kentucky, Lexington.

"I presume . . . Heroine"]   J. M. Brannock to Sarah Brannock, Aug. 7, 1864, James Madison Brannock Papers, Virginia Historical Society.

252–3 "We are . . . theories"]   Joseph Conrad, *Chance* (New York, 1968 [orig. publ. 1912]), 288.

253 "the glamour . . . war"]   Douglas Southall Freeman, *The South to Posterity: An Introduction to the Writing of Confederate History* (New York, 1939), 170.

"There is . . . come"]   *Ohio State Journal* (Columbus), Aug. 12, 1880.

"I think . . . summer"]   J. D. McAdoo to [W. G. McAdoo, Sr.], April 9, 1863, William McAdoo Papers, Library of Congress.

254 Lanier; DeForest]   Sidney Lanier, *Tiger-Lilies* (Chapel Hill, N.C., 1969 [orig. publ. New York, 1867]), 115–121; John William DeForest, *Miss Ravenel's Conversion from Secession to Loyalty,* ed. Gordon S. Haight (New York, 1960 [orig. publ. 1867]), 58.

254 Waterloo] *New York Herald*, Sept. 25, 1861.

"We must . . . peace"] *Richmond Enquirer*, Nov. 29, 1862.

"more blood . . . campaign"] *Cincinnati Commercial*, April 29, 1861.

255 "the *coup de grâce*"] *Harper's Weekly*, VII (April 4, 1863), 210.

"must be *decisive*" and "we can see no results"] Entry of May 24, 1863, George A. Mercer, Diary, University of North Carolina.

"It is time . . . fought"] Reprinted in *Cincinnati Commercial*, July 20, 1864.

"the grand . . . war" and "The loss . . . Austerlitz"] *Cleveland Plain Dealer*, March 1, 1865.

"end . . . thunder"] M[urat] Halstead to John Sherman, April 1, 1863, John Sherman Papers, Library of Congress.

"for the . . . thunder-clap" and "The peculiar . . . results"] *Cincinnati Commercial*, April 11, 1865.

"I think . . . secumb"] Josiah C. Williams to father, June 21, 1862, Josiah C. Williams Papers, Indiana State Library, Indianapolis.

255–6 "The long . . . Arms"] Hugh L. Honnoll to sister, May 15, 1862, Honnoll Family Papers, Emory University.

256 "Society . . . Halleck"] *New York Herald*, May 20, 1862.

257 *Maud*] Alfred Tennyson, *Maud, and Other Poems* (London, 1862), 112–113.

"Charge of the Light Brigade"] See, for example, *Cincinnati Commercial*, Dec. 19, 1862; [Elizabeth Broadwell Lytle] to uncle, Oct. 11, 1863, William Lytle Correspondence, Lytle Papers, Box 31, Cincinnati Historical Society; Thomas [C. Honnell] to Eli and Raney [Honnell], April 6, 1863, Thomas C. Honnell Papers, Ohio Historical Society; [Mrs. J. J. Pringle Smith] to [Mary Lowndes], [July 25, 1861], Cheves-Middleton Papers, Box 12–164, South Carolina Historical Society, Charleston; entry of April 16, 1861, Emilie Quiner, Diary, State Historical Society of Wisconsin; speech by Gerrit Smith, *New York Herald*, Dec. 22, 1862; James Freeman Clarke, *Discourse on the Aspects of the War Delivered . . . April 2, 1863* (Boston, 1863), 9.

257–8 Tennyson and Carlyle] See, for example, entry of Nov. 24, 1864, John R. Thompson's Journal, 1864, John R. Thompson Collection, University of Virginia; T. Carlyle to [John R. Thompson], March 27, 1865, Thomas Carlyle Letters, Princeton University, Princeton, New Jersey.

258 "infusing . . . nation"] *New York Herald*, Oct. 30, 1861.

"I cannot . . . courage"] 3 Hansard CXXXVI (Dec. 12, 1854), col. 74.

"Distinct . . . adventure"] Alexander W. Kinglake, *The Invasion of the Crimea* (New York, 1877 [orig. publ. London, 1863]), I, 281.

"I have felt . . . nation"] Benson J. Lossing to [Sue] Wallace, April 20, 1862, Lew Wallace Papers, Indiana Historical Society, Indianapolis.

"The blood . . . earth"] Carrie to [Charlotte S. Branch], Aug. 14, 1861, Margaret Branch Sexton Collection, University of Georgia. See also James L. Roark, *Masters Without Slaves: Southern Planters in the Civil War and Reconstruction* (New York, 1977), 20.

259 "passed . . . blood"] *Richmond Examiner*, Feb. 4, 1862, reprinted in Moore, ed., *Rebellion Record*, IV, 22.

"True . . . fact"] *Philadelphia Inquirer*, April 13, 1865.

"civil dissolution"] F[rederic] H[enry] Hedge, *The National Weakness: A Discourse Delivered . . . Sept. 26, 1861* (Boston, 1861), 13.

"cannot . . . blood"] Julian M. Sturtevant, *The Lessons of Our National Conflict* (New Haven, Conn., 1861), 16.

260 Gilmer]   Entry of April 13, 1864, Francis W. Gilmer, Notes on the War of 1861 to 65, Francis Walker Gilmer Papers, #8461, University of Virginia. See also Merrill D. Peterson, *The Jefferson Image in the American Mind* (New York, 1960), 168–171.

"The great . . . agencies"]   C. H. Wiley, *Scriptural Views of National Trials: or The True Road to the Independence and Peace of the Confederate States of America* (Greensboro, N.C., 1863), 174.

"We are conservative"]   J. H. Thornwell, *Our Danger and Our Duty* (Columbia, S.C., 1862), 4–5.

"Like a soldier . . . contest"]   *Cincinnati Commercial,* June 12, 1863. See also V. Jacque Voegeli, *Free But Not Equal: The Midwest and the Negro During the Civil War* (Chicago, 1967); James M. McPherson, *The Struggle for Equality: Abolitionists and the Negro in the Civil War and Reconstruction* (Princeton, N.J., 1964); Lawrence J. Friedman, *Gregarious Saints: Self and Community in American Abolitionism, 1830–1870* (Cambridge, 1982), chap. 7; David W. Blight, *Frederick Douglass' Civil War: Keeping Faith in Jubilee* (Baton Rouge, La., 1989), esp. chaps. 3–5, 7.

260–1 "He would . . . preservation"]   Blaine, *Twenty Years of Congress,* I, 438.

261 "to rise . . . men"]   *Cincinnati Commercial,* March 7, 1863. See also Albert [S. Hall] to Cybelia Hall, Sept. 26, 1862, Albert S. Hall Papers, Vertical File, Western Reserve Historical Society, Cleveland, Ohio; Samuel T. Spear, *Radicalism and the National Crisis. A Sermon . . . October 19th 1862* (Brooklyn, N.Y., 1862), 17–19; S. P. Chase to B. F. Butler, July 31, 1862, Salmon P. Chase Papers, Historical Society of Pennsylvania; H. W. B[ellows] to [C. A.] Bartol, Feb. 21, 1862, Bellows Papers, Massachusetts Historical Society; W. G. Snethen to [E. M. Stanton], Jan. 22, 1862, Edwin M. Stanton Papers, Library of Congress; *New York Herald,* Oct. 10, 16, 1863; *Cincinnati Commercial,* April 6, 20, 1863; Sturtevant, *Lessons of Our Conflict,* 21.

"Thank God . . . Republic"]   J[ohn] L[othrop] M[otley] to [William] Amory, Aug. 26, 1865, Massachusetts Historical Society.

262 "while the smoke . . . law"]   George W. Cable, *The Negro Question: A Selection of Writings on Civil Rights in the South,* ed. Arlin Turner (Garden City, N.Y., 1958), 155. On the limits of reconstruction see esp. George C. Rable, *But There Was No Peace: The Role of Violence in the Politics of Reconstruction* (Athens, Ga., 1984); Eric Foner, *Reconstruction: America's Unfinished Revolution, 1863–1877* (New York, 1988); Michael Les Benedict, *A Compromise of Principle: Congressional Republicans and Reconstruction, 1863–1869* (New York, 1974). Compare Herman Belz, *Emancipation and Equal Rights: Politics and Constitutionalism in the Civil War Era* (New York, 1978).

"should deal . . . armory"]   House of Representatives, Feb. 18, 1863, *Congressional Globe,* 37th Congress, 3d Session, 1069.

"passed beyond . . . effective"]   H. W. Bellows to [F. L.] Olmsted, Feb. 12, 1864, Frederick Law Olmsted Papers, Library of Congress.

"with a logic . . . invincible"]   Theo[dore] D. Weld to [Henry] Bellows, Aug. 10, 1862, Bellows Papers, Massachusetts Historical Society. See also, on Phillips, Dicey, *Six Months in the Federal States,* I, 163.

"They are theorists . . . institution"]   Senate, May 2, 1862, *Congressional Globe,* 37th Congress, 2d Session, 1919.

263 Powell and Sumner]   Senate, April 8, 1864, *ibid.,* 38th Congress, 1st Session, 1486–1487.

"War . . . Emancipation"]   Charles Sumner to [Francis Lieber], April 5, 1862, Hitchcock Family Papers, Box 3, Missouri Historical Society, St. Louis. See also David Donald, *Charles Sumner and the Rights of Man* (New York, 1970), 17, 54.

"chicken-heartedness" . . . "success"]   *Chicago Tribune,* Feb. 1, 1865.

265 "excessive prosperity" and "Young . . . fight"]   *New York Herald,* April 29, 1861.

"If the war . . . Ladies"]   Betty [Kemp] to L[ouisa B. Turner], Jan. 29, 1862, Turner Papers, College of William and Mary.

265 "How much . . . humanity"]   S. M. Grimké to [Mrs. H. W. Bellows], Dec. 24, 1863, Bellows Papers, Massachusetts Historical Society.

"A vigorous . . . passed"]   Reprinted in *Cincinnati Commercial,* Nov. 7, 1861.

"from passive . . . exaltation"]   George Washington Williams, *A History of the Negro Troops in the War of the Rebellion, 1861–1865* (New York, 1888), xiii.

"Wagner . . . land"]   *Proceedings of the National Convention of Colored Men, Held in the City of Syracuse, N.Y., October 4, 5, 6, and 7, 1864* (Boston, 1864), 21.

"American . . . undreamed of"]   Stella S. Coatsworth, *The Loyal People of the North-West* (Chicago, 1869), 331–332.

266 "And almost . . . remission"]   Hebrews 9:22.

"Christ-like]   See, for example, John Weiss, *Northern Strength and Weakness. An Address . . . April 30, 1863* (Boston, 1863), 12; C. A. Bartol, *The Recompense. A Sermon for Country and Kindred* (Boston, 1862), 24; Frederic A. Noble, *Blood the Price of Redemption. A Thanksgiving Discourse* (St. Paul, Minn., 1862), 19–20; S. G. Pryor to Penelope, May 18, 1862, Shepard G. Pryor Papers, University of Georgia; J. C. Granbery to [Ella Granbery], Aug. 22, 1863, John Cowper Granbery Manuscripts, University of Virginia; Wiley, *Scriptural Views of National Trials,* 98–99.

"I rejoice . . . Brown"]   Moore, ed., *Rebellion Record,* I, 324. See also Drew Gilpin Faust, *The Creation of Confederate Nationalism: Ideology and Identity in the Civil War South* (Baton Rouge, La., 1988), 26–30; James W. Silver, *Confederate Morale and Church Propaganda* (Tuscaloosa, Ala., 1957), 30–34; James H. Moorhead, *American Apocalypse: Yankee Protestants and the Civil War, 1860–1869* (New Haven, Conn., 1978); George Marsden, *The Evangelical Mind and the New School Presbyterian Experience* (New Haven, Conn., 1970), chap. 10; Paul C. Nagel, *This Sacred Trust: American Nationality, 1798–1898* (New York, 1971), chap. 3; C. C. Goen, *Broken Churches, Broken Nation: Denominational Schisms and the Coming of the American Civil War* (Macon, Ga., 1985); Charles Royster, "Founding a Nation in Blood: Military Conflict and American Nationality," in Ronald Hoffman and Peter J. Albert, eds., *Arms and Independence: The Military Character of the American Revolution* (Charlottesville, Va., 1984), 25–49.

267 "No . . . result"]   Robert L. Dabney, "True Courage. A Discourse Commemorative of Lieut.-General Thomas J. Jackson," in *Discussions by Robert L. Dabney* (Mexico, Mo., 1897), IV, 443.

"Leaving . . . Strasburg" and "Having . . . Turnpike"]   Draft of T. J. Jackson to R. H. Chilton, in Thomas J. Jackson Personal Miscellany, New-York Historical Society.

268 "Our victory . . . fighting" and "No . . . Providence"]   [R. L. Dabney, Notes], "Dr. McGuire's Narrative," Charles William Dabney Papers, Box 31, University of North Carolina. See also T. J. Jackson to [D. H. Hill], March 8, 10, 1862, in [D. H. Hill], "The Haversack," *The Land We Love,* I (June 1866), 119.

"appears . . . State"]   T. J. Jackson to J. T. L. Preston, Dec. 22, 1862, in Allan, *Life and Letters of Margaret Junkin Preston,* 153. See also Jack P. Maddex, "From Theocracy to Spirituality: The Southern Presbyterian Reversal on Church and State," *Journal of Presbyterian History,* LIV (1976), 439–445.

"Thus New Haven . . . freemen"]   George Bancroft, *History of the United States* (Boston, 1853), I, 404. Jackson's copy is at the Virginia Historical Society. See also [R. L. Dabney, Notes], "Rev. B. T. Lacy's Narrative," Charles William Dabney Papers, Box 32, University of North Carolina.

"Christians . . . work"]   J. T. L. Preston to [T. J. Jackson], Feb. 2, 1863, Roy Bird Cook Collection, Series VI, Box 1, West Virginia University. See also T. J. Jackson to Mary Anna Jackson, Dec. 25, 1862, and April 10, 1863, Charles William Dabney Papers, University of North Carolina; T. J. Jackson to E. A. Booles, July 21, 1862, in William Parker Snow, *Southern Generals, Their Lives and Campaigns* (New York, 1866), 192.

"That which . . . ranks"]   Thomas Babington Macaulay, *The History of England* (New York, 1850), I, 113–114. Jackson's copy is at the Virginia Historical Society.

268 "commanded . . . confident"]   [R. L. Dabney, Notes], "Rev. B. T. Lacy's Narrative," Charles William Dabney Papers, Box 32, University of North Carolina.

269 Jackson's regiments]   T. J. Jackson to William S. White, March 9, 1863, in R. L. Dabney, *Life and Campaigns of Lieut.-Gen. Thomas J. Jackson (Stonewall Jackson)* (New York, 1866), 648; Sidney J. Romero, "The Confederate Chaplain," *Civil War History,* I (June 1955), 127–140.

one-third of the soldiers]   Bennett, *Narrative of the Great Revival,* 413. See also Herman Norton, "Revivalism in the Confederate Armies," *Civil War History,* VI (Dec. 1960), 422–423; Bell Irvin Wiley, *The Life of Johnny Reb: The Common Soldier of the Confederacy* (Indianapolis, Ind., 1943), 191. For a different view, see Gardiner H. Shattuck, Jr., *A Shield and Hiding Place: The Religious Life of the Civil War Armies* (Macon, Ga., 1987), chaps. 2, 5.

Jackson's evangelizing]   [Joseph C. Stiles] to [Mrs. Stiles], Nov. 2, 1862, Joseph Clay Stiles Letters, Brock Collection, Huntington Library; [R. L. Dabney, Notes], "Rev. B. T. Lacy's Narrative," Charles William Dabney Papers, Box 32, University of North Carolina; James Power Smith, *The Religious Character of Stonewall Jackson* (Lynchburg, Va., 1897), 8; T. J. Jackson to [R. L. Dabney], Dec. 5, 1862, and Jan. 1, 1863, Robert L. Dabney Papers, Union Theological Seminary in Virginia, Richmond; T. J. Jackson to R. H. Morrison, March 28, 1863, in Mary Anna Jackson, *Life and Letters of General Thomas J. Jackson (Stonewall Jackson)* (New York, 1891), 402; Bennett, *Narrative of the Great Revival,* 67, 140. See also Drew Gilpin Faust, "Christian Soldiers: The Meaning of Revivalism in the Confederate Army," *Journal of Southern History,* LIII (Feb. 1987), 63–90.

"growing . . . army"]   T. J. Jackson to [R. L. Dabney], Dec. 5, 1862, Dabney Papers, Union Theological Seminary in Virginia.

"devise . . . conquests"]   [T. J. Jackson] to [J. T. L. Preston], Feb. 23, 1863, Margaret Junkin Preston Papers, University of North Carolina. See also W. Harrison Daniel, "Southern Presbyterians in the Confederacy," *North Carolina Historical Review,* XLIV (July 1967), 244–245.

"His only . . . Islander"]   D. F. Boyd to P. T. Sherman, March 21, 1891, Sherman Papers, University of Notre Dame.

"mathematical impossibilities"]   W. T. Sherman to [Henry Ward] Beecher, Dec. 7, 1882, Beecher Family Papers, Series I, Box 14, Sterling Library, Yale University. See also W. T. Sherman to Alex[ander McD.] McCook, Dec. 10, 1888, McCook Family Papers, Library of Congress.

"if"]   W. T. Sherman to Miss Middleton, May 18, 1884, William T. Sherman Papers, Missouri Historical Society.

270 "Certainly not . . . agency"]   [Joseph Parrish Thompson], "Major-General William T. Sherman," *Hours at Home,* II (Nov. 1865), 20.

"show . . . oats"]   W. T. Sherman to C. A. Dana, April 21, 1864, Charles A. Dana Papers, Library of Congress.

"that weight of bottled piety"]   W. T. Sherman to Robert Allen, April 8, 1864, *The War of the Rebellion: A Compilation of the Official Records of the Union and Confederate Armies* (Washington, D.C., 1880–1901), Series I, Vol. XXXII, Part III, 301.

"To make . . . path"]   W. T. Sherman to C. A. Dana, April 21, 1864, Dana Papers, Library of Congress.

"mere fiat"]   W. T. Sherman to [Henry Ward] Beecher, Dec. 7, 1882, Beecher Family Papers, Sterling Library, Yale University. See also W. T. Sherman, *Address of General W. T. Sherman to the Officers and Soldiers Comprising the School of Application at Fort Leavenworth, Kansas, October 25, 1882* (n.p., n.d.), 9.

"the war . . . control"]   W. T. Sherman to Ellen [Sherman], Aug. 15, 1864, Sherman Papers, University of Notre Dame.

271 "the bones . . . wheels"]   W. T. Sherman to Geo[rge] Bancroft, Jan. 23, 1875, George Bancroft Papers, Massachusetts Historical Society.

271 "our wounded . . . misery"]   Society of the Army of the Tennessee, *Report of the Proceedings of the Society of the Army of the Tennessee at the Second Annual Meeting . . . November 13th and 14th, 1867* (Cincinnati, Ohio, 1868), 102.

"Wars . . . governed"]   *Banquet at "The Portland," Washington, D.C., February 8, 1883* (n.p., n.d.), 2.

272 "He lived . . . name"]   Frank Moore, *Anecdotes, Poetry and Incidents of the War: North and South* (New York, 1866), 51.

"The subject . . . self-sacrifice"]   Paul H. Hayne to Miss Poyas, July 22, 1864, Lemons-McDermott Papers, South Carolina Historical Society.

"Your suggestions . . . correspondents"]   Albert D. Richardson to Sydney Howard Gay, May 1, 1863, quoted in Louis M. Starr, *Bohemian Brigade: Civil War Newsmen in Action* (New York, 1954), 184.

273 "I pitied . . . borne"]   [Joshua] Lawrence [Chamberlain] to [Sarah B. Chamberlain], April 13, 1865, Joshua Lawrence Chamberlain Papers, Bowdoin College, Brunswick, Maine.

"None . . . whipped us"]   William Roane Aylett, Speech to Veterans of Army of Northern Virginia and Army of the Potomac, [ca. 1895], Aylett Family Papers, Virginia Historical Society.

"political questions"]   Robert Underwood Johnson, *Remembered Yesterdays* (Boston, 1923), 194.

"the humanities of the War period"]   C. C. Buel to Berry Benson, Jan. 3, 1887, Benson Papers, University of North Carolina. See also R. U. J[ohnson] to Jubal Early, April 23, 1884, Jubal Early Papers, Library of Congress; Stephen Davis, " 'A Matter of Sensational Interest': The *Century* 'Battles and Leaders' Series," *Civil War History,* XXVII (Dec. 1981), 338–349; Rayburn S. Moore, "Southern Writers and Northern Literary Magazines, 1865–1890" (Ph.D. diss., Duke University, 1956).

"too military" and "Full . . . armies"]   H. S. Brooks to [Jedediah Hotchkiss], March 2, 1885, Hotchkiss Papers, Library of Congress.

"Around you . . . imagination"]   D. F. Boyd to W. T. Sherman, Feb. 8, 1890, W. T. Sherman Papers, Library of Congress.

274 war generation's writings]   The continuity of attempts at "realism" was noted long ago in Rebecca Washington Smith Lee, "The Civil War and Its Aftermath in American Fiction, 1861–1899" (Ph.D. diss., University of Chicago, 1932), esp. 44. For criticisms of postwar sentimentalizing, see esp. Paul H. Buck, *The Road to Reunion, 1865–1900* (New York, 1937); C. Vann Woodward, *Origins of the New South, 1877–1913* (Baton Rouge, La., 1951), 167–168; Thomas J. Pressly, *Americans Interpret Their Civil War* (New York, 1965 [orig. publ. Princeton, N.J., 1954]), 151–181; George M. Fredrickson, *The Inner Civil War: Northern Intellectuals and the Crisis of the Union* (New York, 1965); Aaron, *Unwritten War;* Rollin G. Osterweis, *The Myth of the Lost Cause, 1865–1900* (Hamden, Conn., 1973); Thomas C. Leonard, *Above the Battle: War-Making in America from Appomattox to Versailles* (New York, 1978); Gerald F. Linderman, *Embattled Courage: The Experience of Combat in the American Civil War* (New York, 1987), epilogue; Gaines M. Foster, *Ghosts of the Confederacy: Defeat, the Lost Cause, and the Emergence of the New South, 1865 to 1913* (New York, 1987); Blight, *Frederick Douglass' Civil War,* chap. 10; Sweet, *Traces of War.*

"I never . . . reversed"]   Hyde, *Following the Greek Cross,* 201–202.

"I see . . . end"]   Willi[am Chunn] to [Lila Land Chunn], Aug. 29, 1862, William Chunn Letters, Emory University.

"hell on earth" and "Nor can . . . experiences"]   Francis Smith Robertson, [Reminiscences], [1926], 1, 10, Virginia Historical Society.

274–5 "Everything . . . awaited us"]   [George M. Vickers], ed., *Under Both Flags: A Panorama of the Great Civil War* (Chicago, 1896), 366.

275 "more like . . . history" and "reckless . . . bleeding"]   John J. Hight, *History of the Fifty-Eighth Regiment of Indiana Volunteer Infantry* (Princeton, Ind., 1895), 69. See also

Bell Irvin Wiley, *The Life of Billy Yank: The Common Soldier of the Union* (Indianapolis, Ind., 1951), 71.

275 "I saw . . . horror"]   William Preston Johnston to [Rosa Johnston], Oct. 14–15, 1863, Johnston Family Papers, Manuscript Department, The Filson Club, Louisville, Kentucky.

275–6 "The ditch . . . skull"]   Entry of July 21, 1863, George A. Mercer, Diary, University of North Carolina. Among published accounts see, for example, Moore, *Anecdotes, Poetry, and Incidents*, 64–65; John Beatty, *The Citizen-Soldier; or, Memoirs of a Volunteer* (Cincinnati, Ohio, 1879), 211; Mary Tucker Magill, *Women, or Chronicles of the Late War* (Baltimore, Md., 1871), 318–319; S. H. M. Byers, *With Fire and Sword* (New York, 1911), 84; William Bircher, *A Drummer-Boy's Diary: Comprising Four Years of Service with the Second Regiment Minnesota Veteran Volunteers, 1861 to 1865* (St. Paul, Minn., 1889), 33; Frank Wilkeson, *Recollections of a Private Soldier in the Army of the Potomac* (Freeport, N.Y., 1972 [orig. publ. New York, 1887]); A. M. Stewart, *Camp, March and Battle-Field; or Three Years and a Half With the Army of the Potomac* (Philadelphia, 1865), 384–385; Wilbur F. Hinman, *The Story of the Sherman Brigade* (Alliance, Ohio, 1897), 461–462; W[illia]m R. Hartpence, *History of the Fifty-First Indiana Veteran Volunteer Infantry* (Cincinnati, Ohio, 1894), 42–43; Horace Porter, *Campaigning With Grant*, ed. Wayne C. Temple (Bloomington, Ind., 1961 [orig. publ. New York, 1897]), 72–73, 110–111; John C. West, *A Texan In Search of a Fight: Being the Diary and Letters of a Private Soldier in Hood's Texas Brigade* (Waco, Tex., 1901), 74–75; Bromfield L. Ridley, *Battles and Sketches of the Army of Tennessee* (Mexico, Mo., 1906), 305; Allen C. Redwood, "With Stonewall Jackson," *Scribner's Monthly*, XVIII (June 1879), 220.

276 "homesick for the field"]   Rufus [Ricksecker] to folks at home, Feb. 14, 1864, Rufus Ricksecker Correspondence, Ohio State University, Columbus. See also Oliver Willcox Norton to brother and sister, July 26, 1862, Oliver Willcox Norton, *Army Letters, 1861–1865* (Chicago, 1903), 107; M. M. C. Pipkin to L. A[nn] C. B. Honnoll, March 23, 1862, Honnoll Family Papers, Emory University; Delos Van Deusen to Hennie, Jan. 27, 1864, Delos Van Deusen Letters, Huntington Library; entry of Jan. 5, 1863, Van S. Bennett, Diary, State Historical Society of Wisconsin; [Horace Lafayette Reed] to parents, May 12, 1863, Horace Lafayette Reed Papers, Barker Texas History Center, University of Texas, Austin.

"knew . . . blood"]   Susan Leigh Blackford, comp., *Memoirs of Life In and Out of the Army In Virginia During the War Between the States* (Lynchburg, Va., 1894), I, 231.

"an elimination . . . action"]   Andrew Hickenlooper, Personal Reminiscences, Vol. I, 54, Andrew Hickenlooper Collection, Box 1, Cincinnati Historical Society.

276–7 "This boy . . . horrors"]   A. C. Haskell to Sophie, Aug. 4, 1863, Haskell Papers, Cheves Collection, South Carolina Historical Society.

277 "Our boys . . . bayonett"]   Entry of Sept. 1, 1864, William Bluffton Miller, Diary, Indiana Historical Society.

"the natural order of events"]   Benton, *As Seen From the Ranks*, 48.

"this is no . . . thick"]   [John S. Casement] to [Frances Casement], July 7, 1864, Casement Collection, Huntington Library.

277–8 DeForest]   J. W. DeForest, "The Brigade Commander," in William Patten, ed., *Short Story Classics (American)* (New York, 1905), II, 335–374. See also DeForest, *Miss Ravenel's Conversion*, ed. Haight, 425, and, in general, John William DeForest, *A Volunteer's Adventures: A Union Captain's Record of the Civil War*, ed. James H. Croushore (New Haven, Conn., 1946).

278 "criminal insanity" and "Is it not . . . picturesque"]   Ambrose Bierce, *The Collected Works of Ambrose Bierce* (New York, 1909), I, 341, 269. See also Ambrose Bierce, *Battlefields and Ghosts* (n.p., 1931); Robert A. Wiggins, "Ambrose Bierce: A Romantic in an Age of Realism," *American Literary Realism*, IV (1971), 1–10; Lawrence I. Berkove, "Arms and the Man: Ambrose Bierce's Response to War," *Michigan Academician*, I (1969), 21–30.

"There is no . . . imagination"]   Cooke quoted in George Cary Eggleston, *Recollections of a Varied Life* (New York, 1910), 70–71.

278 "I write for money"]   [John Esten Cooke] to [G. W. Bagby], July 16, 1879, Bagby Family Papers, Virginia Historical Society. See also William Edward Walker, "John Esten Cooke: A Critical Biography" (Ph.D. diss., Vanderbilt University, 1957), chap. 7.

279 "Life . . . everywhere"]   Quoted in James Turner, *Without God, Without Creed: The Origins of Unbelief in America* (Baltimore, Md., 1985), 205.

"I have seen . . . mutilation"]   Robert [Ingersoll] to brother, June 26, 1863, Robert G. Ingersoll Papers, Box 1, Illinois State Historical Library.

"Men lost . . . destroy" and "Men . . . consecrates"]   Orville J. Victor, ed., *Incidents and Anecdotes of the War* (New York, 1862), 361–362. The *New York Tribune* reporter's account is reprinted in Junius Henri Browne, *Four Years in Secessia: Adventures Within and Beyond the Union Lines* (Hartford, Conn., 1865), 138–146.

280 "He did not . . . demons"]   Joshua Lawrence Chamberlain, *The Passing of the Armies* (New York, 1915), 385–386. See also Linderman, *Embattled Courage,* 73–75.

"He had . . . study"]   *Boston Evening Transcript,* May 31, 1895.

"I was not . . . way"]   O. W. Holmes to [John C. H.] Wu, Jan. 26, 1922, Harry C. Shriver, ed., *Justice Oliver Wendell Holmes: His Book Notices and Uncollected Letters and Papers* (New York, 1936), 154.

"I always . . . type"]   O. W. Holmes to Lewis Einstein, Aug. 20, 1911, Oliver Wendell Holmes, Jr., Collection, Box 1, Library of Congress. Holmes wrote "spere." The word is printed as "spear" in James Bishop Peabody, ed., *The Holmes-Einstein Letters: Correspondence of Mr. Justice Holmes and Lewis Einstein 1903–1935* (New York, 1964), 63.

281 "I do not . . . use"]   Mark DeWolfe Howe, comp., *The Occasional Speeches of Justice Oliver Wendell Holmes* (Cambridge, Mass., 1962), 76.

"sentimental jingoism"]   *The Nation,* LXI (Dec. 19, 1895), 440–441; *Evening Post* (New York), Dec. 17, 1895.

"a metaphor . . . plight"]   Cushing Strout, "Three Faithful Skeptics at the Gate of Modernity," in Howard H. Quint and Milton Cantor, eds., *Men, Women, and Issues in American History* (Homewood, Ill., 1980), 58.

"Certitude . . . not so"]   Oliver Wendell Holmes, Jr., "Natural Law," in *Collected Legal Papers* (New York, 1952 [orig. publ. 1920]), 311.

282 "a race . . . command"]   Howe, comp., *Occasional Speeches of Holmes,* 81.

"that he was . . . right"]   Lewis Einstein, "Introduction," Peabody, ed., *Holmes-Einstein Letters,* xvi.

283 "It means . . . assumptions"]   Harold J. Laski, "The Political Philosophy of Mr. Justice Holmes," *Yale Law Journal,* XL (1931), 685.

"the fighting" . . . "his way"]   Holmes, *Collected Legal Papers,* 310–311. For examples of Holmes's emphasis on force as the basis of law see O. W. Holmes to [Franklin Ford], May 3, 1907, David H. Burton, ed., *Progressive Masks: Letters of Oliver Wendell Holmes, Jr., and Franklin Ford* (Newark, Del., 1982), 43; O. W. Holmes to [Morris R.] Cohen, Nov. 23, 1919, Felix S. Cohen, ed., "The Holmes-Cohen Correspondence," *Journal of the History of Ideas,* IX (Jan. 1948), 17; O. W. Holmes to [Harold J.] Laski, July 17, 1925, Mark DeWolfe Howe, ed., *Holmes-Laski Letters: The Correspondence of Mr. Justice Holmes and Harold J. Laski, 1916–1935* (Cambridge, Mass., 1953), I, 762; O. W. Holmes to [John C. H.] Wu, Aug. 26, 1926, Shriver, ed., *Holmes Book Notices and Uncollected Letters,* 187–188. See also James Fitzjames Stephen, *Liberty, Equality, Fraternity,* 2d ed., ed. R. J. White (Cambridge, 1967 [orig. publ. London, 1874]), 165–166; James Bryce, *The American Commonwealth* (Chicago, 1891), I, 315, 379–380; Frederic Cople Jaher, *Doubters and Dissenters: Cataclysmic Thought in America, 1885–1918* (New York, 1964), 160–161. Compare Arthur Bestor, "The American Civil War as a Constitutional Crisis," *American Historical Review,* LXIX (Jan. 1964), 327–352.

critics]   There is a large literature on "The Soldier's Faith," part of a much larger literature on Holmes. See, for example, Edmund Wilson, *Patriotic Gore: Studies in the*

Literature of the American Civil War (New York, 1962), 743–796; Saul Touster, "In Search of Holmes from Within," *Vanderbilt Law Review,* XVIII (1964–1965), 437–472; Saul Touster, "Holmes a Hundred Years Ago: *The Common Law* and Legal Theory," *Hofstra Law Review,* X (1982), 673–708; Hiller B. Zobel, "The Three Civil Wars of Oliver Wendell Holmes," *Boston Bar Journal,* XXVI (Dec. 1982), 13–22, XXVII (Jan. 1983), 18–23, (Feb. 1983), 18–25; Leonard, *Above the Battle,* 36; G. Edward White, "The Rise and Fall of Justice Holmes," *University of Chicago Law Review,* XXXIX (1971), 51–77; Robert A. Ferguson, "Holmes and the Judicial Figure," *ibid.,* LV (1988), 523–527; David H. Burton, *Oliver Wendell Holmes, Jr.* (Boston, 1980), 30–31, 35, 71; Aaron, *Unwritten War,* 161–162; Fredrickson, *Inner Civil War,* 169–170, 220–222; Linderman, *Embattled Courage,* 281–282; T. J. Jackson Lears, *No Place of Grace: Antimodernism and the Transformation of American Culture, 1880–1920* (New York, 1981), 123–124, 138; John Fraser, *America and the Patterns of Chivalry* (Cambridge, 1982), 231–232; J. Glenn Gray, *The Warriors: Reflections on Men in Battle* (New York, 1970 [orig. publ. 1959]), 223–224. For a recent survey of the Holmes literature see Gary J. Aichele, *Oliver Wendell Holmes, Jr.: Soldier, Scholar, Judge* (Boston, 1989). For a bibliography of Holmes's writings see Sheldon M. Novick, *Honorable Justice: The Life of Oliver Wendell Holmes* (Boston, 1989).

283 "I don't . . . politics" and "I civilly . . . care"]   O. W. H[olmes] to [Frederick] Pollock, Dec. 27, 1895, Mark DeWolfe Howe, ed., *Holmes-Pollock Letters: The Correspondence of Mr. Justice Holmes and Sir Frederick Pollock, 1874–1932* (Cambridge, Mass., 1941), I, 67.

284 William James]   Ralph Barton Perry, *The Thought and Character of William James* (Boston, 1936), II, 250–251; Paul F. Boller, Jr., *American Thought in Transition: The Impact of Evolutionary Naturalism, 1865–1900* (Chicago, 1969), 150–152.

"political . . . South"]   Entry of July 12, 1864, William King, Diary, University of North Carolina.

"a few . . . leaders"]   [George P. Metz] to [?], [ca. July 21, 1863], George P. Metz Papers, Duke University.

"It is not . . . remedy it"]   Samuel Landes to Mary [Embree], July 22, 1862, Lucius C. Embree Papers, Indiana State Library.

"There is . . . somewhere"]   William E. Boggs, *The South Vindicated from the Charge of Treason and Rebellion* (Columbia, S.C., 1881), 6.

"If nations . . . these"]   Alfred Davenport, *Camp and Field Life of the Fifth New York Volunteer Infantry* (New York, 1879), 312.

285 "THE LOTTERY" . . . "PEN"]   Sept. 28, 1864, quoted in Arnold M. Shankman, *The Pennsylvania Antiwar Movement, 1861–1865* (Rutherford, N.J., 1980), 153.

"savage . . . blood"]   House of Representatives, July 1, 1864, *Congressional Globe,* 38th Congress, 1st Session, 3474.

"covered . . . fellow-citizens"]   Speech by John Brough, *Cincinnati Commercial,* Sept. 5, 1864.

"Could not . . . obtained"]   *Detroit Free Press,* March 21, 1865. On Democrats' criticisms see esp. Frank L. Klement, *The Copperheads in the Middle West* (Chicago, 1960); Hubert H. Wubben, *Civil War Iowa and the Copperhead Movement* (Ames, Iowa, 1980); John Niven, *Connecticut for the Union: The Role of the State in the Civil War* (New Haven, Conn., 1965), chap. 11; William Frank Zornow, *Lincoln and the Party Divided* (Norman, Okla., 1954).

"undertaking . . . successfully" and "high crime"]   Joseph E. Johnston, *Narrative of Military Operations Directed During the Late War Between the States* (New York, 1874), 421.

"to avoid . . . war"]   J. E. Johnston, [Address to the People of North Carolina, South Carolina, Georgia, and Florida], May 6, 1865, Schoff Collection, Letters and Documents, Box 4, Clements Library.

286 Grant on Lee]   Young, *Around the World,* II, 627.

286 "The last . . . blood"]   Edward Porter Alexander, *Fighting for the Confederacy: The Personal Recollections of General Edward Porter Alexander,* ed. Gary W. Gallagher (Chapel Hill, N.C., 1989), 433.

"only . . . organized"]   Jacob D. Cox, *The March to the Sea. Franklin and Nashville* (New York, 1902), 169–170.

Lee on "the people"]   R. E. Lee to [John C. Breckinridge], [ca. March 9, 1865], quoted in John B. Gordon, *Reminiscences of the Civil War* (New York, 1904), 391; R. E. Lee to Z. B. Vance, Feb. 24, 1865, *Official Records,* Series I, Vol. XLVII, Part II, 1270–1271; R. E. Lee to A. G. Magrath, Jan. 27, 1865, in Robert Underwood Johnson and Clarence Clough Buel, eds., *Battles and Leaders of the Civil War* (New York, 1888), IV, 683n.

"thought I . . . crisis"]   *Atlanta Herald,* April 28, 1875. See also W. T. Sherman to [Abraham Lincoln], Sept. 28, 1864, *Official Records,* Series I, Vol. XXXIX, Part II, 501; W. T. Sherman, *Memoirs of General William T. Sherman,* 2d ed. (New York, 1886), II, 137–140; Georgia Lee Tatum, *Disloyalty in the Confederacy* (Chapel Hill, N.C., 1934), 77–78. On leaders' guilt see William C. Harris, "The Southern Unionist Critique of the Civil War," *Civil War History,* XXXI (March 1985), 53.

287 "I could not . . . lives"]   Entry of Sept. 23, 1862, Ann R. L. Schaeffer, "Records of the Past [Civil War]," Civil War Papers, MS 1860, Maryland Historical Society Library.

288 "an utterly . . . slaughter"]   *Cincinnati Gazette,* May 30, 1875. For Boynton's activities and writings see the scrapbooks and files of clippings in the Henry Van Ness Boynton Papers, Massachusetes Historical Society, and the Henry Boynton Correspondence in Box 2 of the Ezra Ayres Carman Papers, New York Public Library. See also Richard Allen Andrews, "Years of Frustration: William T. Sherman, the Army, and Reform, 1869–1883" (Ph.D. diss., Northwestern University, 1968).

"the most deliberate . . . perpetrated"]   *Cincinnati Gazette,* April 23, 1881.

"the Shermans . . . manner"]   Donn Piatt to [William Henry] Smith, Dec. 12, 1866, William Henry Smith Papers, Box 18, Ohio Historical Society. See also Thomas Ewing, Jr., to Hugh Ewing, Jan. 22, 1870, Hugh B. Ewing Papers, *ibid.;* E. B. Tyler to John Sherman, March 8, 1865, John Sherman Papers, Library of Congress; Felice A. Bonadio, *North of Reconstruction: Ohio Politics, 1865–1870* (New York, 1970).

"I had . . . sickened me"]   Donn Piatt, *Memories of the Men Who Saved the Union* (New York, 1887), ix.

"He is . . . age"]   A. L. Hough to [Henry M.] Cist, Jan. 8, 1887, Charles E. Cist Papers, Box 22, Cincinnati Historical Society.

288–9 "the darkest . . . history"]   Donn Piatt and Henry V. Boynton, *General George H. Thomas: A Critical Biography* (Cincinnati, Ohio, 1893), 47.

289 "our military . . . troops"]   *Ibid.,* 20.

monuments]   *Ibid.,* 97, 218–219, 242; Piatt, *Memories,* ix.

"the fool of luck"]   *The Capital* (Washington, D.C.), March 24, 1878.

"See . . . ground"]   Piatt, *Memories,* xxiv.

289–90 "man-killer" and "The false . . . ignorance"]   *Ibid.,* 84.

290 Anna Jackson]   Mary Anna Jackson, "Stonewall Jackson—Protest Against Picture as Drawn in 'The Long Roll,' " *Richmond Times-Dispatch,* Oct. 29, 1911. See also James Power Smith, "With Stonewall Jackson in the Army of Northern Virginia," *Southern Historical Society Papers,* XLIII (1920), 77–81; D. G. McIntosh to Editor of Baltimore *Sun,* David Gregg McIntosh Papers, Virginia Historical Society; Elizabeth Randolph Preston Allan, *A March Past: Reminiscences of Elizabeth Randolph Preston Allan,* ed. Janet Allan Bryan (Richmond, Va., 1938), 125.

"She chanted . . . blue"]   Mary Johnston, *The Long Roll* (Boston, 1911), 672.

291 "In writing . . . horrible"]   Mary Johnston to Mrs. Tracy, June 30, 1913, Mary Johnston Collection, #10295, University of Virginia. On Johnston see Anne Goodwyn Jones, *Tomorrow Is Another Day: The Woman Writer in the South, 1859–1936* (Baton Rouge, La.,

1981), chap. 5; Lawrence G. Nelson, "Mary Johnston and the Historic Imagination," in R. C. Simonini, Jr., ed., *Southern Writers: Appraisals in Our Time* (Charlottesville, Va., 1964), 71–102. Robert A. Lively, *Fiction Fights the Civil War: An Unfinished Chapter in the Literary History of the American People* (Chapel Hill, N.C., 1957), 70, groups Johnston with "unreconstructed rebels."

291 "we are . . . war"]   Johnston, *Long Roll,* 138.

"There was . . . horror"]   *Ibid.,* 681.

critic in 1936]   Edward Wagenknecht, "The World and Mary Johnston," *Sewanee Review,* XLIV (April–June 1936), 201–202.

"that the immortals . . . *Drama"*]   Johnston, *Long Roll,* 144.

291–2 "Neither . . . other"]   Roy P. Basler *et al.,* eds., *The Collected Works of Abraham Lincoln* (New Brunswick, N.J., 1953), VIII, 332–333.

292 "God . . . it"]   A. Lincoln to Albert G. Hodges, April 4, 1864, *ibid.,* VII, 282.

"I am . . . same"]   F. B. Carpenter, *Six Months at the White House with Abraham Lincoln* (New York, 1866), 62.

"Men . . . world"]   A. Lincoln to Thurlow Weed, March 15, 1865, Basler *et al.,* eds., *Collected Works of Lincoln,* VIII, 356. See also William L. Barney, *Flawed Victory: A New Perspective on the Civil War* (New York, 1975), 28; George B. Forgie, *Patricide in the House Divided: A Psychological Interpretation of Lincoln and His Age* (New York, 1979), chap. 8.

293 "We are fast . . . evil"]   James Dixon to Leonard Bacon, Dec. 12, 1860, Bacon Family Correspondence, Series I, Box 7, Sterling Library, Yale University.

"Every man . . . define"]   *New York Herald,* Nov. 9, 1860.

294 "Civil war . . . over"]   John Sherman to W. T. Sherman, April 12, 1861, W. T. Sherman Papers, Library of Congress. See also, for example, George Leon Walker, *What the Year Has Done for Us. A Sermon Preached . . . November 21, 1861* (Portland, Me., 1861), 7; Mark W. Summers, *The Plundering Generation: Corruption and the Crisis of the Union, 1849–1861* (New York, 1987), 295.

"still . . . ahead"]   John Sherman to W. T. Sherman, May 7, 1863, W. T. Sherman Papers, Library of Congress. See also Kenneth M. Stampp, *And the War Came: The North and the Secession Crisis, 1860–1861* (Baton Rouge, La., 1950); Goen, *Broken Churches, Broken Nation,* 171–179.

Temple]   Oliver P. Temple, *East Tennessee and the Civil War* (Freeport, N.Y., 1971 [orig. publ. 1899]), 134–137. See also Daniel W. Crofts, *Reluctant Confederates: Upper South Unionists in the Secession Crisis* (Chapel Hill, N.C., 1989); Lacy K. Ford, Jr., *Origins of Southern Radicalism: The South Carolina Upcountry, 1800–1860* (New York, 1988), chap. 10, esp. 371–372; Stephen V. Ash, *Middle Tennessee Society Transformed, 1860–1870: War and Peace in the Upper South* (Baton Rouge, La., 1987), 71–72.

"I am not . . . them"]   *New York Herald,* Aug. 16, 1862. See also Nagel, *This Sacred Trust,* 130–131; Don E. Fehrenbacher, "Lincoln and the Weight of Responsibility," *Illinois State Historical Society Journal,* LXVIII (Feb. 1975), 45–56; David Donald, *Charles Sumner and the Coming of the Civil War* (New York, 1961), 387–388.

CHAPTER SEVEN

Notes for Pages 296–320

My narrative is based on the following sources: J. Cutler Andrews, *The South Reports the Civil War* (Princeton, N.J., 1970), 450; Henry J. Aten, *History of the Eighty-Fifth Regiment, Illinois Volunteer Infantry* (Hiawatha, Kan., 1901), 181–189; Alfred H. Burne, *Lee, Grant and Sherman: A Study in Leadership in the 1864–65 Campaign* (New York, 1939), 95; John K. Shellenberger to editor, May 30, 1881, *Chicago Tribune,* June 4, 1881; *Cincinnati Commercial,* July 2, 4, 12, 1864; James A. Connolly to Mary Dunn Connolly, July 12, 1864, Paul M.

Angle, ed., *Three Years in the Army of the Cumberland: The Letters and Diary of Major James A. Connolly* (Bloomington, Ind., 1959), 234, 236; Alexis Cope, *The Fifteenth Ohio Volunteers and Its Campaigns* (Columbus, Ohio, 1916), 507; Jacob D. Cox, *Atlanta* (New York, 1882), 103–104, 116–129; Jacob Dolson Cox, *Military Reminiscences of the Civil War* (New York, 1900), II, 260–262; Grenville M. Dodge, *Personal Recollections of President Abraham Lincoln, General Ulysses S. Grant, and General William T. Sherman* (Council Bluffs, Iowa, 1914), 77; Samuel G. French, *Two Wars: An Autobiography* (Nashville, Tenn., 1901), 202–211; J[oseph] Grecian, *History of the Eighty-Third Regiment, Indiana Volunteer Infantry* (Cincinnati, Ohio, 1865), 53; J. T. Holmes, *52d O.V.I. Then and Now* (Columbus, Ohio, 1898), 12, 176–201, 236; F. B. James, "McCook's Brigade at the Assault Upon Kennesaw Mountain, Georgia, June 27, 1864," Military Order of the Loyal Legion of the United States, Ohio Commandery, *Sketches of War History, 1861–1865,* ed. W. H. Chamberlin (Cincinnati, Ohio, 1896), IV, 255–277; Perry D. Jamieson, "The Development of Civil War Tactics" (Ph.D. diss., Wayne State University, 1979); Matthew H. Jamison, *Recollections of Pioneer and Army Life* (Kansas City, Mo., 1911), 245–247; William T. Sherman, "The Grand Strategy of the Last Year of the War," in Robert Underwood Johnson and Clarence Clough Buel, eds., *Battles and Leaders of the Civil War* (New York, 1888), IV, 252; Joseph E. Johnston, "Opposing Sherman's Advance to Atlanta," *ibid.,* 272–273; Oliver O. Howard, "The Struggle for Atlanta," *ibid.,* 310–311; Joseph E. Johnston, *Narrative of Military Operations Directed During the Late War Between the States* (New York, 1874), 343; B. H. Liddell Hart, *Sherman: Soldier, Realist, American* (New York, 1929), 265–267; *New York Herald,* July 8, 1864; *New York Tribune,* July 14, 1864; *Daily Chattanooga Rebel* (Griffin, Ga.), June 29, July 14, 1864; *Memphis Appeal* (Atlanta, Ga.), June 29, July 1, 1864; George W. Pepper, *Personal Recollections of Sherman's Campaigns in Georgia and the Carolinas* (Zanesville, Ohio, 1866), 81–85, 105; Judson Kilpatrick to editor, *New York Times,* Feb. 7, 1876; W. T. Sherman, *Memoirs of General William T. Sherman,* 2d ed. (New York, 1886), I, 31, II, 12, 42, 50–67; Nixon B. Stewart, *Dan. McCook's Regiment, 52nd O. V. I. A History of the Regiment, Its Campaigns and Battles* (Alliance, Ohio, 1900), 112–127; Irving A. Buck, *Cleburne and His Command* (New York, 1908), 259–261; B. H. Harmon, "Dead Angle," *Confederate Veteran,* XI (1903), 219; H. K. Nelson, "Dead Angle, or Devil's Elbow, Ga.," *ibid.,* 321–322; George W. Harris, "Dead Angle—Georgia Campaign," *ibid.,* 560; David P. Conyngham, *Sherman's March Through the South* (New York, 1865), 132–141; Wilbur F. Hinman, *The Story of the Sherman Brigade* (Alliance, Ohio, 1897), 43, 544–552; Oliver Otis Howard, *Autobiography of Oliver Otis Howard* (New York, 1908), I, 572–588; John A. Logan, *The Volunteer Soldier of America* (New York, 1979 [orig. publ. Chicago, 1887]), 683–684; Thomas Vernon Moseley, "Evolution of the American Civil War Infantry Tactics" (Ph.D. diss., University of North Carolina at Chapel Hill, 1967); entry of June 28, 1864, *Reminiscences of the Civil War from Diaries of the 103d Illinois Volunteer Infantry* (Chicago, [1905]), 87–91; Henry S. Nourse, "From Young's Point to Atlanta," in *The Story of the Fifty-Fifth Regiment Illinois Volunteer Infantry in the Civil War, 1861–1865* (Clinton, Mass., 1887), 324–331; Arthur L. Wagner, *Organization and Tactics* (Kansas City, Mo., n.d. [orig. publ. 1894]), 98–100; Sam R. Watkins, *"Co. Aytch": A Side Show of the Big Show* (New York, 1962 [orig. publ. 1882]), 156–165; Charles W. Wills, *Army Life of an Illinois Soldier Including a Day by Day Record of Sherman's March to the Sea: Letters and Diary of the Late Charles W. Wills* (Washington, D.C., 1906), 268–271; W. T. Sherman to H. W. Halleck, June 8, 1864, *The War of the Rebellion: A Compilation of the Official Records of the Union and Confederate Armies* (Washington, D.C., 1880–1901), Series I, Vol. XXXVIII, Part I, 61; W. T. Sherman to H. W. Halleck, Sept. 15, 1864, *ibid.,* 66–69; Geo[rge] E. Cooper to Assistant Adjutant General, Oct. 11, 1864, *ibid.,* 181; O. O. Howard to [William D.] Whipple, Sept. 18, 1864, *ibid.,* 199; John Newton to Assistant Adjutant General, Sept. 1864, *ibid.,* 295–296; Nathan Kimball to J. S. Ransom, Aug. 4, 1864, *ibid.,* 304; Tho[ma]s J. Bryan to E[merson] Opdycke, Sept. 1864, *ibid.,* 319–320; Arthur MacArthur, Jr., to [N. P. Jackson], Sept. 12, 1864, *ibid.,* 329; G. D. Wagner to George Lee, Sept. 10, 1864, *ibid.,* 335–336; D. H. Moore to George L. Waterman, Sept. 12, 1864, *ibid.,* 371; Jef[ferson] C. Davis to A. C. McClurg, Sept. 1864, *ibid.,* 632–633; John G. Mitchell to T. Wiseman, Sept. 4, 1864, *ibid.,* 680; Oscar Van Tassell to J. S. Wilson, Sept. 5, 1864, *ibid.,* 685–686; Toland Jones to James S. Wilson, Sept. 10, 1864, *ibid.,* 697–698; James W. Langley to T. Wiseman, Sept. 9, 1864, *ibid.,* 710–711; Geo[rge] W. Cook to Charles Swift, Sept. 6, 1864, *ibid.,* 724–725; J. T. Holmes to Charles Swift, Sept. 7, 1864, *ibid.,* 729, 731; entries of June 22–July 1, 1864, Journal of Joseph S. Fullerton, *ibid.,* 885–889; John A. Logan to William T. Clark, June 28, 1864, *ibid.,* Part III, 84–85; Cha[rle]s C. Walcutt to George

J. Wilkinson, Aug. 10, 1864, *ibid.*, 318; Isaac N. Alexander to [?], Sept. 12, 1864, *ibid.*, 337; William W. Loring to W. W. Mackall, July 30, 1864, *ibid.*, 869–870; Winfield S. Featherston[e] to T. M. Jack, June 30, 1864, *ibid.*, 878–880; S. G. French to W. W. Loring, June 28, 1864, *ibid.*, 900–901; S. G. French to D. West, Aug. 31, 1864, *ibid.*, 901; F. M. Cockrell to D. W. Sanders, June 27, 1864, *ibid.*, 914–915; Sam[ue]l L. Knox to G. Thomas Cox, June 30, 1864, *ibid.*, 933–934; Geo[rge] S. Storrs to D. W. Sanders, June 29, 1864, *ibid.*, 968–969; W. T. Sherman to H. W. Halleck, May 17, 1864, *ibid.*, Part IV, 219; W. T. Sherman to Edwin M. Stanton, May 23, 1864, *ibid.*, 294; W. T. Sherman to [J. B.] McPherson, May 27, 1864, *ibid.*, 327; W. T. Sherman to H. W. Halleck, June 5, 1864, *ibid.*, 408; W. T. Sherman to E. M. Stanton, June 15, 1864, *ibid.*, 480; W. T. Sherman to H. W. Halleck, June 15, 16, 17, 1864, *ibid.*, 480–481, 492, 498; W. T. Sherman to [George H.] Thomas, June 17, 1864, *ibid.*, 499; W. T. Sherman to [U.S. Grant], June 18, 1864, *ibid.*, 507–508; W. T. Sherman to H. W. Halleck, June 18, 1864, *ibid.*, 508; W. T. Sherman to [George H.] Thomas, June 18, 1864, *ibid.*, 508–509; W. T. Sherman to H. W. Halleck, June 21, 23, 1864, *ibid.*, 544, 572–573; W. T. Sherman to [George H.] Thomas, June 24, 25, 1864, *ibid.*, 582, 589; Special Field Orders, June 26, 1864, *ibid.*, 602–606; W. T. Sherman to H. W. Halleck, June 27, 1864, *ibid.*, 607; W. T. Sherman and George H. Thomas messages, June 27, 1864, *ibid.*, 607–612; O. O. Howard to [George H.] Thomas, June 27, 1864, *ibid.*, 612; J. S. Fullerton to [David S.] Stanley, June 27, 1864, *ibid.*, 613; John Newton to J. S. Fullerton, June 27, 1864, *ibid.*, 613; W. T. Sherman to [Joseph D.] Webster, June 28, 1864, *ibid.*, 629; W. T. Sherman to [J. B.] McPherson, June 28, 1864, *ibid.*, 631; W. T. Sherman to [John M.] Schofield, June 30, 1864, *ibid.*, 644; J. W. Ratchford to Division Commanders, June 26, 1864, *ibid.*, 795; J. E. Johnston to [Braxton] Bragg, June 27, 1864, *ibid.*, 795–796; W. T. Sherman to H. W. Halleck, July 9, 1864, *ibid.*, Part V, 91–92; W. T. Sherman to [U.S.] Grant, July 12, 1864, *ibid.*, 123; W. T. Sherman to William Harker, Aug. 9, 1864, *ibid.*, 445–446; J. B. McPherson to W. T. Sherman, June 23, 1864, *ibid.*, 565–566; U. S. Grant to H. W. Halleck, June 28, 1864, John Y. Simon, ed., *The Papers of Ulysses S. Grant* (Carbondale, Ill., 1967–), XI, 141; entry of June 27, 1864, Diary of Edward E. Schweitzer, *Civil War Times Illustrated* Collection, United States Army Military History Institute, Carlisle Barracks, Pennsylvania; entry of June 27, 1864, Diary of Henry G. Shedd, *ibid.*; Silas C. Stevens, [Reminiscences], 86, 88, 95–96, Silas C. Stevens Collection, Box 2, Folder 16, Chicago Historical Society, Chicago, Illinois; [Thomas Edwin Smith] to [Maria Smith], June 28, 29, 1864, Thomas E. Smith Letters, Cincinnati Historical Society, Cincinnati, Ohio; W. T. Sherman to [George H.] Thomas, June 21, 1864, James S. Schoff Civil War Collection, Letters and Documents, Box 7, Clements Library, University of Michigan, Ann Arbor; Mar[tin Gebbart] to Joe, July 1, 1864, Noah L. and Emmanuel Martin Gebbart Papers, Perkins Library, Duke University, Durham, North Carolina; Ira B. Read to aunt, Sept. 18, 1864, Ira Beman Read Papers, *ibid.*; J. T. Bowden to *Confederate Veteran*, Dec. 15, 1903, *Confederate Veteran* Papers, *ibid.*; entries of June 17, 27, 1864, Diary of Albert Quincy Porter, Confederate Miscellany, Box 1b, Woodruff Library, Emory University, Atlanta, Georgia; Eph[raim L. Girdner] to [Mary A. Murphy], June 17, 1864, Ephraim L. Girdner Papers, Union Microfilm Miscellany, *ibid.*; W. T. Sherman to [Silas F.] Miller, June 26, 1864, W. T. Sherman Letters, Filson Club, Louisville, Kentucky; W. J. Hardee, "Memorandum of the Operations of my Corps . . . ," JO 483, Joseph E. Johnston Papers, Henry E. Huntington Library, San Marino, California; W. S. Featherstone to Joseph E. Johnston, Nov. 15, 1867, JO 476, *ibid.*; entries of June 27–29, 1864, Diary of Allen L. Fahnestock, Illinois State Historical Library, Springfield; Fred[erick] Marion to sister, July 7, 1864, Frederick Marion Letters, *ibid.*; Jefferson C. Davis, [Account of Military Service], Jan. 4, 1866, Indiana Historical Society, Indianapolis; John [?] to Cousin Lide, July 2, 1864, James N. Kirkpatrick Letters, *ibid.*; S. K. H[arryman] to [Margaret Moore], June 29, 1864, Samuel K. Harryman Papers, Indiana State Library, Indianapolis; Andrew Bush to Mary Bush, June 28, 1864, Andrew Bush Letters, *ibid.*; entry of June 27, 1864, Diary of Thomas Thomson Taylor, Thomas Thomson Taylor Papers, Louisiana State University, Baton Rouge; [Joseph E. Johnston] to [Lydia McLane Johnston], May 23, 26, 28, 31, June 17, 18, 19, 25, 26, 29, 30, July 1, 2, 1864, McLane-Fisher Family Papers, MS 2403, Manuscripts Division, Maryland Historical Society Library, Baltimore; C. F. M[orse] to Ellen, June 28, 1864, Charles F. Morse Papers, Massachusetts Historical Society, Boston; James A. Kennerly to sister, Aug. 8, 1864, Kennerly Papers, Missouri Historical Society, St. Louis; W. T. Sherman to Hugh B. Ewing, March 10, 1844, W. T. Sherman Papers, Ohio Historical Society, Columbus; W. T. Sherman to P. B. Ewing, Feb. 20, 1844, *ibid.*; Tho[ma]s T. Taylor to [Marie Antoinette Taylor], June 29, July 9, 1864, Thomas T.

Taylor Papers, *ibid.;* [W. T. Sherman], "Abstract of the Georgia & Carolina Campaigns of 1864–5," [Feb. 17, 1867], W. T. Sherman Papers, Library of Congress, Washington, D.C.; John K. Shellenberger to W. T. Sherman, May 10, 1881, *ibid.;* W. T. Sherman to [John Sherman], June 21, 1884, *ibid.;* W. T. Sherman to W[illia]m Lawrence, June 14, 1881, *ibid.;* Josiah Dexter Cotton to Ann Cotton, June 29, 1864, Josiah Dexter Cotton Papers, Library of Congress; John A. Logan to [Mary Logan], June 26, 1864, John A. Logan Papers, Box 33, *ibid.;* C. H. Howard, "Our first view of Atlanta," July 9, 1864, William E. Brooks Collection, *ibid.;* entry of June 27, 1864, Diary of John Wesley Marshall, *ibid.;* Jno. A. Lair to father, mother, sisters, Sept. 14, 1864, John A. Lair Papers, *ibid.;* J. E. Johnston to [Louis T.] Wigfall, June 28, 1864, and T. C. Hindman to L. T. Wigfall, June 26, [1864], Wigfall Family Papers, *ibid.;* W. T. Sherman to Ellen [Sherman], June 12, 26, 30, July 9, 1864, William Tecumseh Sherman Papers, University of Notre Dame, Notre Dame, Indiana; entries of March 3, 18, 1844, Diary of W. T. Sherman, *ibid.;* W. T. Sherman to W. F. Vilas, June 21, 1885, William F. Vilas Papers, State Historical Society of Wisconsin, Madison; entries of June 26, 27, July 5, 1864, Diary of John W. Tuttle, University of Kentucky, Lexington; entry of June 27, 1864, George A. Mercer, "Journal of Campaign with the Army of Tennessee in 1864," Southern Historical Collection, University of North Carolina, Chapel Hill; James Iredell Hall, Notes on the War, Volume II, 28–30, *ibid.;* entry of June 27, 1864, "Journal of Campaign from Dalton to Atlanta," enclosed in Melancton Smith to Abb, Aug. 13, 1867, Benjamin Franklin Cheatham Papers, *ibid.;* [B. F. Cheatham], [Narrative of Atlanta Campaign], *ibid.;* Charles H. Olmstead, Reminiscences, 293–303, Olmstead-Owens Papers, Georgia Historical Society, Savannah; Henry Clinton Parkhurst, "Volume III Civil War. A Sequel to 'On Glory's Path,'" 28–30, Henry Clinton Parkhurst Papers, Box 2, Iowa State Historical Society, Iowa City; [Francis] Wayland [Dunn] to Ransom Dunn, June 24, 1864, Ransom Dunn Papers, Box 33, Michigan History Collection, Bentley Library, University of Michigan, Ann Arbor. For an account of part of the battle see Christopher Losson, *Tennessee's Forgotten Warriors: Frank Cheatham and His Confederate Division* (Knoxville, Tenn., 1989), 152–165.

CHAPTER EIGHT

Notes for Pages 321–404

322 "That we . . . war"]   W. T. Sherman to U. S. Grant, April 10, 1864, *The War of the Rebellion: A Compilation of the Official Records of the Union and Confederate Armies* (Washington, D.C., 1880–1901), Series I, Vol. XXXII, Part III, 312–313.

"Without . . . exist" and "cardinal . . . south"]   "The Condition of the South: By a Citizen of Georgia," *Cincinnati Commercial,* Aug. 25 and 28, 1863.

"you must . . . Carolinas"]   W. T. Sherman to John Sherman, Dec. 29, 1863, W. T. Sherman Papers, Manuscript Division, Library of Congress, Washington, D.C.

323 "never failed . . . seize" and "results . . . course"]   James F. Rusling, *Men and Things I Saw in Civil War Days* (New York, 1899), 146–147.

324 "Grant . . . arm"]   W. T. Sherman to Alex[ander] S. Webb, Dec. 25, 1888, Alexander S. Webb Papers, Box 4, Sterling Library, Yale University, New Haven, Connecticut.

"We will . . . hand"]   W. T. Sherman to Ellen [Sherman], Jan. 28, 1864, William Tecumseh Sherman Papers (consolidated microfilm collection), University of Notre Dame, Notre Dame, Indiana. See also W. T. Sherman to William Sooy Smith, Jan. 27, 1864, *Official Records,* Series I, Vol. XXXII, Part I, 181–182.

"The policy . . . least" and "to create . . . Mississippi"]   Cha[rle]s B. Allan to [?], March 7, 1864, U. S. Army, Officers' and Soldiers' Miscellany, Perkins Library, Duke University, Durham, North Carolina.

railroads]   Robert C. Black III, *The Railroads of the Confederacy* (Chapel Hill, N.C., 1952), 240–242; S. D. Lee, "Sherman's Meridian Expedition and Sooy Smith's Raid to West Point," *Southern Historical Society Papers,* VIII (1880), 59–60. For Sherman's view see H[enry Hitchcock] to Mary [Hitchcock], Nov. 4, 1864, Henry Hitchcock Papers, Library of Congress; Society of the Army of the Tennessee, *Report of the Proceedings of the Society of the Army of the Tennessee at the Second Annual Meeting . . . November 13th and 14th, 1867* (Cincinnati, Ohio, 1868), 101.

324 "raid"] W. T. Sherman's marginalia in S. M. Bowman and E. B. Irwin, *Sherman and His Campaigns: A Military Biography* (New York, 1865), 159, in Jared W. Young's Sherman Collection, Northwestern University Library Special Collections, Evanston, Illinois; W. T. Sherman to John A. Rawlins, March 7, 1864, *Official Records*, Series I, Vol. XXXII, Part I, 176.

325 "Nothing . . . expedition"] Frank Moore, ed., *The Rebellion Record: A Diary of American Events* (New York, 1861–1868), VIII, 472.

"No amount . . . out"] W. T. Sherman to Ellen [Sherman], March 12, 1864, Sherman Papers, University of Notre Dame.

conclusive battle] Joseph E. Johnston to John P. Nicholson, Dec. 1875, *Goodspeed's Catalogue 533,* Item 292; W. T. Sherman to [George H.] Thomas, March 18, 1864, CW 407, Henry E. Huntington Library, San Marino, California; Joseph E. Johnston, "The Dalton-Atlanta Operations: A Review, in Part, of General Sherman's Memoirs," *Annals of the Army of Tennessee and Early Western History,* I (April 1875), 10.

326 "the decisive battle"] W. T. Sherman to Ellen [Sherman], June 12, 1864, Sherman Papers, University of Notre Dame.

"to leave . . . 'Game' "] W. T. Sherman's notes on Bowman and Irwin, *Sherman and His Campaigns,* 184, in Jared W. Young's Sherman Collection, Northwestern University.

"My antagonist . . . position"] [Joseph E. Johnston] to [Lydia McLane Johnston], May 20, 1864, McLane-Fisher Family Papers, MS 2403, Manuscripts Division, Maryland Historical Society Library, Baltimore.

"The necessity . . . with us"] [Joseph E. Johnston] to [Lydia McLane Johnston], May 16, 1864, *ibid.*

Sherman and Johnston on terrain] W. T. Sherman, *Memoirs of General William T. Sherman,* 2d ed. (New York, 1886), II, 49; Joseph E. Johnston, "Opposing Sherman's Advance to Atlanta," Robert Underwood Johnson and Clarence Clough Buel, eds., *Battles and Leaders of the Civil War* (New York, 1888), IV, 267; R[ichard] I[rvine] M[anning] to mother, [May? 1864], Williams-Chesnut-Manning Papers, Box 8, South Caroliniana Library, University of South Carolina, Columbia.

"We have . . . weight"] [Joseph E. Johnston] to [Lydia McLane Johnston], May 20, 1864, McLane-Fisher Family Papers, Maryland Historical Society Library.

"I have . . . rear"] W. T. Sherman to John Sherman, June 9, 1864, W. T. Sherman Papers, Library of Congress. See also Jacob D. Cox, *Atlanta* (New York, 1882), 56.

327 Johnston on what he would have done] Memoirs of Samuel Wragg Ferguson, 142, Samuel Wragg Ferguson Papers, Duke University; John M. Schofield, Notes on Sherman's memoirs, John McAllister Schofield Papers, Library of Congress; J. E. Johnston to [Louis T.] Wigfall, Aug. 27, 1864, Wigfall Family Papers, *ibid.;* Louis T. Wigfall to J. E. Johnston, n.d., *ibid.,* Box 1; Johnston, "Opposing Sherman's Advance," Johnson and Buel, eds., *Battles and Leaders,* IV, 275–276. Compare Thomas L. Connelly, *Autumn of Glory: The Army of Tennessee, 1862–1865* (Baton Rouge, La., 1971), 400–402; Richard M. McMurry, *John Bell Hood and the War for Southern Independence* (Lexington, Ky., 1982), 122.

"I know . . . Lee"] William Swinton, *Campaigns of the Army of the Potomac* (New York, 1866), 495n.

328 "This movement . . . move"] J. E. Johnston to Bev[erley R. Johnston], Oct. 6, 1864, Robert M. Hughes, "Some War Letters of General Joseph E. Johnston," *Journal of the Military Service Institution of the United States,* L (May–June 1912), 323–324. See also J. E. Johnston to [Mansfield Lovell], Oct. 3, 1864, Mansfield Lovell Papers, Library of Congress.

"In Georgia . . . once"] Joseph E. Johnston to [Dabney H. Maury], Oct. 3, 1864, *Joseph Rubinfine, Autographs, Manuscripts, Historical Americana List 70.*

329 "Letters . . . point"]   [D. H. Hill] to [William J.] Hardee, Jan. 26, 1865, Daniel Harvey Hill Papers, Letterbook, North Carolina Division of Archives and History, Raleigh.

"the value . . . done"]   W. T. Sherman to Joseph C. G. Kennedy, Aug. 15, 1865, *Constitutional Union* (Washington, D.C.), Oct. 21, 1865. See also Jos[eph] C. G. Kennedy to [W. T.] Sherman, April 7, 1864, Military Division of the Mississippi, Letters Received, Box 2, Record Group 393, Part 1, No. 2484, National Archives, Washington, D.C.

"No military . . . data"]   W. T. Sherman to Thomas Ewing, Dec. 31, 1864, Thomas Ewing and Family Papers, Library of Congress.

"to induce . . . unavailable"]   Entry of Nov. 30, 1864, Edward Younger, ed., *Inside the Confederate Government: The Diary of Robert Garlick Hill Kean* (New York, 1957), 179.

330 Grant and Beauregard on Hood]   John Russell Young, *Around the World With General Grant* (New York, 1879), II, 294–295; G. T. Beauregard to Cha[rle]s C. Jones, [Jr.], April 1, 1875, William K. Bixby Collection, Missouri Historical Society, St. Louis. Compare McMurry, *Hood*, 158–162, 173.

"wipe out Lee"]   U. S. Grant to W. T. Sherman, Dec. 6 and 18, 1864, W. T. Sherman Papers, Library of Congress.

330–1 "Enemy's . . . determine"]   J. Wheeler to D. H. Hill, Feb. 2, 1865, D. H. Hill Papers, Box 9, Virginia State Library, Richmond.

331 "in violation . . . Art"]   "Notes of conference, had on the 2d day of February A. D. 1865 at Green's-Cut Station Ga.," Feb. 3, 1865, enclosed in G. T. Beauregard to A. H. Stephens, Oct. 15, 1868, Alexander H. Stephens Papers, Series I, Box 7, Woodruff Library, Emory University, Atlanta, Georgia. See also G. T. Beauregard to Cha[rle]s C. Jones, [Jr.], April 1, 1875, Bixby Collection, Missouri Historical Society.

"The necessity . . . affairs"]   Johnson Hagood, *Memoirs of the War of Secession from the Original Manuscripts of Johnson Hagood*, ed. U. R. Brooks (Columbia, S.C., 1910), 331.

"Years . . . there"]   Grenville M. Dodge, *Personal Recollections of President Abraham Lincoln, General Ulysses S. Grant, and General William T. Sherman* (Council Bluffs, Iowa, 1914), 181.

"I deliberately . . . ended"]   W. T. Sherman to John W. Draper, Aug. 17, [1868], John W. Draper Family Papers, Box 6, Library of Congress.

"at Branchville . . . point"]   R. E. Lee to Jefferson Davis, Feb. 4, 1865, Robert E. Lee Papers, Duke University. See also R. E. Lee to Jefferson Davis, Jan. 8, 1865, Douglas Southall Freeman, ed., *Lee's Dispatches: Unpublished Letters of General Robert E. Lee* (New York, 1915), 313.

332 "the vital . . . practicable"]   R. E. Lee to Joseph E. Johnston, Feb. 23, 1865, *Official Records*, Series I, Vol. XLVII, Part II, 1257. See also R. E. Lee to J. C. Breckinridge, Feb. 22, 1865, and R. E. Lee to J. Longstreet, Feb. 22, 1865, *ibid.*, Vol. XLVI, Part II, 1247, 1250; R. E. Lee to Jefferson Davis, Feb. 19 and 23, 1865, *ibid.*, Vol. LIII, 413; R. E. Lee to Z. B. Vance, Feb. 24, 1865, *ibid.*, Vol. XLVII, Part II, 1270; R. E. Lee to W. Porcher Miles, Jan. 19, 1865, William Porcher Miles Papers, Southern Historical Collection, University of North Carolina, Chapel Hill; R. E. Lee to [Mary Anna Randolph Custis Lee], Feb. 21, 1865, Lee Family Papers, Virginia Historical Society, Richmond; Douglas Southall Freeman, *R. E. Lee: A Biography* (New York, 1935), IV, chap. 1.

"As regards . . . Richmond"]   R. E. Lee to W[illia]m S. Smith, July 27, 1868, in G. A. Custer to W. T. Sherman, Dec. 12, 1875, W. T. Sherman Papers, Library of Congress. See also R. E. Lee to Jefferson Davis, March 14, 1865, Clifford Dowdey and Louis H. Manarin, eds., *The Wartime Papers of R. E. Lee* (Boston, 1961), 914–915. On Lee's supplies see Ludwell H. Johnson, "Contraband Trade During the Last Year of the Civil War," *Mississippi Valley Historical Review*, XLIX (March 1963), 635–652. On the importance Lee attached to this source of supplies see R. E. Lee to Z. B. Vance, Jan. 9, 11, 1865, Zebulon B. Vance Papers, Volume 6, North Carolina Archives.

"stopped by the Richd people"]   John Esten Cooke's marginalia in his copy of Swinton, *Campaigns of the Army of the Potomac*, 574, Rare Book Room, Library of Congress.

332 "the necessity . . . capital" and "more . . . enterprises"] Jefferson Davis to the People of the Confederate States of America, April 4, 1865, in Dunbar Rowland, ed., *Jefferson Davis, Constitutionalist: His Letters, Papers, and Speeches* (Jackson, Miss., 1923), VI, 530.

"Lee . . . inevitable"] W. T. Sherman, "The Grand Strategy of the Last Year of the War," Johnson and Buel, eds., *Battles and Leaders,* IV, 259.

333 "would insure . . . Sherman"] U. S. Grant to H. W. Halleck, Aug. 15, 1864, John Y. Simon, ed., *The Papers of Ulysses S. Grant* (Carbondale, Ill., 1967–), XI, 424.

"Lee's . . . also"] U. S. Grant to Geo[rge] G. Meade, April 9, 1864, George Gordon Meade Papers, Historical Society of Pennsylvania, Philadelphia.

"that this fighting . . . resistance"] Entry of June 5, 1864, Diary of Theodore Lyman, III, Lyman Family Papers, Part III, Massachusetts Historical Society, Boston.

Grant's critics] Whitelaw Reid, *Ohio in the War: Her Statesmen, Her Generals, and Soldiers* (Cincinnati, Ohio, 1868), I, 401–402; J. W. Grimes to [W. P.] Fessenden, Aug. 3, 1864, Fessenden Family Papers, Bowdoin College, Brunswick, Maine; Edward A. Pollard, *The Lost Cause; A New Southern History of the War of the Confederates* (New York, 1866), 510; Swinton, *Campaigns of the Army of the Potomac,* 440. See also William S. McFeely, *Grant: A Biography* (New York, 1981), 157, 165; Ludwell H. Johnson, "Civil War Military History: A Few Revisions in Need of Revising," *Civil War History,* XVII (June 1971), 125–127; Edward Hagerman, *The American Civil War and the Origins of Modern Warfare: Ideas, Organization, and Field Command* (Bloomington, Ind., 1988), chap. 10.

"There were brains in those ranks"] Reid, *Ohio in the War,* I, 404.

334 "the slaughtered . . . generalship" and "if it . . . we"] Entry of Aug. 2, 1864, Howard K. Beale, ed., *Diary of Gideon Welles* (New York, 1960), II, 92.

Grant on Virginia Campaign] Young, *Around the World,* II, 307.

"spoke of . . . prevent"] W. G. Bean, ed., "Memoranda of Conversations Between Robert E. Lee and William Preston Johnston," *Virginia Magazine of History and Biography,* LXXIII (Oct. 1965), 475, 478. Compare Bruce Catton, *Grant Takes Command* (Boston, 1969), esp. 170, 215, 274; Herman Hattaway and Archer Jones, *How the North Won: A Military History of the Civil War* (Urbana, Ill., 1983), esp. 527–531, 557–558, 590–593, 693.

335 "a catastrophe"] R. E. Lee to James A. Seddon, June 8, 1863, *Official Records,* Series I, Vol. XXVII, Part III, 868–869. See also R. E. Lee to A. P. Hill, June [?], 1864, Dowdey and Manarin, eds., *Wartime Papers of Lee,* 759–760.

"If we . . . summer"] R. E. Lee to Jefferson Davis, Feb. 3, 1864, *Official Records,* Series I, Vol. XXXII, Part II, 667.

"Genl Grant . . . bull dog"] Entry of May 19, 1864, Creed Thomas Davis, Diary, Virginia Historical Society.

"that this . . . eventually"] E. M. Law, "From the Wilderness to Cold Harbor," Johnson and Buel, eds., *Battles and Leaders,* IV, 144.

"The last . . . Army"] U. S. Grant to J. Russell Jones, July 5, 1864, Simon, ed., *Papers of Grant,* XI, 176.

"inflicted . . . rebellion"] U. S. Grant to E. M. Stanton, July 22, 1865, *Official Records,* Series I, Vol. XXXVIII, Part I, 11.

335–6 "and fighting . . . killed"] Quoted in J. Cutler Andrews, *The North Reports the Civil War* (Pittsburgh, Pa., 1955), 538.

336 "Grant . . . enemy"] Horace Porter, *Campaigning With Grant,* ed. Wayne C. Temple (Bloomington, Ind., 1961 [orig. publ. New York, 1897]), 180–181.

"Oh, for . . . man"] W. P. F[essenden] to [Elizabeth Warriner], Aug. 27, 1864, Fessenden Family Papers, Bowdoin College.

"supposed . . . armies"] Lyman Trumbull to [William Butler], Nov. 20, 1862, William Butler Collection, Chicago Historical Society, Chicago, Illinois. See also Young, *Around the World,* II, 301; Porter, *Campaigning With Grant,* ed. Temple, 26.

336 "Whether . . . to say"]   U. S. Grant to E. M. Stanton, July 22, 1865, *Official Records,*
Series I, Vol. XXXVIII, Part I, 2.

"that until . . . achieved"]   J. Medill to [E. B.] Washburne, May 11, 1864, Elihu B.
Washburne Papers, Library of Congress.

"If you . . . back"]   Henry E. Wing, *When Lincoln Kissed Me: A Story of the Wilderness
Campaign* (New York, 1913), 12–13, 38–39.

337 "I believe . . . purposes"]   Roy P. Basler *et al.,* eds., *The Collected Works of Abraham
Lincoln* (New Brunswick, N.J., 1953), VII, 334.

"I have seen . . . possible"]   A. Lincoln to U. S. Grant, Aug. 17, 1864, *ibid.,* 499.

Smith]   W. F. Smith, "The Genius of Battle," *North American Review,* CLXVI (1888),
144–147.

Rice]   [Allen Thorndike Rice], " 'The Genius of Battle,' " *ibid.,* 334–337; W. T.
S[herman], "Notes for use by A. Thorndike Rice," Jan. 30, 1888, W. T. Sherman Papers,
Library of Congress.

338 "fought . . . persistently" and "knew . . . end"]   W. T. Sherman, "The Grand Strategy
of the War of the Rebellion," *Century Magazine,* XXXV (Feb. 1888), 589, 591. See also
Bruce Catton, "The Generalship of Ulysses S. Grant," in Grady McWhiney, ed., *Grant,
Lee, Lincoln, and the Radicals* ([Evanston, Ill.], 1964), 27–29; Brooks D. Simpson,
"Butcher? Racist? An Examination of William S. McFeely's *Grant: A Biography,"* *Civil
War History,* XXXIII (March 1987), 65–72; Henry M. W. Russell, "The *Memoirs* of
Ulysses S. Grant: The Rhetoric of Judgment," *Virginia Quarterly Review,* LXVI (1990),
189–209.

bloodshed necessary]   "Address of General Sherman," The Society of the Army of the
Potomac, *Report of the Twelfth Annual Reunion at Hartford, Connecticut, June 8, 1881* (New
York, 1881), 51.

"the South . . . mentioning"]   John Fiske, *The Mississippi Valley in the Civil War*
(Boston, 1901), 320.

300,000]   B. F. Scribner, *How Soldiers Were Made; or the War As I Saw It Under Buell,
Rosecrans, Thomas, Grant and Sherman* (New Albany, Ind., 1887), 32; W. T. Sherman
to Philemon B. Ewing, April 21, 1864, in Joseph H. Ewing, "The New Sherman
Letters," *American Heritage,* XXXVIII (July–Aug. 1987), 37.

"awful fact"]   W. T. Sherman to Philip H. Sheridan, Nov. 6, 1864, *Official Records,*
Series I, Vol. XLIII, Part II, 553.

"have fought . . . Richmond" and "move . . . understood"]   Andrew A. Humphreys,
The Virginia Campaign of '64 and '65 (New York, 1883), 7–9.

339 "Grant . . . did"]   Joshua Lawrence Chamberlain, *The Passing of the Armies* (New York,
1915), 381–382.

"they shrugged . . . Confederacy"]   Frank Wilkeson, *Recollections of a Private Soldier
in the Army of the Potomac* (Freeport, N.Y., 1972 [orig. publ. New York, 1887]), 192.

"a morale"]   U. S. Grant to E. M. Stanton, July 22, 1865, *Official Records,* Series I, Vol.
XXXVIII, Part I, 12.

"Immense . . . power"]   W. T. Sherman to Ellen [Sherman], May 20, 1864, Sherman
Papers, University of Notre Dame.

Lincoln's metaphors]   James M. McPherson, "Abraham Lincoln and the Second American Revolution," in John Thomas, ed., *Abraham Lincoln and the American Political
Tradition* (Amherst, Mass., 1986), 152–155.

340 "make Georgia howl"]   W. T. Sherman to [U. S.] Grant, Oct. 9, 1864, *Official Records,*
Series I, Vol. XXXIX, Part III, 162.

"a great . . . Sherman"]   W. T. Sherman to A. J. Smith, Nov. 2, 1864, *ibid.,* 596. See
also W. T. Sherman to [George H.] Thomas, Oct. 29, 1864, *ibid.,* 498.

"He can . . . soon"]   [Edward Barnwell Heyward] to [Katherina Maria Clinch Hey-
ward], Dec. 7, 1864, Heyward Family Papers, University of South Carolina.

340 "break . . . South"]   W. T. Sherman to Ellen [Sherman], March 23, 1865, Sherman Papers, University of Notre Dame.

"that political . . . people"]   W. T. Sherman to R. M. Sawyer, Jan. 31, 1864, *Official Records,* Series I, Vol. XXXII, Part II, 280.

"I propose . . . terms"]   W. T. Sherman to [George H.] Thomas, Oct. 20, 1864, James S. Schoff Civil War Collection, Letters and Documents, Box 7, Clements Library, University of Michigan, Ann Arbor.

"This may . . . statesmanship"]   W. T. Sherman to U. S. Grant, Nov. 6, 1864, *Official Records,* Series I, Vol. XXXIX, Part III, 660.

"a hard" . . . "realities" . . . "indirectly"]   W. T. Sherman to H. W. Halleck, Jan. 1, 1865, *ibid.,* Vol. XLIV, 13.

341 "The lesson . . . organs"]   Henry Hitchcock to Francis Lieber, Jan. 15–16, 1865, Francis Lieber Papers, Huntington Library.

"by virtue" . . . "tenure"]   W. T. Sherman to R. M. Sawyer, Jan. 31, 1864, *Official Records,* Series I, Vol. XXXII, Part II, 279–280.

"You must . . . government"]   W. T. Sherman to H. W. Hill, Sept. 7, 1863, *ibid.,* Vol. XXX, Part III, 402–403.

"vainglory & boasting"]   W. T. Sherman to Ellen [Sherman], April 9, 1865, Sherman Papers, University of Notre Dame.

342 "Then . . . homes"]   Maggie Davis, "Did Sherman Really Sleep in All Those Georgia Homes?" *Atlanta Constitution,* Oct. 18, 1959.

"on almost . . . march"]   Entry of April 5, 1865, Edmund J. Cleveland, Diary, University of North Carolina.

"simple waste and destruction"]   W. T. Sherman to H. W. Halleck, Jan. 1, 1865, *Official Records,* Series I, Vol. XLIV, 13.

343 "that there . . . whiped"]   Y[oung] J. Powell to Ellen [Aumack], March 27, 1865, Ellen Aumack Papers, Duke University. On the army's health see George Worthington Adams, *Doctors in Blue: The Medical History of the Union Army in the Civil War* (New York, 1952), 224.

"There stands" . . . "dad"]   Entry of Nov. 28, 1864, George Sharland, *Knapsack Notes of Gen. Sherman's Grand Campaign through the Empire State of the South* (Springfield, Ill., 1865), 29. On Sherman and his soldiers see Joseph T. Glatthaar, *The March to the Sea and Beyond: Sherman's Troops in the Savannah and Carolina Campaigns* (New York, 1985), chaps. 1, 2.

"Crazy . . . dough-nuts"]   Orville [T. Chamberlain] to [Joseph W. Chamberlain], Dec. 29, 1864, Joseph W. Chamberlain Papers, Indiana Historical Society, Indianapolis.

"the belief . . . so"]   Entry of Nov. 23, 1864, Henry Hitchcock, Diary, Henry Hitchcock Papers, Library of Congress.

344 "Forage liberally!"]   Entry of Nov. 18, 1864, *ibid.* For Sherman's later, somewhat different, account see Sherman, *Memoirs,* 2d ed., II, 181.

"The soldiers . . . has"]   Entry of Nov. 20, 1864, Henry Hitchcock, Diary, Henry Hitchcock Papers, Library of Congress.

"Shermans . . . go"]   S. K. Harryman to Maggie, Jan. 22, 1865, Samuel K. Harryman Papers, Indiana State Library, Indianapolis.

"to do . . . expense"]   T. E. Smith to brother, Dec. 27, 1864, Thomas E. Smith Letters, Cincinnati Historical Society, Cincinnati, Ohio. See also Glatthaar, *March to the Sea,* chaps. 6–8.

"better . . . life"]   Letter XI, Dec. 28, 1864, G. S. Bradley, *The Star Corps; or, Notes of an Army Chaplain, During Sherman's Famous March to the Sea* (Milwaukee, Wis., 1865), 224.

"devastate . . . rights"]   Entries of Dec. 15, 1864, and Jan. 1, 1865, William Bluffton Miller, Diary, Indiana Historical Society.

344 "the torch"]   F. Y. Hedley, *Marching Through Georgia* (Chicago, 1890), 270.

"It *ought* . . . pay for it"]   Entry of Dec. 1, 1864, Henry Hitchcock, Diary, Henry Hitchcock Papers, Library of Congress.

"the delight . . . lash"]   *New York Post,* reprinted in *Cincinnati Commercial,* Dec. 26, 1864.

"Many . . . woods"]   Entry of Nov. 17, 1864, Henry Hitchcock, Diary, Henry Hitchcock Papers, Library of Congress.

345 "Durin' . . . life"]   George P. Rawick, ed., *The American Slave: A Composite Autobiography* (Westport, Conn., 1972), Series I, Vol. III, South Carolina Narratives, Part 4, 92–93.

"said he . . . come" and "I have . . . over"]   Entry of Dec. 27, 1864, George Lawson, Journal, Robert Shaw Collection (George Lawson Letters), Atlanta Historical Society, Atlanta, Georgia.

"Been prayin' . . . come"]   H[enry Hitchcock] to [Mary Hitchcock], Dec. 24–29, 1864, Henry Hitchcock Papers, Library of Congress.

346 "Oh no . . . git out"]   George Ward Nichols, *The Story of the Great March* (New York, 1865), 196.

name of Sherman]   Entry of Dec. 24, 1864, Eliza Frances Andrews, *The War-Time Journal of a Georgia Girl* (New York, 1908), 32; W. T. Sherman to Charles A. Morton, Jan. 9, 1880, *Charles Hamilton Catalog, Auction No. 38* (Dec. 11, 1969), Item 98; C. P. Kingsbury to W. T. Sherman, May 1, 1868, W. T. Sherman Papers, Library of Congress; C. A. B[artol] to [H. W.] Bellows, Jan. 26, 1865, Henry W. Bellows Papers, Massachusetts Historical Society.

"Sherman Cutloose" and "I am . . . Sherman"]   Sam Aleckson, *Before the War and After the Union: An Autobiography* (Boston, 1929), 36. On wartime slavery and resistance see esp. Clarence L. Mohr, *On the Threshold of Freedom: Masters and Slaves in Civil War Georgia* (Athens, Ga., 1986), chaps. 6, 7; Edmund L. Drago, *Black Politicians and Reconstruction in Georgia: A Splendid Failure* (Baton Rouge, La., 1982), chap. 1; Bell Irvin Wiley, *Southern Negroes, 1861–1865* (New Haven, Conn., 1938), 72–83.

"I used . . . presence"]   Entry of Jan. 11, 1865, Andrews, *War-Time Journal,* 64.

"it is . . . fiercest"]   Kate [Crosland] to Bea and Nellie, Dec. 28, 1864, Thomas M. McIntosh Papers, Duke University. See also Mary Elizabeth Massey, *Refugee Life in the Confederacy* (Baton Rouge, La., 1964), 211–214.

"fight . . . road"]   A. G. Magrath, Proclamation, reprinted in *Philadelphia Inquirer,* Feb. 17, 1865.

"It is not . . . people"]   A. G. Magrath to Jefferson Davis, Dec. 25, 1864, Andrew Gordon Magrath Letterbooks, South Carolina Historical Society, Charleston.

347 "most influential . . . army"]   Arthur P. Ford, *Life in the Confederate Army: Being Personal Experiences of a Private Soldier in the Confederate Army* (New York, 1905), 44.

desertion rate]   Freeman, *R. E. Lee,* III, 541.

"many . . . else"]   J[oseph] C. Haskell to Ma, Feb. 15, 1865, Rachel Susan Cheves Papers, Duke University.

"Unmistakeable . . . us"]   S. H. Boineau to Mr. Heyward, Dec. 29, 1864, Heyward Family Papers, University of South Carolina.

"the desire . . . Freedom"]   A. G. Magrath to R. W. Barnwell, Dec. 30, 1864, Magrath Letterbooks, South Carolina Historical Society. See, in general, William James McNeill, "The Stress of War: The Confederacy and William Tecumseh Sherman During the Last Year of the Civil War" (Ph.D. diss., Rice University, 1973).

347–8 Confederate intentions in peace discussions]   J. E. Johnston to [Mansfield] Lovell, May 11, 1865, Mansfield Lovell Papers, Huntington Library; J. E. Johnston to [P. G. T.] Beauregard, Dec. 26, 1867, JO 187, Joseph E. Johnston Papers, *ibid.;* Stephen R. Mallory, Diary and Reminiscences, 68–72, University of North Carolina; J. E. Johnston to A. H. Stephens, April 29, 1868, Alexander H. Stephens Papers, Library of Congress;

Joseph E. Johnston, *Narrative of Military Operations Directed During the Late War Between the States* (New York, 1874), 398–400; Joseph E. Johnston, "My Negotiations with General Sherman," *North American Review,* CXLIII (Aug. 1886), 185–188; Jefferson Davis, *The Rise and Fall of the Confederate Government* (New York, 1881), II, 678–683; John H. Reagan, *Memoirs,* ed. Walter Flavius McCaleb (New York, 1906), 199–200; J. E. Johnston to W. T. Sherman, April 14, 1865, *Official Records,* Series I, Vol. XLVII, Part III, 206–207.

347–8 Sherman-Johnston negotiations]   *Cincinnati Commercial,* April 27, 1865; Johnston, "Dalton-Atlanta Operations," *Annals of the Army of Tennessee and Early Western History,* I (April 1878), 12–13; Johnston, *Narrative,* 402–407; Johnston, "Negotiations with Sherman," *North American Review,* CXLIII (Aug. 1886), 183–197; J. E. Johnston to [Mansfield] Lovell, May 11, 1865, Lovell Papers, Huntington Library; J. E. Johnston to A. H. Stephens, April 29, 1868, Stephens Papers, Library of Congress; Sherman, *Memoirs,* 2d ed., II, 346–362; Synopsis of the Agreement between Generals Johnston & Sherman, Palmer Collection, P-28, Western Reserve Historical Society, Cleveland, Ohio; W. T. Sherman to John W. Draper, Nov. 6, 1868, Draper Family Papers, Library of Congress; W. T. Sherman to John A. Rawlins, May 9, 1865, *Official Records,* Series I, Vol. XLVII, Part I, 29–40; W. T. Sherman to [Joseph Dana] Webster, April 17, 1865, *ibid.,* Part III, 237; W. T. Sherman to U. S. Grant, April 18, 1865, *ibid.,* 243–244; W. T. Sherman to H. W. Halleck, April 18, 1865, *ibid.,* 245; W. T. Sherman to J. E. Johnston, April 21 and 23, 1865, *ibid.,* 265–266, 287; W. T. Sherman to D. L. Swain, April 22, 1865, *ibid.,* 279; *Report of the Joint Committee on the Conduct of the War at the Second Session Thirty-Eighth Congress* (Washington, D.C., 1865), "Sherman-Johnston," 1–23.

348 Sherman on his intentions]   W. T. Sherman to John W. Draper, Oct. 27 and Nov. 6, 1868, Draper Family Papers, Library of Congress; W. T. Sherman to Ellen [Sherman], April 9, 18, 22, 28, May 10, 1865, Sherman Papers, University of Notre Dame; W. T. Sherman to Geo[rge] H. Thomas, May 2, 1865, CW 414, Huntington Library; W. T. Sherman to U. S. Grant, May 10, 1865, HM 21699, *ibid.;* and the sources cited in the preceding notes.

Stanton]   Edwin M. Stanton to [John A.] Dix, April 22, 1865, *New York Herald,* April 23, 1865, *New York Times,* April 23 and 24, 1865; C[harles] S[umner] to [Salmon P.] Chase, April 12, 1865, Salmon P. Chase Papers, Library of Congress; entry of April 22, 1865, James G. Randall, ed., *The Diary of Orville Hickman Browning* (Springfield, Ill., 1933), II, 24; Charles A. Dana, *Recollections of the Civil War* (New York, 1898), 289; Benjamin P. Thomas and Harold M. Hyman, *Stanton: The Life and Times of Lincoln's Secretary of War* (New York, 1962), chap. 19; John F. Marszalek, *Sherman's Other War: The General and the Civil War Press* (Memphis, Tenn., 1981), chap. 7.

Sherman on reconstruction]   For typical expressions of Sherman's often-stated views see W. T. Sherman to P. H. Sheridan, Oct. 7, 1872, Philip H. Sheridan Papers, Library of Congress; W. T. Sherman to C. C. Augur, March 18, 1871, Christopher C. Augur Papers, Illinois State Historical Library, Springfield; W. T. Sherman to [Willard] Warner, Jan. 16, 1866, William Tecumseh Sherman Letters, *ibid;* W. T. Sherman to John Sherman, Dec. 28, 1863, April 11 and Oct. 31, 1866, Jan. 7 and Feb. 3, 1875, W. T. Sherman Papers, Library of Congress; W. T. Sherman to H. W. Walter, Oct. 19, 1874, Harvey Washington Walter Papers, University of North Carolina; W. T. Sherman to [D. F.] Boyd, Jan. 25, 1867, David F. Boyd Family Papers, Louisiana State University, Baton Rouge; W. T. Sherman to [Henry S.] Turner, Dec. 5, 1876, Jan. 11, 1877, W. T. Sherman Papers, Ohio Historical Society, Columbus; W. T. Sherman to Thomas Ewing, Dec. 23, 1865, Ewing Family Papers, Library of Congress; Speech by W. T. Sherman in *Cincinnati Commercial,* June 27, 1865.

349 convention in Little Rock]   Speech on Dec. 11, 1865, reported in newspaper clipping, W. T. and Ellen E. Sherman Scrapbook, Sherman Papers, Box 13, Ohio Historical Society.

"noticed . . . progress"]   W. T. Sherman to H. S. Turner, March 9, 1879, Sherman Papers, *ibid.* See also W. T. Sherman to E. P. Howell, Feb. 4, 1879, W. T. Sherman Papers, Library of Congress; Evan P. Howell to W. T. Sherman, Feb. 1, 1879, *ibid.;* Raymond B. Nixon, *Henry W. Grady: Spokesman of the New South* (New York, 1943),

164; John F. Marszalek, "Celebrity in Dixie: Sherman Tours the South, 1879," *Georgia Historical Quarterly*, LXVI (1982), 368–383.

349 "the best . . . South"] W. T. Sherman to Sidney Herbert, Nov. 22, 1881, W. T. Sherman Papers, Library of Congress. See also W. T. Sherman to H. I. Kimball, Dec. 1, 1881, *ibid.; Cincinnati Commercial*, Nov. 16, 1881.

"Time . . . country"] W. T. Sherman, Comments on Bowman and Irwin, *Sherman and His Campaigns*, April 24, 1866, in Jared W. Young, ed., "General Sherman on His Own Record: Some Unpublished Comments," *Atlantic Monthly*, CVIII (Sept. 1911), 298.

"General . . . fate"] *Philadelphia Inquirer*, April 24, 1865.

"Let us . . . Sherman"] *Ibid.*, April 29, 1865. On the fading of censure see also Reid, *Ohio in the War*, I, 486; H. D. Cooke to [John] Sherman, May 5, 1865, John Sherman Papers, Library of Congress; R. L. Stewart to [C. W. Moulton], June 28, 1865, *ibid.*; Thomas Ewing, Jr., to T[homas] Ewing, Sr., May 1, 1865, Ewing Family Papers, *ibid.*; [Adam Badeau] to [James Harrison Wilson], May 27, 1865, James Harrison Wilson Papers, *ibid.; Cincinnati Commercial*, April 29, 1865; *Cleveland Plain Dealer*, May 15, 1865; *Morning Journal and Courier* (New Haven, Conn.), May 9, 1865; *New York Herald*, April 29 and June 1, 1865; Dana, *Recollections of the Civil War*, 289–290.

350 "Negros . . . labor"] W. T. Sherman to J. E. Johnston, April 21, 1865, Schoff Collection, Letters and Documents, Box 7, Clements Library. Printed in *Official Records*, Series I, Vol. XLVII, Part III, 265–266.

Special Field Order, No. 15] W. T. Sherman to Charles Cowley, May 19, 1881, in [John Page Nicholson], comp., Memoirs of Gen. Sherman: Controversies, Etc. [Scrapbook], Huntington Library; W. T. Sherman to Andrew Johnson, Feb. 1, 1866, W. T. Sherman Papers, Library of Congress; Sherman, *Memoirs*, 2d ed., II, 249–252; Paul A. Cimbala, "The Freedmen's Bureau, the Freedmen, and Sherman's Grant in Reconstruction Georgia, 1865–1867," *Journal of Southern History*, LV (Nov. 1989), 597–632; Willie Lee Rose, *Rehearsal for Reconstruction: The Port Royal Experiment* (New York, 1967 [orig. publ. 1964]), 327–331, 349–361.

"a system of segregation" and "acquire separate property"] W. T. Sherman to Cha[rle]s Anderson, July 28, 1865, Richard Clough Anderson Collection, Huntington Library.

"The conservative . . . against you"] J. M. Corse to W. T. Sherman, Aug. 11, 1865, W. T. Sherman Papers, Library of Congress.

"he has . . . acceptable"] Thomas Ewing, Jr., to T[homas] Ewing, Sr., May 1, 1865, Ewing Family Papers, *ibid.*

Gray] John C. Gray, Jr., to John C. Ropes, May 24, 1865, John Chipman Gray and John Codman Ropes, *War Letters 1862–1865*, ed. Worthington Chauncey Ford (Boston, 1927), 494.

"Sherman . . . conclusions"] Quoted in James E. Sefton, *The United States Army and Reconstruction, 1865–1877* (Baton Rouge, La., 1967), 23.

351 "no special . . . States" and "he utterly . . . war"] *Harper's Weekly*, IX (May 6, 1865), 274.

"obnoxious . . . self government"] W. T. Sherman to H. W. Walter, Oct. 19, 1874, Walter Papers, University of North Carolina.

"beneath a soldiers vocation"] W. T. Sherman to John Sherman, Jan. 7, 1875, W. T. Sherman Papers, Library of Congress.

"hauled . . . Congress"] W. T. Sherman to P. H. Sheridan, Oct. 7, 1872, Philip Henry Sheridan Papers, *ibid.;* Sefton, *United States Army and Reconstruction*, 70.

"the memory" . . . "the rebel element" . . . "prevail"] W. T. Sherman to John Sherman, Feb. 3, 1875, W. T. Sherman Papers, Library of Congress. See also George C. Rable, "William T. Sherman and the Conservative Critique of Radical Reconstruction," *Ohio History*, XCIII (1984), 147–163.

351 "embarrassed"]   W. T. Sherman to [D. F.] Boyd, Jan. 25, 1867, Boyd Family Papers, Louisiana State University.

352 "the new young men"]   W. T. Sherman to John Sherman, Nov. 8, 1888, W. T. Sherman Papers, Library of Congress. On blacks' voting see W. T. Sherman to John Sherman, Sept. 15 and Oct. 15, 1885, *ibid.;* W. T. Sherman, "Old Shady, With a Moral," *North American Review,* CXLVII (Oct. 1888), 365–366.

"the absurd . . . interests"]   W. T. Sherman to [John Eaton] Tourtellotte, Nov. 4, 1884, William T. Sherman Papers, Missouri Historical Society.

353 "war is . . ."]   W. T. Sherman to H. W. Halleck, Sept. 4, 1864, *Official Records,* Series I, Vol. XXXVIII, Part V, 794; W. T. Sherman to James M. Calhoun *et al.,* Sept. 12, 1864, *ibid.,* Vol. XXXIX, Part II, 418; W. T. Sherman to R. M. Sawyer, Jan. 31, 1864, *ibid.,* Vol. XXXII, Part II, 280.

Clausewitz]   Carl von Clausewitz, *On War,* ed. and trans. Michael Howard and Peter Paret (Princeton, N.J., 1976), 75, 87–88. See also Peter Paret, *Clausewitz and the State* (New York, 1976), 364–381; James Turner Johnson, *Just War Tradition and the Restraint of War: A Moral and Historical Inquiry* (Princeton, N.J., 1981), 253–255, 284, 288–289; David Donald, "Refighting the Civil War," in *Lincoln Reconsidered: Essays on the Civil War Era* (New York, 1956), 99–100.

354 "It is reduced . . . destruction"]   W. T. Sherman, Response to Resolutions of the Chamber of Commerce, Jan. 15, 1865, Hitchcock Family Papers, Box 3, Missouri Historical Society.

"When the Congress . . . peace"]   W. T. Sherman, "Our Army and Militia," *North American Review,* CLI (Aug. 1890), 139.

"Many . . . existence"]   W. T. Sherman to R. M. Sawyer, Jan. 31, 1864, *Official Records,* Series I, Vol. XXXII, Part II, 281.

355 "We had . . . behind"]   W. T. Sherman to Daniel M. Martin, Aug. 10, 1864, in Dodge, *Personal Recollections,* 171.

"Reason . . . force"]   W. T. Sherman to John Sherman, April 5, 1864, W. T. Sherman Papers, Library of Congress.

355–6 military men on Sherman]   Jay Luvaas, *The Military Legacy of the Civil War: The European Inheritance* (Chicago, 1959), 70–73, 121–124, 132; Edwin A. Pratt, *The Rise of Rail-Power in War and Conquest, 1833–1914* (London, 1916), 34–37; France James Soady, *Lessons of War As Taught by the Great Masters and Others* (London, 1870), 57–58; V. Derrecagaix, *Modern War,* trans. C. W. Foster (Washington, D.C., 1888), 306–307; Edward Bruce Hamley, *The Operations of War Explained and Illustrated* (Edinburgh, 1922 [orig. publ. 1866]); von Schetika to W. T. Sherman, Aug. 24, 1869, W. T. Sherman Papers, Library of Congress. For a nineteenth-century military writer who understood Sherman's assault on Southern morale, see John Bigelow, *The Principles of Strategy Illustrated Mainly from American Campaigns* (New York, 1968 [orig. publ. Philadelphia, 1894]), 229–233. For a German definition of war similar to Sherman's, citing Clausewitz, see Stanislaus Remak, trans., "Humanity and War," *Army and Navy Quarterly,* I (1885), 125–154.

356 Liddell Hart]   B. H. Liddell Hart, *Sherman: Soldier, Realist, American* (New York, 1929), esp. 425–431; B. H. Liddell Hart, "Foreword to New Edition," in W. T. Sherman, *Memoirs of General William T. Sherman by Himself* (Bloomington, Ind., 1957), vii; B. H. Liddell Hart, *Defence of the West* (New York, 1950), 220–221; B. H. Liddell Hart, *The Liddell Hart Memoirs* (New York, 1965), I, 164–166. On Liddell Hart, see Russell F. Weigley, "American Strategy from Its Beginnings through the First World War," in Peter Paret *et al.,* eds., *Makers of Modern Strategy from Machiavelli to the Nuclear Age* (Princeton, N.J., 1986), 435–436; Russell F. Weigley, *The American Way of War: A History of United States Military Strategy and Policy* (Bloomington, Ind., 1973), 500, n. 52; Brian Bond, *Liddell Hart: A Study of His Military Thought* (New Brunswick, N.J., 1977), 47–49, 222–223; John J. Mearsheimer, *Liddell Hart and the Weight of History* (Ithaca, N.Y., 1988), esp. 43, 91–92.

357 "What the . . . envisage"]   James Truslow Adams, *America's Tragedy* (New York, 1934), 340.

357 "The thing . . . granted"]   Bruce Catton, *America Goes to War* (Middletown, Conn., 1958), 20–22. See also William V. O'Brien, *The Conduct of Just and Limited War* (New York, 1981), 216.

"the concept . . . normal"]   Robert Penn Warren, *Jefferson Davis Gets His Citizenship Back* ([Lexington, Ky.], 1980), 66.

"a straight line of logic"]   Warren, *Jefferson Davis,* 66. See also James Reston, Jr., *Sherman's March and Vietnam* (New York, 1984), 6, 16, 92; Philip Wylie, *Generation of Vipers* (New York, 1942), 266–267; John Bennett Walters, *Merchant of Terror: General Sherman and Total War* (Indianapolis, Ind., 1973), 58; Thomas C. Schelling, *Arms and Influence* (New Haven, Conn., 1966), 17; Robert Leckie, *Warfare* (New York, 1970), 41; Weigley, "American Strategy," in Paret *et al.,* eds., *Makers of Modern Strategy,* 443; Weigley, *American Way of War,* 148–152.

"agonizing uncertainty"]   Catton, *America Goes to War,* 23.

"a war criminal"]   Otto Eisenschiml, "Sherman: Hero or War Criminal?" *Civil War Times Illustrated,* II (Jan. 1964), 36.

358 "It was . . . earth"]   Michael Herr, *Dispatches* (New York, 1977), 43.

"an earlier war crime"]   Mary McCarthy, *The Seventeenth Degree* (New York, 1974), 383. On Vietnam see also Reston, *Sherman's March;* Hamilton DeSaussure, "Comments" on Richard A. Falk, "Methods and Means of Warfare: Counterinsurgency, Tactics, and the Law," in Peter D. Trooboff, ed., *Law and Responsibility in Warfare: The Vietnam Experience* (Chapel Hill, N.C., 1975), 76–77.

359 "the dramatic . . . events"]   Cushing Strout, "Causation and the American Civil War," in *The Veracious Imagination: Essays on American History, Literature, and Biography* (Middletown, Conn., 1981), 40. On Sherman's "cold logic" see also James Truslow Adams's comparison of Sherman and T. J. Jackson in *America's Tragedy,* 328–330. On Sherman's views see also Michael Walzer, *Just and Unjust Wars: A Moral Argument with Historical Illustrations* (New York, 1977), 32–33; John W. Brinsfield, "The Military Ethics of General William T. Sherman: A Reassessment," *Parameters,* XII (June 1982), 36–48; Geoffrey Best, *Humanity in Warfare* (New York, 1980), 206–211; Michael Howard, "*Temperamenta Belli:* Can War Be Controlled," in Michael Howard, ed., *Restraints on War: Studies in the Limitation of Armed Conflict* (Oxford, 1979), 3–4, 9–10; James G. Garner, "General Order 100 Revisited," *Military Law Review,* No. 27–100 (1965), 44–46.

"You gave . . . truth"]   John Mason Loomis to W. T. Sherman, Sept. 24, 1864, W. T. Sherman Papers, Library of Congress.

Burbridge]   W. T. Sherman to [Stephen G.] Burbridge, June 21, 1864, *Official Records,* Series I, Vol. XXXIX, Part II, 135–136. See also W. T. Sherman to Leslie Coombs, Aug. 11, 1864, *ibid.,* 240–241.

"General . . . edge" and "General . . . approves"]   *Harper's Weekly,* VIII (Dec. 10, 1864), 786, (Oct. 18, 1864), 642.

360 "the snivellers and peace men"]   *New York Herald,* Sept. 25 and 30, 1864.

headlines]   *Cincinnati Commercial,* Dec. 12, 1864; *New York Herald,* Dec. 22, 1864, Feb. 19, 1865; *Chicago Tribune,* Feb. 5, 1865; *Philadelphia Inquirer,* Feb. 20, 1865.

engravings]   *Harper's Weekly,* IX (April 1, 8, 1865), 193, 200–201, 204, 217.

"a new principle in our warfare"]   *Cincinnati Commercial,* Nov. 18, 1864.

"moved . . . behind them"]   J. T. Headley, *Grant and Sherman; Their Campaigns and Generals* (New York, 1866), 221.

361 "popularity . . . Savannah"]   Reid, *Ohio in the War,* I, 480.

"To molest . . . weak" and "common sense"]   *Harper's Weekly,* V (Sept. 21, 1861), 594.

"It has . . . war"]   R. E. Carpenter to [C. C. Carpenter], Dec. 19, 1864, Cyrus Clay Carpenter Papers, State Historical Society of Iowa, Iowa City.

361 "When you . . . war"]   [James W. Beekman], [Address to Sherman at the Union League Club], Beekman Papers, New-York Historical Society, New York, New York. Printed in *New York Herald,* June 4, 1865.

362 "War is . . . be so"]   [Samuel] P[owel] to [?], Jan. 29, 1863, John Hare Powel Papers, Powel Collection, Box 22, Historical Society of Pennsylvania. See also *Richmond Whig,* March 14, 1865.

Smyth]   [J.] Adger [Smyth] to Janey, Aug. 7, 1864, J. Adger Smyth Collection, Adger-Smyth[e] Collection, Box 11-408, South Carolina Historical Society.

"When . . . violence"]   *Harper's Weekly,* VI (May 31, 1862), 338.

363 "Let it be . . . burned"]   O. T. Lanphear, *Peace by Power: A Discourse, Preached . . . Oct. 9, 1864* (New Haven, Conn., 1864), 13. See John 15:6.

Stowe]   Harriet Beecher Stowe, *Uncle Tom's Cabin; or, Life Among the Lowly* (Boston, 1852), II, 322. See Malachi 3:2, 4:1, 3:5 and Psalm 72:4. See also Malachi 4:3. On Stowe see Terrie Dopp Aamodt, "Righteous Armies, Holy Cause: Apocalyptic Imagery and the Civil War" (Ph.D. diss., Boston University, 1986), 51–70; Cushing Strout, *The New Heavens and the New Earth: Political Religion in America* (New York, 1974), 182–184; Theodore R. Hovet, "Christian Revolution: Harriet Beecher Stowe's Response to Slavery and the Civil War," *New England Quarterly,* XLVII (Dec. 1974), 535–549. See also James H. Moorhead, "Between Progress and Apocalypse: A Reassessment of Millennialism in American Religious Thought, 1800–1880," *Journal of American History,* LXXI (Dec. 1984), 534–536.

364 Stowe on Sherman]   Harriet Beecher Stowe, *Men of Our Times; or Leading Patriots of the Day* (Hartford, Conn., 1868), 430–431, 442–443, 501–502. See Jeremiah 44:22.

364–5 "I wish . . . tune"]   Henry Watterson, *"Marse Henry": An Autobiography* (New York, 1919), II, 156.

365 "Marching Through Georgia"]   W[illia]m R. Hartpence, *History of the Fifty-first Indiana Veteran Volunteer Infantry* (Cincinnati, Ohio, 1894), 250–251. See also Edwin Tribble, " 'Marching Through Georgia,' " *Georgia Review,* XXI (1967), 423–429.

"No man . . . longer"]   W. H. Van Orden, *General William T. Sherman: A Story of His Life and Military Services* (New York, 1895), 154.

"Those great . . . people"]   *New York Herald,* Sept. 6, 1864.

"General . . . command"]   *Ibid.,* Dec. 22, 1864.

"an important new service"]   A. Lincoln to W. T. Sherman, Dec. 26, 1864, Basler *et al.,* eds., *Collected Works of Lincoln,* VIII, 182.

"I am . . . to me"]   C. E. Bishop to [Levi A.] Ross, Jan. 9, 1865, Levi Adolphus Ross Letters, Illinois State Historical Library.

"I can . . . did it"]   [W. T.] Sherman to Ellen [Sherman], Dec. 31, 1864, Sherman Papers, University of Notre Dame.

366 "has been . . . millions"]   E. P. Powell, *Sermons on Recent National Victories, and the National Sorrow* (Adrian, Mich., 1865), 20.

"making war sustain war" and "the great . . . century"]   *Cincinnati Commercial,* Jan. 10, 1865.

"one . . . time"]   *New York Herald,* Sept. 25, 1864.

"A fortnight . . . Sherman"]   *Cincinnati Commercial,* April 13, 1865.

"coursing . . . speed"]   W. T. Sherman to [Eleanor Mary Sherman Thackara], Jan. 24, 1886, Sherman Papers, Ohio Historical Society.

"he drew . . . ask for"]   L. Catharine Joyner to [?], July 28, 1866, in Daniel Heyward Trezevant, "Burning of Columbia," University of South Carolina. See also Phillip Shaw Paludan, *"A People's Contest": The Union and Civil War, 1861–1865* (New York, 1988), 304–307.

367 "a deep-rooted . . . war" and "He always . . . it"]   Augustus Saint-Gaudens, *The Reminiscences of Augustus Saint-Gaudens* (New York, 1913), I, 367.

367 "Every . . . onward"]   Kathryn Greenthal, *Augustus Saint-Gaudens: Master Sculptor* (New York, 1985), 162. See also John H. Dryfhout, *The Work of Augustus Saint-Gaudens* (Hanover, N. H., 1982), 253–256.

368 "This task . . . War"]   Saint-Gaudens, *Reminiscences*, I, 378.

"grim . . . general" and "the very . . . art"]   Quoted in Burke Wilkinson, *Uncommon Clay: The Life and Works of Augustus Saint-Gaudens* (San Diego, Calif., 1985), 327.

"She is . . . horse"]   Kenyon Cox, "The Sherman Statue," *The Nation,* LXXVI (June 18, 1903), 491.

"For a symbol . . . taste"]   [Henry Adams], *The Education of Henry Adams: An Autobiography* (Boston, 1961 [orig. publ. 1918]), 388.

"art . . . surface"]   Letter No. 130, Aug. 30, 1914, Joseph Hone, ed., *J. B. Yeats: Letters to His Son W. B. Yeats and Others, 1869–1922* (London, 1944), 190.

369 James]   Henry James, *The American Scene,* ed. Leon Edel (Bloomington, Ind., 1968 [orig. publ. 1907]), 173–174.

"One of . . . progress"]   Cox, "Sherman Statue," *The Nation,* LXXVI (June 18, 1903), 491.

370 "vehemence" and "dauntless power"]   James, *American Scene,* ed. Edel, 74.

370–1 Root]   [Elihu] Root, *Speech by the Secretary of War, Mr. Root, Upon the Unveiling of St. Gaudens' Statue of General Sherman in the City of New York, May 30, 1903* (Washington, D.C., 1903), 4, 8, 5.

371–2 "I saw . . . at me"]   P. D. Stephenson, War Autobiography, Vol. 3, pp. 37–39, Louisiana State University.

372 Pond]   J. B. Pond to [W. T.] Sherman, April 13, 1885, W. T. Sherman Papers, Library of Congress; W. T. Sherman to J. B. Pond, Oct. 2, 1885, Sherman Papers, Missouri Historical Society.

"No face . . . Sherman"]   S. H. M. Byers, *Twenty Years in Europe* (Chicago, 1900), 288.

"set up . . . hands" and "his appearance . . . applause"]   *Minneapolis Tribune,* July 4, 1880.

"a healthy . . . flavor" and "He talks . . . instructive"]   *The Capital* (Washington, D.C.), Jan. 25, 1880.

"His personality . . . deeds"]   Newspaper clipping, ca. Nov. 1, 1883, John Sherman's Scrapbook, W. T. Sherman Papers, Ohio Historical Society.

372–3 "He was . . . party"]   Smith P. Galt, "General Sherman's Popularity," in "Reminiscences of Comrades," *The Chaperone,* V (March 1891), 623. See also Clark E. Carr, *My Day and Generation* (Chicago, 1908), 169; [Thomas C. Fletcher], *Life and Reminiscences of General Wm. T. Sherman by Distinguished Men of His Time* (Baltimore, Md., 1891), 324–325; Speech by Chauncey Depew, *The Times* (Philadelphia), Oct. 11, 1890.

373 "the fitting . . . energetic"]   Newspaper clipping, ca. Nov. 1, 1883, John Sherman's Scrapbook, W. T. Sherman Papers, Ohio Historical Society.

"conceived . . . California"]   W. T. Sherman to S. S. L'Hommedieu, July 7, 1862, W. T. Sherman Papers, Library of Congress.

"villainous . . . treason"]   W. T. Sherman to Howell Cobb, Nov. 23, 1857, *ibid.*

"clip . . . enemy"]   W. T. Sherman to U. S. Grant, June 6, 1862, Simon, ed., *Papers of Grant,* V, 141.

popularity among correspondents]   Theo. R. Davis, "With Sherman in His Army Home," *The Cosmopolitan,* XII (Dec. 1891), 200. See also W. T. Sherman to Truman A. Merriman, Nov. 16, 1883, John Davis Batchelder Collection, Vol. 10, Library of Congress.

373 "They are . . . spicy"]   W. T. Sherman to P. H. Sheridan, Jan. 10, 1879, Sheridan Papers, Library of Congress.

Shanks]   William F. G. Shanks, *Personal Recollections of Distinguished Generals* (New York, 1866), 48. See also Louis M. Starr, *Bohemian Brigade: Civil War Newsmen in Action* (New York, 1954), 172; T. Harry Williams, *McClellan, Sherman, and Grant* (New Brunswick, N.J., 1962), 62.

"Sherman . . . like him"]   S. M. Bowman to [W. T. Sherman], Nov. 21, 1868, W. T. Sherman Papers, Library of Congress.

"He hated . . . they said"]   S. H. M. Byers, "Some Personal Recollections of General Sherman," *McClure's Magazine*, III (Aug. 1894), 221.

"I constantly . . . cloth"]   [W. T.] Sherman to [Willard] Warner, March 9, 1879, Sherman Letters, Illinois State Historical Library.

374 "I am . . . New England"]   W. T. Sherman to S[pencer] F[ullerton] Baird, Oct. 25, 1884, William Jones Rhees Collection, Box 52, Huntington Library.

"a few generalities"]   W. T. Sherman to [John T.] Doyle, Nov. 4, 1886, John T. Doyle Papers, California Historical Society, San Francisco.

"I have . . . curiosity"]   Speech on Aug. 29, 1879, in Frederick Cook, ed., *Journals of the Military Expedition of Major General John Sullivan . . . With Records of Centennial Celebrations* (Auburn, N.Y., 1887), 440–441.

"They were . . . in it"]   Entry of Aug. 25, 1883, Malcolm Clark, ed., *Pharisee Among Philistines: The Diary of Judge Matthew P. Deady, 1871–1892* (Portland, Ore., 1975), II, 419.

"frank . . . sentiments" and "the respect . . . people"]   W. T. Sherman to [D. F.] Boyd, July 26, 1875, Boyd Family Papers, Louisiana State University.

"Every day . . . War"]   W. T. Sherman to Ellen [Sherman], Sept. 16, 1883, Sherman Papers, University of Notre Dame.

"His sentences . . . hit"]   Galt, "Sherman's Popularity," *The Chaperone*, V (March 1891), 623.

375 "There will . . . *riot*"]   R. A. Alger to [W. T. Sherman], July 22, 1890, W. T. Sherman Papers, Library of Congress.

"The eyes . . . accountable"]   *Report of the Proceedings of the Society of the Army of the Tennessee, at the Ninth Annual Meeting . . . September 29th and 30th, 1875* (Cincinnati, Ohio, 1875), 387.

"the old . . . unity"]   W. T. Sherman to O. O. Howard, Oct. 24, 1867, Oliver Otis Howard Papers, Bowdoin College. See also Mary R. Dearing, *Veterans in Politics: The Story of the G. A. R.* (Baton Rouge, La., 1952), 321–323.

"but they . . . you"]   [James R. Doolittle] to W. T. Sherman, June 3, 1884, James R. Doolittle Papers, Library of Congress. See also John Sherman to [W. T. Sherman], May 4, 1884, and James G. Blaine to [W. T.] Sherman, May 25, 1884, W. T. Sherman Papers, *ibid.* In his article "Hon. James G. Blaine," *North American Review*, CXLVII (Dec. 1888), 621–623, Sherman misinterpreted Blaine's letter to have been ceding the nomination to him. Blaine was only saying, by implication, that Sherman would be nominated if Blaine were not. See also David Saville Muzzey, *James G. Blaine: A Political Idol of Other Days* (New York, 1934), 272–286.

"Please . . . courteous"]   W. T. Sherman to J. B. Henderson, june 3, 1883 [1884], W. T. Sherman Papers, Library of Congress.

"I will . . . elected"]   Quoted in [P. Tecumseh Sherman], Appendix, *Memoirs of Gen. W. T. Sherman, Written By Himself,* 4th ed. (New York, 1891), II, 466.

"If nominated . . . decline"]   W. T. Sherman to S. I. Crawford, Dec. 9, 1883, W. T. Sherman Papers, Library of Congress.

376 "a mere . . . void"]   W. T. Sherman to J. W. Draper, Jan. 30, 1875, Draper Family Papers, Library of Congress. See also W. T. Sherman to W. G. Eliot, Aug. 3, 1879,

William Greenleaf Eliot Papers, Missouri Historical Society. For a similar view of the presidency see James Bryce, *The American Commonwealth* (Chicago, 1891), I, chaps. 6–7.

376 "I am not . . . curses"]   W. T. Sherman to J. E. Williams, Sept. 21, 1875, *Charles Hamilton Catalog, Auction No. 105* (May 12, 1977), Item 210.

"He talks . . . *manipulated*"]   T. T. Gantt to H. J. Hunt, May 31, 1886, Henry Jackson Hunt Papers, Library of Congress.

"empty honor"]   W. T. Sherman to [Maria Ewing Sherman Fitch], Jan. 7, 1883, Sherman Papers, Ohio Historical Society.

"He was . . . Indians"]   New York, *In Memoriam. William T. Sherman. Proceedings of the Senate and Assembly of the State of New York, on the Life and Services of Gen. William T. Sherman* (Albany, N.Y., 1892), 27.

"his feeling . . . fit"]   "William Tecumseh Sherman," *Illustrated American*, VI (March 7, 1891), 135; *Banquet at "The Portland," Washington, D.C., February 8, 1883* (n.p., n.d.), 4.

377 "Instead . . . construction"]   *Report of the Proceedings of the Society of the Army of the Tennessee at the Second Annual Meeting*, 110. See also John L. Larson, *Bonds of Enterprise: John Murray Forbes and Western Development in America's Railway Age* (Cambridge, Mass., 1984).

"a necessary . . . China" and "a link . . . together"]   W. T. Sherman, "Old Times in California," *North American Review*, CXLVIII (March 1889), 275; W. T. Sherman to Alexander Ramsey, Nov. 10, 1880, *Report of the Secretary of War*, 46th Congress, 3d Session, House Executive Document 1, Part 2, pp. 4–5.

"I honor . . . empire"]   W. T. Sherman to Dan Garrison, Dec. 11, 1888, Sherman Papers, Missouri Historical Society.

"I trust . . . wealth"]   W. T. Sherman to D. R. Garrison, Aug. 16, 1865, Virginia Historical Society. On the army's role in the extension of railroads see William H. Goetzmann, *Exploration and Empire: The Explorer and the Scientist in the Winning of the American West* (New York, 1966), chap. 11; Richard Slotkin, *The Fatal Environment: The Myth of the Frontier in the Age of Industrialization, 1800–1890* (New York, 1985), esp. chap. 15.

377–8 "I know . . . prosperity"]   W. T. Sherman to [Willard] Warner, Feb. 5, 1879, Sherman Letters, Illinois State Historical Library.

378 "the grandest . . . nature" and "wild and desolate"]   [W. T. Sherman], [Address to cadets at the United States Military Academy], W. T. Sherman Miscellaneous Manuscripts, New-York Historical Society.

"waste places"]   W. T. Sherman to [Henry S.] Turner, July 25, 1879, Sherman Papers, Ohio Historical Society.

"absolute desert" and "redeemed"]   *Seventy-Ninth Anniversary Celebration of the New-England Society in the City of New York at Delmonico's, Dec. 22, 1884* (n.p., n.d.), 36.

buffalo]   W. T. Sherman to John N. Dyer, Oct. 31, 1884, St. Louis Mercantile Library, St. Louis, Missouri; Rich[ar]d Dodge to [W. T. Sherman], Nov. 8, 1884, W. T. Sherman Papers, Library of Congress.

"blossom . . . women"]   [W. T. Sherman], [Address at U.S. Military Academy], Sherman Manuscripts, New-York Historical Society.

"The surplus . . . infinite"]   W. T. Sherman's response to a toast, Eads Banquet, March 23, 1875, in newspaper clipping, W. T. and Ellen E. Sherman Scrapbook, Sherman Papers, Ohio Historical Society. On Eads, see Florence Dorsey, *Road to the Sea: The Story of James B. Eads and the Mississippi River* (New York, 1947), chaps. 8–11.

"Every . . . discovered"]   *Seventy-ninth Anniversary Celebration of the New-England Society in New York*, 36.

378–9 "California" . . . "transformation"]   W. T. Sherman to Francis D. Clark, Jan. 15, 1880, W. T. Sherman Papers, Library of Congress.

379 commerce ruled the world] "General Sherman's Speech," *Cincinnati Commercial*, June 12, 1865.

"old . . . town" . . . "railroads . . . enterprise"] W. T. Sherman to [Eleanor Sherman Thackara], Sept. 16, 1883, Sherman Papers, Ohio Historical Society; W. T. Sherman to T. T. Gantt, June 16, 1886, and W. T. Sherman to Joseph G. Breckinridge, June 27, 1887, W. T. Sherman Papers, Library of Congress.

"In N.Y. . . . bored"] T. T. Gantt to H. J. Hunt, April 12, 1886, Hunt Papers, Library of Congress.

"New York . . . world"] W. T. Sherman to Vinnie Ream Hoxie, Sept. 16, 1888, Vinnie Ream Hoxie Papers, *ibid.*

"Let him . . . progress"] *Cincinnati Commercial,* June 12, 1865.

"One feels . . . commerce"] W. T. Sherman to George H. Morgan, Jan. 7, 1889, Sherman Papers, Missouri Historical Society. See also New York, *In Memoriam. William T. Sherman,* 47.

"Impress . . . future"] W. T. Sherman to Mrs. [Paul Octave] Hebert, July 9, 1885, W. T. Sherman–P. O. Hebert Papers, Howard-Tilton Library, Tulane University, New Orleans, Louisiana.

Portland] *Twenty-first Reunion of the Society of the Army of the Potomac . . . July 3d and 4th, 1890,* 34.

380 "the transcendant . . . land"] W. T. Sherman to W. F. Vilas, Jan. 10, 1887, William F. Vilas Papers, State Historical Society of Wisconsin, Madison.

"General . . . Tennessee"] *Report of the Proceedings of the Society of the Army of the Tennessee, at the Twenty-third Meeting,* 533.

381 "What earthly . . . principle"] "Address by General W. T. Sherman at Princeton College, N.J., June 19, 1878," W. T. Sherman Papers, Library of Congress. See, in general, Robert V. Bruce, *The Launching of Modern American Science, 1846–1876* (New York, 1987).

"keeping . . . knowledge" and "In like . . . world"] Address at Washington University, Feb. 22, 1876, in *St. Louis Republican,* Feb. 26, 1876.

"look away" . . . "customs"] "Address at Princeton," June 19, 1878, W. T. Sherman Papers, Library of Congress.

"inevitable . . . greatness"] John William Draper, *Thoughts on the Future Civil Policy of America* (New York, 1865), 85. On Draper see Donald Fleming, *John William Draper and the Religion of Science* (Philadelphia, 1950); James R. Moore, *The Post-Darwinian Controversies: A Study of the Protestant Struggle to Come to Terms with Darwin in Great Britain and America, 1870–1900* (Cambridge, 1979).

382 "I confess . . . source"] W. T. Sherman to J. W. Harper, July 17, 1867, Sherman Papers, Missouri Historical Society.

"I . . . community" and "To find . . . conceive of"] W. T. Sherman to John W. Draper, June 30 and July 17, 1867, Draper Family Papers, Library of Congress.

"Though half . . . resulted"] *Banquet at "The Portland" . . . February 8, 1883,* 4.

382–3 "a bold . . . God"] W. T. Sherman to O. O. Howard, Jan. 1, 1884, Howard Papers, Bowdoin College. On the connection between the war and postwar development see Roger L. Ransom, *Conflict and Compromise: The Political Economy of Slavery, Emancipation, and the American Civil War* (Cambridge, 1989), chap. 8.

383 Draper on Columbia] John William Draper, *History of the American Civil War* (New York, 1867–1870), III, 546–547. See also John W. Draper to [W. T.] Sherman, Sept. 7, 1868, W. T. Sherman Papers, Library of Congress.

"It was . . . were made"] Draper, *History of the Civil War,* III, 537.

"but by . . . South" and "To thoughtful . . . law"] *Ibid.,* 656.

"the Civil War . . . civilization"] W. T. Sherman, *General Sherman's Address to the Grand Army of the Republic* (San Francisco, 1886), 2. The classic study of the concerns shared by Sherman is Walter E. Houghton, *The Victorian Frame of Mind, 1830–1870* (New Haven, Conn., 1957). See also D. H. Meyer, "American Intellectuals and the Victorian Crisis of Faith," *American Quarterly,* XXVII (Dec. 1975), 585–603; Daniel Walker Howe, *The Political Culture of the American Whigs* (Chicago, 1979); John F. Kasson, *Civilizing the Machine: Technology and Republican Values in America, 1776–1900* (New York, 1976); Leo Marx, *The Machine in the Garden: Technology and the Pastoral Ideal in America* (New York, 1964).

383 "one . . . man"] *Banquet at "The Portland" . . . February 8, 1883,* 4.

384 "we remained . . . ourselves"] *Seventy-ninth Anniversary Celebration of the New-England Society in New York,* 38.

"The Civil War . . . OURSELVES"] Sherman, *General Sherman's Address to the Grand Army of the Republic,* 2. See also Rowland Berthoff, *An Unsettled People: Social Order and Disorder in American History* (New York, 1971), 293–296.

"I, the mere soldier"] "Address at Princeton," June 19, 1878, W. T. Sherman Papers, Library of Congress.

384–5 "If there . . . difficulty"] [Harriott Middleton] to Susan [Middleton], [Feb.] 28, [1865], Cheves-Middleton Papers, Box 12-167, South Carolina Historical Society. For another version see Testimony of Rev. A. Toomer Porter, April 15, 1873, *Mixed Commission on British and American Claims, Appendix—Testimony* (Washington, D.C., 1873), XXIII, Book 2, Nos. 228 and 294, p. 15.

385 "How true . . . order"] Draper, *Thoughts on Civil Policy,* 251.

"A proper . . . local"] W. T. Sherman to [whom it may concern], April 19, 1869, Benjamin S. Ewell Papers, University Archives, Swem Library, College of William and Mary, Williamsburg, Virginia. See also Peter D. Hall, *The Organization of American Culture, 1700–1900: Private Institutions, Elites, and the Origins of American Nationality* (New York, 1982), esp. 215–219; John Higham, "Hanging Together: Divergent Unities in American History," *Journal of American History,* LXI (June 1974), 19–22; Robert H. Wiebe, *The Search for Order, 1877–1920* (New York, 1967), chaps. 1–4.

386 "The philosopher . . . hulk"] W. T. Sherman to E. A. Hitchcock, June 18, 1858, Ethan Allen Hitchcock Papers, Library of Congress.

387–8 War Department and army organization] Richard Allen Andrews, "Years of Frustration: William T. Sherman, the Army, and Reform, 1869–1883" (Ph.D. diss., Northwestern University, 1968); Bernard L. Boylan, "The Forty-Fifth Congress and Army Reform," *Mid-America,* XLI (July 1959), 173–186; James Pickett Jones, *John A. Logan: Stalwart Republican from Illinois* (Tallahassee, Fla., 1982), chap. 3; Robert F. Stohlman, Jr., *The Powerless Position: The Commanding General of the Army of the United States, 1864–1903* (Manhattan, Kan., 1975), chap. 3. On Belknap see W. T. Sherman to John W. Draper, March 9, 1876, Draper Family Papers, Library of Congress; W. T. Sherman to [O. M.] Poe, March 10, 1876, Orlando M. Poe Papers, *ibid.;* W. T. Sherman to J. E. Williams, March 10, 1876, *Charles Hamilton Catalog, Auction No. 105* (May 12, 1977), Item 211; W. T. Sherman to [David Dixon] Porter, March 15, 1876, Sherman Papers, Missouri Historical Society; Robert Wooster, *The Military and United States Indian Policy, 1865–1903* (New Haven, Conn., 1988), 102–108; Robert C. Prickett, "The Malfeasance of William Worth Belknap, Secretary of War, October 13, 1869, to March 2, 1876," *North Dakota History,* XVII (Jan. 1950), 5–51, (April 1950), 97–134.

388 "volunteer sore heads"] W. T. Sherman to Geo[rge] H. Thomas, March 23, 1870, *Charles Hamilton Catalog, Auction No. 120* (June 7, 1979), Item 226.

"the smallest men" and "small . . . Congress"] W. T. Sherman to John Welsh, April 4, 1878, W. T. Sherman Papers, Library of Congress. See also W. T. Sherman to [Thomas Ewing Sherman], March 15, 1878, Sherman Papers, University of Notre Dame; Margaret Susan Thompson, *The "Spider Web": Congress and Lobbying in the Age of Grant* (Ithaca, N.Y., 1985); Stephen Skowronek, *Building a New American State: The Expansion of National Administrative Capacities, 1877–1920* (Cambridge, 1982), 30–46.

"officers . . . politic"] W. T. Sherman to [H. W. Benham], Sept. 9, 1874, Benham-McNeill Family Papers, Library of Congress.

388 "Whilst I . . . army"]   W. T. Sherman to P. H. Sheridan, Oct. 7, 1872, Sheridan Papers, *ibid.*

"a skeleton . . . army"]   W. T. Sherman to [Willard] Warner, Jan. 22, 1866, Sherman Letters, Illinois State Historical Library.

389 Continental Army]   W. T. Sherman, [Address to the Graduating Class of 1869, United States Military Academy], W. T. Sherman Papers, Harry L. and Mary K. Dalton Collection, Duke University; [W. T. Sherman], "Centennial Banquet. New York, April 30, 1889. [Response to the] Toast, The Army and the Navy," Sherman Papers, University of Notre Dame; *Second Annual Festival of the New England Society of Pennsylvania . . . December 22, 1882* (n.p., n.d.), 30–32.

Upton]   Stephen E. Ambrose, *Upton and the Army* (Baton Rouge, La., 1964), esp. 76–77; W. T. Sherman to Phillip St. George Cooke, May 10, 1881, Cooke Family Papers, Virginia State Library; Peter D. Skirbunt, "Prologue to Reform: The 'Germanization' of the United States Army, 1865–1898" (Ph.D. diss., Ohio State University, 1983), 69–79; Skowronek, *Building a New American State*, 89–92.

"for good . . . Leavenworth"]   W. T. Sherman to P. H. Sheridan, Oct. 3, 1882, Sheridan Papers, Library of Congress. On West Point see Walter Scott Dillard, "The United States Military Academy, 1865–1900: The Uncertain Years" (Ph.D. diss., University of Washington, 1972), chap. 5. On the School of Application see Timothy K. Nenninger, *The Leavenworth Schools and the Old Army: Education, Professionalism, and the Officer Corps of the United States Army, 1881–1918* (Westport, Conn., 1978), chap. 2. On Sherman's concern for military professionalism see Samuel P. Huntington, *The Soldier and the State: The Theory and Politics of Civil-Military Relations* (Cambridge, Mass., 1957), 229–234; Edward M. Coffman, *The Old Army: A Portrait of the American Army in Peacetime, 1784–1898* (New York, 1986), 269–284.

"my legacy . . . testament"]   W. T. Sherman to P. H. Sheridan, Oct. 3, 1882, Sheridan Papers, Library of Congress; W. T. Sherman, *Address of General W. T. Sherman to the Officers and Soldiers Composing the School of Application at Fort Leavenworth, Kansas, October 25, 1882* (n.p., n.d.).

389–90 "An army . . . whole"]   The Society of the Army of the Potomac, *Report of the Fourteenth Annual Re-union, at Washington, D.C., May 16 & 17, 1883* (New York, 1883), 45.

390 "The regularity . . . salvation"]   W. T. Sherman to H. C. Cameron, Dec. 2, 1879, Barney Collection, Box 28, Huntington Library. See also *Speeches, Correspondence, Etc. at the Tenth Annual Banquet of the Knights of St. Patrick, on Friday Evening, March 17th, 1876* (St. Louis, [1876]), 8–9.

prosperity]   W. T. Sherman to G. Ward Nichols, Jan. 3, 1866, Draper Family Papers, Box 6, Library of Congress.

"the right . . . theorists"]   W. T. Sherman, "General Sherman's Last Speech," *Century Magazine*, XLII (June 1891), 189. See also W. T. Sherman to [Stephen J.] Field, Feb. 27, 1890, HM 31039, Huntington Library. On reformers and military force, see Donald N. Bigelow, *William Conant Church and the Army and Navy Journal* (New York, 1952), chap. 11; Lester D. Langley, "The Democratic Tradition and Military Reform, 1878–1885," *Southwestern Social Science Quarterly*, XLVIII (Sept. 1967), 192–200; John G. Sproat, *The Best Men: Liberal Reformers in the Gilded Age* (New York, 1968), chap. 8; Robert Reinders, "Militia and Public Order in Nineteenth-Century America," *Journal of American Studies*, XI (1977), 91–97; Jerry M. Cooper, *The Army and Civil Disorder: Federal Military Intervention in Labor Disputes, 1877–1900* (Westport, Conn., 1980), chaps. 3–4; Skowronek, *Building a New American State*, chap. 4.

391 "safety and happiness" and "Though peace . . . past"]   W. T. Sherman, *Address of General W. T. Sherman to the Graduating Class of the Michigan Military Academy, at Orchard Lake, June 19, 1879* (n.p., n.d.), 1–2.

"The day . . . peace" . . . "the Army . . . passive"]   Society of the Army of the Potomac, *Report of the Fourteenth Annual Re-union*, 46, 48. See also *St. Louis Post-Dispatch*, July 27, 1877; *Washington Post*, March 4, 1878; W. T. Sherman to [Thomas Ewing Sherman],

Oct. 27, 1877, Sherman Papers, University of Notre Dame; John Swinton to W. T. Sherman, Nov. 29, 1883, W. T. Sherman Papers, Library of Congress; W. T. Sherman to John Swinton, Dec. 2, 1883, Sherman Manuscripts, New-York Historical Society; *New England Society in the City of Brooklyn January 1881 . . . Proceedings at the First Annual Meeting* (n.p., [1881]), 43; W. T. Sherman to John T. Doyle, March 22, 1886, Doyle Papers, California Historical Society.

392 "the hideous . . . politic"] Draper, *Thoughts on Civil Policy,* 252. On postwar fears of revolution see, for example, Paul Boyer, *Urban Masses and Moral Order in America, 1820–1920* (Cambridge, Mass., 1978), chap. 8; Frederic Cople Jaher, *Doubters and Dissenters: Cataclysmic Thought in America, 1885–1918* (New York, 1964); Samuel Rezneck, "Distress, Relief, and Discontent in the United States During the Depression of 1873–1878," *Journal of Political Economy,* LVIII (Dec. 1950), 510; Carl Siracusa, *A Mechanical People: Perceptions of the Industrial Order in Massachusetts, 1815–1880* (Middletown, Conn., 1979), 227; Samuel Bernstein, "The Impact of the Paris Commune in the United States," *Massachusetts Review,* XII (1971), 435–446.

"The armies . . . anarchy"] W. T. Sherman, *General William T. Sherman's Address, New York City, May 30th, 1878* (Philadelphia, 1878), 11. See also W. T. Sherman to [Thomas Ewing Sherman], Oct. 27, 1877, Sherman Papers, University of Notre Dame; W. T. Sherman to T. T. Gantt, May 6, 1878, W. T. Sherman Papers, Library of Congress.

"puffed . . . aristocrat"] *Labor Enquirer* (Denver), Sept. 29, 1883.

"I am not . . . war"] Society of the Army of the Potomac, *Report of the Eighteenth Annual Re-union,* 38–39.

"durable history"] W. T. Sherman to [D. F.] Boyd, June 5, 1875, Boyd Family Papers, Louisiana State University. See also W. T. Sherman to Geo[rge] Bancroft, Nov. 12 and 30, 1874, Jan. 4 and 23, 1875, George Bancroft Papers, Massachusetts Historical Society.

"We had . . . ours"] Sherman, *Memoirs,* 2d ed., I, 209–210.

393 "In times . . . 1861"] *Ibid.,* II, 406.

"The danger . . . perpetuate it"] W. T. Sherman to Thomas M. Anderson, June 29, 1875, Anderson Family Papers, University of Washington, Seattle.

394 "dirty work"] W. T. Sherman to John A. Rawlins, Sept. 21, 1866, quoted in Robert G. Athearn, *William Tecumseh Sherman and the Settlement of the West* (Norman, Okla., 1956), 83.

"inglorious war"] W. T. Sherman to P. H. Sheridan, Oct. 15, 1868, Barney Collection, Box 28, Huntington Library. See also Robert M. Utley, *Frontier Regulars: The United States Army and the Indian, 1866–1891* (Bloomington, Ind., 1973), 119–120; Paul Andrew Hutton, *Phil Sheridan and His Army* (Lincoln, Neb., 1985), 144–146; Coffman, *Old Army,* 255–256; *Cincinnati Enquirer,* Feb. 11, 1886; W. T. Sherman to [John Sherman], June 17, 1868, W. T. Sherman Papers, Library of Congress; W. T. Sherman to Thomas Ewing, March 10, 1867, Ewing Family Papers, *ibid.;* W. T. Sherman to W. C. Church, March 16, 1870, William C. Church Papers, *ibid.;* W. T. Sherman to Herbert A. Preston, April 17, 1873, W. T. Sherman Papers, *ibid.;* W. T. Sherman to [John M. Schofield], Nov. 20, 1868, Barney Collection, Box 28, Huntington Library.

"What the white . . . race"] John Pope to R. M. Sawyer, Aug. 1, 1865, Military Division of the Mississippi, Letters Received, Box 3, Record Group 393, Part 1, No. 2484, National Archives; John M. Corse to W. T. Sherman, Dec. 12, 1865, W. T. Sherman Papers, Library of Congress. See also Richard N. Ellis, "The Humanitarian Generals," *Western Historical Quarterly,* III (April 1972), 169–178.

395 "We must . . . false"] W. T. Sherman to H. B. Carrington, Aug. 30, 1866, Carrington Family Collection, Sterling Library, Yale University.

"We must . . . case"] W. T. Sherman to U. S. Grant, Dec. 28, 1866, quoted in Athearn, *Sherman and the West,* 99.

"I always . . . here"] W. T. Sherman to P. H. Sheridan, May 26, 1869, Sheridan Papers, Library of Congress.

395 "You can . . . want"]   Henry M. Stanley, *My Early Adventures in America* (Lincoln, Neb., 1982 [orig. publ. London, 1895]), 210–211. See also Robert H. Keller, Jr., *American Protestantism and United States Indian Policy, 1869–1882* (Lincoln, Neb., 1983), chap. 6; Francis Paul Prucha, *American Indian Policy in Crisis: Christian Reformers and the Indian, 1865–1900* (Norman, Okla., 1976), chaps. 2, 3; Robert M. Utley, *The Indian Frontier of the American West, 1846–1890* (Albuquerque, N.M., 1984), 164–165; Frederick E. Hoxie, *A Final Promise: The Campaign to Assimilate the Indians, 1880–1920* (Lincoln, Neb., 1984), chap. 1.

"mark . . . Choctaws"]   W. T. Sherman to P. H. Sheridan *et al.*, Dec. 23, 1868, W. T. Sherman Papers, Library of Congress.

396 "cluster" and "till . . . demoralized"]   W. T. Sherman to [C. C.] Augur, Feb. 24, 1869, Augur Papers, Illinois State Historical Library. See also W. T. Sherman to P. H. Sheridan, Nov. 3, 1873, Sheridan Papers, Library of Congress.

"I have . . . people"]   W. T. Sherman to Foster Tappan, July 21, 1876, W. T. Sherman Papers, Library of Congress. See also W. T. Sherman to P. H. Sheridan, Oct. 15, 1868, Barney Collection, Box 28, Huntington Library. On "extermination" compare Utley, *Frontier Regulars*, 51–52; Slotkin, *Fatal Environment*, chap. 15.

"adapt . . . things" and "wild nature"]   W. T. Sherman to [Philemon Ewing], April 9, 1865, Ewing Family Papers, Library of Congress; W. T. Sherman to Ellen [Sherman], April 10, 1865, Sherman Papers, University of Notre Dame. See also W. T. Sherman to Ellen [Sherman], Sept. 14, 1867, *ibid.;* W. T. Sherman to [D. F.] Boyd, May 20, 1867, Boyd Family Papers, Louisiana State University; W. T. Sherman to [Elizabeth] Custer, Jan. 24, 1889, W. T. Sherman Papers, Library of Congress; W. T. Sherman to Richard I. Dodge, Jan. 1, 1882, in Richard Irving Dodge, *Our Wild Indians: Thirty-Three Years' Personal Experience Among the Red Men of the Great West* (New York, 1959 [orig. publ. 1882]), xxxv–xxxix.

"remember . . . ago"]   Charles Allyn, ed., *The Battle of Groton Heights* (New London, Conn., 1882), 361–362.

397 "The process . . . end"]   W. T. Sherman to Robert Clarke, Feb. 29, 1880, Beinecke Library, Yale University.

"We make . . . oppression"]   S. F. Tappan to W. T. Sherman, Nov. 25, 1868, W. T. Sherman Papers, Library of Congress.

"we must . . . insane"]   [W. T.] Sherman to Ellen [Sherman], Aug. 10, 1862, Sherman Papers, University of Notre Dame.

398 "was simply . . . himself"]   *Brooklyn Daily Eagle,* Dec. 21, 1890.

"I thought . . . retirement"]   Oliver O. Howard to W. T. Sherman, Dec. 29, 1883, W. T. Sherman Papers, Library of Congress.

"I suppose . . . raiment"]   *Oil, Paint and Drug Reporter,* [1884], in Scrapbook, Vol. 109, *ibid.*

398–9 "Gold . . . can do"]   W. T. Sherman to Vinnie Ream Hoxie, Sept. 16, 1888, Hoxie Papers, *ibid.*

399 "Nature . . . Indian"]   W. T. Sherman to [John T.] Doyle, May 13, 1888, Doyle Papers, California Historical Society. See also Arthur P. Dudden, "Nostalgia and the American," *Journal of the History of Ideas,* XXII (Dec. 1961), 515–531.

universal suffrage and the propertyless]   See esp. W. T. Sherman to John Sherman, March 4, 1859, and Henry Hitchcock to W. T. Sherman, April 17, 1887, W. T. Sherman Papers, Library of Congress; W. T. Sherman to [Thomas Ewing Sherman], Dec. 18, 1876, Sherman Papers, University of Notre Dame; W. T. Sherman to Geo[rge] Bancroft, July 11, 1872, Bancroft Papers, Massachusetts Historical Society; W. T. Sherman to [P. Tecumseh] Sherman, Sept. 5, 1890, Sherman Papers, Ohio Historical Society.

400 "We are . . . election"]   Byers, *Twenty Years in Europe,* 125.

"Too many . . . prosperous"]   W. T. Sherman to [Robert] Granger, Dec. 8, 1884, Sherman Papers, Missouri Historical Society. See also P. Tecumseh Sherman, "Reminiscences of Early Days," 17–18, Sherman Papers, University of Notre Dame; M. A. Bickerdyke to W. T. Sherman, Feb. 5, 1869, Mary Ann Ball Bickerdyke Papers, Library of Congress; W. T. Sherman to [Felicia Lee Cary Thornton] Shover, Nov. 1, 1873, Thornton Family Papers, Virginia Historical Society. On Ellen Sherman's charities see Anna McAllister, *Ellen Ewing: Wife of General Sherman* (New York, 1936), chaps. 18–21. On veterans as tramps see Dixon Wecter, *When Johnny Comes Marching Home* (Cambridge, Mass., 1944), 182–193, 236; Michael Davis, "Forced to Tramp: The Perspective of the Labor Press, 1870–1900," in Eric H. Monkkonen, ed., *Walking to Work: Tramps in America, 1790–1935* (Lincoln, Neb., 1984), 141–170; John D. Seelye, "The American Tramp: A Version of the Picaresque," *American Quarterly,* XV (1963), 543–544; Allan Pinkerton, *Strikers, Communists, Tramps and Detectives* (New York, 1878), 47–48, 66–67.

400 "by taxation . . . neighbors" and "watch . . . head"] W. T. Sherman to T. T. Gantt, May 6, 1878, W. T. Sherman Papers, Library of Congress.

"labor riots"] W. T. S[herman] to Ellen [Sherman], May 18, 1878, Sherman Papers, University of Notre Dame. See also Thomas E. Sherman to [W. T. Sherman], May 27, 1878, *ibid.*

"with arms and in blood"] W. T. Sherman to T. T. Gantt, May 6, 1878, W. T. Sherman Papers, Library of Congress.

"breakers . . . valorously"] W. T. Sherman to [Henry S.] Turner, May 27, 1878, Sherman Papers, Ohio Historical Society. On the strikes of 1877 see Eric Foner, *Reconstruction: America's Unfinished Revolution, 1863–1877* (New York, 1988), 582–587; Robert V. Bruce, *1877: Year of Violence* (Indianapolis, Ind., 1959); David T. Burbank, *Reign of the Rabble: The St. Louis General Strike of 1877* (New York, 1966); Reinders, "Militia and Public Order," *Journal of American Studies,* XI (1977), 91–97; David Roediger, "America's First General Strike: The St. Louis Commune of 1877," *Midwest Quarterly,* XXI (1980), 196–206; David Roediger, " 'Not only the Ruling Class to Overcome, But Also the So-Called Mob': Class, Skill, and Community in the St. Louis General Strike of 1877," *Journal of Social History,* XIX (1985), 213–239; Cooper, *Army and Civil Disorder,* chaps. 3, 4; Coffman, *Old Army,* 246–254.

401 "If you . . . aeriolytes"] W. T. Sherman to John W. Draper, Sept. 7, 1867, Draper Family Papers, Library of Congress.

"it does look . . . unknown"] Society of the Army of the Potomac, *Report of the Fourteenth Annual Re-union,* 48. On doubts about the nation's future see, for example, Paul C. Nagel, *This Sacred Trust: American Nationality, 1798–1898* (New York, 1971), chap. 4; Bruce Curtis, "William Graham Sumner and the Problem of Progress," *New England Quarterly,* LI (Sept. 1978), 348–369; Robert G. McCloskey, *American Conservatism in the Age of Enterprise, 1865–1910: A Study of William Graham Sumner, Stephen J. Field and Andrew Carnegie* (Cambridge, Mass., 1951), esp. 57–62, 133; Robert Kelley, *The Transatlantic Persuasion: The Liberal-Democratic Mind in the Age of Gladstone* (New York, 1969), 293.

402 "which claimed to be eternal" and "others . . . Indian"] *Report of the Proceedings of the Society of the Army of the Tennessee at the Eighth Annual Meeting,* 278; *St. Louis Republican,* Feb. 26, 1876. See also W. T. Sherman to [Willard] Warner, Jan. 15, 1880, Sherman Letters, Illinois State Historical Library.

"As long . . . succeed"] W. T. Sherman to J. M. Dalzell, Oct. 8, 1881, *The Chaperone,* V (March 1891), 630.

"In treading . . . lands"] W. T. Sherman to Joseph Henry, July 20, 1872, Rhees Collection, Box 43, Huntington Library. See also W. T. Sherman to O. C. Marsh, April 7, 1885, Othniel C. Marsh Papers, Series I, Box 29, Sterling Library, Yale University.

"the laws . . . civilization" and "This drama . . . end"] W. T. Sherman to W[illia]m F. Cody, June 29, 1887, W. T. Sherman Papers, Library of Congress.

"I saw . . . profession"] J. E. Tourtellotte to John Sherman, Feb. 25, 1891, John Sherman Papers, *ibid.*

403 "defunct institution"] W. T. Sherman to [Eleanor Mary Sherman Thackara], May 24, 1881, Sherman Papers, Ohio Historical Society. See, in general, Joseph T. Durkin, *General Sherman's Son* (New York, 1959).

403 "By force . . . others"]   W. T. Sherman to [Henry S.] Turner, June 5, 1878, Sherman Papers, Ohio Historical Society.

"The dream . . . others"]   W. T. Sherman to [Henry S.] Turner, July 7, 1878, *ibid.*

404 "I have neither . . . Amen"]   Newspaper clipping, Mary Elizabeth Sherman Fitch Armstead Scrapbook, Sherman Papers, Box 17, Ohio Historical Society.

"spite . . . about"]   W. T. Sherman to Jarvis, Dec. 9, 1883, Sherman Papers, Missouri Historical Society.

"when . . . nation" and "I sometimes . . . fortunes"]   W. T. Sherman to John T. Doyle, July 7, 1878, Doyle Papers, California Historical Society.

CHAPTER NINE

Notes for Pages 405–417

My account of the review of Sherman's army is based on the following sources: Stanton P. Allen, *Down in Dixie: Life in a Cavalry Regiment in the War Days from the Wilderness to Appomattox* (Boston, 1892), 477–480; Mary Clemmer Ames, *Ten Years in Washington: Life and Scenes in the National Capital, as a Woman Sees Them* (Hartford, Conn., 1879), 270; Henry J. Aten, *History of the Eighty-Fifth Regiment, Illinois Volunteer Infantry* (Hiawatha, Kan., 1901), 321; Charles E. Benton, *As Seen from the Ranks: A Boy in the Civil War* (New York, 1902), 286; William Bircher, *A Drummer-Boy's Diary: Comprising Four Years of Service with the Second Regiment Minnesota Veteran Volunteers, 1861 to 1865* (St. Paul, Minn., 1889), 191–192; Noah Brooks, *Washington in Lincoln's Time,* ed. Herbert Mitgang (New York, 1958), 271–283; Alonzo L. Brown, *History of the Fourth Regiment of Minnesota Infantry Volunteers* (St. Paul, Minn., 1892), 422–423; Joshua Lawrence Chamberlain, *The Passing of the Armies* (New York, 1915), chap. 10; *Cincinnati Commercial,* May 25, 27, 29, 1865; *Cleveland Plain Dealer,* May 25, 1865; Elbridge J. Copp, *Reminiscences of the War of the Rebellion, 1861–1865* (Nashua, N.H., 1911), 524–527; entry of May 24, 1865, Alexander G. Downing, *Downing's Civil War Diary,* ed. Olynthus B. Clark (Des Moines, Iowa, 1916), 277; J[oseph] Grecian, *History of the Eighty-Third Regiment, Indiana Volunteer Infantry* (Cincinnati, Ohio, 1865), 87; W. B. Hazen, *A Narrative of Military Service* (Boston, 1885), 378–379; F. Y. Hedley, *Marching Through Georgia* (Chicago, 1890), chap. 46; entry of May 24, 1865, War Journal, J. T. Holmes, *52d O. V. I. Then and Now* (Columbus, Ohio, 1898), 36; Oliver Otis Howard, *Autobiography of Oliver Otis Howard* (New York, 1908), II, 211; J. W. Anderson, "The Grand Review," in Oscar L. Jackson, *The Colonel's Diary,* ed. David P. Jackson [Sharon, Pa., 1922], 219–221; H. W. Slocum, "Final Operations of Sherman's Army," in Robert Underwood Johnson and Clarence Clough Buel, eds., *Battles and Leaders of the Civil War* (New York, 1888), IV, 758; entry of May 24, 1865, Edwin L. Lybarger, *Leaves From My Diary* (Warsaw, Ohio, n. d.), 15; John G. Nicolay and John Hay, *Abraham Lincoln: A History* (New York, 1890), X, 334; "Recollections of Sherman and Porter," *The Nation,* LII (March 5, 1891), 192–193; Benja[min] Harrison to [Francis C.] Crawford, May 31, 1865, *The War of the Rebellion: A Compilation of the Official Records of the Union and Confederate Armies* (Washington, D.C., 1880–1901), Series I, Vol. XLVII, Part I, 793; Charles A. Page, *Letters of a War Correspondent,* ed. James R. Gilmore (Boston, 1899), 391–397; George W. Pepper, *Personal Recollections of Sherman's Campaigns in Georgia and the Carolinas* (Zanesville, Ohio, 1866), 466; Horace Porter, *Campaigning With Grant,* ed. Wayne C. Temple (Bloomington, Ind., 1961 [orig. publ. New York, 1897]), 506–512; John Sherman, *Recollections of Forty Years in the House, Senate and Cabinet: An Autobiography* (Chicago, 1895), I, 356–357; W. T. Sherman, *Memoirs of General William T. Sherman,* 2d ed. (New York, 1886), II, 376–378; [Hosea Whitford Rood], *Story of the Service of Company E, and of the Twelfth Wisconsin Regiment, Veteran Volunteer Infantry, in the War of the Rebellion* (Milwaukee, Wis., 1893), 444–449; Robert Hale Strong, *A Yankee Private's Civil War,* ed. Ashley Halsey (Chicago, 1961), 210–211; Benjamin P. Thomas and Harold Hyman, *Stanton: The Life and Times of Lincoln's Secretary of War* (New York, 1962), 416–417; Samuel Toombs, *Reminiscences of the War, Comprising a Detailed Account of the Experiences of the Thirteenth Regiment New Jersey Volunteers* (Orange, N.J., 1878), 226–228; Albion W. Tourgée, *The Story of a Thousand: Being a History of the Service of the 105th Ohio Volunteer Infantry* (Buffalo, N.Y., 1896), 381; E. D.

Townsend, *Anecdotes of the Civil War in the United States* (New York, 1884), 245–246;
Theodore F. Upson, *With Sherman to the Sea: The Civil War Letters, Diaries & Reminiscences
of Theodore F. Upson,* ed. Oscar Osburn Winther (Baton Rouge, La., 1943), 175–178; entries
of May 23–24, 1865, Charles S. Wainwright, *A Diary of Battle: The Personal Journals of
Colonel Charles S. Wainwright,* ed. Allan Nevins (New York, 1962), 526–530; *New York
Herald,* May 24, 25, 1865; entry of May 24, 1865, Diary of John W. Bates, Civil War
Miscellaneous Collection, United States Army Military History Institute, Carlisle Barracks,
Pennsylvania; Jasper P. George, "The Autobiography of one of 'Sherman's Men' in the
Rebellion of 1861–5," *ibid;* Samuel A. Craig, "Memoirs of Civil War and Reconstruction,"
Civil War Times Illustrated Collection, *ibid.;* entry of May 24, 1865, Diary of Edward E.
Schweitzer, *ibid.;* [J. R. Zearing] to wife, May 26, 1865, James Roberts Zearing Collection,
Chicago Historical Society, Chicago, Illinois; [Thomas] Edwin Smith to Maria Smith, May
25, [1865], and T. E. Smith to brother, May 27, 1865, Thomas E. Smith Letters, Cincinnati
Historical Society, Cincinnati, Ohio; Roger Hannaford, Memoirs, ff. 337–338, Roger Han-
naford Papers, Box 2, *ibid.;* Andrew Hickenlooper, Personal Reminiscences, Volume I, 349,
Andrew Hickenlooper Papers, *ibid.;* B. F. Fisher to E. V. Gerhart, May 24, 1865, Letter Book,
Benjamin Franklin Fisher Papers, Perkins Library, Duke University, Durham, North Carolina; Sam W. Snow to parents, May 29, 1865, Snow Family Papers, *ibid.;* A. L. Slack to father
and mother, May 31, 1865, Albert L. Slack Letters, Woodruff Library, Emory University,
Atlanta, Georgia; [James Biddle] to wife, May 26, 1865, James Cornell Biddle Papers,
Historical Society of Pennsylvania, Philadelphia; W. T. Sherman to John A. Rawlins, May
19, 1865, HM 23285, Henry E. Huntington Library, San Marino, California; W. T. Sherman
to [J. M. Schofield], May 28, 1865, HM 23216, *ibid.;* Sam Roper to sister, May 25, 1865,
Samuel Roper Collection, *ibid.;* Delos Lake to Calvin Lake, May 26, 1865, Delos W. Lake
Papers, *ibid.;* Charles H. Brush to [H. L. Brush], May 25, 1865, and entry of May 24, 1865,
Diary of Charles H. Brush, Brush Family Papers, Illinois State Historical Library, Springfield; entry of May 24, 1865, Diary of John Batchelor, *ibid.;* Fred[erick] Marion to sister,
May 27, 1865, Frederick Marion Letters, *ibid.;* S. K. Harryman to Maggie [Margaret Moore],
June 4, 1865, Samuel K. Harryman Papers, Indiana State Library, Indianapolis; entry of May
23, 1865, Diary of John Gay, Iowa State Historical Society, Iowa City; Jake [Jacob Ritner]
to [Emeline Ritner], May 28, 1865, Jacob Ritner Letters, *ibid.;* entry of May 24, 1865, Diary
of Charles Berry, Charles Berry, Sr., Papers, *ibid.;* entry of May 24, 1865, Diary of E. P.
Failing, Failing-Knight Papers, Massachusetts Historical Society, Boston; T[h]om[as] [S.
Howland] to sister, May 27, 1865, Thomas S. Howland Letters, *ibid.;* R. Rey to Lizzie, June
3, 1865, Rudolphe Rey Personal Miscellany, New-York Historical Society, New York, New
York; [J. S.] Rob[inson] to Hunt, May 26, [1865], James S. Robinson Papers, Ohio
Historical Society, Columbus; entry of May 24, 1865, Diary of N. L. Parmater, *ibid.;* T. T.
Taylor to M. A. Taylor, May 25, 1865, T. T. Taylor Papers, Box 2, *ibid.;* W. T. Sherman,
"Address of General Sherman," *Twenty-first Reunion of the Society of the Army of the Potomac,*
32–35 [copy corrected in Sherman's hand], Selected Pamphlets, Volume 13, W. T. Sherman
Papers, Ohio Historical Society; M. C. Meigs to [W. T.] Sherman, May 27, 1875, W. T.
Sherman Papers, Library of Congress, Washington, D.C.; David T. Bunker to W. T.
Sherman, July 21, 1875, *ibid.;* W. T. Sherman to James E. Taylor, Aug. 9, 1880, *ibid.;* O.
M. Poe to wife, May 28, 1865, Orlando M. Poe Papers, *ibid.;* John A. Logan to [Mary
Logan], May 26, 1865, John A. Logan Papers, Box 33, *ibid.;* [Adam Badeau] to [James
Harrison Wilson], May 27, 1865, James Harrison Wilson Papers, *ibid.;* entry of May 24, 1865,
Diary of John N. Ferguson, *ibid.;* Sherwood E. Seeley to [Samuel] Glyde [Swain], June 15,
1865, Samuel Glyde Swain Papers, State Historical Society of Wisconsin, Madison; [Adelbert
M. Bly] to Annie [Burdick], May 27, 1865, Adelbert M. Bly Correspondence, *ibid.;* James
M. Sligh to [Eliza W. Sligh], May 29, 1865, Sligh Family Correspondence, Michigan
History Collection, Bentley Library, University of Michigan, Ann Arbor; [Walt Whitman],
"Review," #3829, Walt Whitman Papers, Alderman Library, University of Virginia,
Charlottesville; Ja[me]s Grant Wilson, "General William T. Sherman," Palmer Collection,
Box 17, Western Reserve Historical Society, Cleveland, Ohio.

ACKNOWLEDGMENTS

WHILE working on this book I received help from many people—so many that a full list of them would be tedious, even to those named in it. They all know how much I owe them.

I must record my gratitude for fellowships granted by the John Simon Guggenheim Memorial Foundation, the National Humanities Center, and the Henry E. Huntington Library. Louisiana State University gave me a sabbatical leave, and I received summer grants of aid from Louisiana State University and the University of Texas at Arlington.

The manuscript repositories I visited are mentioned in the Notes; I thank the archivists for their assistance and for permission to quote from materials in their custody.

At the later stages of my work I had the assistance of, in turn, Kathleen Smith, Benjamin Bryant, and Ronald Barr.

As in the past, I have had the benefit of criticisms from E. Wayne Carp, Drew R. McCoy, and W. J. Rorabaugh. Several of my colleagues at Louisiana State University gave me valuable readings and advice: William J. Cooper, Jr., Gaines M. Foster, Sally Graham, Burl Noggle, and Paul F. Paskoff. For the benefit of their insights I also offer special thanks to James Boyden, Robert W. Johannsen, John Kushma, Lewis P. Simpson, and Frank S. Smith.

Jane Garrett was my ideal of an editor ten years ago, and she still is.

I dedicate this book to three good friends—fellow veterans of the annual Hotel Roanoke campaigns, 1980–1989.

INDEX

Permissions Acknowledgments

Special thanks go to the following for permission to reprint material from their collections:

Alderman Library, Manuscripts Division, Special Collections Dept., University of Virginia, Charlottesville, VA; The Archives of The University of Notre Dame, Notre Dame, IN; Arkansas History Commission, Little Rock, AK; Atlanta Historical Society, Library/Archives, Atlanta, GA; Bancroft Library, University of California, Berkeley, CA; Bowdoin College, The Library, Brunswick, ME; California Historical Society, San Francisco, CA; Chicago Historical Society, Chicago, IL; Cincinnati Historical Society, Cincinnati, OH; William L. Clements Library, The University of Michigan, Ann Arbor, MI; Emory University, General Libraries, Atlanta, GA; The Filson Club Historical Society, Louisville, KY; The Historical Society of Pennsylvania, Philadelphia, PA; The Huntington Library, San Marino, CA; Illinois State Historical Library, Springfield, IL; Indiana Historical Society, William Henry Smith Memorial Library, Indianapolis, IN; Indiana State Library, Indianapolis, IN; Louisiana State University, Hill Memorial Library, Baton Rouge, LA; Maryland Historical Society Library, Manuscripts Division, Baltimore, MD; Massachusetts Historical Society, Boston, MA; Missouri Historical Society, St. Louis, MO; The New-York Historical Society, New York, NY; The New York Public Library, Century Company Records, Rare Books and Manuscripts Division, Astor, Lenox and Tilden Foundations, New York, NY; North Carolina State Archives, North Carolina Dept. of Cultural Resources, Raleigh, NC; Ohio Historical Society, Archives-Library Division, Columbus, OH; The Ohio State University, University Libraries, Columbus, OH; William R. Perkins Library, Special Collections Dept., Duke University, Durham, NC; Princeton University, The Library, Princeton, NJ; The South Carolina Historical Society, Charleston, SC; State Historical Society of Iowa, The Historical Division of the Dept. of Cultural Affairs, Iowa City, IA; The State Historical Society of Wisconsin, Madison, WI; Swem Library, University Archives, College of William and Mary, Williamsburg, VA; Tulane University, Howard-Tilton Memorial Library, New Orleans, LA; Union Theological Seminary, The Library, Richmond, VA; The University of Georgia, Hargrett Rare Book and Manuscript Library, Athens, GA; University of Kentucky Libraries, Lexington, KY; The University of North Carolina, Southern Historical Collection, Library, Chapel Hill, NC; University of South Carolina, South Caroliniana Library, Columbia, SC; The University of Texas, The General Libraries, Austin, TX; University of Washington Libraries, Seattle, WA; Virginia Historical Society, Richmond, VA; Virginia Military Institute, Virginia Military Institute Archives, Preston Library, Lexington, VA; Washington University, Olin Library, St. Louis, MO; Washington and Lee University, Special Collections Dept., The University Library, Lexington, VA; The Western Reserve Historical Society, Cleveland, OH; West Virginia and Regional History Collection, West Virginia University, Morgantown, WV; Yale University Library, Manuscripts and Archives, New Haven, CT.